Francis Bacon, Gilbert Watts

Of the Advancement and Proficience of Learning

The partitions of sciences, nine books

Francis Bacon, Gilbert Watts

Of the Advancement and Proficience of Learning
The partitions of sciences, nine books

ISBN/EAN: 9783337886998

Printed in Europe, USA, Canada, Australia, Japan

Cover: Foto ©Andreas Hilbeck / pixelio.de

More available books at **www.hansebooks.com**

SACRATISSIMO DOMINO NOSTRO

CAROLO

DEI GRATIA, MAG. BRITANIÆ,
FRANCIÆ ET HIBERNIÆ REGI:
TERRÆ MARISQ. POTENTISSIMO
PRINCIPI: OCEANI BRITANNICI
AD QUATUOR MUNDI PLAGAS
DISPARTITI IMPERATORI: DOMINO
VIRGINIÆ ET VASTORUM
TERRITORIORUM ADJACENTIUM
ET DISPERSARUM INSULARUM
IN OCEANO OCCIDENTALI.

CHRISTIANÆ FIDEI DEFENSORI,
PACIS INSTAURATORI, PUB.
SECURITATIS AUCTORI
PIO FEL. AUG.

[A 2] *NEC-NON*

NEC-NON

SUB SUI NUMINIS
INFLUENTIA AC CLIENTELA
DUOBUS MAX. MUNDI LUMINARIBUS
PERPETUIS SAPIENTIÆ FLAMMIS
CERTISS. SCIENTIARUM CYNOSURIS
UTRISQ. ANGLIÆ ACADEMIIS

INFIMUS HUMILLIMUS

VERULAMII INTERPRES
HANC PRIMAM INSTAURATIONIS
MAGNÆ PARTEM

D. N. C. Q.

TO THE

PRINCE

OF

GREAT BRITAIN,
FRANCE and *IRELAND;*

THE

GROWING GLORY

OF A

FUTURE AGE.

HE facrifice of my Devotions in the Dedication of thefe Labours (*excellent Prince*) had
gone a more humble way of Ambition, than
through the hands of Kings and Princes,
could I afterwards have juftified fuch humi-
liations. But the Tenure of this work is a Title-Royal,
which no lapfe of time, nor alteration of language can re-
verfe. In the Original entitled to a King; fo continued in the Tranflation, and fo in a direct line de-
fcends upon *Your Highnefs*, as a part of a Royal Patrimony, which I durft not alienate by a lower infcription.
The Author is Sir *Francis Bacon*, a name well known in
the European World; a learned man, happily the

ear-learned'ft, that ever lived, fince the decay of the Grecian and Roman Empires; when Learning was at a high pitch; and which rife and fell with thofe Monarchies; for Scepters and Sciences have the fame revolutions, the fame period. In the vaft fpaces of time between thofe and thefe laft Ages, Philofophy hath been, as it were in a flumber; for many centuries of years. For after the Chriftian Faith grew up, the moft Writers betook themfelves to Theology, and fome miftaking the right limits of Faith and Reafon, fell foul upon *Ariftotle*, and other Philofophers, as Patriarchs of Herefie, which were the Patrons of Reafon. Somewhat awaked from this flumber fhe was, by the *Arabian* Writers, the School-Doctors, and Spanifh Interpreters; made more active by the Chymick Philofophers, but never perfectly recovered until the days of this Author, who is the firft that ever joyn'd Rational and Experimental Philofophy in a regular correfpondence; which before was either a fubtilty of words, or a confufion of matter. He, after he had furveyed all the Records of Antiquity, after the volumes of men, betook himfelf to the ftudy of the volume of the world; and having conquer'd whatever books poffeft (his fpacious fpirit not thus bounded) fet upon the Kingdom of Nature, and carried that victory very far, and which was more than thofe victories, himfelf being mortal, left fuch laws behind him, as may fuffice to fubdue the reft, if Princes encourage men, and men be not wanting to themfelves. This attempt of his was favour'd by the Stars of his Nativity. For it was his felicity to live in the times of two *Great Patrons of Learning*, *King* J A M E S, *Your High-*

nefs

nefs Grand-father of bleffed memory, and Your Royal
Father now Reigning; and it was their glory that he
lived in their times; and will be the eternal honour of
this Nation, that the *Greateſt Kings* and the *Greateſt
Philoſopher* met together in one age, in one Iſland.
By the favour of *his Prince,* who well knew the value of
Learning and Learned men, He was raiſed to the higheſt
dignities in the Civil ſtate; and by his own happy Genius, to the higheſt degree in the ſtate of Learning;
which was the greateſt wonder of the two; being ſuch
incompatible perfections, and divided, enough to fill up
the Sphere of the greateſt ablities alive. Yet with great
applauſe he acted both theſe high parts, of the greateſt
Scholar, and the greateſt States-man of his time: and ſo
quit himſelf in both, as one and the ſame Perſon, in
title and merit; became Lord Keeper of the Great Seal
of *England,* and of the Great Seal of Nature both at
once; which is a Myſtery beyond the comprehenſion of
his own times, and a Miracle requires a great meaſure
of Faith in Poſterity; to believe it. This is the Author
I here preſent unto *Your Highneſs,* this his work,
which by the powerful influence of Your favour ſhall
proſper, and, it may be, be quickned to the regeneration
of another *Phœnix* out of his Aſhes, to adorn your
World: for it is only the benign aſpect, and irradiati-
on of *Princes,* that inſpires the Glob of Learning, and
makes Arts and Sciences, grow up and flouriſh. Heaven
bleſs *Your Highneſs* with bleſſings on the right hand, and
on the left, and make You Heir of all the vertues of
your Royal Progenitors, that the Honour of Princes

begun

begun in them, may be continued in Your person; and that a future age may be so blessed in You, as the present is in Your Royal Father, *the Glory of Kings and their Admiration.*

YOUR HIGHNESS

Most humbly devoted

GILBERT WATS

FA-

FAVOURABLE
READER.

HE *intended* Apologetick, *for the In-stauration of Sciences,* and *the justifi-cation of* this Author, *which should have been prefix'd this work, as a preparation thereto*; *is not publisht. Motives to this resolution, were divers, whereof some are very concerning.* Apologeticks *for such Authors and such enterprises are entertained with jealousies, as if they threatned an innovation in the state of Learning*; *by reversing the judgements of* Antiquity, *and the Placits of the* Modern ; *and by bringing in a new* Primum Mobile, *into the Intellectual Globe of Sciences , to the subversion of the Arts received. But these are groundless fears, fancied by such, who either understand not the intention of this at-tempt* ; *or, engag'd in a* Professory *way, suspect their pro-fit and reputation to be in danger, if such designs should take effect.* Our Author *protests against such daring vanities,* the raising *of any new* Sect, *upon the ruins of* Antiquity ; *and every where endeavours to improve the labours of Ancient and Modern Writers, and so must he do who defends him, if he understands the business he goes about.* The *point is not, touch-ing what is already done* ; *nor of the Abilities of the Agents*; *nor of the capacity of their Instruments* ; *which could not be undertaken without emulous comparisons, both of Persons,* A-*ctions and Things* : *but the point is touching* propagation *and* advancement *of* Knowledges; *the improvement, and not the conservation only of the Patrimony of our Ancestors* : *and that by opening to the* understanding *a different way, than hath been known to former Ages*; *and clearing that glass to the letting in of a more plentiful light.* The *ways and ends of these two knowledges (I mean of what we have, and of what we may have) thus different*; *and the princi-*

ples,

ples upon which they proceed so divers; both may consist
without contradictions and confutations; or the invasions
upon their distinguisht rights : and so the propagation of
Knowledge, by the assistance, of the Father of Lights, may
be pursued, with the reservation of the honour of Ancient
and Modern Authors, and the Arts in use, which respecting the end whereto they were instituted, Disputation, Redargution, and the like, are very conducent, and in their
way of perfection highly exalted. And this is the first
motive of deliberating the publication of my Apologetick,
the difficulty of the business. Another is this. The times
into which we are fallen, are learned Times, as ever were
since the Grecian Philosophers, and, their seconds, the Arabian Writers, which also through the great advantages of
the experiments of later Ages, and the directions of Antiquity, in many particulars have out-gone their Predecessors;
so as he that dare adventure, as, some do, to intrude unstudied
thoughts upon so learned an Age as this is, neither reve-
rences the age as he ought, nor wisely consults his own reputation with Posterity. And as the Times are learned, so
(which too frequently falls out) somewhat confident. Great
Wits, and which have fortified their conceptions by books
and study, are strongly prepossest with almost impregnible anticipations; and not so easily induced, as more inconcerned
and disengaged natures are; to know or unknow any thing,
that either should be farther inquired into, or should be forgotten. And much within these two Orbs our Apology moves;
in discovery of Ignorance, and of Error; of what we know
not, and of what we should not know. For certainly much
knowledge remains yet conceal'd, and the way to this discovery is by foregoing many unprofitable subtilties; and by a
learn'd ignorance falling off from many aery speculations
to the solid simplicity of the Ancients. Were we to
compass a Panegirick in praise of the perfections of the
learning of our days; which indeed merits such a sacrifice, the labour were but half what it is, for laudato-
ry hymns seldom come out of season; they need no
preparations, and what might be wanting in the
weight of speech, would be supplied by an aptitude
to accept and believe. But in the business in hand, the

mind

mind of man, *the principal subject to be wrought upon, and* her speculations, *both which we so admire, are so immur'd and blockt up with corrupt notions, either from the placits of Philosophers, the depraved Laws of Demonstration, or from inherent qualities in the general nature of man, or individuate temperature of particulars; that nothing can be done until these be convinced; at least, subjected to examination : which is another motive that stays me upon the Land.* An other Reason (*which is the last I will trouble the Reader withall*)*is this. Time the measure of all our Actions, without whose assistance our best conceptions are* Abortives, *by the intercurrence of other engagements (which I might have dispenced withall, had I rightly understood the servile tenure of secular contracts)hath surpriz'd me. I conceive, which I pronounce with some passion, that a Scholar for his studies had been the master of his own hours; but he that traficks with the world shall find it otherwise. Time which I presum'd I could command,and stay as I do my Watch, hath commanded me. And these diversions were seconded* (Humane Reader) *by a sad Accident. It pleased God in the heat of my attendance on this business, to take away, by one of the terrors of mortality, the* Stone, *my dear brother Sir* Richard Scot, *servant to the most eminent* Lord, *the* Lord Deputy General *of* Ireland; *beloved of his dear* Lord *to the latest minute of life; honour'd with his presence to the farthest confines of mortality; and there, by his Noble Piety, deliver'd up, with as much solemnity, as a Kingdom could confer, unto the immortality of another* World. *This deadly shaft passing through him, so wounded me, that I my self was arrived within few paces of the land of darkness. In his silent Marble, the best part of that small portion of joy I had in the World; but all my* hopes *are entombed. This pensive casualty so took me off from books and business, as for some months after, I could relish no thoughts but what were mingled with the contemplations of mortality.*

      Sic fugit intercà fugit irrevocabile tempus.

These were the impediments to my APOLOGETICK; .   [B 2]   *which*

which (*if what is done be accepted*) *shall be prefixt the*
NOV. ORG. *For of this Translation this is the*
first part (Reader.) *if it please thee ; if it please thee*
not, the last. But before I take my leave , here are some
tacite objections, which I would meet half way, and
and so weaken their approaches, left they fall too heavy
upon me. The first is, *touching the* Division *of the first*
book into Chapters, *contrary to the mind of the Author,*
and the intention of the work. This exception may be thus
satisfied, That profit is to be preferred before artificial con-
trivance, where both cannot so conveniently be had ; and to
this end, discretion to be followed before rule. Were the
Author now alive and his vast designs going on, this altera-
tion had been somewhat bold : but the inimitable Architect
now dead , having perfected little more than the outward
Courts, as it were, of his magnificent Instauration ; and the
whole summ of Sciences, and the stock of Arts in present
possession, not able to defray the charges of finishing this Fa-
brick ; I thought fit, by compartitions and distributions into
several rooms, to improve what we have, to our best advan-
tage, so it might be done without prejudice to the Authors
procedure, and apt coherence, which I hope it is : Having
respect herein rather to accommodation than decoration ; for
Houses (*as our Author says*) are built to live in, and not to
look on, *and therefore use to be preferred before* uniformity. *Another exception may be made against the draught*
of the Platform *into* Analitick Tables, *which seems some-*
what pedantick, and against that common rule, Artis eft dif-
fimulare Artem. *To this I answer thus.* Order *and de-*
pendance is, as it were, the soul of the World, of the Works
of Nature and Art, and that which keeps them united ,
without which all would fall asunder, and become like the
first Chaos before the production of light. And of all Methods *that ever were, at least that ever came to our hands,*
our Authors is the most natural, and most dependent. For
Truth, *as it reflects on us, is a congruent conformity of the*
Intellect *to the* Object *; and of the different faculties thereof*
to the difference of things : wherefore the truest Partition *of*
humane Learning, is that, which hath reference to humane
faculties ; when the Intellectual Globe, *and the Globe of*

the

the World, *intermix their beams and irradiations in a direct line of projection, to the Generation of Sciences. This our Author hath perform'd to admiration; and in this gone beyond all Antiquity, yet upon their grounds; wherein he can never be out-gone, unless followed by Posterity. The Ancients indeed were men of most profound speculations, but in the delivery of themselves, somewhat involv'd, as appears by* Plotinus, Proclus, Trismegistus *and others; and many of* Platoes *School writ Dialogue-wise, which is no doctrinal way. As for* Aristotle, *his precepts touching* Method *(if any such book was written) they are perisht, saving where he scatters such rules here and there, which should have been silenced, and are not so well followed by himself. And for the* Methods *of the Moderns,* Ramus *and others, by the improvement of* German *Writers, impair'd; they knit the limbs of knowledge too soon; have bedwarfed Sciences, and are become an Art (as learned* Hooker *expresses it) which teaches the way of speedy discourse, and restrains the mind of man, that it may not wax over-wise. The Excellency therefore of our Authors* Partitions, *induced me to these delineations, for their use only, who have not the leasure, or patience to observe it according to the merit; that by this* Anatomy, *the junctures and arteries, as it were, of this great body might more visibly appear.* Another objection is, *touching the* Allegations in the Margin, *contrary to the solemn custom of Antiquity, and the most of graver Authors. For this I had these reasons. It pleased our Author, though he was himself a living fountain of Knowledge, and had a wealthy stock of his own, yet to taste of other waters, and to borrow from Antiquity, and to acknowledge such borrowings;* He thus naming his Authors, *I thought fit to note them. And as he was a man of a most elevated phansie and choice conceptious, so was he in the selection of his Authors, and the passages he pleas'd to make use of: and it is worth the labour to know with whom such great Wits use to converse; to point to the Mines where they dig their Ore; and to the shadows where they repose at noon. And as his selection of Authors was very choice, so was his application of their sayings, very curious; and in a strain beyond the vulgar reach. Places out of* Sacred Scriptures *are so explicated*
cated

cated, *so applyed, as you may search all the Commenters that are extant, and not find the like expositions, as you shall find in him. As for humane Authors he betters his borrowings from them; teaching the allegations out of them, a sence above the meaning of him that lent it him; and which he repairs too with double interest for what he borrowed. These considerations invited me to Marginal Citations. These Reasons set apart, I cannot approve this weak ambition; and do, not without censure, read Modern Authors prostitute to humane allegations; as if the Truth they deliver, were to be tryed by voices; or having lost its primitive Innocence, must be cover'd with these fig-leaves; or as if the Authors themselves were afraid that it should make an escape out of their Text, if it were not beset in the Margin with Authorities as with a Watch. The last exception is, touching the Prefaces, and other Introductions prefix'd this work, that make the Gates and Entries so wide, as they seem to invite the City to run away. This is thus answer'd. It must be remembred that this work in the Design was very spacious; and is in the performance of what is done so ample, that when the second and third Parts shall be added, (as added they will be) the Porches and Ingresses, in the judgement of any good Architect, are proportionable enough. And if our Authors rule hold, that every fair Fabrick should have three Courts; a green Court, a second Court more garnisht, and a third to make a square with the Front; then have you here this Epistle as the mean Court; Judgements upon this Author living and dead, as the middle Court; and the Authors own excellent Preface to confront with the work it self. Now I should say something touching Translation; and as it is mine. The very Action is somewhat obnoxious to censure; being of the nature of those, the falling whereof may disgrace more, than the carrying of it through, credit the undertaker. But, besides the conscience of the deed done; for other ends I could not have; (the Author now dead; and alive* mihi nec injuriis nec beneficiis notus) *and that to be a* Translator *is more than to be an* Author, *some such as there be; and that it is no such mean office, to bear a light before a* Lord *Chancellor of* England : *I should excuse it, were the example mine : so, writes learned* Sa-
vil

vil ; *so, eloquent* Sandys ; *so,* Malvezzi's Noble Interpreter ; *with whom conferred I am less than a shadow : So, ma-*
ny able and eminent names of France *and* Italy *, and other*
Nations ; So the Ancients of former Ages and of all Argu-
ments. : But if any be so solemn, so severe, and of such
primitive tastes, they can away with no waters, which come
not from the spring-head ; nor endure to drink of Tiber*,*
that passes through Thames *; They may give over here, if*
they so please, and proceed no farther. This interpretation
was not meant for such fastidious palates, and yet, it may be,
for as distinguishing as theirs are. Now if this very acti-
on be thus liable to exception, much more must my perfor-
mance be. Certainly books by Translation *commonly take*
wind in the effusion ; and for strength fall short of their O-
riginals ; as reflexed beams are weaker than direct : but
then it must be understood of Originals *, truly so. For if*
a Writer *deliver himself out of his Native Language, I*
see not why a Translator *rendring him in it, may not come*
near him : and in this case, the Author himself is the Interpreter*, being he* translates *his own thoughts, which ori-*
ginally speak his mother tongue. Yet for all this, Errors
I know there are, and some lapses, which require a con-
nivence ; and a Reader hath this advantage, that he may
stay upon one period, as long as an Interpreter did on one page ;
besides his peculiar Genius to some studied passages. Some
Errors (passing but a trasient eye upon what is done) I see
already ; and could note them ; but I would not willingly
gratifie some kind of Readers so far. They that are Ju-
ditious and Ingenious too (for I would have no Readers that
have not these two ingredients in their compositions, though
sometimes I name but one, which I would then, should be
predominant) will in their judgement find them, and in their
mercy pardon them. As for Sophists *and* Satyrists*, a dege-*
nerate Race of men, that sit upon the lives and learning
of all that write ; who resolv'd to do nothing themselves,
may with more security censure others : and them too, who,
as Learned Don *deciphers them, forbid not books, but*
men ; damning what ever such a name, hath, or shall
write : *they are things below the merit of my indignation ;*
objects of scorn ; which a little slighted, and not inflamed
by

by opposition, or countenanced to a reply by confutation, will within a while, of themselves, extinguish and vanish : like some dispersed roving winds, which without encounter are dispirited and die. And it concerns me, *Courteous Reader,* to put on such a confidence as this; for being I am likely to appear in mine own person, as I do now in the person of another; to be too tender-fronted were to invite injuries, and to prostitute such unseasonable modesty to abuse. He that will to sea, must look for some cloudy days; and to be too scrupulous or Ceremonious touching Times or Persons, *is the bane of business, and of all well-meant* endeavours : according to that of Solomon, Qui observat ventum non seminat, & qui considerat nubes, nunquam metet.

TESTI-

To the

MERIT

OF THE

INCOMPARABLE · PHILOSOPHER .

Sir *FRANCIS BACON*,

B Y

Some of the Beſt-learn'd of this inſtant Age.

 Lthough *ſevere Inquiſitors of truth*, and ſuch who by their learned Labours ſtand upon publick Record in the approv'd Archives of Eternity, may, in an humble diſtance, lay claim and title to that ſacred Prerogative— *Ego autem ab homine Teſtimonium non Capto* ; *ipſa enim Opera quæ facio teſtantur de me* ; —— yet becauſe ſuch *Great Authors*, in their high flight, are ſo leſſen'd in the air of unfrequented contemplations; and take ſuch unbeaten ways, as they become the *weak wonder* of common Capacities, accuſtom'd to popular opinions, and authoriz'd Errors : and in this admiring Ignorance, the *prejudicate objects* of Emulation, Envy, Jealouſies, and ſuch like impotent paſſions : It ſeems (in a ſort) neceſſary, that the way be clear'd before ſuch Writers ; and that they enter the Theatre, as well with the ſuffrage of *voice* , to gain upon the *will*; as with the ſtrength of *Reaſon*, to convince the *Underſtanding*.

Wherefore, not ſo much for the honour of this Author, (though that is intended too) as for the aid of ſome anticipate Readers, not yet manu-miſſed from a ſervile belief to the liberty of their own judgements, (ſuch, I mean, as are yet under the minority of an implicite faith,) I thought good to deliver this imperfect liſt of *Deponents*, which the precipitancy of this Edition, would not permit to fill up with ſome other *great Names*, both of this Kingdom, and of forreign Nations. What is wanting here to the accompliſhment of this *Catalogue*, Time, *the Parent of Truth*, ſhall conſummate.

Le Sieur Maugars Counſellor and Secretary to the King of *France*,

[C]

in

in the Epiſtle to his Tranſlation of a Part of this Work, gives our Author this Teſtimony.

Amongſt whom every one knows that Sir Francis Bacon, by many degrees off, holds the firſt rank, both for the vivacity of his Spirit, eminency of his Learning, Elegancy of his ſtile. I have ſtudied with diligence all his writings; and preſume I may do a performance of ſome merit and acceptation, in preſenting to my Country his Books of the Advancement of Learning, a Work hath not been ſeen in our Language. This is the Book which I have cauſed to paſs the Seas; not as the gold of the Indies, to cheriſh vice, and corrupt our Manners; but as a ſoveraign Plant of ſingular vertue, to cure the wounds which ignorance and Pedantiſm have given humane Sciences.

Mr. Peirre D' Ambois. Sr de la Magdelaine, in his juſt and elegant diſcourſe upon the life of our Author, delivers his cenſure thus:

Judgement and Memory never met in any man in that height and meaſure they met in him; ſo as in ſhort time he became Maſter of all thoſe Knowledges which are learnt in Schools.

A page after; but as he ever valued himſelf, rather born for other men, than himſelf; now that he could not, for want of imployment, any longer endow the publick with his Active perfections; he was deſirous at leaſt to become profitable in a Contemplative way, by his writings and by his books, monuments certainly meriting to find entertainment in all the Libraries of the world; and which deſerve to be ranged with the faireſt works of Antiquity.

The ſame noble French-man in his Advertiſement to our Authors *Nat. Hiſtory* thus expreſſes him.

For this Natural Hiſtory, where the quality of Metals, the Nature of Elements, the Cauſes of Generation and Corruption, the divers actions of Bodies one upon another, and ſuch like impreſſions, are diſcourſed with ſuch life and light, that he may ſeem to have learn'd his knowledge even in the School of the Firſt Man. And though herein he may be thought to have paſs'd upon the breaches of Ariſtotle, Pliny and Cardan; yet notwithſtanding he borrows nothing from them: as if he had a deſign to make it appear, that thoſe great men have not ſo entirely poſſeſt themſelves of this ſubject, but that there remains much to be diſcover'd. For my part, though it be far from my intention, to raiſe the reputation of this Author upon the ruins of Antiquity; yet I think it may be avouched upon the grounds of reaſon, that in this preſent Argument he hath ſome advantage of them: being that the moſt of the Ancients which have written of things Natural, have ſatisfied themſelves in reporting things, as the information of others hath given them intelligence; and conſidering, that oftentimes that which is deliver'd them for Hiſtory, is far eſloign'd from all verity; they have choſen rather, by reaſons to confirm the reſolutions of another, than to make an exact enquiry, and diſcovery themſelves. But Monſieur Bacon not relying upon the meer word and credit of ſuch as went before him, will have Experience joyn'd with Reaſon; and examines the receiv'd principles of the Schools, by the effects of Nature; the ſpeculations of the Intellectual Globe, by the

operation

operations of the Corporal. *By this means he hath found out so many rare secrets, whereof he hath bequeath'd us the invention; and made many axioms acknowledged for false, which hitherto have gone current amongst* Philosophers, *and have been held inviolable.*

Tob. Adami, in his Preface to the *Realis Philosophia,* of that excellent Philosopher *Campanella* (who lives to enjoy that Fame, which many eminent for their Learning, rarely possess after death) speaks his opinion thus.

We erect no Sect, establish no Placits of Heresie, but endeavour to transcribe universal and ever-veritable Philosophy out of the Ancient Original Copy of the World: not according to variable and disputable speculations, but according to the Conducture of sense and irrefragable depositions of the Architect himself, whose hands in works, dissents not from his word in writing. And if the great Instauration *of the deepmining Philosopher,* Francis Bacon, Lord Verulam, Chancellor of England, *a work of high expectation, and most worthy, as of consideration, so of assistance, be brought to perfection, it will perchance appear, that we pursue the same ends; seeing we tread the same foot-steps in tracing, and, as it were, hounding nature, by* Sence *and* Experience, *&c.*

Sr. *Tob. Mathews,* in his Epistle to the Duke of *Florence* prefixt his Italick Translation of my *Lord Bacon's Essays,* amongst other Elogies decyphers him thus.

St. Austin *said of his illegitimate son,* Horrori mihi erat illud ingenium, *and truly I have known a great number whom I much value, many whom I admire, but none who hath so astonisht me, and, as it were, ravisht my senses, to see so many and so great parts, which in other men were wont to be incompatible, united, and that in an iminent degree in one sole Person. I know not whether this truth will find easie belief, that there can be found a man beyond the* Alpes, *of a most ready wit; most faithful memory; most profound judgement; of a most rich and apt expression; universal in all kinds of knowledge, as in part may be seen by that rare incomparable piece, the* Advancement of Learning, *which future Ages shall render in different languages: But be the faith of other Nations what it will in this point, the matter I report is so well understood in* England, *that every man knows and acknowledges as much, nay, hath been an eye and ear-witness thereof; nor, if I should expatiate upon this subject, should I be held a flatterer, but rather a suffragan to truth.*

Mr. *George Sandys* in his excellent Commentaries on his inimitable Translation of the stately *Metamorphosis,* rendred, in an equal felicity of expression, to the eternal fires of that *sweet-tongu'd Roman;* often cites the judgement of our Author, from whose sentence he never appeals, but rather adores as an Oracle; and in an ingenious acknowledgement of assistance from him, thus delivers him to posterity.

Of Modern writers I have receiv'd the greatest light from Geraldus, Pontanus, Ficinus, Vives, Comes, Scaliger, Sabinus, *and the Crown of the later, the Vicount of St.* Albans; *assisted, though less constantly*

con-

conſtantly,by other Authors, almoſt of all Ages and Arguments. Having been true to my firſt purpoſe, in making choice, for the moſt part, of thoſe interpretations, which either bear the ſtamp of Antiquity, *or receive eſtimation from the* honour of the Author.

Marin Merſenne, An able man, but a declar'd adverſary to our Authors deſign (whoſe Arguments I ſhall encounter in my Apologetick for the *Inſtaur. of Sciences*) in his Book of the *Verity of Sciences* againſt the *Scepticks* and *Pyrrhonians, Lib.* I. *Cap.* XVI. acknowledges thus much, which coming from an Adverſary is therefore more valid.

Verulam, ſeems to have no other intention in his New Method, *then to eſtabliſh the* Verity of Sciences; *wherefore you muſt not anticipate, as granted, that he makes for you, or that he is of your opinion; he confeſſes we know little, but he ſubverts not the Authority of* Senſe *and of* Reaſon, *no, he labours to find out proper and proportionable inſtruments, whereby to conduct the underſtanding to the knowledge of Nature and her effects.*

The Authors Cenſure upon himſelf.

For in my judgement, it is a matter which concerns not only the Benefit of others; but our own Repetition alſo; that no man imagine that we have projected in our minds ſome ſlight ſuperficial notion of theſe Deſigns; *and that they are of the nature of thoſe things, which we could* Deſire, *and which we accept only as good wiſhes. For they are ſuch as without queſtion, are within the power and poſſibility of men to compaſs, unleſs they be wanting to themſelves; and hereof, we for our parts, have certain and evident demonſtration; for we come not hither,* as Augures, to meaſure Countries in our mind, for Divinations; but as Captains, to invade them for conqueſt.

His anſwer to ſome Tacite Objections.

I do foreſee that many of thoſe things which I ſhall regiſter as Deficients *will incur divers cenſures; as that ſome parts of this enterprize were done long ago, and are now extant; others, that they taſte of curioſity and promiſe no great fruit; others, that they are impoſſible to be compaſſed by humane induſtries.* For the two firſt, *let the particulars ſpeak for themſelves.* For the laſt touching impoſſibilities, *I determine thus. All thoſe things are to be held poſſible and performable which may be accompliſht by ſome perſon, though not by every one; and which may be done by the united labours of many, though not by any one apart, and which may be effected in a ſucceſſion of Ages, though not in the ſame Age; and in brief, which may be fimſht by the care and charge of the publick, though not by the abilities and induſtry of private perſons. If for all this there be any, who would rather take to himſelf that of* Solomon, Dicit Piger, Leo eſt in via, *than that of* Virgil

Poſſunt quia poſſe videntur——

it is enough for me, if my labours may be eſteemed as votes, yet the better ſort of wiſhes: for as it asks ſome knowledge to demand a Queſtion not impertinent; ſo it requires ſome underſtanding, to make a wiſh not abſurd. *Proem. lib.* 2.

IN HONOREM

ILLUSTRISSIMI DOMINI

FRANCISCI

DE

VERULAMIO

Vice-Comitis S^{cti} *ALBANI:*

Poſt Editam ab eo INSTAUR. MAG.

Qvis iſte tandem? non enim vultu ambulat
   Quotidiano. Neſcis Ignare? audies:
Dux Notionum; veritatis Pontifex;
Inductionis Dominus; & Verulamii;
Rerum Magiſter unicus, at non Artium:
Profunditatis Pinus; atq; Elegantiæ:
Naturæ Aruſpex intimus: Philoſophiæ
Ærarium: Sequeſter Experientiæ,
Speculationiſq; Æquitatis Signifer:
Scientiarum ſub pupillari ſtatu
Degentium olim Emancipator: luminis
Promus: Fugator Idolûm, atq; Nubium:
Collega Solis: Quadra Certitudinis:
Sophiſmatum Maſtix: Brutus Literarius,
Authoritatis exuens Tyrannidem:
Rationis & ſenſus ſtupendus Arbiter;
Repumicator Mentis: Atlas Phyſicus,
Alcide ſuccumbente Stagiritico:
Columba Noæ, quæ in vetuſtis Artibus
Nullum locum, requiemve Cernens, præſtitit,
Ad ſe ſuamq; Matris Arcam regredi.
Subtilitatis terebra; Temporis nepos
Ex veritate matre: Mellis Alveus.

Mundiq;

Mundiq; & Animarum, facerdos unicus :
Securis Errorum : inq; Natalibus
Granum finapis, acre aliis, Crefcens fibi.
O me, propè Laffum ; Juvate Pofteri.

GEOR. HERBERT Orat. Pub.
in Academ. Cantab.

MANES

MANES

VERULAMIANI:

SIVE

IN OBITUM

INCOMPARABILIS

FRANCISCI

DE

VERULAMIO, &c.

EPICEDIA.

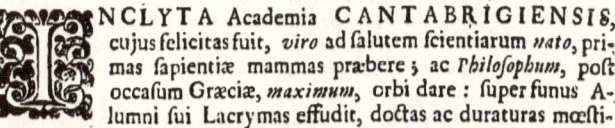NCLYTA Academia CANTABRIGIENSIS, cujus felicitas fuit, *viro ad salutem scientiarum nato*, primas sapientiæ mammas præbere; ac *Philosophum*, post occasum Græciæ, *maximum*, orbi dare : super funus Alumni sui Lacrymas effudit, doctas ac duraturas mœstitias. Ex hoc integro Musarum fonte, modica hæc sed facunda fluenta, collegit *interpres*; ut quod, viventi, seculum dederat decus, gliscente adhuc invidiâ; & morienti dedisse constaret, cessante nunc adulatione. Reliqua sui nominis æternitati consecranda, continuatâ seculorum serie ad ultimas usq; mundi favillas, rependet posteritas : Quis supremam suis laudibus manum imponet, novit tantum *Fundator ille, ac simul eversor Seculorum.*

Adhuc

ADhuc superbis insolente purpurâ
Feretri rapinis Inclitos in tot viros
Sterile Tribunal ? cilicio dicas diem,
Saccúmq; totam facito luxuriem fori.
A Themide libra nec geratur pensilis,
Sed urna, pragravis urna Verulamii.
Expendat. Eheu ! Ephorus haud lancem premit,
Sed Areopagus; nec minor tantus sophos,
Quàm Porticus bracchata. Nam vester, scholæ,
Gemiscit axis, tanta dum moles ruit.
Orbis soluta cardo litterarii,
Ubi studio coluit togam & trabeam pari.
Qualis per umbras Ditis Euridice vagans
Palpare gestiit Orphëum, quali Orphëus,
Saliente tandem (vix prius crispâ) Styge,
Alite fibras lyræ titillavit manu;
Talis plicata Philologon ænigmatis
Petiit Baconum vindicem, tali manu
Lactata cristas extulit Philosophia,
Humiq; soccis reptitantem Comicis
Non proprio Ardelionibus molimine
Sarsit, sed Instauravit. Hinc politiùs
Surgit cothurno celsiore, & Organo
Stagirita Virbius reviviscit Novo.
    Calpen superbo Abylámq; vincit remige
Phoebi Columbus, artibus novis, Novum
Daturus Orbem; promovit conamina
Juvenilis ardor, usq; ad invidiam trucem
Fati minacis. Quis Senex vel Hannibal,
Oculi superstitis timens caliginem,
Signis Suburram ventilat victricibus ?
Quis Milo inultus quercubus bilem movet,
Senecta tauro gibba cùm gravior premit ?
Dum noster Heros traderet scientias
Æternitati, prorsus expeditior
Sui Sepulchri comperitur artifex.
Placida videtur Ecstasis speculatio,
Quâ mens tueri volucris Idæas boni
In lacteos properat Olympi tramites.
His immoratur sedibus Domestica,
Peregrina propriis. Redit. Jocularitèr
Fugax; vagatur rursus, & rursus redit.
Furtiva tandem seriò, se subtrahit
Totam; gementi, morbido cadaveri
Sic desuescit anima, sic jubet mori.
    Agite lugubres Musæ, & à Libani jugis
Cumulate thura, Sydus in pyram illius
Scintillet omne; scelus si accendi rogum
Regum Prometheo culinari foco.

Et si qua fortè ludat in cineres sacros
Aura petulantior, fugamq; suadeat,
Tunc flete ; lacrymis in amplexus ruent
Globuli sequaces. Denuò fundamine
Ergastuli everso radicitùs tui
Evehere fœlix anima, Jacobum *pete,*
Ostende, & illuc, civicam fidem *sequi.*
E Tripode juris, dictites oracula
Themidos *alumnis. Sic (Beati cœlites)*
Astræa *pristino fruatur vindice,*
Vel cum Bacono *rursus* Astræam *date.*

R. P.

---

*A*Udax *exemplum qnò Mens humana feratur,*
  Et Sæcli vindex ingeniose tui ;
Dum senio macras recoquis fœliciter artes,
  Subtrahis & prisco libera colla jugo ;
Quo deflenda modo veniunt tua funera ? quales
  Exposcunt lacrymas; quid sibi fata valunt ?
An timuit Natura parens ne nuda jaceret,
  Detraxit vestem dum tua dextra sacram ?
Ignotiq; oculis rerum patuere Recessus,
  Fugit & aspectum Rimula nulla tuum ?
An verò, Antiquis olim data Sponsa Maritis,
  Conjugis amplexum respuit illa novi ?
An tandem damnosa piis atq; invida cœptis,
  Corripuit vitæ fila (trahenda) tuæ ?
Sic ultra vitreum Siculus *ne pergeret orbem*   Atchim.
  Privati cecidit militis ense Senex.
*Tùq; tuos manes ideò (*Francisce*) tulisti,*
  Ne, non tentandum, perficeretur opus.

---

*S*Unt qui defuncti vivant in marmore, & ævum*
  Annosis credant postibus omne suum :
Ære micant alii, aut fulvo spectantur in auro,
  Et, dum se ludunt, ludere fata putant.
Altera pars hominum, numerosâ prole superstes,
  Cum Niobe *magnos temnit iniqua* Deos.
At tua cælatis hæret nec Fama Columnis,
  Nec tumulo legitur, Siste viator iter :
Si qua Patrem proles referat, noncorporis illa est,
  Sed quasi de cerebro nata Minerva Jovis.
Prima tibi virtus monumenta perennia præstat,
  Altera, nec citiùs corruitura, Libri :
Tertia Nobilitas ; ducant jam fata triumphos,
  *Quæ (*Francisce*) tui nil nisi corpus habent.*

i   **[D]**   Utraq;

Utraq; pars melior, Mens & bona Fama superſunt,
Non tanti ut redimas vile cadaver habes.

T. Vincent. T. C.

MUſæ fundite nunc aquas perennes
  In Threnos, Lacrymáſq; Apollo fundat
Quas vel Caſtalium tenet Fluentum:
Nam Letho neq; convenire tanto
Poſſint nænia parva, nec coronent
Immenſa hæc modicæ ſepulchra guttæ:
Nervus ingenii, Medulla ſuadæ
Dicendiq; Tagus, reconditarum
Et gemma pretioſa Literarum,
Fatis concidit, (heu trium Sororum
Dura ſtamina) Nobilis Baconus.
O quam te memorem Bacone ſumme
Noſtro carmine! & illa glorioſa
Cunctorum monumenta ſeculorum,
Excuſa ingenio tuo, & Minervâ!
Quam doctis, elegantibus, profundis,
Inſtauratio. Magna, plena rebus!
Quanto lumine tineas Sophorum;
Diſpellit veterum tenebricoſas
Ex chao pocreans novam ſοφίαν:
Sic ipſe Deus inditum ſepulchro
Corpus reſtituet manu potenti:
Ergo non moreris (Bacone) nam te
A morte, & tenebris, & a ſepulchro,
Inſtauratio Magna vindicabit.

R. C. T. C.

PArcite:. Noſter amat facunda ſilentia luctus,
  Poſtquam obiit ſolus dicere qui potuit:
Dicere, quæ ſtupeat Procerum generoſa corona,
  Nexaq; ſollicitis ſolvere Jura reis.
Vaſtum opus. At noſtras etiam Verulamius artes
  Inſtaurat veteres, condit & ille novas.
Non quâ majores: Penitus verum ille receſſus
  Naturæ, audaci provocat ingenio.
Aſt Ea, ſiſte gradum, ſeriſq; nepotibus, (inquit,)
  Linque quod inventum ſæcla minora juvet.
Sit ſatis, his ſeſe quod nobilitata Juventis,
  Jactent ingenio tempora noſtra tuo.

Eſt

Est aliquid, quo mox ventura superbiet ætas;
  Est, soli notum quod decet esse mihi:
Sit tua laus pulchros Corpus duxisse per artus,
  Integra cui nemo reddere membra queat:
Sic opus artificem infectum commendat Apellem,
  Cum pingit reliquam nulla manus Venerem.
Dixit, & indulgens cæco Natura *furori,*
  Præsecuit vitæ Filum Operisq; simul.
At Tu, qui pendentem audes detexere telam,
  Solus quem condant hæc monumenta scies.

                    H. T. Coll. Trin. Socius.

Dum moriens tantam nostris Verulamius Heros
  Tristitiam Musis, *luminaq; uda facit:*
Credimus heu nullum fieri post fata beatum,
  Credimus & Samium desipuisse senem.
Scilicet hic miseris, fælix nequit esse, Camænis,
  Nec se quàm Musas plus amat iste suas.
At luctantem animam Clotho imperiosa coëgit
  Ad cælum, invitos traxit in astra pedes.
Ergone Phœbeias jacuisse putabimus artes?
  Atq; herbas Clarii nil valuisse Dei?
Phœbus idem potuit, nec virtus abfuit herbis,
  Hunc artem, atq; illas vim retinere putes:
At Phœbum (ut metuit ne Rex foret iste Camænis)
  Rivali medicam crede negâsse manum.
Hinc dolor est; quod cum Phœbo Verulamius Heros
  Major erat reliquis, hâc foret arte minor.
Vos tamen ô, tantum Manes àtq; Umbra, Camænæ,
  Et pœnè inferni pallida turba Jovis,
Si spiratis adhuc, & non lusistis ocellos,
  Sed neq; post illum vos superesse putem:
Si vos ergo aliquis de morte reduxerit Orpheus,
  Istaq; non aciem fallit imago meam:
Discite nunc gemitus, & lamentabile carmen,
  Ex oculis vestris lacryma multa fluat.
En quam multa fluit? veras agnosco Camænas
  Et lacrymas, Helicon vix satis unus erit;
Deucalionæis & qui non mersus in undis
  Pernassus (mirum est) hisce latebit aquis.
Scilicet hic periit, per quem vos vivitis, & qui
  Multâ Pierias nutriit arte Deas.
Vidit ut hic artes nullâ radice retentas,
  Languere ut summo semina sparsa solo;
Crescere Pegaseas docuit, velut Hasta Quirini
  Crevit, & exiguo tempore Laurus erat.

                    [D 2]   *Ergo*

Ergo Heliconiadas *docuit cùm crescere* divas,
  Diminuent hujus secula nulla decus.
Nec ferre ulterius generosi pectoris æstus
  Contemptum potuit, Diva Minerva, *tuum.*
Restituit calamus solitum divinus honorem,
  Dispulit & nubes alter Apollo *tuas.*

Dispulit & tenebras sed quas obfusca vetustas,
  Temporis & prisci lippa senecta tulit;
Atq; alias methodos sacrum instauravit acumen,
  Gnossiaq; eripuit, sed sua fila dedit.
Scilicet antiquo sapientûm vulgus in ævo
  Tam claros oculos non habuisse liquet;
Hi veluti Eoo *surgens de littore* Phœbus,
  Hic velut in mediâ fulget Apollo *die:*
Hi veluti Typhis *tentârunt æquora primùm,*
  At vix descruit littora prima ratis,
Pleiadas hic Hyadasq; *atq; omnia sidera noscens,*
  Syrtes *atq; tuos, improba* Sylla, *canes;*
Scit quod vitandum est, quo dirigat æquore navem,
  Certiùs & cursum nautica monstrat acus:
Infantes illi Musas, *hic gignit adultas;*
  Mortales illi, gignit at iste Deas.
Palmam ideò reliquis Magna Instauratio *libris*
  Abstulit, & cedunt squalida turba sophi.
Et vestita novo Pallas *modo prodit amictu,*
  Anguis depositis ut nitet exuviis.
Sic Phœnix *cineres spectat modò nata paternos,*
  Æsonis *& rediit prima juventa senis.*
Instaurata suos & sic Verulamia *muros*
  Jactat, & antiquum sperat ab inde decus.

Sed quanta effulgent plus quam mortalis ocelli
  Lumina, dum regni mystica sacra canat?
Dum sic naturæ leges, arcanâq; Regum,
  Tanquam à secretis esset utrisque, canat:
Dum canat Henricum, *qui Rex, idemq; Sacerdos,*
  Connubio stabili junxit utramq; Rosam.

Atqui hæc sunt nostris longè majora Camænis,
  Non hæc infœlix Granta, *sed Aula sciat:*
Sed cum Granta *labris admoverit ubera tantis*
  Jus habet in laudes (maxime Alumne) tuas.
Jus habet, ut mæstos lacrymis extingueret ignes,
  Posset ut è medio diripuisse rogo.
At nostræ tibi nulla ferant encomia Musæ,
  Ipse canis, laudes & canis inde tuas.
Nos tamen & laudes, quâ possumus arte, canemus,
  Si tamen ars desit, laus erit iste dolor.

Tho. Randolph. T. C.

Sic cadit Aonii rariſſima Gloria cœtûs ?
  Et placet Aoniis credere ſemen agris ?
Frangantur Calami, diſrumpantúrq; libelli,
  Hoc poſſint tetricæ ſi modo jure Deæ.
Heu quæ lingua ſilet, quæ jam facundia ceſſat;
  Quò fugit ingenii Nectar & Eſca tui ?
Quomodo Muſarum nobis contingit Alumnis
  Ut caderet noſtri præſes Apollo chori ?
Si nil cura, fides, labor, aut vigilantia poſſint,
  Siq; feret rapidas, de tribus una, manus ;
Cur nos multa brevi nobis proponimus ævo ?
  Cur putri excutimus ſcripta ſepulta ſitu ?
Scilicet ut dignos aliorum à Morte labores
  Dum rapimus, nos Mors in ſua jura trahat,
Quid tamen incaſſum nil proficientia fundo
  Verba? quis optabit, te reticente, loqui ?
Nemo tuum ſpargat violis fragrantibus urnam,
  Nec tibi Pyramidum mole ſepulchra locet ;
Nam tua conſervant operoſa volumina famam,
  Hoc ſatis, hæc prohibent te monumenta mori.

Williams.

ORdine ſequeretur deſcriptio Tumuli VERULAMIANI, monumentum Nobiliſſ. MUTISII, in honorem domini ſui conſtructum ; quâ pietate, & dignitatem Patroni ſui, quem (quod rari faciunt, etiam poſt cineres Coluit) conſuluit ; Patriæ ſuæ opprobrium diluit ; ſibi nomen condidit. Buſta hæc nondum in viſit Interpres, ſed inviſurus : Interim Lector tua cura Commoda, & abi in rem tuam.

Creſcit occulto velut Arbor ævo
Fama BACONI.——

FRAN-

FRANCISCUS

BARO DE *VERULAMIO*

Vice-Comes S^{ti} *ALBANI*.

ALMÆ MATRI	INCYTÆ
Inclytæ Acad.	Academiæ.
CANTABRIGIENSI. S.	*OXONIENSI.* S.

DEbita Filii qualia poſſum perſolvo; quod vero facio, idem & vos hortor, ut *Augmentis Scientiarum* ſtrenuè incumbatis : & in Animi modeſtia libertatem ingenii retineatis : Neq; talentum à veteribus concreditum in ſudario reponatis. Aſſuerit proculdubiò & affulſerit Divini Luminis Gratia, ſi humilia-
tâ

CUm *Almæ Matri* meæ inclytæ *Academiæ Cantabrigienſi* Scripſerim, deeſſem ſanè officio, ſi ſimule Amoris pignus ſorori ejus non deferrem. Sicut autem eos hortatus ſum, ita & vos hortor ut *Scientiarum Augmentis* ſtrenuè incumbatis, & veterum labores, neq; nihil, neq; omnia eſſe putetis ; ſe vires etiam

tâ & fubmiſsâ *Religioni Philoſophia* am proprias modeſte perpenden-
clavibus ſenſûs legitimè & dex- tes, ſubinde tamen experiamini,
trè ûtamini : & amoto omni con- omnia cedent quam optimè; ſi
tradiƈtionis ſtudio, Quiſq; cum Arma non alii in alios vertatis ſed
alio, ac ſi ipſe ſecum diſputet, junƈtis copiis in Naturam rerum
Valete. impreſſionem faciatis, ſufficit quip-
pe illa Honori & Viƈtoriæ, *Valete.*

FRAN-

FRANCIS Lord *VERULAM*
Confulted thus,

And thus concluded with Himfelf; the publication whereof he conceiv'd did concern the prefent
and future AGE.

Eing it was manifeftly known unto him, that humane underftanding creates it felf much trouble ;
nor makes an apt and fober ufe of fuch Aids, as
are within the Command of Man ; from whence
infinite ignorance of Things ; and from the ignorance of Things , innumerous difadvantages ; his opinion was, that with all our induftry we fhould endeavour, if
happily that fame Commerce of the Mind and of Things
(than which a greater bleffing can hardly be found on Earth,
certainly of earthly Felicities) might by any means be entirely reftored ; at leaft brought to terms of nearer correfpondence. But that Errors, which have prevailed, and
would prevail for ever, one after another, (if the mind
were left free to it felf) fhould rectifie themfelves, either
by the inbred power of the underftanding, or by the aids and
affiftances of Logick, there was no hope at all; becaufe that
the Primitive Notions of Things, which the mind with a
too facile and fupine attractive faculty receives in , treafures up and accumulates, from which all the reft are derived , are unfound, confufed, and rafhly abftracted from
things. The like luxuriant vanity and inconftancy there is in
the fecond and fequent Notions ; whence it comes to pafs,that
all that humane Reafon which we employ, as touching the Inquifition of things, is not well digefted and built ; but like
fome magnificent Pile without foundation. For whilft men
admire and celebrate the counterfeit forces of the mind ; her
true powers which might be raifed (were right directions adminiftred, and fhe taught to become obfequious to things ,
and not impotently to infult over them) they pafs by and
lofe. This one way remaineth that the bufinefs be wholly
reattempted

[E]

reattemped with better preparations ; and that there be throughout, An Inſtauration of Sciences and Arts, and of all Humane Learning rais'd from ſolid foundations. And this, though it may ſeem in a ſort an infinite enterprize, and above mortal abilities, yet the ſame will be found more ſound and adviſed, than thoſe performances which hitherto have been atchieved : for in this there is ſome iſſue ; but in the endeavours now undertaken about Sciences, a perpetual Wheeling, Agitation and Circle. Neither is he ignorant how unfrequented this Experience is, how difficil and incredible to perſwade a belief ; yet he thought not to deſert the deſign, nor himſelf ; but to try and ſet upon the way, which alone is pervious and penetrable to the mind of Man. For it is better to give a beginning to a thing which may once come to an end, than with an eternal contention and ſtudy to be enwrapt in thoſe mazes which are endleſs. And the ways of Contemplation for the moſt part reſemble thoſe celebrated ways of Action ; the one, at the firſt entrance hard and difficult, ends in an open plain ; the other at firſt ſight ready and eaſie, leads into by-ways and down-falls : And being he was uncertain when ſuch conſiderations ſhould hereafter come into any man's mind, induced eſpecially from this argument, that there hath none hitherto appear'd, who hath applied his mind to ſuch cogitations, he reſolv'd to publiſh, ſeparately, the Fiſt parts as they could be perfected. Neither is this an ambitious but ſollicitous feſtination ; that if in the mean ſpace he ſhould depart this mortal ſtation ; there might yet remain a deſignation and deſtination of the thing he comprehended in his mind ; and withall ſome Demonſtration of his ſincere and propenſe affection to promote the good of Mankind. Truly he eſteemed other ambition whatſoever, inferior to the buſineſs he had in hand : For either the matter in conſultation, and thus far proſecuted, is nothing ; or ſo much as the conſcience of the merit it ſelf, ought to give him contentment without ſeeking a recompence from abroad.

THE

The PREFACE.

Of the State of Learning , *that it is not* Proſperous, *nor greatly* Advanced; *and that a far different way, than hath been known to former Ages,
muſt be opened, to man's* Underſtanding ; *and o-
ther Aids procured; that the* Mind *may practice
her own power the* nature of things.

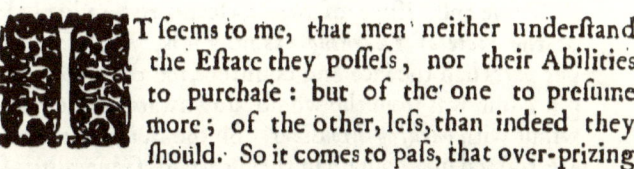T ſeems to me, that men neither underſtand
the Eſtate they poſſeſs , nor their Abilities
to purchaſe : but of the one to preſume
more ; of the other, leſs, than indeed they
ſhould. So it comes to paſs, that over-prizing
the Arts received, they make no farther Inquiry ; or undervaluing themſelves, more than in equity they ought,
they expend their Abilities upon matters of ſlight conſequence, never once making experiment of thoſe things
which conduce to the ſumm of the buſineſs. Wherefore,
Sciences alſo have , as it were, *their Fatal Columns* ; being
men are not excited, either out of Deſire or Hope, to penetrate farther. And ſeeing *the* Opinion *of* Wealth *is one
of the cheif cauſes of* Want ; and that out of a confidence of what we poſſeſs in preſent, true aſſiſtances are
deſpiſed for the future , it is expedient, nay, altogether
neceſſary, that the exceſſive Reverence and Admiration
conceived of thoſe *Sciences* , which hitherto have been
found out, ſhould in the Front and Entrance of this work,
(and that roundly and undiſſemblingly) by ſome wholſome premonition, be taken off, leſt their Copy and U-
tility be too much Magnified and Celebrated. For he that

ſurveys

surveys with diligence all the variety of Books, wherein
Arts and *Sciences* triumph; fhall every where find infinite repetitions of the fame matter, for manner of Delivery divers, but for Invention ftale and preoccupate; fo
as what at firft view feem'd numerous, after examination
taken, are found much abated. § As for profit, I may confidently avouch it, That the wifdom we have extracted,
chiefly from the Grecians, feems to be a Child-hood of
Knowledge, and to participate that which is proper to
children, namely, *that it is apt for talk; but impotent and
immature for propagation:* for it is of Controverfies rank
and fertile, but of works barren and fruitlefs. So that
the Fable and Fiction of *Scylla*, feems to be a lively Image
of the *State of Learning,* as now it is, which for the upper parts had the face and countenance of a comely Virgin; but was from the womb, downward circled and enwrapt with *barking Monfters.* So the *Sciences* wherein we
are trained up, contain in them certain Generalities fpecious and plaufible; but when you defcend unto particulars, as to the Parts of Generation, expecting folid effects,
and fubftantial operations, then, Contentions and Barking
Altercations arife, wherein they clofe, and which fupply
the place of a fruitful womb. § Again, if thefe kinds
of Sciences were not altogether a mere livelefs Thing,
methinks it fhould not have faln out, which now for many
Ages hath continued, that *they* fhould thus ftand at a ftay,
in a manner immoveable in their firft Footings, without any
Augmentation worthy the Race of Mankind, in fuch a
dull Improficience, that not only Affertion remains Affertion, but Queftion refts ftill, Queftion, which by Dif-
putes is not determined, but fixt and cherifht: and all
Tradition and Succeffion of Difcipline delivered from
hand to hand, prefents and exhibits the Perfon of Teacher
and Scholar, not of inventor, or of one fhould add fomething of note to what is invented. § But in Arts Mecha-
chanical we fee the contrary hath come to pafs, which as
if they were infpired by the Vital breath and prolifick influence of a thriving Air, are daily *Propagated* and *Perfected;* and which in their firft Authors appear'd, for the
moft part rude and even burthenfome and Formlefs, have
                                              afterward

afterward acquir'd new-refin'd vertues, and a certain apt Propriety and ufeful Accommodation, fo infinitely fruitful, that fooner may mens ftudies and defires languifh and change, than thefe *Sciences* arive at their full height and perfection. § Contrariwife *Philofophy*, and *Sciences Intellectual*, like *States* are ador'd and celebrated, but nothing *Advanc'd*; nay, commonly of moft vigor in their firft Author, and by Time Degenerate and become embafed. For fince the time men became *devoted*, and as (*Pedary Senators*) refigned over to the Placits and Definitions of one, they do not add any *Amplitude to Sciences*, but are wholly taken up in a fervile duty of *Polifhing or Protecting* certain Authors. § And let no man here alleage, that *Sciences* growing up by degrees, have at length arrived to a juft period or perfect Stature, and fo (as haveing filled up the juft fpaces of *Augmentation*) have fetled and fixt themfelves in the works of fome few Authors; and now that nothing more accomplifht can be found out, there remains no more to do, but that the *Sciences* already extant be improved, and adorned. Indeed it could be wifht that the *ftate of Learning were thus profperous*; but the very truth is, thefe mancipations and fervile refignations of *Sciences*, is nothing elfe but a peccant humour, bred out of daring luft and confidence in fome few, and a languifhing floth and Pufillanimity in the reft. For when *Sciences* (for fome parts it may be) have been tilled and laboured with diligence, then perchance hath there rifen up fome bold-undertaking wit, for Compendious brevity of Method popular and plaufible, who in fhew hath conftituted a *Science*, but indeed depraved the *Labours of the Ancients*: Yet thefe Abridgments find acceptation with Pofterity, for the expedite ufe of fuch a work, and to avoid the trouble and impatience of a new *Inquiry*. § And if any ftand upon *Confent now inveterate*, as the Judgement and teft of Time, let him know he builds upon a very deceivable and infirm Foundation. Nor is it, for the moft part, fo revealed unto us, what in *Arts* and *Sciences* hath been difcovered and brought to light in divers ages, and different Regions of the World; much lefs what hath been experimented, and ferioufly laboured by particular

Perfons

Perfons in private ; *For neither the Births, nor the Abortions of Time have been Regiftred.* § Nor is Confent it felf, nor the long continuation thereof, with fuch reverence to be adored : for however there may be many kinds of *States* in *Civil Government* ; yet *the State of Sciences is but one*, which always was, and fo will continue, *Popular* ; and with the People the Difciplines moft in requeft are either *Pugnacious* and *Polemical* ; or *Specious* and *Frivolous* ; namely fuch as either *illaqueate* or *allure* the *affent.* Wherefore without queftion, the greateft Wits in every age have been over-born, and in a fort tyrannized over, whilft men of Capacity and Comprehenfion above the vulgar, (yet confulting their own Credit and Reputation) have fubmitted themfelves to the over-fwaying Judgement of *Time* and *Multitude.* Therefore if in any *Time* or *Place*, more profound Contemplations have perchance emerged and revealed themfelves, they have been forthwith toft and extinguifht by the Winds and Tempefts of *Popular opinions :* fo that *Time like a River carries down to us that which is light and blown up ; but finks and drowns that which is weighty and folid.* § Nay, the very fame Authors, who have ufurpt a kind of *Dictature in Sciences*, and with fuch confidence paft cenfure upon matters in doubt, have yet (the heat once over) in the *Intervals*, from thefe peremptory fits of Affeveration, changed their note, and betaken themfelves to complaints, upon the *fubtility of Nature*, the *fecret Receffes of Truth*, the *Obfcurity of Things*, the *Implication of Caufes*, the *Infirmity of Mans Difcerning Power :* Yet nothing the more modeft for all this, feeing they chufe rather to charge the Fault upon the *common condition of Man and Nature*, than to acknowledge any Perfonal deficience in themfelves. Yea, it is a thing ufual with them, that what they cannot compafs by *Art*, their way applied, to conclude the fame impoffible to be attained by the fame *Art* : and yet for all this, *Art* muft not be condemned, being fhe is to examine and judge ; wherefore the aim and intention of fuch accufations is only this, *That Ignorance may be delivered from Ignominy.* § So likewife what is already commended unto us, and entertained hitherto, is for moft part fuch a kind of *Knowledge*, as is

full

full of Words and Queſtions ; but barren of Works and
real Improvements ; for *Augmentation* backward and heartleſs ; pretending perfection in the whole, but ill-filled up
in the Parts ; for choice Popular, and of the Authors themſelves ſuſpected, and therefore fortified and countenanced
by artificious evaſions. § And the Perſons who have entertained a deſign to make trial themſelves, and to give
ſome *Advancement* to *Sciences* , and to *Propagate their
bounds*, even theſe Authors durſt not make an open departure from the Common received Opinions ; nor viſit
the Head-ſprings of Nature, but take themſelves to have
done a great matter, and to have gained much upon the
Age, if they may but *interlace*, or *annex* any thing of their
own ; providently conſidering with themſelves, that by
theſe middle courſes, they may both conſerve the *modeſty
of Aſſenting* ; and the *liberty of Adding*. But whilſt they
thus cautiouſly conform themſelves to Opinions and Cuſtoms, theſe *Plauſible moderations*, redound to the great
prejudice and detriment of Learning ; For *at once to Admire and go beyond Authors* , *are habits ſeldom compatible :
but it comes to paſs here after the manner of Waters, which
will not aſcend higher than the level of the firſt Spring-head,
from whence they deſcend* ; wherefore ſuch writers amend
many things, but promote little or nothing, making a
Proficience in *Melioration*, not in *Augmentation*. § Neither hath there been wanting *undertaking Spirits* , who
with a more reſolute confidence, preſuming nothing yet
done, take themſelves to be the men, muſt rectifie All ;
and imploying the ſtrength of their wits in crying down,
and reverſing all former judgements, have made paſſage
to themſelves, and their own *Placits* ; whoſe buſie Cla-
mor, hath not much advanced *Knowledge*, ſince their aim
and intention hath been, not to enlarge the *bounds of Philoſophy* and *Arts*, by a *ſincere* and *ſolid Enquiry* ; but only
to change the *Placits*, and tranſlate the Empire of *Opinions*, and ſettle it upon themſelves , with little advantage
to *Learning* ; *ſeeing amongſt oppoſite Errors, the Cauſes of
Erring are commonly the ſame*. § And if any inconcerned natures, not mancipate to others, or their own opinions, but affecting liberty, have been ſo far animated, as to
deſire

defire that others together with themfelves, would make
farther *Inquiry* ; thefe furely have meant well, but performed little , for they feem to have proceeded upon probable grounds only, being wheeled about in a vertiginous
maze of Arguments, and by a promifcuous *licenfe of Inquiry,* have indeed loofned the finews of *fevere Inquifition* : nor hath any of all thefe with a juft patience, and fufficient expectance attended the *Operations of Nature,* and
the *fucceffes of Experience.* § Some again have embarqu'd
themfelves in the *Sea of Experiments,* and become almoft
Mechanical ; but in the *Experience* it felf, they have practifed a roving manner of *Inquiry,* which they do not in
a regular courfe conftantly purfue. § Nay, many propound to themfelves , certain petty Tasks, taking themfelves to have accomplifht a great performance, if they can
but extract fome one Invention by a manage as poor as impertinent ; for none rightly and fuccefsfully fearch the
nature of any thing to the life in the Thing it felf ; but after a painful and diligent variation of Experiments, not
breaking off there, proceeds on, finding ftill emergent
matter of farther *Difcovery.* § And it is an Error of fpecial note, that the induftry beftowed in Experiments, hath
prefently, upon the firft accefs into the Bufinefs, by a too
forward and unfeafonable Defire, feifed upon fome defign'd operation ; I mean fought after, *Fructifera non Lucifera, Experiments of Ufe and not Experiments of Light
and Difcovery :* not imitating the divine method which
created the firft day *Light* only, and allowed it one entire
Day, producing *no Materiate work the fame day*, but de-
fcended to their Creation the days following. § As for
thofe who have given the preeminence unto *Logick,* and
are of opinion that the fureft Guards for *Sciences* muft
be procur'd from *thence* ; they have truly and wifely
difcerned, that the mind of man, and Intellective Faculty
left unto it felf, may defervedly be fufpected. But the
remedy is too weak for the difeafe, and is it felf not exempt
from Diftemperature ; for the *Logick* in force, though it
may be rightly accommodated unto *Matters Civil and Popular Sciences,* which confift in *Difcourfe* and *Opinion* ; yet
it comes far fhort of penetrating the *fubtilty of Nature* ;
and

and undertaking more than it can master, *seems rather to establish and fix Errors than to open a way to Truth.* § Wherefore to recollect what hath been said, it seems that neither *Information from others*, *nor mens Inquiries* touching *Sciences*, have hitherto successfully shined forth, especially seeing there is so little *certainty in Demonstration* and *Infallibility* of Experiments thus far discovered. And the Fabrick of the Universe to the contemplative eye of the Mind, for the frame thereof, is like some Labyrinth or intricate Maze, where so many doubtful passages; such deceiveable resemblances, of Things and Signs; such oblique and serpentine windings, and intricate knots of Nature every where present themselves, as confounds the understanding. And withall, we must continually make our way, through the woods of Experiences, and particular Natures, by the incertain Light of Sense, sometimes shining, sometimes shadowed: yea, and the guides, which (as hath been toucht) offer their assistance, they likewise are entangled, and help to make up the number of Errors, and of those that Err. In matters of such perplext difficulty, there is no relying upon *the Judgement of men* from their own abilities; or upon the *Casual Felicity of Particular events*; for neither the *capacity of Man*, how excellent soever; nor the *chance of Experience*, never so often iterated and essayed, is of force to conquer these Mysteries: we must march by line and level, and all the way, even from the first perception of Senses, must be secured, and fortified by a certain Rule, and constant Method of proceeding. § Yet are not these things so to be understood, as if, in so many Ages, and so much Industry, nothing at all hath been performed to purpose; nor is their any cause why it should repent us of the *Discoveries* already made; for certainly the Ancients, in those speculations which consist in strength of Wit, and abstract Meditation, have approved themselves men of admirable comprehensions: But as in the *Art of Navigation*, the men of former Ages, directing their course by observation of Stars only, could edge along the coast of the known Continent, and it may be, cross some narrow Seas or the

[F] Me-

Mediterranean ; but before the Ocean could be thus commanded, and the Regions of the new world difcovered, it was requifite that the ufe of the *Mariners Needle*, as a more fure and certain guide fhould be firft found out ; even fo what difcoveries foever have been hitherto made in *Arts* and *Sciences*, they are of that quality, as might have been brought to light by Practice, Meditation, Obfervation and Difcourfe, as things nearer the fenfes, and for moft part, under the command of common Notions ; but before we can make our approaches, to the remote and hidden fecrets of Nature, it is necefarily requifite, that a better and more perfect ufe, and practick-operation of the Mind and Underftanding Faculty be introduc'd. § As for us, furely we,(vanquifh'd with an immortal love of Truth) have expos'd our felves to doubtful,difficult and defert Paths ; and by the protection and affiftance of the Divine Power, have born up and encouraged our felves againft the violent Affaults and prepared Armies, as it were, of Opinions, and againft our own private and inward hefitations and fcruples, and againft the clouds and darknefs of Nature, and every where flying fancies ; that fo we might procure the prefent and future Age more fafe and found Indications and Impreffions of Truth. If in this high and arduous attempt, we have made any *Proficience*, furely by no other means have we cleared our felves a way, than by a fincere and juft *humiliation of the fpirit of Man , to the laws and operations of Nature.* For all they that went before us, who applied themfelves to the finding out of *Arts* , cafting a tranfient eye upon Things, Examples, and Experience, have prefently (as if Invention were nothing elfe but a meer Agitation of Brain) invoked in a manner their own fpirits, to divine, and utter Oracles unto them : but we being chaftely and perpetually converfant with the operations of Nature, divorce not the Intellect from the Object farther than that the Images and Beams of things (as in fenfe)may meet and concentrate ; by which manner of proceeding, there is not much left to the ftrength and excellency of Wit. The fame fubmiffion of fpirit we have practifed in difcovery, we have followed in delivery :

Nor

Nor have we endeavour'd to set off our selves with Glory;
or draw a Majesty upon our Inventions, either by Triumphs of Confutations, or Depositions of Antiquity;
or an usurpation of Authority; or the vail of Obscurity; which are Arts he may easily find out, whose study is
not so much the Profit of others, as Applause to himself. I say we neither have practised, nor go we about,
by force or fraud to circumvent mens Judgements, but conduct them to the things themselves, and to the league and
confederacy of things, that they may see what they have,
what they reprehend, what they add and contribute to the
Publick. And if we have been too credulous, or too dormant, & not so intentive upon the matter, or languisht in the
way, or broken off the thread of the *Inquiry*, yet notwithstanding we present things after such a manner open and
naked, that our Errors may be detected and separated before they can spread themselves, or insinuate their contagion into the mass of Sciences; and after such a Method
as the continuation of our labours, is a matter facile and
expedite. By this means we presume we have establisht
for ever, *a true and legitimate Marriage, between the Em-*
pirical and Rational faculty; whose fastidious and unfortunate Divorce and Separation, hath troubled and disor-
dered the whole Race and Generation of Man-kind.
§ And seeing these performances are not within the compass of our meer natural Power and command, we do here,
in the Access to this work, *Pour forth humblest and most*
ardent supplications to God the Father, God the Word, God
the Spirit, that they being mindful of the Miseries of Man-
kind, and of the Pilgrimage of this life, wherein we wear
out few and evil days, they would vouchsafe to endow Man-
kind, by my hand, with new Donatives. And moreover,
we humbly pray, that Humane knowledges, may no way im-
peach, or prejudice Divine Truths; nor that from the dif-
closing of the ways of sense, and the letting in of a more
plentiful Natural Light, any mists of Incredulity or clouds
of Darkness arise in our minds, touching Divine Myste-
ries; but rather that from a purified Intellect, purged from
Fancies and Vanity; and yet yielded and absolutely rendred

up to *Divine Oracles* ; *the Tributes of Faith may be rendred to* Faith. *In the laſt place, that the venome of knowledge infuſed by the Serpent , whereby the mind of man is ſwelled and blown up, being voided; we may not be too aſpiringly wiſe, or above ſobriety, but that we may improve and propagate Verity in Charity.* § Now we have performed our vows to heaven, converting our ſelves to men, we admoniſh them ſomethings that are Profitable , and requeſt of them ſome things that are equal. Firſt we admoniſh (which thing we have alſo prayed for,) that we keep humane Reaſon within due Limits in matters Divine,

Philo.Jud. and Senſe within compaſs : *For ſenſe like the Sun, opens and reveals the face of the Terreſtial Globe , but ſhuts up and conceals the face of the Celeſtial.* Again, that men beware that in flight from this error, they fall not upon a contrary extreme , *of too much abaſing Natural Power;* which certainly will come to paſs, if they once entertain a conceit, *that there are ſome ſecrets of Nature ſeperate and exempt, as it were by injunction, from Humane Inquiſition.* For it was not that *pure and immaculate Natural Knowledge, by the light whereof* Adam *gave names unto the Creatures, according to the propriety of their Natures , which gave the firſt motion and occaſion to the Fall; but it was that proud and Imperative Appetite of Moral Knowledge, defining the laws and limits of Good and Evil, with an intent in man to revolt from God, and to give laws unto himſelf, which was indeed the project of the Primitive Temptation.* For, of the knowledges which contemplate the works of Nature, the

Prov. 25. holy Philoſopher hath ſaid expreſly ; *That the glory of God is to conceal a thing; but the glory of the King is to find it out* : as if the Divine Nature, according to the innocent and ſweet play of Children, which hide themſelves to the end they may be found, took delight to hide his works, to the end they might be found out ; and of his indulgence and goodneſs to mankind, had choſen the ſoul of man to be his Play-fellow in this game. § In ſumm, I would adviſe all in general, that they would take into ſerious conſideration the true and Genuine ends of *knowledge* ; that they ſeek it not either for Pleaſure, or Contention, or Contempt

tempt of others, or for Profit, or Fame, or for Honour and Promotion ; or such like adulterate or inferior ends : but for the merit and emolument of Life, and that they regulate and perfect the same in charity : *For the defire of Power, was the fall of Angels ; the defire of Knowledge, the fall of Man ; but in charity there is no excefs, neither Men nor Angels ever incurred danger by it.* § The Requefts we make are thefe ; (To fay nothing of our felves touching the matter in hand) we *Requeft* thus much, *That men would not think of it as an opinion ; but as a work, and take it for Truth, that our aim, and ends is not to lay the foundation of a Sect or Placit, but of Humane Profit and Proficience.* § Again, that refpecting their own Benefit, and putting off Partialities and Prejudices, they would all contribute in one for the publick Good : and that being freed and fortified by our Preparations and Aids, againft the Errors and Impediments of the ways, they likewife may come in, and bear a part in the burden, and inherit a portion of the Labours that yet remain behind. § Moreover that they chear up themfelves, and conceive well of the enterprife ; and not figure unto themfelves a conceit and fancy, *that this Our Inftauration is a matter infinite, and beyond the power and compafs of Mortality* ; feeing it is in truth the right and legitimate end and period of *Infinite Errors* ; and not unmindful of Mortality, and Humane Condition, being it doth not promife that the *Defign* may be accomplifht within the Revolution of an Age only, but delivers it over to Pofterity to Perfect. In a word, *it feeks not Sciences arrogantly in the cells of man's wit, but fubmiffively in the greater world :* And commonly, *Empty things are vaft and boundlefs, but Solids are contracted and determined within a narrow compafs.* § To conclude, we thought good to make it our laft fuit, (left peradventure through the difficulty of the Attempt, any fhould become unequal Judges of our Labours) that men fee to it, how they do, from that which we muft of neceffity lay down as a ground (if we will be true to our own ends) affume a liberty to cenfure, and pafs fentence upon our labours ; feeing we reject all this *premature and Anticipated humane*

mane Reafon, rafhly and too fuddenly departed from *Things*, (as touching the *Inquifition of Nature*) as a thing various, difordered and ill-built : Neither in equity can it be required of us, *to ftand to the Judgement of that* Reafon, *which ftands it felf, at the Bar of Judicature.*

The

The Diſtribution of the Work into Six Parts.

P. I. Partitiones Scientiarum, Or *a ſummary Survey and* partition *of* Sciences.

P. II. Novum Organum, Or *True Directions for the Interpretation of Nature.*

P. III. Phænomena Universi, Or *Hiſtory Natural and Experimental,* for *the building up Philoſophy.*

P. IV. Scala Intellectus, Or *the Intellectual Sphere rectified to the Globe of the World.*

P. V. Prodromi, Or *The Anticipations of* ſecond Philoſophy *emergent upon Practice.*

P. VI. Secunda Philosophia, Or *Active Philoſophy, from intimate Converſe with Nature.*

The A R G U M E N T *of the ſeveral* P A R T S.

IT is one point of the Deſign we have in hand, *That every thing be delivered with all poſſible Plainneſs and Perſpicuity :* for *the nakedneſs of the Mind, as once of the Body, is the* companion *of Innocence and Simplicity.* Firſt therefore, *the order and Diſtribution of the work,* with the reaſon thereof, muſt be made manifeſt. The *Parts of the Work* are, by us aſſigned, *Six.*

¶ *The* Firſt *Part exhibits the* ſumm *or univerſal deſcription of that Learning and Knowledges in the poſſeſſi-* P. I.
on

on whereof, men have hitherto been eſtated. For we thought good to make ſome ſtay even upon *Sciences received,* and that, for this conſideration ; that we might give more advantage to the *Perfection of ancient knowledges, and to the introduction of new :* For we are carried, in ſome degree, with an equal temper of Deſire, *both to improve the labours of the Ancients , and to make farther progreſs.* And this makes for the faith and ſincerity of

Prov. 18.

our meaning, according to that of the wiſe, *The unlearned Man receives not the words of knowledge, unleſs you firſt interpret unto him the conceptions of his heart :* Wherefore we will not neglect to ſide along (as it were in paſſage) the Coaſts of *accepted Sciences and Arts* ; and to import thither, ſomethings uſeful and profitable. § Nevertheleſs we adjoyn *ſuch Partitions of Sciences, as comprehend, not only ſuch things that are found out and obſerved already, but ſuch alſo as are thereto pertaining, and have been hitherto pretermiſs'd.* For their are found *in the Intellectual Globe, as in the Terreſtial, ſoyls improved and Deſerts.* Wherefore let it not ſeem ſtrange, if now and then we make a departure from the *uſual Diviſions* , and forſake the beaten path of ſome Partitions : *for Addition whilſt it varies the whole, of neceſſity varies the Parts and the Sections thereof* ; and the *accepted Diviſions,* are accommodated only to the *accepted ſumm of Sciences,* as it is now caſt up. § Concerning thoſe *Parts,* which we ſhall note as *Pretermitted,* we will ſo regulate our ſelves, as to ſet down more than the naked Titles, or brief Arguments of *Deficients.* For where we deliver up any thing as a *Deſiderate,* ſo it be a matter of merit ; and the reaſon thereof may ſeem ſomewhat obſcure ; ſo as, upon good conſideration, we may doubt, that we ſhall not be ſo eaſily conceived what we intend, or what the contemplation is we comprehend in our mind, and in our mediation, there it ſhall ever be our preciſe care, to annex either *precepts,* for the performing of ſuch a Work ; or a Part of the Work it ſelf, performed by us already, for *Example* to the whole : that ſo we may in every Particular, either by *Operation or Information,* promote the buſineſs. For in my judgement, it is a matter which concerns not only the benefit of others, but

our

our own Reputation alſo, that no man imagine that we
have projected in our minds ſome ſlight ſuperficial notion
of theſe *Deſigns*; and that they are of the nature of thoſe
things, which we could *Deſire*, and which we accept only as *good wiſhes.* For they are ſuch as without queſtion,
are within the power and poſſibility of men to compaſs;
unleſs they be wanting to themſelves; and hereof, we for
our parts, have certain and evident demonſtration; *for
we come not hither, as Augures, to meaſure Countries in
our mind, for Divination; but as Captains, to invade
them, for a conqueſt. And this is the Firſt Part of our
Works.*

¶ Thus having paſſed over Ancient Sciences, in the
next place we enable humane Intellect to ſail through.
*Wherefore to the Second Part is deſigned the Doctrine touch-
ing more ſound, and perfect uſe of Reaſon, in the inquiry
of Things, and the true aſſiſtances of the underſtanding;*
that hereby (ſo far as the condition of humanity and mortality will ſuffer) the Intellect, may be elevated; and amplified with a faculty, capable to conquer the dark, and
deeper ſecrets of Nature. And the *Art*, we here ſet down,
which we are wont to call, The *Interpretation of Nature*,
is a kind of *Logick*, though very much, and exceeding
different. That *vulgar Logick* profeſſes the Preparation
and Contrivance of aids and forces for the underſtanding,
herein they conſpire, but it clearly differs from the Popular, ſpecially in three things, namely, *in the end, in the
order of Demonſtrating, and, in the firſt diſcloſures to Inquiry.* § For *the End* propounded in this our Science is, that
there may be found out not Arguments, but Arts; not
things Conſentaneous to Principles, but even Principles
themſelves; not probable reaſons, but deſignations and
indications of works; wherefore from a different intention follows a different effect: for there, an Adverſary is
diſtreſſed and vanquiſht by Diſputation, here by nature,
the thing done. § *And with this End accords the nature
and order of their Demonſtrations* : For in *vulgar Logick,*
almoſt all the pains is imployed about *Syllogiſm* : as for
Induction, the *Dialecticks* ſeem ſcarce ever to have taken
it into any ſerious conſideration, ſlightly paſſing it over

P. II.

and

and haftning to the forms of Difputing. But we reject *Demonftration by Syllogifm*, for that it proceeds confufed-ly; and lets Nature efcape our hands. For though no man call into doubt, but that *what are coincident in a mid-dle term are in themfelves coincident*, (which is a kind of Mathematick Certitude) yet here lies the Fallax, *that Syllogifm confifts of Propofitions, Propofitions of words, and words are the tokens and marks of things*. Now if thefe fame *notions* of the mind, (which are, as it were, *the foul of words*, and the Bafis of this manner of Structure and Fabrick) be rudely and rafhly divorc'd from things, and roving; not perfectly defin'd and limited, and alfo many other ways vicious; all falls to ruine. Wherefore we reject *Syllogifm*, not only in regard of *Principles* (for which nor do they make ufe of it but in refpect alfo of *Mid-dle Propofitions*, which indeed *Syllogifm*, however, infers and brings forth; but barren of operations and remote from practice; and in relation to the Active Part of Sciences, altogether incompetent. Although therefore we may leave to *Syllogifm*, and fuch celebrated and applauded *Demonftrations*, a jurifdiction over Arts Popular and O-pinable (for in this kind we move nothing) yet for the nature of things, we every where, as well in *Minor as Ma-jor Propofitions*, make ufe of *Inductions:* for we take *In-duction* to be that form of *Demonftration*, which fupports fenfe; prefles Nature, and is inftanced in Works, and in a fort mingled therewith. Wherefore the order alfo of *Demonftration* is altogether inverted. For hitherto the bu-finefs ufed to be thus managed; from fenfe, and fome few Particulars, fuddenly to fly up to the higheft Generals, as to fixt Poles, about which Difputations may be turned; from which the reft of intermediate Axioms may be de-rived. A way compendious indeed, but precipitate; and to Nature inpervious; but for Difputations ready, and accommodate. But according to *our Method, Axioms* are raifed by a fequent continuity and graduat dependan-cy, fo as there is no feifing upon the higheft Generals, but in the laft place; and thofe higheft Generals in quality not notionals; but well terminated, and fuch as Nature acknowledges to be truly near allied unto her; and which

cleave

cleave to the individual intrinsicks of things. § *But touching the form it self of Induction and Judgement made by it,* we undertake a mighty work. For the *Form, whereof Logicians speak, which proceeds by simple enumeration, is a childish thing,* and concludes upon admittance; is exposed to peril from a contradictory instance; looks only upon common operations; and is in the issue endless. But to the knowledges of *Induction,* such a *Form* is required, as may solve and separate *experience*; and by due exclusion and rejection necessarily conclude. And if that publick and popular *Judgement of Dialecticks,* be so laborious, and hath exercised so many and so great Wits; how much greater pains ought we to take in this other; which not only out of the secret closets of the mind, but out of the very entrails of Nature is extracted? Nor is this all; for we more firmly settle, and solidate the foundation of Sciences, and take the first rise of our inquiry deeper than hitherto hath been attempted; submitting to examinations those Principles, which *vulgar Logick* takes up on the credit of another. For the *Dialecticks* borrow, as it were, from all other Sciences, the Principles of Sciences; again, adore the prime Notions of the mind: Lastly, rest satisfied with the immediate informations of sense rightly disposited. But our judgement is this, that true Logick should visit every particular Province of Sciences, with greater command than their principles possess; and that those same *putative Principles* be enforc'd to give an account, and be liable to examination, until such time as their validity and tenure clearly appeared. And as touching the *Prime Notions of the Intellect,* there is nothing of those, (the understanding left at liberty to it self) hath congested, but matter to be suspected; nor any way warrantable, unless it be summon'd, and submit it self to a new Court of Judicature; and that sentence pass according thereto. Moreover we many ways sift and sound the information of sense it self; for the Senses deceive; yet withall they indicate their Errors: but Errors are at hand, Indications to be sought for a far off. § *The guilt of Sense is of two sorts, either it destitutes us, or else deceives us.* For first, there are many things which escape the cognizance of sense, even when it is well disposed, and no way impedite : either by reason of the subtility of the entire body, or the minutness of the parts thereof, or the distance of place, or the slowness, and likewise swiftness of motion; or the familiar converse with the object, or some other causes. Again, nor where sense truly apprehends its object, are her Precepts so very firm : *for the testimony and information of sense, is ever from the Analogy of Man, and not from the Analogy of the World*; and it is an error of dangerous consequence to assert, *that sense is the measure of things.* Wherefore to encounter these inconveniences, we have with painful and faithful service every where sought out, and collected assistances, *that Supplements to Deficients*; *to Variations, Rectifications, may be ministred.* Nor do we undertake this so *muchby instruments, as by experiments*; for the subtilty of *Experiments*, is far greater than of sense it self, though assisted with exact instruments; we mean *such experiments,* which to the intention of the thing inquired, are skilfully according to Art invented and accommodated. Wherefore we do not attribute much to the immediate and particular perception of sense; but we bring the matter to this issue, that sense may judge only of the experiment, the experiment of the thing. We conceive therefore, that of *sense*, (from which all knowledge in things natural must be derived, unless we mean wilfully to go a witless way to work) we are become the religious Pontifs; and the not inexpert interpreters of her Oracles; so as others may seem in outward profession; but we in deed and action, to protect and honour *sense.* And of this kind are they which we prepare; for the light of Nature, the actuating, and immission thereof, which of themselves were sufficient, were humane Intellect equal, and a smooth inanticipated Table. But when the minds of men are after such strange ways besieged, that for to admit the true beams of things, a sincere and polisht Area is wanting; it concerns us, of necessity to bethink our selves of seeking out some remedy for this distemperature. The *Idolaes*, wherewith the mind is preoccupate are either *Attracted, or Innate*; Attracted have slid into mens minds;

either

either by the *Placits and Sects of Philosophers*; or by *depraved laws of Demonstrations*. But the *Innate* inhere in the nature of the Intellect, which is found to be far more liable to error, than *sense*. For however men may please themselves, and be ravisht into admiration, and almost adoration of the mind of man, this is most certain: *as an inequal looking-glass*, changes the rays of objects, according to its own figure, and cutting; even so the mind, when it suffers impression from things by sense, in encogitating and discharging her notions, doth not so faithfully insinuate and incorporate her nature, with the nature of things. And those two first kinds of *Idolaes* can very hardly; but those latter, by no means be extirpate. It remains only that they be disclosed; and that same treacherous faculty of the mind be noted and convinced; left from the unsound complection of the mind, upon the extermination of ancient, perchance new shoots of Errors spring in their place; and the business be brought only to this issue, that errors be not extinguisht, but changed: but on the contrary, now at last, it be for ever decreed and ratified, *That the intellect cannot make a judgement but by induction*, and by *a legittimate form thereof*. Wherefore *the Doctrine of purifying the Understanding*, that it may become receptive of truth, is perfected by *three Reprehensions*; *Reprehension of Philosophy*; *Reprehension of Demonstrations*; and *Reprehension of Native humane Reason*. These explicated, and then the case cleared, what the nature of things, what the nature of the mind is capable off; we presume (the Divine goodness being President at the Rites) that we have prepared and adorned, *the Bride-chamber of the Mind and of the Universe*. Now may the vote of the Martiage-song be, *that from this conjunction, Humane Aids, and a Race of Inventions may be procreated, as may in some part vanquish and subdue mans miseries and necessities*. And this is the second Part of the Work.

¶ But our purpose is not only to point out and munite the way; but to enterprise it: *Wherefore the third Part of the Work compriseth*, Phænomena Universi, as to say, *all kind of Experience, and Natural History*, of such kind

P. III.

kind as may be fundamental for the building up of *Na-tural Philosophy*. For neither can any exact way of *De-monstration or Form of interpreting Nature*, both guard and support the mind from error and lapse; and withal present and minister matter for knowledge. But they who proposed to themselves not to proceed by Conjectures and Divinations, but to find out, and to know, whose end and aim is not to contrive Fictions and Fables, but to search with diligence into the nature of, and, as it is were, *anatomize this true world*; must derive all from the very things themselves. Nor can the substitution and compen-sation of Wit, or Meditation, or Argumentation suffice to this travail, inquisition, and mundane perambulation; no not if all the Wits in the World should meet together. Wherefore we must either take a right course, or desert the business for ever: and to this day the matter hath been so managed, that it is no marvail, if nature hath not dis-closed her self. For first, defective and fallacious infor-mation of sense; negligent, inequal, and as it were, casu-al observation; vain Tradition, and from idle Report; Pra-ctice, intent on the Work, and Servile; *Experimental at-tempt*, ignorant, dull, wild, and broken: lastly, slight and poor *Natural History*; have towards the raising of Philo-sophy, congested most depraved matter for the under-standing. After this, preposterous subtilty of arguing, and ventilation, hath essayed a late remedy to things plainly desperate; which doth not any way recover the business, or separate errors. § *Wherefore there is no hope of greater advancement and progress, but in the Restaurati-of Sciences.* And the commencements hereto must, by all means, be derived from *Natural History*; and that too, of a new kind and provision: for to no purpose you polish the Glass, if Images be wanting: not only faithful guards must be procured, but apt matter prepared. And this our *History*, as our *Logick*, differs from that in use, in many particulars: *in the end or office, in the Mass and Congeries; then in the subtilty, also in choice, and in constitution in re-ference to those things that follow.* § *For first we propound such a Natural History,* as doth not so much either please for the variety of things, or profit for present improve-ment

ment of Experiments, as it doth disperse a light to the invention of causes; and gives, as it were, the first Milk to the nourishing up of Philosophy. For though we principally pursue operation, and the Active part of Sciences; yet we attend the due season of Harvest; nor go about to reap the green herb or the blade. For we know well that Axioms rightly invented, draw after them the whole troup of Operations; and not sparsedly, but plenfully exhibit Works. But we utterly condemn and renounce, as *Atalantaes Apple* which retards the Race, that unseasonable and childish humour of accelerating early Pledges of new Works. And this is the Duty of our *Natural History*. § As for the *Mass, we compile* a History, not only of Nature at Liberty, and in Course; I mean, when without compulsion she glides gently along, and accomplishes her own work: (as is the *History of the Heavens, Meteors, Earth and Sea; of Minerals, Plants, Animals:*) but much rather of *Nature straitned and vext*; when by the provocations of Art, and the ministry of Man, she is put out of her common road; distressed and wrought. Wherefore, all the experiments of Arts Mechanical; all of the Operative part of Liberal; all of many Practical, not yet conspired into a peculiar Art (so far as any discovery may be had, and so far as is conducent to our intention) we will set down at large. So likewise (not to dissemble the matter) nothing regarding mens pride and bravades, we bestow more pains, and place more assurance in this Part than in that other; being the nature of things, more discloses her self in *the vexation of Art*, than when it is at its own liberty § Nor do we present the *History of Substance only*, but also we have taken it as a part of our diligence, to prepare a separate *History of their vertues*, we mean, such as in nature may be accounted Cardinal, and wherein the Primordials of Nature are expresly constituted; as matter invested with her Primitive qualities and appetites; as *denfe, rare, hot, cold, confiftent, fluid, ponderous, light,* and others not a few. § For indeed, to speak of *subtilty, we search out with choice diligence, a kind of Experiments, far more subtile and simple than those commonly met with.* For we educe and extract many out

of

of darkneſs, which had never come into any mans mind to
inveſtigate, ſave his who proceeds by a certain and conſtant path, to the invention of cauſes : whereas in themſelves they are of no great uſe ; that it is clearly evident,
that they were not ſought after, for themſelves, but that
they have directly the ſame reference to things and works,
that the Letters of the Alphabet have to ſpeech and
words ; which, though ſingle by themſelves, they are
unprofitable, yet are they the Elements of all Language.
§ *And in the choice of Reports and Experiments, we pre-*
ſume that we have given in better ſecurity, than they who
hitherto have been converſant in Natural Philoſophy : for
we admit nothing but by oculate faith, at leſt evident
proof ; and that after moſt ſevere enquiry : ſo as nothing
is reported hightned to the abuſive credit of a miracle ;
but what we relate are chaſte and immaculate from Fables
and Vanity. So alſo all thoſe received and ventilated current fictions and lies, which by a ſtrange neglect, have for
many ages been countenanced, and are become inveterate ;
we do by name proſcribe, and preciſely note, that they may

Plut de Ed.
P. ex Plat.
de Rep. be no longer prejudicial to Sciences. For what one wiſely
obſerves, *That Fables, Superſtitions, and idle Stories, which*
Nurſes inſtill into young Children, do in good earneſt deprave
their minds : ſo the ſame reaſon moved us, to be ſo religious
and careful, left at the entrance, where we handle and take
the charge *of the Infancy, as it were, of Philoſophy, under*
natural Hiſtory ; ſhe ſhould be initiated in any vanity.
§ But *in every new and ſomewhat more ſubtile experiment,*
in our opinion, certain and tryed, we yet apertly adjoyn
the manner of the experiment we have practiſed, that after
it is made apparent what the ſucceſs of every particular
was with us ; men might ſee the error which might lurk
and cleave thereto ; and be awaked to proofs, if any
ſuch be, more exact and ſecure. § *In brief*, we every where ſparſedly inſert monitions and ſcruples and
conjectures ; ejecting and interdicting, as it were, by a ſacred adjuration and exorciſm, all Phantaſms. § *Laſtly,*
being it is a thing moſt liquid unto us, how exceedingly
Experience and Hiſtory diſperſe the beams of the ſight of
humane Intellect ; and how hard a matter it is, ſpecially

to

to minds tender and preoccupate, at firſt entrance, to become familiar with nature; we therefore many times add
our own obſervations, as certain firſt converſions and inclinations, and as it were, *Aſpects of Hiſtory to Philoſophy*;
to the end that they may be both pledges to men, that they
ſhall not ever be detained in the waves of Hiſtory; as alſo
that when they are once arrived to the operation of the
underſtanding, all may be in a more preparedneſs. And
by this kind of *Natural Hiſtory*, as here we deſcribe, we
ſuppoſe that there may be a ſecure and eaſie acceſs unto
Nature; and ſolid and prepared matter preſented unto the
Underſtanding.

¶ *Now we have* both fortified and environed the un- P. IV.
.derſtanding with faithful Auxiliaries and forces, and by
a ſtrict Muſter raiſed a compleat Army of Divine Works,
*there ſeems nothing remaining but that we ſet upon Philoſophy
it ſelf.* But in ſo deficile and dubious an enterpriſe, there
are ſome particulars, which ſeem neceſſarily to be interpoſed partly for inſtruction, partly for preſent uſe. § *Of
theſe the firſt is, that the examples of Inquiſition, and of Invention,* he propounded according to our Rule and Method repreſented in particular Subjects; chiefly making
choice of ſuch Subjects, which amongſt other things to
be enquired, are the moſt noble, and in mutual relation,
moſt adverſe; that there may not want an *example* in every kind. Nor do we ſpeak of thoſe *examples,* which for
illuſtration ſake, are annexed to every particular Precept
and Rule (for we have ſufficiently quit our ſelves hereof
in the *Second Part of the Work,*) but we mean directly
the Types and Platforms which may preſent, as it were,
to the eye, the whole Procedure of the Mind, and the
continued Fabrick and Order of Invention, in certain ſelected ſubjects; and they various and of remark. For it
came into our mind, that in *Mathematicks,* the frame
ſtanding, the Demonſtration inferred is facile and perſpicuous; on the contrary, without this accommodation and
dependency, all ſeems involved, and more ſubtile than indeed they be. *Wherefore to examples of this ſort we aſſign the Fourth Part of our Work:* which indeed is nothing
elſe, but a particular, and explicite application of the Second Part. [H] ¶ *But*

P. V.

¶ *But the* **fifth** *Part* is added only for a time, and paid as interest until the Principal be raised. For we are not so precipitantly bent upon the end, as too slightly to pass over what we casually meet with by the way. Wherefore the *Fifth Part of the Work*, is composed of such things as we have, or found out, or experimented, or superadded ; nor yet do we perform this, by the *reason and rules of Interpretation*, but by the same application of the understanding, which others in enquiry and invention use to practice. For seeing from our perpetual converse with nature, we hope greater matters from our meditations, than we can promise to our selves from the strength of our own wit ; these observations may be as tents pitched in the way, into which the mind, in pursuit of more certain Collections, may turn in, and for a while repose her self. Yet in the mean, we promise not to engage our selves upon the credit of those Observations ; because they are not found out, nor tried by the right *form of Interpretation.* § And there is no cause why any should distast or entertain a jealousie, *at that suspension of Judgement in knowledge, which asserts not absolutely, that nothing can be known ; but that nothing, without a certain Order, and a certain Method, can be known ; and yet withal, lays down for use and ease, certain Degrees of certitude, until the mind be fixt upon the explication of*

Academ.
Ver. Nov.

causes. For neither those very Schools of Philosophers, who down right maintained *Acatalepsie* or *Incomprehensibility,* have been inferiour to those, who usurp *a liberty of*

Dogmat.

pronouncing sentence : but they provided not assistances to the sense and understanding, as we have done, but utterly took away all *credit* and *authority*, which is a far different case and almost opposite.

P. VI.

¶ *Now the sixth Part of our Work, whereto the rest are subservient and ministrant, doth altogether disclose, and propound that Philosophy, which is educed, and constituted out of such a legitimate sincere and severe enquiry, as we have already taught and prepared.* But to consummate and perfect this *last Part*, is a thing exalted above our strength, and beyond our hopes. We have given it, as we trust, not contemptible beginnings ; the prosperous success of mankind shall give it issue ; and

per-

peradventure fuch, as men, in this prefent ftate of mind
and imployments, can not eafily conceive and comprehend. And the cafe concerns not contemplative felicity
alone, but indeed mens affairs and fortunes, and all the
power of Works: *For Man, Natures minifter and interpreter, doth, and underſtands ſo much, as he hath by Operation or Contemplation obferved of Natures Order; nor can
know or do any more:* For neither can any forces unloofe
and break afunder the chain of Caufes; nor is nature o-
therwife, than by obedience unto it, vanquifht.   Wherefore thefe two main Intentions, *Humane Sciences, and Humane Potencies,* are indeed in the fame point coincident:
and the fruftration of Works, for moſt part, falls out from
the ignorance of Caufes. § But herein the fumm and perfection of all confifts, if a man, never taking off the eye
of his mind from the things themfelves; throughly imprint their images to the life. For God defend, that we
fhould publifh the ayery dreams of our own Fancy, for the
real *Ideas of the World!* But rather may he be fo graci-
oufly propitious unto us, that we may write the *Apocalypfe,*
and true vifion of the impreffions and fignets of the Creator, upon the Creature !

*Wherefore thou, O Father, who haſt conferred vifible
Lights as the* Primitiæ *on the Creature; and breathed into
the face of Man Intellectual Light, as the accomplifhment of
thy Works; protect and conduct this Work, which iffuing
from thy Goodnefs, returns to thy Glory! Thou, after thou
hadſt furveyed the works thy hands had wrought, faw that
all was exceeding Good, and haſt refted : but Man furveying
the works his hands had wrought, faw that all was vanity
and vexation of Spirit, and found no Reſt : Wherefore if
we labour with diligence, and vigilance in Thy works;
thou wilt make us Participants of thy Vifion, and of thy
Sabbath. We humbly fupplicate, that we may be of this
refolution, and infpired with this mind; and that thou wouldſt
be pleafed to endow humane Race, with new Donatives by our
hands; and the hands of others, in whom thou ſhalt implant
the fame Spirit.*

[H 2]   THE

THE
GENERAL ARGUMENT
Of the
Nine Books.

LIB. I. Is Proemial to the Inftauration of Sciences. § Reports the DISCREDITS of LEARNING. § The DIGNITY of LEARNING.

LIB. II. Declares the ADVANCEMENT of LEARNING. § In-ftrumental. § Effential , in the Partition of Sciences, into HISTORY. § POESY. § PHILOS. § Partit. of HIST. § POESY.

LIB. III. Partitions of PHILOSOPHY , into § SUMMARY. § SPECIAL, into DIVINE. § NATURAL. § HUMANE. § Partitions of NATURAL PHILOSOPHY.

LIB. IV. Partitions of HUMANE PHILOSOPHY into § PHI-LOSOPHY of HUMANITY. § CIVIL. § Partitions of the PHILOSOPHY of HUMANITY.

LIB. V. Partitions of SCIENCES , from the Ufe and Objects of of the MIND, into § LOGICK, § ETHICK. § Of LO-GICK into INVENTION. § JUDGEMENT. § MEMORY. § TRADITION.

LIB. VI. Partitions of TRADITION or ELOCUTION into the ORGAN of SPEECH. § METHOD of SPEECH. § ILLU-STRATION of SPEECH.

LIB. VII. Partitions of ETHICK or MORAL KNOWLEDGE, into the Doctrine of the PLATFORM of GOOD. § Of the CULTURE of the MIND.

LIB.

LIB. VIII. Partitions of CIVIL KNOWLEDGE, into the Doctrine of CONVERSATION. § Of NEGOTIATION. § Of GOVERNMENT of STATES.

LIB. IX. Partitions of THEOLOGY omitted, DEFICIENTS Three. § I. THE RIGHT USE OF HUMANE REASON in DIVINITY. § II. The DEGREES OF UNITY IN THE CITY OF GOD. § III. The EMANATIONS OF SS. SCRIPTURE.

The

THE
ARGUMENT
OF THE
CHAPTERS
OF THE
First Book.

CAP. I.

THE *Confecration of this Work unto the moft Learned of Princes, King* James. § *Who in high , but juft conceptions is here admired.* § *The Diftribution into the Dignity and Proficiency of Learning.* I. *Difcredits of Learning from the objections of Divines; That the afpiring unto Knowledge was the firft Sin.* That *Learning is infinite and full of anxiety.* That *Learning inclines the Mind to Herefie and Atheifm.* II. *The Solution. Original Guilt was not in the Quantity, but in the Quality of Knowledge.* § *The Corrective hereof, Charity.* III. *Againft Infinity, Anxiety, and Seducement of Knowledge, Three prefervatives.* § *That it inftruct us in our Mortality.* § *That it gives us content.* § *That it foar not too high.* § *And fo Philofophy leads the Mind by the Links of Second Caufes unto the Firft.*

CAP. II.

I. *Difcredits caft upon Learning from the objections of Politicks; That Learning foftens Mens natures, and makes them unfit for Exercife of Arms.*

Arms. That Learning perverts mens minds for matter of Govern-
ment. Other particular indispositions pretended. II. The solution;
Learning makes not men unapt for Arms. III. Learning inables
men for Civil Affairs. IV. Particular seducements imputed to
Learning: As curious incertainty. § Pertinacious Regularity. § Mif-
leading Book-Presidents. § Retired slothfulness. § Relaxation of
Discipline; are rather cured than caused by Learning.

C A P. III.

I. *Discredits of Learning from Learned mens Fortunes; Manners;*
Nature of Studies. II. Derogations derived from Fortune are these;
Scarcity of Means. § Privateness of Life. § Meanness of Imploy-
ment. III. From their Manners; these too Regular for the times.
§ Too sensible of the good of others; and too neglective of their own.
§ A defailance in applying themselves to Persons of Quality. § A
Failing in some lesser Ceremonies of demeanure. § Gross Flattery
practised by some Learned men. § Instanced, in the Modern De-
dication of Books. § Discreet Morigeration allowed.

C A P. IV.

I. *Distempers of Learning from Learned mens Studies, are of three*
sorts; Phantastical Learning; Contentious Learning; Delicate
Learning. II. Delicate Learning a curiosity in words, through pro-
fuseness of speech. § Decent expression commended. § Affected
brevity censured. III. Contentious Learning, a curiosity in matter,
through Novelty of Terms or strictness of Positions. § A vanity
either in Matter; or in Method. IV. Phantastical Learning hath
two branches, Imposture; Credulity. § Credulity a Belief of Histo-
ry; or a Belief of Art; or Opinion: and that either Real, in the
Art it self. § Or Personal in the Author of such an Art or Science.

C A P. V.

Peccant Humours in Learning. I. Extreme affection to two extremes;
Antiquity: Novelty. II. A distrust that any thing New, should now
be found out. III. That of all Sects and Opinions, the best hath
still prevailed. IV. An over-early reduction of Knowledge into Arts
and Methods. V. A neglect of Primitive Philosophy. *VI. A*
Divorce of the Intellect from the Object. VII. A contagion of Know-
ledge in General, from Particular inclinations and tempers. VIII. An
impatience of suspense; haste to positive assertion. IX. A Magistral
manner of Tradition of Knowledge. X. Aim of Writers, Illustra-
tion, not Propagation of Knowledge. XI. End of Studies, Curiosity,
Pleasure, Profit, Preferment, &c.

CAP.

CAP. VI.

The Dignity of Learning from Divine Arguments and Testimonies.
I. From Gods Wisdom. § *Angels of Illumination.* § *The first*
Light. § *The first Sabbath.* § *Mans imployment in the Garden.*
§ *Abels contemplation.* § *The Invention of Musick.* § *Confusion*
of Tongues. II. *The excellent Learning of Moses.* § *Job.* § *So-*
lomon. § *Christ.* § *St. Paul.* § *The Ancient Doctors of the*
Church. § *Learning exalts the Mind to the Celebration of Gods Glo-*
ry; and is a preservative against Error and Unbelief.

CAP. VII.

The Dignity of Learning from humane Arguments and Testimonies.
I. *Natural Inventors of new Arts, for the Commodity of Man's life,*
consecrated as Gods. II. *Political, Civil Estates and Affairs ad-*
vanced by Learning. § *The best and the happiest times under Learn-*
ed Princes and others. § *Exemplified in six continued succeeding*
Emperours from the death of Domitian. III. *Military : The Con-*
currence of Arms and Learning. § *Exemplified in* Alexander *the*
Great. § Julius Cæsar *the Dictator.* § Xenophon *the Philosopher.*

CAP. VIII.

The Merit of Learning, from the influence it hath upon Moral vertues.
§ *Learning a Sovereign remedy for all the Diseases of the Mind.*
§ *The dominion thereof greater than any Temporal Power, being a*
Power over Reason and Belief. § *Learning gives Fortunes, Honours*
and Delights, excelling all other as the soul the sense. § *Durable*
monuments of Fame. § *A prospect of the Immortality of a future*
World.

The second BOOK.

THE PROEM.

T*He Advancement of Learning commended to the Care of Kings.*
I. *The Acts thereof in general three, Reward, Direction, Assi-*
stance. II. *In special, about three Objects, Places, Books, Persons.* § *In*
Places four Circumstances, Buildings, Revenues, Priviledges, Laws of
Discipline. § *In Books two, Libraries, good Editions.* § *In Persons*
two, Readers of Sciences extant; Inquirers into Parts non-extant.
III. *Deficients in the Acts of Advancement, six, want of Foundations*
for Arts at large. § *Meanness of Salary to Readers.* § *Want of al-*
lowance for experiments. § *Preposterous Institutions : unadvised*
practises in Academical studies. § *Want of Intelligence between the*
Universities of Europe. § *Want of Enquirers into the Defects of Arts.*
§ *The Authors particular design.* § *Modest defence.*

[1]   CAP.

CAP. I.

I. *An Universal Partition of Humane Learning into,* § *History.* **II.** *Poefie.* **III.** *Philosophy.* § *This Partition is drawn from the three Intellective Faculties ; Memory ; Imagination ; Reason.* § *The same distribution is agreeable unto Divine Learning.*

CAP. II.

I. *The Partition of History, into Natural and Civil. (Ecclesiastical, and Literary comprehended under Civil.)* **II.** *The Partition of Natural History, into the History of Generations.* **III.** *Of Preter-Generations.* **IV.** *Of Arts.*

CAP. III.

I. *A Second Partition of Natural History from the Use and End thereof, into Narrative, and Inductive. And that the most noble end of Natural History is, that it minister and conduce to the building up of Philosophy ; which end, Inductive History respecteth.* **II.** *The Partition of the History of Generations, into the History of the Heavens ; The History of the Meteors ; The History of the Earth, and Sea ; The History of Massive Bodies,or of the greater Collegiats ; The History of Kinds, or of the lesser Collegiats.*

CAP. IV.

I. *The Partition of History Civil, into Ecclesiastical and Literary ; and (which retains the general name) Civil.* **II.** *Literary* Deficient. § *Precepts how to compile it.*

CAP. V.

Of the Dignity and Difficulty of Civil History.

CAP. VI.

The first Partition of Civil History, into § *Memorials.* § *Antiquities.* § *Perfect History.*

CAP. VII.

The Partition of Perfect History, into Chronicles of Times ; Lives of Persons ; Relation of Acts. § *The explication of the History of Lives.* § *Of Relations.*

CAP. VIII.

The Partition of the History of Times ; into universal and particular History. The advantages and disadvantages of both.

CAP. IX.

The Second Partition of the History of Times,into Annals,and Journals:

CAP. X.

A Second Partition of Special-Civil History into History Simple & Mixt.
CAP.

The Third BOOK.

*nick, and Magick: reſpondent to the Parts of Speculative knowledge ;
Mechanick to Phyſick; Magick to Metaphyſick.* § *A purging of the word
Magia.*II.*Two Appendices to Operative knowledge: An Inventory of the
eſtate of Man.* § *A Catalogue of Polychreſts, or things of multifarious uſe.*

CAP. VI.

*Of the great Appendix of Natural Philoſophy, as well Speculative as Ope-
rative ; Mathematick knowledge: and that it ought to be placed rather amongſt Appendices ; than amongſt ſubſtantial Sciences.* § *The
Partition of Mathematicks into Pure, and Mixt.*

The fourth BOOK.

CAP. I.

I. **T**He *Partition of the Knowledge of Man, into the Philoſophy of
Humanity, and Civil.* § *The partition of the knowledge of Humanity, into the knowledge touching the Body of Man ; and into the
knowledge touching the Soul of Man.* II. *The conſtitution of a general knowledge, touching the Nature and Eſtate of Man.* § *The partition of the knowledge concerning the Eſtate of Man, into the knowledge touching the Perſon of Man ; and into the knowledge touching
the League of Soul and Body.* § *The partition of the knowledge touching the Perſon of Man into the knowledge of Man's miſeries.*
§ *And of Man's prerogatives.*III. *The partition of the knowledge, touching the League, into the knowledge of Indications,* § *And of Impreſſions.* § *The aſſignment of Phyſiognomy.* § *And of Interpretation of
Natural Dreams: unto the Doctrine of Indications.*

CAP. II.

I. *The partition of the knowledge reſpecting the Body of Man, into Art Medicinal.* § *Coſmetick.* § *Athletick.* § *And Voluptuary.* II. *The partition of Medicine, into three duties.* § *Conſervation of Health.*
III. *Cure of Diſeaſes.* IV. *And Prolongation of life: and that the
laſt Part, Prolongation of life, ſhould be ſeparate from the other two.*

CAP. III.

I. *The partition of Humane Philoſophy touching the Soul, into the knowledge of the Inſpired Eſſence ; and into the knowledge of the ſenſible,
or traduced Soul.* § *The ſecond partition of the ſame Philoſophy, into
the knowledge of the Suſtance and Faculties of the Soul · And into
the knowledge of the Uſe, and Objects of the Faculties.* II. *Two Appendices of the knowledge, concerning the Faculties of the Soul, the
knowledge of Natural Divination.* § *And the knowledge of Faſcination.* III. *The Diſtribution of the Faculties of the ſenſible Soul, into
Motion, and Senſe.*

The fifth BOOK.

CAP. I.

I. **T**He *partition of the knowledge which reſpecteth the uſe and objects of
the Faculties of the Mind of Man, into Logick, and Ethick.* II.*The
Diviſion of Logick, into the Arts of Invention, of Judgement, of Memory, and of Tradition.*   CAP.

I. The partition of the Art of Invention, into the Inventive of Arts, and of Arguments. § The former of these which is the more eminent, is Deficient. **II.** The partition of the Inventive Art of Arts, into Literate Experience. § And a New Organ. **III.** A delineation of Literate Experience.

CAP. III.

I. The partition of the Inventive Art of Arguments, into Promptuary, or Places of Preparation: And Topick, or Places of Suggestion. **II.** The partition of Topicks, into General, § And particular Topicks. **III.** An Example of particular Topick in the Inquiry, De Gravi & Levi.

CAP. IV.

I. The partition of the Art of Judging, into Judgement by Induction, § And by Syllogism. Of the first a Collection is made in the Novum Organum. § The first partition of Judgement by Syllogism into Reduction, Direct, and Inverst. § The second partition thereof, into Analytick Art, and the knowledge of Elenches. **II.** The division of the knowledge of Elenches, into Elenches of Sophisms, § Into Elenches of Interpretation of Terms, § And into Elenches of Images or Idolaes. **III.** The division of Idolaes, § Into Impression from the general nature of Man, or Idola Tribûs. § Into Impressions from the Individual temper of Particulars, or Idola specûs. § Into Impressions by words and Communicative nature, or Idola Fori. **IV.** An Appendix to the Art of Judging; namely of the Analogy of Demonstration according to the nature of the subject.

CAP. V.

I. The Partition of Art Retentive, or of Memory, into the Knowledge of the Helps of Memory. § And the Knowledge of Memory it self. **II.** The Division of the Doctrine of Memory, into Prenotion, and Emblem.

The sixth BOOK.

CAP. I.

I. THe Partition of the Art of Tradition, into the Doctrine of the Organ of Speech. The Doctrine of the Method of Speech, and the Doctrine of the Illustration of Speech. § The partition of the Doctrine of the Organ of Speech, into the knowledge of the Notes of things; of Speaking, and of Writing: Of which the two last constitute Grammer, and the Partions thereof. § The Partition of the knowledge of the Notes of Things, into Hieroglyphicks; and into Characters Real. **II.** A second Partition of Grammer into Literary; and Philosophycal. **III.** The aggregation of Poesie referring to Measure, to the knowledge of Speech. § An aggregation of the knowledge of Ciphers to the knowledge of Scripture.

CAP. II.

I. The Doctrine of the Method of Speech is assigned a substantial and principal Part of Traditive knowledge: it is stiled the Wisdom of Delivery. **II.** The divers kinds of Methods are enumerated; their Profits and Disprofits annext. § The Parts of Method.

CAP. III.

I. The Grounds and Office of Rhetorick. **II.** Three Appendices which appertain only to the preparatory Part. The Colours of Good and Evil, as well simple as compared. **III.** The Anti-theta of Things. **IV.** Lesser stiles or usual Forms of Speech.

CAP.

CAP. IV.

I. *Two general Appendices of Traditive knowledge : Art Critical.* II. *And Pedagogical.*

The seventh BOOK.

CAP. I.

I. *The Partition of Moral Philosophy, into the knowledge of the Exemplar, or Platform; and into the Georgicks or Culture of the Mind. § The division of the Exemplar (namely of Good) into Good Simple, and Good Compared.* II. *The Partition of Good Simple, into Individual Good; and Good of Communion.*

CAP. II.

I *The Partition of individual or private Good, into Good Active; and Good Passive.* II. *The Partition of Passive Good, into Conservative Good; and perfective Good.* III. *The Partition of the Good of Communion, into General. § And into Respective Duties:*

CAP. III.

I. *The Partition of the Doctrine of the Culture of the Mind, into the knowledge of the Characters of the Mind.* II. *Of the Affections.* III. *Of the Remedies and Cures thereof.* IV. *An Appendix to the same Doctrine touching the Congruity between the Good of the Mind, and the Good of the Body.*

The eighth BOOK.

CAP. I.

The Partition of Civil knowledge, § Into the knowledge of Conversation. § The knowledge of Negociation. § And the knowledge of Empire or State-Government.

CAP. II.

I. *The Partition of the knowledge of Negociation into the knowledge of dispersed Occasions.* II. *And into the knowledge of the Advancement of life. § Examples of the knowledge of scattered Occasions from some of Solomons Parables. § Precepts concerning the Advancement of Fortune.*

CAP. III.

The Partition of the Art of Empire or Government is omitted, only access is made to two Deficients. I. *The knowledge of enlarging the Bounds of Empire.* II. *And the knowledge of universal Justice, or of the Fountains of L*

The ninth BOOK.

CAP. I.

The Partitions of inspired Theology are omitted, only way is made unto three Desiderates. I. *The knowledge of the right Use of Humane Reason in matters Divine.* II. *The knowledge of the degrees of unity in the City of God.* III. *The Emanations of SS. Scripture.*

FRAN-

FRANCISCI

DE

VERVLAMIO

ARCHITECTURA

Scientiarum.

THE

GENERAL IDEA

AND

PROJECT

OF THE

LORD *VERVLAM'S*

Inſtauratio Magna.

Repreſented in the

PLATFORM

OF THE

DESIGN

Of the Firſt Part thereof,

As it was conceiv'd in the Mind of the Author
and is expreſſed in the Model of the Work.

DEUS OMNIA
IN MENSURA, ET NUMERO, ET ORDINE,
DISPOSUIT.

The Emanation of SCIENCES, from the Intellectual Faculties of MEMORY, IMAGINATION, REASON.

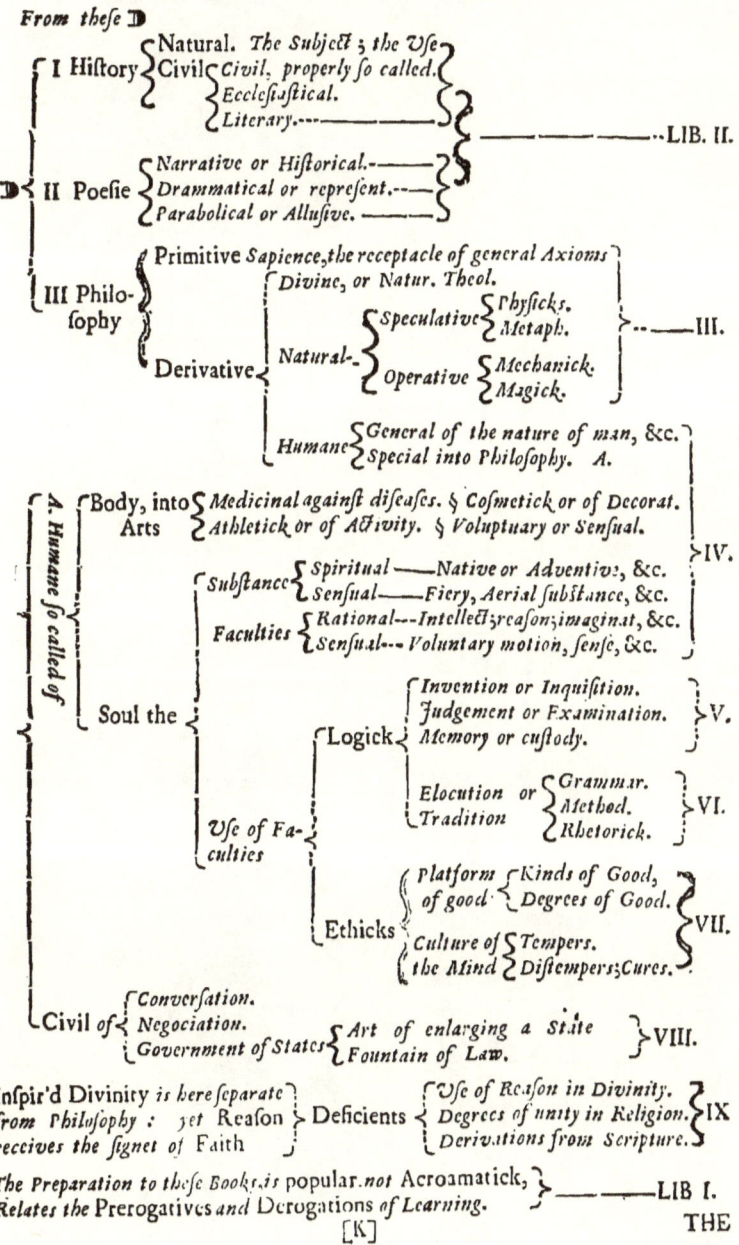

From these 𝕯

I History ⎰ Natural. *The Subject ; the Use*
⎱ Civil ⎰ *Civil, properly so called.*
⎱ *Ecclesiastical.*
⎱ *Literary.* ——————————————————————————————**LIB. II.**

II Poesie ⎰ *Narrative or Historical.*—
⎱ *Drammatical or represent.*—
⎱ *Parabolical or Allusive.*

III Philosophy ⎰ Primitive *Sapience, the receptacle of general Axioms*
⎱ ⎰ *Divine,* or *Natur. Theol.*
⎱ Speculative ⎰ *Physicks.*
⎱ *Metaph.* ⎱ **III.**
Derivative ⎰ *Natural* ⎰ Operative ⎰ *Mechanick.*
⎱ *Magick.*
Humane ⎰ *General of the nature of man, &c.*
⎱ *Special into Philosophy. A.*

A. Humane so called of

Body, into Arts ⎰ *Medicinal against diseases.* § *Cosmetick or of Decorat.*
⎱ *Athletick or of Activity.* § *Voluptuary or Sensual.*

⎰ Substance ⎰ *Spiritual* ——*Native or Adventive, &c.*
⎱ *Sensual* ——*Fiery, Aerial substance, &c.* **IV.**
Faculties ⎰ *Rational* ---*Intellect;reason;imaginat, &c.*
⎱ *Sensual* --- *Voluntary motion, sense, &c.*

Soul the ⎰ Logick ⎰ *Invention or Inquisition.*
⎱ *Judgement or Examination.* **V.**
⎱ *Memory or custody.*

Use of Faculties ⎰ *Elocution* or ⎰ *Grammar.*
⎱ *Tradition* ⎱ *Method.* **VI.**
⎱ *Rhetorick.*

Ethicks ⎰ Platform of good ⎰ *Kinds of Good,*
⎱ *Degrees of Good.* **VII.**
Culture of the Mind ⎰ *Tempers.*
⎱ *Distempers;Cures.*

Civil of ⎰ *Conversation.*
⎱ *Negociation.*
⎱ *Government of States* ⎰ *Art of enlarging a State* ⎰ **VIII.**
⎱ *Fountain of Law.*

Inspir'd Divinity is here separate ⎰ *from Philosophy :* yet Reason ⎰ Deficients ⎰ *Use of Reason in Divinity.*
receives the signet of Faith ⎱ *Degrees of unity in Religion.* **IX**
Derivations from Scripture.

The Preparation to these Books is popular. *not* Acroamatick, ⎰ ———**LIB I.**
Relates the Prerogatives *and* Derogations *of Learning.* ⎱

[K]   THE

LIB. I. THE DIGNITY OF LEARNING.

Reporting the — **Difhonours & Derogations of Learning in the**

Difcredites from

Divines Cap. 1.
- Defire of Knowledge the firſt ſin,
- Knowledge an Infinite : an Anxious thing.
- Learning the cauſe of Hereſie and Atheiſm.

Objected, Anſwered.

Politicks C. 2.
- Learning makes men unapt for Arms.
- Difables men for Civil Affairs.
- Particular indifpoſitions pretended.

Objected, Anſwered:

Learned Mens Cap. 3.

Fortunes
- Scarcity of means.
- Privateneſs of life.
- Meanneſs of imployment.

Manners
- Too incompatible with the times.
- Too ſenſible of the common good.
- Not applying to Perſons of quality.
- A failing in points of behaviour.
- Groſs flattery practiſed by ſome.

Studies in ſome impertinents.

Diſtempers in ſtudies Cap. 4.
- Phantaſtical Learning.
- Contentious Learning.
- Delicate Learning.

Peccant Humors Cap. 5.
- Affection to two extremes, *Antiquity, Novelty.*
- A diſtruſt that any thing *New* ſhould now be found out.
- A conceit that the beſt Opinions ſtill prevail.
- A too peremptory reduction of Sciences into Methods.
- A neglect of *Primitive Philoſophy.*
- A divorce of the Intellect from the Object.
- A contagion of Knowledge from particular inclinations.
- An impatience of ſuſpenſe : haſte to Poſitive Aſſertion.
- A Magiſtral manner of Tradition of Knowledge.
- Aim of Writers, Illuſtration, not Propagation.
- End of Studies, Curioſity, Pleaſure, Profit, Promotion, &c.

Honors, and Prerogatives of Learning from Arguments

Divine Cap. 6.
- Wiſdom of God. § Angels of Illumination.
- Firſt light. § *Adams'.* § *Abel's,* Contemplation, &c.
- The Learning of *Moſes, Job, Solomon,* &c.

Humane cap. 7. 8.
- Inventors of Arts conſecrated as Gods.
- Civil Eſtates advanc'd by Learning.
- The concurrency of Arms and Letters.
- The Dominion. § Donations of Learning.

LIB. II. THE ADVANCEMENT OF LEARNING.

```
                          ⎧ Amplitude of Reward.
          General by the ⎨ Wisdom of Direction.
                          ⎩ Conjunction of Labours.

Personal,
in Proem.
lib.                                ⎧ Places, ⎧ Buildings.   § Revenews.
                                    ⎪ as      ⎩ Priviledges. § Discipline.
                        ⎧ Promoted ⎨
                        ⎪    by     ⎪ Books,  ⎧ Libraries.
                        ⎪           ⎨ as      ⎩ Good Editions.
                        ⎪           ⎪
            Special ⎨              ⎩ Personi ⎧ Lectures for Arts extant.
                        ⎪            as       ⎩ Inquirers into Arts non-extant.
                        ⎪
                        ⎪           ⎧ Want of foundations for Arts at large.
                        ⎪ Preju-   ⎪ Want of sufficient Salary to Lecturers.
                        ⎩ diced    ⎨ Want of allowance for Experiments.
                           for      ⎪ Want of a right course of proceding in studies.
                                    ⎪ Want of Intelligence between Universities.
                                    ⎩ Want of Inquiries into Arts Deficient.


                                               ⎧ Genera- ⎧ Heaven.  § Meteors.
                                               ⎪ tions.  ⎨ Earth.   § Sea.
                                               ⎪         ⎩ Elements. § Specificks.
                                    ⎧ Subject ⎨ Preter-  ⎧ Monsters. § Marvels.
                                    ⎪ Cap. 2. ⎨ Gener.   ⎩ Magick, &c.
                        ⎧ Natural ⎨           ⎪ Arts me- ⎧ Agriculture.
                        ⎪  the      ⎪           ⎩ chanick  ⎩ Alchimy, &c.
                        ⎪           ⎩ Use and end ⎧ Narrative.
                        ⎪             Cap. 3.     ⎩ Inductive.

           1 History ⎨                           ⎧ Memorials.
           referr'd    ⎪           ⎧ Civil in spe- ⎧ 1 ⎨ Antiquities.  ⎧ Chronicles.
Real, by a to Me-      ⎨           ⎪ cial. C.5.6,  ⎨   ⎩ Perfect History ⎨ Lives.
right Par- mory        ⎪           ⎪ 7,8,9,10.     ⎪                     ⎩ Relations.
tition of             ⎪ Civil ⎨              ⎩ 2 Pure.  § Mixt.
Learning              ⎪ into    ⎪ Ecclesiastical ⎧ General of the Church.
Into                  ⎩           ⎨ Cap. 11.     ⎨ Special ⎧ Prophesie.
Cap. 1.                             ⎪                       ⎩ Providence.
                                    ⎪ Literary ⎧ Ages. § Climates. § Declinations,
                                    ⎩ Cap. 4.  ⎩ Instaurations, &c. of Learning.

                        ⎧ Append. to History.   Orations. Epistles. § Apothegms.
                        ⎩ Cap. 12.

                                   ⎧ Narrative or Historical.
           2 Poesie referred to the ⎨ Drammatical or Representative.
           Imagination, Cap. 13.    ⎩ Parabolical or Allusive.
           3 Philosophy, referring to Reason and the will. Lib. seqq.
```

**LIB. III. THE PARTITION OF KNOWLEDGES IN GE-
NERAL INTO**

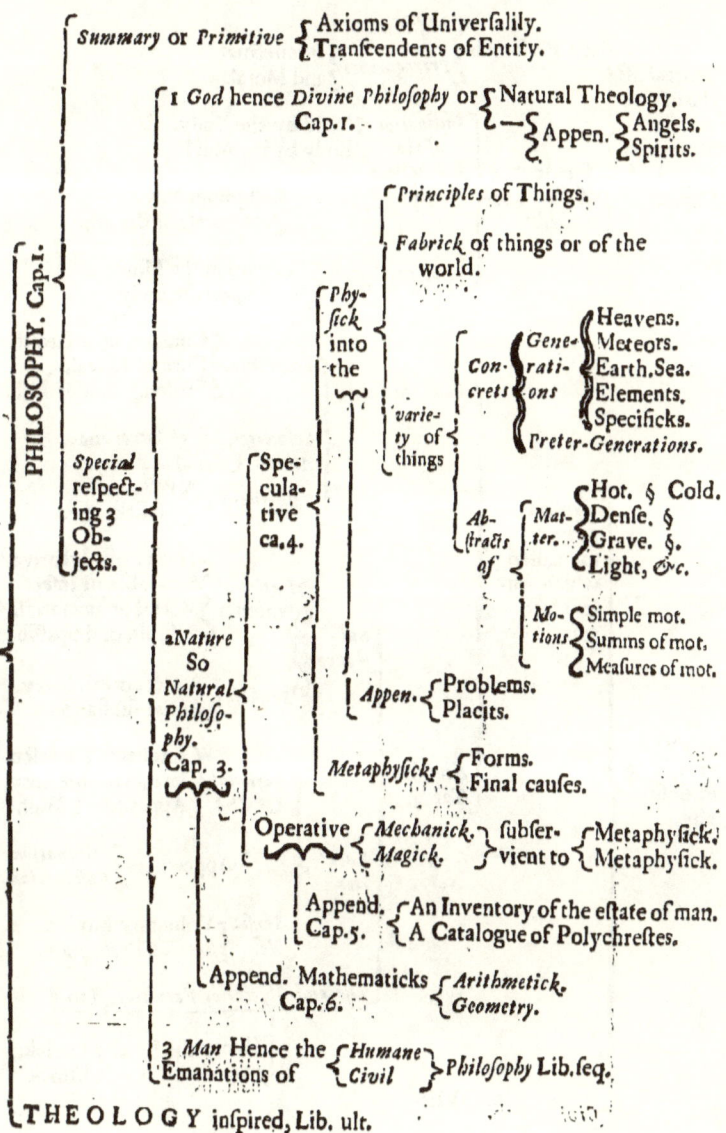

Summary or *Primitive* { Axioms of Univerſality.
Tranſcendents of Entity.

PHILOSOPHY. Cap.1.

1 *God* hence *Divine Philoſophy* or { Natural Theology.
Cap.1. — { Appen. { Angels,
Spirits.

Principles of Things.

Fabrick of things or of the
world.

Special
reſpect-
ing 3
Ob-
jects.

Phy-
ſick
into
the
varie-
ty of
things

Con-
crets { Gene-
rati-
ons { Heavens.
Meteors.
Earth.Sea.
Elements.
Specificks.

Preter-Generations.

Spe-
cula-
tive
ca.4.

Ab-
ſtracts
of { Mat-
ter. { Hot. § Cold.
Denſe. §
Grave. §.
Light, &c.

a Nature
So
Natural
Philoſo-
phy.
Cap. 3.

Mo-
tions { Simple mot.
Summs of mot.
Meaſures of mot.

Appen. { Problems.
Placits.

Metaphyſicks { Forms.
Final cauſes.

Operative { *Mechanick.*
Magick. } ſubſer-
vient to { Metaphyſick.
Metaphyſick.

Append.
Cap.5. { An Inventory of the eſtate of man.
A Catalogue of Polychreſtes.

Append. Mathematicks { *Arithmetick.*
Cap.6. { *Geometry.*

3 *Man* Hence the { *Humane*
Emanations of { *Civil* } *Philoſophy* Lib.ſeq.

THEOLOGY inſpired, Lib. ult.

LIB. IV. THE PARTITION OF HUMANE KNOWLEDGE, OR THE KNOWLEDGE OF HUMANITY.

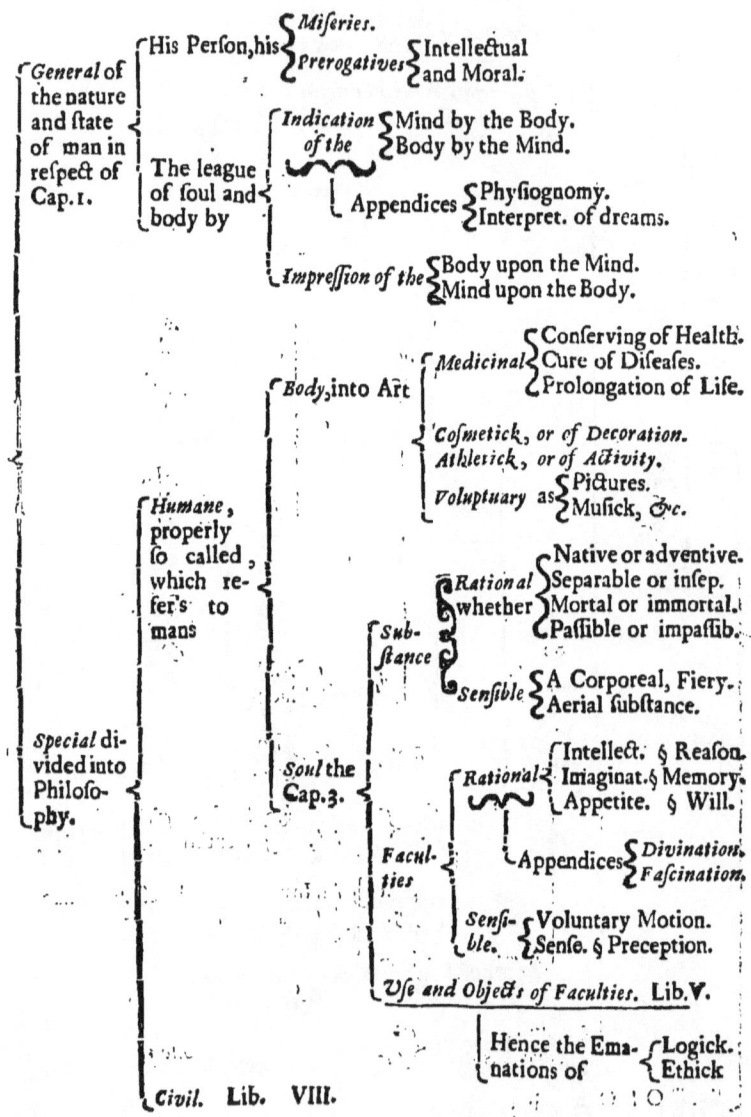

General of the nature and ſtate of man in reſpect of Cap. 1.

His Perſon, his
- *Miſeries.*
- *Prerogatives* Intellectual and Moral.

The league of ſoul and body by
- *Indication of the* Mind by the Body. / Body by the Mind.
- Appendices Phyſiognomy. / Interpret. of dreams.
- *Impreſſion of the* Body upon the Mind. / Mind upon the Body.

Special divided into Philoſophy.

Humane, properly ſo called, which refer's to mans

Body, into Art
- *Medicinal* Conſerving of Health. / Cure of Diſeaſes. / Prolongation of Life.
- *Coſmetick,* or of Decoration. / *Athletick,* or of Activity. / *Voluptuary* as Pictures. / Muſick, &c.

Soul the Cap. 3.
- *Subſtance*
  - *Rational whether* Native or adventive. / Separable or inſep. / Mortal or immortal. / Paſſible or impaſſib.
  - *Senſible* A Corporeal, Fiery. / Aerial ſubſtance.
- *Faculties*
  - *Rational* Intellect. § Reaſon. / Imaginat. § Memory. / Appetite. § Will.
  - Appendices Divination. / Faſcination.
  - *Senſible.* Voluntary Motion. / Senſe. § Preception.
- *Uſe and Objects of Faculties.* Lib. V.
- Hence the Emanations of Logick. / Ethick

Civil. Lib. VIII.

LIB. V. THE PARTITION OF THE USE AND OBJECTS OF THE FACULTIES OF THE MIND, INTO

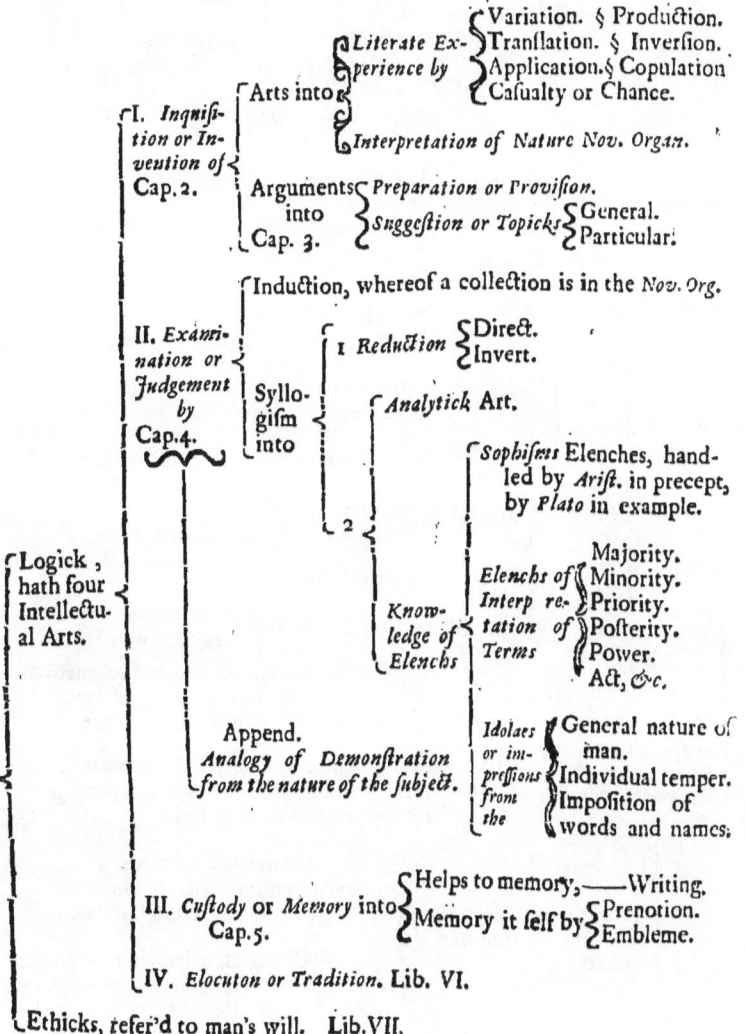

Logick, hath four Intellectual Arts.

I. *Inquisition or Invention of* Cap. 2.

Arts into *Literate Experience by*
- Variation. § Production.
- Translation. § Inversion.
- Application. § Copulation
- Casualty or Chance.

Interpretation of Nature Nov. Organ.

Arguments into Cap. 3.
- *Preparation or Provision.*
- *Suggestion or Topicks* — General. Particular.

II. *Examination or Judgement by* Cap. 4.

Induction, whereof a collection is in the *Nov. Org.*

Syllogism into
- 1 *Reduction* — Direct. Invert.
- 2 *Analytick* Art.

Sophismes Elenches, handled by *Arist.* in precept, by *Plato* in example.

Knowledge of Elenchs
- *Elenchs of Interpretation of Terms* — Majority. Minority. Priority. Posterity. Power. Act, &c.
- *Idolaes or impressions from the* — General nature of man. Individual temper. Imposition of words and names.

Append. *Analogy of Demonstration from the nature of the subject.*

III. *Custody or Memory into* Cap. 5.
- Helps to memory, — Writing.
- Memory it self by — Prenotion. Embleme.

IV. *Elocution or Tradition.* Lib. VI.

Ethicks, refer'd to man's will. Lib. VII,

LIB. VI. THE PARTITION OF THE ART OF ELOCUTION OR OF TRADITION INTO THE

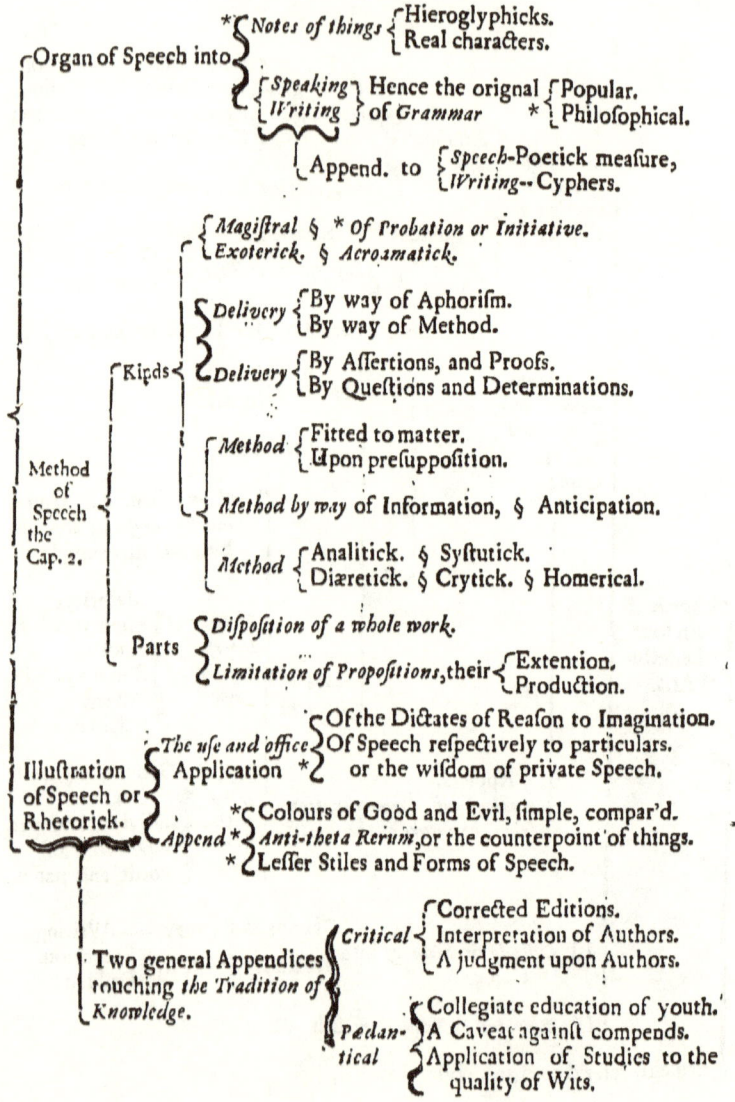

Organ of Speech into

* *Notes of things* { Hieroglyphicks.
Real characters.

Speaking *Writing* } of *Grammar* Hence the orignal { Popular.
* Philofophical.

Append. to { *Speech*-Poetick meafure,
Writing-- Cyphers.

Method of Speech the Cap. 2.

Kinds

{ *Magiftral* § * Of Probation or *Initiative*.
Exoterick. § *Acroamatick*.

Delivery { By way of Aphorifm.
By way of Method.

Delivery { By Affertions, and Proofs.
By Queftions and Determinations.

Method { Fitted to matter.
Upon prefuppofition.

Method by way of Information, § Anticipation.

Method { Analitick. § Syftutick.
Diæretick. § Crytick. § Homerical.

Parts { *Difpofition of a whole work.*
Limitation of Propofitions, their { Extention.
Production.

Illuftration of Speech or Rhetorick.

The ufe and office Application *

{ Of the Dictates of Reafon to Imagination.
Of Speech refpectively to particulars.
or the wifdom of private Speech.

Append *

* { Colours of Good and Evil, fimple, compar'd.
Anti-theta Rerum, or the counterpoint of things.
Leffer Stiles and Forms of Speech.

Two general Appendices touching *the Tradition of Knowledge*.

Critical { Corrected Editions.
Interpretation of Authors.
A judgment upon Authors.

Pedantical { Collegiate education of youth.
A Caveat againft compends.
Application of Studies to the quality of Wits.

LIBVII.

Platform of Good. Cap. I.
{
  Simple or the kinds of Good Cap. 2.
  {
    Individuals, or vertues
    {
      Active from a desire of { Perpetuity. Certainty. Variety. }
      Passive { Conservative Good. Perfective Good. }
    }
    Of Communion, or Duties
    {
      General. Duties of { Professions, &c. Oeconomical; Political duties. }
      Respective Vices { Impostures, frauds, cautils, &c. Of professions. }
    }
    Individ. & common
    {
      Simply and irrespectively taken.
      Comparatively between { Man and Man. Case and Case. Publick and Private. Time and Time. }
    }
  }
  Compared, or the Degrees of Good of { Honesty. § Profit. § Pleasure. Body. § Mind. § Fortune. Contemplative. Active Good. }
}

Culture of the Mind in the Cap. 3.
{
  Characters or tempers.
  {
    Impressed by Nature to { Arms. § Letters. Contemplative. § Active course of life. }
    Impos'd by { Chance of { Sex. § Age. § Region. Health. § Beauty, &c. } Fortune { Nobility. § Honours. Riches. § Poverty. } }
  }
  Affections or distempers, their.
  {
    Names { Pleasure, pain, fear, hope. Anger, Patience, Love, Hate. }
    Nature { How stirr'd. How still'd. How secreted? How disclosed? What operations they produce? What turns they take? How enwrapt? How they encountre? }
  }
  Cures, or Remedies. { Custom, Exercise, Habit, Education. Emulation, Company, Friends, Fame, Reproof, Exhortation, Laws, Books. Study, Brief Precepts hereof. }
}

Append. *The Congruity between the Good of* { Body and Mind. }

[L]

LIB. VIII. THE PARTITION OF CIVIL KNOWLEDGE INTO

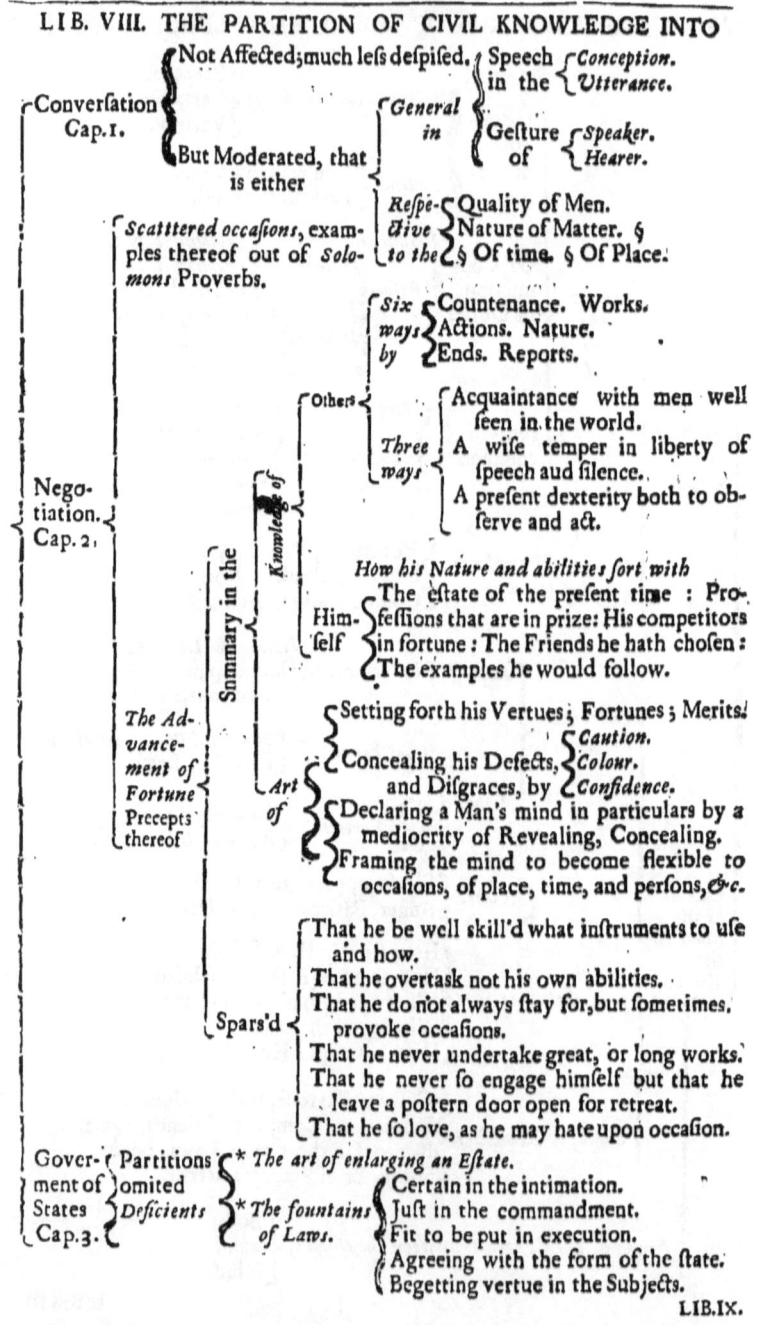

Conversation
Cap. 1.
{
Not Affected; much lefs defpifed.
But Moderated, that is either

Speech in the { Conception. Utterance.

General in { Gefture of { Speaker. Hearer.

Negotiation.
Cap. 2.
{
Scatttered occafions, examples thereof out of Solomons Proverbs.

Refpective to the { Quality of Men. Nature of Matter. § Of time. § Of Place.

Summary in the Knowledge of

Others { Six ways by { Countenance. Works. Actions. Nature. Ends. Reports.

Three ways {
Acquaintance with men well feen in the world.
A wife temper in liberty of fpeech aud filence.
A prefent dexterity both to obferve and act.

The Advancement of Fortune Precepts thereof

Himfelf {
How his Nature and abilities fort with
The eftate of the prefent time : Profeffions that are in prize: His competitors in fortune : The Friends he hath chofen : The examples he would follow.

Art of {
Setting forth his Vertues; Fortunes; Merits.
Concealing his Defects, and Difgraces, by { Caution. Colour. Confidence.
Declaring a Man's mind in particulars by a mediocrity of Revealing, Concealing.
Framing the mind to become flexible to occafions, of place, time, and perfons, &c.

Spars'd {
That he be well skill'd what inftruments to ufe and how.
That he overtask not his own abilities.
That he do not always ftay for, but fometimes, provoke occafions.
That he never undertake great, or long works.
That he never fo engage himfelf but that he leave a poftern door open for retreat.
That he fo love, as he may hate upon occafion.

Government of States Cap. 3.
{
Partitions omitted { * The art of enlarging an Eftate.
Deficients { * The fountains of Laws.
{
Certain in the intimation.
Juft in the commandment.
Fit to be put in execution.
Agreeing with the form of the ftate.
Begetting vertue in the Subjects.

LIB. IX.

LIB. IX. INSPIRED THEOLOGY.

The Partition of Inspired Divinity is omitted, only an entrance is made unto three DEFICIENTS.

Deficients

I * *The Limits and Use of HUMANE REASON in Matters DIVINE.*

The

Use it self { Explication of Divine Mysteries.
{ Inferences thence deduced.

Excesses in that Use { Mining into things not revealed by a too Curious inquiry.
{ Attributing equal Authority to *Derivations,* as to *Principles* themselves.

II * *The Degrees of Unity in the City of God.*

In Points { Fundamental ; one Lo. one Faith, &c.
{ Superstructive or of perfection.

☾ { A dissent *in Fundamental Points,* discorporates men from the Church of God ; not so *in superstructive Points.*

III * *Emanations from Scripture wherein are observed*

Errors in Interpretation { In supposing that all Philosophy is derived from Scripture, as the School of *Paracelsus* did, and some others now do.
{ In Interpreting Scripture as one would a humane Author ; whereas two things were known to God which are not known to Man { Secrets of the Heart.
The { Succession of Times.

A Desiderate { A Collection of Positive Divinity upon particular Texts in brief observations.
{ Prejudiced

by { Dilating into commmon places.
{ Chasing after Controversies
{ Reducing to Methods.

FRAN=

OF THE
Dignity and Advancement
OF
LEARNING.

CHAP. I.

The Confecration of this Work unto the moft learned of Princes, K. James, who in high, but juft, conceptions is here admired. § The Diftribution, into the Dignity and the Proficiency of Learning. I. Difcredits of Learning, from the objections of Divines : That the afpiring unto Knowledge was the firft Sin. That Learning is a thing infinite, and full of Anxiety. That Knowledge enclines the Mind to Herefie and Atheifm. II. The folution : Original Guilt was not in the Quantity, but in the Quality of Knowledge. § The Corrective hereof, Charity. III. Againft Infinity, Anxiety, and Seducements of Sciences ; three Prefervatives : That we forget not our mortality. § That Learning give us content. § That it foar not too high. § And fo Philofophy leads the mind by the Links of Second Caufes, unto the Firft.

Here were under the Old Law (Excellent *King*) both *Free-will-offerings,* and *Daily Sacrifices* ; the one proceeding upon ordinary obfervance ; the other upon a devout Chearfulnefs. Certainly, in my opinion, fome fuch kind of Homage belongs to *Kings* from their fervants ; namely, That every one fhould tender, not only Tributes of his Duty, but Prefents of Affection. In the former of thefe, I hope, I fhall not be wanting ; for the latter I was in fufpenfe what I fhould moft principally undertake, and in conclufion I thought it more refpective to make choice of fome Oblation, which might reſet, rather to the propriety and excellency of your individual Perfon, than to the bufinefs of your Crown and State.

§ Reprefenting your Majefty, as my duty is, many times unto my mind; (leaving afide the other parts, whether of your Vertue, or of your Fortune) I have been poffeft with extreme wonder, when I confider the

A   excellency

excellency of thofe Vertues and Faculties in you,which the Philofophers call intellectual; the capacity of your Mind comprehending fo many and fo great Notions, the faithfulnefs of your Memory, the fwiftnefs of your Apprehenfion, the penetration of your Judgment, the order and facility of your Elocution.   In truth *Plato*'s Opinion fometimes comes into my

In Phædo. mind, which maintains, *That knowledge is nothing elfe but remembrance; and that the mind of man by nature knows all things, once redimed and reftored to her own native light, which the cloudy vault or gloomy tabernacle of the body had orefpread with darknefs.* For certainly the beft and cleareft Inftance for this Affertion fhines in your Majefty, whofe mind is fo ready to take flame from the leaft occafion prefented, or the leaft fpark of anothers Knowledge delivered.   Wherefore as the facred Scripture faith of

1 Reg.4. the wifeft King, *That his heart was as the fands of the fea :* which though it be one of the largeft Bodies, yet it confifteth of the fmalleft portions; fo hath God given your Majefty a compofition of Underftanding exceeding admirable, being able to compafs and comprehend the greateft matters, and neverthelefs, to apprehend the leaft, and not to fuffer them to efcape your Obfervation; Whereas it fhould feem very difficult, or rather an impoffibility in nature, for the fame Inftrument to make it felf fit for great and fmall works.   And for your gift of Speech, I call to mind

Annal.13. what *Cornelius Tacitus* faith of *Auguftus Cæfar, Augufto* (faith he) *prompta ac profluens, quæ deceret principem, eloquentia fuit.*   In truth if we note it well, Speech that is *Elaborate,* or *Affectate,* or *Imitating,* although otherwife excellent, hath fomewhat fervile in it and holding of the fubject; but your Majefties manner of Speech is indeed Prince-like,flowing as from a Fountain, and yet ftreaming and branching it felf into Natures Order, full of Facility and Felicity,*Imitating none,and Inimitable of any.* And as in your Civil eftate, refpecting as well your Kingdom as your Court,there appeareth to be an Emulation and Contention of your Majefties Vertue with your Fortune, namely,excellent moral Endowments with a fortunate Regiment; a pious and patient expectation when time was, of your greater Fortune, with a profperous and feafonable poffeffion of what was expected; a holy obfervation of the Laws of Marriage, with a bleffed and happy fruit of Marriage in a moft fair Progeny; a godly Propenfion and moft befeeming a Chriftian Prince to Peace, with a fortunate concurrence of the like inclination in your neighbour Princes : So likewife in your intellectual Abilities, there feemeth to be no lefs Contention and Emulation; if we compare your Majefties gifts of Nature with the rich Treafury of multiplicious Erudition and the knowledge of many Arts. Neither is it eafie to find any *King* fince Chrifts time, which may be compared with your Majefty for variety and improvement of all kind of Learning Divine and Humane: Let who will revolve and perufe the Succeffion of Kings and Emperours, and he fhall find this judgement is truly made. For indeed it feemeth much in Kings, if by the compendious Extraction of other mens Wits and Labours, they can take hold of knowledge, or attain any fuperficial ornaments or fhews of Learning, or if they countenance and prefer learned men; but for a King, and a King born, to drink indeed the true Fountains of Learning, nay, to be himfelf a Fountain of Learning, is almoft a Miracle.   And this alfo is an accefs to your Majefty, that in the fame Clofet of your Mind, there are treafured up as well Divine and Sacred Literature, as Prophane and Humane; fo that your Majefty

jefty ftands invefted with that triplicity of Glory, which was afcribed
to that famous *Hermes Trifmegiftus, The Power of a King, the Illumination
of a Prieft, the Learning of a Philofopher.* Wherefore fince in thefe glorious Attributes of Learning, fo inherent and individual in your Perfon,
your Majefty fo far excels all other Kings, it is very meet that fuch rare
endowments of Nature and Art fhould be celebrated, not only in the fame
or admiration of the prefent time, or in light of Hiftory conveyed o-
ver to Pofterity, but be engraven in fome folid Work, which both
may exprefs the Power of a great King, and bear a Character or Signa-
ture of fo excellent a learned King. Now (to return to our intended
purpofe) I concluded with my felf that I could not make to your Majefty a better oblation, than of fome Treatife tending to that end.

§ The Sum and Argument hereof will confift of *two Parts : In the former,* which is more flight and popular (yet may not be paft over) we fhall
entreat of the *excellency of Knowledge and Learning, through all the parts
thereof;* and likewife of the *merit of thofe who have worthily and wifely
imployed and placed their bounties and induftries in the Augmentation, and
Propagation thereof. In the latter Part* (which is the main and fum of this
work) *I fhall propound and fet down what in this kind hath been embraced,
undertaken and accomplifht hitherto, for the Advancement of Learning :
and again briefly touch at fuch particulars as feem deficient in this enterprize;*
to the end that though I dare not prefume pofitively to feparate and felect what I would chiefly commend unto your Majefty; yet by reprefenting many and different Obfervations, I may excite your Princely Cogitations to vifit the peculiar Treafures of your own Mind, and thence to
extract what is moft conducent to the *amplifying and enlarging of the
bounds of Arts and Knowledges,* agreeable to your Magnanimity and
Wifdom.

I. In the entrance to the *former Part,* to clear the way, and as it were,
to make filence, to have the teftimonies concerning the *Dignity* of Learning to be better heard, without the interruption of tacit Objections, I
think good firft to deliver Learning from the Difcredits and Difgraces
which Ignorance hath caft upon it, but Ignorance feverally difguifed; ap-
pearing and difcovering it felf fometime in the *zeal of Divines,* fometime
in the *arrogancy of Politicks,* and fometimes *in the errors of Learned men
themfelves.* I hear the former fort fay, *That Knowledge is of the nature and
number of thofe things, which are to be accepted with great Limitation and
Caution; That the afpiring to overmuch Knowledge, was the original temptation and fin, whereupon enfued the Fall of Man; And that even at this
day Knowledge hath fomewhat of the Serpent in it, and therefore where it
entreth into a man, it makes him fwell, Scientia inflat;* That *Solomon*   1 Cor. 8.
gives a cenfure, *That there is no end of making Books, and that much rea-*   Ecclef.12.
ding is a wearinefs to the flefh; and again in another place, *That in fpaci-*   Ecclef.1.
ous knowledge there is much contriftation, and that he that encreafeth know-
ledge, encreafeth anxiety; That *St. Paul* gives a caveat, *That we be not fpoil'd*   Colof. 2.
through vain Philofophy ; And that experience demonftrates how the
Learnedft men have been Arch-hereticks; How Learned times have
been inclined to Atheifm, and how the Contemplation of fecond Caufes
doth derogate from the Authority of the firft.

II. To difcover then the error and ignorance of this Opinion, and the
mifunderftanding in the grounds thereof, any man may fee plainly that

theſe

these men do not obserue and confider, That it was not that *Pure and Primitive Knowledge of Nature*, by the light whereof man did giue names to other Creatures in Paradife, as they were brought before him, according to their Proprieties, which gaue the occafion to the Fall; but it was that proud Knowledge of *Good and Evil*, with an intent to fhake off God and to giue Law vnto himfelf. Neither is it any *Quantity of Knowledge*, how great foeuer, that can make the mind of man to fwell; for nothing can fill, much lefs extend the Soul of man but God, and the contemplation of God: therefore *Solomon* fpeaking of the two Principal Senfes of. Inquifition, the Eye and the Ear, affirms, *That the Eye is never fatisfied with feeing, nor the Ear with hearing;* and if there be no fulnefs, then is the Continent greater than the Content. So of Knowledge it felf and the Mind of Man, whereto the Senfes are but Reporters, he defines likewife in the Words plac'd after the Calendar or Ephimerides which he makes of the diuerfity of times and feafons for all Actions and Purpofes, concluding thus, *God hath made all things beautiful and decent in the true return of their feafons; alfo he hath placed the world in mans heart, yet cannot man find out the work which God worketh from the beginning unto the end:* By which words he declares, not obfcurely, that God hath framed the Mind of Man, as a Mirror or Glafs capable of the Image of the uniuerfal world, and as joyful to receiue the Impreffions thereof, as the Eye joyeth to receiue Light; and not only delighted in the beholding the variety of things and the viciffitudes of times, but raifed alfo to find out and to difcern the inuiolable Laws and infallible Decrees of Nature: And although he feem to infinuate that the fupreme or fummary Law of Nature, which he calleth *the work which God worketh from the beginning to the end*, is not poffible to be found out by Man; yet that doth not derogate from the Capacity of the Mind, but may be referred to the impediments of Knowledge, as the fhortnefs of life, the ill conjunction of labours deprav'd, and unfaithful Tradition of Knowledge over from hand to hand; and many other inconueniencies wherewith the condition of Man is enfnared and inuolued. For that no parcel of the World is denied to Man's enquiry or inuention he clearly declares in another place, where he faith, *The fpirit of a man is as the Lamp of God wherewith he fearcheth the inwards of all fecrets.* If then fuch be the capacity and receipt of the Mind of Man, it is manifeft that there is no danger at all from the *Proportion* or *Quantity* of *Knowledge* how large foeuer, left it fhould make it fwell or out-compafs it felf but; merely in the *Quality*, which being in Quantity more or lefs, if it be taken without the true Correctiue thereof, hath in it fome nature of malignity, or venom full of flatuous fymptoms. This Antidote, or Correctiue fpice, the mixture whereof tempers Knowledge and makes it fo fouereign, is *Charity*, which the Apoftle immediately adds in the former claufe, faying, *Knowledge blows up, but Charity builds up;* Not vnlike to that which he deliuers in another place, *If I fpake* (faith he) *with the tongues of Men and Angels and had not Charity, it were but as a tinkling Cymbal:* Not but that it is an excellent thing to fpeak with the tongues of Men and Angels, but becaufe if it be feuer'd from *Charity*, and not refer'd to the publick good of Mankind, it rather exhibits a vain and empty glory, than any fubftantial and folid fruit.

As for that Cenfure of *Solomon*, concerning the excefs of writing and
reading

Ecclef. 1.

Ecclef. 3.

1 Cor. 8.

1 Cor. 13.

reading Books, and the anxiety of spirit which redoundeth from Knowledg, and that admonition of S. *Paul, that we be not seduced by vain Philosophy;* if those places be rightly understood, they do very excellently set forth the true bounds and limitations, whereby humane knowledge is confin'd and circumscribed, yet so as without any such contracting and coarctation, it may comprehend all the universal nature of things. These limitations are three : *The first, that we do not so place our felicity in Knowledge, as we forget our Mortality: The second, that we make application of our Knowledge, to give our selves repose and contentment and not distaste or repining: The third, that we do not presume by the contemplations of Nature to attain the Mysteries of God.* § For as touching *the first, Solomon* doth excellently expound himself in the same Book ; *I saw well,* saith he, *that knowledge recedes as far from ignorance as light doth from darkness, and that the wise mans eyes keep watch in his head, whereas the fool roundeth about in darkness; but withal I learned that the same mortality involves them both.* | Ecclef. 2.

§ *For the second,* certain it is, no anxiety, or perturbation of mind resulteth from knowledge, otherwise than merely by accident : For all knowledge and wonder (which is the seed of knowledge) is an impression of pleasure in it self; but when we fall to framing conclusions out of our Knowledge, which obliquely applied to our particular purposes, either minister weak fears or vast desires, then there grows that vexation and trouble of Mind, whereof we speak : for then Knowledge is no more *Lumen siccum,* as *Heraclitus* the *Profound* would have it, *Lumen siccum optima anima,* but it becomes *Lumen madidum,* or *maceratum,* being steeped and infused in the humours of the Affections.

§ *The third rule* deserves a little to be stood upon, and not to be lightly passed over : For if any man shall think by view and enquiry into these sensible and material things, to attain that light whereby he may reveal unto himself the Nature and Will of God, then indeed, *is he spoil'd through vain Philosophy.* For the Contemplation of the Creatures, having regard to the Creatures themselves, produceth Knowledge, but having regard to God, wonder only, which is a broken Knowledge. And therefore it was most aptly said by one of *Plato's* School, *That the sense of man carries a resemblance with the sun, which opens and reveals the terrestrial Globe, but conceals and seals up the stars and celestial Globe :* So | Philo Jud, deSomniis. doth the Sense discover natural things, but it darkens and shuts up divine. And hence it hath proceded, that some of the chosen rank of the more learned have fallen into Heresie, whilst they have sought to fly up to the secrets of the Deity, by the waxen wings of the Senses.

§ As for the conceit of those who are of opinion that *too much knowledge should encline the mind to Atheism, and that the ignorance of the second Causes, should be, as it were a Midwife to our Piety towards the first.* I would willingly charge these in the language of *Job, Will you lye for God* | Job 13. *as one man doth for another to gratifie him?* For certain it is that God works nothing in Nature according to ordinary course but by second Causes ; and if they would have it otherwise believed, it is mere imposture, under colour of Piety to God, and nothing else but to offer unto the Author of Truth the unclean sacrifice of a Lye. But farther, it is an assured truth and a conclusion of Experience, That a little or superficial taste of *Philosophy,* may perchance incline the Mind of Man to *A-theism*

*theifm;*but a full draught thereof brings the Mind back again to Religion. For in the entrance of Philofophy, when the fecond Caufes, which are next unto the Senfes, do offer themfelves to the mind of man, and the mind it felf cleaves unto them and dwells there, an oblivion of the higheft Caufe may creep in ; but when a man paffeth on farther and beholds the dependency, continuation and confederacy of Caufes, and the works of Providence, then according to the Allegory of the Poets, he will eafily believe that the *higheft link of Natures chain muſt needs be tied to the foot of* Jupiter's *chair.* To clofe in a word ; Let no man, upon a weak conceit of fobriety or ill applied moderation, think or maintain that a man can fearch too far, or be too well ſtudied *in the Book of God's word,* or in *the Book of God's works; Divinity* or *Philofophy* ; but rather let men awake themfelves and chearfully endeavour, and purfue an endlefs progrefs or proficiency in both : only let them beware leſt they apply Knowledge to *fwelling,* not to *charity* ; to *oſtentation* not to *uſe* : and again, that they do not unwifely mingle and confound thefe diſtinct Learnings of *Theology* and *Philofophy,* and their feveral waters together.

Homer.
Iliad.9.

Chap. II.

I. Difcredits of Learning from the objections of Politicks, *That Learning foftens mens Natures, and makes men unfit for the exercife of Arms. That it perverts mens difpofitions for matter of Government.* § *Other particular indifpofitions pretended.* II. The Solution. *Learning makes not men unapt for Arms.* III. *Learning enables men for Civil affairs.* IV. Particular feducements imputed to Learning ; As, *Curious Uncertainty,* § *Pertinacious Regularity,* § *Mifleading Precedents,* § *Retired flothfulnefs,* § *Relaxation of Difcipline,* are all rather cured than caufed by Learning.

I.  Ow let us defcend to the Difgraces whereby *Politicks* defame *Learning* ; They be thefe, *That Learning doth foften mens manners, and makes them more unapt for the honour and exercife of Arms : That it doth marr and pervert mens difpofitions for matter of Government and Policy ;* which the ſtudy of Arts makes either too *Curious by vanity of Reading* ; Or too peremptory *by the ſtrict rigour of Rules* ; Or too overweening, *by reafon of the greatnefs of examples* ; Or too incompatible with the times, *by reafon of the diffimilitude of examples* ; Or at leaſt it doth divert and alienate mens *minds from bufinefs and action, inſtilling into them a love of leifure and privatenefs.*

§ *And that it doth bring into* States *a relaxation of Difcipline, whil_eſt every man is more ready to argue than obey.* Out of this conceit *Cato* furnamed the *Cenfor,* one of the wifeſt men indeed that ever liv'd, when *Carneades* the *Philofopher* came in Embaffage to *Rome,* and that the young men of *Rome* began to flock about him, being allured with the fweetnefs and Majefty of his eloquence, gave counfel in open Senate, *That they fhould give him his difpatch with all fpeed, leſt he fhould infect and inchant the minds*

Plato in
M.Cato.

minds of the youth, and at unawares bring in an alteration of the manners and customs of the State.   This same conceit or humor mov'd *Virgil*, preferring the honour of his country, before the reputation of his own Profession, to make a kind of separation between the *Arts of Policy*, and the *Arts of Literature*, challenging the one to the *Romans*, yielding the the other to the *Grecians*, in the verses so much renowned,

> *Tu regere imperio populos · Romane memento,*
> *Hæ tibi erunt Artes———*

<small>Virgil. Æn. 6.</small>

And we see that *Anytus* the accuser of *Socrates*, laid it as an article of charge and accusation against him, that he did with the variety and power of discourses and disputation, embase, in the minds of young men, the Authority and Reverence of the Laws and Customs of their Country; and that he did profess a pernicious and dangerous Science, wherein, whoever was instructed, might make the worse matter seem the better, and to suppress Truth by force of Eloquence.

<small>Plato A- pol. Socr.</small>

II. But these and the like imputations have rather a countenance of Gravity, than any sincerity of Truth : For experience doth witness that the self-same persons, and the self-same times, have flourisht in the *glory of Arms and Learning*. As for men, we may instance in that noble pair of Emperors *Alexander the Great*, and *Julius Cæsar the Dictator*; the one was *Aristotle's* Scholar in Philosophy; the other *Cicero's Rival* in Eloquence.   But if any man had rather call for Scholars that have become great Generals, than Generals that were great Scholars, let him take *Epaminondas* the Theban, or *Xenophon* the Athenian; whereof the one was the first that abated the power of *Sparta*, and the other was the first that made way to the overthrow of the *Monarchy of Persia*. And this conjunction of *Arms and Letters*, is yet more visible in times than in persons, by how much an Age is a greater object than a Man : For the self-same times with the *Ægyptians, Assyrians, Persians, Grecians* and *Romans*, that are most renowned for *Arms*, are likewise most admired for *Learning*; so that the gravest Auctors and Philosophers, the greatest Captains and Governors have lived in the same Ages.   Neither indeed can it otherwise be ; for as in man the ripeness of the strength of the body and the mind comes much about one age, save that the strength of the body comes somewhat the more early ; so in States, the glory of Arms and *Learning* (whereof the one correspondeth to the body, the other to the soul of man) have a concurrence, or a near sequence of Time.

III. Now for *matter of Policy and Government*, that *Learning* should rather be an *impediment than an adjunct* thereunto is a thing very improbable.   We all confess that it is an unadvised act to commit a natural Body, and the cure of Health; to *Emperique Physitians*, who commonly have a few receipts which seem to them to be universal Remedies; whereupon they are confident and adventurous, when yet they neither know the causes of Diseases, nor the Complexions of Patients, nor the peril of Symptomes, nor the Method of Cures. We see it a like error in those, who for expedition of their Causes and Suits rely upon petty Advocates and Lawyers, which are only men of Practice, and not grounded in their Books, who are many times easily surpriz'd, when a new case falls out besides the common Road of their experience : So by

like

like reafon, it cannot but be a matter of doubtful confequence, if States be managed by Emperique Statef-men. On the contrary, it is almoft without inftance, that ever any Government was difaftrous, that was in the hand of Learned Governours. For howfoever it hath been ordinary with Politick men to extenuate; and difable Learned men by the name of Pedants, yet Hiftory, which is the miftrefs of Truth, makes it appear in many particulars, that the Government of Princes in minority, hath far excelled the Government of Princes of mature age, even for that reafon which Politicks feek to traduce, which is, that by that occafion the State hath been in the hands of Pedants. Who knows not that for the firft five years fo much magnified during the minority of *Nero,* the Burden of the State was in the hands of *Seneca* a *Pedant?* So likewife *Gordianus* the younger owes the ten years applauded government to *Mifitheus* a *Pedant.* And with the like happinefs *Alexander Severus* govern'd the State in his minority, in which fpace women rul'd all, but by the advice and counfel of Preceptors and Teachers. Nay, let a man look into the Government of the *Bifhop of Rome,* as by name, into the Government of *Pius Quinctus* or *Sextus Quinctus* in our times, who were both at their entrance efteemed but as *Pedantical Friars* ; and he fhall find, that fuch *Popes* do greater things, and procede upon truer Principles, than thofe which have afcended to the Papacy from an education and breeding, in affairs of eftate and Courts of Princes. For though men bred in learning are, perchance, not fo quick and nimble in apprehending occafions, and accommodating for the prefent to points of convenience, which the Italians call *Raggioni di Stato,* the very name

Piston. whereof *Pius Quintus* could not hear with patience, but was wont to fay, *That they were the inventions of wicked men, and repugnant to Religion and the moral Vertues* ; yet in this there is made ample recompence, that they are perfect and ready, in the fafe and plain way of Religion, Juftice, Honefty, and the Moral Vertues ; which way, they that conftantly keep and purfue, fhall no more need thofe other Remedies, than a found body needs Phyfick. And befides, the fpace of one mans life can not furnifh prefidents enough to direct the event of but one mans life. For as it hapneth fometimes that the great Grand-child, Nephew or Pro-nephew, refembleth the Grand-father, or great Grand-father more than the Father; fo many times it comes to pafs, that the occurrences of prefent times may fort better with ancient examples, than with thofe of later or immediate times. Laftly, the wit of one man can no more countervail the latitude of Learning, than one mans means can hold way with a common purfe.

IV. And were it granted that thofe *feducements* and *indifpofitions* imputed to Learning, by Politicks, were of any force and validity, yet it muft be remembred withal, that *Learning* miniftreth in every of them, greater ftrength of medicine or remedy, than it offereth caufe of *indifpofition* or *infirmity.* For if that *Learning* by a fecret influence and operation makes the mind *irrefolute and perplext,* yet certainly by plain precept it teacheth how to unwinde the thoughts, how far to deliberate, when to refolve ; yea, it fhews how to protract, and carry things in fufpenfe without Prejudice till they refolve.

§ Be it likewife granted that *Learning makes the minds of men more peremptory and inflexible,* yet withal it teacheth what things are in their
nature

nature demonſtrative, and what are conjectural; and propounds as well, the uſe of diſtinctions, and exceptions, as the ſtability of rules and principles.

§. Be it again, *that learning miſleads and wreſteth mens minds, whether by diſproportion, or diſſimilitude of examples,* I know not, yet I know well, that it unfoldeth, and laies open as well the force of circumſtances, as the errors of compariſons, and the cautions of applications; ſo that in all theſe it doth more rectifie mens minds, then pervert them. And theſe remedies *Learning* doth every way convey and inſinuate by the quick penetration, and forcible variety of examples. Let a man look into the errors of *Clement* VII, ſo lively deſcribed by *Guicciardine,* who ſerved under him; or into the errors and waverings of *Cicero,* painted to the life by his own penſill, in *his Epiſtles to Atticus,* and he will fly a pace from being inconſtant and irreſolute in his deſigns. Let him look into the errors of *Phocion,* and he will beware how he be obſtinate or inflexible. Let him read the fable of *Ixion,* and it will diſpel vaporous hopes and ſuch like fumes and clouds. Let him behold *Cato* the *Second,* and he will never be one of the *Antipodes,* to tread oppoſite to the preſent world.

§ Now for the conceit, *That learning ſhould be a friend to ſloth, and ſhould oreſpread the mind with a ſweet ſlumber of repoſe and retiredneſs;* it were a ſtrange thing, if that which accuſtometh the mind to a perpetual agitation, ſhould be the *Patroneſs to ſlothfulneſs :* whereas contrariwiſe it may be truly affirmed, that no kind of men love buſineſs for it ſelf, but thoſe that are *Learned*; for other Perſons love affairs and buſineſs for the *Profit,* as hirelings the work, for the wages; others for *Honor,* for while they are in Action, they live in the eyes of men and refreſh their reputation, which othewiſe would wear; others for *Power* and the *Priviledges of Fortune,* that they may pleaſure their friends, and diſpleaſure their foes; others that they may *exerciſe ſome faculties wherein they take a pride,* and in this imagination, entertain their thoughts in a good humour and pleaſing conceit towards themſelves; others *to advance other ends :* ſo that as it is ſaid of untrue valours, that ſome mens valours are in the eyes of thoſe that look on, ſo the induſtry and courage of theſe men ſeems to aim at this, that other may applaud them, or they hugg themſelves in the contemplation of their own deſignments : only *Learned men* love buſineſs and imployment, as actions agreeable to nature, and no leſs healthful to the mind than exerciſe is to the body; taking pleaſure in the Action it ſelf, and not in the purchaſe: ſo that, of all men living, they are the moſt indefatigable, if it be towards any buſineſs, which can repleniſh and detain the mind according to the dignity thereof. And if there be found ſome laborious in reading and ſtudy, and yet idle in buſineſs, and action, this grows not from learning, but from ſome weakneſs or ſoftneſs of body or mind, ſuch as *Seneca* ſpeaks of, *Quidam* (ſaith he) *tam ſunt umbratiles ut putent in turbido eſſe quicquid in luce eſt.* Well may it be, that ſuch a point of a mans nature may make him give himſelf to learning, but it is not learning that breeds, or implants any ſuch point in his nature. But if any man notwithſtanding reſolvedly maintaineth, *that Learning takes up too much time which might otherwiſe be better imployed*; I anſwer, that no man can be ſo ſtraitned and oppreſt with buſineſs, and an active courſe

Controv. lib. 4. Prov.

of

of life, but may have many vacant times of leasure, whilst he expects the returns and tides of businefs, except he be either of a very dull temper and of no difpatch ; or ambitious (little to his credit and reputation) to meddle and ingage himfelf in imployment of all natures and matters above his reach. It remaineth therefore to be enquired, in what matter, and how, thofe fpaces and times of Leasure, fhould be filled up and fpent ; whether in pleafures or study ; fenfuality ; or contemplation, as was well anfwered by *Demofthenes* to *Æfchines* , a man given to pleafure, who when he told him by way of reproach, *that his orations did*

Plut. in Demoft.

fmell of the Lamp, indeed (faid *Demofthenes*) *there is great difference between the things that You and I do by lamp-light:* Wherefore let no man fear left learning fhould *expulfe bufinefs* ; nay rather it will keep and defend the poffeffions of the mind, againft idlenefs and pleafure, which otherwife, at unawares, may enter, to the prejudice both of Bufinefs and Learning.

§ Again, whereas they object, *That learning fhould undermine the reverence of Laws and Government,* it is a meer calumny without all fhadow of truth: For to fay that a blind obedience fhould be a furer obligation then an ocular duty, is all one to fay, that a blind man may tread furer by a guide, then a feeing man can with the ufe of a light and his eyes. Nay it is without all controverfie that Learning doth make the mind of man, gentle, ductile, maniable and pliant to government ; whereas ignorance makes them churlifh, thwart, and mutinous ; which the Records of time do clearly manifeft, confidering that the moft unlearned, rude and barbarous times have been moft fubject to feditions, tumults and changes. As for the judgement of *Cato* the *Cenfor* ,

Plut. in M. Cato.

he was well punifht for his *blafphemy againft learning*: For when he was paft threefcore years old, he was taken with an extreme defire to go to the fchool again, and to *learn the greek tongue* ; which doth well demonftrate that his former cenfure of the Grecian Learning was rather an affected gravity, than the inward fenfe of his own opinion. As for *Virgil's verfes,* though it pleafed him to brave the world in taking to the *Romans* the *Art of Empire,* and leaving to others all other *Arts,* as popular and fervile ; yet fo much is manifeft, that the Romans never afcended to that *hight of Empire,* till the time they had afcended to the *hight of Arts.* For in the time of the two firft *Cæfars,* Perfons moft perfect in the State-principles of Government, there lived contemporaries, *the beft Poet, Virgilius Maro* ; *The beft Hiftoriographer, Titus Livius* ; *the beft Antiquary, Marcus Varro* ; *the beft or fecond Orator Marcus Cicero* ; without queftion the chiefeft, every one in their feveral faculty, that to the memory of man are known. Laftly, as for the *accufation of Socrates,* only this I fay, The time muft be remembred when it was profecuted, namly under the *thirty Tyrants,* of all mortals the bloodieft, bafeft and moft unworthy of Government: which revolution of State and Time was no fooner over, but *Socrates,* whom they had made a Perfon Criminal, was made a Perfon Heroical, and his Memory accumulate with all honours divine and humane ; and thofe Difcourfes of his, which were then termed Corrupting of Manners, were after celebrated by all Pofterity for moft foveraign medicines of Mind and Manners. And let this ferve for anfwer to *Politiques,* which in their humorous feverity, or in their feigned gravity , have prefumed to throw

imputations

imputations upon Learning; which redargution neverthelefs, fave that we know not whether our labours may extend to other ages, feems not fo needful for the prefent, feeing the afpect and favour of two moft learned Princes (*Queen* Elizabeth *and Your Majefty*, being as *Caftor* and *Pollux*, *Lucida Sidera*, Stars of a moft benign influence) hath wrought in us of Britain, *fo much love* and *reverence towards Learning*.

CHAP. III.

I. *Difcredits of Learning from* Learned mens Fortunes, Manners, Nature of ftudies. II. In the Fortunes *fcarcity of Means*, § *Obfcurity of life*. § *Meannefs of Imployment*. III. In their Manners, *Too Regular for the times*, §. *Too fenfible of the good of others, and neglective of their own*. § *They fail in applying themfelves to Particular Perfons*. §. *They fail in fome points of Behaviour*. § *Grofs Flattery practis'd by fome Learned*; § *Inftanced in the Modern Dedication of Books*. §. *Difcreet Morigeration allowed*.

I. **N**Ow come we to the third fort of Difcredit or Diminution of Credit, that redounds upon Learning from learned men themfelves, which commonly cleaveth fafteft. It is derived either from *their Fortune*, or from *their Manners*, or from *the Nature of their ftudies*; whereof the firft is not in their power; the fecond is not to the point; fo as the third alone feemeth properly to fall into enquiry: but becaufe we are not in hand with the true value of things, but with popular eftimation, it will not be amifs to infinuate fomewhat alfo of the two former.

II. The Derogations therefore, or Diminutions of Credit which grow to Learning *from the fortune of the Learned men*, are taken either from their *Poverty and fcarcity of Means*; or from their *obfcure and private courfe of Life*; or from the *meannefs of imployment wherein they are converfant*.

§. As concerning *Want*, and that ufually is the cafe of Learned men, that they are *poor*, and commonly begin with little, and grow not rich fo faft as other men, which convert their labours cheifly to lucre and encreafe; it were good to leave the common Place in Commendation of *Poverty* to fome *Frier Mendicant* to handle, (if by their leaves I may be fo bold) to whom much was attributed by *Machiavell* in this point, when he faid, *that the Kingdom of the clergie had been long before at an end, if the reputation and reverence towards the poverty of Friers and Monks, had not born out the fcandals of the fuperfluities and exceffes of Bifhops and Prelates :* fo a man might fay that the felicity and magnificence of Princes and great Perfons, had long fince turned to Barbarifm and Rudenefs, if the *Poverty of Learning* had not kept up civility and honour of life. But without fuch advantages of hunting after the praife thereof, it is worthy obfervation, what a facred and reverend thing *Poverty of Fortune* was, for fome ages in the Roman State, which yet was a State without Paradoxes: For thus faith *Titus Livius* in his in-

Dell. Hiſt. Fior.lib.1.

Præf.lib.
I.
troduction, *Either my affection to the work I have undertaken deceives me, or there was never State more great, more religious, more richly furnish'd with good presidents, nor which avarice and riot conquered so late, nor where so great reverence to Poverty and Parcimony continued so long.* So likewise after the State of *Rome* was now degenerate, we read that when *Cæsar* the *Dictator* took upon him a Restauration of the collapsed state, one of his *confidents* gave him this counsel, That of all Points the most summary to such a designment, as he went about, was by all means to take away the estimation of wealth, *For* (saith he)

Orat.ad C.
Cæsar.
Salust, im-
putata.
these and all other evils, together with the reputation of mony shall cease, if neither publique Officers nor any other Dignity, which commonly are so coveted, were exposed to sale. To conclude this point, as it was truly

Laert. in
Diog.
Cyn.
said that *Rubor est virtutis Color,* though sometimes it come from vice; so you may truly say, *Paupertas est virtutis fortuna,* though sometimes it may proceed from misgovernment and improvidence. Surely this is

Prov. 28.
Prov. 23.
Solomons Censure, *Qui festinat ad divitias non erit insons,* and Precept, *Buy the truth and sell it not;* So wisdom and knowledge judging it right and equal that means should be imployed to get Learning, and not Learning be applied to gather up means.

§ To what purpose should we speak of the *privateness and obscureness of life,* which is objected to learned men? It is a Theme so common and so frequently handled by all, to extol *Leasure* and *retiredness,* not taxed with sensuality and sloth, before a Civil and Active life; for safety, liberty, sweetness, dignity, or at least freedom from indignities, as no man handles this subject, but handles it well: such a consonancy it hath to mens conceptions in the expressing; and to mens consent in the allowing. This only I will add, that Learned men forgotten in States, are like the Images of *Cassius* and *Brutus* in the funerals of *Junia,* of which, not to be represented as others were, *Tacitus* saith, *Eo*

Annal.3.
ipso præfulgebant quod non visebantur.

§ For *Meanness of imployment assigned to Learned men,* that which is most traduced to contempt is, That the government of childhood and youth is commonly allotted to them, the contempt of which age is transferred upon the Preceptors or Tutors. But how unjust this traducement is, if you will reduce things from popularity of opinion, to measure of reason, may appear in that we see men are more careful what they put into new vessels, than into a vessel season'd; and more curious what mould they lay about a young plant, than a plant corroborate: So as it is manifest that the weakest terms and times of all things, use to have the best applications and helps. Harken, if you please, to

Joel 2.
the Hebrew Rabbins, *Your young men shall see visions, your old men shall dream dreams;* from this Text they collect, that youth is the worthier age, by so much as Revelation is more clear by visions, than by dreams. And it is worth the noting that however *Pedants* have been the derision and scorn of *Theaters,* as the Apes of *Tyranny,* and that the modern looseness or negligence hath taken no due regard to the choice of *School-masters* and *Tutors;* yet it hath been an ancient complaint drawn down from the best and wisest times, even to our age, that States were too busie with their *Laws* and too negligent in point of *Education.* Which excellent part of Ancient Discipline hath been in some sort revived of late times *by the Colleges of the Jesuits,* whose pains and diligence

gence when I confider, as well in the culture of knowledge, as information of manners, the faying of *Agefilaus* touching *Pharnabazus* comes
into my mind, *Talis cum fis utinam nofter effes.* And thus much concerning the difcredits drawn from the *Fortunes and Condition of Learned men.* Plut. in Agefil.

III. As touching the *Manners of Learned men,* it is a thing belonging
rather to their individual Perfons, than their ftudies and point of learning : No doubt there is found among them, as in all other Profeffions,
and Conditions of life, men of all temperatures, as well bad as good,
but yet fo, as it is not without truth that is faid, *abire ftudia in mores ;*
and that Learning and Studies, unlefs they fall upon very depraved
difpofitions, have an influence and operation upon the manners of
thofe that are converfant in them, to reform nature and change it to
the better.

§ But upon an attentive and indifferent review, I for my part, can
not find any difgrace to learning can proceed from the *Manners of
Learned men, adherent unto them as they are Learned ;* unlefs peradventure it be a fault (which was the fuppofed fault of *Demofthenes, Cicero,
Cato* the *fecond, Seneca,* and many more) that becaufe the times they
read of, are commonly better, than the times they live in ; and the
duties taught, better than the duties practifed ; they *contend too far, to
reduce the corruption of manners to the honefty of precepts, and prefcripts,
of a too great hight, and to impofe the Laws of ancient feverity upon dif-
folute times :* and yet they have Caveats enough touching this aufterity
out of their own fprings : For *Solon,* when he was asked *Whether he had
given his Citizens the beft laws ? the beft* (faid he) *of fuch as they would
receive.* So *Plato,* finding that his own heart could not agree with the
corrupt manners of his Country, refufed to bear place or office, faying,
*That a mans Country is to be ufed as his Parents were, that is, with per-
fwafion and not with violence, by entreating and not by contefting :* And
Cæfars counfelor put in the fame caveat, faying, *non ad vetera inftituta
revocans quæ jampridem corruptis moribus ludibrio funt :* And *Cicero*
notes this error directly in *Cato* the *fecond,* writing to his friend *Atticus, Cato optime fentit fed nocet interdum Reipub. loquitur enim tanquam
in Repub. Platonis, non tanquam in fæce Romuli.* The fame *Cicero* doth
excufe and expound the Philofophers for going too far, and being too
exact in their Prefcripts , *Thefe fame Præceptors and Teachers,* (faith he)
*feem to have ftretched out the line and limits of Duties fomewhat beyond the
natural bounds, that when we had laboured to reach the higheft point of Perfection, we might reft where it was meet :* and yet himfelf might fay, *Mo-
nitis fum minor ipfe meis ;* for he ftumbled at the fame ftone , though
in not fo extreme a degree. Plut. in Solon. In vita. in epift. ali-bi. Crat. ad C. Cæf. Saluft. ad fcripta. Ad Attic. lib.2. ep.1. Pro L. Muræna.

§ Another fault which perchance not undefervedly is objected a-
gainft Learned men, is this, *that they have preferr'd the honour and profit of
their Country, and Mafters before their own fortunes and fafeties.* So *Demofthenes* to his Athenians, *My Counfels* (faith he) *if you pleafe to note
it, are not fuch whereby I fhould grow great amongft you, you become little amongft the Grecians ; but they be of that nature as are fometimes not
good for me to give, but are always good for you to follow.* So *Seneca* after he had confecrated that *Quinquennium Neronis* to the eternal glory
of Learned Governors, held on his honeft and loyal courfe of Good
and Oratio: de Corona.

and Free Counsel, after his Master grew extremely corrupt to his great peril and at last to his ruine. Neither can it be otherwise conceived; for Learning endues mens minds with a true sense of the frailty of their Persons; the Casualty of fortune; the Dignity of the soul; and their vocation: which when they think of, they can by no means perswade themselves that any *advancement of their own fortunes,* can be set down as a true and worthy end of their being and ordainment. Wherefore they so live, as ever ready to give their account to God, and to their Masters under God, whether they be Kings or States they serve, in this

Mat.25.

stile of words, *Ecce tibi Lucrifeci,* and not in that *Ecce mihi Lucrifeci.* But the corrupter sort of Politiques, that have not their minds instituted and establish'd in the true apprehension of Duties, and the contemplation of good in the universality, *refer all things to themselves,* as if they were the *worlds Center,* and that the *concurrence of all lines should touch in them and their fortunes*; never caring in all tempests, what becomes of the Ship, so they may retire and save themselves in the Cock-boat of their own fortune. On the contrary, they that feel the waight of Duty, and understand the limits of self love; use to make good their places, and duties, though. with peril: and if they chance to stand safe in seditions and alterations of times and Government, it is rather to be attributed to the reverence which honesty even wresteth from adversaries, than any *versatile or temporizing advantage in their own carriage.* But for this point of tender sense, and fast obligation of duty, which without doubt Learning doth implant in the mind, however it may be taxed and amerced by Fortune; and be despised by Politiques in the depth of their corrupt principles, as a weak and improvident virtue, yet it will receive an open allowance, so as in this matter there needs the less disproof or excusation.

§ Another fault there is incident to Learned men, which may sooner be excused than denied, namely this; *That they do not easily apply and accommodate themselves to persons with whom they negociate and live:* which want of exact application ariseth from two causes; *The first is, the largeness and greatness of their minds, which can hardly stoop and be confined within the observation of the nature and custom of one person.* It is the

Seneca.

speech of a Lover, not of a wise man, *Satis magnum alter alteri theatrum sumus.* Nevertheless I shall yield that he that cannot contract the light of his mind, as he doth the eye of his body, as well as disperse and dilate it, wants a great faculty for an active course of life. *The second cause is the honesty and integrity of their nature,* which argueth no inhability in them, but a choice upon judgement; for the true and just limits of observance towards any person extend no farther, than so to understand his inclination and disposition, as to converse with him without offence; or to be able, if occasion be offered, to give him faithful counsel, and yet to stand upon reasonable guard and caution, in respect of our selves: but to be speculative into others, and to feel out a mans disposition, to the end to know how to work him, winde him and govern him at pleasure; is not the part of an ingenious nature, but rather of a heart double and cloven; which, as in friendship, it is want of integrity, so towards Princes and Superiours it is want of Duty. For the Custom of the *Levant,* whereby it was accounted a hainous offence, to gaze and fix their eyes upon Princes, is indeed, in the outward ceremony

mony

mony, barbarous, but good in the moral; for it becomes not Subjects
by bent and inquisitive observations, to penetrate into the *hearts of*   Prov.25.
Kings, which the Scripture hath declared to be *inscrutable*.

§ There is yet another fault with which I will conclude this Part ,
which is often noted in Learned men; namely , *that in small and out-*
ward matters of behaviour and carriage (as in countenance, gesture,
march, ordinary discourse, and the like)*they do many times fail to observe*
decensie and discretion; so as the vulgar sort of capacities make a judgement of them in greater matters, by that which they find wanting in
small and ordinary points of Action.   But this prejudication doth oftentimes deceive them: nay let them know, they have their answer
from *Themistocles*, who being invited to touch a Lute, said, arrogantly
enough, being applyed to himself, but pertinently to the purpose in
hand, *That he could not indeed fiddle, but he knew how to make a small*   Plut in
Town, a great State.   And there are , no doubt, many well seen in the   Themist.
Arts of Government, and Policy, which are to seek in ordinary conversation and punctual occasions.   I refer such scoffers to the Elogie *Al-*   Plato '
cibiades gave of his Master *Socrates*, whom he compar'd to the *Galli-*   Conv:
pots of the Apothecaries, which on the outside were drawn with Apes, Owls,
and Antiques, but contained within precious liquors and soveraign con-
fections; acknowledging that to vulgar capacity and popular report,
he was not without some superficial levites, and deformities, but was inwardly replenisht with excellent powers and virtues.   And so much
touching the Point *of Manners of learned men.*

§ In the mean time I thought good to advertise, that I have no purpose to give allowance to some *base and unworthy Conditions of some*
Professors, whereby they have discredited both Themselves and Learning : such were those *trencher Philosophers*, which in the later age of
the Roman state; were usually in the houses of great Persons; whom
not improperly you may call *solemn Parasites :* of which kind *Lucian*
makes a merry discription of the Philosopher, that the great Lady took
to ride with her in the Coach, and would needs have him carry her
little Dog *Melitæns*; which he doing officiously and yet uncomely, the
Page scoffing said, *I doubt our Philosopher of a Stoick will turn Cynique.*   De Merc.
But above all the rest, the gross and palpable flattery whereunto ma-   conduct:
ny not unlearned have abased and abused their wits and pens, turning
as *Du Bartas* saith *Hecuba* into *Helena*, and *Faustina* into *Lucretia*, hath
diminisht the prize and estimation of Learning.

§ Neither is the *Modern Dedication of Books to Patrons to be Com-*
mended; for that Books, such as are worthy the name of Books, ought
to have no *Patron* but *Truth* and *Reason.*   The custom of the Ancients
was better, who were wont to *dedicate their writings only to private and*
equal friends , or to entitle the Books with the names of such friends;
or if they Dedicated their Books to Kings or great Persons, it was
to some such as the Argument of the Book was fit and proper
for.   These and the like Courses may deserve rather apprehension than
defence.

§ Nor say I this, as if I condemned the *Morigeration and application*
of Learned men, to men in fortune and place; for the answer was good
that *Aristippus* made to one that askt him in mockery, *How it came to pass*   Laert. in
that Philosophers were followers of Rich men, and not Rich men of Philo-   Aristip.
sophers ?

sophers? He answered soberly and yet sharply, *That it was because Philosophers knew well what they had need of, but Rich men did not.* Of like nature was the answer which the same Philosopher made when having a Petition to *Dionysius* and no ear given to him *he fell down at his feet in manner of a Worshipper, whereupon* Dionysius *staid and gave him the hearing, and granted it :* but a little after, some person tender of the honour and credit of Philosophy, *reproved Aristippus that he would offer the Profession of Philosophy such an indignity as for a private suit to fall to a Tyrants feet ?* to whom he replyed ; *That was not his fault, but it was the fault of* Dionysius *that had his ears in his feet.* Neither was it accounted weakness, but a discretion in him that would not dispute his best with *Adrianus Cæsar,* excusing the fact, *That it was reason to yield to him that commanded thirty Legions :* These and such like *applications and stoopings of Learned men below the terms of Gravity,* at the command of necessity or the advantage of occasion, cannot be condemned ; for though they may seem, at first sight, somewat base and servile, yet in a judgement truly made, they are to be accounted *submissions* to the *Occasion* and not the *Person.*

Ibid.

Spartian. in Hadrian.

C H A P. IV.

I. *Distempers of Learning from* Learned mens studies, *are of three sorts.* Phantastical Learning, Contentious Learning, Delicate Learning. II. Delicate Learning, *a Curiosity in words through Profuseness of speech.* § *Decent expression commended.* § *Affected Brevity censured.* III. Contentious Learning, *a Curiosity in matter, through the novelty of terms, or strictness of Positions.* § *A vanity either in Matter or in Method.* IV. Phantastical Learning *hath two branches,* Imposture, Credulity. § *Credulity is a belief of History.* § *Or a belief of Art or Opinion ; and that either* Real *in the Art it self.* § *Or Personal in the Author of such an Art, or Science.*

L Et us now proceed to those *Errors, and Vanities, which have intervened amongst the studies of Learned men, and therewith are intermingled ;* which is the principal point and proper to the present Argument ; wherein my purpose is not to patronize errors, but by a Censure and separation of the errors, to sift out that which is found and solid, and to deliver the same from aspersion. For we see it is the manner of men, especially of envious persons, to scandalize, and deprave that which retains the State and Virtue, by taking advantage upon that which is corrupt and degenerate ; as the Heathens in the Primitive Church us'd to blemish and taint the Christians, with the faults and corruptions of Heretiques : Nevertheless I have no meaning to make any exact animadversion of the *Errors, and Impediments in matters of Learning,* which are more secret and remote from vulgar opinion, but only to speak of such as do fall under a common and popular observation, and known, or at least, which recede not far off therefrom.

I. I find

I. I find therefore chiefly three vanites, and vacuities in Learning, which have given occasion to the reproach and disgrace thereof. For *those things* are esteemed *vain* which are either *false*, or *frivolous*; namely, wherein there is, either no truth, or no use : *those Persons* we esteem vain, which are either *Credulous* in things false, or *Curious* in things of little use. And *Curiosity* is either in *matter* or in *words*; that is when either labour is spent in *vain matters*, or time is wasted in the delicacy of *fine words :* so that it is agreeable as well to true reason as approved experience, to set down three distempers of Learning : The first is *Phantastical Learning*; The second *Contentious Learning*; The third *Painted* and *Delicate Learning :* or thus, *vain Imaginations, vain Alter-cations, vain affectations.* And with the last I will begin.

II. This Distemper seated in the *superfluity and profuseness of speech* (though in times past by turns, it was in some price) about *Luthers* time, got up mightily into credit, and estimation. The heat and efficacy of Preaching, to win and draw on the people, began chiefly about that time to flourish; and this required a popular kind of ex-pression. This was furthered by the Enmity and Opposition concei-ved in that same age against the *School-men*; whose writings were alto-gether in a differing stile and form of expression; taking liberty to coyn and frame new and rude terms of Art, without any regard to the pureness and elegancy of speech, so they might avoid circuit of words, and deliver their sense and conceptions, in a precise exact ex-pression : and so it came to pass a little after, that a greater care was taken for Words, than Matter; and many affected rather Comptness of stile; a round and clean Period; the sweet falling of the clauses; and illustrations by Tropes and Figures; than the waight of Matter, soundness of Argument, life of Invention, or depth of Judgment. Then sprang up the *flowing and watery vein of Osorius*, the Portugal Bishop, to be in price and request : Then did *Sturmius* spend such in-finite and curious pains upon *Cicero* the Orator, and *Hermogenes* the Rhetorician. Then did our *Carre* and *Ascham* in their Lectures and Writings almost Deifie *Cicero*, and *Demosthenes*, and allure young Students to that polisht and flourishing kind of Learning. Then did *Erasmus* take occasion to make that scoffing kind of Eccho, *Decem an-nos consumpsi in Legendo Cicerone*, to which the Echo answered, *One, Asine.* Then grew the Learning of the Schoolmen to be utterly despi-sed, as rude and barbarous. In sum, the whole inclination and bent of those times was, rather about *Copy* than *Weight*. Here we see the first *Distemper of Learning*, when, as we have said, *men study Words and not Matter.* Whereof though I have represented examples of late times only, yet such vanities have been accepted, in some degree or o-ther, in ancient times, and will be so hereafter. . Now it is not possi-ble but that this should have an operation to discredit and debase the reputation of Learning, even with vulgar capacities; when they see Learned mens Works, like the first letter of a Patent, which though it be limmed and set out with large flourishes, yet it is but a letter. And it seems to me that *Pigmalions frenzie* is a good Emblem and Por-traicture of this vanity; for what are words but the Images of matter, and except they be animated with the spirit of reason, to fall in Love with them, is all one as to fall in love with a Picture.

C   §. But

§. But yet notwithſtanding it is a thing not haſtily to be condemned to illuſtrate and poliſh the obſcurity and roughneſſ of Philoſophy, with the *ſplendor of words* and *ſenſible elocution,* For hereof we have great examples in *Xenophon, Cicero, Seneca, Plutarch,* and even in *Plato* himſelf;and the uſe hereof is great: For though to the ſevere inquiſition of Truth, and the deep progreſſ into Philoſophy, it is ſome hinderance, becauſe it is too early ſatisfactory unto the mind, and quencheth the thirſt and deſire of farther ſearch ; yet if a man be to have any uſe of ſuch knowledge in Civil occaſions (of *Conference, Counſel, Perſwaſion, Diſcourſe, and the like*) he ſhall find all that he deſireth prepar'd and ſet out to his hand in thoſe Auctors. But the exceſſ of this is ſo juſtly contemptible, that, as *Hercules,* when he ſaw the Image of *Adonis, Venus minion,* in the Temple, ſaid, *nil ſacri es* ; ſo there is none of *Hercules* his followers in Learning, I mean, the more induſtrious and ſevere inquirers into Truth, but will deſpiſe thoſe *Delicacies* and *Affectations,* as indeed capable of no Divineneſſ.

§ Little better is that kind of ſtile (yet neither is that altogether exempt from vanity) which neer about the ſame time ſucceeded this *Copy* and *ſuperfluity of ſpeech.* The labour here is altogether, *That words may be aculeate, ſentences conciſe, and the whole contexture of the ſpeech and diſcourſe, rather rounding into it ſelf, than ſpread and dilated :* So that it comes to paſs by this Artiſice, that evey paſſage ſeems more witty and weighty than indeed it is. Such a ſtile as this we find more exceſſively in *Seneca* ; more moderately in *Tacitus* and *Plinius Secundus* ; and of late it hath been very pleaſing unto the ears of our time. And this kind of expreſſion hath found ſuch acceptance with meaner capacities, as to be a dignity and ornament to Learning ; nevertheleſſ, by the more exact judgments, it hath been deſervedly deſpiſed, and may be ſet down *as a diſtemper of Learning,* ſeeing it is ·nothing elſe but a hunting after words, and fine placing of them. And thus much of the firſt *Diſeaſe* or *Diſtemper* of Learning.

III. Now followes the diſtemper *ſetled in Matter,*which we ſet down as a *ſecond diſeaſe of Learning,*and have deſigned it by the name of *contentious ſubtilty* ; and this is in nature ſomewhat worſe than that whereof we ſpake even now. For as the ſubſtance of Matter,is better than the beauty of words ; ſo on the contrary, *vanity of Matter* is more odious than *vanity of words.* Wherein it ſeemeth that the reprehenſion of St. *Paul* was not only proper for thoſe times, but Prophetical for the times following ; and not only reſpective to Divinity, but extenſive ı. Tim. 6. to all knowledge, *Devita prophanas vocum novitates :* For in theſe words he aſſigns two Markes and Badges of ſuſpected and falſiſied ſcience ; The firſt is the *Novelty* and *Strangeneſſ of Terms* ; The other, the *ſtrictneſſ of Poſitions* ; which of neceſſity induce oppoſition and ſo Alterations and Queſtions. Certainly like as many ſubſtances in nature, which are ſolid and entire, doe many times putrifie and corrupt into worms ; ſo good and ſound Knowledge doth often putrifie and diſſolve into a number of ſubtle, idle, unwholſome, and (as I may terme them) *vermiculate* Queſtions, which ſeem indeed to have a kind of Motion and Quickneſs in them, and yet they are unſound and hollow, and of no ſolid uſe. This kind of *Degenerate Learning* corrupting it ſelf, did chiefly reign amongſt the *Schoolmen* ; who having abundance of of Leifure, fharp, and ftrong wits, and fmall variety of reading, (for their wits were fhut up within the writing of a few Authors, chiefly *Ariftotle*, their Dictator, as their Perfons were fhut up in the cells of Monafteries and Colleges) and for moft part ignorant of the Hiftory either of Nature, or of Time, did out of no great Quantity of Matter, but infinite agitation of their Wit and Phancy, as of the fpindle, fpin out unto us thofe laborious webs of Learning, which are extant in their Books.   For the Wit and Mind of Man, if it work upon Matter, by contemplating Nature and the Works of God, worketh according to the ftuff, and is limited thereby ; but if it worketh upon it felf, as the *fpider works his web*, then it is endlefs, and brings forth *Cobwebs of Learning*, indeed admirable for finenefs of thred and work, but of no Subftance and Profit.

§ This fame unprofitable *fubtilty* or *Curiofity*, is of two forts ; and it is difcerned either in the fubject and *Matter* it felf, fuch as is fruitlefs *Speculation* or *Controverfie*, whereof there are no fmall number, both in Divinity and Philofophy ; Or in the *Manner* and *Method of handling*, which amongft School-men was this ; Upon every Pofition or Affertion they framed objections, then folutions of thofe objections, which folutions, for the moft part , were only diftinctions, whereas indeed, the ftrength of all fciences, *like the Old mans Fagot*, confifteth not in every ftick afunder, but in them all together united in the band. For the *Harmony of fciences*, that is when each part fupports the other, is and ought to be the true and brief way of confutation and fuppreffion of all the fmaller fort of objections : but on the other fide, if you draw out every Axiom, as the fticks of a Fagot, one by one, you may eafily quarrel with them, and bend and break them at your pleafure. So that as it was faid of *Seneca, verborum Minutiis rerum frangit pondera*, may truly be faid of the School-men, *Quæftionum Minutiis fcientiarum frangunt pondera*.   For were it not better for a man, in a fair room to fet up one great light, or branching candleftick of lights, whereby all may be feen at once, than to go up and down with a fmall watch candle into ever corner ? And fuch is their *Method*, that refteth not fo much upon evidence of Truth proved by Arguments, Authorities, Similitudes and Examples ; as upon particular Confutations, and Solutions of every fcruple, cavillation, and objection ; thus breeding queftion upon queftion ; even as in the former refemblance, *when you carry the light into one corner, you darken the reft*. So that the *fable of Scylla* feems to be a lively image of this kind of Philofophy or knowledge , which for the upper part had the fhape of a comely Virgin, but below, *Candida fuccinctam latrantibus inguina monftris* ; So you fhall find fome generalities of the School-men, fair and well proportioned, and invented to fome good purpofe ; but then when you defcend to diftinctions and decifions , in ftead of a fruitful womb for the ufe and benefit of mans life, they end in monftrous and barking *Queftions*.   Wherefore it is no marvail, if this quality of Knowledge fall under, even popular contempt, the people being apt to contemn Truth upon occafion of Controverfies, and altercations ; and to think they are all out of their way ; which never meet and agree among themfelves ; and when they fee the digladiations of Learned men, about matters of no ufe or moment, they eafily fall upon that judgement of *Dionyfius* of Syracufa, *verba ifta funt*

*Æfop.
Fab. Pict.
Mor.*

*Fabius
Quintili.
X.*

*V. 13. Buc.
Ecl. 3.*

fenum

Laertius
in Plato. *fenum otioforum.* Notwithstanding it is most certain, that if the School-
men, to their great thirst of Truth, and unwearied travail of wit, had
joyn'd variety, and universality of reading, and contemplation, they
had certainly proved excellent lights to the great *advancement of
all Arts and Sciences.* And thus much of the second Disease of
Learning.

IV. For the third Disease of Learning which concerns *Deceit or Un-
truth,* it is of all the rest the foulest, as that which doth destroy the Nature
and essential form of Knowledge, which is nothing but a representation of Truth. For the *Truth of Being,* and the *Truth of Knowing* are
all one, differing no more than the direct beam, and the beam reflected.
This vice therefore brancheth it self into two sorts, *Imposture* and *Credulity;* the one deceives, the other is deceived; which although they
appear to be of a diverse nature; the one seeming to proceed of Cunning, and the other of Simplicity; yet for the most part they do concur, for as the verse noteth,

Horat.
Epi.   *Percontatorem fugito nam garrulus idem est:*

Intimating that an *Inquisitive man is a Pratler;* so upon the like reason,
a *Credulous man is a deceiver.* As we see it in Fame and Rumors, that
he that will easily believe Rumors, will as easily augment Rumors;
Tacit.
Hist. l.1. which *Tacitus* wisely notes in these words, *Fingunt simul creduntq;*
such affinity there is between a propensity to *Deceive* and a facility to
Believe.

§ This *facility of Crediting* and accepting all things, though weakly authorized, is of two kinds, according to the nature of the Matter
handled, for it is either *belief of History,* or (as the Lawyers speak) *matter of Fact,* or *matter of Opinion.* In the former kind, we see with what
loss and detriment of Credit and Reputation, this error hath distain'd
and embased much of the *Ecclesiastical History,* which hath two easily
received and registred Reports and Narrations of Miracles wrought by
Martyrs, Hermites, or Monks of the Desert, Anchorites, and other holy men; and of their Reliques, Sepulchers, Chappels, Images and
Shrines. So in *Natural History,* we see many things have been rashly,
and with little choice or judgement received and registred, as may appear in the writings of *Plinius, Cardanus, Albertus,* and diverse of the
Arabians, which are every where fraught with forged and fabulous Reports, and those not only uncertain and untried; but notoriously untrue and manifestly convicted, to the great derogation of *Natural Philosophy* with grave and sober men. Wherein in truth the wisdom and
integrity of *Aristotle* doth excellently appear, that having made so diligent and exquisite a *History of living Creatures;* hath mingled it so
sparingly with any vain or feigned matter; but hath rather cast all
De Mirab.
Aufcult. *Prodigious Reports,* which he thought worthy the recording into one
commentary; wisely discerning that matter of manifest Truth (which
might be the experimental ground-work whereupon Philosophy and
Sciences were to be built) ought not unadvisedly, to be mingled with
matter of doubtful faith: and yet again things rare and strange, which
to many seem incredible, are not wholly to be suppressed or denyed to
be recorded to Posterity.

                                                                    But

§ But that other *Facility of Credit*, which is yielded, not to *History* and *Reports*, but to *Arts* and *Opinions*, is likewise of two sorts ; either when too much belief is attributed to *Arts* themselves, or to certain *Authors* in any Art.   The Sciences themselves, which hold more of the fancy and of belief, than of Reason and Demonstration, are chiefly three *Astrologie*, *Natural Magique* and *Alchimy* ; of which Sciences nevertheless the end and pretences are noble ; For *Astrology* professeth to discover the influence and domination of the superiour Globe, over the inferiour : *Magique* proposeth to it self to call and reduce Natural Philosophy from variety of speculations, to the magnitude of works: *Alchimy* undertakes to make a separation and extraction of all heterogeneous and unlike parts of bodies, which in mixture of Nature are Implicate and Incorporate; and to refine and depurate bodies themselves, that are distained and soiled; to set at liberty such as are bound and imprisoned ; and to bring to perfection such as are unripe.   But the derivations and prosecutions, which are presumed to conduce to these ends, both in the Theory and in the Practise of *these Arts*, are full of *Errors* and *Vanity*.   Nor is the Tradition and manner of Delivery for most part ingenious and without suspition, but vail'd over and munited with devises and impostures.   Yet surely to *Alchimy* this right is due, that it may truly be compared to the Husbandman whereof *Æsope* makes the Fable, *that when he died, told his sons he had left unto them a great mass of Gold buried under ground in his Vineyard, but did not remember the particular place where it was hidden* ; who when they had with spades turn'd up all the Vineyard ; gold indeed they found none ; but by reason of their stirring and digging the Mold about the Roots of their Vines, they had a great Vintage the year following : so the painful search and stir of *Alchimists* to make Gold, hath brought to light a great number of good and fruitful experiments, as well for the disclosing of nature, as the use of mans life.

§ As for the *overmuch Credit that hath been given to Authors in Sciences, whom they have invested with the power of Dictators, that their words should stand, and not of Consuls to give advice* ; the damage is infinite that Sciences have received thereby, as a Principal cause that hath kept them low at a stay, and that they have lien heartless, without any notable *Groweth or Advancement*.   For hence it hath come to pass, that in *Arts Mechanical*, the first deviser cometh short, and time supplies and perfects the rest ; but in *Siences*, the first Author goeth farthest, and time looseth and corrupteth.   So we see *Artillery*, *Sailing*, *Printing*, were imperfect, formless, and grosly managed at first, but in progress of time accommodated and refined.   But contrariwise the *Philosophy* and *Sciences* of *Aristotle*, *Plato*, *Democritus*, *Hypocrates*, *Euclide*, *Archimedes*, were of most vigor in their Authors, and in process of time, became rather degenerate and embased, and lost much of their lustre ; whereof the reason is no other, but that in *Arts Mechanical, many wits and industries have contributed in one, in liberal Arts and Sciences, many wits and industries have been spent about, and yielded to the art of some one* ; whom (notwithstanding many times) his sectators have rather depraved than illustrated.   For as water will not ascend higher than the level of the first Spring-head, from whence it descendeth ; so knowledge derived from *Aristotle*, will never rise higher than the knowledge of
Aristotle.

Ariſtot.
de Rep.
Soph. lib.
1.

Ariſtotle.   And therefore although the poſition be good, *Oportet diſcen-tem credere,* yet it muſt be coupled with this, *Oportet jam edoctum judicio ſuo uti.*   For Diſciples owe unto Maſters, only a *temporary belief,* and a ſuſpenſion of their judgment, until they be fully inſtructed, and not an abſolute reſignation of their liberty, and a perpetual captivity of their judgements.   Therefore, to conclude this point, I will ſay no more but this. *Let great Authors ſo have their due, as we do not derogate from Time, which is the Author of Authors and Parent of Truth.*

Chap. V.

Peccant Humours in Learning.   I. *Extreme affection to two extremes, Antiquity, Novelty.*   II. *A diſtruſt, that any thing New, ſhould now be found out.*   III. *That of all Sects and Opinions, the beſt hath ſtill prevailed.*   IV. *An over early reduction of Knowledge into Arts and Methods.*   V. *A neglect of* Primitive Philoſophy.   VI. *A Divorce of the Intellect from the Object.*   VII. *Infection of Knowledge in general from individual inclinations.*   VIII. *An impatience of Doubt, haſt to Aſſertion.*   IX. *A Magiſtral manner of Tradition of Knowledge.*   X. *Aim of writers, Illuſtration, not Propagation of Knowledge.*   XI. *End of ſtudies, Curioſity, Pleaſures, Profit, Preferments,* &c.

Thus have we at length gone over three Diſtempers or Diſeaſes of Learning; beſides the which, there are other, rather *peccant Humours,* than *confirmed Diſeaſes,* which nevertheleſs are not ſo ſecret and intrinſique, but that they fall under a popular ſenſe and reprehenſion, and therefore are not to be paſſed over.

I. The firſt of theſe is an *extreme affection of two extremities, Antiquity and Novelty;* wherein the daughters of *Time,* do take after the Father; for as Time devoureth his children, ſo theſe, one of them ſeeketh to depreſs the other; while *Antiquity* envieth there ſhould be *new Additions;* and *Novelty* can not be content to add things *recent,* but it muſt deface and reject the *old.*   Surely the advice of the Prophet is the true direction in this caſe, *State ſuper vias antiquas & videte quænam ſit via recta & bona & ambulate in ea.   Antiquity* deſerveth that reverence, that men ſhould make a ſtay a while, and ſtand thereupon, and look about to diſcover which is the beſt way; but when the diſcovery is well taken, then not to reſt there, but cheerfully to make progreſſion.   Indeed to ſpeak truly, *Antiquitas ſeculi, Juventus Mundi,* Certainly our times are the Ancient times, when the world is now Ancient, and not thoſe which we count Ancient, *ordine retrogrado,* by a computation backward from our own times.

II. An other error induced by the former is, *a ſuſpition and diffidence, that any thing ſhould be now to be found out, which the world ſhould have miſt and paſt over ſo long time:* as if the ſame objection might be made to *Time,* wherewith *Lucian* reproacheth *Jupiter,* and other the Heathen
                                                                              then

Jerem.6.

Sen. ait.
Lact. Inſt.
Lib. 1.

then Gods, *For he wonders that they begat so many children in old time, and begot none in his time?* and asks in scoffing manner, *whether they were now become Septuagenary, or whether the Law Papia; made against old mens marriages, had restrained them?* So it seems men doubt least time is become past children and generation. Nay rather the levity and inconstancy of mens judgements, is hence plainly discovered, which until a matter be done, wonder it can be done. So *Alexander's* expedition into *Asia* was prejudg'd as a vast impossible enterprize; yet afterwards it pleased *Livie*, so to slight it as to say of *Alexander, Nil aliud* Hist.lib.9. *quam bene ausus est vana contemnere :* The same hapned unto *Columbus* in the western Navigation. But in intellectual matters it is much more common, as may be seen in many propositions in *Euclid*, which till they be demonstrate, they seem strange to our assent ; but being Demonstrate, our mind accepteth of them by a kind of Recognisance or Retractation,(as the Lawyers speak)as if we had understood and known them before.

III. Another error which hath some affinity with the former is, *a conceit That all sects and ancient opinions, after they have been discussed and ventilated ; the best still prevail'd and suppress the rest:* Wherefore they think that if a man should begin the labour of a new search and examination, he must needs light upon somewhat formerly rejected, and after rejection, lost, and brought into oblivion : as if the *multitude,* or the wisest, to gratifie the *multitude,* were not more ready to give passage to that which is popular and superficial; than to that which is substantial and profound. *For Time* seemeth to be of the nature of a River, which carrieth down to us that which is light and blown up, and sinketh and drowneth that which is waighty and solid.

IV. Another error of divers nature from the former is, *The over-early and Peremptory reduction of Knowledge into Arts and Methods ; which once done, commonly Sciences receive small or no augmentation.* For as young men, when they knit and shape perfectly, do seldom grow to a farther stature : so knowledge while it is disperst into *Aphorisms,* and *Observations,* may grow and shoot up; but once inclosed and comprehended in Methods, it may perchance be farther polisht and illustrate , and accommodated for use and practice, but it increaseth no more in bulk and substance.

V. Another error which doth succeed that which we last noted, is, *That after distribution of particular Arts and Sciences into their several places, many men have presently abandoned the universal notion of things,* or Philosophia Prima, *which is a deadly enemy to all Progression.* Prospects are made from Turrets and high places ; and it is impossible to discover the more remote and deeper parts of any Science, if you stand but upon the flat and level of the same Science, and ascend not as into a watch-Town to a higher Science.

VI. Another error hath proceeded *from too great a reverence, and a kind of Adoration of the mind and understanding of man , by means whereof men have withdrawn themselves, too much, from the contemplation of Nature, and the observations of experience ; and have tumbled up and down in their own speculations and conceits ;* bur of these surpassing *Opinators,*and(if I may so speak)*Intellectualists.*(which are notwithstanding, taken for the most sublime and divine Philosophers) *Heraclitus* gave a

just

N. I. juſt cenſure, ſaying, *Men ſeek truth in their own little world, and not in the great common world*, for they diſdain the Alphabet of nature, and *Primer-Book* of the Divine works; which if they did not, they might perchance by degrees and leaſure, after the knowledge of ſimple letters, and ſpelling of Syllables, come at laſt, to read perfectly the Text and Volume of the Creatures. But they, contrariwiſe, by continual meditation and agitation of wit, urge, and as it were invocate their own ſpirits to divine, and give *Oracles* unto them, whereby they are deſervedly and pleaſingly deluded.

VII. Another Error, that hath ſome connexion with this latter, is, *That men do oftentimes imbue and infect their meditations and doctrines with the infuſions of ſome Opinions, and conceptions of their own, which they have moſt admired; or ſome Sciences to which have moſt applyed and conſecrated themſelves, giving all things a Dye and Tincture, though very deceivable, from theſe favorite ſtudies.* So hath *Plato* intermingled his Philoſophy with Theology; *Ariſtotle* with Logick; The ſecond School of *Plato, Proclus* and the reſt, with the Mathematicks. Theſe Arts had a kind of *Primo-geniture* with them, which they would ſtill be kiſſing and making much of, as their firſt born ſons. But the *Alchimiſts* have forged a new Philoſophy out of the Fire and Furnace; and *Gilbert* our Country-man, hath extracted another Philoſophy out of a Load-ſtone. So *Cicero*, when reciting the ſeveral opinions of the nature of the ſoul, he found a Muſitian that held the ſoul was but a harmony, ſaith pleaſantly, *Hic ab arte ſua non receſſit:* But of theſe errors *Ariſtotle* ſaith aptly and wiſely, *Qui reſpiciunt ad pauca de facili pronunciant.*

Tuſc lib.1.
De Gen.
& Cor.
lib.1. &
alibi.

VIII. Another error is, *An impatience of Doubt, and an unadviſed haſte to Aſſertion without due and mature ſuſpenſion of judgement:* For the two ways of contemplation are not unlike the two ways of action, commonly ſpoken of by the Ancients; of which the one was a plain and ſmooth way in the beginnining, but in the end impaſſible; the other rough and troubleſome in the entrance, but after a while fair and even; ſo is it in contemplations, if a man will begin in certainties, he ſhall end in doubts; but if he can be content to begin with doubts, and have patience a while, he ſhall end in certanties.

IX. The like error diſcovereth it ſelf in the *manner of Tradition and Delivery of knowlege, which is, for the moſt part, imperious and magiſtral, not ingenious and faithfull; ſo contrived, as may rather command our aſſent, than ſtand to examination.* It is true that in compendious Treatiſes deſigned for Practice, that Form of Writing may be retained; but in a juſt and compleat handling of knowledge, both extremes are to be avoided, as well the vein of *Vellieus* the Epicurean, *who feared nothing ſo much as to ſeem to doubt of any thing;* as that of *Socrates* and the Academy, leaving all things in doubt and incertainty: Rather men ſhould affect candor and ſincerity, propounding things with more or leſs aſſeveration, as they ſtand in their judgement proved, more or leſs.

Cic. de
Nat. Dier.
l.b.

X. Other errors there are *in the ſcope that men propound to themſelves whereunto they bend their endeavours and ſtudies:* For whereas the moſt devout Leaders and noted Profeſſors of Learning, ought chiefly to propound to themſelves to make ſome notable addition to the Science they

they profefs; contrariwife, they convert their labours to afpire to certain fecond prizes, as to be a *profound interpreter*, or commentator; a fharp and ftrong champion or *Defender*; a Methodical compounder or *Abridger* : fo the Revenues and Tributes of Sciences come to be improved, but not the Patrimony and Inheritance.

◦ XI. But the greateft error of all the reft is, *the miftaking or mifplacing the laft and fartheft end of knowledge* : For many have entred into a defire of Learning and Knowledge, fome upon an inbred and reftlefs *Curiofity*; others to entertain their minds with variety and *delight*; others for *ornament and reputation*; others for *contradiction* and victory in difpute; others for *Lucre* and living; few to improve the gift of reafon given them from God, to the benefit and ufe of men. As if there were fought in knowledge, a *couch*, whereupon to reft a reftlefs and fearching fpirit, or a *Tarrafs* for a wandring and variable mind to walk up and down in at liberty unreftrained; or fome high and eminent *Tower of State*, from which a proud and ambitious mind, may have a Profpect; or a *Fort* and commanding ground for ftrife and contention; or a *fhop* for profit and fale; and not rather a rich *ftore-houfe and Armory* for the glory of the Creator of all things, and the relief of mans eftate. For this is that which indeed would dignifie and exalt Learning; if contemplation and action were more nearly and ftraitly, than hitherto they have been conjoyn'd and united together : which combination, certainly would be like unto that conjunction of the two higheft Planets, when *Saturn* which hath the Dominion over reft and contemplations, confpires with *Jupiter* the Lord of Civil fociety and Action. Howbeit I do not mean when I fpeak of Ufe and Action, Profeffory or Lucretive Learning; for I am not ignorant how much that diverts and interrupteth the *Progreffion and advancement of knowledge*; like indeed the *Golden apple*, thrown before *Atalanta*, which while fhe goes afide and ftoopeth to take up, the race is hindred:

Declinat curfus, aurumq; volubile tollit.   Ovid. Met. 10.

Neither is it my meaning, as was fpoken of *Socrates*, to call Philofophy down from heaven, to converfe upon the earth; that is to lay *Natural Phylofophy* afide, and to celebrate only *Moral Phylofophy* and *Policy*. But as Heaven and Earth do confpire and contribute, to the ufe and benefit of the life of Man; fo indeed this fhould be the end of *both Phylofophies*; that vain fpeculations, and what ever is empty and barren, being rejected; that which is folid and fruitful may be preferved and augmented; that fo Knowledge may not be a Courtezan for Pleafure, or as a bond-woman for gain; but as a fpoufe for generation, fruit and honeft folace.

§ Now me thinks I have defcribed and opened, as by a kind of diffection, thofe *Peccant Humours*; or at leaft, the Principal of them, *which have not only given impediment to the Proficience of Learning, but have given alfo occafion to the traducement thereof.* Wherein if I have come too near the quick, it muft be remembred, *Fidelia vulnera amantis do* Pfal. 145. *lofa ofcula malignantis* : however this furely I think I have gained, that I ought to be the better believed, concering the *Commendations of Learning* in that which follows, becaufe I have proceeded fo freely concerning

D   cenfure

censure, in that which went before.   And yet I have no purpose to enter into a *Landative of Learning*, or to make a *Hymn to the Muses*;
though I am of opinion, that it is long since their Rites were duely celebrated : but my intent is, without varnish or amplification, to take the
just waight, and to ballance the *Dignity of Knowledge* in the scales with
other things ; and to search out the true values thereof, *from testimonies Divine and Humane.*

C H A P. VI.

The Dignity of Learning from Divine Arguments and Testimonies.
I. *From Gods wisdom.* § *Angels of Illumination.* § *The first Light
and first Sabbath.* § *Mans imployment in the Garden.* § *Abels
contemplative life.* § *The invention of Musick.* § *Confusion of
Tongues.* II. *The excellent Learning of* Moses. § Job. § Solomon. § Christ. §. St. Paul. § *The Ancient Doctors of the Church.*
§ *Learning exalts the Mind to the Celebration of Gods glory ; and is
a Preservative against Error and Unbelief.*

I.   FIrst therefore let us seek the Dignity of Knowledge , in the
Arch-Type or first Platform, which is in the *Attributes*, and in
the *Acts of God*, as far as they are revealed to man, and may be observed with sobriety. Wherein we may not seek it by the name of
Learning ; for all *Learning* is Knowledge acquired, and no knowledge
in God is *acquired*, but *Original* : and therefore we must look for it by
another name, that is *wisdom* or *sapience*, as the sacred Scriptures call it.
It is so then ; In the *works* of the *Creation* , we see a double emanation

Gen. 1. of Divine virtue from God ; whereof the one is referr'd to *Power*, the
other to *Wisdom*, that is chiefly exprest in making the *Mass* and substance of the *Matter* ; this in disposing the beauty of the *Form*.   This
being supposed, it is to be observed, that for any thing which appears in
the History of the *Creation*, the confused Mass and Matter of *Heaven* and
Earth was made in a moment of Time ; yet the *Order* and *Disposition* of
that *Chaos* or Mass, was the work of six days : such a note of difference
it pleased God to put upon the works of *Power*, and the works of *Wisdom* ; wherewith concurs, that in the Creation of the *Matter* ; it is
not recorded that God said *Let there be Heaven and Earth*, as it is said
of the works following ; but simply and actually, *God made Heaven
and Earth* : so that the *Matter* seems to be as a *Manufacture*, but the
Form carries the stile of a *Law* or *Decree*.

§ Let us proceed *from God to Angels or Spirits*, whose nature in or-
der of Dignity is next Gods. We see, so far as credit is to be given to the
Celestial Hierarchy, set forth under the name of *Dionysius Areopagita*,
Dion.
Aveo. that in the order of Angels, the first place or degree is given to the
Seraphim, that is, *Angels of Love* : the second to the *Cherubim*, that is,
Angels of Illumination : the third, and so following, Places to *Thrones*,
Principalities and the rest, which are Angels of Power and Ministry.
So

So as from this order and diftribution, it appears, that *the Angels of Knowledge and Illumination*, are placed before *the Angels of Office and Domination.*

§ To defcend from Spirits and Intelleftual Forms, to Senfible and Material Forms; we read *that the firft of Created forms was Light*; which hath a relation and correfpondence in nature and Coporeal things, to knowledge in Spirits and Incorporeal things. So in the diftribution of *Days*, we fee the *day* wherein God did reft and contemplate his own works, was bleft above all the *days* wherein the Fabrick of the *Univerfe* was Created and Difpofed.

§ After the Creation was finifht, we read that *Man was plac'd in the Garden to work therein*; which work fo appointed to him, could be no other than the *work of Contemplation*, that is, the end hereof was not for neceffity, but for delight and exercife without vexation or trouble: For there being then no reluftation of the Creature, no fweat of the brow; mans imployment muft of confequence have been matter of *delight* and *contemplation, not of Labour and Work.* Again, the firft Afts that man perform'd in *Paradife*, comprehended the two fummary parts of *knowledge*; thofe were the *view of Creatures, and the impofition of names.* For the *knowledge* which introduc'd the Fall, it was (as we have toucht before) not the *Natural Knowledge concerning the Creatures*; but the *Moral Knowledge of Good and Evil*, where the fuppofition was, *that Gods Commandments or Prohibitions were not the Originals of Good and Evil, but that they had other beginnings*, which man afpired to know, to the end to make a total defeftion from God, and to depend wholly upon himfelf, and his Freewill.

§. To pafs to the firft event or occurrence after the Fall of Man, we fee (as the Scriptures have infinite Myfteries, not violating at all the truth of the ftory or letter) *an image of the two States, the Contemplative and Aftive, figur'd in the Perfons of Abel and Cain*, and in their Profeffions and Primitive trades of life; whereof the one was a Shepherd, who by reafon of his leifure, reft in a place, and free view of Heaven, *is a lively image of a Contemplative life*; the other a Husbandman, that is, a man toil'd and tired with working; and his countenance fixt upon the earth: *where we may fee the favour and Eleftion of God went to the Shepherd, and not to the tiller of Ground.* Gen. 4:

§ So in the Age before the Flood, the holy Records (with in thofe few Memorials which are there entred and regiftred, touching the occurrences of that age) have vouchfafed to mention and honour *Inventors of Mufick and works in Metals.* Gen. 4:

§ In the next Age after the Flood, the great judgement of God upon the ambition of Man was the *Confufion of Tongues*; whereby the *open trade and intercourfe of Learning and Knowledge was chiefly embraced.* Gen. 11:

II. Let us defcend to *Mofes* the Law-giver, and Gods firft Notary, he is adorn'd in Scripture with this commendation, *That he was feen in all the Learning of the Ægyptians*; which Nation, we know, was one of the moft ancient Schools of the world; for fo *Plato* brings in the Ægyptian Prieft faying unto *Solon, You Grecians are ever children*, Acts 7:

In Timæo *you have no knowledge of Antiquity, nor Antiquity of Knowledge :* Let us take a view of the *Ceremonial Law of Moses,* and we fhall find (befides the prefiguration of Chrift, the Badge or Difference of the people of God, from the profane Race of the world ; the exercife and impreffion of obedience,and other facred ufes and fruits of the fame Law) that fome of the moft learned Rabbins, have travelled profitably and profoundly in the fame, intentively to obferve and extract, fometimes *a Natural, fometimes a Moral fence of the Ceremonies and Ordinances :* For example, where it is faid of the Leprofie, *If the whitenefs have over-fpread the flefh, the Patient may pafs abroad for clean ; but if there be any whole flefh remaining, he is to be fentenced unclean, and to be feparated at the difcretion of the Prieft.* From this Law one of them collects a Principle in Nature ; *That Putrifaction is more contagious before maturity then after.* Another raifeth a Moral inftruction ; *That men are fpread with vice, do not fo much corrupt publick Manners, as thofe that are half evil and but in part only.* So that from this and other like places in that Law, there is to be found, befides Theological fence, much afperfion of Philofophy.

§ So likewife that *excellent Book of Job,* if it be revolved with diligence, it will be found full and pregnant with the fecrets of *Natural Philofophy* ; as for example, of *Cofmography,* and the roundnefs of the Earth in that place, *Qui extendit Aquilonem fuper vacuum, & appendit Terram fuper nihilum,* where the Penfilenefs of the Earth ; the Pole of the North ; and the Finitenefs or convexity of Heaven, are manifeftly touched. Again, *of Aftronomy and Conftellations,* in thofe words, *Spiritus ejus ornavit Cælos, & obftetricante manu ejus eductus eft coluber tortuofus :* And in another place, *Canft thou bind the fweet influences of Pleiades, or loofe the bands of Orion ;* where the fetled and immoveable configuration of the firft Stars, ever ftanding at equal diftance, is with great elegancy defcribed. So in another Place, *Which maketh Arcturus, Orion and Pleiades and the fecret chambers of the South :* Where he again points at the depreffion of Southern Pole, defigning it by the name of *the fecrets of the South,* becaufe the Southern Stars are not feen upon our Hemifphere. Matter of Generation of living Creatures, *Haft thou not poured me out like milk, and condenfed me like Curds ?* Matter of Minerals, *Surely there is a Mine for Silver,and a place wherein Gold is fined ; Iron is digged up out of compacted duft, and Brafs extracted from ftone diffolved in the furnace,* and fo forward in the fame Chapter.

§ So likewife in the perfon of *Solomon the King, we fee the endowments of wifdom, both in his Petition and Gods affent thereunto, preferred before all terrene and temporal felicity.* By virtue of which Donative and Grant, *Solomon* being fingularly furnifht and enabled, not only writ thofe *excellent Parables or Aphorifms* concerning Divine and Moral Philofophy ; but alfo compiled a *Natural Hiftory* of all verdure or vegetables *From the Cedar upon the Mountain, to the Mofs upon the Wall ;* which is but the rudiment of a plant, between putrifaction and an Herb ; and *alfo of all things that breath or move.* Nay the fame *Solomon the King,* although he excell'd in treafure and the magnificence of Building, of Shipping, and Navigation, of Service and Attendance, of Fame and Renown, and the like train of Glory, he reaps

Margin notes:
In Timæo
Levit. 13.
Job 26.
Ibid.
Job 38.
Job 9.
Job 10.
Job 28.
1 Reg. 4.

reaps and makes claim to himſelf of nothing ; but only the Honour of
the Inquiſition, and Invention of Truth, for ſo he ſaith expreſly, *The
Glory of God is to conceal a thing, but the Glory of a King is to find it* Prov.25.
out. As if according to that innocent and affectionate play of Children, the Divine Majeſty took delight to hide his works, to the end
to have them found out ; and as if *Kings* could not obtain a greater
Honour, than to be Gods play-fellows in that game ; eſpecially conſidering the great command they have of wits and means, whereby the
inveſtigation of all things may be perfected.

§ Neither did the diſpenſation of God vary in the times after our
Saviour came into the world ; *For our Saviour himſelf did firſt ſhew his
power to ſubdue Ignorance, by his conference with the Doctors of the Law,* Luc 2.
and the Prieſts in the Temple, before he ſhewed his power to ſuddue Nature, by his great and ſo many Miracles. *And the coming of the Holy* Acts A-
Ghoſt was chiefly figur'd and expreſt in the ſimilitude and guiſt of Tongues, poſt.2.
which are the *vehicula ſcientiæ.*

§. So in the election of *thoſe inſtruments which it pleaſed God to uſe in
the Plantation of the Faith,* at the firſt he imployed perſons altogether
Unlearned, otherwiſe than by inſpiration from the holy Spirit ; whereby more evidently he might declare his immediate and divine working, and might abaſe all humane Wiſdom and Knowledge : yet nevertheleſs that counſel of his in this reſpect was no ſooner perform'd, but
in the next viciſſitude and ſucceſſion of time he ſent his divine Truth
into the world, waited on with other Learning, as with ſervants and
hand-maids ; therefore we ſee *St. Pauls pen , (who was only learned* Acts A-
amongſt the Apoſtles) was chiefly imployed by God, in the Scriptures of poſt.12.
the new Teſtament.

§ So again we know, *that many of the Ancient Biſhops and Doctors
of the Church were excellently read and ſtudied in all the Learning of
the Heathen,* in ſo much that the Edict of the *Emperour* Julian, *where-* Epiſt. ad
by it was interdicted unto Chriſtians to be admitted into Schools, or ex- Jambl.
erciſes of Learning , was eſteemed and accounted a more pernitious
Engine and Machination againſt the Chriſtian Faith , than were all the
ſanguinary proſecutions of his Predeceſſors. Neither could the emu- P. Diac.1.
lation and jealouſie of *Gregory the Firſt,* (otherwiſe an excellent man) 3. Parag.
who deſigned to extinguiſh and obliterate Heathen Authors and Antiquity, 33.
ever obtain the opinion of Piety and Devotion amongſt holy men.
But contrariwiſe it was the Chriſtian Church, which amidſt the inundations of the Scythians from the North-weſt ; and the Saracens from
the Eaſt, did preſerve in the ſacred Lap and Boſom thereof the *precious
relicks of Heathen Learning,* which otherwiſe had utterly periſht and
been extinguiſht. And of late in our age we may likewiſe ſee the *Je-
ſuits,* who partly in themſelves, and partly by emulation and provocation of Adverſaries, *have much quickned and ſtrengthened the ſtate of
Learning* ; we ſee, I ſay, what notable ſervices they have done, and
what helps they have brought in, to the repairing and eſtabliſhing of
the Roman Sea.

§. Wherefore to conclude this Part, there are two principal Duties
and Services beſides ornament and illuſtration, which humane Learning
doth perform to Faith and Religion : *The one, becauſe they are effectual incitements to the exaltation and celebration of the Glory of God :* for

Pſal. XIX. as the Pſalms, and other Scriptures, do often invite us to the contemplation, and publication of the magnificent and wonderful works of God ; ſo if we ſhould reſt only in the outward form, as they firſt offer themſelves unto our ſenſes ; we ſhould do the like the injury to the Majeſty of God, as if we ſhould judge of the ſtore and wealth of ſome excellent Jeweller, by that only, which is ſet out towards the ſtreet Mat. 22. in his ſhop. *The other, becauſe they* |*miniſter a ſingular help and preſervative againſt unbelief,* and errors : *You err, not knowing the Scriptures nor the Power of God.* Where he lays before us, two books or volumes to ſtudy, if we will be ſecur'd from errors : Firſt the *volume of Scriptures,* which reveal the will of God ; then the *volume of Creatures,* which expreſs his power ; whereof the latter is as a key to the former, not only opening our underſtanding to conceive the true ſence of Scriptures, by the general rules of Reaſon and Laws of ſpeech ; but beſides, chiefly opening our belief, in drawing us unto a due meditation of the omnipotency of God ; the characters whereof are chiefly ſigned and engraven upon his works. Thus much for *Divine Teſtimonies and Evidences,* concerning the true Dignity and value of Learning.

CHAP. VII.

The Dignity of Learning from humane Arguments *and* Teſtimonies. I. Natural, *Inventors of New Arts for the Commodities of Mans life, conſecrated as Gods.* II. Political, *Civil Eſtates and affairs advanced by Learning.* § *The beſt and happieſt times under Learned Princes and others.* § *Exemplified in the immediate ſucceeding Emperours, from the death of* Domitian. III. Military, *The concurrence of Arms and Learning.* § *Exemplified in* Alexander *the* Great. § Julius Cæſar *the Dictator.* § Xenophon *the Philoſopher.*

AS for *Humane Teſtimonies and Arguments,* it is ſo large a field, as in a diſcourſe of this compendious nature and brevity, it is fit rather to uſe choice, than to imbrace the variety of them.

    I. Firſt, therefore in the degrees of Honour amongſt the Heathens, it was the higheſt, to attain to a Veneration and Adoration as a God ; this indeed to the Chriſtians is as the forbidden fruit ; but we ſpeak now ſeparately of Humane Teſtimony. Therefore, (as we were ſaying) with the Heathens, that which the Grecians call *Apotheoſis* ; and the Latines *Relatio inter Divos* ; was the Herodia. l. 4 Dio. Reliqui. ſupreme Honour which man could attribute unto man : ſpecially, when it was given, not by a formal Decree or Act of Eſtate, (as it was uſed amongſt the Roman Emperours,) but freely by the aſſent of Men and inward belief. Of which high Honour there was a certain degree and middle term : For there were reckoned above *Humane Honours, Honours Heroical* ; and *Divine* ; in the Diſtribution whereof, Antiquity obſerved this order. Founders of States ; Lawgivers ; Extirpers of
Tyrants ;

Tyrants ; Fathers of their Country, and other eminent Perſons in Civil Merit, were honour'd with the title of *Worthies* only, or *Demi-Gods* ; ſuch as were *Theſeus, Minos, Romulus,* and the like : on the other ſide ſuch as were *Inventors and Authors of new Arts* ; *and ſuch as endowed mans life with new Commodities, and acceſſions, were ever conſecrated among the Greater and Entire Gods* ; which hapned to *Ceres, Bacchus, Mercury, Apollo,* and others, which indeed was done juſtly and upon ſound judgment : For the *merits of the former,* are commonly confined within the circle of an Age, or a Nation, and are not unlike ſeaſonable and favouring ſhowers, which though they be profitable and deſirable, yet ſerve but for that ſeaſon only wherein they fall, and for a Latitude of ground which they water : *but the beneſices of the latter,* like the influences of the Sun, and the heavenly bodies, are for time, permanent, for place, univerſal : thoſe again are commonly mixt with ſtrife and perturbation ; but theſe have the true character of Divine preſence, and come in *Aura leni* without noiſe or agitation.

II. Neither certainly is the *Merit of Learning in Civil affairs, and in repreſſing the inconveniences which grow from man to man, much inferiour to the other, which relieve mans neceſſities, which ariſe from Nature.* And this kind of merit was lively ſet forth in that feigned relation of *Orpheus his Theatre,* where all beaſts and birds aſſembled, which forgetting their proper natural appetites of Prey, of Game, of Quarrel, ſtood all ſociably and lovingly together liſtening unto the Airs and accords of the harp ; the ſound whereof no ſooner ceaſed, or was drown'd by ſome louder noiſe, but every beaſt returned to his own nature. In which Fable is elegantly deſcribed, the nature and condition of men, who are toſſed and diſordered with ſundry ſavage and unreclaim'd deſires, of Profit, of Luſt, of Revenge ; which yet as long as they give ear to precepts, to the perſwaſion of Religion, Laws, and Magiſtrates, eloquently and ſweetly couch'd in Books, to Sermons and Harangues ; ſo long is ſociety and peace maintain'd, but if theſe inſtruments be ſilent, or that ſeditions and tumults make them not audible, all things diſſolve and fall back into Anarchy and Confuſion.

Philoſ. in Orph.

§ But this appeareth more manifeſtly, *when Kings or Perſons of Authority under them, or Governours in States, are endowed with Learning :* For although he might be thought partial to his own profeſſion that ſaid, *Then ſhould People or States be happy when either Kings were Philoſophers or Philoſophers Kings* ; yet ſo much is verified by experience, *that under wiſe and Learned Princes and Governours of State, there hath been ever the beſt and happieſt times.* For howſoever Kings may have their errors and imperfections ; that is, be liable to Paſſions and depraved cuſtoms, like other men, yet if they be illuminated by Learning, they have certain anticipate notions of Religion, Policy, and Morality, which preſerve and refrain them from all ruinous and peremptory errors and exceſſes, whiſpering evermore in their ears, when Councellours, and Servants ſtand mute and ſilent. So likewiſe *Senators and Councellours which be Learned, do proceed upon more ſafe and ſubſtantial principles than Councellours which are only men of experience :* Thoſe ſeeing dangers a farre off, and repulſing them betimes ; whereas theſe are wiſe only near at hand, ſeeing nothing, but what is imminent and ready to fall upon them, and then truſt to the agility of their wit, in the point of dangers, to ward and avoid them.   § Which

Plato. de Rep.5.

§ Which felicity of times under *Learned Princes* (to keep ſtill the law of brevity by uſing the moſt ſelected and eminent examples) doth beſt appear, in the Age which paſſed from the death of *Domitianus* the Emperour, untill the reign of *Commodus, comprehending a ſucceſſion of ſix Princes, all Learned, or ſingular favourers and advancers of Learning, and of all ages (if we regard temporal happineſs) the moſt flouriſhing that ever Rome ſaw, which was then the Model and Epitome of the world :* A
Suet. in
Dom. pa-
rag. 23.
matter revealed and preſigur'd unto *Domitian* in a dream, the night before he was ſlain, *for he ſeem'd to ſee grown behind upon his ſhoulders a neck and a head of gold* ; which Divination came indeed accordingly to paſs, in thoſe golden times which ſucceeded ; of which we will make ſome particular, but brief commemoration. *Nerva* was a Learned Prince, an inward acccquaintance, and even a Diſciple to *Apollonius*
Nerva tuis
Dion. l. 68.
Plin. Pan.
the Pythagorean ; who alſo almoſt expired in a verſe of Homers,

Telis Phœbe tuis, lachrimas ulciſcere noſtras.

Trajan was for his Perſon not Learned, but an admirer of Learning, and a munificent benefactor to the Learned, a Founder of Librarics, and in whoſe Court (though a warlike Prince) as is recorded, Profeſ-
Dion. in
Adriano.
ſours and Preceptors were of moſt credit and eſtimation. *Adrian* was the moſt curious man that lived, and the inſatiable inquirer of all variety and ſecrets. *Antonius* had the patient and ſubtile wit of a
Dion. in
Anton. P.
School-man, in ſo much as he was called *Cymini-Sector, a Carver, or a divider of Cummin-ſeed :* And of the *Divi fratres, Lucius Commodus* was delighted with a ſofter kind of Learning ; and *Marcus* was ſurnam'd the *Philoſopher. Theſe Princes as they excel'd the reſt in Learning, ſo they excel'd them likewiſe in virtue and goodneſs. Nerva* was a moſt mild
Plin. Pan.
Aur. vict.
c. 13.
Emperour, and *who* (if he had done nothing elſe) *gave Trajan to the World. Trajan,* of all that reigned, for the Arts, both of Peace and War, was moſt famous and renowned : the ſame Prince enlarged the bounds of the Empire ; the ſame, temperately confin'd the Limits and
Xyphil. ex
Dion.
Trajan.
Power thereof ; he was alſo a great Builder in ſo much as *Conſtantine* the Great, in emulation was was wont to call him, *Parietaria, Wall-Flower,* becauſe his name was carved upon ſo many walls. *Adrian* was Times rival for the victory of perpetuity, for by his care and munificence in every kind, he repaired the decaies and ruines of Time.
Capitol.
In Ant. P.
Antoninus, as by name, ſo nature, a man exceeding *Pious* ; for his nature and inbred goodneſs, was beloved and moſt acceptable to men of all ſorts and degrees ; whoſe reign, though it was long, yet was it
§
In Vero.
In M. Ant.
peaceful and happy. *Lucius Commodus* (exceeded indeed by his brother) excel'd many of the Emperours for goodneſs. *Marcus* formed by nature to be the pattern and Platform of virtue, againſt whom that *Ieſter* in the banquet of the Gods had nothing to object, or carpe at, *ſave his patience towards the humours of his wife.* So in this continued ſequence of *ſix Princes, a man may ſee the happy fruits of Learning in So-*
Juliani
Cæſars.
veraignty, Painted forth in the greateſt Table of the world.

III. Neither hath *Learning an influence or operation upon Civil merit and the Arts of peace only,* but likewiſe it hath no leſs Power & Efficacy in *Martial and Military virtue,* as may notably be repreſented in the examples of *Alexander* the Great ; and *Iulius Cæſar* the *Dictator,* mention'd, by the

way

way before, but now in fit place to be refumed ; of whofe *Military ver-tues and Acts in war*, there needs no note or recital, having been the wonders of the world in that kind ; but, of *their affection and propension towards Learning, and peculiar perfection therein*, it will not be imper-tinent to fay fomething.

§ *Alexander* was bred and taught under *Ariftotle*, (certainly a great Philofopher) who dedicated divers of his Books of *Philofophy* unto him : he was attended with *Califthenes*, and divers other Learned perfons that followed him in Camp, and were his perpetual affociates, in all his Travels and Conquefts. *What Price and Eftimation he had Learn-ing in*, doth notably appear in many particulars ; as in the envy he ex-preffed towards *Achille's* great fortune, in this, *That he had fo good a Trumpet of his Actions and prowefs as* Homer's *verfes*. In the judgment he gave touching the *precious Cabinet of Darius*, which was found a-mongft the reft of the fpoils ; whereof, when queftion was mov'd, what thing was worthy to be put into it, and one faid one thing, ano-ther, another, *he gave fentence for* Homer's *works*. His reprehenfory letter to *Ariftotle*, after he had fet forth his *Book of Nature*, wherein he expoftulates with him, for publifhing the fecrets or myfteries of Philo-fophy, and gave him to underftand, *That himfelf efteemed it more to excel others in Learning and Knowledge, than in Power and Empire*. There are many other particulars to this purpofe. *But how excellently his mind was endowed with Learning*, doth appear, or rather fhine in all his *Speeches* and *anfwers*, full of of knowledg and wifdom ; whereof though the Remains be fmall, yet you fhall find deeply impreffed in them, the foot-fteps of all fciences in Moral knowledge ; *Let the fpeech of Alexander* be obferved *touching Diogenes*, and fee (ifye pleafe) if it tend not to to the true eftate of one of the greateft queftions in moral Philofophy ? *Whether the enjoying of outward things, or the contemning of them, be the greater happinefs*. For when he faw *Diogenes contented with fo little*, turning to thofe that ftood about him, that mock'd at the Cynicks condition, he faid, *If I were not* Alexander, *I could wifh to be* Diogenes. But *Seneca*, in this comparifon, prefers *Diogenes*, when he faith, *Plus erat quod Diogenes nollet accipere, quàm quod Alexander poffet dare, There were more things which Diogenes would have refufed, than thofe were which Alexander could have given*. In *Natural knowledg*, obferve that fpeech that was ufual with him, *That he felt his mortality chiefly in two things, Sleep, and Luft :* which fpeech, in truth, is extract-ed out of the depth of *Natural Philofophy*, tafting rather of the concep-tion of an *Ariftotle*, or a *Democritus*, than an *Alexander* ; feeing as well the indigence, as redundance of nature, defign'd by thefe two Acts, are, as it were, the inward witneffes and the earneft of Death. In *Poefy*, let that fpeech be obferved, when upon the bleeding of his wounds, he called unto him one of his Flatterers, that was wont to a-fcribe unto him divine honour ; *look* (faith he) *this is the bloud of a man, not fuch liquor as* Homer *fpeaks of, which ran from* Venus *hand, when it was pierced by* Diomedes: with this fpeech checking both the *Poets*, and his flatterers, and himfelf. In *Logick* obferve that reprehenfion of *Dialectick Fallacies*, in repelling and retorting Arguments, in that fay-ing of his wherein he takes up *Caffander*, confuting the informers againft his father *Antipater*. For when *Alexander* hapned to fay, *Do you think thefe*

Plut. in Alexand.

Plut. ut fupra.

Ut fupra.

Ut fupra.

De Ben. 5.

Plut. in Alexand.

E   *men*

Plut.in A-
lexand. *men would come so far to complain, except they had just cause?* Caſſander
anſwered, *Yea, that was it that made them thus bold, becauſe they hoped
the length of the way would dead the diſcovery of the aſperſion;* See (ſaith
the King) *the ſubtilty of Ariſtotle wreſting the matter both waies,* Pro and
Contra, Yet the ſame Art which he reprehended in another, he knew
well how to uſe himſelf, when occaſion required, to ſerve his own
turn. For ſo it fell out that *Caliſthenes,* (to whom he bare a ſecret
grudge, becauſe he was againſt the new ceremony of his adoration)
being mov'd, at a banquet, by ſome of thoſe that ſate at table with
him, that for entertainment ſake (being he was an eloquent man) he
would take upon him ſome Theme, at his own choice, to diſcourſe
upon, which *Caliſthenes* did, and chuſing the Praiſes of the Macedonian Nation, performed the ſame with the great applauſe of all that

Plutarch.
ut ſupra. heard him: whereupon *Alexander,* nothing pleaſed, ſaid, *That upon
a good ſubject it was eaſie for any man to be eloquent,* but turn, ſaid he,
your ſtile, and let us hear what you can ſay againſt us. *Caliſthenes* undertook the charge, and performed it, with that ſting and life, that
Alexander was fain to interrupt him, ſaying, *An ill mind alſo, as well as
a good cauſe might infuſe eloquence.* For *Rhetorick,* whereto Tropes and
Ornaments appertain; ſee an elegant uſe of Metaphor, wherewith he
taxed *Antipater,* who was an Imperious and Tyrannous Governour.
For when one of *Antipaters* friends commended him to *Alexander* for
his moderation. and that he did not degenerate, as other Lievtenants

Plutarch.
Dict.Not. did, into the Perſian Pride, in uſing Purple, but kept the ancient Ma-
cedon habit, *But Antipater* (ſaith *Alexander*) *is all Purple within.* So
likewiſe that other Metaphor is excellent; when *Parmenio* came unto
him in the plain of *Arbella;* and ſhewed him the innumerable multitude
of enemies which viewed in the night, repreſented, by the infinite
number of lights, a new Firmament of ſtarres; and thereupon adviſed

Plut.in
Alexan. him to aſſail them by night, *I will not,* ſaid *Alexander, ſteal a victory.*
For matter of Policy, weigh that grave and wiſe diſtinction, which all
ages have embraced, whereby he differenced his two chief friends, E-

Ut ſupra. pheſtion and *Craterus,* when he ſaid, *That the one loved Alexander, and
the other loved the King,* Deſcribing a Difference of great import, a-
mongſt even the moſt faithful ſervants of Kings, *that ſome in ſincere
affection love their Perſons, others in duty love their Crown.* Obſerve
how excellently he could tax an error, ordinary with Counſellors of
Princes, who many times give counſel, according to the model of their

Plut.in
Alex. own mind and fortune, and not of their Maſters. For when *Darius*
had made great offers to *Alexander* : I, ſaid *Parmenio, would accept theſe
conditions, If I were as Alexander* : ſaid *Alexander, ſurely ſo would I,
were I as parmenio.* Laſtly, weigh that quick and acute reply, which
he made to his friends asking him, *what he would reſerve for himſelf, giving
away ſo many and great gifts?* Hope, ſaid he; as one who well knew

Ut ſupra. that when all accounts are caſt up aright, *Hope* is the true portion and
inheritance of all that reſolve upon great enterprizes. This was *Julius
Cæſar's* portion when he went into *Gaul*, all his eſtate being exhauſted
by profuſe Largeſſes. This was likewiſe the portion of that noble

S.Fran.
Bacon.
Apol. Prince, howſoever tranſported with Ambition, *Henry Duke of Guyſe,*
of whom it was uſually ſaid, *That he was the greateſt uſurer in all France,
becauſe that all his wealth was in names, and that he had turned his*
whole

whole eſtate into obligations. But the admiration of *this Prince,* whilſt
I repreſent him to my ſelf, not as *Alexander the Great,* but as *Ariſtotles
Scholar,* hath perchance carried me too far.

§ As for *Iulius Cæſar, the excellency of his Learning,* needs not to be ᴄⁱᶜ. ᵈᵉᶜˡᵃ
argued, either from his education, or his company, or his anſwers; ᴏʳᵃᵗ.
For this, in a high degree, doth declare it ſelf in his own writings, ᶜⁱᶜ.ᵈᵉ ᴏ-
and works, whereof ſome are extant, ſome unfortunately periſh't. ⁱᵘˡ.
For firſt, there is left unto us *that excellent Hiſtory of his own wars, which
he entitled only a Commentary;* wherein all ſucceeding times have ad- ˢᵘᵉᵗ.ⁱⁿ
mired the ſolid weight of matter; and lively images of Actions and ᵖᵃʳᵃᵍ. ⁵⁵.
Perſons expreſt in the greateſt propriety of words, & perſpicuity of Narration, that ever was. Which endowments, that they were not infuſed by nature, but accquired by *Precepts and inſtructions of Learning,*
is well witneſſed by that work of his entitled *De Analogia,* which was ᵖᵃʳᵃᵍ.⁵⁵.
nothing elſe but a *Grammatical Philoſophy,* wherein he did labour, to
make this *vox ad Placitum,* to become *vox ad Licitum,* and to reduce
cuſtome of ſpeech, to congruity of ſpeech; that words, which are the
the images of things, might accord with the things themſelves, and not
ſtand to the Arbitrement of the vulgar. So likewiſe we have by his
edict, *a reformed computation of the year,* correſpondent to the courſe ˢᵘᵉᵗ.ⁱⁿ
of the Sun; which evidently ſhews, that he accounted it his equal glo- ᵖᵃʳᵃᵍ. ⁴⁰.
ry, to find out the laws of the ſtars in heaven; as to give laws to men
on earth. So in that Book of his entitled *Anti-Cato;* it doth eaſily ap- ᴾˡᵘᵗ ⁱⁿ
pear, that he did aſpire, as well to victory of wit, as victory of war; ᶜᵃꜱⁱ
undertaking therein a Conflict againſt the greateſt Champion with the
Pen, that then lived, *Cicero the Oratour.* Again in his Book of *Apophthegms,* which he collected, we ſee he eſteemed it more honour, to
to make himſelf but a pair of Tables, or Codicils, wherein to regiſter
the wiſe and grave ſayings of others; than if his own words were hal-
lowed as Oracles, as many vain Princes, by cuſtom of Flattery, delight
to do. But if I ſhould report divers of his *Speeches,* as I did in *Alexander,* they are truly ſuch, as Solomon notes, *Verba ſapientum ſunt tan-* ᴱᶜᶜˡᵉꜰ.¹²,
quam aculei, & tanquam clavi in altum defixi : wherefore I will here only
propound three, not ſo admirable for elegancy, as for vigour and efficacy : As firſt, it is reaſon he be thought *a maſter of words,* that could
with one word appeaſe a mutiny in his army : the occaſion was this;
The *Romans,* when their Generals did ſpeak in their Army, did uſe
the word, *Milites,* when the Magiſtrates ſpake to the people, they
did uſe the word, *Quirites : Cæſars* ſouldiers were in a tumult, and ſe-
ditiouſly prayed to be caſſed, not that they ſo meant, but by expoſtu-
lation thereof, to draw *Cæſar* to other conditions; *He,* nothing daun-
ted and reſolute, after ſome ſilence began thus, *Ego, Quirites,* which ˢᵘᵉᵗ.ⁱⁿ
word did admit them already caſhiered; wherewith the ſouldiers were ⁱᵘˡ.ᵖᵃʳᵃᵍ.
ſo ſurprized, and ſo amazed; as they would not ſuffer him to go on in ⁷⁰.
his ſpeech; and relinquiſhing their demands of *Diſmiſſion,* made it now
their earneſt ſuit, that the name of *Milites,* might be again reſtored
them. *The ſecond ſpeech* was thus; *Cæſar* did extreamly affect the name
of *King;* therefore ſome were ſet on, as he paſſed by, in popular accla-
mation to ſalute him *King :* he finding the cry weak and poor, put off ˢᵘᵉᵗ.ᵖᵃ-
the matter with a jeſt, as if they had miſt his ſir-name, *Non Rex ſum,* ʳᵃᵍ.⁷°,
(ſaith he) *ſed Cæſar;* indeed ſuch a ſpeech, as if it be exactly ſearch't,

the life and fulnefs of it can fcarce be exprest. For first it pretended a refufal of the name, but yet not ferious. Again, it did carry with it an infinite confidence, and magnanimity; as if the Appellation *Cæfar* had been a more eminent Title, than the name of King; which hath come to pafs, and remaineth fo till this day. But, that which moft made for him, this fpeech by an excellent contrivance, advanced his own purpofe; for it did clofely infinuate, that the Senate and People of *Rome* did ftrive with him about a vain fhadow, a name only, (for he had the power of a King already) and for fuch a name, whereof mean families were invefted; for the Sir-name *Rex*, was the title of many families; as we alfo have the like in our Dialect. The laft fpeech, which I will mention in this place, was this; When *Cæfar*, after the war was declared, did poffefs himfelf of the City of *Rome*, and had broke open the inner *Treafury*, to take the mony there ftored up, for the fervice of the war, *Metellus*, for that time Tribune, withftood him;

Plut. in Cæfar. to whom *Cæfar*, *If thou doft perfift* (faith he) *thou art dead*; prefently taking himfelf up, he added, *Young man, it is harder for me to fpeak this, than to do it*; *Adolefcens, durius eft mihi hoc dicere quam facere*; A fpeech compounded of the greateft terror, and the greateft clemency, that could proceed out of the mouth of man. But, to purfue *Cæfars* Abilities in this kind no farther, it is evident, that he knew well *his own perfection in Learning,* as appears, when fome fpake, what a ftrange refolution it was in *Lucius Scylla* to refign his *Dictature*; he fcoffing at him, anfwered, *That Scylla could not skill of Letters, and therefore*

Suet. in Jul. *knew not how to Dictate.*

§. 77. § Now it were time to leave this point touching *the ftrict concurrance of Military virtue and Learning,* (for what example in this kind, can come with any grace, after *Alexander* and *Cæfar?*) were it not that I am tranfported with the height and rarenefs of one other particular inftance, as that which did fo fuddenly pafs from fcorn to wonder;

Xen. Hift. de Exp. Cyri. and it is of *Xenophon the Philofophor,* who went from *Socrates* his School into *Afia* with *Cyrus* the younger, in his expedition againft King *Artaxerxes.* This *Xenophon,* at that time was very young, and never had feen the wars before; neither had then, any command in the Army, but only followed the war as a voluntary, for the love and converfation of *Proxenus* his friend. He was by chance prefent when *Falinus* came in meffage from the great King, to the Grecians, after that *Cyrus* was flain in the field, and the Grecians, a handful of men, having loft their General, left to themfelves in the midft of the Provinces of *Perfia,* cut off from their Country by the interception of many miles, and of very great and deep Rivers. The Meffage did import that they fhould deliver up their Arms, and fubmit themfelves to the Kings mercy: to which meffage before publick anfwer was made, divers of the Army conferr'd familiarly with *Falinus,* amongft whom *Xenophon*

Hift. de Cy. Ex. l 2. hapned to fay thus, *Why,* (faid he) *Falinus we have now but thefe two things left, our Arms and our Virtue, if we yield up our Arms, how fhall we make ufe of our Virtue?* whereto *Falinus* fmiling faid, *If I be not deceived, Young Gentleman, you are an Athenian, and ftudy Philofophy, and it is pretty that you fay, but you are much abufed, if you think your Virtue can withstand the Kings Power;* here was the fcorn, the wonder followeth. This *young Scholar or Philofopher,* after all the Captains

tains and Commanders were murthered by treafon, conducted ten thoufand Foot, through the heart of all the Kings high Countries, from
Babylon to *Grecia*, in defpite of all the Kings forces; to the aftonifh-
ment of the world, and the encouragement of the Grecians in time
fucceeding, to make invafion upon the *Perfian Monarchy* and to fubvert
it. Which indeed foon after, *Jafon* the *Theffalian* conceiv'd and defign'd; *Agefilaus* the *Spartan* attempted and commenced; *Alexander*
the *Macedonian* at laft atchieved, all being ftirred up, by this *brave leading Act of that young Scholar.*

Chap. VIII.

The Merit of Learning from the influence it hath upon Moral Virtues.   § *Learning a foveraign remedy for all the difeafes of the
   Mind.*   § *The Dominion thereof greater than any Temporal Power, being a Power over Reafon and Belief.*   § *Learning gives Fortunes, Honours, Delights excelling all others, as the foul the fenfe.*
   § *Durable Monuments of Fame.*   § *A Profpect of the immortality
   of a future world.*

TO proceed now, *from Imperial and Military Virtue, to Moral, and
   that which is the Virtue of Private men:* Firft, that of the Poet
is a moft certain truth,

> *Scilicet ingenuas didiciffe fideliter Artes*   Ovid. de
> *Emollit mores nec finit effe feros.*   Pont.

For *Learning doth reclaim mens minds from Wildenefs and Barbarifm;*
but indeed, the accent had need be put upon *Fideliter;* for a fuperficial confufed knowledge doth rather work a contrary effect. I fay,
Learning takes away levity, temerity, and infolency, whilft it fuggefts all
dangers and doubts, together with the thing it felf; ballanceth the
weight of reafons and arguments on both fides; turns back the firft
offers and *placits* of the mind as fufpect, and teacheth it to take a tried
and examin'd way: The *fame doth extirpate vain and exceffive admiration,* which is the root of all weak advifement. For we *admire*
things, either becaufe they are *New,* or becaufe they are *Great:* As
for *novelty,* no man that wades in Learning, and contemplation of things
throughly, but hath this printed in his heart, *Nil novi fub fole:* nei-   Ecclef.1.
ther can any man much marvail at the *play of Puppets,* that thrufts but
his head behind the curtain; and advifeth well of the organs and
wires that caufe the motion. As for *Magnitude,* as *Alexander the
Great,* after he was ufed to great Battles, and conquefts in *Afia;* when
at any time he received Letters out of *Greece,* of fome fights and fervices there, which were undertaken commonly for fome Bridge, or a
Fort, or at moft for the befiege of fome City; was wont to fay, *It
feemed to him, that he was advertifed of the Battles of* Homers *Frogs and
Mice:* So certainly, if a man meditate upon the world and the Fabrick
thereof;

thereof; to him the Globe of the Earth, with men marching upon it, (the Divineneſs of ſouls excepted) will not ſeem much other, than *a Hillock of Ants whereof ſome creep, and run up and down with their Corn, others with their Eggs, others empty ; all about a little heap of Duſt.*

§ Again, *Learning takes away, or at leaſt, mitigates the fear of death, and adverſe Fortune; which is one of the greateſt impediments to Virtue or Manners.* For if a mans mind be ſeaſoned and *imbued* with the contemplation of Mortality, and the corruptible nature of things, he will, in his apprehenſion, concur with *Epictetus*, who going forth one day ſaw a woman weeping for her Pitcher of Earth; and going forth the next day ſaw another woman weeping for her ſon, ſaid, *Heri vidi fragilem frangi, hodie vidi mortalem mori :* Therefore *Virgil* did excellently and profoundly couple the knowledge of the cauſe and the conqueſt of fears together, as concomitants :

Felix qui potuit rerum cognoſcere cauſas;
Quiq; metus omnes & inexorabile fatum,
Subjecit pedibus, ſtrepitumq; Acherontis avari.

It were too long to go over the particular Remedies, *which Learning doth miniſter to all the diſeaſes of the Mind* ; ſometimes purging the ill Humours, ſometimes opening the obſtructions, ſometimes helping digeſtion, ſometimes exciting appetite, often healing the wounds and exulcerations thereof, and the like. Therefore I will conclude with that, which ſeems to be the ſum of all, which is, *that Learning ſo diſpoſeth and inclineth the mind, as that it is never wholly ſetled and fixt in the defects thereof, but ever awakes it ſelf and breaths after a Growth and Perfection :* For the unlearn'd man knows not what it is to *deſcend into himſelf, or to call himſelf to account, or what a ſweet life it is ſenſibly to feel, that he is every day better.* If he chance to have any good parts, he will be boaſting theſe ; and every where expoſe them to the full view ; and it may be uſe them dexterouſly to his own advantage and reputation ; but not much improve or encreaſe them. Again, what faults ſoever he hath, he will uſe art and induſtry to hide and colour them, but not to amend them ; like an ill Mower that mowes on ſtill and never whets his Sythe : Contrariwiſe, *a learned man doth not only imploy his mind and exerciſe his good parts, but continually reforms himſelf, and makes Progreſſion in virtue :* Nay, to ſay all in a word. Certain it is, that *Veritas* and *Bonitas* differ but *as the Seal and the Print* ; for goodneſs *is Truth's impreſſion* ; and on the contrary the ſtorms and tempeſts of Vice and Paſſions break from the Clouds of *error* and *faſhood.*

11. *From Morality,* let us paſs on to matter of *power and commandment,* and conſider, *whither there be any ſoveraignty or empire comparable to that wherewith Learning inveſts and crowns names.* We ſee the Dignity of commanding, is according to the dignity of the commanded : Commandment over Beaſts and Cattle, ſuch as Heardmen and Shepherds have, is a thing contemptible ; Commandment over children, ſuch as School-maſters and Tutors have, is a matter of ſmall honour ; commandment over ſlaves, is a diſparagement, rather than a honour ; neither

Sen. Nat. Q. lib. 1. præf.

Enchir. C. 33. Arr. l. 3. c. 24.

Geor. 2

Plat. Alcib. Porph. in Stob. Sen. Epiſt. Plut. Mor.

ther is the commandment of Tyrants much better, over a fervile People, difmantled of their Spirits and generofity of mind; therefore it
was ever held, that honours in free Monarchies and Common-wealths
had a fweetnefs more than in Tyrannies; becaufe a command over the
willing is more honourable than over the forced and compelled:
Wherefore *Virgil*, when he would out of the higheft ftrain of his Art
exprefs the beft of Humane honours, that he could attribute to *Cæfar*, he
doth it in thefe words,

——victorq; volentes
——Per Populos dat jura, viamq; affectat Olympo.

Georg. 4.

*But the Commandment of knowledge is far higher than the Commandment
over the will, though free, and not enflaved and vaffal'd: For it is a Dominion over Reafon, Belief, and the Underftanding, which is the higheft part
of man, and gives Law to the will it felf:* For without Queftion there is no
power on earth, which advanceth and fets up a Throne, and, as it were,
a Chair of eftate, in the fouls of men and their Cogitations, Affents, and
Belief, *but Knowledge and Learning:* And therefore we fee, the detefta-
ble and extreme pleafure that *Arch-Hereticks, falfe Prophets,* and *Impoftors* are ravifht, and tranfported withal, when once they find that they
begin to have a Dominion, and Superiority over the faith and confci-
ences of men; indeed fo great, as he that hath once tafted it, it is feldom feen that any perfecution or torture can make them relinquifh this
Soveraignty: But as this is that which the Divine Author of the Revelations calls, *The depth or profoundnefs of Satan;* fo on the contrary, the
juft and lawful Soveraignty over mens minds, eftablifht by the clear e-
vidence, and fweet commendation of Truth, approacheth certainly
neareft to the fimilitude of the Divine Rule.

Apo: 2.

§ *As for Fortunes and Honours, the magnificence of Learning doth not
fo enrich and adorn whole Kingdoms and Common-wealths, as it doth not
likewife amplifie and advance the Fortunes and Eftates of particular perfons;*
For it is an ancient obfervation, that *Homer hath given more men their
living, than either* Scylla, *or* Cæfar, *or* Auguftus *ever did,* notwithftanding
their great Largeffes, fuch infinite donatives, and diftributions of much
Land. No doubt, it is hard to fay, whether Arms or Learning have advanced greater numbers: But if we fpeak of Soveraignty, we fee, *that
if Arms have carried away the Kingdom, yet Learning hath born away
the Priefthood,* which ever hath been in fome competition with
Empire.

§ Again, *If you contemplate the Pleafure and Delight of Knowledge and
Learning, affuredly it far furpaffes all other pleafure:* For what? Shall,
perchance, the pleafures of the Affections fo far excel the pleafures of
the fenfes, as a happy obtaining of a defire, doth a fong or a dinner;
and muft not by the fame degrees of confequence, the pleafure of the
Intellect tranfcend thofe of the Affections? In all other pleafures there
is a finite fatiety, and after they grow a little ftale, their flower and
verdure vades and departs; whereby we are inftructed, that they were
not indeed pure and fincere pleafures, but fhadows and deceits of *Pleafures;* and that it was the Novelty which pleas'd, and not the Quality: therefore voluptuous men often turn Fryars, and the declining

age of ambitious Princes is commonly more sad and besieged with Melancholy; *But of Knowledge there is no satiety*; but viciffitude, perpetually and interchangeably, returning of fruition and appetite; so that the good of this delight muft needs be simple, without Accident or Fallacy. Neither is that *Pleasure* of small efficacy and contentment in the mind of man, which the Poet *Lucretius* describeth elegantly, *Suave, mari* De Rer. *magno turbantibus aequora ventis,* &c. *It is a view of delight* (faith he) *to* Nat.lib. 2. *ftand or walk upon the fhore, and to fee a fhip toft with tempeft upon the fea : a pleafure to ftand in the window of a Caftle, and to fee two Battails joyn upon a plain : but it is a pleafure incomparable, for the mind of man, by Learning to be fetled and fortified in the Tower of Truth, and from thence to behold the errors and wandrings of other men below.*

§ Laftly, leaving the vulgar arguments., *That by Learning man excels man, in that wherein man excels beafts*; that by the help of Learning, man afcends in his underftanding, even to the heavens, whither in body he can not come, and the like; let us conclude this difcourfe concerning *the dignity and Knowledge of Learning*, with that good, whereunto mans nature doth moft afpire, *Immortality and continuance.* For to this tendeth Generation, raifing of Houfes and Families, Buildings, Foundations, Monuments, Fame, and in effect the fum and height of humane defires. *But we fee how far the monuments of Wit and Learning, are more durable than the Monuments of materiate Memorials and Manufactures.* Have not the *verfes of Homer* continued xxv Centuries of years and above, without the lofs of a fyllable, or letter ? during which time, infinite number of Places, Temples, Caftles, Cities, have been decayed or been demolifht. The *Pictures* and *Statues* of *Cyrus, Alexander, Caefar,* no nor of the Kings and Princes of much later years, by no means poffible are now recoverable; for the Originals, worn away with age, are perifht; and the Copies daily lofe of the life and Primitive refemblance; *But the images of mens wits, remain unmaimed in books for ever, exempt from the injuries of time, becaufe capable of perpetual renovation.* Neither can they properly be called Images, becaufe, in their way, they generate ftill and caft their feeds in the minds of men; raifing and procreating infinite Actions and Opinions in fucceeding ages. So that if the invention of a fhip, was thought fo noble and wonderful, which tranfports Riches and Merchandice from Place to Place; and confociates the moft remote regions in participation of their fruits and commodities; *how much more are letters to be magnified, which as fhips, paffing through the vaft fea of time, to counite the remoteft ages of Wits and Invention in mutual Trafique and Correfpondency?*

§ Furthermore, we fee fome of the Philofophers which were moft immerfed in the fenfes and leaft divine, and which peremptorily denyed the immortality of the foul, yet convicted by the power of truth came to this point, *That whatfoever Motions and Acts the fpirit of man could perform without the Organ of the body, it was probable that thofe remained after death*; fuch as were the motions of the underftanding, but not of the affections; *fo immortal and incorruptible a thing did knowledge feem to them to be.* But we, illuminated with divine Revelation, difclaiming thefe rudiments and delufions of the fenfes, know that not only the mind, but the affections purified; not only the foul, but the body fhall be advanced in its time to immortality. But it muft be remembred,

remembred, both now and other times, as the nature of the point may require, that in the proofs, of the dignity of Knowledge and Learning, I did at the beginning separate Divine Testimonies, from Humane; which method I have constantly pursued, and so handled them both a-part.   Although all this be true, neverthelesse I do not take upon me, neither can I hope to obtain by any Perorations, or pleadings of this case touching Learning, to reverse the judgement either of *Æsops Cock,* that preferred the *Barley-corn before the Gemm*; or of *Midas,* that being chosen *Judge between* Apollo, *President of the Muses, and* Pan *President of Sheep,* judg'd for plenty; or of *Paris, that judged for Pleasure* and love, against wisdom and power; or of *Agrippina's* choice, *Occidat matrem, modo imperet!* preferring Empire with any condition never so dete-stable; or of *Ulysses, qui vetulam prætulit immortalitati*; being indeed figures of those that prefer custom before all excellency; and a number of the like popular judgements: for these things must continue as they have been, but so will that also continue, whereupon Learning hath ever relied as on a firm foundation which can never be shaken: *Justi-ficata est sapientia à Filiis suis.*

Ovid. Met.XI.

Eurip. in Troad.

Tac. An. XIV.

Mat.XI.

F   THE

THE
Second Book
OF
FRANCIS L. VERULAM
VICOUNT St *ALBAN*,

OF THE

Dignity and Advancement

O F

LEARNING.

To the KING.

THE PROEM

The Advancement of Learning commended unto the care of Kings. I. The
Acts thereof in general, three, *Reward, Direction, Assistance.*
II. In special, about three objects, *Places, Books, Persons.* § In
places four Circumstances, *Buildings, Revenues, Priviledges, Laws of
Discipline.* § In Books two, *Libraries, good Editions.* § In
Persons two, *Readers of Sciences Extant; Inquirers into Parts non-
extant.* III. Defects in these Acts of Advancement, six; *Want of
Foundations for Arts at large.* § *Meanness of Salary unto Professors.* § *Want of allowance for Experiments.* § *Preposterous institutions, and unadvised practices in Academical Studies.* § *Want
of Intelligence between the Universities of* Europe. § *Want of Inquiries into the Deficients of Arts.* § *The Authors Design.* § *Ingenious Defence.*

 T might seem to have more convenience, although it
come often otherwise to pass, (Excellent King,) that
those that are fruitful in their Generation, and have,
this way, a fore-sight of their own immortality in their
Descendants, should above all men living, be careful
of the the estate of future times, unto which they cannot but know that they must at last transmit their dearest Pledges.
Q. *Elizabeth* was a sojourner in the world, in respect of her unmarried life, rather than an inhabitant: she hath indeed adorned her own
F 2   tims

time, and many ways enrich it ; but in truth, to Your Majefty, whom God hath bleft with fo much Royal Iffue worthy to perpetuate you for ever ; whofe youthful and fruitful Bed, doth yet promife more children ; it is very proper, not only to irradiate, as you do, your own times, but alfo to extend your Cares to thofe Acts which fucceeding Ages may cherifh, and Eternity it felf behold : Amongft which, if my affection to Learning do not tranfport me, there is none more worthy, or more noble, *than the endowment of the world with found and fruitful Advancements of Learning ;* For why fhould we erect unto our felves fome few Authors, to ftand like *Hercules Columns,* beyond which there fhould be no difcovery of knowledge ; feeing we have *your Majefty,* as a bright and benign Star, to conduct and profper us in this Navigation.

I. To return therefore unto our purpofe, let us weigh and confider with our felves, what hitherto hath been performed, what pretermitted by Princes and others, for the *Propagation of Learning:* And this we will purfue clofely and diftinctly, in an Active and Mafculine Expreffion, no where digreffing, nothing dilating. Let this ground therefore be laid, which every one may grant, that the greateft and moft difficult works are overcome, either by the *Amplitude of Reward,* or by the *wifdom and foundnefs of Direction,* or by *conjunction of Labours ;* whereof the firft, *encourageth our endeavours ;* the fecond, *takes away Error and Confufion ;* the third, *fupplies the frailty of Man.* But the Principal amongft thefe three, is the *wifdom and foundnefs of Direction,* that is, a Delineation and Demonftration of a right and eafie way to accomplifh any enterprize : *Claudus enim,* as the saying is, *in via antevertit Curforem extra viam ;* and *Solomon* aptly to the purpofe, *If the Iron be blunt, and he do not whet the edge, then muft he put too more ftrength ; but wifdom is profitable to Direction :* By which words he infinuateth, that *a wife election of the Mean, doth more efficacioufly conduce to the perfecting of any enterprize, than any enforcement or accumulation of endeavours.* This I am preffed to fpeak, for that (not derogating from the Honour of thofe who have any way deferved well of Learning) I fee and obferve, that many of their Works and Acts, are rather matter of *Magnificence* and *Memory* of their own *names,* than of *Progreffion and Proficience of Learning ;* and have rather encreafed the *number of Learned men,* than much promoted the *Augmentation* of *Learning.*

II. The Works or Acts pertaining to the *Propagation of Learning,* are converfant about three objects ; about the *Places of Learning ;* about the *Books ;* and about the *Perfons of Learned men.* For as *water,* whether falling from the Dew of Heaven, or rifing from the fprings of the earth, is eafily fcattered and loft in the ground, except it be collected into fome *receptacles,* where it may by union and Congregation into one body comfort and fuftain it felf ; for that purpofe the induftry of man hath invented Conduits, Cifterns and Pools, and beautified them with divers accomplifhments, as well of Magnificence and State, as of Ufe and Neceffity : fo this moft excellent *liquor of Knowledge,* whether it diftil from a divine infpiration ; or fpring from the *fenfes,* would

Ecclef. 10.

would foon perifh and vanifh, if it were not conferved in *Books, Traditions, Conferences,* and in *Places* purpofely defigned to that end; as *Univerfities, Colledges, Schools,* where it may have fixt *ftations* and Power and Ability of uniting and improving it felf.

§ And firft, the works which concern the *Seats of the Mufes,* are four, Foundations of *Houfes;* Endowments with *Revennes;* Grant of *Priviledges; Inftitutions, and ftatutes for Government;* all which chiefly conduce to privatenefs and quietnefs of life, and a difcharge from cares and troubles, much like the *ftations Virgil* defcribeth for the Hiving of Bees.

Geor. 4.

> *Principio Sedes Apibus ftatioque petenda,*
> *Quo neque fit ventis aditus, &c.*

§ But the works touching *Books* are chiefly two: Firft *Libraries,* wherein, as in famous fhrines, the Reliques of the Ancient Saints full of virtue, are repofed. Secondly, *new Editions of Authors, with corrected impreffions; more faithful Tranflations, more profitable Gloffes, more diligent Annotations;* with the like train furnifh't and adorned.

§ Furthermore, the works pertaining to the *Perfons of Learned men,* befides the *Advancing and Countenancing of them* in general, are likewife two; the *Remuneratioon* and *Defignation of Readers,* in *Arts and Sciences* already extant and known; and the *Remuneration and Defignation of writers concerning thofe parts of Knowlege, which hitherto have not been fufficiently till'd and labour'd.* Thefe briefly are the works and Acts, wherein the Merit of many renowned Princes and other illuftrious Perfons, hath been famed, *towards the ftate of Learning.* As for particular Commemoration, of any that hath well deferved of Learning, when I think thereof, that of *Cicero* comes into my mind, which was a motive unto him after his return from banifhment to give general thanks, *Difficile non aliquem; ingratum, quenquam præterire:* Let us rather according to the advice of Scripture, *Look unto the part of the race which is before us, than look back unto that which is already attained.*

Cic. Orat. poft redit. Epift. ad Phil. 3.

III. Firft therefore, amongft fo many *Colledges* of Europe, excellently founded, I find ftrange, *that they are all deftinated to certain Profeffions and none Dedicated to Free and Univerfal ftudies of Arts and Sciences:* For he that judgeth, that all Learning fhould be referred to ufe and Action, judgeth well; but yet it is eafie this way to fall into the error taxt in the Ancient Fable, in which, *the other parts of the Body entred an Action againft the ftomach, becaufe it neither perform'd the office of Motion, as the Limbs do; nor of fenfe, as the head doth;* but yet all this while it is the ftomach, that concocteth, converteth, and diftributeth nourifhment into the reft of the body: So if any man think *Philofophy and univerfal contemplations a vain and idle ftudy,* he doth not confider that all Profeffions and Arts from thence derive their fap and ftrength. And furely I am perfwaded that this hath been a great caufe *why the happy progreffion of Learning hitherto hath been retarded;* becaufe thefe Fundamentals have been ftudied but only in paffage, and deeper draughts have not been taken thereof: *For if you will have a Tree bear more fruit than it hath ufed to do,* it is not any thing you can do to the Boughs,

Liv. lib. 2. 7.c. 260. Æfop. Fab.

by

but it is the stirring of the earth about the root, and the application of new mould, or you do nothing. Neither is it to be passed over in silence, *that this dedicating of Colledges and Societies, only to the use of Professory Learning, hath, not only, been an enemy to the growth of Sciences; but hath redounded likewise to the prejudice of States and Government: :* For hence it commonly falls out that Princes, when they would make choice of Ministers fit for the Affairs of State, find about them such a marvellous solitude of able men; because there is no education Collegiate design'd to this end, where such as are fram'd and fitted by nature thereto, might give themselves chiefly to *Histories,* Modern *Languages,* Books and *discourses of Policy,* that so they might come more able and better furnish't to service of State.

§ And because *Founders of Colledges do Plant, and Founders of Lecturers do water,* it followeth now in order to speak of the Defects which are in publick Lectures; *the smalness of stipends* (especially with us) *assigned to Readers of Arts or of Professions:* For it doth much import to the *Progression and Proficiency of Sciences,* that Readers in every kind be chosen out of the ablest and most sufficient men; as those that are ordained, not for transitory use, but for to maintain and propagate the seeds of Sciences for future Ages; This cannot be, except the Rewards and Conditions be appointed such, as may sufficiently content the most eminent man in that Art, so as he can be willing to spend his whole Age in that function and never desire to practice. Wherefore that *Sciences may flourish, Davids* Military Law should be observed, *That those that stayed with the Carriage should have equal parts with those that were in the Action;* else will the Carriages be ill attended. So *Readers in Sciences* are, as it were, Protectors and Guardians of the Provision of Learning, whence the Action and services of Sciences may be furnish't, Wherefore it is reason that the *Salaryes of Speculative men, should be equal to the gains of Active men;* otherwise if allowances to Fathers of Sciences be not in a competent degree ample and condign, it will come to pass,

1 Sam. 30.

Virg. Geor. 3.
Ut Patrem invalidi referent jejunia Nati.

§ Now I will note another *Defect,* wherein some Alchymist should be called unto for help; for this Sect of Men advise Students to sell their Books and to build furnaces; to quit *Minerva* and the Muses, as Barren Virgins, and to apply themselves to *Vulcan.* Yet certainly it must be confest, that unto the depth of *Contemplation,* and the fruit of *Operative studies* in many Sciences, especially *Natural Philosophy,* and *Physick;* *Books are not the only subsidiary Instruments,* wherein the Munificence of men, hath not been altogether wanting; for we see *Spheres, Globes, Astrolabes, Maps,* and the like, have been provided, and with industry invented, as Helps to *Astronomy* and *Cosmography;* as well as *Books.* We see likewise some places dedicated to the study of *Phisick,* to have *Gardens for the inspection and observation of simples* of all sorts; and to be authorized the use of *Dead Bodies for Anatomy-Lectures.* But those do respect but a few things; in the generality set it down for Truth, *That there can hardly be made any main Proficience in the disclosing of the secrets of Nature, unless there be liberal Allowance for Experiments;* whether

ther *of* Vulcan *or of* Dædalus; *I mean of Furnace, or of Engine, or any o-*
ther kind : And therefore *as Secretaries and Spials of State,* are allowed to bring in Bills for their diligence in the inquiry and discovery of
New Occurrences and Secrets in Foreign Estates; *so you must allow In-*
telligencers and Spials of Nature their bills of Expences; else you shall never be advertised of many things most worthy to be known. For if *A-*
lexander made *such a liberal Assignation of Treasure unto Aristotle,* for
Hunters, Fowlers, Fishers, and the like, that he might compile a History of living Creatures; certainly much more is their merit, who
wander not in wild forrests of Nature, but make themselves a way
through the Labyrinths of Arts.

§ Another Defect to be observed by us (indeed of great import) is,
A neglect, in those which are Governours in Universities, of Consultation;
and in Princes and superior Persons, of visitation; to this end, that it
may with all diligence be considered and consulted of, whether the Readings,
Disputations and other Scholastical exercises, anciently instituted, will be
good to continue, or rather to antiquate and substitute others more effectu-
al : For amongst Your Majesties most wise maxims, I find this, *That in* Iacobus.R.
all usages and Præsidents, the times be considered wherein they first began;
which if they were weak or ignorant, it derogateth from the Authority of
the usage and leaves it for suspect. Therefore in as much as the usages
and orders of Universities, were for most part derived from times more
obscure and unlearned than our own, it is the more reason that they be
re-examined. In this kind I will give an instance or two for examples
sake, in things that seem most obvious and familiar. *It is an usu-*
al practice (but in my opinion somewhat preposterous) that Scholars
in the Universities , are too early entred in Logick and Rhetorick;
Arts indeed fitter for Graduats than Children and Novices. For these
two (if the matter be well weighed) are in the number of the gravest Sciences, being the *Arts of Arts, the one for Judgment , the other*
for Ornament. So likewise they contain Rules and Directions, either for
the Disposition or Illustration of any subject or material Circumstance
thereof; and therefore for minds empty and unfraught with matter,
and which have not as yet gathered that which *Cicero* calls *Sylva* and
Supellex, that is stuff and variety of things, to begin with those Arts,
(as if one would learn to weigh, of measure, or paint the wind) doth
work but this effect, that the virtue and strength of these Arts, which
are great and Universal, are almost made contemptible, and have de-
generated either into *Childish Sophistry or ridiculous Affectation;* or at
least have been embased in their reputation. And farther, the untime-
ly and unripe accession to these Arts, hath drawn on, by necessary consequence, a watery and superficiary delivery and handling thereof, as
is fitted indeed to the capacities of Children. Another instance which
I will set down as an Error now grown inveterate, long agoe in the Universities, and it is this; *That in Scholastical exercises, there useth to be*
a divorce, very prejudicious, between Invention and Memory : for there
the most of their speeches are either, altogether premeditate, so as they are ut-
tered in the very precise form of words they were conceived in, and nothing
left to invention; or meerly extemporal, so as very little is left to Memory;
Whereas in Life and Action, there is very little use of either of these a-
part, but rather of their intermixture; that is, of notes or memorials;
and

and of extemporal speech : So as by this course, exercises are not accommodate to practice, nor the Image answereth to the Life : And it is ever a true rule in *exercises, that all, as neer as may be, should represent those things which in common course of life use to be practised ;* otherwise they will pervert the motions and faculties of the mind, and not prepare them.   The truth whereof is plainly discovered, when Scholars come to the Practice of their Professions, or other Actions of Civil life, which when they set into, this defect, whereof we speak, is soon found out by themselves, but sooner by others.   But this part, *touching the amendment of the Institutions of the Universities,* I will conclude,

Cic. Epist.
Ad Att.
lib. IX.

with the clause of *Cæsars* letter to *Oppius, Hoc Quemadmodum fieri possit, nonnulla mihi in mentem veniunt & multa reperiri possunt, de iis rebus, rogo vos, ut cogitationem suscipiatis.*

§ Another *Defect* which I note, ascends a little higher than the precedent : *For as the progression of Learning consisteth much in the wise Government and institution of Universities in particular ; so it would be more advanced, if the Universities in general, dispersed through all Europe, were united in a neerer conjunction and correspondence by mutual Intelligence :* For there are, as we see, many Orders and Societies, which, though they be divided under several Soveraignties and spacious Territories, yet they do contract and maintain a Society and a kind of *Fraternity* one with another ; in so much that they have their *Provincials* and *Generals,* to whom all the rest yield obedience.   And surely as nature creates *Brother-hoods* in *Families ;* and Arts Mechanical contract *Brotherhoods in Communalties ;* the Anointment of God super-induceth a *brother-hood in Kings and Bishops * ; Vows and Canonical rules unite a *Brother-hood in Orders ;* in like manner, there cannot but intervene *a Noble and Generous Fraternity between men by Learning and Illuminations ;* reflecting upon that relation which is attributed to God, who himself is

Isc. 1.

called, *The Father of Illuminations or Lights.*

§ Lastly, this I find fault with, which I somewhat toucht upon before, *that there hath not been, or very rarely been, any publick designation of able men, who might write or make inquiry of such parts of Learning as have not been hitherto sufficiently laboured and subdued.*   Unto which point it will be very available, if there were erected a kind of *visitation of Learning ;* and a Cense or Estimate taken, what parts of Learning are rich and well improved ; what poor and destitute.   For *the opinion of Plenty is amongst the Causes of want ;* and the multitude of Books makes a shew rather of superfluity, than penury.   Which surcharge, nevertheless, if a man would make a right judgement, is not remedied by suppressing or extinguishing books heretofore written, but by publish-

Exod. 7.

ing good new books, which may be of such a right kind, *That, as the Serpent of Moses, may devour the Serpents of the Enchanters.*

§ The Remedies of these *defects* now enumerate, except the last, and of the last also, in respect of the Active part thereof, which is the *Designation of writers,* are *opera Basilica,* towards which the endeavours and industry of a private man, are commonly but as an Image in a cross way, which may point at the way, but cannot go it : But the *speculative part, which pertaineth to the examination of knowledges,* namely, *what is deficient in every particular Science,* is open to the industry of a private man.   *Wherefore my designment is to attempt a general and faithful*

faithful perambulation and visitation of Learning; specially with a diligent and exact enquiry, what parts thereof lye fresh and waste, and are not yet improved and converted to use by the industry of men; to the end that such a plot made and recorded to memory, may minister light both to publick Designations, and the voluntary labours of private endeavours. Wherein neverthelefs my purpose is, at this time, *to note only Omiffions and Deficiencies, and not to make redargution of Errors and Over-fights:* For it is one thing to fet forth what ground lieth unmanur'd, and another thing, to correct ill husbandry in that which is manured.

§ In the undertaking and handling of which work I am not ignorant what a businefs I move, and what a difficult province I fuftain, and alfo, how unequal my abilities are unto my will: yet I have a good hope, that if my extreme love to Learning carry me too far, I may obtain the excufe of affection, for that, it is *not granted to man, To love and to be wife.* I know well that I muft leave the fame liberty of judgement to others, that I ufe my felf; and intruth, I fhall be indifferently glad, to accept from others, as to impart that duty of humanity; *Nam qui erranti comiter monftrant viam,* &c. I do fore-fee likewife, that many of thofe things which I fhall enter and regifter as *Omiffions* and *Deficients,* will incur divers cenfures; *as,* that fome parts of this enterprife were done long-ago and now are extant; *others,* that they tafte of curiofity, and promife no great fruit; *others,* that they are too difficult and impoffible to be compaffed by humane induftries. For the two firft, let the particulars fpeak for themfelves: For the laft, touching *impoffibility,* I determine thus; All thofe things are to be held poffible and performable, which may be accomplifht by fome perfon, though not by every one; and which may be done by the united labours of many, though not by any one apart; and which may be effected in a fuccef'on of ages, though not in the fame age; and in brief, which may be finifht by the publick care and charge, though not by the ability and induftry of particular perfons. If, notwithftanding, there be any man who would rather take to himfelf that of *Solomon, Dicit Piger, Leo eft in via,* than that of *Virgil.*

Poffunt quia poffe videntur: It is enough to me, if my labours may be efteemed as votes, and the better fort of wifhes: for as it asketh fome knowledge to demand a queftion not impertinent; fo it requireth fome fenfe to make a wifh not abfurd.

(margin: Cic. Offic. 1. ex Ennio.)

(margin: Prov. 22;)

(margin: Æn. 5.)

CHAP. I.

I. *An univerfal Partition of Humane Learning into,* § *Hiftory.* II. *Poetry.* III. *Philofophy.* § *This Partition is taken from the triplicity of Intellective Faculties: Memory: Imagination: Reafon.* § *The fame Partition is appropriate to Divine Learning.*

I. THat is the trueft Partition of humane Learning, which hath reference to the *three Faculties* of Mans foul, which is the feat of Learning. *History* is referred to *Memory*, *Poesie* to the *Imagination*, *Philosophy* to *Reason*. By *Poesie*, in this place, we understand nothing else, but *feigned History*, or Fables. As for *Verse*, that is only a stile of expression, and pertains to the *Art of Elocution*, of which in due place.

§ *History is properly of Individuals circumscribed within time and place :* for although *Natural History* seem to be conversant about *universal Natures* ; yet this so falls out, because of the promiscuous similitude in things Natural comprehended under one kind ; so that if you know one, you know all of that species. But if any where there be found Individuals, which in their kind are either singular, as the *Sun* and the *Moon* ; or which do notably digress from their kind, as *Monsters* ; these are as aptly handled in *Natural History*, as particular men are in *Civil History*. All these are referred unto *Memory*.

II. *Poesie*, in that sence we have expounded it, *is likewise of Individuals, fancied to the similitude of those things which in true History are recorded*, yet so as often it exceeds measure ; and those things which in Nature would never meet, nor come to pass, *Poesie* composeth and introduceth at pleasure, even as *Painting* doth : which indeed is the work of the Imagination.

III. *Philosophy* dismisseth Individuals and comprehendeth, not the first Impressions, but the abstract Motions thereof, and conversant in compounding and dividing them according to the Law of Nature, and of the things themselves :   And this is wholly the office and operation of *Reason*.

§ And that this *Distribution* is truly made, he shall easily conceive that hath recourse to the Originals of Intellectuals. Individuals only strike the sense, which is the port or entrance of the understanding. The Images or Impressions of those Individuals accepted from the *sense*, are fixt in the *Memory*, and at first enter into it entire, in the same manner they were met : afterwards the *understanding* ruminates upon them, and refines them, which then it doth either meerly *review* ; or in a wanton delight counterfeit and *resemble* ; or by compounding and dividing digest and endue them. So it is clearly manifest, that from these three fountains of *Memory*, of *Imagination* and of *Reason*, there are these three Emanations, of *History*, of *Poesie*, and of *Philosophy*, and that there can be no other nor no more : for *History* and *Experience*, we take for one and the same, as we do *Philosophy* and *Sciences*.

§ Neither do we think any other Partition than this is requisite to *Divine Learning*. Indeed the informations of *Oracle* and of Sense be divers ; both in the matter and manner of Conveying, but the spirit of Man is the same, the Cells and Receptacles thereof the very same. For it comes to pass here, as if divers Liquors, and that by divers Funnels, should be receiv'd into one and the same vessel. Wherefore *Theology* also consists either of *Sacred History* ; of *Parables*, which are a kind of *Divine Poesie* ; or of *Precepts* and *Doctrines*, as an *eternal Philosophy*. As for that part which seems supernumerary, which is *Prophecy*, that is a branch of *History :* however *Divine History* hath that prerogative over *Humane*, that the Narration may be before the Fact as well after.

CHAP.

Chap. II.

I. The Partition of History into *Natural and Civil* (*Ecclesiastical and Literary comprehended under Civil.*)   II. The Partition of *Natural History, into the History of Generations.*   III. *Præter-Generations.*   IV. *Of Arts.*

I. **H**Istory is either *Natural or Civil :* in *Natural* the operations of Nature are recorded ; in *Civil* the Actions of men.   In both these without question, the Divine Workings are translucent, but more conspicuous in *Acts Civil* ; in so much as they constitute a peculiar kind of History, which we usually stile *Sacred* or *Ecclesiastical :* And in truth to us such seems the Dignity of Learning and of Arts to be, that there ought to be reserv'd a *Particular History* for them apart from the rest ; which yet we understand to be comprehended, as *Ecclesiastick History* also is, under *History Civil.*

II. The Partition of *Natural History* we shall raise out of the state and condition of *Nature* herself, which is found subject to a triple state, and under a three-fold regiment : For *Nature is either Free and displaying her self in her ordinary course* ; as in the Heavens, living Creatures, Plants, and the Universal furniture of the world ; or *put out of her usual course and depos'd from her state, by the pravities and insolencies of contumacious Matter, and the violence of Impediments,* as in Monsters : or lastly, she is *Comprest and fashioned, and as it were new cast,* as in Artificial Operations : Let therefore the partition of *Natural History,* be made into the History of *Generations* ; of *Præter-Generations,* and of *Arts* ; whereof the last we use to call *History Mechanical,* or *Experimental.*   The first of these handles the *Liberty of Nature* ; the second the *Errors* ; the third the *Bands* thereof.   And we are the rather induced to assign the *History of Arts,* as a branch of *Natural History,* because an opinion hath long time gone currant, as if *Art* were some different thing from *Nature,* and *Artificial* from *Natural.*   From this mistake this inconvenience arises, that many writers of *Natural History* think they have quit themselves sufficiently, if they have compiled a History of *Creatures,* or of *Plants,* or of *Minerals;* the experiments of Mechanical Arts past over in silence.   But there is yet a more subtile deceit which secretly steals into the minds of Men, namely, that *Art* should be reputed a kind of *Additament* only to *Nature,* whose virtue is this, that it can indeed either perfect *Nature inchoate, or repair it when it is decayed, or set it at liberty from impediments ; but not quite alter, transmute, or shake it in the foundations :* which erroneous conceit hath brought in a too hasty despair upon mens enterprises.   But on the the contrary, this certain truth should be throughly setled in the minds of men, *That Artificials differ not from Naturals in Form and Essence, but in the Efficient only* ; for man hath no power over *Nature,* save only in her *Motion* ; that is, to mingle or put together Natural bodies, and to separate or put them asunder ; wherefore, where there is *Apposition and Separation of Bodies,* Natural conjoyning (as they term it) *Active with Passive,* man may do all things ; this not done, he can do nothing.   Nor is it

material

material so things be managed in a right order, for the production of such an effect, whether this be done by the Art of Man or without the Art of Man. Gold is sometimes digested and purged from crudities and impurities, by fire; sometimes found pure in small sands, Nature performing her own work. So the Rain-Bow is formed of a dewy cloud in the Air above; form'd also by aspersion of water by us below. Therefore Nature commandeth all, and these three are her substitute Administrators, *The course* of *Nature; the Expatiation of Nature and Art; or the Cooperation of Man with Nature in particulars.* Wherefore it is very proportionable, that these three be comprized in Natural History, which C. *Plinius* for most part performed, who alone comprehended *Natural History* according to the dignity thereof; but what he thus comprehended he hath not handled as was meet, nay rather foully abused.

C. Plin.
Nat. Hist.

III. The first of these is extant in some good perfection : *The two latter are handled so weakly and so unprofitably, that they may be referr'd to the list of Deficients.* For you shall find no sufficient and competent collection of those works of *Nature which have a Digression and Deflection from the ordinary course of Generations, Productions and Motions;* whether they be the singularities of certain Countries and Places, or the strange events of times; or the wit of chance, or the effects of latent proprieties; or *Monodicals of Nature* in their kind. It is true, there are a number of Books more than enough, full fraught with fabulous Experiments, forged Secrets, and frivolous Impostures, for pleasure and strangeness; but a substantial and severe *Collection of Heteroclites,* and of the *wonders of Nature,* diligently examined and faithfully described, *this, I say, I find not,* especially with due rejection, and, as it were, publick proscription of untruths and fables, which have got up into credit. For as the matter is now carried, if any untruths touching *Nature* be once on foot and celebrated (whether it be the Reverence of Antiquity, that can thus far countenance them; or that it is a trouble to call them unto a re-examination; or that they are held to be rare ornaments of speech, for similitudes and comparisons) they are never after exterminate and called in. The use of this work honour'd with a President in *Aristotle,* is nothing less than to give contentment to curious and vain wits, as the manner of *Mirabilaries* and the *spreaders of invented Prodigies* is to do; but for two reasons serious and grave; the one to correct the partiality of Axioms, which are commonly grounded upon common and popular examples; the other because from the *wonders of Nature,* a fair and open passage is made to the *wonders of Art.* For the business in this matter is no more than by quick sent to trace out the footings of nature in her wilful wandrings; that so afterward you may be able at your pleasure, to lead or force her to to the same place and postures again.

De Mirab.

§ Neither do I give in precept, that superstitious Narrations of Sorceries, Witch-crafts, Inchantments, Dreams, Divinations, and the like, where there is clear evidence of the fact and and deed done, be altogether excluded from this *History of Marvails.* For it is not yet known, in what cases, and how far, effects attributed to superstition, do participate of Natural Causes; and therefore, howsoever the use and practice of these Arts, in my opinion, is justly to be condemned; yet from the
speculation

speculation and confideration of them, (if they be clofely purfued) we may attain a profitable direction; not only for the right difcerning of offences in this kind of guilty perfons; but for the farther difclofing of the fecrets of Nature. Neither furely ought a man to make fcruple of entring and penetrating the vaults and receffes of thefe Arts, that propofeth to himfelf only the inquifition of *Truth,* as your Majefty hath confirmed in your own example: For you have with the two clear and quick-fighted eyes of *Religion and Natural Philofophy,* fo wifely and throughly enlightened thefe *fhadows,* that you have proved your felf moft like the *Sun* which paffeth through polluted places, yet is not diftained. But this I would admonifh, that thefe *Narrations* which have mixture with *Superftition,* be forted by themfelves, and not be mingled with the *Narrations,* which are purely and fincerely Natural. As for the Narrations touching the *Prodigies* and *Miracles* of *Religions,* they are either not true; or no way Natural, and therefore pertain not to *Natural Hiftory.*

K. Iames; his Dæmonelogy.

IV. For Hiftory of Nature, wrought and fubdued by the hand, which we are wont to call *Mechanical,* I find indeed fome collections made of Agriculture, and likewife of many *Manual Arts*; but commonly (which in this kind of knowledge is a great detriment) with a neglect and rejection of *Experiments familiar and vulgar*; which yet, to the *interpretation of Nature,* do as much, if not more, conduce, than Experiments of a higher quality. But it is efteemed a kind of difhonour and afperfion unto Learning, if learned men fhould, upon occafion perchance, defcend to the Inquiry or Obfervation of *Matters Mechanical,* except they be reputed for *Secrets of Art, or Rarities, or Subtilties.* Which humour of vain and fupercilious arrogance, *Plato* juftly derideth, where he brings in *Hippias* a vaunting Sophift, difputing with *Socrates* a fevere and folid inquifitor of Truth; where the fubject being of Beauty, *Socrates* after his wandring and loofe manner of difputing, brought in firft an example of a fair Virgin, than of a fair Horfe, than of a fair Pot well glaz'd; at this laft inftance *Hippias* fomewhat mov'd faid; *Were it not for courtefie fake, I fhould difdain to difpute with any that alledged fuch bafe and fordid inftances*; to whom *Socrates, Tou have reafon, and it becomes you well, being a man fo trim in your veftments, and fo neat in your fhooes*; and fo goes on in an Irony. And certainly this may be averr'd for truth, that they be not the higheft inftances, that give the beft and fureft information. This is not unaptly expreft in the Tale, fo common, of the Philofopher, *That while he gaz'd upward to the ftars fell into the water:* for if he had lookt down, he might have feen the ftars in the water; but looking up to heaven he could not fee the water in the ftars. In like manner it often comes to pafs that fmall and mean things conduce more to the difcovery of great matters, than great things to the difcovery of fmall matters; and therefore *Ariftotle* notes well, *that the Nature of every thing is beft feen in his fmalleft Portions.* For that caufe he enquires the Nature of a Common-wealth, firft in a Family and the fimple conjugations of Society, Man and Wife; Parents and Children; Mafter and Servant, which are in every cottage. So likewife the Nature of this great City of the world, and the Policy thereof, muft be fought in every firft Concordances and leaft Portions of things. So we fee that fecret of Nature (efteemed one of the great myfteries)

In Hipp. Major.

Laert. in Thalete.

Pol. lib. 1.

myſteries) of the turning of Iron toucht with a Loadſtone towards the Poles, was found out in needles of Iron, not in bars
of Iron.

§ But if my judgement be of any weight, I am wholly of this mind,
that the uſe of *Mechanical Hiſtory*, to the raiſing of *Natural Philoſophy*,
is of all other the moſt radical and fundamental ; ſuch Natural Philoſophy, I underſtand, as doth not vaniſh into the fumes of ſubtile and
ſublime ſpeculations, but ſuch, as ſhall be effectually operative to the
ſupport and aſſiſtance of the incommodities of mans life : For it will
not only help for the preſent, by connecting and transferring the obſervations of one Art, into the uſe of others, which muſt needs come
to paſs, when the experiences of divers Arts ſhall fall into the conſideration and obſervation of one man ; but farther, it will give a more
clear illumination, than hitherto hath ſhined forth, for the ſearching
out of the cauſes of things, and the deducing of Axioms. For *like as
you can never* well know and prove the diſpoſition of another man, unleſs you provoke him ; nor *Proteus* ever changed ſhapes, until he was
ſtraitned and held faſt with cords ; ſo nature provoked and vexed by
Art, doth more clearly Appear, than when ſhe is left free to her ſelf. But
before we diſmiſs this part of *Natural Hiſtory*, which we call *Mechanical*
and *Experimental*, this muſt be added ; That the body of *ſuch a Hiſtory*, muſt be built not only of *Mechanical Arts themſelves*, but the *operative part of Liberal Sciences*, as alſo many practices not yet grown up
into Art, that nothing profitable may be omitted, which avails to the
information of the underſtanding. And ſo this is the firſt Partition of
Natural Hiſtory.

C H A P.   III.

I. The Second Partition of *Natural Hiſtory*, from the uſe and end
thereof into *Narrative and Inductive*. And that the moſt noble end
of *Natural Hiſtory is, that it miniſter and conduce to the building up
of Philoſophy : which end Inductive Hiſtory reſpecteth.* II. The Partition of the *Hiſtory of Generations into the Hiſtory of the Heavens :
The Hiſtory of the Meteors : The Hiſtory of the Earth and Sea : The
Hiſtory of Maſſive Bodies, or of the greater Corporations : The
Hiſtory of Kinds, or of the leſſer Corporations.*

I. N *Atural Hiſtory*, as in reſpect of the *ſubject, it is of three ſorts*, as
we obſerved before ; ſo in reſpect of the *uſe, of two :* for it is
applied, either for the knowledge of things themſelves recorded in *Hiſtory* ; or as the Primitive matter of *Philoſophy*. The former of theſe,
which either for the pleaſure of the Narrations is delightful, or for the
practice of experiments is uſeful, and for ſuch pleaſure or profits ſake is
purſued, is of far inferiour quality, compared with that which is the
Materials and Proviſion of a *true and juſt induction*, and gives the
firſt ſuck to *Philoſophy*, wherefore let us again divide *Natural Hiſtory*,
into *Hiſtory Narrative*, and *Inductive ; this latter we report as Deficient.* Nor do the great names of Ancient Philoſophers, or the mighty
volumes

volumes of Modern writers fo aftonifh my fenfe; for I know very well that *Natural Hiftory*, is already extant, ample for the Mafs, for variety delightful, and often curious for the diligence: but if you take from thence *Fables* and *Antiquity*, and *Allegations of Authors*, and *vain Contro-verfies*, *Philofophy* and *Ornaments*, which are accommodate to Table-talk, or the *night-difcourfes* of Learned men, then will the fequel, for the *Inftaurations* of *Philofophy*, come to no great matter: And to fpeak truth, this is far fhort of the variety which we intend. For firft thofe two parts of *Natural Hiftory*, whereof we have fpoken, The Hiftory of *Præter-generations*, and *of Arts*, matters of great confequence, are there *Deficient*: then in that third general Part mentioned before, namely of *Generations*, of five parts thereof, the *Natural Hiftory* extant gives fatisfaction only to one.

II. For the *Hiftory of Generations* hath Five fubordinate Parts; The firft is of *Celeftial Bodies*, which comprehends the *Phænomena* fincere, and not dogmatiz'd into any peremptory affertions: The fecond of *Meteors* with the *Comets*, and of the *Regions*, as they call them, of the *Air*; neither is there extant any Hiftory concerning *Comets*, *Fiery Meteors*, *Winds*, *Rain*, *Tempefts*, and the reft, of any value: The third is of the *Earth* and *of the Water* (as they are integral parts of the World) of *Mountains*, of *Rivers*, of *Tydes*, of *Sands*, of *Woods*, as alfo of the *Figure* of the continents, as they are ftretcht forth: in all thefe particulars the Inquiries and Obfervations are *rather Natural*, *than Cofmographical*: Fourthly, touching the *general Maffes of Matter*, which we ftile the *Greater Collegiats*, commonly called the *Elements*: Neither are there found any narrations touching *Fire*, *Air*, *Water*, and of their Natures, Motions, Workings, Impreffions, which make up any complete body: The fifth and the laft Part is of *the Perfect and exact Collections*, which we entitle the *leffer Collegiats*, commonly called *Kinds* or *Specificks*. In this laft part only the induftry of writers hath appeared, yet fo as was prodigally wafted in fuperfluous matter, fwelling with the outward defcriptions of living Creatures, or of Plants and fuch like; than enricht with folid and diligent obfervations, which in *Natural Hiftory* fhould every where be annext and interferted. And to fpeak in a word, all the *Natural Hiftory* we have, as well in regard of the Inquifition, as of the Collection, is no way proportionable in reference, to that end whereof we fpeak, namely the *Raifing and advancing of Philofophy*: Wherefore we pronounce *Inductive Hiftory Deficient*. And thus far of *Natural Hiftory*.

C H A P. IV.

I. The Partition of *Civil History, into Ecclesiastical and Literary,* and, which retains the general name, *Civil.* II. *Literary Deficient.* § Precepts how to compile it.

I. *C*Ivil *History,* in our Judgement, is rightly divided into three kinds; first into *Sacred* or *Ecclesiastical*; then into that which retains the general name *Civil*; lastly, into that of *Learning* and *Arts.* We will begin with that kind we set down last, because the other are extant, *but this I thought good to report as Deficient*; it is the *History of Learning.* And surely the *History of the world* destitute of this, may be thought not unlike the statue of *Polyphemus,* with his eye out, that part of the Image being wanting, which doth most shew the nature and spirit of the Person. And though we set down this as *Deficient,* yet we are not ignorant, that in divers particular Sciences of Juris-consults, Mathematicians, Rhetoricians, Philosophers, there are made some slight Memorials and small relations of Sects, Schools, Books, Authors, and such like successions of Sciences. There are likewise extant, some weak and barren discourses touching the *Inventors of Arts and Usages*; but a Just and General *History of Learning,* we avouch that none hitherto hath been publisht. Wherefore we will propound the Argument; the way how to contrive it, and the use thereof.

II. *The Argument is nothing else but a recital from all Times, what Knowledges and Arts, in what Ages and Climates of the world have flourisht.* Let there be made a commemoration of their *Antiquities, Progressions* and *Peragrations,* through divers parts of the World: (for Sciences shift and remove, as people do.) Again, of their *Declensions, Oblivions,* and *Instaurations.* Let there likewise be observations taken through all *Arts,* of the *occasion and original of their Invention*; of their *Manner of delivery,* and the discipline of their managings, *Course of study* and exercises. Let there also be added the *Sects,* then on foot; and the *more famous controversies* which busied and exercised Learned men; the scandals and reproaches to which they lay open; the Lauds and Honours wherewith they were grac'd. Let there be noted the *Chiefest Authors,* the *best Books, Schools, Successions, Universities, Societies, Colledges, Orders,* and whatsoever else belongs to the State of Learning. But above all, let this be observed (which is the **Grace and Spirit of** *Civil History,*) that the Causes and Consultations be Connexed with the events: namely, that *the nature of Countries and People be recorded, the dispositions apt and able; or inept and inable for divers disciplines; the Occurrences of time Adverse, or Propitious to Learning; the zeals and mixtures of Religions; the Discountenances, and favours of Laws; and lastly, the eminent virtues and sway of Persons of note, for the promoting of Learning; and the like.* But our advice is, that all these points be so handled, that time be not wasted in praise and censure of particulars, after the manner of *Criticks*; but that things be plainly and historically related, and our own judgements very sparingly interposed.

§ *As*

§ *As for the manner. of compiling. such a History,* we do especially admonish thus much ; *that the Matter and Provision thereof be drawn, not only from Histories and Criticks; but also that through every century of years or lesser Intervals, by a continued sequence of time, deduced from the highest antiquity; the best Books written within those distinguisht spaces of time be consulted with* ; that from a taste and observation of the argument, stile and method thereof, and not a through a perusal, for that *were an infinite work, the learned spirit of that age, as by a kind of charm, may be awakt and rais'd up from the dead.*

§ *As touching the use of this Work,* it is design'd to this end; not ; that the Honour and State of Learning usher'd in by so many Images and Ghosts of the Learned, should be celebrated, or that for the earnest affection we bear to Learning, we desire, even to a curiosity, to enquire and know, and to conserve whatsoever to the state of Learning may any way appertain; but chiefly, for a more serious and grave purpose. It is, in few words this, *For that such a Narration, as we have described, in our opinion, may much confer to the wisdom and judgement of Learned men, in the use and administration of Learning : and that the passions and perturbations; the vices and virtues; as well about, Intellectual matters, as Civil may be observed; and the best Presidents for practice may be deduced therefrom.* For it is not Saint *Austins*, nor Saint *Ambrose* his works, (as we suppose) that will make so wise a Bishop or a Divine, as *Ecclesiastical story* throughly read and observed : which without question may befal Learned men from the History of Learning. For whatsover is not munited and sustained by Example and Records, is exposed to imprudency and ruine. Thus much of the *History of Learning.*

Chap. V.

Of the Dignity. § *And difficulty of Civil History.*

Civil *History* properly so called comes now to be handled ; The *Dignity* and *Authority whereof,* is very eminent among secular writings : For upon the credit of *this History,* the examples of our Ancestors ; the vicissitudes of Affairs; the grounds of Civil Prudence; and the Name and Fame of men depend.

§ But the *Difficulty is as great as the Dignity*; for to draw back the mind in writing, to the contemplation of matters long ago passed ; and thus, as it were, to make it aged ; to search out with diligence ; and to deliver with faith and freedom, and with the life and height of expression ; to represent unto the eyes, the changes of times ; the chatacters of Persons ; the incertainties of Counsels ; the Conveyances of Actions (as of waters,). the subtilties of Pretentions, the secrets of State, is a task of great pains and judgements ; especially seeing Ancient reports, are subject to incertainty ; Modern liable to danger : Wherefore the errors are many which attend *Civil History*; whilst some write poor and popular Relations, the very reproach of History ;

others patch up, in a rash haste, and unequal contexture, particular Reports, and brief Memorials, others slightly run over the heads of actions done; others on the contrary pursue every trivial Circumstance, nothing belonging to the sum and issue of things; some out of a too partial indulgence to their own wit, take confidence to fain many things; but others add and imprint upon affairs the Image, not so much of their own wit, as of their affections; mindful rather of their own parts, than to become Religious deponents for truth; others every where interlace such Politick observations; as they most fancy, and seeking occasion of digression for ostentation, too slightly break off the contexture of the discourse; others for want of moderation and judgement over do things, by the prolixity of their speeches, Harangues or other performances, so as it is sufficiently manifest, that in the writings of men, *there is not any kind more rare than a just History, and in all points complete and perfect.* But our purpose at this present is, to set down a partition of knowledge, *for the observation of parts omitted; and not a censure of parts erroneous.* Now we will proceed *to the Partitions of Civil History*, and those of divers sorts; for the particular kinds will be less intangled, if divers partitions be propounded; than if one partition by divers members be curiously drawn out.

•

C H A P. VI.

The first Partition of Civil History, *into § Memorials, § Antiquities. § And Perfect History.*

Ivil History is of three kinds, not unfitly to be compared to the three sorts of Pictures or Images: for of Pictures and Images we see, some are unperfect and unfinisht; others perfect; and others decayed and defaced with Age. In like manner we will divide *Civil History, which is the Image of Actions and Times*, into three kinds, agreeable to those of Pictures; namely, *Memorials; Perfect History;* and *Antiquities. Memorials are Histories unfinisht*, or the first and rough draughts of History : *Antiquities are Histories defaced*, or the Remains of History, which have casually escaped the shipwrack of Time.

§ *Memorials or Preparations to History*, are of two sorts, whereof one may be termed *Commentaries;* the other *Registers. Commentaries* set down a naked Continuance and Connexion of Actions and Events, without the Causes and Pretexts of Business; the beginnings and Motives thereof; also the Counsels and Speeches, and other preparations of Actions : For this is the true nature of *Commentaries*, though *Cæsar* in modesty mixt with greatness, did for his pleasure apply the name of *Commentaries*, to the best History that is extant. But *Registers* are of two sorts, for either they comprehend the titles of Matter and Persons in a continuation of Times, such as are *Calendars* and *Chronologies: or Solennities of Acts;* of which kind are the Edicts of Princes; the Decrees of Councils; the Proceedings of Judgements;

Pub-

Publick Orations; Letters of Eſtate, and the like ; without the Contexture or Continued thred of the *Narration.*

§ *Antiquities,* or the *Remains of Hiſtories,* are as we ſaid, *tanquam*
Tabula Naufragii ; when induſtrious and underſtanding perſons (the
memory of Things being decayed, and almoſt overwhelmed with oblivion) by a conſtant and ſcrupulous diligence, out of Genealogies,
Calendars, Inſcriptions, Monuments, Coyns, Proper Names and Styles ;
Etymologies of words, Proverbs, Traditions, Archives and Inſtruments,
as well publick as private ; Fragments of ſtories, ſcattered paſſages of
Books that concern not Hiſtory ; out of all theſe, I ſay, or ſome of them,
they recover and ſave ſomewhat from the Deluge of Time. Certainly
a painful work, but acceptable to all ſorts of Men, and atttended
with a kind of Reverence, and indeed worthy (all Fabulous Originals of Nations defac'd, and extinguiſht) to be ſubſtituted in the room
of ſuch counterfeit ſtuff: but yet of the leſs Authority; becauſe what
is proſtitute to the licenſe of private deſigns, loſes the honour of publick regard.   In theſe kinds of *Imperfect Hiſtories,* I deſign no Deficience, ſeeing they are *tanquam imperfectè miſta,* ſo as ſuch Defects are
but their nature. As for *Epitomes the corruptions, certainly, and the*
Moths of Hiſtories, we would have them baniſht (wherein we concur with many of moſt ſound judgement) as thoſe that have fretted
and corroded the ſound bodies of many excellent Hiſtories ; and
wrought them into baſe and unprofitable dregs.

CHAP. VII.

The Partition of Perfect Hiſtory, into *Chronicles of Times* ; *Lives*
of Perſons ; *Relations of Acts.* § The Explication *of the Hiſtory of*
Lives. § *Of Relations.*

JUſt or *Perfect Hiſtory* is of three kinds, according to the nature of the
object which it propounds to repreſent ; for it either repreſents a
portion of Time ; or ſome memorable Perſon ; or ſome Famous Act: The
firſt we call *Chronicles* or *Annals* ; the ſecond *Lives* ; the third *Relations.*
Of theſe, *Chronicles* ſeem to excel, for Celebrity and Name ; *Lives,*
for profit and examples ; *Relations,* for ſincerity and verity. *For Chro-*
nicles, repreſent the magnitude of publick Actions, and the extern faces of
Men, as they regard the publick, and involve in ſilence ſmaller Paſſages,
which pertain either to Matter or Men. And ſeeing it is the workman-
ſhip of God alone, *to hang the greateſt weight upon the ſmalleſt wyers* ; it
comes many times to paſs, that ſuch a Hiſtory purſuing only the greater
occurrences, rather ſets forth the Pomp and Solemnity, than the true
reſorts, and the intrinſick contextures of buſineſs. And although it
doth add and intermix the Councils themſelves ; yet affecting greatneſs, it doth beſprinkle mens actions with more ſolemnneſs and wiſdom, than indeed is in them ; *that a Satyre may be a truer table of a*
Mans life, than many ſuch Hiſtories. Contrariwiſe ; *Lives,* if they be
well written with diligence and judgement (for we do not ſpeak of
Elogies, and ſuch ſlight commemorations) although they propound un-

to themfelves fome particular perfon, in whom Actions, as well commune as folemn; fmall as great; private as publick, have a compofition and commixture; yet, certainly, they exhibit more lively and faithful Narrations of Matters; and which you may more fafely and fuccefsfully transferr into example. But *fpecial Relations of Actions*, fuch as are the *wars of Peloponnefus*; the *Expedition of Cyrus*; the *Confpiracy of Cataline*, and the like, ought to be attired with a more pure and fincere Candor of Truth than the *Perfect Hiftories of Times*; becaufe in them may be chofen au Argument more particular and comprehenfible; and of that quality, as good notice and certitude, and full information, may be had thereof: whereas, on the contrary, the *ftory of Time* (fpecially more ancient than the age of the writer) doth often fail in the memory of things, and containeth blank fpaces, which the wit and conjecture of the writer (confidently enough) ufeth to feize upon and fill up, Yet this which we fay, touching the fincerity of *Relations*, muft be underftood with refervation, for indeed it muft be confeffed (fince all mortal good laboureth of imperfection, and conveniences with difconveniences are ufually connext) that fuch kind of *Relations*, fpecially if they be publifhed about the times of things done; feeing very often they are written with paffion or partiality, of all other narrations, are defervedly moft fufpected. But again, together with this inconvenience, this remedy groweth up; that thefe fame *Relations*, being they are not fet out by one fide only, but through faction and partiary affections are commonly publifhed by fome or other on both fides; they do by this means open and hedge in a middle way between extremes to truth: and after the heat of paffions is over, they become, to a good and wife writer of Hiftory, not the worft matter and feeds of a perfect Hiftory.

§ As touching thofe points which feem *deficient* in thefe three kinds of Hiftory, without doubt there are many particular Hiftories (of fuch I fpeak as may be had) of fome dignity or mediocrity, which have been hitherto paffed by, to the great detriment of the honour and fame of fuch Kingdoms and States, to which they were due, which would be too tedious here to obferve. But leaving the ftories of forreign Nations, to the care of Forreign Perfons; left I fhould become *Curiofus in aliena Repub*. I cannot fail to reprefent unto Your Majefty the indignity and unworthinefs of the *Hiftory* of *England*, as it now is, in the main continuation thereof, as alfo the partiality and obliquity of that of *Scotland*, in the lateft and largeft author thereof: fuppofing that it would be honour to Your Majehy, and a work acceptable with Pofterity, if this Ifland of *Great Britany*, as it is now joyned in a Monarchy for the Ages to come, fo were joyned in one Hiftory for the times paft, after the manner of the facred Hiftory, which draweth down the ftory of the Ten Tribes, and of the two Tribes as Twins together. And if it fhall feem that the weight of the work; (which certainly is great and difficult) may make it lefs exactly, according to the worthinefs thereof, performed; behold an excellent period of much fmaller compafs of time, as to the ftory of *England*; that is to fay, from the uniting of the Rofes to the uniting of the Kingdoms; a fpace of time, which in my judgment containsmore variety of rare events, than in like number of fucceffions ever was known in an Hereditary Kingdome.

For

For it begins with the mixt Title to a Crown, partly by might partly by right: An entry by Arms; an establishment by marriage; so there followed times answerable to these beginnings; like waves after a great tempest, retaining their swellings and agitations, but without extremity of storm; but well past through by the wisdom of the Pilot, *being* Hen. VII. *one of the most sufficient Kings of all his Predecessors.* Then followed a King whose Actions conducted rather by rashness, than counsel, had Hen. VIII. much intermixture with the affairs of Europe; ballancing and inclining them according as they swayed; In whose time began that *great Alteration in the Ecclesiastical State*; such as very seldom comes upon the Stage. Then followed the Reign of a Minor; then an Offer of an Usurpation, though it was very short, *like a Fever for a day:* Then the Reign Ed. VI. of a woman matcht with a Forreigner: Again, of a woman that liv'd Maria solitary and unmarried. And the close of all was this happy and glo-Elisa. rious event; that is, that this Island divided from all the world, should be united in it self; by which that ancient Oracle given to *Æneas,* Virg. Æn. which presaged rest unto him; *Antiquam exquirite Matrem*; should be 3. fulfill'd upon the most noble Nations of England and Scotland, now united in that name of *Britannia, their ancient Mother*; as a Pledge and Token of the Period and Conclusion, now found of all Wandrings and Peregrination. *So that as massive bodies* once shaken, feel certain Trepidations before they fix and settle; so it seems probable, that by the Providence of God, it hath come to pass, *That this Monarchy, before it should settle and be establish'd in your Majesty and your Royal Progeny,* Iacobus. R. Caro- (in which I hope it is firm fixt for ever) *it should undergoe so many chan-* lus. R. *ges, and vicissitudes, as prelusions of future Stability.*

§ As *for Lives,* when I think thereon, I do find strange that these our Times have so little known, and acknowledged their own virtues; *being there is so seldom any Memorials or Records of the lives of those who have been eminent our times.* For although Kings and such as have absolute soveraignty, may be few; and Princes in free Common-wealths (so many States being collected into Monarchies,) are not many; yet however, there hath not been wanting excellent men (though living under Kings,) that have deserv'd better, than an uncertain and wandring Fame of their memories; or some barren and naked Elegie. For herein the invention of one of the late Poets, whereby he hath well enricht the ancient Fiction, is not inelegant: *He fains that at the end of the Thread of every mans life, there was a Medal or Tablet, whereon the name of the Dead was stampt*; and that time waited upon the shears of the fatal Sister, and as soon as the Thread was cut, caught the Medals, and carrying them away; a little after threw them out of his Bosom into the River Lethe. And that about the Bank there were many Birds flying up and down, that would get the Medals; and after they had carried them in their beaks a little while, soon after, through negligence suffered them to fall into the River. Amongst these Birds there were a few *swans* found, which if they got a Medal with a name, they used to carry it to a certain *Temple consecrate to Immortality.* But such *swans* are rare in our Age: And although many men more mortal in their vigilances and studies, than in their bodies, despise the *Memory of their Name,* as if it were fume or air, *Animæ nil magnæ laudis egentes:* Plin. iun. namely whose Philosophy and severity springs from that root, *Non pri-* alicubi in Epist.

H5

us laudes contempsimus quam laudanda facere descivimus. Yet that will
Prov. 10: not with us, prejudicate *Salomon's* Judgment, *The memory of the Iust
is with Benediction ; but the name of the wicked shall putrifie :* The one
perpetually flourishes; the other instantly departs into Oblivion; or
dissolves into an ill Odour. And therefore in that stile and form of
speaking, which is very well brought in use, attributed to the Dead,
of *Happy Memory* ; of *Pious Memory* ; of *Blessed Memory* ; we seem to
acknowledge that which *Cicero* alledgeth ; borrowing it from *Demosthenes, Bonam Famam propriam esse possessionem defunctorum* ; which
possession I cannot but note that in our age it lyes much wast and neglected.

§ *As concerning Relations* it could be in truth, wish'd, that there
were a greater diligence taken therein : For there is no Action more e-
minent, that hath not some able Pen to attend it, which may take and
transcribe it. And because it is a Quality not common to all men to
write a *Perfect History* to the life and Dignity thereof; (as may well
appear by the small number, even of mean Writers in that kind) yet if
particular Actions were but by a tolerable Pen reported, as they pass,
it might be hoped that in some after Age, Writers might arise, that
might compile a *Perfect History* by the help and assistance of such *Notes :*
For such *Collections* might be as a *Nursery Garden*, whereby to Plant a
fair and stately Garden, when time should serve.

Chap. VIII.

The Partition of the *History of Times*, into History *Universal* ; and *Particular*. The Advantages and Disadvantages of both.

THE *History of Times* is either *Universal* ; or Particular : This comprehends the affairs of some Kingdom ; or State ; or Nation : That,
the affairs of the whole world. Neither have there been wanting those,
who would seem to have composed a *History of the world*, even from the
Birth thereof; presenting a miscellany of matter and compends of *Reports*
for *History*. Others have been confident that they might comprize, as
in a Perfect *History*, the Acts of their own times, memorable throughout the world ; which was certainly a generous attempt, and of singular use. For the actions, and negotiations of men, are not so divor-
ced through the division of Kingdoms, and Countries; but that they
have many coincident Connections : wherefore it is of great import to
behold the fates, and affairs destinate to one age or time drawn, as it
were, and delineate in one *Table*. For it falls out that many writings not
to be despised (such as are they whereof we spake before, *Relations*)
which perchance otherwise would perish ; nor often come to the Press ;
or at least the chief heads thereof might be incorporated into the body
of such a *General History*, and by this means be fixed and preserved.
Yet notwithstanding if a man well weigh the matter, he shall perceive
that the Laws of a *Just History* are so severe and strict, as they can hardly be observ'd in such a vastness of Argument ; so that the Majesty of
History is rather minisht, than amplified by the greatness of the Bulk.
For

For it comes to pass that he who every where pursueth such variety of matter; the precise strictness of Information by degrees slackned; and his own diligence dispersed in so many things, weakned in all, takes up popular Reports and Rumours; and from *Relations* not so authentick, or some other such like slight stuff, compiles a *History*. Moreover he is forced (lest the work should grow too voluminous) purposely to pass over many occurrences worth the relating; and many times to fall upon the way of Epitomes and abridgments. There is yet another danger of no small importance, which such a work is liable unto, which is directly opposed to the profitable use of *Universal History*; for as General History preserves some *Relations*, which, it may be, otherwise would be lost; so contrarywise many times it extinguishes other fruitful *Narrations* which otherwise would have lived through *Breviaries*, which are ever accepted in the world.

Chap. IX.

Another Partition *of the History of Times* into Annals and *Journals*.

THE Partition *of the History of Time* is likewise well made into *Annals*; and *Journals*: Which Division, though it derive the names from the *Period of Times*, yet pertains also to the choice of Business. For *Tacitus* saith well, when falling upon the mention of the magnificence of certain structures, presently he adds; *Ex dignitate Populi Ro. repertum esse, res illustres, Annalibus; Talia, Diurnis urbis Actis mandari:* Applying to *Annals*, Matters of State; to *Diaries* Acts and Accidents of a meaner nature. And in my judgment a Discipline of Heraldry would be to purpose in the disposing of the merits of Books; as of the merits of Persons. For as nothing doth more derogate from Civil Affairs, than the confusion of Orders and Degrees; so it doth not a little embase the authority of a grave *History*, to intermingle matters of trivial consequence, with matters of State; such as are Triumphs, and Ceremonies, Shews, and Pageants, and the like. And surely it could be wisht that this distinction would come into Custom. In our Times *Journals* are in use only in Navigations, and Expeditions of war. Amongst the Ancients it was a point of Honour to Princes to have the Acts of their Court referr'd to *Journals*. Which we see was preserv'd in the reign of *Ahasuerus* King of *Persia*, who, when he could not take rest, call'd for the Chronicles; wherein he reviewed the Treason of the Eunuches past in his own time. But in the *Diaries* of *Alexander* the Great, such small Particularities were contained, that if he chanc'd but to sleep at the Table, it was Registred. For neither have *Annals* only compriz'd grave matters; and *Journals* only light; but all were promiscuously, and cursorily taken in *Diaries*; whether of greater, or of lesser Importance.

Annal. 19.

*Lib. Esth;
Cap 6.*

*Plutarch
Symp. 1.*

C H A P. X.

A Second Partition of History Civil, *into* Simple, *and* Mixt. § Cosmography *a mixt History.*

THE laſt Partition of *Civil Hiſtory* may be this.. *Hiſtory Simple*, and *Mixt.* The Commune Mixtures are two, the one from *Civil Knowledge* ; the other ſpecially from *Natural* : For there is a kind of writing introduc'd by ſome, to ſet down their Relations, not continued according to the Series of the *Hiſtory* ; but pickt out, according to the choice of the Author, which he after re-examines, and ruminates upon ; and taking occaſion from thoſe ſelected pieces, diſcourſes of Civil Matters. Which kind of *Ruminated Hiſtory*, we do exceeding well allow of ; ſo ſuch a Writer do it indeed, and profeſs himſelf ſo to do. But for a man reſolvedly writing a *Juſt Hiſtory*, every where to ingeſt *Politick inter-lacings* ; and ſo to break off the thread of the *ſtory*, is unſeaſonable and tedious. For although every wiſe Hiſtory be full, and as it were impregnant with Political Precepts and Counſels ; yet the Writer himſelf ſhould not be his own *Mid-wife* at the delivery.

§ *Cofmography* likewiſe, is a *mixt-Hiſtory*, for it hath from *Natural Hiſtory*, the Regions themſelves, and their ſite, and commodities ; from *Civil Hiſtory*, Habitations, Regiments and Manners ; from the *Mathematicks*, Climates, and the Configurations of the Heavens, under which the Coaſts and Quarters of the World do lye. In which kind of *Hiſtory* or Knowledge, we have cauſe to Congratulate our Times ; for the world in this our age, hath through-lights made in it, after a wonderful manner: The Ancients certainly had knowledge of the *Zones*, and of the *Antipodes* ;

Virg.
Geor. 1.

(*Nofq; ubi Primus Equis Oriens afflavit anhelis,*
Illic ſera Rubens accendit Lumina veſper)

and rather by Demonſtrations than by Travels. But for ſome ſmall keel to emulate Heaven it ſelf ; and to Circle the whole Globe of the Earth, with a more oblique and winding Courſe, than the Heavens do ; this is the glory and prerogative of our Ages. So that theſe Times may juſtly bear in their *word*, not only *Plus ultra*, whereas the Ancients uſed *non ultra* ; and alſo *imitabile fulmen*, for the Ancients *non imitabile fulmen.*

Virg. Æn.
6.

Demens qui Nimbos & non imitabile Fulmen.

But likewiſe that which exceeds all admiration *imitabile Cœlum*, our voyages ; to whom it hath been often granted to wheel and roſe about the whole compaſs of the Earth, after the manner of Heavenly Bodies. *And this excellent felicity in Nautical Art, and environing the world, may plant alſo an expectation of farther Proficiencies and Augmen-*
tations

tations of Sciences ; specially seeing it seems to be decreed by the Divine Council, that these two should be Coevals, for so the Prophet *Daniel* speaking of the latter times fore-tells, *Plurimi pertransibunt & Cap.12; augebitur Scientia :* as if the through Passage, or Perlustration of the World, and the various propagation of knowledge were appointed to be in the same Ages ; as we see it is already performed in great part ; seeing our times do not much give place for Learning to the former two *Periods*, or *Returns* of Learning ; the one of the *Grecians* ; the other of the *Romans* ; and in some kinds far exceed them.

CHAP. XI.

I. The Partition of *Ecclesiastical History*, into the *General History of the Church*. II. *History of Prophesie*. III. *History of Providence*.

HIstory *Ecclesiastical* falls under the same division commonly with *Civil History* ; for there are *Ecclesiastical Chronicles* ; there are *Lives* of *Fathers* ; there are *Relations of Synods*, and the like, pertaining to the *Church*. In proper expression this kind of History is divided, *into the History of the Church by a general name, History of Prophesie ; and History of Providence.* The first recordeth the times and different state of the *Church Militant* ; whether she flote as the *Ark in the Deluge* ; or sojourn *as the Ark in the Wilderness* ; or be at the rest *as the Ark in the Temple* ; that is, the State of the Church in *Persecution* ; in *Remove* ; and in *Peace*. In this Part I find no *Deficience* ; but rather more things abound therein, than are wanting ; only this I could wish, that the virtue and sincerity of the Narrations were answerable to the greatness of the Mass.

II. The Second Part which is the *History of Prophesie*, consisteth of two Relatives ; the *Prophesie it self* ; and the *accomplishment thereof :* wherefore the design of this work ought to be, that every *Prophesie of Scripture* be sorted with the truth of the event ; and that throughout all the ages of the world ; both for Confirmation of Faith ; as also to plant a *Discipline* ; and skill in the Interpretation of *Prophesies*, which are not yet accomplisht. But in this work, that latitude must be allowed which is proper, and familiar unto *Divine Prophesies* ; that their accomplishments may be both perpetual and punctual : For they resemble the nature of their Author, *to whom one day is as a thousand years, Psal.90; and a thousand years are but as one day :* And though the fulness and height of their complement be many times assigned to some certain age, or certain point of time, yet they have nevertheless many stairs and scales of Accomplishment throughout divers Ages of the world. This work I set down as *Deficient* ; but it is of that nature as must be handled with great wisdom, sobriety, and reverence, or not at all.

III. The third Part which is the *History of Providence* hath fallen indeed upon the Pens of many pious Writers, but not without siding

I   of

of Partiaries ; and it is imployed *in the obſervation of that divine Correſpondence which often interveneth between Gods revealed Will, and his ſecret Will.* For though the Counſels and Judgements of God be ſo obſcure, that they are *inſcrutable to the Natural man* ; yea, many times withdraw themſelves even from *their* eyes, that look out of the Tabernacle : Yet ſometimes by turns it pleaſeth the Divine wiſdom for the Confirmation of *this* ; and Confutation of thoſe which are *as without God in the world* ; to purpoſe them to be ſeen written in ſuch Capital Letters, that, as the Prophet ſpeaketh, *Every one that runs by, may read them* ; that is, *that men meerly Senſual and Carnal* ; *who make haſte to poſt over thoſe divine Judgements* ; *and never fix their cogitations upon them : yet though they are upon the ſpeed, and intend nothing leſs, they are urg'd to acknowledge them.* Such as are late, and unlooked for Judgements ; unhoped for Deliverances ſuddenly ſhining forth ; the divine Counſels, paſſing through ſuch Serpentine windings, and wonderful mazes of things ; at length manifeſtly diſintangling and clearing themſelves. Which ſerve not only for the Conſolation of the minds of the Faithful ; but for the Aſtoniſhment and Conviction of the Conſciences of the Wicked.

1 Cor. 2.

Ad Epheſ. 2.

Habac. 2.

CHAP. XII.

The Appendices of Hiſtory Converſant about the words of Men, as Hiſtory it ſelf about the Deeds : The Partition thereof into, Orations. § Letters. § And Apophthegms.

BUt not the *Deeds only, but the Words alſo of Men, ſhould be retained in Memory.* It is true that ſometimes *Words* are inſerted into the Hiſtory it ſelf, ſo far as they conduce to a more perſpicuous, and ſolemn Delivery of *Deeds.* But *the ſayings and words of men,* are preſerved properly in Books of *Orations* ; *Epiſtles* ; and *Apophthegms.* And certainly the *Orations,* of wiſe men made touching buſineſs, and matters of grave and deep importance, much conduce, both to the knowledge of things themſelves ; and to Elocution.

§ But yet greater Inſtructions for Civil Prudence, are from the *Letters of great Perſonages* , touching the Affairs of State. And of the *words of men,* there is nothing more ſound and excellent, than are *Letters* ; for they are *more natural than Orations* ; *more adviſed than ſuddain Conferences.* The ſame *Letters,* when they are continued according to the ſequel of times (as is obſerved in thoſe ſent by Embaſſadors, Governours of Provinces, and other Miniſters of Eſtate) are without Queſtion of all other *the moſt precious proviſion for Hiſtory.*

§ Neither are *Apophthegms* only for delight , and ornament ; but for real Buſineſſes ; and Civil Uſages, for they are, as he ſaid, [a] *Secures aut mucrones verborum,* which by their ſharp edge cut and penetrate the knots of Matters and Buſineſs : And Occaſions run round in a Ring ; and what was once profitable, may again be practis'd ; and again be effectual , whether a man ſpeak them as ancient ; or make them his own.

a Cic. Epiſt. Fam. L. IX.

own. Neither can it be doubted but that is useful in Civil negotiations, which a *Cæsar* himself hath honour'd by his own example ; it is pity his book is lost, seeing what we have in this kind, seems to be collected with little choice. *Thus much of History*, namely of that part of Learning, which answereth to one of the Cells, or Domicils of the understanding, which is, *Memory*.

a Etiam &: tu Inclite Heros;

CHAP. XIII.

The Second Principal Part of Humane Learning Poesie; 1. *The Partition of* Poesie into Narrative. II. Dramatical. III. And Parabolical. § *Three Examples of* Parabolical Poesie *propounded;* IV. Natural. V. Political. VI. Moral.

NOw let us proceed to *Poesie*. *Poesie is a kind of Learning in words restrained; in matter loose and licens'd;* so that it is referred , as we said at first, to the *Imagination* ; which useth to devise, and contrive, unequal and unlawful Matches and Divorces of things. And *Poesie* , as hath been noted, is taken in a double sence ; *as it respects Words ;* or *as it respects Matter.* In the *first sence*, it is a kind of Character of speech ; for *Verse*, is a kind of Stile and Form of Elocution, and pertains not to *Matter ;* for a *true Narration* may be composed in *Verse ;* and a *Feigned in Prose.* In the *latter sence* , we have determined it, a *Principal member of Learning,* and have placed it next unto *History ;* seeing it is nothing else than *Imitation of History at pleasure.* Wherefore searching and pursuing in our Partition the true veins of Learning; and in many points, not giving place to custom, and the *received Divisions ;* we have dismissed *Satyrs,* and *Elegies,* and *Epigramms,* and *Odes,* and the like, and referred them to *Philosophy* and *Arts of Speech.* Under the name of *Poesie,* we treat only of *History Feigned at Pleasure.*

I. The truest *Partition of Poesie,* and most appropriate, besides those Divisions common to it with History (for there are *feign'd Chronicles, feign'd Lives,* and *feign'd Relations*) is this, *that it is either Narrative ; or Representative, or Allusive: Narrative is a meer imitation of History,* that in a manner deceives us; but that often it extols matters above belief. *Dramatical or Representative , is as it were a visible History ;* for it sets out the Image of things, as if they were Present ; and *History,* as if they were Past. *Parabolical or Allusive is History with the Type; which brings down the Images of the understanding to the Objects of Sense.*

§ As for *Narrative Poesie,* or if you please *Heroical,* (so you understand it of the *Matter,* not of the *Verse*) it seems to be raised altogether from a noble foundation ; which makes much for the Dignity of mans Nature. For seeing this sensible world, is in dignity inferiour to the soul of Man; *Poesie* seems to endow Humane Nature with that which *History* denies; and to give satisfaction to the Mind, with, at least, the shadow of things, where the substance cannot be had. For if the matter be throughly considered ; a strong Argument may be drawn from *Poesie,* that a more stately greatness of things; a more per-

fect

fect Order; and a more beautiful variety delights the foul of Man, than any way can be found in Nature, since the Fall. Wherefore seeing the Acts and Events, which are the subject of true *History*, are not of that amplitude, as to content the mind of Man; *Poesie* is ready at hand to feign *Acts* more *Heroical*. Because *true History* reports the successes of business, not proportionable to the merit of Virtues and Vices; *Poesie* corrects it, and presents Events and Fortunes according to desert, and according to the Law of Providence : because *true History*, through the frequent satiety and similitude of Things, works a distaste and misprision in the mind of Man; *Poesie* cheereth and refreshes the soul; chanting things rare, and various, and full of vicissitudes. So as *Poesie* serveth and conferreth to Delectation, Magnanimity and Morality; and therefore it may seem deservedly to have some Participation of Divineness; because it doth raise the mind, and exalt the spirit with high raptures, by proportioning the shews of things to the desires of the mind; and not submitting the mind to things, as *Reason* and *History* do. And by these allurements, and congruities, whereby it cherisheth the soul of man; joyned also with consort of Musick, whereby it may more sweetly insinuate it self, it hath won such access, that it hath been in estimation even in rude times, and Barbarous Nations, when other Learning stood excluded.

II. *Dramatical, or Representative Poesie , which brings the World upon the stage*, is of excellent use, if it were not abused. For the Instructions, and Corruptions of the *Stage*, may be great; but the corruptions in this kind abound; the Discipline is altogether neglected in our times. For although in Modern Common-wealths, *stage-playes* be but esteemed a sport or pastime, unless it draw from the Satyr, and be mordent; yet the care of the Ancients was, that it should instruct the minds of men unto virtue. Nay, wise men and great Philosophers have accounted it, as the Archet, or musical Bow of the Mind. And certainly it is most true, and as it were, a secret of nature , *that the minds of men are more patent to affections , and impressions, Congregate, than solitary.*

III. But *Poesie Allusive, or Parabolical, excels the rest, and seemeth to be a sacred and venerable thing ; especially seeing Religion it self hath allowed it in a work of that nature, and by it, traficks divine commodities with men.* But even *this* also hath been contaminate by the levity and indulgence of mens wits about *Allegories*. And it is of ambiguous use, and applied to contrary ends. For it serves for *Obscuration* ; and it serveth also for *Illustration :* in this it seems, there was sought a way how to teach; in that an Art how to conceal. And this way of teaching, which conduceth to *Illustration*, was much in use in the Ancient times : for when the inventions and conclusions of humane reason, (which are now common and vulgar) were in those ages strange and unusual; the understandings of men were not so capable of that subtilty, unless such discourses, by resemblances and examples, were brought down to sense. Wherefore in those first ages all were full of *Fables*, and of *Parables*, and of *Ænigmaes*, and of *Similitudes* of all sorts. Hence the *Symboles* of *Pythagoras* ; the *Ænigmaes* of *Sphynx* ; and the *Fables* of *Æsop* ; and the like. So the *Apophthegmes* of the Ancient sages, were likewise expressed by *similitudes*. So *Menenius Agrippa*, amongst

Liv. Hist.
l. 1. 2.

amongſt the Romans, a Nation in that Age not learned, repreſſed a ſe-
dition by a Fable. *And as Hieroglyphicks were before letters ; ſo Parables were before Arguments.* So even at this day, and ever, there is
and hath been much life, and vigour in *Parables* ; becauſe Arguments
cannot be ſo ſenſible, not examples ſo fit. *There is another uſe of Parabolical Poeſy, oppoſite to the former, which tendeth to the folding up of thoſe
things ; the dignity whereof, deſerves to be retired, and diſtinguiſht, as
with a drawn Curtain : That is, when the ſecrets and myſteries of Religion,
Policy, and Philoſophy are veiled, and inveſted with Fables, and Parables.* But whether there be any miſtical ſence couched under the ancient *Fables* of the *Poets*, may admit ſome doubt : and indeed for our part
we incline to this opinion, as to think, that there was an infuſed myſtery in many of the ancient *Fables* of the *Poets*. Neither doth it move
us that theſe matters are left commonly to School-boys, and Grammarians, and ſo are embaſed, that we ſhould therefore make a ſlight judgement upon them : but contrarywiſe becauſe it is clear, that the *writings*
which recite thoſe *Fables*, of all the writings of men, next to ſacred writ,
are the moſt ancient ; and that the *Fables* themſelves, are far more ancient than they (being they are alledged by thoſe writers, not as exco-
gitated by them, but as credited and recepted before) they ſeem to be
like a thin fine rarified Air, which from the traditions of more Ancient
Nations, fell into the Flutes of the Grecians. And becauſe that whatſoever hath hitherto been undertaken for interpretation of theſe *Parables*, namely by unskilful men, not learned beyond common places, gives
us no ſatisfaction at all ; we thought good to refer Philoſopy according
to *ancient Parables*, in the number of *Deficients*.

§ And we will annex an example or two of this work : not that the
matter perhaps is of ſuch moment : but to maintain the purpoſe of our
deſign. That is this ; that if any portion of theſe works, which we report as *Deficient*, chance to be more obſcure than ordinary ; that we
always propoſe, either Precepts, or Examples, for the perfecting of
that work ; left perchance ſome ſhould imagine, that our conceit
hath only comprehended ſome light notions of them ; and that we like
Augures, only meaſure Countries in our mind, but know not how to
ſet one foot forward thither. As for any other part defective in *Poeſy*,
we find none ; nay rather, *Poeſy* being a plant coming, as it were, from
the luſt of a rank ſoil, without any certain ſeed, it hath ſprung up, and
ſpread abroad above all other kind of Learning. But now we will
propound examples, in number only three ; one from things *Natural* ;
one from *Political* ; and one from *Moral*.

The firſt example of Philoſophy, according to Ancient Parables in
things Natural. *Of the* Univerſe, *according to
the Fable of* Pan.

IV. The Original of *Pan*, the Ancients leave doubtful ; for ſome ſay
that he was the *Son of Mercury*, others attribute unto him a far different
beginning : For they affirm that all *Penelopes* ſuitors had to do with her,
and from this promiſcuous Act *Pan* deſcended, a common offſpring to
them all. There is a third conceit of his birth, not to be paſſed over :
for ſome report that he was the ſon of *Jupiter* and *Hybris*, which ſignifies

con-

contumelie. But however begotten, the *Parcæ*, they fay, were his fi-
fters, who dwelt in a cave under ground; but *Pan* remained in the open
Air. The figure and form, Antiquity reprefented him by, was this.
He had on his head a pair of Horns, rifing in a fharp, acuminate to heaven; his body fhagged, and hairy; his beard very long; his fhape bi-
formed; above like a man, below like a beaft; finifht with the feet of
a Goat. He bare thefe enfigns of Jurifdiction; in his left hand a pipe
of feven Reeds; in his right a fheep hook or a ftaff, at the upper end
crooked or inflexed: he was clad with a Mantle made of a Leopards
skin. *The dignities* and offices attributed unto him were thefe; that
he was the God of Hunters; of Shepherds; and of all Rural Inhabitants: Lo. Prefident Mountains; and next to *Mercury*, the Embaffa-
dour of the Gods. *Moreover* he was accounted the Leader, and Commander of the Nymphs; which were always wont to dance the Rounds,
and frisk about him: his train were the Satyrs, and the old *Sileni:* He
had power alfo to ftrike men with terrors, and thofe efpecially vain,
and fuperftitious, which are termed *Panick fears.* His *Acts* recorded
are not many; the chiefeft was, that he challenged *Cupid* at wreftling,
in which conflict he had the foil; caught *Typhon* in a net, and held him
faft. *Moreover* when *Ceres* being fad and vext for the Rape of *Proferpi-
na*, had hid her felf, and that all the Gods took pains, by difperfing themfelves feveral ways, to find her out; it was only *Pans* good fortune, as
he was hunting, to lite on her, and to give the firft intelligence where
fhe was. *He prefumed* alfo to put it to the trial, who was the better mu-
fician he or *Apollo*, and by the judgment of *Midas* was preferred; for
which judgment, *Midas* had a pair of Affes ears fecretly imped to his
head. Of the Love-tricks of *Pan*, there is nothing reported, or at leaft
not much; a thing to be wondred at, efpecially being among a Troop
of Gods fo profufely amorous. This alfo is faid of him, •That he loved
the Nymph *Eccho*, whom he took to wife; and one pretty wench more
called *Syrinx*, towards whom *Cupid* (in an angry revengeful humour
becaufe fo audacioufly he had challenged him at wreftling) inflamed his
defire. *So he* is reported once to have follicited the Moon apart into
the high Woods. *Moreover* he had no iffue (which is a marvel alfo,
feeing the Gods, fpecially thofe of the male-kind, were very Generative)
only he was the reputed Father of a little Girl called *Iambe*, that with
many pretty tales was wont to make ftrangers merry; and fome thought
that fhe was begotten of his wife *Eccho*. The *Parable* feemeth to be
this.

§ *Pan* as the very name imports reprefents, or layeth open the world,
or the world of things. *Concerning* his Original there are only two o-
pinions that go for Currant : For either he came of *Mercury*, that is the
Word of God, which the holy Scriptures, without all Controverfie, affirm; and the Philofophers, fuch as were the more Divine, faw; or elfe
from the confufed feeds of things. For fome of the Philofophers
held, that the Seeds and Principles of Nature, were even in the fubftance infinite, hence the opinion, of *Similary Parts primordial*, was
brought in; which *Anaxagoras* either invented, or celebrated. Some
more acutely and foberly, think it fufficient to falve the variety of Nature, if feeds, the fame in fubftance, be only diverfified in form and
figure; certain and definite; and placed the reft in the inclofure, and
                                                              bofom

[margin notes:]
Cic. Epift. ad Act. l. 5.

Claud. de R. Profer.

Ovid. Met. XI.

Laert. in Anaxag.

Laert in vitis eo- rum.

boſom of the ſeeds.   From this ſpring, the opinion of Atomes is derived, which *Democritus* maintain'd; and *Lucippus* found out.   But o-   Laert. in
thers, though they affirm only one Principle of Nature (*Thales* water;   vitis.
Anaximenes Air; *Heraclitus* Fire) yet they have defined that Principle,
which is one in Act, to be various and diſpenſable in power; as that
wherein the ſeeds of all natural eſſences lie hidden.   *They* who have
introduced the firſt Matter every way diſarayed, and unformed, and   *In Timæi*
indifferent to any form (as *Plato* and *Ariſtotle* did) came to a far nea-   *phyſ.I.*
rer, and natural reſemblance of the *Figure* of the *Parable*.   For they conceiv'd the Matter as a common Courtezan; and the Forms as Suitors.
So as all the Opinions touching the beginnings of things come to this
point, and may be reduc'd to this diſtribution; that the world took
beginning either from *Mercury*; or from *Penelope*; and all her ſuitors.
The third conceit of *Pans* Original is ſuch, as it ſeems that the Grecians
either by intercourſe with the Ægyptians; or one way or other, had
heard ſomething of the Hebrew myſteries.   For it points to the ſtate
of the World not conſidered in the abſolute production; but as it ſtood
after the fall of *Adam*, expos'd and made ſubject to Death aud Corruption: For in that ſtate it was, and remains to this day; the off-ſpring
of God; and of Sin, or *Contumely* : For the *like* ſin of *Adam* was a kind   Gen. 3;
of Contumely, when *he would be like God*.   And therefore all theſe three
Narrations concerning the manner of *Pans* Birth, may ſeem true; if they
be rightly diſtinguiſht according to things and times.   For this *Pan*,
as we now behold and comprehend it, took beginning from the word
of God, by the means of confuſed matter, which yet was the work of
God, and the entrance of Prevarication, and through it of corruption.

§ The *Deſtinies* may well be thought the ſiſters of *Pan*, or *Nature* :
for the beginnings, and continuances, and diſſolutions; the Depreſſi-
ons alſo, and eminencies, and labours, and felicities of things; and
whatſoever conditions of a particular Nature, are called *Fates* or *Deſtinies* : which yet, unleſs it be in ſome noble individuate ſubject, as a
Man, a City, or a Nation, commonly are not acknowledged.   But
Pan, that is, the *Nature of things*, is the cauſe of theſe ſeveral ſtates,
and qualities in every particular; ſo as in reſpect of Individuals, the
Chain of nature, and the thread of the *Deſtinies*, is the ſame.   Moreover the Ancients ſeigned, that *Pan* ever lived in the open Air; but
the *Parcæ*, or *Deſtinies*, in a mighty ſubterraneous Cave; from whence
with an infinite ſwiftneſs they flew to men : becauſe the nature and common face of the *Univerſe* is apert, and viſible; but the individual *Fates*
of Particulars are ſecret, ſwift, and ſuddain.   But if *Fate* be taken in
a more general acception, as to ſignifie the more notable only, and not
every common event; yet in that ſenſe alſo, the ſignification is correſpondent to the univerſal ſtate of things; ſeeing from the order of Na-
ture, there is nothing ſo ſmall which comes to paſs without a Cauſe;
and nothing ſo abſolutely great, as to be independent; ſo that the very Fabrick of *Nature* comprehendeth in the lap and boſom thereof, every event, ſmall or great; and by a conſtant rule diſcloſeth them in due
ſeaſon.   Wherefore no marvel if the *Parcæ* be brought in, as the legitimate Siſters of *Pan* : For *Fortune* is the daughter of the fooliſh vulgar;
and found favour only with the more unſound Philoſophers.   Certainly

ly the words of Epicurus favour lefs of Dotage than of prophanenefs where he faith ; *Præftare, credere fabulam Deorum, quam Fatum affere-re,* As if any thing in the frame of nature could be like an Ifland, which is feparate from the connection of the continent. But *Epicurus* (as it is evident from his own words) accommodating, and fubjecting his *Natural Philofophy* to his *Moral* ; would hear of no opinion which might prefs and fting the confcience ; or any way difcalm, and trouble that *Euthymia,* or *Tranquillity of mind,* which he had receiv'd from *Democritus.* Wherefore being more indulgent to the delufions of his own fancyes, than patient of truth ; he hath fairly caft off the yoak, and abandon'd as well the *Neceffity* of *Fate,* as the *Fear* of the *Gods.* And thus much concerning the Fraternity of *Pan* with the *Deftinies.*

§ *Horns* are attributed unto the *World,* broad at the root, fharp at the top ; the nature of all things being like a Pyramis leffening upwards. For *Individuals* in which the Bafe of nature is fpread out ; being infinite, are collected into Species, which are many alfo ; Species again rife up into Generals ; and thefe afcending are contracted into more Univerfal Generalities ; fo that at length, nature may feem to clofe in a *unity* ; which is fignified by the Pyramidal Figure of *Pans Horns.* Neither is it to be wondr'd at, that *Pan* toucheth heaven with his *horns* ; feeing the tranfcendentals *of Nature,* or *Univerfal Ideas,* do in fome fort reach things Divine. Wherefore Homers *famous Chain of Natural*

Caufes, tyed to the foot of Iupiters *Chair,* was celebrated. And it is plain, that no man converfant in *Metaphyfick* ; and thofe things which in Nature are *Eternal,* and immoveable ; and that hath never fo little withdrawn his mind from the fluid ruin of fublunary things, which doth not at the fame inftant fall upon *Natural Theology :* fo direct and compendious a paffage it is, from the top of the *Pyramis,* to matters Divine.

§ The body of *Nature* is elegantly and and lively drawn *Hairy,* reprefenting the beams of things ; for beams are, as it were, the hairs or briftles of nature ; and every Creature is more or lefs Beamy ; which is moft apparent in the faculty of feeing ; and no lefs in every magnetick virtue, and operation upon diftance ; for whatfoever worketh upon any thing upon Diftance, that may rightly be faid to dart forth rays. Moreover *Pans beard* is faid to be exceeding long, becaufe the beams or influences of the Heavens ; and fpecially of the Sun, do operate, and pierce fartheft of all ; fo that not only the furface, but the inward bowels of the earth have been turn'd ; fubduc'd ; and impregnate, with the mafculine Spirit of the heavenly influence. And the form of *Pans beard* is the more elegant ; becaufe the *Sun,* when his higher part, is fhadowed with a Cloud, his beams break out in the lower ; and fo appears to the eye as if he were *bearded.*

§ Nature is alfo moft expreffively fet forth with a *bi-formed Body* ; in reference to the Differences between fuperiour and inferiour bodies. For the one part, by reafon of their beauty ; and equability ; and conftancy of motion ; and dominion over the earth ; and earthly things ; is aptly fet out by the fhape of man : And the other part in refpect of their perturbations ; and irregular motions ; and that they are for moft part commanded by the Celeftial ; may be well fitted with the figure of a *bruit beaft.* Again this fame *bi-formed* defcription of his *body,* pertains

tains to the participation of the ſpecies or kind; for no ſpecies of Nature, ſeems to be ſimple; but, as it were participating aud compounded of two, Eſſential Ingredients. For Man hath ſomething of a Beaſt: a Beaſt ſomething of a Plant: a Plant ſomething of an inanimate Body: and all natural things are indeed bi-formed; and compounded of a ſuperiour and inferiour kind.

§ It is a witty Allegory that ſame, of the *feet of the Goat*; by reaſon of the upward tending motions of Terreſtrial bodies towards the regions of the air; and of the heaven; where alſo they become penſile; and from thence are rather forc'd down, than fall down. For the Goat is a mounting Animal, that loves to be hanging upon rocks, and precipices, and ſteep hills: And this is done alſo in a wonderful manner, even by thoſe things which are deſtinated to this inferiour Globe; as may manifeſtly appear, in *Clouds* and *Meteors,* And it was not without the grounds of reaſon, that *Gilbert,* who hath written a painful and an experimental work, touching a *Loadſtone,* caſt in this, doubt, *Whether or no ponderous bodies, after a great diſtance, and long diſcontinuance from the earth, may not put off their motion towards the inferiour Globe.?* De Magn.

§ The two enſigns which *Pan* bears in his hands, do point, the one at *Harmony,* the other at *Empiry:* for the *Pipe of ſeven Reeds,* doth evidently demonſtrate the conſent and *Harmony*; or diſcordant concord of Nature, which is cauſed by the motion of the ſeven wandring ſtars: for there are no other Errors, or manifeſt Expatiations in heaven, ſave thoſe of the ſeven Planets; which being intermingled, and moderated with the equality of the fixed ſtarrs; and their perpetual and invariable diſtance one from the other, may maintain and excite both the conſtancy in ſpecifical; and the fluency of Individual Natures. If there be any leſſer Planets which are not conſpicuous; or any greater Mutation in heaven (as in many ſuperlunary Comets) they ſeem but like Pipes, either altogether mute, or only ſtreperous for a time, becauſe their influence either doth not ſtream down ſo low as to us; or doth not long interrupt the Harmony of the *ſeven Pipes of Pan.* And that *Staff of Empiry,* may be excellently applied to the order of Nature, which is partly right, partly crooked. And this ſtaff or rod is eſpecially crooked at the upper end; becauſe all the works of Divine Providence are commonly fetcht about by circuits, and windings; ſo that one thing may ſeem to be done, and yet indeed a clean contrary brought to paſs; as *the ſelling of Joſeph into Egypt,* and the like. Beſides in all wiſe humane Government, they that ſit at the helm, do more happily bring their purpoſes about, and inſinuate more eaſily things fit for the people, by pretexts, and oblique courſes; than by down-right dealing. Nay, (which perchance may ſeem very ſtrange) in things meerly natural, you may ſooner deceive nature, than force her; ſo improper, and ſelf-impeaching are open direct proceedings; whereas on the other ſide, an oblique and an inſinuating way, gently glides along, and compaſſeth the intended effect. Gen. 42.

§ *Pans Cloak or Mantle,* is ingeniouſly feigned to be the *Skin of a Leopard,* becauſe it is full of ſpots: ſo the Heavens are ſpotted with Stars; the Sea with Iſlands; the Land with Flowers; and every particular creature alſo, is for moſt part garniſhed with divers colours about the ſuperficies; which is, as it were, a Mantle unto it.

K

§ Thy

§ The office of *Pan* could be by nothing so conceived; and exprest to the life, as by feigning him to be the *God of Hunters*; for every natural Action, and so by consequence, motion and progression, is nothing else but a *Hunting*. Arts and Sciences have their works; and humane Councils their ends, which they they earnestly *hunt* after. All natural things have either their food, as a *prey*; or their pleasure, as a recreation; which they seek for; and that in a quick-discursive, and discerning way,

Virg. B. 1.   *Torva leæna Lupum sequitur, Lupus ipse Capellam,*
Florentem Cythisum sequitur lasciva Capella.

§ *Pan* is also said to be the God of the *Country Swains*; because men of this condition lead lives more agreeable unto Nature, than those that live in the Cities and Courts of Princes; where Nature by too much Art is corrupted: so as the saying of the Poet (though in the sence of love) may be here verified:

Mart. Ep.   ——*Pars minima est ipsa puella sui.*

§ *Pan* was held to be *Lord President of the Mountains*; because in high Mountains and Hills *Nature* lays her self most open, and is most displayed to the view and contemplation of men.

. § Whereas *Pan* is said to be (*next unto Mercury*) the *Messenger* of the Gods; there is in that a Divine Mystery contained; because, next unto the word of God, the *Image* of the world proclaims the Divine power and wisdom; as records the sacred Poet, *The Heavens proclaim the*
Psal. 19.   *Glory of God, and the vast Expansion reports the works of his hands.*

§ The *Nymphs*, that is the Souls of living things, give great delight to *Pan*: for the souls of the living are the Minions of the World. The *Conduct* of these Nymphs is with great reason attributed to *Pan*, because these Nymphs, or Souls of the living, do follow their natural disposition, as their guides; and with infinite variety every one of them after the fashion of his Country, doth leap and dance with uncessant mo-
N. L.   tion about her. *Wherefore one of the Modern* very ingeniously hath reduced all the power of the Soul into Motion; noting the misprision, and precipitancy of some of the ancients; who fixing their eyes and thoughts with unadvised haste, upon Memory; Imagination and Reason have past over the *Cogitative faculty* untoucht; which hath a chief part in the order of conception. For he that calleth a thing into his mind, whether by impression or recordation, *cogitateth* and *considereth*; and he that imployeth the faculty of his phansie, also *cogitateth*; and he that reasoneth doth in like manner *cogitate* or advise: and to be brief, the Soul of man, whether admonisht by sense, or left to her own liberty; whether in functions of the Intellect, or of the affections and of the will, dances to the musical Airs of the *cogitations*; which is that *tripudiation* of the *Nymphs*.

§ The *Satyres*, and *Sileni*, are perpetual followers of *Pan*, that is old age and youth: for of all natural things, there is a lively, jocund, and (as I may say) a dancing age; and a dull, flegmatick age: the carriages and dispositions of both which ages, may peradventure seem to a
man

man which ferioufly obferves them, as ridiculous and deformed as thofe of the *Satyrs*, or of the *Sileni*.

§ Touching the *Terrors which* Pan *is faid to be the Author of*, there may be made a wife inftruction ; namely, *that Nature hath implanted in every living thing, a kind of care and fear, tending to the prefervation of its own life, and being ; and to the repelling and fhunning of all hurtful encounters.* And yet Nature knows not how to keep a mean, but always intermixeth vain and empty fears, with fuch as are difcreet and profitable ; fo that all things (if their infides might be feen) would appear full of *Panick frights* ; but fpecially Men ; and above all other men, the people which are wonderfully travailed and toffed with fuperftition ; fpecially in hard, and formidable , and adverfe times ; which indeed is nothing elfe but a *Panick terror.* Nor doth this fuperftition reign only in the vulgar ; but from popular opinons, breaks out fome times upon wife men ; as Divinely *Epicurus* (if the reft of his difcourfes touching the Gods, had been conformable to this rule) *Non Deòs vulgi negare prophanum ; fed vulgi opiniones diis applicare prophanum.*   Laert. in Epicur.

§ Concerning *the audacity of* Pan; *and his combate upon challenge with* Cupid ; *the meaning of it is, that matter wants not inclination , and defire, to the relapfing and diffolution of the World into the old Chaos ; if her malice and violence were not reftrained and kept in order, by the prepotent concord of things ; fignified by* Cupid, *or the God of Love.* And therefore it fell out well for man, by the fatal contexture of the world ; or rather the great goodnefs of the Divine Providence, that *Pan* was found too weak, and overcome. To the fame effect may be interpreted, *his catching of* Typhon *in a net :* for howfoever there may fometimes happen vaft, and unwonted tumors (as the name of *Typhon* imports) either in the Sea, or in the Air, or in the Earth ; yet nature doth intangle in an intricate toil, and curb, and reftrain, as it were with a chain of Adamant, the exceffes and infolencies of thefe kind of Bodies.

§ As touching the *finding out of* Ceres, *attributed to this God, and that as he was hunting and thought little of it*, which none of the other Gods could do, though they did nothing elfe but feek her, and that with diligence ; it gives us this true and grave admonition ; that is, *that men do not expect the invention of things neceffary for life and manners, from abftract Philofophies, as from the greater Gods; though they fhould apply themfelves to no other ftudy ; but only from* Pan, *that is, from difcreet experience, and from the univerfal obfervation of the things of the World ;* where oftentimes by chance (and as it were going a hunting) fuch inventions are lited upon. For the moft profitable inventions, are the off-fpring of experience ; and, as it were, certain Donatives diftributed to men by chance.

§ His conteftation with *Apollo* about *Mufick* ; and the event thereof, contains a wholefome inftruction , which may ferve to reftrain mens reafons, and judgements, with the reins of fobriety, from boafting and and glorying in their gifts. For there feems to be a two-fold *Harmony* or *Mufick* ; the one of Divine Wifdom ; the other of Humane Reafon ; for, to humane judgement, and as it were, the ear of mortals ; the adminiftration of the world ; and of Creatures therein ; and the   Addas & Incompar. Sandifii comment. ad Ovid. Met. X.

more

more ſe●●et judgements of God, found ſomewhat hard and harſh : Which rude ignorance, albeit it be well proclaim'd by Aſſes ears ; yet notwithſtanding theſe ears are ſecret, and do not openly appear ; neither is it perceived, or noted as a Deformity by the Vulgar.

§ Laſtly, it is not to be wondered at, that there is nothing attributed unto *Pan* concerning *Loves*, but only of the marriage with *Eccho* ; for the world doth injoy it ſelf, and in it ſelf all things elſe. Now he that loves would enjoy ſomething : but where there is enough, there is no place left to deſire. Wherefore there can be no wanton love in *Pan*, or the *World*, nor deſire to obtain any thing, (ſeeing it is contented with it ſelf) but only *Speeches* ; which (if plain) are pronounced by the Nymph *Eccho*, a thing not ſubſtantial, but only vocal ; if more accurate by *Syringa* ; that is, when *words* and *voices* are regulated by certain numbers ; Poetical, or Oratorical, as by muſical meaſures. It is an excellent invention, that amongſt *ſpeeches* and *voices*, only *Ecoho* ſhould be taken in marriage by the *World* ; *for that alone is true Philoſophy, which doth faithfully render the very words of the world ; and which is written, no otherwiſe, than the world doth dictate ; and is nothing elſe than the image and reflection thereof* ; and addeth nothing of its own, but only iterates, and reſounds.

§ And whereas *Pan is reported to have called the Moon aſide into a high-ſhadowed wood* ; ſeems to appertain to the convention between ſence and heavenly, or divine things : For the caſe of *Endymion*, and *Pan* are different ; the *Moon* of her own accord came down to *Endymion*, as he was aſleep : *For that Divine illuminations oftentimes gently ſlide into the underſtanding, caſt aſleep, and retired from the ſenſes* ; but if they be called, and ſent for by *Senſe*, as by *Pan* ; then they preſent no other light than that,

> *Quale ſub incertam lunam ſub luce malignâ*
>   *Eſt iter in ſylvis.———*

It belongs alſo to the ſufficiency, and perfection of the world, that it begets no iſſue : For the world doth generate in reſpect of its parts ; but in reſpect of the whole, how can it generate, ſeeing there is no body beyond the bounds of the Univerſe ? *As for that Girl Iambe,* father'd upon *Pan,* certainly it is a wiſe adjection to the fable ; for by *her* are repreſented thoſe *vain and idle Paradoxes concerning the nature of things,* which have been frequent in all ages, and have filled the world with novelties, for the matter, fruitleſs ; ſpurious for the Race ; by their garrulity, ſometimes pleaſant ; ſometimes tedious and unſeaſonable.

An other example of Philoſophy according to Ancient Parables
in Politicks *of War,* according to the
Fable of *Perſeus.*

Herod.
Polym.
Ovid.
Met. 4.

V. Perſeus *a Prince of the Eaſt is reported to have been imployed by* Pallas *for the deſtroying of* Meduſa, who was very infeſtious to the Weſtern parts of the World, about the utmoſt Coaſts of *Hiberia.* A
                 Monſter

Monſter huge and fierce, of an aſpect ſo dire and horrid, that with her ^{Paus.} very looks ſhe turn'd men into ſtones . Of all the *Gorgons* this *Meduſa* ^{Strab.} alone was mortal, the reſt not ſubject to death : *Perſeus* therefore preparing himſelf for this noble enterpriſe, had Arms and gifts beſtowed on him by three of the Gods : *Mercury* gave him wings fitted for his feet not his arms ; *Pluto* a helmet ; *Pallas* a ſhield, and a Looking-glaſs. *Notwithſtanding* although he was thus well furniſht, he went not directly to *Meduſa*, but turned into the *Greæ*, which by the Mothers ſide were ſiſters to the *Gorgons*. Theſe *Greæ* from their birth were hoary-headed, reſembling old women. They had but one only *eye*, and one *tooth* among them all ; both which as they had occaſion to go abroad, they were wont in courſe to take with them, and at their return to lay them down again. This *eye* and *tooth* they lent to *Perſeus* ; ſo finding himſelf completely appointed for the Action deſigned, with winged ſpeed he marches towards *Meduſa*. Her he found ſleeping ; yet durſt not venture himſelf a front to her aſpect, if ſhe ſhould chance to awake ; but turning his head aſide, beholding her by reflection in *Pallas* her *Mirror*, and ſo directing his blow, cut off her head ; from whoſe bloud guſhing out, inſtantly there emerged *Pegaſus* the flying Horſe. Her head thus ſmitten off, *Perſeus* transfers and inſerts into *Pallas* her ſhield ; which yet retained this virtue, that whoſoever lookt upon it, as one blaſted or Plannet-ſtruck, he ſhould ſuddenly become ſenſeleſs.

§ *This Fable* ſeems to be deviſed for direction to the preparation, ^{Sandys} and order that is to be obſerved in making of war. And firſt the un- ^{Comment, In} dertaking of any war ought to be as a commiſſion from *Pallas* ; cer- ^{Ovid.} tainly not from *Venus*, (as the Trojan war was) or ſome ſuch ſlight ^{Met. 4.} motive ; becauſe the Deſigns of War, ought to be grounded upon ſo- ^{Renoyard.} lid counſels. Then for the choice of War ; for the nature and quality thereof ; the Fable propounds three grave and wholſome Precepts. *The firſt is, that a Prince do not much trouble himſelf about the conqueſt of neighbour Nations : nor is the way of enlarging a Patrimony, and an Empiry, the ſame ; for in the augmentation of private poſſeſſions, the vicinity of Territories is to be conſidered ; but in the amplification of publick Dominions, the occaſion and facility of making war, and the fruit to be expected, ought to be inſtead of propinquity.* Therefore *Perſeus*, though an Eaſtern Prince, makes the expedition of his War a far off, even in the remoteſt parts of the Weſtern World. *There is a notable* preſident of this Caſe, ^{Plut. in} in the different manner of warring, practiſed by two Kings, the Father ^{Alex. Id.} and the Son, *Philip* and *Alexander*. For *Philip* warred upon Borderers ^{de Fort.} only, and added to the Empire ſome few Cities, and that not without ^{Alex.} great contention and danger ; who many times, but eſpecially in a *Theban* war, was brought into extreme hazard : But *Alexander* carried the Actions of his War a far off ; and with a proſperous boldneſs undertook an expedition againſt the *Perſian* ; conquered infinite Nations ; tired, rather with travel than war. This point is farther cleared in the propagation of the *Roman Empire*, what time their conqueſts towards the *Weſt* ſcarce reacht beyond *Liguria*, did yet in the *Eaſt*, bring all the Provinces, as far as the mountain *Taurus*, within the compaſs of their Arms and command. So *Charles* the Eighth, King of *France*, find- ^{Hiſt. Ff in.} ing the War of Britain (which afterward was compounded by marrige) ^{Seriy a.} ^{lii.}

not

not so feasible, pursued his enterprize upon *Naples*, which he accomplisht
with wonderful facility and felicity.   Certainly wars made upon Nations far off, have this advantage, that they are to fight with those who
are not practised in the discipline and Arms of the Aggressor: but in a
war made upon Borderers, the case is otherwise.   Besides the preparation for such an expedition is commonly better appointed; and the terror to the enemy from such a bold and confident enterprize, the greater.   Neither can there usually be made, by the enemy to whom the
war is brought so far off, any retaliation or reciprocal invasion; which
in a war upon borderers often falls out.   But the chief point is, that in
subduing a neighbour state, the election of advantages is brought to a
streight; but in a foreign expedition,a man may turn the race of the war
at pleasure, thither, where military discipline is most weakned; or
the strength of the Nation much wasted and worn; or Civil discords are
seasonably on foot; or such like opportunities present themselves.

Cic.1.de Off.
Bacon de jure Belli cont.
Hisp.

§ *The second precept is, that the motives of war be just; and Religious;
and Honourable; and Plausible:* for that begets alacrity, as well in the
Souldiers that fight, as in the people that afford pay: it draws on and
procureth aids; and hath many other advantages besides.   Amongst
the just grounds of war, that is most favourable, which is undertaken
for the extirpation of Tyrants; under whom the people loose their
courage, and are cast down without heart and vigour, *as in the sight of
Medusa:* which kind of heroick Acts, procured *Hercules* a divinity a-
mongst the Gods. ,Certainly it was a point of Religion amongst the
Romans, with valour and speed, to aid and succour their confederates
and allies, that were any way distressed.   So just vindictive wars have
for most part been prosperous; so the war against *Brutus* and *Cassius,*
for the revenge of *Cæsars* death; of *Severus* for the death of *Pertinax*;
of *Junius Brutus* for the revenge of the death of *Lucretia :* and in a word,
whosoever relieve and revenge the calamities and injuries of men, bear
arms under *Perseus.*

§ *The third precept is, that in the undertaking of any war, a true estimate of the forces* be taken; and that it be rightly weighed whether the
enterprise may be compact and accomplisht; lest vast and endless designs be pursued.   *For amongst the Gorgons,* by which war is represented, *Perseus* wisely undertook her only, that was mortal; and did not
set his mind upon impossibilities.   Thus far the fable instructs touching
those things that fall in deliberation, about the undertaking of a war;
the rest pertain to the war it self.

§ *In war those three gifts of the Gods do most avail,* so as commonly
they govern, and lead fortune after them : for *Perseus received speed,
from Mercury;* concealing *of his Counsels, from* Orcus; *and* Providence
from Pallas.   Neither is it without an Allegory, and that most prudent,
that those wings of *speed* in dispatch of affairs (for quickness in war is of
special importance) were fastened unto his heels, and not unto his Arm-
holes; to his feet, and not to his shoulders; because *celerity* is required,
not so much in the first aggressions and preparations; as in the pursuit
and the succours that second the first assaults : for there is no errors in
war more frequent, *than that prosecution, and subsidiary forces, fail to
answer the alacrity of the first onsets.   Now the Helmet of Pluto,* which
hath power to make men invisible, is plain in the Moral : for the *secret-
ing*

ting of Counsels next to *Celerity,* is of great moment in War ; whereof Celerity it self is a great part ; for *speed,* prevents the disclosure of Counsels. *It pertains to* Pluto's *Helmet,* that there be one General of the Army in War, invested with absolute authority ; for consultations communicated with many, partake more of the *Plumes* of *Mars,* than of the *Helmet* of *Pluto.* To the same purpose are various pretensions, and doubtful designations, and emissary reports ; which either cast a cloud over mens eyes, or turn them another way, and place the true aims of Counsels in the dark : for diligent and diffident cautions touching Letters, Ambassadors, Rebels, and many such like Provisoes, adorn and begirt the *Helmet* of *Pluto.* But *it importeth no less,* to discover the Counsels of the enemy, than to conceal their own : wherefore to the *Helmet* of *Pluto,* we must joyn the *Looking-glass* of *Pallas,* whereby the strength, the weakness, the secret abettors, the divisions and factions, the proceedings and counsels of the enemy may be discerned and disclosed. *And because the casualties of war are such,* as we must not put too much confidence, either in the concealing our own designs, or the dissecreting the designs of the enemy, or in celerity it self ; we must especially take the *Shield* of *Pallas,* that is of *Providence* ; that so, as little, as may be, be left to Fortune. Hitherto belong the sending out of Espials, the fortification of Camps, (which in the Military Discipline of this latter age, is almost grown out of use : for the Camps of the Romans were strengthened as if it had been a City, against all adverse events of War) a setled and well ordered Army, not trusting too much to the light Bands, or to the Troops of Horsemen, and whatsoever appertains to a substantial and advised defensive War : seeing in Wars the *Shield* of *Pallas* prevails more than the *sword of* Mars,

§ But *Perseus* albeit he was sufficiently furnisht with forces and courage, yet was he to do one thing of special importance, before he enterprized the Action ; and that was, to have some *intelligence with the* Greæ. These *Greæ are treasons,* which may be termed the *sisters of War* ; not descended of the same stock, but far unlike in nobility of Birth : *so Wars are Generous and Heroical ; but Treasons base and ignoble.* Their description is elegant, for they are said to be gray-headed, and like old women from their birth ; by reason that Traitors are continually vext with cares and trepidations. But all their strength, before they break out into open Rebellions, consists either in an *eye, or in a tooth,* for every faction alienated from any state, hath an *evil eye, and bites.* Besides, this *eye and tooth* is, as it were, common ; for whatsoever they can learn or know, runs from hand to hand amongst them. And as concerning the *tooth,* they do all bite alike, and cast the same scandals ; so that hear one, and you hear all. *Perseus* therefore was to deal with these *Greæ,* and to engage their assistance for the loan of their *Eye and Tooth :* their *Eye for Discoveries* ; their *Tooth for the sowing and spreading of Rumors* ; and the stirring up of envy ; and the troubling of the minds of men. *After all things are well, and preparedly disposed for war* ; that is first of all to be taken into consideration, which *Perseus* did, *that* Medusa *may be found asleep :* for a wise Captain ever assaults the enemy unprepared ; and when he is most secure. *Lastly, in the very action and heat of war,* the looking into *Pallas* her *Glass,* is to be put in practice : for most men, before it come to the push, can with diligence

and

and circumspection dive into, and discern the state and designs of the enemies; but in the very point of danger, either are amazed with fear; or in a rash mood fronting dangers too directly, precipitate themselves into them; mindful of victory; but forgetful of evasion, and retreat. Yet neither of these should be practised, but they should look with a reversed countenance into *Pallas Mirror*; that so the stroak may be rightly directed, without either terror or fury.

§ After the war was finisht, and the victory won, there followed two Effects; *The procreation and raising of Pegasus*; which evidently denotes Fame, that flying through the world proclaims victory; and makes the remains of that war easy and feasible· *The second is the bearring of Medusa's head in his shield*; because there is no kind of defence for excellency comparable to this: For one famous and memorable Act prosperously enterpriz'd and atchieved; strikes the Spirit of insurrection in an enemy, into an amazing terror; and blasts envy her self into an astonishment and wonder.

The third Example of Philosophy according to Ancient Parables in *Morality*. Of *Passion according to the Fable of Dionysius.*

Orph.in
Hym.
Ov.Met.3.
Eurip.in
Bacc.
Nonn.in
Dion.

VI *They say that Semele Jupiters Minion*, having bound her Paramour, by an inviolable oath, to grant her one request which she would ask, desir'd that he would accompany her in the same form, wherein he came into *Juno:* So she perisht with lightning. But the *Infant* which she bare in her Womb, *Jupiter* the Father took out, and sowed it in his thigh till the months were accomplisht, that it should be born. *This burden* made *Jupiter* somewhat to limp; wherefore the child, because it vext and pinched *Jupiter*, while it was in his flank, was called *Dionysius*. *Being born* he was committed to *Proserpina* for some years to be nurst; and being grown up, he had such a maiden face, as that a man could hardly judge whether it were a boy, or a girl. *He was dead also*, and buried for a time, but afterwards revived. *Being but a youth* he invented the planting and dressing of vines; the making and use of wine; for which becoming famous and renowned, he subjugated the world even to the utmost bounds of *India*. *He rode in a Chariot drawn with Tygers*. There danced about him certain deformed *Hobgoblins* called *Cobali*; *Acratus* and others; yea, even the *Muses* also were some of his followers. *He took to wife Ariadne*, forsaken and left by *Theseus*. The *tree sacred unto him was the Ivy*. He was held the *Inventor* and In-

Pans: in
Bœot.
Eurip.in
Bac.

stitutor of *sacrifices* and *Ceremonies*, but such as were frantick and full of corruptions and cruelties. *He had likewise power to strike men with madness:* For it is reported that at the Celebration of his *Orgyes*, two famous Worthies, *Pentheus* and *Orpheus*, were torn in pieces by certain mad-enraged women; the one because he got upon a tree, out of a curiosity to behold their Ceremonies in these Sacrifices; the other because he played sweetly and cunningly upon the harp. *And for the Gests of* this God, they are in a manner the same with *Jupiters.*

V.Com-
ment.in
Ovid.Met
3.G. San-
ctis.Re-
noard.

§ *There is such excellent Morality coucht in this fable*, as Moral Philosophy affords not better. *For under the Person of Bacchus is described the nature of Passion; or of Affections and Perturbations of the mind. First*
there-

therefore touching the birth and parentage of *Passion* ; the beginning of all Passion, though never so hurtful, is nothing else than *good Apparent :* For as the Mother of virtue is *good Existent* ; so the Mother of Passion is *good Apparent.* The one of these (under which Person, the soul of man is represented) is *Jupiters* lawful wife ; the other his Concubine : which yet affecteth the honour of *Juno,* as *Semele* did. *Passion* is conceiv'd in an unlawful desire, rashly granted, before rightly understood, and judged : And after when it begins to grow fervent, the *Mother* of it, which is the Nature and Species of *Good,* by too much inflammation is destroyed and perisheth. The proceeding of *Passion* from the first conception thereof is after this manner : It is nourisht and concealed by the mind of man, (which is the Parent of *Passion,*) specially in the inferiour part of the mind, as in the thigh ; and so vexeth, and pulleth, and depresseth the mind ; as those good determinations and actions, are much hindred and lamed thereby : but when it comes to be confirmed by consent and habit ; and breaks out into Act, that it hath now, as it were, fulfill'd the months, and is brought forth and born ; first, for a while it is brought up by *Proserpina* ; that is, it seeks corners and secret places, and lurks, as it were, under ground ; until the reigns of shame and fear laid aside, and boldness coming on ; it either assumes the pretext of some virtue, or becomes altogether impudent and shameless. *And it is most true that every vehement Passion is of a doubtful sex :* being masculine in the first motion ; but feminine in prosecution. *It is an excellent fiction, that of dead* Bacchus, *reviving* ; for *Passions* do sometimes seem to be in a dead sleep, and extinct ; but we must not trust them, no though they were buried : For let there be but matter and opportunity offer'd, they rise again.

§ *The invention of the Vine is a wise Parable* ; for every affection is very quick and witty in finding out that which nourisheth and cherisheth it ; and of all things known to men, *wine is most powerful and efficacious to excite and inflame passions* ; of what kind soever ; as being, in a sort, a common incentive to them all.

§ *Again, affection or passion is elegantly set down to be a subduer of Nations, and an undertaker of infinite expedition :* For desire never rests content with what it possesseth ; but with an infinite and unsatiable appetite still covets more ; and harkens after a new purchase.

§ *So Tigers* Stable *by affections* ; *and draw their Chariot :* For since the time that *Affection* began to ride in a Coach ; and to go no more a foot ; and to captivate *Reason* ; and to lead her away in triumph ; it grows cruel ; unmanageable and fierce, against whatsoever withstands or opposeth it.

§ *And it is a pretty device, that those ridiculous* Demons, *are brought in dancing about* Bacchus *his Chariot :* For every vehement affection doth cause in the eyes, face, and gesture, undecent and subseeming, apish, and deformed motions ; so that they who in any kind of Passion, (as in anger, arrogance, or love,) seem glorious and brave in their own eyes ; do appear to others mishapen and ridiculous.

§ *The Muses are seen in the company of passion :* and there is almost no affection so depraved and vile, which is not soothed by some kind of *Learning :* And herein the indulgence and arrogancy of Wits doth ex-

L.   ceedingly

ceedingly derogate from the Majesty of the Muses ; that whereas they should be the Leaders and Ancient-bearers of life ; they are become the foot-pages, and bnffoons to lusts and vanity.

§ *Again, where* Bacchus *is said to have engaged his affections on her that was abandoned and rejected by another :* it is an Allegory of special regard ; for it is most certain, that *passion* ever seeks and sues for that which experience hath relinquisht ; and they all know, who have paid dear for serving and obeying their *lusts ;* that whether it be honour, or riches, or delight, or glory, or knowledge, or any thing else, which they seek after ; they pursue things cast off, and by divers men in all ages, after experience had, utterly rejected and repudiate.

§ *Neither is it without a Mystery , that the Ivy was sacred to* Bacchus ; the application holds two ways: *First,* in that the *Ivy* remains green in Winter; *Secondly,* in that it creeps along, imbraceth, and advanceth it self over so many divers bodies, as trees, walls, and edifices. *Touching the first,* every *passion* doth through renitence and prohibition, and as it were, by an *Antiperistasis,* (like the *Ivy* through the cold of Winter) grow fresh and lively. *Secondly,* every predominant affection in mans soul, like the *Ivy,* doth compass and confine all Humane Actions and Counsels ; neither can you find any thing so immaculate and inconcern'd, which affections have not tainted and clinched, as it were, with their tendrels.

§ *Neither is it a wonder, that superstitious ceremonies were attributed unto* Bacchus, seeing every giddy-headed humour keeps, in a manner, Revel-rout in false Religions ; so that the pollutions and distempers of Hereticks, exceed the Bacchanals of the Heathens ; and whose superstitions have been no less barbarous, than vile and loathsome. *Nor is it a wonder, that madness is thought to be sent by* Bacchus, seeing every affection in the Excess thereof, is a kind of *short fury ;* and if it grow vehement and become habitual ; it commonly concludes in *Madness.*

§ *Concerning the rending and dismembring of* Pentheus *and* Orpheus, *in the celebration of the Orgies of* Bacchus ; the Parable is plain. For every *prevalent affection* is outragious against two things ; *whereof the one is curious enquiry into it ;* *the other free and wholsome admonition.* Nor will it avail, though that *inquiry* was only to contemplate and to behold, as it were going up into a tree, without any malignity of mind ; nor again, though that *admonition* was given with much art and sweetness ; but howsoever, the *Orgies* of *Bacchus* cannot endure either *Pentheus* or *Orpheus.*

§ *Lastly, that confusion of the persons of* Jupiter *and* Bacchus, may be well transferred to a Parable ; seeing noble and famous Acts, and remarkable and glorious merits, do sometimes proceed from virtue and well ordered reason, and magnanimity ; and sometimes from a secret affection, and a hidden passion ; howsoever both the one and the other, so affect the renown of Fame and Glory ; that a man can hardly distinguish between the Acts of *Bacchus ;* and the Gests of *Jupiter.*

But we stay too long in the *Theatre ;* let us now pass on to the *Palace* of *the Mind ;* the *entrance* whereof we are to approach with more veneration and attention.

THE

THE
Third Book
OF
FRANCIS L. VERULAM
Vicount St. *ALBAN,*
OF THE
Dignity and Advancement
OF
LEARNING.

To the KING.

Chap. I.

I. *The Partition of Sciences,* into Theology and Philosophy. II. *Partition of Philosophy into three Knowledges.* Of God ; of Nature ; of Man. III. *The Constitution of* Philosophia Prima, *or* Summary Philosophy ; *as the Commune Parent of all.*

LL *History* (Excellent King) treads upon the Earth, and performs the office of a Guide, rather than of a light ; and *Poesie* is, as it were, the dream of Knowledge ; a sweet pleasing thing, full of variations ; and would be thought to be somewhat inspired with Divine Rapture ; which Dreams likewise pretend : but now it is time for me to awake, and to raise my self from the Earth, cutting the liquid Air of *Philosophy* and *Sciences.*

I. *Knowledge is like waters ; some waters descend from the Heavens, some spring from the Earth,* so the Primary *Partition* of Sciences, is to be derived from their fountains ; some are seated above ; some are here beneath. For all knowledge proceeds from a twofold information ; *either from divine inspiration, or from external Sense ;* As for that knowledge which infused by instruction ; that is Cumulative, not Original ; as it is in waters, which besides the Head-springs, are encreased by the

reception

reception of other Rivers that fall into them. *Wherefore we will divide Sciences, into Theology ; and Philosophy ;* by *Theology* we understand *Inspired or Sacred Divinity ;* not Natural, of which we are to speak anon. But this *Inspired Theology,* we reserve for the last place, that we may close up this work with it ; seeing it is the Port and Sabbath of all Humane Contemplations.

II. *The Object of Philosophy is of three sorts ; God ; Nature ; Man ;* so likewise there is a Triple *Beam* of things ; *for Nature darts upon the understanding with a direct Beam ; God because of the inequality of the medium, which is the Creature, with a refract Beam ; and man represented and exhibited to himself, with a beam reflext.* Wherefore Philosophy may fitly be divided into three knowledges ; the *knowledge of God ;* the *knowledge of Nature ;* and the *knowledge of Man.*

III. And because the Partition of Sciences are not like several lines that meet in one angle ; but rather like branches of trees that meet in one stemm, which stemm for some dimension and space is entire and continued, before it break, and part it self into arms and boughs, ; therefore the nature of the subject requires, before we pursue the parts of the former distribution, to erect and constitute *one universal Science,* which may be the mother of the rest ; and that in the progress of Sciences, a Portion, as it were, of the common high-way may be kept, before we come where the ways part and divide themselves. *This Science we stile Primitive Philosophy or Sapience,* which by the Ancients was defin'd to be, *The Science of things divine and humane.* To this *Science* none of the rest is opposed, being it is differenced from other Knowledges, rather in the limits of latitude ; than in the things and subject ; that is, handling only the tops of things. Whether I should report this as *Deficient,* I stand doubtful, yet I think I very well may. For I find a certain kind of Rhapsody, and confused masse of knowledge, namely of *Natural Theology ;* of *Logick :* of particular parts of *Natural Philosophy* (as of the Principles of Nature, and of the soul) composited and compiled : and by the height of terms, from men who love to admire themselves advanced, and exalted, as it were, to the vertical point of Sciences. But we, without any such stately loftiness, would only have thus much, *That there might be design'd a certain Science, that should be the receptacle of all such Axioms, as fall not within the compass of any special part of Philosophy ; but are more common to them all, or most of them.*

§ That there are many of this kind, needs not to be doubted. For example, *Si inæqualibus æqualia addat ; omnia erunt inæqualia ;* is a rule in the Mathematicks : and the same holds in the Ethicks concerning *Attributive Justice ;* for in *Justice Expletive,* the reason of equity requires, *That equal Portion be given to unequal Persons ; but in Attributive, unless unequal be distributed unto unequal, it is a great injustice. Quæ in eodem tertio conveniunt, & inter se conveniunt ;* is likewise a rule taken from the Mathematicks ; but so potent in *Logick* also, as all Syllogisms are built upon it. *Natura se potissimum prodit in minimis,* is a rule in Natural Philosophy so prevalent, that it hath produced *Democritus* his Atomes ; yet hath *Aristotle* made good use of it in his *Politicks,* where he raiseth his contemplations of a City or State, from the Principles of a Family. *Omnia mutantur nil interit ;* is also a maxime in Natural Philosophy thus expressed, that the *Quantum* of Nature is neither diminisht

Euclid.
El. lib. 1.

Euclid. El.
Arist.

Arist. de
Part. Animal. 1.

Polit. 1.

nisht nor augmented : The same is applied to Natural Theology thus varied; *That they are the works of the same Omnipotence, to make nothing somewhat; and to make somewhat nothing;* which the Scriptures likewise testifie : *I have found by experience that all the works of God do persevere for ever: nothing can be put unto them, nor any thing taken from them. Interitus rei arcetur per reductionem ejus ad Principia,* is a rule in Natural Philosophy; the same holds also in the Politicks (as *Machiavel* hath wisely observed) because the means which must specially preserve States from ruine, are commonly nothing else than reformation, and a reduction of them to their Ancient customes. *Putredo serpens magis contagiosa est quam matura;* is a ground in Natural Philosophy; the same is an excellent Maxime in Moral Philosophy; because professedly wicked, and desperately impious persons, do not corrupt publick manners so much, as they do, who seem to have some soundness and goodness in them; and are diseased but in part. *Quod conservativum est formæ majoris, id activitate potentius;* is a ground in natural Philosophy: for it makes for the conservation of the fabrick of the universe; that the chain and contexture of nature, be not cut asunder or broken; and that there be not *vacuum,* as they call it, or *empty discontinuity* in the world; and that heavy bodies should be congregate and assembled to the massy pile of the earth, makes for the conservation of the Region of gross and compacted natures: wherefore the first and universal motion commands, and subdues, the latter and more particular. *The same rule* holds in the *Politicks,* for those things which conduce to the conservation of the whole *Body Politick* in its entire nature and absence, are more potent, than those things are, which make only for the well-fare and existence of particular members, in a State or Civil Government. *So the same rule* takes place in Theology; for amongst Theological virtues, *Charity,* a virtue most communicative excells all the rest. *Augetur vis agentis per anti-peristasin contrarii :* is a rule in Natural Philosophy; the same works wonders in Civil states, for all faction is vehemently moved, and incensed at the rising of a contrary faction. *Tonus discors in concordem attritum desinens, concentum commendat : To fall suddenly from a Discord upon a Concord commends the Air :* it is a rule in Musick: the like effect it worketh in Morality, and the Affections. That *Trope of Musick,* to fall or slide softly, from the close or cadence (as they call it) when it seemed even to touch it, is common with the Trope of Rhetorick, *of deceiving expectation.* The Quavering upon a stop in Musick, gives the same delight to the ear; that the playing of light upon the water, or the sparkling of a Diamond gives to the eye.

Splendet tremulo sub lumine Pontus.

Organa sensuum cum Organis reflexionum conveniunt : This hath place in *Perspective Art;* for the eye is like to a Glass, or to waters : and in *Acoustick Art;* for the Instrument of hearing is like to the straits and winding within a Cave. These few instances may suffice for examples. And indeed the Persian Magick, so much celebrated, consists chiefly in this; *to observe the respondency in the Architectures, and Fabricks of things Natural; and of things Civil.* Neither are all these whereof we have spoken, and others of like nature *meer Similitudes* only, as men of narrow obser-

Marginal notes:
Ecclcs. 3.

Disc. so-
pra li. 1.
Dec. di
liu. lib. 3.
Avicenna
Hippoc.
Epid.

Arist. al-
cubi.

Arist. Me-
teor. 1.
Problem,
§. 11.

V. Boet. de
Musica.
&c.

Virg. Æn.

Alhaz.
Opt. 4. Vi-
tello. Pas-
sim.

obſervation perchance may conceive; but one & the very ſame footſteps, and ſeals of Nature, printed upon ſeveral ſubjects or matters. *This kind of Science,* hath not been hitherto ſeriouſly handled: You may peradventure find in the Writings coming from the pens of the profounder ſorts of wits, Axioms of this kind, thinly and ſparſedly inſerted, for the uſe and explication of the Argument which they have in hand; but a complete body *of ſuch Maximes, which have a Primitive and Summary force and efficacy in all Sciences , none yet have compoſed;* being notwithſtanding a matter of ſuch conſequence, as doth notably conduce to the unity of Nature; which we conceive to be the office and uſe of *Philoſophia Prima.*

§ There is alſo an other part of this, *Primitive Philoſophy,* which, if if you reſpect *terms,* is Ancient; but, if the *matter* which we deſign, is new, and of an other kind; and it is an Inquiry concerning the *Acceſſory Condition of Entities,* which we may call *Tranſcendents;* as *Multitude, Paucity; Similitude; Diverſity; Poſſible,* and *Impoſſible; Entity; Non-entity;* and the like. For being *Tranſcendents* do not properly fall within the compaſs of *Natural Philoſophy;* and that Dialectical diſſertation about them is rather accommodated to the Forms of Argumentation, than the Nature of things; it is very convenient that this Contemplation , wherein there is ſo much dignity and and profit, ſhould not be altogether deſerted; but find at leaſt ſome room in the *Partitions of Sciences:* but this we underſtand to be perform'd far after an other manner, than uſually it hath been handled. *For example,* no man who hath treated of *Paucity* or *Multitude,* hath endeavour'd to give a reaſon, *Why ſome things in Nature are and may be ſo numerous and large; others ſo few and little.* For certainly it cannot be, that there ſhould be in nature as great ſtore of Gold, as of Iron; as great plenty of Roſes, as of Graſs; as great variety of determin'd and ſpecifick Natures, as of imperfects, and non-ſpecificates. *So* none in handling *Similitude* and *Diverſity,* hath ſufficiently diſcovered the Cauſe, why betwixt divers ſpecies there ſhould, as it were perpetually, be interpoſed, *Participles of Nature ,* which are of a doubtful kind and reference; *as Moſs* betwixt Putrefaction and a Plant : *Fiſhes* which adhere and move not, betwixt a Plant and a living Creature : *Rats* and *Mice,* and other vermine between living Creatures generated of Putrefaction, and of ſeed : *Bats* or Flitter-miſe between Birds and Beaſts; *Flying Fiſhes,* now commonly known, between Fowls and Fiſh : Sea-calfs between Fiſhes and four-footed Beaſts; and the like. Neither hath any made diligent inquiry of the Reaſon how it ſhould come to paſs, *being like delights to unite to like,* that Iron draws not Iron, as the Loadſtone doth; nor Gold allures and attracts unto it Gold, as it doth Quickſilver. Concerning theſe and the like adjuncts of things, there is, in the common Diſceptation about *Tranſcendents* a deep ſilence : *For men have purſued Niceties of Terms, and not ſubtilties of things.* Wherefore we would have this *Primitive Philoſophy* to contain a ſubſtantial and ſolid inquiry of theſe *Tranſcendents, or Adventitions Conditions of Entities,* according to the Laws of *Nature,* and not according to the Laws of *Words.* So much touching *Primitive Philoſophy, or Sapience,* which we have juſtly referr'd to the Catalogue of *Deficients.*

CHAP.

Chap. II.

I. Of *Natural Theologie:* § *Of the Knowledge of Angels, and of Spirits; which are an Appendix thereof.*

THe *Commune Parent* of Sciences being first placed in its proper Throne like unto *Berecynthia,* which had so much heavenly Issue.

Omnes Cælicolæ, omnes supera alta tenentes.   Virg. Æn. 6. i.

We may return to the former Division of the three Philosopies, *Divine, Natural and Humane.*

I. *For Natural Theology,* is truly called *Divine Philosophy.* And this is defined to be a Knowledge, or rather a spark and rudiment of that Knowledge concerning God; such as may be had by the light of Nature; and the Contemplation of the Creature : which Knowledge may be truly termed *Divine* in respect of the Object ; and *Natural* in respect of the Light. The Bounds of this Knowledge are truly set forth, that they may extend to the Confutation and Conviction of Atheism; the Information of the Law of Nature ; but may not be drawn out to the Confirmation of Religion. *Therefore there was never Miracle wrought by God to convert an Atheist, because the light of Nature might have led him to confess a God ; but Miracles are designed to convert Idolaters, and the Superstitious, who have acknowledged a Deity, but erred in his Adoration ; because no light of Nature extends to declare the Will and true Worship of God.* For as works do shew forth the power and skill of the workman, but not his Image : So the works of God, do shew the Omnipotency and Wisdom of the Maker ; but no way express his Image. And in this the Heathen opinion differs from the sacred Truth ; For they defined the World to be the Image of God ; Man the Image of the World ; but Sacred Scriptures never vouchsafed the World that honour, as any where to be stiled the Image of God, but only, *the works of his hands :* but they substitute man, *the immedate Image of God.* Wherefore, that there is a God ; that he reigns and rules the World ; that he is most potent, wise, and provident : that he is a Rewarder, a Revenger; that he is to be adored ; may be demonstrated and evinced even from his works; and many wonderful secrets touching his Atributes, and much more touching his Regiment and dispensation over the world, may likewise with sobriety be extracted, and manifested out of the same works; and is an Argument hath been profitably handled by divers. *But out of* the contemplation of Nature, and out of the Principles of Humane Reason, to discourse, or earnestly to urge a point touching the Mysteries of Faith; and again, to be curiously speculative into those secrets, to ventilate them ; and to be inquisitive into the manner of the Mystery, is , in my judgement not safe : *Da Fidei quæ Fidei sunt.* For the Heathens themselves conclude as much, in that excellent and divine Fable of the golden Chain, *That Men and Gods*

Psal. 8. Gen. 1,

were

were not able to draw Jupiter *down to the Earth*; *but contrariwise* Jupiter *was able to draw them up to Heaven.* Wherefore he laboureth in vain, who shall attempt to draw down heavenly Mysteries to our reason; it rather becomes us to raise and advance our reason to the adored Throne of Divine Truth. And in this part of *Natural Theologie,* I am so far from noting any deficience, as I rather find an excess; which to observe I have somewhat digressed, because of the extreme prejudice, which both Religion and Philosophy have received thereby; as that which will fashion and forge a heretical Religion, and an imaginary and fabulous Philosophy.

§ *But as concerning the nature of Angels and Spirits,* the matter is otherwise to be conceived; which neither is inscrutable, nor interdicted; to which knowledge, from the affinity it hath with mans soul, there is a passage opened. The Scriptnre indeed commands, *let no man deceive you with sublime discourse touching the worship of Angels, pressing into that he knows not*; yet notwithstanding if you observe well that precept, you shall find there only two things forbidden; namely *Adoration of Angels,* such as is due to God; and *Phantastical Opinions of them,* either by extolling them above the degree of a creature; or to extol a mans knowledge of them farther than he hath warrantable ground. But the sober enquiry touching them, which by the gradations of things corporal, may ascend to the nature of them; or which may be seen in the Soul of Man, as in a Looking-glass, is in no wise restrained. *The same may be concluded of impure and revolted spirits*; the conversing with them, and the imployment of them, is prohibited; much more any veneration towards them; but the Contemplation or Science of their Nature; their Power; their Illusions; not only from places of sacred Scripture, but from reason or experience; is a principal part of Spiri- tual Wisdom. For so the Apostle saith, *we are not ignorant of his stratagems.* And it is no more unlawful to enquire, in natural Theology, the nature of *evil Spirits*; than to enquire the nature of Poysons in Physick, or of vices in the Ethicks. But this part of Science touching *Angels* and degenerate spirits, I cannot note as *Deficient*; for many have imployed their pens in it : Rather most of the Writers in this kind may be argued either of vanity, or superstition, or of unprofitable subtilty.

Chap. III.

This Partition of Natural Philosophy into Speculative, and Operative. § *And that these two, both in the intention of the writer; and in the body of the Treatise, should be seperated.*

Leaving therefore *Natural Thologie* (to which we have attributed the enquiry of *Spirits,* as an Appendix) we may proceed to the second Part, namely that of *Nature, or Natural Philosophy.* *Democritus* saith excellently, *That the knowledge concerning Nature, lies hid in certain deep Mines and Caves.* And it is somewhat to the purpose, that the

the Alchimists do so much inculcate, *That Vulcan is a second Nature, and perfects that compendiously which Nature useth to effect by ambages and length of time:* why then may we not divide Philosophy into two parts; the *Mine, and the Fornace;* and make two professions, or occupations of *Natural Philosophers;* Pyoners or workers in the Mine; and *Smiths,* or Refiners? Certainly however we may seem to be conceited, and to speak in jest; yet we do best allow of a division in that kind, if it be proposed in more familiar and Scholastical terms; namely, that the *knowledge of Nature,* be divided into *the Inquisition of Causes;* and the *Production of Effects;* Speculative, and Operative; the one searcheth the bowels of Nature; the other fashions Nature, as it were, upon the Anvile.

§ Now although I know very well with what a strict band, causes and effects are united; so as the explication of them, must in a sort be coupled and conjoyned: yet because all solid and fruitful Natural knowledge hath a double, and that distinct, scale or ladder; *Ascendent and Descendent;* From *Experiments to Axioms,* and from *Axioms to the new Experiments.* I judge it most requisite, that these two parts, *Speculative* and *Operative,* be separate, both in the intention of the Writer, and the Body of the Treatise.

Paracel.
de Philos.
sagaci.

Chap. IV.

I. *The Partition of the* Speculative knowledge *of Nature into* Physick special, and Metaphysick: *Whereof* Physick *enquires the Efficient Cause, and the Matter :* Metaphysick *the final Cause and the Form.* II. *The Partition of* Physick, into the knowledges of the Principles of Things; of the Fabrick of Things, or of the World: And of the variety of things. III. *The Partition of* Physick, *touching the variety of things,* into the Doctrine of Concretes; and into the Doctrine of Abstracts. *The Partition of the* knowledge of Concretes, *is referred over to the same Partition which Natural History Comprehends.* IV. *The Partition of the* knowledge of Abstracts, into the knowledge of the Schemes of Matter; and into the knowledge of Motions. V. *Two Appendices of* Speculative Physick; Natural Problems: *And the* Placits of Ancient Philosophers. VI. *The Partition of* Metaphysick , *into the* Doctrine of Forms; *And into the* Doctrine of the Final Causes.

I. THat part of *Natural Philosophy* which is *Speculative and Theorical,* we think convenient to divide into *Physick special, and Metaphysick.* And in this Partition I desire it may be conceiv'd, that we use the *Metaphysick* in a different sence from that, that is received. And here it seems to fall out not unfitly, to advertise in general of our purpose and meaning touching the use of words, and terms of Art. *And it is this,* that as well in this word *Metaphysick* now delivered, as in other terms of Art, wheresoever our conceptions and notions are new, and differ from the received; yet with much reverence, we retain the

Ancient

Ancient terms : For being we hope, that the method it felf, and a perfpicuous explication of the Matter, which we labour to annex, may redeem us from an incongruous conception of the words we ufe, we are otherwife zealous (fo far as we can without prejudice of Truth and Sciences) to depart as little as may be, from the opinions and expreffions of Antiquity. And herein I cannot but marvail at the confidence of *Ariftotle,* who poffeft with a fpirit of contradiction; and denouncing war againft all Antiquity, not only ufurpt a licenfe to coyn new terms of Arts at pleafure; but hath endeavoured to deface and extinguifh all ancient wifdom. In fo much as he never names any ancient Authors; or makes any mention of their opinions, but to reprehend their Perfons; or to redargue their Placits, and Opinions. Certainly if he affected glory, and drawing difciples after him, he took the right courfe : For the fame comes to pafs in the afferting and receiving a Philofophical Truth, that doth in a Divine Truth; *veni in nomine Patris, nec recipitis me, fi quis venerit in nomine fuo eum recipietis.* But Ioan.5. from this divine Aphorifm, if we confider whom fpecially it hath defigned (namely Antichrift the greateft Impoftor of all times) we may collect, *that the coming in a mans own name,* without any regard of *Antiquity,* or (if I may fo fpeak) of *Paternity,* is no good Augury of Truth, however it be joyned with the fortune and fuccefs of an *eum recipietis. But for* Ariftotle, *certainly an excellent man, and of an admirable profound wit, I fhould eafily be induced to believe; that he learned this ambition of his Scholar, whom perhaps he did emulate : that if one conquered all Nations; the other would conquer all Opinions, and raife to himfelf a kind of Monarchy in contemplations.* Although it may fo fall out, that he may at fome mens hands, that are of a bitter difpofition, and biting language, get a like title, as his Scholar did.

Lucan.1. 10.

Fœlix terrarum Prædo, non utile Mundo Editus exemplum.—— So

Fœlix Doctrinæ Prædo, &c. But to us on the other fide that do defire, fo much as lies in the power of our pen, to contract a league and commerce between Ancient and Modern knowledge; our judgement ftands firm, *to keep way with Antiquity.ufq; ad Aras ;* and to retain the Ancient terms, though fometimes we alter their Sence, and Definitions : according to the modern and approved manner of Innovation, in Civil Government; where the ftate of things being changed, yet the folemnity of words and ftiles is obferved which *Tacitus* notes; *Eadem* Annal.1. *Magiftratuum vocabula.*

§ To return therefore to the acception of the word *Metaphyfick,* in our fence. It appears, by that which hath been already faid, that we diftinguifh *Primitive Phylofophy,* from *Metaphyfick,* which heretofore hath been confounded and taken for the fame thing. The one we have fet down as a *commune Parent of all Sciences ;* the other, as a portion of *Natural Philofophy.* We have affign'd Common and Promifcuous *Axioms* of Sciences, to *Primitive Philofophy.* Likewife all *Relative and Adventive Conditions and Characters of Effences,* which we have named *Tranfcendents ;* as *Multitude, Paucity, Identity, Diverfity,* *Poffible,*

Poſſible, Impoſſible, and ſuch like ; we have attributed to the ſame, only with this Proviſo, that they be handled as they have efficacy in nature ; and not Logically.   *But we have referred* the inquiry concerning
God ; Unity, Bonity, Angels, Spirits, to *Natural Theology.* Wherefore now it may rightly be demanded, what after all this is remaining
to *Metaphyſick!* certainly beyond nature, nothing ; but of nature it
ſelf the moſt excellent part.   And indeed without prejudice to Truth,
we may thus far concur with the opinion and conceit of Antiquity ;
that *Phyſick* only handleth that which is inherent in matter, and
is moveable ; *Metaphyſick* things more abſtracted and fixt.   *Again that*
Phyſick ſuppoſeth exiſtence only and Motion ; and natural Neceſſity :
but *Metaphyſick* the Mind alſo ; the Idea or platform.   For to this point
perchance the matter comes, whereofwe ſhall diſcourſe.   But we will
propound this difference, (leaving aſide the ſublimity of ſpeech) per-
ſpicuouſly and familiarly.   We have divided *Natural Philoſophy* into the
Inquiſition of cauſes ; and the production of effects.   The inquiry of
cauſes we have referred to the Theorical part of *Philoſophy* ; which we
have divided into *Phyſick and Metaphyſick* ; wherefore by neceſſary conſequence the true difference of theſe two Theories, muſt be taken
from the nature of the Cauſes which they enquire ; ſo without all obſcurity or circuit, *Phyſick* is that which enquires of the *efficient cauſe* ;
and of the *Matter* ; *Metaphyſick,* that which enquires of the *Form and*
end.

II *Phyſick* therefore comprehends Cauſes variable and incertain, and
according to the nature of the ſubject moveable and changing, and at-
tains not a fixt conſtancy of Cauſes.

> *Limus ut hic dureſcit, & hæc ut cæra liqueſcit*
> *Uno eodemque igni——*   Virg. Æn.
>   8.

Fire is cauſe of induration, but reſpective to clay ; Fire is cauſe of col-
liquation, but reſpective to wax.   We will divide *Phyſick* into three
Knowledges : For Nature is either united and collected into one ; or
diffuſed and diſtributed : Nature is collected into one either in reſpect
of the *common Seeds and Principles of all things* ; or in reſpect of the *en-*
tire, total Fabrick of the univerſe.   This union of Nature hath brought
forth two Parts of *Phyſick,* one of the *Principles of Things* ; the other of
the *Fabrick of the Univerſe,* or of the World ; which we uſe to call the
Doctrines of *Summs* or *Totals.*   The *Third Knowledge* which handles Nature *diffuſed,* or *ſcattered,* exhibits *all the variety of things,* and the leſſer *Summs* or *Totals.*   Wherefore from theſe contemplations it is plainly manifeſt, that there are three Knowledges touching *Natural Philoſo-*
phy, of the Principles of things ; of the world ; or of the Fabrick of things
Of Nature *multiplicious or ſparſed* ; which laſt Part, (as we have ſaid)
contains all the variety of things ; and is, as it were, the firſt Gloſs, or
Paraphraſe touching the *Interpretation of Nature,* Of theſe three Parts,
none is wholly *Deficient* ; but in what truth and Perfection they are
handled, I make not now my judgment.

III. But we will again divide *Phyſick diſtinctively ſorted,* or of the *va-*
riety of things, into two Parts ; *into Phyſick of concretes* ; *and into Phyſick*
of Abſtracts : or into *Phyſick of Creatures* ; and into Phyſick of *Na-*
tures

tures. The one (to ufe the terms of Logick) inquires of *Subftances* with all the variety of their Adjuncts; the other of *Accidents,* or Adjuncts through all the variety of fubftances. *For example,* if the inquiry be of a *Lion,* or of an *Oak,* thefe are fupported by many and divers Accidents: Contrarywife if the enquiry be made of *Heat,* or *Heavineß,* thefe are in many diftinct fubftances. And feeing all *Phyfick or Natural Philofophy* is fituate in a middle term, between *Natural Hiftory and Metaphyfick*; the firft part (if you obferve it well) comes nearer to *Natural Hiftory*; the latter part nearer to *Metaphyfick*; *Concrete Phyfick* hath the fame divifion which *Natural Hiftory* hath; fo that it is a knowledge either concerning the *Heavens*; or concerning *Meteors*; or concerning the *Globe of the earth and Sea*; or concerning the *greater Collegiates,* which they call the *Elements*; or concerning the *leſſer Collegiates, or natures fpecifick*; fo likewife concerning *Pretergenerations*; and concerning *Mechanicks.* For in all thefe, *Natural Hiftory* inquires and reports the fact it felf; but *Phyfick,* the Caufes likewife; but you muft conceive this of fluid, not fixt Caufes, that is, of matter and of the efficient.

§ Amongft thefe Portions of *Phyfick, that part is altogether maimed and imperfect which enquires of Cœleftial bodies*; which notwithftanding, for the excellency of the Subject, ought to be taken into fpecial confideration. For *Aftronomy,* it is indeed not without fome probability and ufe grounded upon the *Phænomena,* but it is vulgar; bafe, and no way folid: But *Aftrology* in many Circumftances hath no ground at all. *In truth Aftronomy* prefents fuch a facrifice to Mans underftanding, as once *Prometheus* did, when he went about to couzen *Jupiter*; for inftead of a true, fubftantial *Ox,* he prefented the *hide* of a great and fair *Ox* ftuft, and fet out with ftraw, leaves, and Ofier twigs; fo in like manner *Aftronomy* exhibiteth the extrinfick Parts of Celeftial Bodies, (namely the Number, Scituation, Motion, and Periods of the ftars) as the *Hide of Heaven*; fair and artificially contrived into Syftems, and Schemes: but the Entrals are wanting, that is, *Phyfical reafons,* out of which (adjoyning Aftronomicall Hypothefes) the Theory ſhould be extracted, not fuch grounds and fuppofitions as ſhould only fave the *Phænomena* (of which kind a number may be wittily devifed) but fuch as propound the fubftance, motion and influx of the Heavens, as they truly are in nature. For thofe Dogmaes and Parodoxes are almoft vanifht, and long agoe exploded, namely, the *Rapture of the Firſt Mover :* and the *Solidity of Heaven (ſtars being there fixt as nails in the Arched Roof of a Parlour).* And other opinions, not much better, as, *that there are divers Poles of the Zodiack*; *and of the world*; *that there is a ſecond moveable of Kenitency, contrary to the rapture of the firſt moveable*; *that all parts of the firmament are turned about by perfect circles*; *that there are Eccentricks and Epicycles, to ſave the conſtancy of Motion by perfect circles*; *that the Moon hath no force or influence upon a body ſuperior to it,* and the like. And the abfurdity of thefe fuppofitions, hath caſt men upon that opinion, *of the Diurnal Motion of the Earth*; *an opinion which we can demonſtrate to be moſt falſe.* But fcarce any man can be found, who hath made enquiry *of the Natural Cauſes of the ſubſtance of the heavens, as well Stellare, as Inter-ſtellare*; fo of the *ſwiftneß and ſlowneß of heavenly bodies, referr'd one to another*; alſo *of the various incitation of Motion in the ſame Planet*; likewife *of the perpetuated courſe of Motion from*

Raptus 1. mobilis. Soliditas cœli. Motus renitentia. Poli adverſi. Epicycli. Excent. Motus Terræ diurn: &c.

Hypotheſis imaginaris. vide digreſs.

from Eaſt to Weſt, and the contrary: Laſtly of *Progreſſions, ſtations and Retrogradations, of the Elevation and Declination of Motions, by the Apogée, or middle point; and* Perigée *or loweſt point of heaven; ſo of the oblique windings of Motions, either by flexuous Spires, weaving and unweaving themſelves, as they make their approach or receſs from the Tropicks; or by ſerpentine ſinuations, which they call Dragons, ſo of the fixt Poles of Rotations or wheeling motions, why they ſhould be placed in ſuch a point of the heavens, rather than in any other; ſo of the alligation of ſome Planets at a certain diſtance from the Sun:* I ſay an inquiry of this kind, hath ſcarce been attempted, ſave that ſome labour hath been taken therein, only in Mathematical obſervations and Demonſtrations. But theſe obſervations only ſhew how wittily all theſe motions may be contrived, and cleared from oppoſition; not how they may truly ſubſiſt in Nature; and repreſent only ſeeming Motions, and their fictitious Fabrick, and framed at pleaſure, not their cauſes, and the real truth of Things. Wherefore *Aſtronomy,* ſuch as now it is made, may well be counted in the number of *Mathematical Arts,* not without great diminution of the Dignity thereof; ſeeing it ought rather (if it would maintain its own right) be conſtitute a branch, and that moſt principal of Natural Philoſophy. For whoever ſhall reject *the feigned Divorces of ſuperlunary and ſublunary bodies; and ſhall intentively obſerve the appetencies of Matter, and the moſt univerſal Paſſions, (which in either Globe are exceeding Potent, and transverberate the univerſal nature of things) he ſhall receive clear information concerning celeſtial matters from the things ſeen here with us: and contrarywiſe from thoſe motions which are practiſed in heaven; he ſhall learn many obſervations which now are latent, touching the motions of bodies here below: not only ſo far as theſe inferiour motions are moderated by ſuperiour, but in regard they have a mutual intercourſe by paſſions common to them both.* Wherefore this part of *Aſtronomy* which is *natural* we ſet down as *Deficient.* And this we will call *Living Aſtronomy,* to diſtinguiſh it from *Prometheus Ox* ſtuft with ſtraw, which was an Ox in outward ſhape only.

§ But *Aſtrology* is corrupted with much ſuperſtition, ſo as there is hardly to be found any ſound part therein. Yet in our judgment it ſhould rather be purged, than clean caſt away. But if any contend, that this ſcience is not grounded upon reaſon, and Phyſical contemplations; but in blind experience, and the obſervation of many Ages; and therefore reject a trial by natural Arguments (which the Chaldee Aſtrologers boaſted) he may by the ſame reaſon revoke Auguries, Divination, and Predictions from beaſts entrals, and ſwallow down all kind of Fables; for all theſe ſuperſtitious vanities were avoucht, as the Dictates of long experience, and of Diſcipline delivered over by tradition. But we do both accept *Aſtrology,* as a Portion of Natural Philoſophy; and yet attribute unto it no more credit, than reaſon and the evidence of Particulars do evince; ſetting aſide ſuperſtitions and fictions. And that we may a little more ſeriouſly conſider the matter.

§ *Firſt what a vain fancy is this, that every Planet ſhould reign for certain hours by turn, ſo as in the ſpace of twenty four hours, they ſhould reſume their Dominions thrice over, three ſupernumerary hours reſerved?* Yet this conceit brought forth unto us the Diviſion of the week, a computation very ancient, and generally received, as from the interchangeable

changeable courſe of days moſt manifeſtly it appears; when in the beginning of the day immediately ſucceeding, the fourth Planet from the
Planet of the firſt day, enters upon his Government; by reaſon of the
three ſupernumerary hours, whereof we have ſpoken.

§ *Again we are confident to reject, as an idle fiction, the doctrine of
Genethliacal Poſitures of the heavens, to preciſe points of time; with the
Diſtribution of the Houſes;* thoſe ſame darlings in Aſtrology, which have
made ſuch mad work in the Heavens; nor can I ſufficiently wonder that
many excellent men, and for Aſtrology of Principal note, ſhould ground
themſelves upon ſo ſlight reaſons, to avouch ſuch opinions. For they
ſay, ſeeing that experience it ſelf diſcovers as much, that *ſolſtices, Æ-
quinoctials, new Moons, full Moons,* and the like *greater revolutions* of
ſtars, do manifeſtly and notably work upon natural Bodies; it muſt
needs be, that the more exact, and ſubtile aſpect and poſture of the
ſtars, ſhould produce effects more exquiſite and occult. But they ſhould
firſt except the Suns operations by manifeſt heat; and likewiſe, the
magnetick influence of the Moon, upon the *increaſe of Tides every half
Moon* (for the daily Flux and Reflux of the Sea is another thing:) But
theſe ſet aſide; the other power of the Planets upon natural bodies
(ſo far as they are confirmed by experience) is ſlender and weak; and,
which they ſhall find, latent in the *greater Revolutions.* Wherefore they
ſhould rather argue the other way, namely, that ſeeing thoſe *greater
Revolutions,* have ſo ſmall influence, *thoſe exact and minute differences
of Poſitures* have no force at all.

§ *Thirdly, Thoſe Fatalities, that the hour of Nativity or conception governs the Birth; The hour of inception, the fortune of the thing begun;
the hour of Queſtion, the fortune of the thing enquired; and, in a word,
the ſcience of Nativities, Elections, Queſtions, and ſuch like levities; in
our judgment, have no certainty or ſolidity in them; and may by natural
reaſons be plainly redargued and evinced.* The point to be ſpoken of rather, is, what that is which we retain and allow of in Aſtrology; and
in that which we do allow, what is deficient? for, for this end, that is,
for the obſervation of *Deficients,* we undertook this work; not intend-
ing (as we have often ſaid) matter of cenſure. And indeed amongſt
the receiv'd parts of *Aſtrology,* the Doctrines of *Revolutions* we judge
to have more ſoundneſs in them, than the reſt. But it may be to good
purpoſe, to ſet down and preſcribe certain Rules, by the ſcale and ſquare
whereof, *Aſtrological* Obſervations may be examined; that what is
fruitful may be retain'd; what is frivolous rejected.

§ *The firſt Precept* may be that whereof we have admoniſht already;
let the greater *Revolutions be retained; the leſſer Horoſcopes and Houſes caſhiered.* Thoſe, like Great Ordnance may diſcharge their influences, at
a ſpacious remoteneſs; theſe like ſmall Bows, are for a ſhort diſtance,
and carry not their forces far. *The ſecond rule is; That the operation of
the Heavens workes not on all bodies but only upon the more tender and
penetrable;* ſuch as are Humours, Air, Spirits : but here we except the
Operations *of the heat of the Sun, and of the Heavens,* which without
queſtion pierce even to Mettals, and many ſubterraneous Bodies. *The
third rule is, that the Operation of the Heavens extends rather to the Maſs
of things and Nature in groſs; than unto individual eſſences, and particularities;* yet obliquely it reacheth to many Individuals, namely,
                                                             thoſe

those Individuates which of the same species are most *Passible*, and are
like soft wax: even as when a Pestilential air seizeth on bodies more
open and less resistent ; and passeth by Bodies more compact and strong.
The fourth rule is, somewhat like the precedent ; *That the Operation of
the Heavens hath its influx and dominion not in points and narrow minutes of times ; but in greater spaces.* Therefore *Prognostications* of the
temperatures of the year may be true ; but upon particular days, are
worthily accounted vain and idle. *The last rule,* (which by the more
wise Astrologers hath been ever embraced) is, *That there is no fatal necessity in the stars, but that they do incline rather, than enforce.* We add
this moreover (wherein we plainly take part with *Astrology,* if it were
rectified) and which we know to be most certain: *That Celestial bodies
have other influences besides heat and light :* which influences are of force
according to the Rules we have prescribed, and no otherwise : But
these lie hid in the profound Parts of Natural Philosophy, and require
a larger dissertation. Wherefore we think good (that which we have
said being rightly conceived) to set down, *Astrology* agreeable to our
Principles, amongst *Deficients,* and as we have named *Astronomy* grounded upon natural reasons, *Living Astronomy,* so we think fit to call *A-
strology* ascertain'd upon the same reasons, *Sound Astrology.* As for the
right way how to frame and make this Art, although what we have
said, doth not a little conduce thereto, yet according to our manner,
we will add a few more observations which shall clearly propound, out
of what materials it should be collected, and to what end it should be
referred.

§ *First, let the knowledge touching the Commixtures of Beams be receiv'd into sound Astrology,* that is of Conjunctions, and of Oppositions,
and the rest of the constellations, or Aspects of Planets, one on another. *Also we assign* to this part concerning the Commixtures of Beams,
the passing of the Planets through the signs of the Zodiack, and Posi-
tion under the same signs : For the location of a Planet under any sign,
is a kind of Conjunction of the same Planet with the Stars of the signs :
Moreover as Conjunctions, so likewise Oppositions and other Constellations of Planets towards the Stars of the signs, are to be noted, which
hitherto hath not perfectly been accomplisht. *But the interchangeable
Commixtures* of the Rays of the fixt stars, are indeed profitable to the
Contemplation of the Fabrick of the world ; and of the Nature of the
Regions lying under them ; but not unto *Predictions,* because these As-
pects are ever the same.

§ *Secondly, let there be taken into Astrology the Accessions of every particular Planet nearer to the Perpendicular, and Recessions from it, according to the Climates of Regions.* For all the Planets as well as the Sun,
have their Summers, their Winters; wherein they dart down more forcible, or more feeble rays, according to their Posture in respect of the *Perpendicular.* For without question, *the Moon in Leo* works more forcibly upon natural bodies here below, than when she is in *Pisces :* Not
because the *Moon* placed in *Leo,* hath reference to the Heart, and under
Pisces respects the Feet, (as the vulgar Fable goes) ; for their Elevation towards the Perpendicular and Approximation towards the greater
Stars, just after the same manner as the *Sun.*

§ *Thirdly, let the Apogæa, and Perigæa of the Planets be received with*
                                                                    due

*due inquiry, to what the vigor of a Planet appertains in respect of himself;
and to what in his vicinity to us.* For a Planet in his *Apogæa,* or exaltation is more chearful and active; but in his *Perigæa* or declension more
communicative. " *So the Sun* in his Elevation, when he enters the
" Tropick of *Cancer,* is in heat more recollected and vigorous; but
" when he falls off from the Meridian, as in *Capricorn,* he is more faint,
" yet more dispersed in his influence. For in his Ascension, he is not only
" nearer to the fixed Stars; but his beams then falling at more equal
" and right angles; become more united; and by a direct resultance
" from the earth intermix, and so reduplicate their force; whereas in
" his declension, they are oblique, and therefore feeble and errant in
" reflection. Wherefore with the Inhabitants under the Equator, the
" heat is more intense; than it is with Northern Confiners, where the
" Sun daily keeps his circuit near about the Horizon: But yet in this
" Perigean motion, the Suns beams are more communicative, though
" less active; because departing from the point of their incidence in the
" rebound, their reflection is oblique and dispersed. This enquiry
" touching the projection of beams in a right or oblique line, would
" be made with diligence, for it concerns all the influences of the hea-.
" vens upon terrene bodies; the general constitution of the year; the
" divers temperatures of the air in the five Zones; the complexion of
" different Climates and the like.

§ Fourthly, to be brief, *let there be taken in all the remaining Accidents of the motion of Planets; as what are the Accelerations, Retarda-
tions, Progresses, Stations, Retrogradations,* of every one of them in
their course, what their distance from the *Sun,* their *Combustions, Encrease,* and *Diminutions of Light, Eclipses,* and whatsoever else of this
nature. For all these cause, that the *Beams* of the *Planets* do work
more strongly, or more weakly, and after divers ways and distinct
virtues: And these four observations, belong to the Radiations of
Star.

§ Fifthly, let there be received in, whatsoever may any way, open
and disclose the natures of Stars *Errant* or *Fixt,* in their proper essence and activity; as what is their *Magnitude;* of what *colour* and *a-
spect;* what *Scintillation* and *Vibration* of light; what *Situation* towards the *Poles* or *Æquinoctial;* what *Asterisms;* which are more *mingled*
with other Stars; which are more *solitary;* which are *superiour,* which
inferiour; which of the fixt Stars are within the line and course of the
Sun and Planets (namely within the Zodiack) which without; which
of the Planets is *more swift;* which *more slow;* which may *move in
the Ecliptick line;* which may *expatiate in latitude* from it; what Planet may be *retrograde, which not;* what Planet may be at any distance
from the Sun, which is tyed to attend the Sun; which moves swifter in
Apogéo, which in *Perigéo;* to conclude the Irregularities of *Mars;* the
expatiations of *Venus,* the wonderful Labours or Passions, which are
often found in the *Sun,* and in *Venus,* and the like?

§ Last of all, let there be taken into *Astrologie,* even from tradition the particular Natures, and Inclination of Planets, as also of fixt
Stars; which seeing they are delivered over with such an universal consent, they are not lightly to be rejected; but where they cross the
grounds and reasons of natural Principles. And of such observations

as

as these, *found Astrologie* is compiled; and according to these only, should Schemes and configurations of Heaven, be composed and interpreted. *Sound Astrologie* is likewise applied and referred with more confidence to *Predictions*; to *Elections*, with more *Caution*, within due limits to both. *Predictions* may be made of future *Comets*, which as we conjecture may be foretold; and of all sorts of Meteors; of Deluges; Droughts, Heats, Conglaciations, Earth-quakes, overflowing of Waters; breaking out of Fires, Winds, great Rains, divers Tempests, and strange seasons of the Year; Pestilences, Epidemical diseases; Plenty and dearth of Grain; Wars, Seditions, Sects, Plantations of new Colonies: lastly, of all Commotions and greater Innovations, either in *Nature*, or in *State-Government*: so these predictions may be drawn down (though not with like certainty) to more *special occurrences*, and perchance to *singularities*; if the general inclinations of such times and seasons, being first discovered and found out, these be applied by a sharp piercing judgement Philosophical or Political, to special or more particular events, which may be most subject to such *Accidents*. As for example, a man shall find out from a fore-sight of the seasons of the year, such temperatures of Weather, as are propitious or pernitious rather to Olives, than to Vines; rather to *Phthisicks*, and ulcerations of Lungs, than to *Hepaticks* and obstructions of the Liver; more to the inhabitants of high and mountainous, than low and champain Countries; more to Monks than Courtiers, by reason of their different kind of diet: Or if one from the knowledge he hath of the influence, the Heavens have over the spirits of men, should find out a man to be of such a complexion and disposition; to affect or distast rather the people than Princes; rather learned and curious, than couragious and warlike dispositions; rather sensual and voluptuous, than active and politick natures. Such instances as these are infinite, but (as we have said) they require not only that general knowledge, taken from the Stars, which are active; but also a particular knowledge of Subjects which are Passive. Nor are *Elections* altogether to be rejected, but more sparingly to be credited, than *Predictions*. For we see in Planting, and in Sowing, and in Grafting, that the observation of the *age* of the *Moon* is a matter, not altogether vain and frivolous. But these *Elections*, are by our rules more restrained than *Predictions*: and this must ever be observed, that *Elections* are of force, in such cases alone, where both the *Influx* of the Heavens is such, as doth not suddenly pass over; and likewise the *Action* of *inferiour Bodies* such, as is not presently perfected: for neither the *Encreases* of the *Moon*, nor of the Planets are accomplisht in an instant: but *punctuality* of time, is by all means to be rejected. There are found many of the like precise observations (which a man would hardly believe) in *Elections* about Civil affairs. But if any man in this case shall except against us, saying, that we have indeed made some remonstrance out of what this *reformed Astrologie* should be deduced; and likewise to what it may with profit be referred: but the manner how it is to be deduced, we have given no precept at all; he should not deal equally with us, to exact at our hands the Art it self, which we never promised, or purposed to handle. Yet notwithstanding touching such a point of Demand, thus much we will admonish; that there are only four means, which may prepare the way

N

to this knowledge. *Firſt, by Experiments future, then by Experiments paſt :* Again, *by Tradition* ; laſt of all, *by natural Reaſons. Now for future Experiments,* to what end ſhould we ſpeak much of them ? ſeeing to make up a competent number of Inſtances, ſo many ages are requiſite, as it were, but loſt labour, to think to comprehend it ? *As for Experiments paſt,* they indeed are within the compaſs and reach of men, although it is a matter will require much labour, and much leiſure to accompliſh. For *Aſtrologians* (if they be not wanting to their Profeſſion) may make a collection from the faithful reports of Hiſtory, of all greater contigences ; as *Inundations, Peſtilences, Wars, Seditions,* and (if the ſtate ſo require) *the deaths of Kings :* and may contemplate the *ſituation of the Heavens,* not according to the ſubtilty of *Figures* ; but according to thoſe general rules which we have already ſet down, to know in what poſtures the Heavens were, at thoſe times, when ſuch effects came to paſs ; that ſo where there is a clear, and evident conſent, and concurrence of events ; there a probable rule of *Prediction* may be inferred. *As for Traditions,* they ought to be ſo examined and ſifted, that ſuch as manifeſtly oppugn *Phyſical Reaſons,* ſhould be diſcarded ; but ſuch as well conſent, ſhould be valid even of their own authority. *Laſtly, as for Phyſical or Natural reaſons,* they are the apteſt for this inquiry ; which make inquiry of the Catholick, and more univerſal inclinations and Paſſions of Matter, and of the ſimple and genuine motions of Bodies ; for by theſe wings we ſafely ſoar and mount up to thoſe celeſtial materiare ſubſtances. Thus much concerning *Aſtrologia ſana.*

§ *There is another Portion of Aſtrological Frenzie* (beſides thoſe figments which we have noted at the beginning) which is wont to be ſeperate from *Aſtrologie,* and to be transferred into *Celeſtial Magick,* as they call it. This hath purchaſed a ſtrange Gloſs, from the working fancie of mans wit ; namely, *That a benevolent ſituation or aſpect of Stars, may be taken in ſeals and ſignet-rings (be it of Metals, or of any Gemms, capable of ſuch impreſſion) which may arreſt the felicity of that hour, which otherwiſe would ſwiftly paſs away, and as it were, fix it, being volatilous.* As the Poet paſſionately complains of this ſo noble Art, among the Ancients, now long ago buried in oblivion.

C. Agrip. de Occult. Ph.1.

N.L.

> *Annulus infuſo non vivit mirus Olympo,*
> *Non magis ingentes humili ſub lumine Phœbos*
> *Fert Gemma, aut Celſo divulſas cardine lunas.*

Indeed the Church of *Rome* hath imbraced the *Reliques of Saints,* and their virtues, (for in Divine and immateriate things, the flux of time hath no power to abate the force and efficacy) but that the *Reliques of Heaven* ſhould be ſo lodged, as that the hour which is paſt, and, as it were, dead, ſhould revive and be continued ; is a meer ſuperſtition, and impoſture. Wherefore let us let go theſe idle fancies, unleſs the Muſes be grown doting old Wives.

IV. *Abſtract Phyſick in our judgement, may very well be divided into two Parts, into the Doctrine of the Schemes of Matter ; and into the doctrine of Appetites or Motions.* We will run them both over briefly, from whence the delineations of the true Phyſick of Abſtracts may be

drawn

drawn.   The *Schemes of Matter* are ; *Denfe, Rare* ; *Grave, Light* ; *Hot, Cold* ; *Tangible, Pneumatick* ; *Volatile, Fixt* ; *Determinate, Fluid* ; *Humid, Dry* ; *Fat, Crude* ; *Hard, Soft* ; *Fragile, Tenfile* ; *Porous, United* ; *Spirituous, Languid* ; *Simple, Compofite* ; *Abfolute, imperfectly Mixt* ; *Fibrous and full of veins, of a fimple Pofiture or equal* ; *Similar, Diffimilar* ; *Specificate, Non-fpecificate* ; *Organical, Inorganical* ; *Animate, Inanimate.* Neither do we extend the figurations of Matter any farther, for *Senfible and Infenfible* ; *Rational and Irrational,* we refer to the knowledge of Man.

§ *Appetites and Motions,* are of two forts ; either *motions fimple,* which contain in them the Roots of all natural Actions ; but yet according to the *Schemes and habitudes of Matter :* or *Motions compofited and produced* ; from which laft, the received Philofophy of the Times (which comprehends little of the Body of Nature) takes its beginning. But fuch *Compound Motions* (as *Generation Corruption,* aud the reft) fhould be taken for the *fumms* and *products* of fimple Motions ; rather than for *Primitive Motions. Motions fimple,* are Motions of *Antitypie,* commonly called *Motion oppofing Penetration* of Dimenfions ; *Motion of Connexion, or Continuity,* which they call, Motion to avoid vacuity ; *Motion of Liberty,* left there fhould be any compreffion or extenfion preternatural ; *Motion into a new fphere,* or to Rarefaction and Condenfation ; *Motion of a fecond connexion,* or a motion left there fhould be a folution of continuity ; *Motion of greater Congregation,* or to the Mafs of their connaturals, which is commonly called Natural Motion ; *Motion of leffer Congregation,* ufually ftiled, Motion of Sympathy and of Antipathy ; *Motion Difponent,* or that parts may be rightly placed in the whole ; *Motion of Affimilation,* or of Multiplication of its Nature upon another ; *Motion of Excitation,* where the more noble and vigorous agent awaketh, and ftirs up Motion latent and dormant in another ; *Motion of the Seal or of Impreffion,* that is, Operation without Communication of Subftance ; *Motion Regal,* or a Cohibition of other Motions from a Motion Predominant ; *Motion without Termination,* or Spontaneous Rotation ; *Motion of Trepidation,* or of Contraction and Dilatation of Bodies placed betwixt things good for them, and obnoxious to them ; *laftly, Motion of Reft or abhorrency of Motion,* which is the Caufe of many things.   Of this kind are *fimple Motions* which truly iffue forth out of the inward bowels of Nature ; which complicate, continuate, interchang'd repreff'd, repeated, and many ways aggregated, do conftitute thofe *Compofite Motions* or *Summs* of Motions, which are receiv'd, and fuch other of the fame kind.   *The Summs of Motions* are thofe Celebrated Motions, *Generation, Corruption, Augmentation, Diminution, Alteration and Lation, fo Mixtion, Separation, Verfion.*

§ *There remains only as Appendices of Phyfick, the Meafures of Motions* ; of what efficacy the *Quantity,* or Dofe of Nature is ? *What diftance* can do, which is called, not unproperly, the orb of Virtue or Activity ? *What incitation, or Tardity,* can effect ? *What a long or fhort delay ?* *What the force or rebatement* of a thing ? *What the inftigation of Periftafie* or circumambient inclofure ?   And thefe are the natural and genuine Parts of true natural Philofophy, touching *Abftracts.* For in the *figurations, or Schemes of Matter* ; *in Motions fimple* ; *In fumms or Aggre-*

gations of Motions; *and in Measures of Motions, the Physick of Abstracts is accomplisht.* As for voluntary Motion in Animals; Motion in the Actions of Senses; *Motion of the Imagination*; *of the Appetite,* and of *the will*; *Motion of the mind*; *of the discerning faculty,* or Practick Judgement;and of the *Intellectuals,*we refer over to their proper Knowledges. *Yet thus much again* we advertise, that all these Particulars we have delivered, are no farther to be handled in *Physick,* than the enquiry of their *Matter* and *Efficient*; for according to their Forms and Ends they are revised and re-examined in *Metaphysick.*

V. *We will here annex two notable Appendices,* which have reference not so much to the Matter, as to the Manner of Inquiry; *Natural Problems*; *and Placits of Ancient Philosophers.* The first is the *Appendix of multiplied or sparsed Nature*; the second *of Nature united or of summs.* Both these belong to a grave and circumspect *moving of doubts,* which is no mean part of Knowledge : For *Problems* comprehend *particular Dubitations*; *Placits,* general; about *Principles* and the *Fabrick.* Of *Problems* there is an excellent example in the writing of *Ari-*
stole; which kind of work certainly deserv'd not only to have been celebrated by Posterity; but by their labours to have been continued; seeing new *doubts* arise daily. But in this point Caution is to be taken, and that of great Importance. The recording and proposing of *Doubts* hath in it a two-fold use : *One,* that it munites and fortifies Philosophy against errors; when that which is not altogether so clear and evident is not defin'd and avouched, (left error should beget error)but a judgement upon it is suspended, and is not definitive. *The other,* that the entry of *Doubts,*and recording of them,are so many Sponges which continually suck and draw in unto them an increase and improvement of Knowledge; whereby it comes to pass that those things, which without the suggestion of Doubts•had been slightly, and without observation passed over,are by occasion of such *Dubitations,*more seriously and attentively considered. But these two utilities scarce recompence one discommodity, which unless it be carefully lookt unto, insinuateth it self; namely, *That a doubt once acknowledged as justly made, and become, as it were, authentick*; *presently stirs up defendants both ways*; *who in like manner commend over the same liberty of doubting to Posterity*; *so that men bend and apply their wits, rather to keep a doubt still on foot, than to determine and solve it.* Instances of this case we have every where, both in Jurisconsults; and in Students in the Universities; who if they have once entertain'd a *Doubt,* it goes ever after authoriz'd for a *Doubt,* assuming unto themselves a priviledge, as well of *Dubitation,* as of *Assertion* : *Whereas the right use of Reason is, to make things doubtful certain*; *and not to call things certain, into doubt* : *Wherefore I report as Deficient a Calendar of Dubitations,* or *Problems* in Nature, and approve the undertaking of such a work, as a profitable pains; so care be had, that as knowledge daily grows up, (which certainly will come to pass, if men hearken unto us) such *Doubts* as be clearly discust, aud brought to resolution, be rased out of the *Catalogue of Problems.* To this *Calendar,* I would have another annext no less useful : *For seeing that in all Enquiries, there be found these three sorts of things*; *things manifestly true*; *Doubtful*; *manifestly false* : It would be a very profitable course to adjoyn to the *Calendar of Doubts,* and *Non-liquets*; a *Calender of Falshoods,*
and

Aristot. Probl.

and of *popular Errors*, now paſſing unargued in Natural Hiſtory, and
in Opinions ; that Sciences be no longer diſtemper'd and embaſed by
them.

§ *As for the Placits of Ancient Philoſophers*, as were thoſe of *Pythago-*
ras, Philolaus, Xenophon, Anaxagoras, Parmenides, Leucippus, Demo-
critus, and others, (which men uſe diſdainfully to run over *)* it will not
be amiſs to caſt our eyes with more reverence upon them. *For al-*
though Ariſtotle,after the manner of the race of the Ottomans, thought he   Ariſtot,
could not ſafely reign , unleſs he made away all his Brethren ; yet to thoſe
who ſeriouſly propound to themſelves the inquiſition and illuſtration
of *Truth*, and not *Dominion* or *Magiſtrality*, it cannot but ſeem a matter of great profit, to ſee at once before them, the ſeveral opinions of
ſeveral Authors touching the Natures of things. Neither is this for a-
ny great hope conceiv'd,that a more exact truth can any way be expected from theſe or from the like Theories.For as the ſame *Phænomena*;the
ſame *Calculations* are ſatisfied upon the Aſtronomical Principles both of
Ptolomy and *Copernicus :* So the popular experience we embrace ; and
the ordinary view and face of things, may apply it ſelf to many ſeveral Theories ; whereas a right inveſtigation of truth requires another
manner of ſeverity and ſpeculation. For as *Ariſtotle* ſaith elegantly,   Phyſ.1
That Children at firſt indeed call all men Fathers, and women Mothers,
but afterwards they diſtinguiſh them both : So certainly experience in
Childhood, will call every *Philoſophy, Mother* ; but when it comes to
ripeneſs, it will diſcern the true Mother. In the mean time it is good
to read over divers *Philoſophies*, as divers Gloſſes upon Nature ; whereof, it may be,one in one place ; another in another , is more corrected. Therefore I could wiſh a collection made, but with diligence and   De Anti-
judgment, *De Antiquis Philoſophiis*, out of the lives of Ancient Philo-   quis Phi-
ſophers ; out of the Parcels of *Plutarch* of their *Placits* ; out of the Ci-   loſophiis,
tations of *Plato* ; out of the Confutations of *Ariſtotle* ; out of a ſparſed
mention found in other Books as well of Chriſtians, as of Heathens, (as
out of *Lactantius, Philo, Philoſtratus*, and the reſt) : *For I do not yet*
ſee extant a work of this Nature. But here I muſt give warning,that this
be done diſtinctly, ſo as the *Philoſophies*, every one ſeverdly, be compoſed and continued,and not collected by titles and handfuls, as hath
been done by *Plutarch. For every Philoſophy while it is entire in the*
whole piece, ſupports it ſelf ; *and the opinions maintained therein give*
light, ſtrength, and credence mutually one to the other ; *whereas if they*
be ſimple and broken, it will ſound more ſtrange and diſſonant. In truth
when I read in *Tacitus* the Actions of *Nero*, or of *Claudius* inveſted   Tacit;
with Circumſtances of Times, Perſons, and inducements : I find them
not ſo ſtrange, but they may be true : but when I read the ſame Actions in *Suetonius Tranquillus*, repreſented by titles and common places,
and not in order of Time, they ſeem monſtrous and altogether incre-   Sueton;
dible : *So is Philoſophy when it is propounded entire* ; *and when it is ſli-*
ced and articled into fragments. Neither do I exclude out of this *Ca-*
lendar of the Placits, or Sects of Philoſophy, the Theories and opinions
of later times, as that of *Theophraſtus Paracelſus* eloquently reduced into a body and Harmony of Philoſophy by *Severinus* the Dane, or of
Teleſius of Coſenze, who reviving the Philoſophy of *Parmenides* hath
turn'd the weapons of the Peripateticks upon themſelves, or of *Patri-*
cius

cius the *Venetian* ; who hath sublimated the fumes of the *Platonists* ; or of *Gilbert* our Countryman, who hath restored to light the opinions of *Philolaus* ; or of any other whatsoever, if he be of merit. And because the volumes of these Authors are wholly extant, there may be abridgements made only of them, and so annext, by way of reference to the rest. And thus much of *Natural Philosophy*, and the *Appendices* thereof.

VI. *As for* *Metaphysick*, *we have assigned unto it, the inquiry of* Formal *and* Final *causes* ; *which application, as to* Forms, *may seem to be nugatory and void.* For an opinion hath prevailed ; and is grown inveterate, that the *essential Forms* and *true Differences* of things, can by no diligence of Man be found out. Which opinion in the mean, gives and grants us thus much ; that the *Invention of Forms*, is of all other parts of knowledge the worthiest to be sought ; if it be possible they may be found. And as for Possibility of Invention, there are some fainthearted discoverers ; who when they see nothing but Air and Water, think there is no farther Land. But it is manifest that *Plato*, a man of an elevated wit, and who beheld all things as from a high cliff, in his doctrine of Ideas, did descry, *that forms were the true object of knowledge, however he lost the real fruit of this most true opinion, by contemplating and apprehending* Forms, *as absolutely abstract from matters ; and not confined and determined by matter : whereupon it came to pass that he turned himself to Theological speculations, which infected and distained all his Natural Philosophy.* But if we keep a watchful, and a severe eye upon Action and Use, it will not be difficult, to trace and find out what are the *Forms* ; the disclosure whereof would wonderfully enrich and make happy the estate of man. *For the Forms of substances,* (man only except, of whom it is said, *Formavit hominem de limo terræ, & spiravit in faciem ejus spiraculum vitæ* ; not as of all other kinds, *Producat aqua, producat terra*) I say the species of creatures, as they are now multiplied by compounding and transplanting, are so perplext and complicate, as it is either altogether lost labour to make enquiry of them, or the inquisition thereof, such as as may be had, should be suspended for a time, and when the *Forms* of nature, in her more simple existence are rightly sought and found out, then to be determin'd and set down. For, as it were not a thing easie, nor any way useful, *to seek the Form of that sound, which makes a word* ; being that words through composition, and transposition of letters are infinite : *but to enquire the Form of sound, which expresseth some simple letter* (namely with what collision, with what application of the instruments of voice it is made) is a thing comprehensible and easie ; *which form of letters once known, presently leads us to the form of words.* In the same manner to enquire the form of a Lyon, of an Oak, of Gold, nay of Water, of Air, is a vain pursuit ; but to enquire the *Forms* of *Dense, Rare* ; *Hot, Cold* ; *Heavy, Light* ; *Tangible, Pneumatick* ; *Volatile, Fixt* ; and the like, both of *Figurations* and of *Motions* ; whereof the most of them we have enumerated when we handled *Physick*, and are wont to call them, *Forms of the first rank or order* ; and which (as the letters of the Alphabet) are not so many in number, and yet build up and support the *Essences and Forms* of all substances. And this is that very point, which we aim at, and endeavour to compass ; and which constitutes and defines that part
of

Forma. Rerum.
In Timeo alibi.
Gen.2.
Gen.i.

of *Mataphysick*, whereof we now enquire. Not doth this so prejudicate or hinder, but that *Physick* may consider the same Natures also (as hath been said) bnt only according to the fluid and mutable causes. *For example*, if the cause of *whiteneß in Snow* or *in Froth* be enquired, it is well rendred, *that it is the subtile intermixture of Air with water.* But this is far from being the *Form of whiteneß*; being that Air intermixt with the dust, or powder of Glaß, or Chrystal, doth likewise produce *whiteneß*, as well as if it were mingled with water; but this is the efficient cause only, which is no other than *vehiculum Formæ.* But if the enquiry be made in *Metaphysick*, you shall find some such rule as this, *That two diaphanous bodies being intermixt, their optick Portions in a simple order, or equally placed, do determine and constitute whiteneß.* This part of *Metaphysick I find deficient :* and no marvail, because by the course of enquiring, which hitherto hath been practised, the *Forms of things* will never appear, while the world endures. *The root of this error, as of all other, is this ; that men in their contemplations of nature are accustomed to make too timely a departure, and too remote a receß from experience and particulars ; and have yielded and resigned themselves wholly over to the fumes of their own fancies, and popular Argumentations.* But the use of this part of *Mntaphysick*, which I report as deficient, is of the rest the most excellent in two respects.

§ *First*, because it is the duty and peculiar virtue of all Sciences, to abridge (as much as the conception of truth will permit) the ambages and long circuits of Experience, and so to apply a remedy to the ancient complaint of *vita brevis, ars longa.* And this is excellently perfor-   Hipp. med, *by collecting and uniting the Axioms of Sciences, into more general   Aphor. heads and conceptions ;* which may be agreeable to all Individuals. For *Sciences, are the Pyramids supported by History ; and Experience as their only and true Basis ; and so the Basis of Natural Philosophy is Natural History ; the stage next the Basis is Phisick ; the stage next the vertical point is Metaphysick :* as for the *Cone* and *vertical point* it self (*opus quod ope-   Eccles. 3 ratur Deus à principio usque ad finem;* the *summary law of Nature*) we do justly doubt, whether mans enquiry can attain unto it. But these three be the true *stages of Sciences ;* and are, to men swelled up with their own knowledge, and a daring insolence, to invade Heaven, like the three hills of the *Giants.*

Ter sunt Conati imponere Pelion Oßæ,   Virg.
Scilicet atque Oßæ frondosum involvere Olympum.   Geor. 1.

But to those that disabling themselves, and discharging their pride, refer all to the glory of God, they are the three acclamations, *Sancte,*   Apoc. 4. *Sancte, Sancte :* for *God is holy in the multitude of his works, Holy in the   In Parm. order of them, Holy in the union.* And therefore the speculation was excellent in *Parmenides* and *Plato;* although but a speculation in them, *That all things by scales did ascend to unity.* So then, that science is the worthiest, which least chargeth mans understanding with multiplicity ; and it is evident, that that is *Metaphysick,* as that which principally speculates those *simple Forms of things ;* (which we have stiled *Forms of the first degree* or order) which though they be few in number, yet in their Commensurations and Co-ordinations, they make all kinds of variety.
§ *The*

§ *The Second* respect which enobles this part of *Metaphysick* touching *Forms*, is, that of all other sciences, it doth most enfranchise, and set at liberty the Power of Man; and brings it forth into a most ample and open field to exercise in. For *Physick* directs mans labour and diligence through narrow and restrained ways, imitating the flexious courses of ordinary Nature; But *latæ undique sapientibus viæ,* to *sapience* (which was anciently defined to be, *Rerum divinarum & humanarum scientia*) there is ever copy and variety of means. For Physicall causes give light and occasion to new inventions in *simili materia*; but whosoever knows any *Form*, knows also the *utmost possibility of superinducing that nature upon any variety of matter*; and so is less restrained and tied in operation, either to the Basis of the *matter*, or to the condition of the *Efficient*; which kind of knowledge, though in a more divine sence, *Solomon* elegantly describes, *Non arctabuntur gressus tui, et Currens non habebis offendiculum*; his meaning is, that the ways of *sapience*, are not liable to streights, nor perplexities.

Plat. in Phæd. Cic. de Fin. 2. Tusc. 4.

Prov. IV.

§ *The second part of Metaphysick,* is the enquiry of *Final Causes*; which we note not as omitted, but as misplaced: for the enquiry of them usually is made amongst the *Physicks,* and not in the *Metaphysicks.* And yet if this were a fault in *order* only, I should not much stand upon it; for *order* is a matter of Illustration, and pertains not to the substance of *Sciences:* but this inversion of *order,* hath caused a notable *deficience,* and brought a great decay upon Philosophy. For the handling of *Final Causes* in the *Physicks,* hath intercepted, and banisht the enquiry of *Physical Causes*; and hath given men occasion to rest satisfied in such specious, and umbratilous Causes; and not thorowly to urge and press the enquiry of *real and truly Physical Causes.* For this I find done not only by *Plato,* who ever Ancreth upon that Shore; but also by *Aristotle*; *Galen,* and others, who usually likewise fall upon these Flats. For to say, *That the eye-lids furnisht with hairs are for a quick-set and fence to fortifie the the sight: or that the firmness of skins, and hides of living Creatures, is to repel the extremities of heat and cold: or that Bones are ordained by Nature for Columns and Beams whereupon the frame of the Body is to be built: or that Trees shoot forth leaves to shadow and protect the fruit from the Sun and the wind: or that the Clouds are ingendred above, to water the earth below: or that the Earth is close, compact and solid, that it may be a Station and Mansion for living Creatures*; is properly enquired in *Metaphysick*; but in *Physick* they are impertinent. Nay, (to pursue this point) *such discoursing Causes as these, like the Remoraes (as the fiction goes) adhering to ships, stay and stug the sayling, and the Progress of Sciences, that they could not hold on their Course, and advance forward to further Discoveries: And now long ago it is so brought to pass, that the search of Physical Causes, thus neglected, are decayed and passed over in silence.* And therefore the *Natural Philosophy* of *Democritus,* and some others, who removed God and a Mind from the frame of things; and attributed the structure of the world to infinite Preludiums, and Essays (which by one name they term'd *Fate* or *Fortune*; and have assigned the Causes of Particulars to the necessity of Matter, without intermixture of *Final Causes*) seemeth to us (so far as we can conjecture from the Fragments and Remains of their Philosophy) in respect of *Physical Causes,* to have been far more solid, and to have penetrated more profoundly into Nature;

Arist. Probl.

than

than that of *Aristotle* and *Plato* for this reason alone, *that those Ancient Philosophers never wasted time in final Causes; but these perpetually press and inculcate them.*   And in this point *Aristotle* is more to blame than *Plato,* seeing he hath omitted the fountain of all final Causes, *God* ; and in the place of *God* substituted Nature ; and hath imbraced *final Causes* rather as a lover of *Logick,* than an adorer of Divinity.   Nor do we therefore speak thus much, because those *final Causes* are not true, and very worthy the enquiry in *Metaphysick Speculations* ; but because, while they sally out, and break in upon the Possessions of *Physical Causes,* they do unhappily depopulate and waste that Province: For otherwise, if they keep themselves within their precincts and borders, they are extremely deceiv'd, who ever think that there is an enmity or repugnancy between *them* and *Physical Causes.*   For the cause render'd, *That the hairs about the eye-lids, are for the safe-gard of the sight,* doth not indeed impugn that other Cause ;   *That pilositie is incident to Orifices of Moisture,*

Muscosi Fontes, &c.———

Virg. Buc.

Nor the Cause render'd, *that the firmness of Hides is in Beasts for armor against the injuries of extreme weather,* doth impugn that other Cause; *That that firmness is caused by the contraction of pores in the outward parts of the body through cold, and depredation of Air* ; and so of the rest : both causes excellently conspiring, save that, the one declares an intention, the other a consequence only : Neither doth this call in question, or derogate from divine *Providence* ; but rather wonderfully confirms and exalts it.   For *as in* Civil Actions, that Politick wisdom will be more deep, and admired, if a man can use the service of other men to his own ends and desires ; and yet never acquaint them with his purpose (so as they shall do what he would they should do, and yet not understand what they do) ; then if he should impart his counsels to those he imploys : So the wisdom of God shines more wonderfully, when Nature intends one thing, and *Providence* draws forth another ; then if the Characters of Divine *Providence* were imprest upon every particular habitude and motion of Nature.   Surely *Aristotle,* after he swelled up Nature with *Final Causes* ; *Naturam nihil frustra facere* ; *suique voti semper esse compotem* (*si impedimenta abessent*) ; and had set down many such tending to that purpose ; *had no farther need of God :* But *Democritus* and *Epicurus,* when they publisht and celebrated their *Atoms* ; were thus far by the more subtile wits listned unto with Patience : but when they would avouch, that the Fabrick and Contexture of all things in Nature, knit and united it self without a *Mind,* from a fortuitous Concourse of those *Atoms,* they were entertain'd with laughter by all.   So that *Physical Causes* are so far from withdrawing mens minds from *God* and *Providence* ; as rather contrariwise those Philosophers which were most exercised in contriving those Atoms, found no end and issue of their travail, until they had resolved all at last into *God* and *Providence.* Thus much of *Metaphysick,* a part whereof touching *Final Causes* I deny not to have been handled both in the Physicks and Metaphysicks ; in these truly, in those improperly ; for the inconvenience hath ensued thereupon.

De Cœlo,
lib. 1, &
lib. de
part. a.
nimal.

CHAP. V.

I. The Partition of the Operative Knowledge of Nature into *Mechanick and Magick* : Respondent to the parts of Speculative Knowledge ; *Mechanick to Physick* ; *Magick to Metaphysick.* § A purging of the word *Magia.* II. Two Appendices to Operative Knowledge, *An Inventary of the Estate of man. A Catalogue of Polychrests, or things of multifarious use.*

I. THE *Operative knowledge of Nature,* we will likewise divide into two Parts ; and that from a kind of Necessity. For this *Division* is subordinate to the former *Division of Speculative Knowledge* ; for *Physick, and the Enquiry of Efficient and Material Causes , produces Mechanick : but Metaphysick, and the enquiry of Forms produces Magick :* As for Final Causes, the enquiry is barren , and as a Virgin consecrate to *God brings forth nothing.* Nor are we ignorant that there is a *Mechanical Knowledge,* which is meerly *emperical,* and *operary,* not depending on *Physick* ; but this we have referr'd to *Natural History,* and separate it from *Natural Philosophy :* Speaking here only of that *Mechanical* Knowledge which is connext with *Causes Physical.* But yet there falls out a certain *Mechanical,* or experimental Knowledge which neither is altogether *Operative,* nor yet properly teaches so high as speculative *Philosophy :* For all the Inventions of Operations which have come to mens Knowledge , either have fallen out by casual incidence ; and afterwards deliver'd from hand to hand, or were sought by a purposed experiment. Those which have been found out by intentional experiment, they have been disclosed either by the light of *Causes,* and *Axioms* ; or found out by extending, or transferring, or compounding former inventions ; which is a matter more sagacious and witty, than Philosophical. And this part which by no means we despise, we shall briefly touch hereafter, when we shall treat of *Literate experience* amongst the parts of *Logick.* As for the *Mechanick* now in hand, *Aristotle* hath handled it promiscuously ; *Hero in spiritalibus* ; as likewise *Georgius Agricola* a modern Writer, very diligently in his *Minerals* ; and many others in particular Treatises on that subject ; so as I have nothing to say of *Deficients* in this kind ; but that the *promiscuous Mechanicals* of Aristotle, ought to have been with more diligence continued, by the pens of recent Writers ; especially with choice of such experimentals, of which either the Causes are more obscure, or the Effects more noble. But they who insist upon these, do, as it were, only coast along the shoar, *Premendo littus iniquum.* For in my judgement there can hardly be any radical alteration, or novation in Nature ; either by any fortuitous adventures ; or by essays of Experiments ; or from the light of Physical Causes ; but only through the invention of *Forms.* Therefore if we have set down that part of *Metaphysick* as *Deficient,* which entreateth of *Forms* ; it follows that *Natural Magick* also, which is a Relative unto it, is likewise *Defective.*

§ But

§ But it feems requifite in this place that the word *Magia*, accepted for a long in the worfe part, be reftored to the ancient and honourable fence. *Magia amongft the Perfians*, was taken for a fapience, and a Science of the harmony and contents of univerfals in Nature ; fo thofe three *Eaftern Kings* which came to adore *Chrift*, are ftiled by the name of *Magi:* and we underftand it in that fence, as to be, *a Science which deduceth the knowledge of hidden forms to ftrange and wonderful effects and operations ; and as it is commonly faid, by joyning Actives with Paffives, which difclofeth the great wonders of Nature.* As for the *Natural Magick*, (which flies abroad in many mens books) containing certain credulous and fuperftitious traditions, and obfervations of *Sympathies, and Antipathies*, and of hidden and fpecifick proprieties, with fome experiments commonly frivilous ; ftrange, rather for the art of conveyance and difguifement, than the thing it felf ; furely he fhall not much err, who fhall fay, that this kind of Magick, is as far differing in truth of Nature, from fuch a knowledge as we require ; as the Books of the Gefts of *Arthur* of *Britain*, or of *Hugh* of *Burdeaux*, differs from *Cæfars* Commentaries in truth of ftory. For it is manifeft, that *Cæfar* did greater things *de vero*, than they durft feign of their *Heroes* ; but he did them not in that fabulous manner. *Of this kind of Learning, the Fable of* Ixion *was a figure* ; who projecting with himfelf to enjoy *Juno* the Goddefs of Power, had copulation with a *cloud*, of which he begot *Centaurs* and *Chimeræs*. So whoever are carried away with a frantick and impotent paffion, and vaporous conceit to thofe things, which only, through the fames and clouds of Imagination, they fancy to themfelves to fee, in ftead of fubftantial operations ; they are delivered of nothing but airy hopes, and certain deformed and monftrous apparitions. The operation and effect of this fuperficiary, and degenerous *Natural Magick* upon Men, is like fome foporiferous drugs, which procure fleep ; and withal exhale into the fancy, merry and pleafant dreams in fleep. *Firft*, it cafts mans underftanding into a fleep, ftill chanting and fuggefting fpecifick proprieties, and fecret virtues ; and fet down, as it were, from heaven, to be delivered, and to be learned only by auricular traditions ; whence it comes to pafs, that men are no more ftirred up and awaked to fearch with diligence, and to force out the true caufes ; but fit down fatisfied with thefe frivolous and credulous opinions : and then inftills an infinite number of pleafing fictions, in the manner of dreams, and fuch as one would moft wifh to be true. And it is worth the pains to note, that in thefe Sciences, which hold fo much of *imagination* (as are that *adulterate Magick*, whereof we now fpeak, *Alchymie*, *Aftronomy*, and the like) the means and Theory are ever more monftrous, than the end and pretences. *The turning of Silver* or *Quick-filver*, or any other metal into Gold, as a hard thing to believe : yet it is a thing far more probable, to a man well skilled, and experimented in the natures of weight, yellow, colour, malleable and extenfible ; as alfo fixt and volatile : and likewife to one who hath exactly fearcht into the firft feeds and menftruous Purgings of Minerals ; that Gold by an induftrious and curious wit, may, at laft, be produced ; than that a few grains of *Elixir*, or of the power of Production, fhould be of force ;

in a few Minutes, to turn Metals into Gold, by the activity of the same *Elixir* ; which is able to perfect Nature, and to deliver it from all impediments. *So the retarding of Age*, or the restoring of some degree of youth, doth not easily. purchase a belief : yet it is far more likely to a man that knows perfectly the nature of *Arefaction*, and the depredations of the spirits ; upon the solid parts of the body ; and hath throughly observed the nature of Assimulation, and of Alimentation ; either more perfect or more peccant ; also the nature of the Spirits and of the Flame (as it were) of the body, assigned sometimes to consume, sometimes to repair ; may by Diets, Bathings, Anointings, proper Medicines, and accommodate Motions, and the like , *prolong life* , or renew some degrees of youth, or vivacity : then that this should be effected , by a few drops or scruples of *some precious Liquor* or Quintessence. *Again, that Fates may be drawn from the Stars*, men will not suddenly, and easily assent unto ; but these, that the hour of Nativity (which oftentimes through many natural accidents, is either accelerated or differed) should govern the fortune of the whole life, or that the hour of Question is co-fatal with the thing it self which is sought, you will say are meer impostures. But such a rash impotency and intemperance, doth possess and infatuate the whole race of man ; that they do not only presume upon, and promise to themselves what is repugnant in nature to be performed ; but also, are confident that they are able to conquer even at their pleasure, and that by way of recreation, the most difficult passages of nature, without trouble or travail. *And of Magick* thus much ; the name whereof we have vindicated from reproach , and separated the true and noble kind from the base and counterfeit.

II. *Of this operative part of Nature there are two Appendices*, both of much importance. *The first is , that there be made an Inventory of the estate of Man* ; in which there should be taken and compendiously cast up, the summ of all the wealth and fortunes of men (whether they arise from the fruits and revenues of Nature, or of Art) which are now extant, and whereof men are already possest, adding such inventions, as is manifest have been in times past celebrated , but are now perisht. To this end and purpose, that he who addresseth himself to the search of new Inventions, may not be arrested in his inquest, nor waste time and study in those things which are already invented, and are now extant. *And this Inventary* will be more artificial, and more serviceable, if you add those things which in popular conceit are reputed *impossible* ; and together with them couple such inventions, as are nearest in degree to *impossibles*, and yet are extant ; that the one may set an edge on mans enquiry, the other may in a sort direct it : and that from these *Optatives*, and *Potentials*, mans *Actives* may be more readily conducted.

★
CATA-
LOGUS
POLY-
CHRE-
STO-
RUM.
§ *The second is, that there be made a Calendar of those experiments*, which are *Polychrests*, things of a multifarious use ; and most universal consequence ; and which conduce and direct to the *Invention* of other *experiments*. For example ; the artificial experiment of *conglaciation of Water by Ice with black salt*, pertains to infinite purposes and essays ; for this discloseth the secret and abstruse

ſtruſe manner of Condenſation, than which nothing is more commodious for men. *As for fire*, that is a ready and known Agent for *Rarefaction*, but the myſtery of *Condenſation*, is not yet fully diſcovered : and it makes much for the abridgement of invention, if *Polychreſts* of this nature were collected into a particular Catalogue.

CHAP. VI.

Of the great Appendix of Natural Philoſophy Speculative, *as* Operative, Mathematick knowledge ; *and that it ought rather to be placed amongſt Appendices, than amongſt ſubſtantial Sciences.* § *The Partition of* Mathematicks *into* Pure *and* Mixt.

A Riſtotle ſaith well; *Phyſick and Mathematick ingender practical or*   Metaph.1, *mechanical knowledge :* Wherefore now we have handled, both   & 12. the *ſpeculative* and *operative* part of the *knowledge of Nature* ; order requires that we ſpeak of *Mathematick*, which is an auxiliary Science to to them both. *For*, in the received Philoſophy, *Mathematick is annext, as a third part, to Phyſick and Metaphyſick*; but it ſeems to us, who have undertaken to reexamine, and Till over again theſe things, (if we had deſigned this as a ſubſtantive and principal Science) more agreeable both in reſpect of the nature of the thing, and the light of order, to place it as a branch of *Metaphyſick*. For *Quantity*, which is the ſubject of *Mathematick Science*, applied to Matter, is the Doſe, as it were, of Nature, and productive of a number of effects in things natural ; and therefore is to be reckoned in the number of *eſſential forms*. For the   Laert. in Power of *Figure and Number*, ſeemed to be of ſuch force amongſt   Dem. the Ancient Philoſophers, that *Democritus* placed the ſeeds of the variety of things, principally, in the *Figures of Atoms* ; and *Pythagoras* aſſerted, the Natures of things, to be conſtituted of *Numbers*. In   Iambl. de the mean, this is true, that of Natural *Forms*, (as we underſtand forms)   vita Pyth. *Quantity* is of all moſt abſtracted and ſeparable from Matter : which was the reaſon why it hath been more painfully laboured, and exactly inquired by men, than any other *Form* whatſoever, which are all more immerſed in Matter. For being it is the nature of Man (certainly to the great prejudice of knowledge) to delight *in the open Fields of Generals* ; rather than in the *Woods* and *Incloſures of Particulars*; there was nothing found more acceptable and delightful, than the *Mathematicks*; wherein that appetite of expatiating and meditating might be ſatisfied. *And* though all this be true, yet to us, who provide not only for truth and order, but likewiſe for the uſe and profit of men; it ſeemed at laſt better, to deſign *Mathematicks*; being they are of ſuch efficacy, both in *Phyſick*, and in *Metaphyſick*, and in *Mechanicks*, and in *Magick*, as the *Appendices* and Auxiliary Forces of them all : which in a ſort we are compelled to do for the wantonneſs and arrogancie of the *Mathematicians*, who
could

could be content, that *this Science*, might even command and over-rule *Phyfick*. For it is come to paſs, by what fate I know not, that *Mathematick* and *Logick*, which ſhould carry themſelves as hand-maids to *Phyſick*, boaſting their certainty above it, take upon them a command and Dominion. But we do not ſo much ſtand upon the rank and dignity of this Science, let us confider the thing it ſelf.

§ *Mathematicks are either Pure or Mixt*; *to Pure Mathematicks*, thoſe Sciences are referred, which handle *Quantity* altogether abſtracted from Matter, and Phyſical Axioms. *They are two, Geometry,* and *Arithmetick; the one handling Quantity continued, the other diſſe-vered.* Which two Arts have indeed been inquired into, with ſub-tilty and induſtry, but neither to the labours of *Euclid* in *Geometry,* hath there been any thing of any worth added by poſterity, in ſo many centuries of years ſince he flouriſht; nor hath the Doctrine of *Solids,* for the uſe and excellency of the knowledge, been laboured and advanced by Writers Ancient or Modern. And in *Arithmetick* there hath not been found out apt and ſufficient variety of compendious ways for *ſupputations;* eſpecially about *Progreſſions;* whereof there is great uſe in the Phyſicks. Nor is the *Algebra, or Art of Equation* well perfected; but that *Pythagorical* and *Myſtical A-rithmetick,* which is begun to be revived out of *Proclus,* and ſome Remains of *Euclid;* is a ſpacious field of ſpeculation : *For ſuch is the nature of Man, that if it be not able to comprehend ſolids, it waſtes it ſelf in unprofitable niceties.*

§ *Mixt Mathematick,* hath for ſubject *Axioms,* and *portions of Phy-ſick;* and confiders *Quantity,* as it is auxiliary to enlighten, demon-ſtrate, and actuate them. For many parts of Nature can never be with ſufficient ſubtilty comprehended, nor demonſtrated with ſuf-ficient perſpicuity, nor accommodated to uſe with ſufficient dexterity and certainty, without the Aid and intervening of the *Mathema-ticks.* Of which ſort are *Perſpective, Muſick, Aſtronomy, Coſmogra-phy, Architecture, Ingenarie,* and divers others. But in *Mixt Mathe-maticks,* I can now report no entire portions *Deficient;* I rather make this prediction, that there will be more kinds of them invented by poſterity, if men be not wanting to themſelves. For as Phyſical knowledge daily grows up, and new Axioms of nature are diſ-cloſed, there will be a neceſſity of new Mathematick inventions, and ſo at laſt more *Mixt Mathematicks* will be contrived. *And now we have paſſed through the knowledge of Nature, and have no-ted the Deficients therein.* Wherein if we have departed from the Ancient and received opinons, and thereby have moved contradi-ction; for our part, *as we affect not to diſſent, ſo we purpoſe not to contend.* If it be *truth,*

Virg. Bu-col.   *Non Canimus ſurdis, reſpondent omnia ſylvæ;*

The voice of nature will cry it up, though the voice of man ſhould cry it down. And as *Alexander Borgia* was wont to ſay, of the Ex-vid. Hiſt. Gal. pedition of the *French* for *Naples, that they came with chalk in their hands* ha..ls *to mark up their Lodgings, and not with weapons to fight* ; fo we lik⸱ better, that entry of truth, which comes peaceably, where the *Minds* of men, capable to lodge fo great a gueft, are figned, as it were, with *chalk*; *than that which comes with Pugnacity*; *and forceth it felf a way by contentions and controverfies.* Wherefore having finiſht two parts of Philoſophy, *concerning God, and concerning nature*; the third remains *concerning* Man.

THE

THE
Fourth Book
OF
FRANCIS L. VERULAM
Vicount St ALBAN,
OF THE
Dignity and Advancement
OF
LEARNING.

To the KING.

CHAP. I.

I. The Partition *of the Knowledge of Man into the Philosophy of Humanity ; and Civil.* § The Partition of the Knowledge of *Humanity into the Knowledge touching the Body of Man ; and into the Knowledge touching the Soul of Man.* II *The Constitution of a general Knowledge of the Nature, or of the State of man.* § The Division *of the Knowledge of the State of Man, into the Knowledge of the Person of Man ; and of the League of the Mind, and the body.* § The Division *of the Knowledge of Mans Person, into the Knowledge of Mans Miseries.* § And *of his Prerogatives.* III. The Division *of the Knowledge of the League, into the Knowledge of Indications.* § And *of Impressions.* § The Assignment of Physiognomy. § And *of the Interpretation of Natural Dreams, to the Knowledges of Indications.*

F any Man (*Excellent King*) shall assault, or wound me for any of those *Precepts* I have delivered, or shall hereafter deliver (besides that I should be safe, being under the Protection of *Your Majesty*) let him know, that he doth that which is against the Custom and Law of Arms: For I am a Trumpeter only, I do not begin the fight ; perchance one of those of whom *Homer*, &c.

Hom.Il.4. Καλεετε κήρικας διος Ἄγγελοι, ἠδὲ κỳ ἀνδρῶν:

For thefe even between Mortal and enraged enemies paft to and fro ever inviolated. Nor doth our Trumpet fummon, and incourage men to tear and rend one another with contradictions; and in a civil rage to bear Arms, and wage War againft themfelves; but rather, a peace concluded between them, they may with joynt forces direct their ftrength againft *Nature her felf;* and take her high Towers, and difmantle her fortified Holds; and thus enlarge the Borders of mans Dominion, fo far as Almighty God of his goodnefs fhall permit.

Plat. in Alcib. 1. I. Now let us come to that Knowledge, whereunto the Ancient O- racle directeth us, which is *the knowledge of our felves :* which deferves Cic. de LL. lib. 1. the more accurate handling by how much it toucheth us more nearly. *This knowledge is to man the end and term of Knowledges ; but of Nature her felf, a portion only.* And generally let this be a rule, that all Di- Sen. Epift. § 89. vifions of Knowledges be fo accepted and applied, *As may rather de- fign forth and diftinguifh Sciences into Parts; than cut and pull them afun- der into pieces; that fo the continuance and entirenefs of Knowledges may ever be preferved.* For the contrary practice hath made particular Sci- ences to become barren, fhallow, and erroneous; while they have not been nourifht, maintain'd and rectified from the common Fountain and Cicero de Orat. Nurfery. So we fee *Cicero* the Orator complained of *Socrates,* and his School ; *That he was the firft that feparated Philofophy and Rhetorick;* whereupon Rhetorick became a verbal, and an empty Art. And it is alfo evident, that the opinion of *Copernicus,* touching *the Rotation of the Earth* (which now is maintain'd) becaufe it is not repugnant to the *Phænomena,* cannot be revinced by Aftronomical Principles; yet by the Principles of Natural Philofophy, truly applied, it may. So we fee alfo that the *Science of Medicine,* if it be deftituted and forfaken of *Natural Philofophy,* it is not much better than *Empirical Practice.*

§ *This being laid as a ground,* let us proceed to the *Knowledge of man.* This hath two parts: *For it either confidereth man fegregate, or diftri- butively; or congregate, and in fociety: the one we call Philofophy of Hu- manity; the other Philofophy Civil.* The *Philofophy of Humanity, or Hu- mane,* confifteth of the fame Parts, whereof man himfelf confifteth; that is, of knowledges which refpect the *Body;* and of knowledges which refpect the *Mind.*

II. *But before* we purfue particular Diftributions, let us conftitute ; *One general Knowledge of the Nature and State of Man :* For indeed it is very fit that this *Knowledge* be emancipate, and made a knowledge by it felf. It is compos'd of thofe *Sympathies* and *Concordances* commune between the *Body* and the *Mind.*

§ *Again, this Knowledge of the Nature and State of man* may be di- ftributed into two Parts ; attributing to the one *the undivided Nature of man;* to the other *the Combination between the Mind and the Body:* The firft of thefe we will call *the knowledge of the Perfon of man;* the fecond *the knowledge of the League.* And it is plain that all thefe feve- ral Branches of Knowledge, being they are common and commixt, could not be affigned to that firft Divifion of Knowledge, converfant about

about the *Body* ; and of Knowledges conversant about the *Mind.*

§ *The Knowledge concerning the Person of man*, comprehends specially two things ; namely the Contemplations of the *Miseries of Mankind* ; and of the *Prerogatives*, or *Excellencies of the same.* But the *bewailing of mans miseries* hath been elegantly and copiously set forth by many in the writings, as well of Philosophers, as divines. And it is both a pleasant and a profitable Contemplation.

§ As for that other touching *Mans Prerogatives*, it is a point may well be set down among the *Deficients. Pindar* when he would extol *Hiero*, speaks (as usually he doth) most elegantly, *That he cropt off the tops, or summities of all virtues.* For I suppose it would much conduce to the Magnanimity, and Honour of Man ; if a Collection were made of the *Ultimies* (as the Schools speak) or *Summities* (as *Pindar*) of *Humane Nature*, principally out of the faithful reports of History : That as ; *What is the last and highest pitch, to which mans Nature of it self hath ever reach'd in all the Perfections both of Body and Mind.* What a strange ability was that which is reported of *Cæsar, that he could dictate at once to five Secretaries!* So the Exercitations of the Ancient Rhetoricians, *Protagoras* ; *Gorgias* ; likewise of Philosophers.; *Calisthenes* ; *Possidonius* ; *Carneades* ; who were able to discourse *extempore* upon any Subject *Pro* and *Con*, with fluency and elegancy of expression, do much ennoble the Powers of mans wit and natural endowments. And that which *Cicero* reports of his Master *Archias* is little for use, but perchance great for Ostentation and Faculties ; that he was able upon the sudden to alledge a great number of excellent verses pertinent to the purpose of such Discourses as were then in hand. It is a singular commendation to that faculty of the Mind, the *Memory* ; that *Cyrus* or *Scipio* could call so many thousands of men by their Particular Names. But the Trophies of Moral virtues, are no less famous than those of intellectual virtues. What a great example of patience doth that common story of *Anaxarchus* present unto our thoughts, who put to the Rack and Torture, bit out his own tongue, the hoped Instrument of some Discovery, and spit it in the Tyrant's face? Nor is that inferiour for tolerance though much for the merit and Dignity, (which fell out in our time) of a certain Burgundian, who had committed a Murder upon the Person of the Prince of Orange ; this slave being scourged with iron whips ; and his flesh torn with burning Pincers, gave not so much as a groan ; howbeit when a broken piece of the Scaffold fell by chance upon the head of one that stood by, the scorcht stigmatiz'd varlet laught, even in the midst of his torments, who a little before wept at the cutting off of his curled hair. In like manner the serenity and security of Mind hath appeared wonderful in many, even at the instant approaches of Death ; as that of a Centurion recorded by *Tacitus* ; who being commanded by the executioner to stretch forth his neck valiantly. *I would* (saith he) *thou wouldst strike as valiantly.* But *John Duke* of Saxonie when the commission was brought him, as he was playing at chess, wherein his death was commanded the next day, call'd to one that stood by, and smiling, said ; *See, whether I have not the better hand of this Game* ; *He* (pointing towards him with whom he played) *will boast when I am dead, that he was the fairer of the set.* And our *More*, Chancellour of England, when the day before he was to die, a Barber came unto him (sent for this end, left perchance the grave and reverend fight of his long hair

might move compaffion in the People, and asked him whether it was his pleafure to have his hair cut) he refufed, and turning to the Barber ; *The King* (faid he) *is at fuit with me for my head, and untill that Controverfie be ended I mean to beftow no coft upon it.* And the fame Perfon at the very point of Death, after he had laid his head upon the fatal Block raifeth up himfelf a little again ; and having a fair large Beard gently removed it, faying, *Yet I hope this hath not offended the King.* But not to infift too long upon this point, it is evident what we mean, namely, that *the wonders of Humane Nature, and the ultimate Powers, and virtues as well of Mind as of Body, fhould be collected into a Volume, which might ferve as a Kalendar of Humane Triumphs.* For a work of this Nature, we approve the Purpofe, and Defigne of *Valerius Maximus,* and C. *Plinius* ; but it could be wifht they had us'd more choice and Diligence.

III *As touching the knowledge of the league, or mutual Alliance between the Body and the Mind* ; that may be diftributed into two Parts. For as all *leagues and Amities* confift of mutual intelligence, and mutual offices ; fo this *league* of *Mind* and *Body,* is in like manner comprifed in thefe two circumftances ; that is, to defcribe *How thefe two, namely, the Mind and the Body, difclofe one to the other ; and how one worketh upon the other, by difcovery or Indication* ; and by *Impreffion.* The former of thefe (namely a defcription what difcovery may be made of the Mind, from the habit of the Body, or of the Body from the Accidents of the Mind) hath begotten unto us two Arts, both of prediction ; where-

of the one is honoured with the Inquiry of *Ariftotle* ; and the other of *Hippocrates.* And although the modern times, have polluted thefe Arts with fuperftitious and Phantaftical mixtures, yet being purged and reftored to their true ftate, they have both a folid ground in nature, and a profitable ufe in life.

§ *The firft is Phyfiognomy, which difcovers the difpofitions of the mind, by the lineaments of the Body. The fecond is the expofition of Natural dreams, which difcovereth the ftate and Difpofition of the Body, from the Palfions and Motions of the mind.* In the Former of thefe, I note a Deficience : for *Ariftotle* hath very ingeniously and diligently handled the Po-

ftures of the Body, while it is at Reft ; but not the Geftures of the Body when it is in Motion ; which are no lefs comprehenfible by Art, and of Greater ufe. For the lineaments of the Body, do difclofe the Inclinations and Proclivities of the Mind in general ; but the Motions and Geftures of the Face and Parts, do not only fo, but further declare the Acceffes, and Seafons, and Prognofticks of the prefent difpofition, and of the will. For, to ufe your Majefties moft apt and elegant expreffion, *The tongue*

fpeaks to the ear, but the Gefture fpeaks to the eye. And therefore a number of old fubtile and crafty Perfons, whofe eyes do dwell upon the faces and fafhions of Men, do well know this obfervation ; and can turn it to their own advantage, as being a great part of their ability and wifdom, Neither indeed can it be denied, but that this is a great difcovery of diffimulation in an other, and a great direction, for the election of feafons, and opportunities of approaching to perfons ; which is not the meaneft part of Civil Prudence. And let no man think, that fuch dexterity may fomewhat avail, in refpect of fome Particular perfons, but cannot be comprehended under rule : for we all laugh, and weep,

and

and blush, and bend the brow much after the same manner; and so for most part it is in other more subtile motions. As for *Chiromancy,* it is a meer imposture.

§ *And as touching the exposition of Dreams*; it is a subject handled in some mens writings, but foild with many idle vanities; only thus much for the present I do Insinuate that this knowledge of *interpreting Dreams,* wants the support of a solid Base; and that foundation is this, *where the same effect is wrought, by an inward cause, that useth to be wrought by an outward; that extern Act is transformed into a Dream.* The surcharge of the stomack from a gross vapour, and from the poise of some outward weight, are alike; wherefore they that labour of the *Night-mare* do dream, that a weight is put upon them, with a great preparation of circumstances. The fluctuation or pensility of the Bowels, from the agitation of the waves in the sea, and from the wind gathered about the *Diaphragma,* are alike: therefore such as are troubled with the Hypocondriack wind, do often dream of Navigations, and Agitations upon the waters. There are an infinite number of such like instances.

§ The other branch of the *knowledge of the league* (which we have called *Impression*) hath not as yet been collected into Art, but hath sometimes intervened among other Treatises sparsedly, and as in passage only. It hath the same Antistrophe with the former: for the consideration is double; *either how, and how far the humours and temperament of the body, do alter or work upon the mind:* Or again, *How and how far, the Passions and Apprehensions of the mind do alter or work upon the Body.* The former of these we see sometimes handled in the Art of Physick; but the same hath by strange ways insinuated it self into Religion. For the Physician prescribes Remedies to cure the Maladies of the mind; as in the cures of Frenzies and Melancholy: they do also administer Physick to exhilerate the Mind; to munite and strengthen the heart, and so to increase the courage, to sharpen and clarifie the wits, to corroborate the Memory, and the like. But Diets, and choice of Meats, and Drinks, and other observances touching the Body, in the sect of the *Pythagoreans*; in the Heresie of the *Manichees,* and in the law of *Mahomet* do exceed all measure. So likewise *the ordinances of the Ceremonial Law, interdicting the eating of the bloud; and the Fat:* and *distinguishing between beasts clean and unclean,* so far as they are for meat, are many and strict. Nay the Christian faith it self, though clear and sincere from all clouds of ceremonies; yet retains the use of Fastings; Abstinences; and other observances, which tend to the maceration and humiliation of the Body; as things not meerly Figurative; but also Fruitful. The root and life of all such prescripts as these, (besides the Ceremony it self, and the practice of Canonical obedience,) consists in this whereof we speak, namely, *that there may be a mutual sufferance and humiliation of the Soul with the Body.* And if any man of weaker judgement do conceive, that these impressions of the Body upon the Mind, do either question the immortality, or derogate from the soveraignty of the soul over the Body; to an easie doubt, an easie answer is sufficient. Let him take these instances; *either from an Infant in the Mothers wombe, which is compatible with the Accidents and Symptomes; of the mother, and yet separable in its season, from the Body of the mother:* Or from Monarchs, who though they have absolute power, are sometimes inclined

Deut. 12.

clined by the fway of their Servants; yet without fubjection of their Perfons or diminution of their Power.

§ *Now as for the reciprocal part, the operations of the Soul, and of the Effects and Paffions thereof upon the Body;* that alfo hath found a place in Medicine. For all wife Phyficians do ever confider and handle, *Accidentia Animi,* as a Matter of great moment, for their Cures; and which are of great force to further or hinder all other Remedies. But there is another obfervation pertinent to this fubject, which hath been very fparingly inquired into, and nothing to the depth and dignity of the thing; that is, (fetting afide the affections) *how far the Imagination of the Mind, or a thought deeply fixt, and exalted as it were, into a belief, is of Power to alter the Body of the Imaginant?* For though it hath a manifeft power to hurt, it follows not, that it hath the fame degree of power to help: No more indeed, than if a man fhould conclude, that becaufe there be peftilent Airs able fuddenly to kill a man in health; therefore there fhould be Soveraign Airs, able fuddenly to cure a man in ficknefs. *This Inquifition* would certainly be of excellent ufe, but Laert. in V. as *Socrates* faid, it *needs a Delian Diver,* being covered with darknefs and obfcurity. *Again,* of all thefe Knowledges, *de Fœdere;* or of the *Concordances between the mind and the body,* there is no part more neceffary than the difquifition of the *Seats* and *Domicils,* which the feveral faculties of the mind do take and occupate in the Body, and the Organs thereof. Which kind of knowledge hath not wanted Sectators, but what is found in many fuch Writers is either controverted, or flightly inquired; and would be fearcht into with more diligence and per-Plat. in Ti- fpicacity. For the opinion introduced by *Plato* placing the underftand-mæo. ing in the brain, as in a high Tower; *Animofity* (which he unfitly cal-Arift. de leth *Anger,* being it is nearer to Tumor and Pride) in the *Heart;* Con-Gen. A- nim. 4. *cupifcence* and *Senfuality* in the *Liver,* deferves not altogether to be de-Gal. fpifed; nor yet too haftily embrac'd. So the placing of the *Intellectu-*de plac. *al Faculties; Imagination, Reafon, Memory;* according to the ventri-Plat. cles of the Brain, is not without error. Thus have we explicated the Knowledge touching the *individed nature of man,* as alfo touching the *League of the Body and the Mind.*

Chap. II.

I. The Partition *of the Knowledge refpecting the Body of Man into Art Medicinal.* §. *Cofmetick.* §. *Athletick.* §. *And Voluptuary.* II. The Partition *of Medicine, into three duties.* §. *Confervation of Health.* III. *Cure of Difeafes.* IV. *And Prolongation of Life:* And that the laft part, *Prolongation of Life,* fhould be feparate from the other two.

THE *Knowledge that concerns mans body,* is divided, as the *Good* of *Mans Body* is divided, unto which it is referr'd. *The Good of Mans Body,* is of four kinds; *Health; Form, or Beauty; Strength; Pleafure.* Wherefore there are fo many *Sciences; Medicine,* or the *Art of of Cure; Cosmetick, or the Art of Decoration; Athletick, or the Art of Activity; and Art Voluptuary,* which *Tacitus* calls *Eruditus Luxus.*

§ *Medicine* is a noble Art, and according to the Poets descended of a most generous race; for they have brought in *Apollo,* as the chief God of Medicine, to whom they have assigned *Æsculapius* for his son; a God too, and a Professor of *Physick: Because in things natural the Sun is the Author, and Fountain of Life; the Physician the Conserver of Nature; and as it were a second spring of Life.* But the greatest glory to *Physick* is from the works of our Saviour, who was a Physician both of Soul and Body. And as he made the Soul the peculiar object of his heavenly Doctrine; so he design'd the Body the proper subject of his miracles. For we never read of any miracles done by him respecting Honour or Wealth, (besides that one when Tribute was to be given to *Cæsar*) but only respecting the Body of man; or to preserve, or to sustain, or to cure it.

§ *The Subject of Medicine* (namely *mans Body*) is, of all other things which nature hath brought forth, most capable of Remedy; but then that Remedy is most capable of Error: For the same subtility, and variety of the subject, as it affords great possibility of Cure, so it gives great facility to error. Wherefore as that Art (such as now it is) may well be reckon'd amongst Arts conjectural; so the enquiry thereof may be placed in the number of the most difficult, and axactest Arts. Neither yet are we so senseless, as to imagine with *Paracelsus,* and the Alchymists; *That there are to be found in mans Body certain Correspondences, and Parallels to all the variety of specifick Natures in the world* (as *Stars, Minerals,* and the rest) as they foolishly fancy and Mythologize; straining, but very impertinently, that emblem of the Ancients, *That man was Microcosmus, an abstract, or model of the whole world,* to countenance their fabulous, and fictious invention. Yet notwithstanding this is an evident truth, (which we were about to say) *That amongst all Bodies Natural, there is not found any so multipliciously compounded as the Body of man.* For we see Herbs, and Plants, are nourished by earth and water; Beasts by Herbs and Fruits: But man by the flesh of living Creatures; as Beasts, Birds, Fish; and also of Herbs, Grains, Fruits, Juice, and divers Liquors; not without manifold commixtures, seasoning, and Preparation of these Bodies before they come to be mans meat, and aliment. Add hereunto, that Beasts have a more simple order of life, and less change of affections to work upon their Bodies, and they commonly working one way; whereas man in his Mansions, Exercises, Passions, Sleep, and Vigilances is subject to infinite vicissitudes of changes. So that it is most evident that of all other natural substances, the Body of man is the most fermentated, compounded, and incorporated Mass. The soul, on the other side, is the simplest of substances, as it is well exprest;

—————*Purumq; relinquit*
Æthereum sensum, atq; Aurai simplicis ignem.

So that it is no marvail, though the soul so placed, enjoy no rest; according to that Principle, *Motus rerum extra locum est rapidus, placidus in loco:* But to the purpose, this various and subtile composition and fabrick of mans body hath made it, as a curious and exquisite instrument,

[marginal notes: Homer. Hym. Paean. fan. alii,]

[marginal notes: Paramir. lib. 4. Rob. Flud. pass. sim.]

[marginal notes: Virg. Æn. 6. Arist. Phys. & de cæl.]

Paufan.in
Elincis.
Ov.Met.1.
ment, eafie to be diftemper'd; therefore the Poets did well *to conjoyn Mufick and Medicine in* Apollo; *becaufe the Genius of both thefe Arts is almoft the fame*; and the office of a Phyfician confifteth meerly in this, to know how to tune, and finger this Lyre of mans body; that the Harmony may not become difcordant and harfh. So then this incon-ftancy, and variety of the fubject, hath made the Art more conjectu-ral : And the Art being fo conjectural had given more large fcope, not only to error, but even to impofture. *For almoft all other Arts and Sciences are judg'd by their power and operation; and not by their fuccefs and work. The Lawyer is judg'd by the virtue of his pleading ; and not by the iffue of the Caufe; the Mafter in the Ship approves his Art, by the directing his courfe aright, and not by the fortune of the voyage : But the Phyfician, and perhaps the Politick hardly have any porper particular Acts, whereby they may make a clear demonftration of their Art and abilities ; but bear away honour or difgrace principally from the event which is ever an unequal judicature.* For who can tell, if a Patient dye or recover; or if a State be preferved or ruin'd; whether it be by Art or Accident ? Therefore it often falls out, that the Impoftor bears away the Prize, Virtue the Cenfure. Nay, the weaknefs and credulity of men is fuch, *As they often prefer a Mountebank, or Witch, before a Learn'd Phyfician.* There-fore the Poets were clear and quick-fighted, when they made Æfcula-pius and *Circe*, Brother and Sifter; both children of the Sun, as in the Verfes; of Æfculapius the Suns Son,

Virg. Æn.
7.
> *Ille repertorem Medicinæ talis, & Artis,*
> *Fulmine Phœbigenam Stygeas detrufit ad undas;*

And likewife of *Circe* the Suns Daughter,

Ibid.
> *Dives inacceffos ubi folis filia lucos*
> *Affiduo refonat cantu : tectifq; fuperbis*
> *Urit odoratam nocturna in lumina Cedrum.*

For in all times in the reputation and opinion of the Multitude, Witches, and old Women, and Impoftors have been rival Competi-tors with Phyficians; and have even contended with them for the fame of Cures. And what I pray you follows ? Even this, that Phyfitians fay to themfelves, as *Solomon* expreffeth it upon a higher occafion, *If it befals*
Ecclef.2. *to me, as it befals to the fool, why fhould I labour to be more wife ?* And therefore I cannot much blame Phyficians, if they ufe commonly to intend fome other Art, or Practice, which they fancy more than their Profeffion : For you fhall have of them Poets, Antiquaries, Criticks, Rhetoricians, Politicks, Divines, and in thefe Arts better feen, than in
Agrip. de
vanitcien. their own profeffion. Nor doth this come to pafs, as I fuppofe, be-caufe (as a certain Declaimor againft Sciences, objects againft Phyfici-ans) they have ever Converfant before their eyes fuch loathfome and fad fpectacles, that they muft needs retire their minds from thefe ob-jects, to fome other contemplations ; for as they are men, *Nihil Hu-mani à fe alienum putent,* but for this reafon, whereof we now fpeak; namely, that they find, *that Mediocrity, and excellency in their Art, maketh no difference in profit or reputation towards their Perfons or For-tunes.*

tunes.   For the vexations of ſickneſs; the ſweetneſs of life; the flattery hope; the commendation of friends; maketh men to depend upon Phyſicians with all their defects : But if a man ſeriouſly weigh the matter, theſe things rather redound to the imputation of Phyſicians, than their excuſation : who ſhould not for theſe prejudices caſt away hope; but encreaſe their pains and diligence.   For whoſoever pleaſeth to excite and awake his obſervation, and a little look about him, ſhall eaſily deprehend even from common and familiar examples, what a command and ſoveraignty the ſubtilty and ſharpneſs of the underſtanding hath over the variety either of matter,or of the form of things. *Nothing is more variable than mens faces* and countenances; yet the memory retains the infinite diſtinctions of them : Nay, a Painter with a few ſhells of Colours; the benefit of his eye; the habit of his imagination; and the ſteadineſs of his hand; can imitate and draw with his pencil all faces that are, have been, or ever ſhall be; if they were brought before him : *Nothing more variable than mans voice;* yet we can eaſily diſcern their differences in every particular perſon; nay, you ſhall have a Buffoon, or a Pantomimus will render and expreſs to the life, as many as he pleaſeth.   *Nothing more variable than articulate ſounds of words,* yet men have found a way to reduce them to a few Letters of the Alphabet. And this is moſt certain, *that it is not the inſufficiency, or incapacity of mans mind; but rather the remote ſtanding, or placing of the object that breeds theſe Mazes, and Incomprehenſions.*   For as the ſenſe a far off is full of miſtaking; but within due diſtance errs not much; ſo it is in the underſtanding.   *For men uſe commonly to take a proſpect of Nature, as from ſome high Turret, and to view her a far off; and are too much taken up with generalities, whereas if they would vouchſafe to deſcend and approach nearer to particulars; and more exactly and conſiderately look into things themſelves; there might be made a more true and profitable diſcovery and comprehenſion.*   Now the remedy of this error, *is not alone this, to quicken or ſtrengthen the Organ; but withal to go nearer to the object :* And therefore there is no doubt but if Phyſicians, letting Generalities go for a while, and ſuſpending their aſſent thereto, would make their approaches to Nature; they might become Maſters of that Art,whereof the Poet ſpeaks,

> *Et quoniam variant morbi, variabimus Artes;*
> *Mille mali ſpecies, mille ſalutis erunt.*

Ovid R.
A. l.2.

Which they ought the rather to endeavour becauſe the Philoſophers themſelves, upon the which Phyſicians, whether they be Methodiſts, or Chymiſts, do relye (*for Medicine not grounded upon Philoſophy is a weak thing*) are indeed very ſlight and ſuperficial. *Wherefore if* too wide Generalities, though true, have this defect, that they do not well bring men home to Action; certainly there is greater danger in thoſe Generals, which are in themſelves falſe, and inſtead of directing to truth, miſlead the mind into the by-paths of Error.

§ *Medicine therefore* (as we have ſeen) hitherto hath been ſuch, as hath been more profeſſed, than laboured; and yet more laboured than advanced; ſeeing the pains beſtowed thereon, hath been rather in circle;

cle, than in progreſſion. *For I find much Iteration but ſmall Addition in Writers of that Faculty.*

II. We will divide it into three Parts, which we will call the three Duties thereof: *The firſt is Conſervation of Health, ſecond the Cure of Diſeaſes; the third Prolongation of Life.*

§ But for this laſt duty, Phyſicians ſeem not to have acknowledg'd it as any principal part of their Art; but have (ignorantly enough) mingled and confounded it as one and the ſame with the other two. *For* they ſuppoſe, that if Diſeaſes be repelled before they ſeize upon the body; or be cured after they have ſurpriz'd the body; that *Prolongation of Life* muſt naturally follow. Which though it be ſo, without all queſtion, yet they do not ſo exactly conſider; that theſe two offices of *Conſervation* and *Curation,* only pertain to Diſeaſes; and to ſuch *Prolongation of Life* alone, which is abbreviated and intercepted by Diſeaſes: But *to draw out the thread of Life,* and to prorogue Death for a ſeaſon, which ſilently ſteals upon us by natural reſolution, and the A-trophy of Age; is an argument, that no Phyſician hath handled it according to the Merit of the ſubject. *Neither let that ſcruple trouble the* *minds of Men, as if this thing committed to the diſpenſation of Fate, and* *the divine providince , were now by us firſt repealed and commended to the* *charge and office of Art.* For without doubt Providence doth diſpoſe and determine all kind of deaths whatſoever , whether they come of violence, or from Diſeaſes, or from the courſe of Age; and yet doth not therefore exclude Preventions and Remedies: For Art and humane induſtry do not command and rule Fate, and Nature; but ſerve and adminiſter unto them. *But* of this part we ſhall ſpeak anon: Thus much in the mean time by way of anticipation, leſt any ſhould unskilfully confound this *third office* of medicine, with the two former, which uſually hitherto hath been done.

Fatum, Stoic. horr. Dogma.

§ *As for the duty of preſervation of Health,* the firſt duty of the three, many have written thereof, as in other points very impertinently, ſo (in our judgment) in this particular; in attributing too much to the quality of meats, and too little to the quantity thereof: and in the quantity it ſelf, they have diſcourſed like Moral Philoſophers, exceſſively praiſing Mediocrity; whereas both *faſting* changed to cuſtome, and *full feeding,* to which a man hath inured himſelf, are better *regiments of health,* than thoſe *Mediocrities* which commonly enervate Nature, and make her ſlothful, and impatient, if need ſhould be, of any extremity, exceſs, or indigence. And for the divers kinds of *Exerciſe,* which much conduce to the *conſervation of health,* none of that profeſſion hath well diſtinguiſht or obſerved; whereas there is hardly found any diſpoſition to a diſeaſe, which may not be corrected by ſome kind of exerciſe proper to ſuch an infirmity: As bowling is good againſt the weakneſs of the Reins; ſhooting againſt the obſtruction of the Lungs; walking and upright deport of the Body, againſt the Crudities of the ſtomach; and for other diſeaſes other exercitations. But ſeeing this part touching *the conſervation of health,* hath been in every point after a ſort handled, it is not our purpoſe to purſue leſſer deficiencies.

III. *As concerning the cures of Diſeaſes;* that is a Part of Medicine, whereon much labour hath been beſtowed, but with ſmall profit. It comprehendeth in it the *knowledge of Diſeaſes,* to which mans body is
subject

ſubject, together with the *Cauſes, Symptomes,* and *Cures* thereof. In this ſecond Duty of Medicine, many things are *deficient,* of theſe we will propound a few, which are more remarkable, which to enumerate without preciſe order or Method, we ſuppoſe ſufficient.

§ *The firſt is the diſcontinuance,* of that profitable and accurate diligence of *Hippocrates,* whoſe cuſtom was to ſet down a *Narrative* of the ſpecial caſes of his Patients, what the Medicament, what the event. Therefore having ſo proper and notable a precedent from him, who was accounted the Father of the Art, we ſhall not need to alleage any example forreign, fetcht from other Arts ; as from the wiſdom of the Lawyers, with whom nothing is more uſual, than to ſet down and enter more notable caſes, and new diciſions, whereby they may the better furniſh and direct themſelves for the definition of future caſes. *Wherefore I find this continuation of Medicinal Reports deficient,* ſpecially digeſted into one entire body , with diligence and judgement , which yet I underſtand not to be made ſo ample, as to extend to every common caſe that daily falls out (for that were an infinite work, and to ſmall purpoſe) nor yet ſo reſerved and contracted as to admit none, but Prodigies and Wonders, as many have done : for many things are new in the *manner* and circumſtances of the thing, which are not *new* in the *kind* ; and he that ſhall give his mind to obſerve, ſhall find many things even in matters vulgar worthy obſervation.

*NARRA-TIONES MEDICI-NALES.

§ So in *Diſquiſitions Anatomical* , the manner is , that thoſe parts which pertain in general to Mans body, are moſt diligently enquired and obſerved even to a curioſity, and that in every leaſt filet : *but as touching the variety which is found in divers bodies, there the diligence of Phyſicians fails.* And therefore I grant that *ſimple Anatomy* hath been moſt clearly handled ; *Comparative Anatomy, I define to be deficient.* For men have made a good enquiry into all the parts, and into their conſiſtencies, figures, and collocations : but the divers figure, condition, and poſture of thoſe parts in divers men, they have not ſo well obſerved. The reaſon of this omiſſion I ſuppoſe is no other than this , that the firſt inquiry may be ſatisfied in the view of one or two Anatomies ; but the latter, being *Comparative* and Caſual , muſt ariſe from the attentive and exact obſervation of many *Diſſections :* and the firſt is a matter, wherein learned Profeſſors in their Lectures, and the preſs of ſpectators ſtanding about them, may vaunt themſelves ; but the ſecond kind of *Anatomy,* is a ſevere knowledge, which muſt be acquired by a retired ſpeculation, and a long experience. Nevertheleſs, there is no doubt but that the Figure and Structure of the inward parts is very little inferiour, for variety and lineaments, to the outward members ; and that Hearts and Livers, and Ventricles are as different in men, as are either their Foreheads, or Noſes, or Ears.

*ANATO-MIA COMPA-RATA.

§ *And in theſe differences of inward parts,* there are often found the *Cauſes continent* of many Diſeaſes ; which Phyſicians not obſerving, do ſometime accuſe the Humours which are not delinquent, the fault being in the very Mechanick Frame of ſome part. In the cure of which Diſeaſes, to apply *Alterative Medicines* , is to no purpoſe (becauſe the part peccant is incapable of ſuch alteration,) but the matter muſt be mended, and accommodated, or palliated by a preſcript Diet and familiar Medicines. So likewiſe to *Comparative Anatomy* appertain ac-

curate

curate obfervations, as well of all kind of humours, as of the footſteps
and impreſſions of difeafes in divers bodies diffected : for the Humours
in Anatomies are commonly paſt by, as if they were fuperfluous Purga-
ments and Excrements ; whereas it is a point very uſeful and neceſſary, to note of what nature, and of how various kinds there be of different humours (not relying herein too much upon the received diviſions,) which fometimes may be found in the body of Man ; and in what
Cavities and Receptacles, every humour uſeth for moſt part to lodge
and neſtle, and with what advantage or prejudice, and the like. In like
manner the *Footſteps* and *Impreſſions* of *Difeafes*, and the leſions and de-
vaſtations of the inward parts by them, are to be obſerved with diligence in divers *Anatomies* ; as impoſthumes, ulcerations, folutions of
continuity, putrefactions, corroſions, confumptions, luxations, difloca-
tions, obſtructions, repletions, tumors ; together with all perternatural
excreſcencies, found in mans body (as ſtones, carnoſities, wens, worms,
and the like ;) I fay all thefe, and fuch other, ſhould be with great diligence inquired, and digeſted by that *Comparative Anatomy*, whereof
we ſpeak, and the experiments of many Phyſicians collected and col-
lated together. *But this variety of Accidents*, is by Anatomiſts, either
handled perfunctorily, or elfe paſt over in filence.

§ *Touching that other defect in Anatomy, (namely, that it hath not been*
ufed to be practifed upon living bodies;) to what end ſhould we ſpeak of
it ? for this is an odious and an inhumane experiment , and by *Celfus*

juſtly condemned : yet notwithſtanding, that obfervation of the Ancients is true, That many Pores, Paſſages and Pertuſions, which are more
ſubtile than the reſt, appear not in *Anatomical diffections*, becaufe they
are ſhut and latent in Dead *Bodies* ; whereas they are open and manifeſt in *Live*. Wherefore to confult both for uſe and humanity, this *A-*
natomia vivorum, is not altogether to be relinquiſht, or referred (as
Celfus did) to the cafual infpections of Surgions, feeing this may well
be performed, being diverted upon the *Diffection of Beaſts a-*
live, which , notwithſtanding the diffimilitude of their parts with
mans, may fufficiently fatisfie this enquiry, being done with judgement.

§ *Likewife in their inquiry of Difeafes*, they find many *Difeafes which*

they decern and judge to be incurable ; fome, from the firſt acceſs of the
Difeafe, others, after fuch a certain period : fo that the Profcriptions of
L. *Scylla*, and the *Triumvirs*, were nothing to the *Profcriptions of Phyfici-*
ans, by which, by their moſt unjuſt Edicts ; they deliver over fo many
men to death ; whereof numbers do efcape with lefs difficulty, than
they did in the Roman Profcriptions. Therefore I will not doubt
to fet down among *Deficients a work of the cures of Difeafes held incura-*
ble ; that fo fome excellent Generous Profeſſors in that faculty, may be
awakt and ſtirred up, to fet to this work(fo far as the latent operations of
Nature, by mans induſtry, may be difclofed) feeing this very fentence of *Pronouncing Difeafes to be incurable*, enacts a Law, as it were,
for floath and negligence, and redeems ignorance from Difcredit and
Infamy.

§ *Nay farther, to infift a little upon this Point, I eſteem it the office of*

a Phyfician, not only to reſtore health, but to mitigate dolours, and tor-
ments of Difeafes ; and not only when fuch mitigation of pain, as of a
dangerous

dangerous symptome, may make and conduce to recovery; but even when all hope of recovery being gone, it may serve to make a fair and easie passage out of life.   For it is no small felicity, which *Augustus Cæ-* Sueton. in Aug. *far was wont to wish to himself, that same Euthanasia*; which was also no-ted in the Death of *Antonius Pius,* who seemed not so much to dye, as to be cast into a sweet and deep sleep.   And it is written of *Epicurus* that he procured this same easie departure unto himself; for after his, disease was judged desperate, he drowned his stomach and senses with a large draught, and ingurgitation of wine; whereupon the Epigramm was made ——*hinc Stygias ebrius hausit aquas, He took away by these* Lucr: in Epicuro, *draughts of wine, the bitter taft of the Stygian water.*   But in our times Physicians make a kind of scruple and nicety of it, to stay with a pati-ent after the disease is past hope of cure; whereas in my judgment, if they would not be wanting to their profession, and to humanity it self, they ought both to enquire the skill, and to give the attendance, *for the facilitating and assuaging of the Pains and Agonies of Death at their departure.*   And this part, the enquiry *de Euthanasia Exteriori,* (which we so call to distinguish it from that *Euthanasia,* or *sweet-calm Dying,* procured by a due preparation of the soul) we refer to the number of *De-ficients.*

§ *So in the Cures of Diseases,* I find generally this *Deficience*; that the Physicians of the time, though they do not impertinently pursue the ge- * DE ME-DICINIS AV-THEN-TICIS. neral intentions and scope of Cures; yet for particular Receipts, which by a kind of propriety respect the cures of specifical diseases; either they do not well know them, or they do not religiously observe them. For the Physicians have frustrated and taken away the fruit of Traditions, and approved experience, by their *Magistralities*; in adding and taking out, and changing ingredients of Receipts at their pleasure; and almost after the manner of Apothecaries, putting in *Quid pro Quo*; comman-ding so presumptuously over Medicine, as the Medicine can no longer command the disease.   For except *Treacle,* and *Mithridatum,* and of late,*Dioscordium,* and the confection of *Alkermes,* and a few more Me-dicines; they commonly tie themselves to no receipts severely and strictly.   For the confections of sale, which are in the shops, they are in readiness rather for general purposes, than accommodate and proper for particular cures; for they do not exactly refer to any disease in spe-cial; but generally to the opening of obstructions, comforting conco-ction, altering Distemperatures.   And this is the cause why *Empericks* and *Old women* are more happy many times in their Cures, than Lear-ned Physicians; because they are faithful, aud scrupulous in keeping themselves to the confection and composition of approved *Medicines.* *I remember that a Physician* with us here in England , famous for pra-ctice, in religion half Jew, and almost an Arabian for his course of stu-dy,wont to say, *your European Physicians are indeed Learned men, but they know not the Particular Cures of Diseases.*   And the same person u-sed to jest, but unreverently, saying, *That our Physicians were like Bishops, they had the Keys of binding and loosing, and nothing else.*   But to speak the truth in earnest; in our opinion it would be a matter of good con-sequence, if some Physicians of Note for Learning and Practice, would compile *a work of Probations, and experimented Medicines for the cure of Particular Diseases.*   For that any man, induced by some specious rea-

fon, fhould be of opinion, that it is the part of a learned Phyfician (refpecting the complections of Patients, their Age, the feafon of the year,
Cuftomes and the like, rather to accommodate his Medicines as occafions fuggeft, than to infift upon fome certain Prefcripts, is a deceivable
affertion, and which attributes too little to experience, too much to
judgment. *Certainly* as in the ftate of *Rome* they were the men moft
ufeful, and of the beft compofition, which either being Confuls favou-
red the People, or being Tribunes inclined to the Senate : So in the matter we now handle, they be the beft of Phyficians, which either in
their great Learning, do much value the Traditions of Experience ; or
being famous for Practice, defpife not Methods and Generalities of Art.
As for qualifications of Medicines (if at any time that be expedient) they
are rather to be practis'd upon the Differents of Phyfick, than incorporated into the Receipt, wherein nothing fhould be innovated without apparent neceffity. *Wherefore this Part which handleth Authentick*
and Pofitive Medicines, we report as *Deficient :* but it is a matter not
to be attempted or undertaken without a fharp and piercing judgment ;
and as it were, in a Synod of felect Phyficians.

IMITA-
TIO
THER-
MARVM
NATU-
RALI-
UM.

§ Alfo in the *Preparations of Medicines* I do find it ftrange (fpecially
confidering how *Mineral Medicines* have been fo extolled, and celebrated by Chymifts ; and that they are fafer for the outward than inward
Parts) *that no man hitherto hath endeavoured by Art to imitate Natural*
Baths, and Medicinable Fountains ; and yet it is confeffed that *thofe*
Baths and Fountains receive their virtues from mineral veins through
which they pafs : and for manifeft proof hereof mans induftry knows
well how to difcern and diftinguifh from what kind of Minerals fuch
waters receive their tinctures; as whether from Sulphur ; Vitriol ; Steel,
or the like : *which natural tincture of waters,* if it may be reduced to
compofitions of Art, it would be in mans power, both to make more
kinds of them, as occafion required ; and to command, at pleafure, the
temperament thereof. *Therefore this Part of the imitation of Nature in*
Artificial Baths (a thing without queftion both profitable and eafie to
be done) we take to be *Deficient.*

FILUM
MEDICI-
NALE.

§ *But left I fhould purfue the particulars more precifely,* than is agreeable
to our intention, or to the proportion of this Treatife ; I will clofe and
conclude *this Part* with a note of one *Deficience* more, which feems to
us to be of great confequence ; which is, *that the Prefcripts in ufe are too*
compendious to effect any notable or difficult cure. For in our judgment
it is a more vain and flattering, than true opinion, to think that any
Medicine can be fo fovereign, or fo happy, as that the fimple ufe thereof fhould be of force fufficient for fome great cure. It were a ftrange
fpeech which fpoken, or fpoken oft, fhould reclaim a man from a vice
deeply rooted and inveterate, certainly it is far otherwife : *But it is*
● *order, Purfuit, Sequence, Artificial interchange, that are potent and*
mighty in nature : Which although they require more exact judgment
in prefcribing ; and more precife obedience in obferving, yet this is
amply recompenced in the greatnefs of effects. And although a man
would think, by the daily diligence of Phyficians, their Vifitations,
Seffions, and Prefcriptions, which they perform to the fick ; that they
did painfully purfue the Cure ; and go on in a certain courfe : Yet let
a man exactly look into their prefcripts, and miniftrations, he fhall find
many

many of them full of wavering, inconftancy, and every days devifes; and fuch as came into their minds without any certain, or advifed courfe of Cure. *For they fhould even from the beginning, after they have made a full and perfect difcovery of the difeafe, meditate and refolve upon an orderly fequence of Cure ; and not without important reafons depart therefrom.* And let Phyficians know for certain, that (for example) three perchance, or four receipts, are rightly prefcribed for the Cure of fome great difeafe; which taken *in due order, and in due fpaces of time perform the Cure ; which if they were taken fingle, or by themfelves alone; or if the Courfe were inverted, or the entervals of time not obferved, would be hurtful.* Nor is it yet our meaning that every fcrupulous and fuperftitious way of Cure in eftimation fhould be the beft; no more than that every ftreight way is the way to Heaven, but that the way fhould be right as well as ftreight and difficult. *And this Part* which we call *Filum Medicinale* we fet down as *Deficient.* So thefe are the Parts which in the *Knowledge of Medicine,* touching the cure of Difeafes, are *defiderate,* fave that there remains yet one part more of more ufe than all the other, which is here wanting, *A true and Active natural Philofophy, upon which the fcience of Medicine fhould be built :* but that belongs not to this Treatife.

IV. *The third part of Medicine* we have fet down to be that of the *Prolongation of Life,* which is a part new and *Deficient,* and the moft noble of all : For if any fuch thing may be found out, Medicine fhall not be practis'd only in the impurities of Cures, nor fhall Phyficians be honour'd only for Neceffity, but for a gift, the greateft of earthly Donations that could be confer'd on mortality, whereof men, next under God, may be the Difpenfers and Adminiftrators. *For although the world to a Chriftian man, travelling to the land of Promife, be as it were a wildernefs, yet that our fhooes and veftments (thas is our Body, which is as a coverture to the foul,) be lefs worn away while we fojourn in this wildernefs, is to be efteemed a gift coming from the divine goodnefs.* Now becaufe this is one of the choiceft parts of Phyfick, and that we have fet it down amongft *Deficients,* we will after our accuftomed manner give fome Admonitions, Indications, and Precepts thereof.

§ *Firft we advertife,* that of Writers in this Argument there is none extant that hath found out any thing of worth, that I may not fay, any thing found touching this fubject. *Indeed Ariftotle* hath left unto pofterity a fmall brief Commentary of this matter; wherein there is fome acutenefs, *which he would have to be all can be faid, as his manner is :* But the more recent Writers have written fo idly, and fuperftitioufly upon the point, that the Argument it felf, through their vanity, is reputed vain and fenflefs.

§ *Secondly, we advertife,* that the intentions of Phyficians touching this Argument are nothing worth : and that they rather lead men away from the point, than direct them unto it. For they difcourfe *that Death is a deftitution of Heat and Moifture, and therefore natural heat fhould be comforted and radical moifture cherifht ;* as if it were a matter to be effected by Broaths, or Lettuces, and Mallows, or * Jujubs, or fine Wafer-cakes, or elfe with hot fpices, generous wine, or the fpirits of wine, or chymical oyls ; all which do rather hurt, than help.

§ *Thirdly,* we admonifh men that they ceafe to trifle, and that they be

[margin: DE PROLONGAN-DO CUR-RICULO VITÆ.]

[margin: De longitud.& Brev.vlt.]

*[margin: * Arabian Plums.]*

be not so credulous as to think that such a great work as this is, *to retard and turn back the course of Nature*, may be brought to perfection by a morning draught, or the use of some precious Receipt; no not with *Aurum Potabile*, or the substances of Pearls, or such like toys; but that they take it for a grounded truth, that the *Prolongation of Life*, is a great work, and which consists in many kinds of Receipts; and of an orderly course and connexion of them: And let no man be so stupid as to believe, *that what never yet was done, can be now effected, but by means yet never attempted.*

Fourthly, we admonish men, that they rightly observe and distinguish touching those Receipts which conduce to a *healthful life*, and those which confer to a *long life*. For there are many things which exhilarate the spirits, strengthen the active powers of nature, repel diseases, which yet subduct from the sum of life, and without sickness accelerate aged *Atrophie*. And there are other Receipts which conduce to the *Prolongation of life*, and the *retardation of the Atrophie of old-age*; but yet are not us'd without hazard of health: So that they who use these remedies for the *prorogation of life*, must likewise provide against such inconveniences as upon their usage may unexpectedly fall out. And thus much by way of Admonition.

§ *As for Indications*, the image, or Idea we have conceiv'd in our mind hereof, is this: Things are conserv'd and continued two ways; either in their own Identity, or by *Reparation*. *In their proper Identity*, as a Fly or an Ant in *Amber*; a Flower, an Apple or Wood in Conservatories of Snow; a dead corps in Balsam. By *Reparation*, as in Flame, and Mechanicks. He that goes about the work of *Prolongation of Life*, must put in practice both these kinds, (for disunited, their strength is weakned) and *Mans body* must be *conserv'd* after the same manner *inanimate Bodies* are conserved: and again, as *Flame* is conserved; and lastly, even as *Mechanicks* are conserved. *Wherefore there are three intentions for the Prolongation of Life; the Retardation of Consumption; the Integrity of the Reparation; and the Renovation of that which begun to decay and grow old.* Consumption is caus'd by two *Depredations*, *Depredation* of *innate Spirit*; and *Depredation* of *ambient Air*. The resistence of both is two-fold, either when the *Agents* (that is, the succ and moistures of the Body) become less *Predatory*; or the *Patients* are made less depredable. The *Spirit* is made less *Predatory*, if either it be condensed in substance, as in the use of Opiates, and nitrous application, and in contristations; or be *diminished in Quantity*, as in spare, Pythagorical or Monastical Diets: or is sweetned and *refresht with motion*, as in ease and tranquility. *Ambient Air* is made less *Predatory*, either when it is *less heated with the beams of the Sun*, as in colder Countries; in Caves, in Hills, and in the Pillars or Stations of Anchorites; or when it is repell'd from the Body, as in dens-close skin; in the Plumage of birds, and the use of oyl and unguents without Aromatick ingredients. *The juice and succulencies of the Body, are made less depredable*, if either they be made more indurate, or more *dewy*, and *oyly*: Indurate as in *austere course Diet*; in a life accustomed to cold, by *strong exercises*; by certain *Mineral Baths*: Roscide or dewy, as in the use of Sweet-meats, and abstinence from Meats, Salt and Acid; but especially in such a mixture

ture of drinks, as is of parts very tenuious and fubtil , and yet without all acrimony or tartnefs.   *Reparation is done by Aliments* ; and Alimentation is promoted four ways : *By the Concoction of the inward Parts*
for the fending forth of the nourifhment ; as in *Confortatives* of the
Principal Bowels ; *by Excitation of the outward parts,* for the attraction of nourifhment,as in *due exercifes* and frications ; and fome kind of
Unctions and appropriate Baths;*by preparation of the Aliment it felf* ; that
it may more eafily infinuate it felf , and in a fort anticipate Digeftions,
as in divers and artificial kinds of *feafoning meat, mingling drink, leaven-*
ing bread, and reducing the virtues of all thefe three into one ; by *com-*
forting, the laft act of *Affimilation,* as in *feafonable fleep,* and outward
or *Topick Applications : the Renovation of that which began to wax old,*
is performed two ways, either by *inteneration of the habit of the body*
it felf, as in the ufe of fuppling or foftning applications by Baths , emplaifters and unctions, of fuch quality as may foak or infinuate into the
parts, but not extract from it ; or by *expurgation of the old moifture,*
and fubftitution of new moifture, as in feafonable and often purging ; letting of blood ; attenuating Diets, which reftore the Flower of the
Body, and fo much for *Indications.*

§ *As for Precepts,* although many of them may be deduced from the
Indications, yet we thought good to fet down three of the moft principal.   *Firft,* we give in *Precept* that the *Prolongation of Life,* muft be
expected from a prefcript fet Diet, rather than from any familiar regiment of Food, or the excellency of particular Receipts : for whatfoever are of fuch virtue, as they are able to make nature *retrograde,* are
commonly more ftrong and potent to *alter,* than that they can be compounded together in any Medicine , much lefs be intermingled in familiar food.   It remain therefore that fuch Receipts be adminiftred
regularly, and fucceffively, and at fet appointed times, returning in
certain courfes.

§ *Our fecond Precept is, that the Prolongation of life be expected, ra-*
ther from working upon fpirits, and from a malaciffation or inteneration
of Parts, than from any kinds of Aliment or order of Diet.   For feeing
the Body of Man, and. the Frame thereof (leaving afide outward accidents) three ways becomes Paffive , namely, *from the fpirits ; from*
the parts ; *and from aliments* ; the way of *prolongation of life,* by means
of aliment is a long way about , and that by many ambages and circuits ; but the ways by working upon the fpirits, and upon the parts,
are more compendious , and fooner brings us to the end defired ; becaufe the fpirits are fuddenly moved , both from vapours and paffions, which work ftrangely upon them : and the Parts, by Baths, Unguents, Emplaifters , which in like manner make way by fudden impreffions.

§ *Our third Precept is, that Malaciffation or inteneration of Parts by*
outward Topicks, muft be performed by applications Confubftantial, Pene-
trating, and Stringent.   Confubftantials are willingly entertained with
a kindly imbrace, and properly intenerate and fupple ; *Penetrating*
and infinuating remedies are the Deferents, as it were, of Malaciffant
and mollifying qualities, and convey more eafily and impreffedly the
virtue thereof ; and do themfelves fomewhat expand and open the
Parts.   *Reftringents* keep in the virtue of them both, and for a time

fix it, and also cohibite and reprefs perfpiration; which is a thing repugnant to *Malaciſſation or ſuppling*, becauſe it ſends forth the moiſture; wherefore by theſe three (but diſpoſed in order, and ſucceeding than intermixt) the matter is effected. *In the mean* time we give this caveat, that it is not the intention of *Malaciſſation* by outward Topicks to nouriſh Parts; but only to render them more capable of nouriſhment: for whafoever is more dry, is leſs active to aſſimilate. And thus much of the *prolongation of life*, which is a third part newly aſſigned to Medicine.

§ *Come we now to Coſmetick medicaments, or the Art of Decoration;* which hath indeed, parts Civil, and parts effeminate. For cleanneſs, and the *civil beauty* of the Body was ever eſteemed to proceed from a modeſty of behaviour, and a due reverence *in the firſt place* towards God, whoſe creatures we are, then towards ſociety, wherein we live; and then towards our ſelves, whom we ought no leſs, nay, much more to revere, than we do any others. *But that Adulterate decoration by Painting and Ceruſs*, it is well worthy of the imperfections which attend it; being neither fine enough to deceive, nor handſome to pleaſe, nor ſafe and wholſome to uſe. And it is a wonder that this corrupt cuſtom of *painting*, hath ſo long eſcaped penal Laws, both of the Church and of the State; which yet have been very ſevere againſt the exceſſive vanity of Apparel, and the effeminate trimming of hair. *We read indeed of* Jeſabel *that ſhe painted her face; but of* Eſther *and* Judith, *no ſuch matter is reported.*

2 Reg.9.

§ *Let us proceed to Athletick*, which we take in a ſomewhat more large ſence than uſually it is. For to this we refer any point of *Ability*, whereunto the body of man may be brought, or any aptitude thereto, whether it be of *Activity*, or of *Patience* whereof *Activity* hath two parts, *ſtrength* and *ſwiftneſs*; and patience likewiſe hath two parts, *Indurance* of *Natural wants*, and *Fortitude* in *torments*. Of all theſe we ſee many times notable Inſtances in the practice of Tumblers; in the hard fare of ſome Salvages; in the wonderful ſtrength of Lunaticks; and in the conſtancy of many in the midſt of exquiſite torments. Nay, if there be any other faculty, which falls not within (as in thoſe that Dive, that obtain a ſtrange power of containing Reſpiration, and the like) we refer it to this part. And that ſuch things may ſometimes be done, is moſt certain: but the Philoſophy and enquiry of cauſes touching them, is commonly neglected; for this reaſon, as we ſuppoſe, becauſe men are perſwaded, that ſuch maſteries and commands over Nature, are obtained either by a peculiar inbred aptneſs of ſome men, which falls not within the rules of diſcipline; or from a continual cuſtom from childhood, which rather is commanded than taught. Which though it be not altogether ſo true, yet to what end ſhould we note any *Deficience*? for the *Olympick games* are down long ſince; and a mediocrity in theſe things is enough for uſe; but an excellency in them ſerveth commonly but for Mercenary oſtentation.

§ *In the laſt place we come to Arts of Pleaſure:* They, as the ſenſes to which they refer are of two kinds, *Painting* delights the eye, eſpecially, with an infinite number of ſuch Arts appertaining to Magnificence about Buildings, Gardens, Garments, Veſſels, Cups, Gemms, and the like. *Muſick delights the ear*, which is ſet out with ſuch variety and
preparation

preparation of Voices ; Airs and Inftruments. In ancient time water-Inftruments were efteemed the chief Organs of that Art which now are almoft grown out of ufe. *Thefe Arts* belonging *to the eye and the ear*, are principally above the reft accounted *Liberal* ; thefe two fenfes are more chafte ; the Sciences thereof more learned , as having in their train the Mathematick Art as their Hand-maid : So the one is referr'd to Memory and Demonftrations ; the other unto Manners,and the Paffions of the Mind. The delight of the other fenfes and the Arts about which they are converfant , are in lefs reputation and credit, as drawing nearer to fenfuality than magnificence. Unguents ; Odors ; Dainties ; Delicious fare , and Incitements to Lufts ; need rather a Cenfor to reprefs them , than a Doctor to inftruct them. And it is well obferved by fome , *That while States and Commonwealths have been in their growth and rifing, Arts military have flourifht ; when they have been fetled and ftood at a height, Arts liberal ; and drawing to their declenfion and ruin, Arts voluptuary.* And it is to be fear'd that this age of the world being fomewhat upon the defcent of the wheel, inclines to *Arts voluptuary :* Wherefore we pafs them over. With *Arts voluptuary* I couple *Practices Joculary* ; for the deceiving of the fenfes, may be fet down as one of the delights of the fenfes.

§ *And now we have gone through the Knowledges concerning the Body of man (Phyfick, Cofmetick, Athletick* and *Voluptuary)* we admonifh thus much by the way ; that feeing fo many things fall into confideration about the *Body of man,* as *Parts, Humours, Functions, Faculties, Accidents* ; and feeing (if we could aptly do it) an entire Body fhould be made touching the *Body of man* , which might comprehend all thefe, (like to that of *the knowledge of the Soul,* whereof we fhall fpeak anon) notwithftanding left Arts fhould be too much multiplied, or the ancient Limits of Arts tranfpos'd, more than need muft ; we receive into the Body of Medicine , *the knowledge of the Parts of mans Body , of Functions, of Humours ; of Refpiration, of Sleep ; of Generation ; of the fruit of the Womb, of Geftation in the Womb ; of Growth ; of the flower of Age ; of what Hairs ; of Impinguation,* and the like ; although they do not properly pertain to thofe three duties of *Confervation of Health ; Cure of Difeafes ; Prolongation of Life :* But becaufe mans body is every way the Subject of Medicine. *As for voluntary motion,* and fenfe, we refer them to the *knowledge concerning the Soul* ; as two principal Parts thereof. And fo we conclude *the knowledge which concerns mans Body,* which is but the *Tabernacle of the Soul.*

C H A P. III.

I. The Partition of *Humane Philofophy concerning the Mind, into knowledge of the inspired Essence; and into the knowledge of the senfible, or producted Soul.* § A fecond Partition of *the fame Philofophy, into the knowledge of the Substance and Faculties of the Soul, and the knowledge of the use and objects of the Faculties.* II. Two Appendices of *the knowledge concerning the Faculties of the Soul.* § *The knowledge of Natural Divination;* § *And the knowledge of Fafcination.* III. The Diftribution of *the Faculties of the senfible Soul.* § *Into Motion;* and § *into Senfe.*

I. **N**Ow *let us proceed to the Knowledge which concerns the Mind or Soul of man,* out of the treafures whereof all other Knowledges are extracted. *It hath two Parts, the one entreateth of the Reafonable Soul, which is a thing Divine; the other of the unreafonable Soul, which is common to us with Beafts.* We have noted a little before (where we fpeak of Forms) thofe two different *Emanations of Souls,* which in the firft Creation of them both, offer themfelves unto our view, that is, that one hath its original from the *Breath of God;* the other from the *Matrices of the Elements;* for of the Primitive Emanation of the Rational Soul; thus fpeaks the Scripture, *Déus formavit*

Gen.2.   *hominem de limo terrá, & fpiravit in faciem ejus fpiraculum vitæ :* But the Generation of the unreafonable Soul, or of Beafts, was accom-

Gen.1.   plifht by thefe words; *Producat Aqua, Producat Terra :* And this irrational Soul, as it is in man, is the Inftrument only to the *Reafonable Soul;* and hath the fame original in us, that it hath in Beafts; namely, *from the flime of the earth;* for it is not faid *God form'd the Body of man, of the flime of the earth, but God formed man,* that is the whole man *that Spiraculum* excepted. Wherefore we will ftile that part of the general knowledge concerning *man's foul,* the knowledge of the *fpiracle, or inspired fubftance;* and the other Part, the knowledge *of the Senfible* or *Product Soul.* And feeing that hitherto we handle Philofophy only (placing *facred Theologie* in the clofe of this work) we would not have borrowed this Partition from *Divinity,* if it had not here concurr'd with the Principles of *Philofophy. There are many and great Precellencies of the foul of man, above the fouls of beafts,* evident unto thofe who philofophize even according to fenfe : And wherefoever the concurrent Characters of fuch great excellencies are found, there fhould ever, upon good reafon, be made *a fpecifick Difference.* Wherefore we do not altogether fo well allow the Philofophers promifcuous, and confufe Difcourfes touching *the Functions of the Soul; as if the Soul of man was differenced gradually, rather than fpecifickly; from the foul of Beafts;* no otherwife than the Sun amongft the Stars, or Gold amongft Metals.

§ *There remains another partition alfo to be annexed to the Knowledge in General concerning the foul or mind of man,* before we fpeak at large of the kinds: For what we fhall fpeak of the *fpecies* hereafter, comprehendeth

prehendeth both the partitions; as well that which we have set down already, as this which we shall now propound. *Wherefore the second Partition may be, into the knowledge concerning the Substance and Faculties of the Soul;* and into the knowledge *concerning the use and objects of the Faculties.*

§ This two-fold Partition of the Soul thus premis'd, let us now come unto the species or kinds. The knowledge of the *Spiraculum,* or *inspired Essence,* as that concerning the substance of the Reasonable Soul, comprehends these Inquiries touching the Nature thereof; as whether, *it be Native, or Adventive; Separable, or Inseparable; Mortal, or Immortal; how far it is tied to the Laws of Matter, how far, not, and the like?* What other points soever there are of this kind, although they may be more diligently, and soundly inquired even in Philosophy, than hitherto they have been; yet for all this, in our opinion, they must be bound over at last, unto Religion, there to be determined and defined; for otherwise they still lye open to many errors and illusions of sense. *For seeing that the substance of the Soul was not deduced and extracted in her Creation from the Mass of Heaven and Earth, but immediately inspired from God; and seeing the Laws of Heaven and Earth are the proper subjects of Philosophy; how can the knowledge of the substance of the Reasonable Soul be derived or fetch'd from Philosophy? But it must be drawn from the same inspiration from whence the substance thereof first flowed.* _{Animæ Origo Mylleri-um.}

§ The Knowledge of the *sensible* or *produced Soul,* as touching the substance thereof is truly enquired into; but this enquiry seems to us to be *Deficient:* For what makes these terms of *Actus Ultimus;* and *Forma Corporis;* and such like wild logical Universalities, to the knowledge of the Souls substance? For the *sensible Soul,* or the soul of Beasts, must needs be granted, *to be a Corporal substance attenuated by heat and made Invisible: I say, a thin gentle gale of wind swell'd and blown up from some flamy and airy Nature, indeed with the softness of Air to receive impression, and with the vigor of fire to embrace action; nourished partly by an oily, partly by a watery substance; spread over the Body; residing (in perfect Creatures) chiefly in the head; running through the nerves; refresht and repair'd by the spirituous blood of the Arteries;* as *Bernardinus Telesius,* and his Scholar, *Augustinus Donius* in some points, not altogether unprofitably, have delivered it. Let there be therefore made a more diligent enquiry touching this knowledge, and the rather for that this point, not well understood hath brought forth superstitious and very contagious opinions, and most vilely abasing the Dignity of the *soul of man;* of *Transmigration of souls out of one body into another; and Lustrations of souls by Periods of years; and finally of the too near affinity in every point of the soul of man, with the souls of beasts.* This soul in *Beasts is a principal soul,* whereof the body of Beasts is the Organ; but *in man this soul is it self an Organ* of the Soul Rational and may rather be called by the appellation of a *Spirit,* than of a *Soul.* And thus much of the *substance of the Soul.* _{* DE SUB-STANTIA ANIMÆ SENSIBI-LIS} _{Teles. de Rer. Nat. lib. 5. Donius.}

§ *The Faculties of the Soul are well known, to be Understanding; Reason; Imagination; Memory; Appetite; Will,* and all those Powers, about which the Sciences of *Logick* and *Ethick* are conversant. But in the *knowledge concerning the soul, the Original of these Faculties* ought to be handled

handled, and that Physically, as they are connatural with the Soul, and adhere to it : Only their *uses* and *objects* are designed to other Arts. And in this part (in our opinion) there hath been no extraordinary performance hitherto ; although we do not report it as *Deficient.*

II This Part *touching the faculties of the Soul* hath *two Appendices,* which as they have been handled have rather presented us with smoak, than any lucid flames of truth ; one of these is the Knowledge of *Natural Divination* ; the other of *Fascination.*

§ *Divination* hath been anciently and fitly divided into two Parts ; *Artificial* and *Natural. Artificial* by arguing from the Indication of signs, collects a *Prediction : Natural* from the internal *Divination* of the mind without the assistance of signs, makes a Presage. *Artificial is of two sorts* ; one argueth from *Causes* ; the other from *Experiments* only, by a blind way of Authority ; which later is for the most part superstitious, such as was the Heathen Discipline upon the *inspection of the Intrals of Beasts* ; the *Flight of Birds* ; and the like: So the solemn Astrology of the Chaldeans was little better. Both the kinds of *Artificial Divination* are distributed amongst divers Sciences. The Astrologer hath his *Predictions* from the situation of the stars ; the Physician hath his *Predictions*, of the approach of Death ; of Recovery ; of ensuing Symptoms of Diseases ; from Urines ; Pulses ; aspect of Patients, and the like. The Politick hath his *Predictions* ; *O urbem vænalem & cito perituram, si emptorem invenerit,* The truth of which *Prophesie* staid not long, being first accomplisht in *Sylla,* after in *Cæsar.* Wherefore Predictions of this Nature are not pertinent to the present purpose, but are to be referred over to their proper Arts. But the *Divination Natural,* which springeth from the internal Power of the Soul, is that which we now speak of. *This is of two sorts, the one Native* ; *the other by Influxion. Native* is grounded upon this supposition, *that the mind when it is withdrawn and collected into it self, and not diffused into Organs of the Body, hath from the natural Power of its own Essence, some Prenotion of things future.* And this appears most in sleep ; Extasies ; Propinquity of Death ; more rare, in waking, or when the Body is healthful and strong. And this state of the mind is commonly procured and furthered by abstinencies, and those observances which do most of all retire the *Mind* unto it self from the practick functions of the *Body :* that thus redeem'd from the incumbrances of exterior ingagements, it may possess and enjoy its own Nature. *But Divination by Influxion* is grounded upon another supposition, *That the Mind as a Mirror or Glass should take a secondary kind of Illumination from the fore-knowledge of God and Spirits* ; *unto which the same State and Regiment of the Body which was to the first, doth likewise conduce.* For the same sequestration of the mind causeth it more severely to employ its own Essence ; and makes it more susceptive of *Divine Influxions :* save that the soul, in *Divinations by Influction* is rapt with a kind of fervency and impatiency, as it were of the Deity, wherewith it is possest (which the Ancients noted by the name of *sacred Fury* ; but in *Native Divination,* the mind is enfranchis'd and neerer to a repose rather, and an immunity from labour.

§ *Fascination is the Power and intensive Act of the Imagination upon the Body of another,* (for of the Power of the *Imagination* upon the Body

Salust. in Jugurth.

of

of the imaginant, we have spoken before). In this kind the *school of Paracelsus*, and the Disciples of pretended *Natural Magick*, have been so intemperate, as they have only not equall'd the force and apprehension of the *Imagination*, with the Power of *miracle-working faith*. Others, drawing nearer to the similitude of truth, when they had more intentively considered the secret energies and impressions of things; the Irradiations of the senses; the transmissions of cogitations from Body to Body; the conveyances of *Magnetick* virtues; came to be of opinion, that much more might such impressions; Informations; and Communications be made, from spirit to spirit; being that a spirit of all other things is more powerful and strong to work, and more soft and penetrable to suffer: whence the conceits have grown, made almost popular, of the Mastering spirit; of men ominous and unlucky; of the strokes of love and envy; and of others of like Nature. Incident unto this, is the enquiry, *How the Imagination may be intended and fortified?* For if the *Imagination* fortified be of such great power, then it is material to know by what ways it may be exalted, and made greater than it self? And here comes in crookedly, and as dangerously a Palliation and Defence of a great part of *Ceremonial Magick*. For it may be a specious pretence, that Ceremonies; Characters; Charms; Gesticulations; Amulets, and the like, *do work not by any tacit or sacramental contract with evil spirits; but serve only to strengthen and exalt the imagination of him that useth them; even as the use of Images in religion hath prevail'd for the fixing of mens minds in the Contemplation of things, and the raising of the devotion of them that Pray.* But for my own judgment, if it be admitted, that the force of *Imagination* is so Potent, and that Ceremonies exalt and fortifie that Power; and be it granted, that Ceremonies are used sincerely to that intention, and as a Physical Remedy, without the least thought of inviting the assistance of Spirits by them; yet for all this, I should hold them unlawful, because they impugn and contradict that divine Edict pass'd upon man for sin, *In sudore vultus comedes panem tuum.* For this kind of *Magick* propounds those noble fruits, (which God hath set forth to be bought at the price of Labour) to be purchas'd by a few easie and slothful observances,

III. There remain two knowledges, which refer specially to the *Faculties of the inferior or sensible Soul,* as those which do most Communicate with corporal Organs; the one is of *Voluntary Motion,* the other of *sense and sensibility.*

§ In the former of these the Inquiry hath been very superficial, and one entire part almost quite left out. For concerning the office and apt fabrick of the Nervs and Muscles, and of other parts requisite to *this Motion,* and which part of the Body rests whilst another is moved, and that the Governour and Chariot-driver, as it were, of this *Motion,* is the *Imagination;* so as dismissing the *Image* to which the *Motion* was carried, the *Motion* it self is presently intercepted and arrested (as when we walk, if another serious and fixed thought come into our mind, we presently stand still) and many other such subtilties not to be slighted, have now long ago come into Observation and Enquiry. *And how Compressions,* and *Dilatations,* and *Agitations of the Spirit* (which without question is the spring of *Motion,* should incline, excite, and enforce the

(marginal notes:)
Par. In Param.
Crollij Præf.
Gen. 3.
*
DE NIXIBUS SPIRITUS IN MOTU VOLUNTARIO.

the corporal and ponderous Maſs of the Parts, *hath not yet been enqui-*
red into, and handled with diligence; and no marvail, ſeeing the ſenſible ſoul it ſelf hath been hitherto taken for an *entelechie,* or *ſelf-moving*
Facultie, and ſome Function, rather than a ſubſtance. But now it is
known to be a corporal and materiate Subſtance; it is neceſſary to be
enquired, by what efforts ſuch a puſil and a thin ſoft air ſhould put in
motion, ſuch ſolid and hard bodies. Therefore ſeeing this part is *De-*
ficient let *enquiry* be made thereof.

§ *But of ſenſe and ſenſibility* there hath been made a far more plentiful and diligent enquiry, both in General Treatiſes about them, and in
Particular Sciences; as in *Perſpective,* and *Muſick*; how truly, is not
to our purpoſe to deliver. Wherefore we cannot ſet them as *Deficients :*
Notwithſtanding there are two noble and remarkable Parts, which in
this knowledge we aſſign to be *Deficient*; the one concerning *the diffe-*
rence of Perception and Senſe; the other concerning the *Form* of
Light.

§ *As for the Difference between Perception and Senſe,* Philoſophers
DE DIFFE-
RENTIA
PERCEP-
TIONIS
ET SEN-
SUS
ſhould in their writings *de ſenſu & ſenſibili* have premis'd a ſolid and
found diſcovery thereof, as a matter Fundamental. For we ſee that
there is a manifeſt power of *Perception* even in all Bodies Natural; and
a kind of Election to embrace that which is any way allied in nature, and
favourable to them; and to fly what is adverſe and foreign. Neither
do we mean of more ſubtile *Perceptions* only, *as when the Loadſtone*
draws unto it Iron; *Flame leaps to Bituminous Mould*; one Bubble of
water near another Bubble, cloſeth and incorporates with it; Rays
glance from a white object; the Body of a living Creature aſſimilates
that which is good for it, excerneth what is unprofitable; a piece of
ſpunge even when it is rais'd above the ſurface of the water, ſucks in
water, expels air; and the like. For to what end ſhould we enumerate ſuch inſtances, ſeeing no body, plac'd neer to another, changeth
the other, or is changed of it, unleſs a reciprocal *Perception* precede
the operation. Every Body hath a *Perception* of the Pores and Paſſages by which it inſinuates it ſelf; it feels the invaſion of another Body, to which it yieldeth; it *perceivs* the remove of another Body, by
which it was detained; when it recovers it ſelf, it *perceivs* the divul-
ſion of its continuance, which for a time reſiſteth; and in a word, *Per-*
ception is diffuſed through the whole body of Nature. Air doth ſo
exactly *Senſe* Hot and Cold, that the *Perception* thereof is far more ſubtile than mans Touch, which yet is taken for the diſcerning Rule of
Hot and Cold. *Two faults* therefore are found concerning this knowledge; that men have for moſt part paſt it over untouch'd, and unhand-
led; which notwithſtanding is a moſt noble ſpeculation: The other
is that they who perchance have addicted their minds to this contem-
Campa-
nella, ulij.
plation, have in the heat of this Purſuit gone too far, and attributed
Senſe to all Bodies, that it is almoſt a piacular crime to *pull of a bow from*
a Tree, leſt it ſhould groan and complain as Polydore did. But they ſhould
Virg. Æn.
3.
explore with diligence the difference of *Perception* and *Senſe,* not only in comparing of *Senſibles* with *Inſenſibles* according to the entire body (as of Plants, and living Creatures) but alſo to obſerve in the ſenſible Body, what ſhould be the cauſe that ſo many Actions ſhould be
diſcharg'd, and that without any *Senſe* at all? Why Aliments are digeſted,

gefted, egefted: Humours and fucculent Moiftures carried upwards and downwards ; the Heart and Pulfe beat ; the Guts as fo many Shops, or Work-houfes fhould every one accomplifh his proper Work; and yet all thefe, and many fuch like are performed without *Senfe* ? But men have not with fufficient enquiry fearcht or found out of what Nature the Action of *Senfe* is; and what kind of Body ; what delay ; what Conduplication of Impreffion are required to this, that pain or pleafure fhould follow ? To clofe this Point they do feem to be altogether ignorant of the difference betwixt *fimple perception and fenfe ; how far perception may be made without fenfe* ? Nor is this enquiry a controverfie of words, but a matter of great and important moment. *Wherefore let* there be made a better *inquiry* of this knowledge, as of a matter very profitable, and of manifold ufe. Confidering alfo that the ignorance of fome of the ancient Philofophers touching this matter, fo far obfcured the light of reafon, as that they thought, *there was, without any difference, a Soul infufed into all Bodies* ; nor did they conceive how *Motion*, with a difcerning inftinct, could be made with *Senfe* ; or *Senfe* exift without a *Soul.*

§ *As for the Form of Light*, that there hath been made a due enquiry thereof (fpecially feeing men have fo painfully employ'd their Studies in the *Perfpectives*) may well be cenfur'd as a ftrange overfight. For neither in the *Perfpectives*, nor elfewhere, is there any thing inquired concerning *Light*, of any worth or weight : The Radiations of it are handled, the Originals not : *But the placing of Perfpectives amongft the Mathematicks hath begotten this defect ; and others of like nature ; becaufe men have made a too early departure from Phyfick.* So on the other fide the handling of *Light*, and the Caufes thereof, in *Phyficks* is commonly fuperftitious, as of a thing of a middle nature, betwixt natural and Divine ; in fo much as fome of *Plato's* School have introduced *Light* as a thing more ancient than *Matter it felf* : For when the empty fpace was fpread abroad they affirm'd, in a vain imagination, that it was firft fill'd with *Light* ; and afterwards with a *Body* ; whereas Holy Writ fets down plainly *the Mafs of Heaven and Earth to be a dark Chaos before the Creation of Light.* But what are handled Phyfically, and according to fenfe, of this fubject, prefently defcendeth to *Radiations* ; fo as there is very little Philofophical enquiry extant touching this point. And men ought to fubmit their Contemplations a while, and to enquire what is common to all *Lucid Bodies*, as of the *Form* of *Light* : For what an immenfe difference of Body is there (if they may be confidered according to their dignity) betwixt the Sun and the rotten Wood, or the putrid fcales of Fifh? They fhould likewife make enquiry, what fhould be the Caufe why fome things take fire, and once throughly heated caft forth a *Light* ; others not ? Iron, Metals, Stones, Glafs, Wood, Oyl, Tallow by fire, either caft forth a *Flame*, or at leaft grow *Red* : But *Water* and *Air* heated with the fury of the hotteft Flames, to the higheft degree they are capable of, acquire no fuch Light, nor caft forth any Splendor. If any man think, it therefore thus comes to pafs, becaufe it is the property of fire to *give light* ; but *Water* and *Air* are utter enemies to *Fire* ; fure he was never rowed with Oars in a dark night upon falt waters, and in a hot feafon ; where he might have feen fmall drops of water rebounding from the clafhing of the Oars, to

RADIX PERSPECTIVÆ SIVE DE FORMA LUCIS.

Ficin. Card. de Cufa.

Gen. 1.

S   *fparkle*

sparkle and cast forth a *light:* Which is likewise seen in the fervent froath of the Sea which they call the *Sea-longs.* And what affinity with flame and fired matter have the *Cicindulæ,* the *Luciolæ,* and the *Indian Fly,* which cast a light over a whole arched Room; or the eyes of certain living Creatures in the dark; and Sugar, as it is grated or broken; or the sweat of a horse hard ridden, in a soultry night; and many more? Nay, *many have understood so little in this point, as many have thought the sparks from a flint to be attrited Air.* But when the Air is not fired with heat, and apparently *conceives Light,* how comes it to pass, that Owls and Cats, and many other Creatures see in the night? *So that it must needs be (seeing vision cannot be conveyed without light) that there is a native and inbred light in Air, although very feeble and weak; yet such as may be proportioned to the Optick Beams of such Creatures, and may suffice them for sight.* But the cause of this evil, as of many more, that men have not drawn forth the *common Forms of things Natural,* from *particular Instances;* which is that we have set down as the proper subject of *Metaphysick;* which is it self a part of *Physick,* or of the knowledge of *Nature.* Therefore let there be *enquiry* made of the *Form and Originals of Light,* and in the mean time, it may be placed among *Deficients.* And thus much of the *Knowledge concerning the substance of the Soul, Rational and Sensible,* with their *Faculties,* and of the *Appendices* of the same *Knowledge.*

THE

THE
Fifth Book
OF

FRANCIS L. VERULAM
Vicount S.t *ALBAN*,

● OF THE

Dignity and Advancement
OF

LEARNING.

To the KING.

CHAP. I.

I. The Partition *of the Knowledge, which respecteth the Use, and Objects of the Faculties of the Mind of Man, into Logick, and Ethick.* II. The Division of *Logick into the Arts, of Invention; of Judgement; of Memory; and of Tradition.*

HE Knowledge respecting the *understanding of Man* (*Excellent King*) and that other respecting *his Will*, are, as it were, Twins by Birth: For the *Purity of Illumination*, and the Liberty of *will began together; fell together: Nor is there in the Universal Nature of things so intimate a Simpathy, as that of Truth and Goodness.* The more shame for Learned Men, if they be for Knowledge like *winged Angels*; for base Desires, they be like *Serpents* which crawl in the Dust, carrying indeed about them Minds like a Mirror or Glass; but menstruous and distain'd.

§ *We come now to the Knowledge which respecteth the use and objects of the Faculties of the Mind of Man.* This hath *two Parts*, and they well known, and by general consent received, *Logick and Ethick:* Save that we have a little before set at liberty *Civil Knowledge*, which commonly was taken in as a Part of *Ethick*; and have made it an entire *Knowledge of man congregate or in society*; handling here *only man segregate*

S 2 *gate*

gate. Logick intreateth of the Understanding *and* Reason ; Ethick *of the* Will, Appetite *and* affections ; the one produceth *Decrees* ; the other *Actions.* It is true that the *Imagination* in both Provinces, Judicial and Ministerial, performs the Office of an Agent or Nuncius, or common Atturney. For *Sense* sends over all sorts of Ideas unto the *Imagination,* upon which, Reason afterwards sits in Judgement : And *Reason* interchangeably sends over selected and approved Ideas to the *Imagination,* before the Decree can be acted. For *Imagination* ever precedes voluntary motion and incites it ; so that *Imagination* is a common reciprocal Instrument to both : Saving that this *Janus* is bifronted, and turns faces : For the face towards *Reason* hath the print of *Truth* ; but the face towards *Action* hath the print of *Goodness :* which nevertheless are faces, ●

Ovid.
Met.

————*Quales decet esse sororum.*

Neither is the *Imagination* a meer and simple Messenger, but is invested with, or at leastwise usurpeth no small Authority, besides the duty of the message : For it is well said by *Aristotle, That the Mind hath over the* **Polit.1,** *Body that command which the Lord hath over a bond-man ; but the* Reason *hath over the* Imagination *that command which a Magistrate hath over a free Citizen,* who may come also to rule in his turn. For we see that in matters of *Faith* and *Religion,* the *Imagination* mounts, and is elevated above *Reason* ; not that *Divine Illumination* resideth in the *Imagination* ; (nay, rather in the high Tower of the mind, and understanding) but, *as in virtues Divine, grace makes use of the motion of the will ; so in Illuminations Divine, grace makes use of the Imagination :* Which is the Cause that Religion sought ever an access, and way to the *Mind,* by *Similitudes, Types, Parables, Visions, Dreams.* Again, it is no small Dominion the *Imagination* hath in perswasions, insinuated by the power of Eloquence : for where the minds of men are gently intreated, inflamed, and any way forcibly won by the smooth Artifice of speech, all this is done by exalting the *Imagination,* which growing hot and impatient, not only triumphs over *Reason* ; but in a sort offers violence unto it ; partly by blinding, partly by extimulating it. Nevertheless I see no reason why we should depart from the former Division : For the *Imagination* commonly doth not produce Sciences ; for *Poesie* which hath ever been attributed to the *Imagination,* is to be esteemed rather a play of the wit, than a knowledge. As for the power of the *Imagination in things Natural,* we have assigned that, a little before, to the *Doctrine de Anima.* And for the affinity it hath with *Rhetorick,* we think it fit to refer it to the Art it self, whereof we shall intreat hereafter.

§ *This Part of Humane Philosophy which is Rational or respecting Logick,* is to the Taste and Palate of many Wits, not so delightful ; and **Sen.alicu-** seemeth nothing else but a net and snare of thorny subtilty. For as it **bi.** is truly said. *that knowledge is animi Pabulum;* so in the nature of mens appetites, and election of this *food,* most men are of the taste and stomach of the Israelites in the Desert, that would fain have turned *ad ollas Carnium,* and were weary of *Manna* ; which though it were Celestial, yet seemed it less nutritive and comfortable. So generally those *Knowledges* relish best, that have an infusion somewhat more esculent of flesh in them ; such

such as are *Civil History, Morality, Policy,* about the which mens affections; Praiſes, Fortunes do turn, and are converſant : But this ſame *lumen ſiccum,* doth parch and offend moſt mens watry and ſoft natures.
But if we would meaſure and value things according to their proper
worth, *Rational Sciences are the keys of all other Arts ; and as the Hand
is the Inſtrument of Inſtruments ; the Mind , the Form of Forms ; ſo
theſe knowledges are to be eſteemed the Art of Arts.* Neither do they
direct only; but likewiſe ſtrengthen and confirm; as the uſe and habit
of ſhooting, doth not only enable to ſhoot a nearer ſhoot ; but alſo
to draw a ſtronger Bow.

II. *Arts Logical or intellectual are four in number ,* divided according
to the ends whereunto they are referred : For mans labour in *Rational Knowledges* is, either to *invent that which is ſought ; or to judge what
is invented ; or to retain that which is judg'd ; or to deliver that which is
retained :* So as there muſt needs be ſo many *Rational Sciences ;* Art of
Inquiry or *Invention ;* Art of *Examination* or *Judgement ;* Art of *Cuſto-
dy* or *Memory ;* and Art of *Elocution* or *Tradition ;* whereof we will
ſpeak, of every particular apart.

CHAP. II.

I. The Partition *of the* Art of Invention *into the* Inventive of Arts :
and of Arguments. § The former of theſe, which is the more
eminent, is *Deficient.* II. The Diviſion *of the* Inventive Art of
Arts, *into literate Experience.* § And a new Organ. III. A Delineation *of Experience Literate.*

I. *I*Nvention *is of two kinds, much differing ; the one of Arts and Sciences ; the other of Arguments and Speeches.* The former of theſe
I report to be wholly *Deficient,* which ſeems to me to be ſuch a *Defi-
ence,* as if in the making of an *Inventory,* touching the eſtate of a *De-
funct,* it ſhould be ſet down, *of ready money nothing :* For as *money*
will fetch all other commodities ; ſo all other *Arts* are purchas'd by
this *Art.* And *as the Weſt Indies* had never been diſcovered, if the uſe
of the *Mariners Needle* had not firſt been diſcovered, though thoſe *Regions* be vaſt , the *Verſor* is a ſmall Motion : So it cannot be found
ſtrange , if *in the diſcovery and advancement of Arts,* there hath not
been made greater Progreſſion, ſeeing the *Art of Invention and Perlu-
ſtration* hitherto was unknown.

§ *That this part of knowledge is wanting ſtands plainly confeſſed.*
For firſt *Logick* doth not profeſs, nay, not pretend to *invent* either Arts
Mechanical, or Arts (as they call them) *Liberal ;* nor to elicite the
Operations of the one, or the *Axioms* of the other ; but ſpeaks to men
as it were in Paſſage, and ſo leaves them with this inſtruction, *cuiq; ſuâ
arte credendum.* *Celſus* a wiſe man, as well as a Phyſician (though it
be the cuſtom of all men to be copious in the commendation of their
own Profeſſion) acknowledgeth it gravely and ingeniouſly, ſpeaking of
the Emperical and Dogmatical Sects of Phyſicians, *That Medicines and*
Cures

* EXPERI-
ENTIA LI-
TERATA,
SIVE VE-
NATIO
PANIS.

Ariſt. Mo-
ral. 1.

De Re
Medica. Cures were first found out, and then after the Reasons and Causes were discovered: not the other way, that the Causes first extracted from the nature of things, gave light to the invention of Remedies. But *Plato* often notes InTimæo.
Philib. a-
libi. it; *That particulars are infinite;* again, *that the highest Generalities give no sufficient Direction;* and *that the Pyth of all Sciences,whereby the Arts-man is distinguisht from the Inexpert, consisteth in middle Propositions, which experience hath delivered and taught in every particular Science.* And therefore we see, that they which discourse of the first *Inventors of things,* and the *Originals of Sciences,* have celebrated rather *Chance* than *Art;* and have brought in *Beasts,Birds,Fishes,Serpents,* rather than *Men,* as the first Doctors of Sciences.

Virg. Æn.
12.
Dictamnum Genetrix Cretâ carpit ad Ida,
Puberibus Caulem foliis & flore comantem
Purpureo, non illa feris incognita Capris
Gramina, cum tergo volucres hæsere sagittæ.

So that it was no marvail (the manner of Antiquity being for to consecrate *Inventors* of things profitable) that the Ægyptians, an ancient Nation, to whom many Arts owe their Beginnings, had their Temples full of the Idols of Brutes, but almost empty of the Idols of men,

Virg.
Æn.8.
Omnigenumq; Deûm monstra & Latrator Anubis,
Contra Neptunum; & Venerem, contraq; Minervam, &c.

And if you like better, from the Tradition of the Grecians, to ascribe the *first invention of Arts to men;* yet you cannot say that *Prometheus* applied his contemplation on set purpose to the invention of Fire; Ovid.Me-
tam.&c. or that when he first stroak the flint he expected Sparks; but that he fell upon this experiment by chance, and as they say, ——*furtum Jovi fecisse;* so as for the *Invention of Arts* we are more beholding to a wild Goat for *Chirurgery;* or to a Nightingal for modulations of Musick; Pamirol.
li Rer.
M. .Pa.2. the *Ibis* for *Clysters;* to a Potlid that flew open for Artillery; and to say in a word, to *Chance,* or any thing else more than to *Logick.* Neither is the form of *Invention,* which *Virgil* describes,much other,

Virg.G.1.
Et varias usus meditando extunderet Artes
Paulatim ——

For here is no other method of *Invention* propounded, than that which brute Beasts are capable of, and often put in ure, *which is a first intentive sollicitude about some one thing, and a perpetual practice* Oratio.
pro L.
Cor. Bal-
bo. *thereof; which the necessity of their Conservation imposeth upon such Creatures;* for *Cicero* saith very truly, *usus uni rei deditus, & naturam & artem sæpe vincit,* Therefore if it be said of men,

Virg.G.1.
.
Labor omnia vincit
Improbus, & duris urgens in rebus egestas.

It is likewife faid of Beafts,

Quis expedivit Pfittaco fuum Καῖρε 3

Who taught the Raven in a droughth to throw Pebbles into a hollow
tree, where by chance fhe fpied water, that the water might rife fo as
fhe might come to it ? Who taught the Bee to fail through fuch a vaft
fea of Air, to the Flowers in the Fields 3 and to find the way fo far
off to her Hive again? Who taught the Ant to bite every grain of
Corn that fhe burieth in her Hill, left it fhould take root and grow, and
fo delude her hope ? And if you obferve in *Virgil's* verfe, the word *ex-
tundere*, which imports the *Difficulty*, and the word *Paulatim*, which
imports the *flownefs* 3 we are where we were, even amongft the *Egyptian
Gods*, feeing hitherto men have made little ufe of the faculty of
Reafon, none at all of the *duty of Art*, for the *difcovery of Inventions.*

§ Secondly, if this which we affirm, be well confidered, it is de-
monftrated by the *Form of Induction* which Logick propounds, namely by that *Form of Inference*, whereby the Principles of Sciences are
found out and proved 3 which, as it is now framed, is utterly vitious
and incompetent, and fo far from perfecting nature, that it rather perverts and diftorts it. For he that fhall exactly obferve how this *Æthe-
real Dew of Sciences* 3 like unto that the Poet fpeaks of,

Aerei mellis Cæleftia dona,

is gather'd (feeing that even Sciences themfelves are extracted out of
particular examples, partly Natural, partly Artificial, or from the
Flowers of the Field and Garden) fhall find that the mind, of her own
nature and inbred difpofition, doth more ingenioufly, and with better Invention, Act an *Induction*, than Logicians defcribe it. For from
a *nude enumeration of Particulars* (as Logicians ufe to do) without an
Inftance Contradictory, is a vitious Conclufion 3 nor doth fuch an *Induction* infer more than a probable Conjecture. For who will take
upon him, when the particulars which a man knows, and which he
hath mention'd, appear only on one fide, there may not lurk fome
particular which is altogether repugnant? As if *Samuel* fhould have
refted in thofe fons of *Ifhay*, which were brought before him in the
houfe 3 and fhould not have fought *David*, which was abfent in the
field. And this *Form of Induction* (to fay plainly the truth) is fo grofs
and palpable, that it might feem incredible, that fuch acute and fubtil
wits as have exercis'd their meditations in thefe things, could have ob-
truded it upon the world 3 but that they hafted to Theories, and Dog-
maticals 3 and from a kind of pride and elation of mind defpifed *particulars*, fpecially any long ftay upon them. *For they have ufed thefe
examples and particular inftances, but as Sergeants and Whifflers, ad fum-
movendam turbam, to make way and room for their opinions 3 and never
advis'd with them from the beginning 3 that fo a legitimate and mature deliberation, concerning the truth of things, might be made.* Certainly it is
a thing hath touch'd my mind with a pious and religious wonder, to
fees

see the fame fteps leading to error, troden in divine and humane enquiries. For as in the apprehending of divine truth, men cannot endure to become as a child; fo in the apprehending of humane truth, for men come to years, yet to read, and repeat, the firft Elements *of Inductions,* as if they were ftill children, is reputed a poor and contemptible employment.

§ Thirdly if it be granted, that the *Principles* of Sciences may be rightly inferr'd from the *Induction,* which they ufe, or from fenfe and experience; yet neverthelefs, certain it is, that inferiour Axioms, cannot rightly and fafely be deduced, by Syllogifm from them, in things of nature, which participate of matter. For in *Syllogifm* there is a reduction of Propofitions to *Principles* by middle Propofitions: And this Form, whether for *Invention,* or for *Proof,* in Sciences Popular, as *Ethicks, Politicks, Laws,* and the like, takes place; yea, and in Divinity; feeing it hath pleafed God of his goodnefs, to accommodate himfelf to mans capacity: but in Natural Philofophy where nature fhould be convinc'd and vanquifht by deeds, and not an Adverfary, by Argument; truth plainly efcapes our hands: *becaufe that the fubtilty of the operations of Nature, is far greater than the fubtilty of words.* So that the *Syllogifm* thus failing, there is every way need of help and fervice, of true and rectified *Induction,* as well for the more general Principles, as inferiour Propofitions. *For Syllogifms* confift of Propofitions, Propofitions of words, words are the currant tokens or marks of the Notions of things; wherefore *if thefe Notions (which are the fouls of words)* be groffely, and variably abftracted from things, the whole building falls. Neither is it the laborious examination either of Confequences, Arguments, or the verity of Propofitions, that can ever repair that ruine; being the error is, as the Phyficians fpeak, in the *firft digeftion;* which is not rectified by the fequent functions of Nature. And therefore it was not without great and evident Caufe, that many of the Philofophers, and fome of them, fome of fingular note, became *Academicks;* and *Scepticks;* which took away all *certainty of knowledge* or of *Comprehenfions;* and denyed that the knowledge of man extended further than apparence and probability. It is true that fome are of opinion, that *Socrates,* when he put off certainty of fcience from himfelf,

Cic. in A-
cad.

did this but by a form of *Irony, & fcientiam diffimulando fimulaffe;* that is, that by renouncing thofe things which he manifeftly knew, he might be reputed to know even that which he knew not; neither in the later Academy, which *Cicero* embraced, was this opinion of *Acatalepfie* held fo fincerely: For all thofe which excell'd for eloquence, commonly

In Acad.
Q.

made choice of this Sect, as fitter to give glory to their copious fpeech, and variable difcourfe both ways; which was the caufe they turn'd afide from that ftreight way by which they fhould have gone on to truth, to pleafant walks made for delight and paftime. *Notwithftanding* it appears that there were many fcatter'd in both Academies, the old and new (much more among the *Scepticks*) that held this *Acatalepfie* in fimplicity and integrity: But here was their chief error, that they charged the *Perceptions* of the *Senfes,* whereby they did extirpate and pluck up Sciences by the roots. For the fenfes although they many times deftitute and deceive men, yet affifted by much induftry they may be fufficient for Sciences; and that not fo much by the help of *Inftruments* (though thefe

are

are in some sort useful) as of experiments of the same kind, which may produce more subtil objects, than for the faculty of sense, are by sense comprehensible. And they ought rather to have charged the defects in this kind upon the errors, and contumacie of the mind, which refuseth to be pliant and morigerous to the Nature of things; and to crooked demonstrations and rules of arguing and concluding, ill set down and propounded from the *Perception of Sense*. This we speak not to disable the mind of man; or that the business should be abandoned; but that apt and proper assistances may be accquired; and applied to the understanding, whereby men may subdue the difficulties of things, and the obscurity of Nature. *For no man hath such a steadiness of hand by nature or practice, that he can draw a strait line or make a perfect circle with his hand at liberty, which yet is easily done by rule or compass.* This is that very business which we go about and with great pains endeavour, *that the mind by the help of Art might be able to equal Nature;* and that there might be found out an Art of Discovery, or Direction, which might disclose, and bring to light other Arts, and their Axioms and Works. This upon good ground we report *Deficient.*

II This Art of *Discovery* (for so we will call it) hath two parts; for either the Indication is made from *Experiments to Experiments;* or from *Experiments to Axioms;* which may likewise design *new Experiments;* whereof the former we will term, *Experientia Literata;* the later, *Interpretatio Naturæ,* or *Novum Organum.* Indeed the former (as we have touched heretofore is not properly to be taken for an *Art,* or a part of Philosophy, but a kind of *sagacity;* wherefore we sometimes call it *Venatio Panis,* borrowing the name from the Fable. *But as a man may go on his way after a three-fold manner; either when himself feels out his way in the dark; or being weak-sighted is led by the hand of another; or else when he directs his footing by a light:* So when a man essays all kind of *Experiments* without sequence or method that is a meer palpation; but when he proceeds by direction and order in *Experiments,* it is as if he were led by the hand; and this is it which we understand by *Literate Experience:* For the *light it self,* which was the third way, is to be derived from the *Interpretation of Nature, or the New Organum.*

[margin note: ⋆ EXPERIENTIA LITERATA sive VENATIO PANIS]

III. *Literate Experience, or the Hunting of Pan* shews the divers ways of making *Experiments:* This (seeing we have set it down as *Deficient,* and that it is a matter not altogether so plain and perspicuous) we will according to our manner and design give some light touches and shadows of it. The manner of *making Experiment* chiefly proceeds; either by *variation of the experiment;* or by *Production of the Experiment;* or by *translation of the Experiment;* or by *inversion of the Experiment;* or by *compulsion of the experiment;* or by *Application of the Experiment;* or by *Copulation of the Experiment;* or else by the *lots and chance of the Experiment.* And all these are limited without the terms of any *Axiom* of *Invention:* For that other part of the *New Organ* takes up and containeth in it all *Transition of Experiments into Axioms; or of Axioms into Experiments.*

§ *Variation* of *Experience* is first practis'd upon *Matter;* that is when the *Experiment* in things already known commonly adhereth to such a *kind of matter;* and now it is tried in other things of like kind; as

the

the *making of Paper* is only tried in linen, and not in silk, (unless perchance amongst the Chineses; nor yet in stuffs intermixt with hair and bristles, of which is made that which we call chame-lot; nor yet in woollen, cotton, and skins, although these three last seem to be more Heterogeneous, and so rather may become useful mingled, than separate: So insition in fruit-Trees, is practis'd, but rarely tried in Trees wild; although it is affirm'd that an Elm grafted upon an Elm, will produce wonderful shades of leaves. Insition likewise in flowers, is very rare, though now the Experiment begins to be made upon musk-Roses, which are successfully inoculate upon common Roses. So we place the *variation in the Part of a thing amongst the variations in Matter.* For we see a scion, or young slip grafted upon the trunk of a tree, to shoot forth more prosperously, than if it had been set in earth: And why, in like manner, should not the seed of an Onion inserted into the head of another Onion while it is green, germinate more happily than if it had been sown in the bare earth? And here the *Root* is varied for the *Trunk*, that the thing may seem to be a kind of insition in the root. *Secondly, the variation of an Experiment may be made in the efficient.* The *beams of the Sun* through burning-Glasses are so fortified, and intended to such a degree of heat, that they are able to set on flame any matter, which is apt easily to conceive fire: Now whether *may the beams of the Moon*, by the same Glasses be actuated by some weak degrees of warmth; that we may see whether all heavenly Bodies be hot in power? So *bright and radiant heats* are exalted by Glasses: Whether are *gloomy and opaque heats* (as of stones and mettals, before they be made burning hot by the force of fire) subject to the same impression, or are they rather in this some portions of light? So Amber, and Jet, or an Aggat chafed draw unto them straw; whether warmed at the fire will they do the like? *Thirdly, the variation of an Experiment may be made in Quantity*, concerning which a very diligent care is to be taken, being it is encompassed with many errors. For men are of opinion *that if the Quantity be augmented and multiplied, the virtue is proportionably augmented and multiplied;* and this commonly is with them a Postulatum, and a supposed truth, as if the matter were a Mathematical certitude; which is utterly untrue. *A globe of Lead, or a pound in weight* let fall from a Tower, say, it descends to the earth in the space of ten Pulses; whether will *a Globe of two pound weight* (in which that force of Motion, which they call Natural, should be doubled,) light upon the earth in the space of five Pulses? But that Globe shall come down almost in an equal space of time with this, and shall not be accelerated according to the measure of *Quantity.* So (imagine,) one dragm of Sulphur mingled with half a pound of Steel, it will make it fluid and liquid; Will therefore an ounce of Sulphur suffice to the dissolving of four pounds of Steel? But that follows not; *For it is certain that the obstinacy of the matter in the Patient is more encreas'd by Quantity, than the Activity of the virtue in the Agent.* Besides, too much, as well as too little frustrates the effect: For in the excoctions and depurations of Mettals it is a familiar error, that to advance excoction, they augment the heat of the Furnace, or the *Quantity of the Injection;* but if these exceed due proportion, they hinder the operation; because through their force and acrimony, they turn much of
the

the pure Metal into fumes, and carry it away; so as there is a loss in the Mettal; and the mass which remains through the emission of the Spirits becomes more obstinate and indurate. *Men should* therefore remember the mockery of *Æsop's* housewife, who conceited that by doubling her measure of Barley, her Hen would daily lay her two eggs: *Æsop: Fab.* But the Hen grew fat and laid none. It is not altogether safe to rely upon any Natural experiment, before proof be made *both in a lesser, and greater Quantity.*

§ *Production of an Experiment is of two sorts, Repetition and Extension; namely when the Experiment either is iterated; or driven to a kind of subtilty.* Example of *Repetition* may be this; *the spirit of wine* is made of wine once distilled, and it is much more quick and strong than wine it self; will likewise the spirit it self of wine distilled, or sublimated, proportionably exceed it self in strength? *But Repetition* also is not without deceit; for neither doth the second exaltation equal the excess of the first; and many times by *iteration of the Experiment* after a certain state, and height of operation, Nature is so far from a further progression, as she rather falls into a relapse. Wherefore the *experiment* must be made with Caution and judgment. So *Quick-silver* in linen, or else in the midst of moulten Lead when it begins to grow cold, the Quick-silver inserted is stupified, and is no longer fluid; will the same *Quick-silver* if it be often so practis'd upon, become so fixt as to be made malleable? The example of extension may be this, *water placed upwards*, and made pensile; and by a long neb of a glass dipt in wine, mixt with water, will unmingle, the water from the wine, the wine leasurely ascending, and setling in the top; the water descending, and setling in the bottom: Now as wine and water which are two divers bodies are separate by this device; may the more subtil parts of wine in like manner, which is an entire body, be separate from the more gross, that so there may be a distillation, as it were, by weight; and that there may be found floating in the top, a substance nearest to the spirit of wine, but perchance more delicate? So the Loadstone draweth Iron solid, and entire, unto it; will a piece of a Loadstone, plunged into dissolv'd parcels and fragments of Iron, allure the Iron unto it, and cover it self with it? So *the versor of a Mariners needle* applies it self to the Poles of the world: Doth it do this after the same manner, and upon the same consequence whereby Celestial Bodies move? Namely if you should place the Needle in a contrary posture, that is, in the South-point, and there stay it a while, and then cease your forcing it, and leave it to it self; would this *Needle* turn it self perchance to the North; and chuse rather to wheel about by the West into its desired natural site, than by the East? *So gold imbibeth* Quicksilver which is contiguous to it; doth the gold ingulf, and suck up this Quicksilver into it self without extension of its substance, that it becomes a Mass more ponderous than gold it self? *So some men subminister helps to their memories* by setting up Images and Pictures of Persons in certain rooms; would they attain the same end, if (setting aside such Images) they should effigiate to themselves an Idea of their gests and habits. And thus much of the Poduction of an experiment.

§ *The translation of an experiment is three-fold, either from Nature, or chance into Art; or from Art, or one Practice into another; or from*

T 2   *4.*

a part of some Art, into a diverse part of the same Art. Of Translation from Nature, or chance into Art, there are innumerable examples; for that almost all Mechanical Arts owe their originals from slender beginnings presented by *Nature* or *Chance.* It is a receiv'd Proverb, *That Grapes consorted with Grapes sooner come to maturity:* Which from the Nature of mutual assistance and friendship grew popular. But our makers of Syder, which is a wine of Apples, do well imitate this: For they provide that they be not stampt or prest, before, by being cast into heaps for a time; they mature by mutual contact; whereby the acidity and tartness of the liquor is corrected. So the *imitation of Artificial Rainbows* by the spiss aspersion of little drops, is by an easie derivation from natural Rain-bows composed of a dewy Cloud. *So the manner of distilling* might be taken either from above, as from showers or dew; or from that homely experiment of Drops adhering to Covers put upon Pots of boyling water. *And a man would have been a-fraid to have imitated Thunder and Lightning,if the Pot-lid of that chymick Monk had not,by being tost up into the air, instructed him.* But the more plentiful *this experiment* is of examples, the fewer we need to produce. And if men would be at leisure to imploy their studies in the inquiry of things profitable; they should view attentively, by degrees and of set purpose all the workmanship, and the particular workings of Nature; and perpetually, and thoroughly meditate with themselves, which of those may be transfer'd to Arts, *For Nature is the Mirror of Art :* And the experiments are as many which may be *translated from Art into Art*; *or from one Practice into another,* though this is not so much in use: For nature every way is obvious to all men; but Arts appropriate to particular Professors, are only known to them. *Spectacles* are invented to help a weak sight; might there be contrived an instrument which fastned to the ear, might help such as are thick of hearing? So *embalming, and honey conserve dead Corps*; might not some of those ingredients be transfer'd into a medicine, which might be useful to bodies alive? So the practice of Seals upon wax; cements for walls,and upon Lead is ancient; but this invention shewed the way to Impression upon Paper, or the Art of Printing. *So in the Art of Cookery, salt seasons flesh,* and that better in Winter, than in Summer: Might not this be profitably translated to Baths and their temperament, as occasion shall require; either to impress some good moisture, or extract some peccant humour. *So salt* in the new-found experiment of *Artificial Conglaciations* is found to have great power to condense: Might not this be transfer'd to the condensation of Metals; seeing it is known long since that strong-waters,being composited of some kinds of salts, have a power to deject and precipitate small sands of Gold out of certain Metals, not so dense and compact as Gold ? *So painting revives the memory of a thing,by the Image of a Picture:* Is not this traduced into an Art, which they call *the Art of Memory?* Let this in general serve for admonition; that nothing can so much conduce to the drawing down, as it were, from heaven, a whole showr of new and profitable Inventions, as this, that the experiments of many Mechanick Arts, may come to the knowledge of one man, or some few, who by mutual conference may whet and sharpen one another; that so by this which we call *Translation of Experiments,* Arts may nourish, and as

it

Pancirol-lus par.2.

it were by a commixture, and communication of Rayes, inflame one the other. For although the rationall way by an artificial *Organum*, promise far greater matters; yet neverthelefs this *fagacity by literate experience*, may in the mean project and fcatter to the benefit of man (as miffive Donatives amongft the Ancients) many rudiments to know-ledge, which may be had at hand. *There remains the Tranflation of a Part of Art into another part diverfe from it*, which little differs from the *Tranflation of Art into Art.*: But becaufe many *Arts* exercife great fpaces, fo as they may very well fuftain a *Tranflation* within the limits of their own operations; we thought good to annex this kind of *Tran-flation*; fpecially feeing it is in fome Arts of very great import. For it maketh much to the advancement and amplification of the Art of Phyfick; if the *Experiments* of that part of Medicine *concerning the Cures of Difeafes*, be transfer'd to thofe Parts concerning the *Regiment of Health*, and the *Prolongation of Life.* For if fome excellent *Opiate* be of that force and virtue, as to reprefs and affwage the raging infla-mation of the fpirits, in a peftilential Fever; let no man queftion, but that a like receipt by a due proportioned Dofe made familiar, may in fome degree put back and retard inflamation, which grows and creeps upon us by age. Thus much for the *Tranflation of Experiments.*

§ *Inverfion of Experiment* is, when the contrary to that which is by *Experiment* manifeft, is tried: For example, *Heat by Glaffes is inten-ded*; is cold fo too? So *Heat* when it diffufeth it felf is yet rather car-ried upwards: Is cold likewife in diffufing it felf carried rather down-wards? For inftance, take a fmall Bar of Iron, and heat it on one end, then fet it upright, (that end which is heated placed downwards) lay-ing your hand upon the end, it will prefently burn your hand; but now inverfe the Bar, placing the hot part upwards, and your hand up-on the part which is downwards, and you fhall not feel the heat fo foon by many Pulfes: Whether or no, if the Bar was heated all over, and one end fhould be moiftned with fnow, or with a fponge dipt in cold water; if the fnow or fponge were applied to the part which is upward, would (I fay) the cold fooner pierce downward, than if the fnow or fponge placed at the lower end, the cold would fhoot upward. *So the Beams of the Sun* rebound from a white upon a black are congregate: Whether are fhadows alfo difperfed upon white, and united upon black? The Experiment we fee made in a dark room, the light being let in thorow a narrow chink only, where the Images of things which are without, are taken upon white Paper, not upon black. So a vein is opened in the fore-head for the Megrim, or Head-ach. Muft alfo the Hemicrane be fcarified for the *Soda*; or the pain of the head in gene-ral? So much for the *Inverfion of Experiment.*

§ *Compulfion of Experiment, is when Experiment is urged, and exten-ded to annihilation, or privation of the vertue.* For in other kinds of hunting, the game is only taken, but in this kill'd. Example of *Com-pulfion* is this; *The Loadftone draws Iron*, inforce therefore the Iron, or vex the Loadftone, fo as the virtue of attraction be ftifled or expir'd: As, fuppofe the Loadftone were burnt or macerate in ftrong waters, whether will it forego, or abate its virtue? Contrarywife, *if fteel or Iron be reduced into Crocum Martis*, or into prepar'd fteel, as they call it; or be diffolved in *Aqua Fortis*; will the Loadftone ftill allure them?

Again,

Again, the Loadstone draws Iron through all interpos'd Bodies that we know, as Gold ; Silver ; Glaſs, &c. Fix therefore ſome medium upon it (if it may be) that may intercept, and arreſt its virtue. Make a trial of Quickſilver ; of Oyl ; Gums ; a burning coal ; and the like, which yet have not been experimented. *So there have* been brought in of late *certain Perſpectives,* which multiply after a ſtrange manner the minuteſt viſibles: Preſs the uſe of them, either upon ſmall objects, as they may not be able to work upon ; or upon ſo vaſt, as they may be confounded in working: As whether they can clearly diſcover thoſe moats in Urine, which otherways could not be diſcern'd ? Whether in Iewels, every way pure and ſpotleſs, they can make the grains and imperceptible clouds to become viſible ? *Whether* can they expoſe to view the moats in the Sun (which are untruly charged upon *Democritus*

for his Atoms, and the Principles of Nature) as if they were great Bodies ? Can they ſo diſtinguiſh to the ſight the groſſer duſt made of Ceruſs, and Vermilion, that the ſmall grains may appear ; here the red, there the white ? *Again, can* they multiply greater Figures (imagine a face ; an eye, or ſo) to the ſame bigneſs they can a flea, or a little worm ? *Can they* make a piece of Cypreſs, or Cobweb-Lawn appear ſo full of holes, as if it were a Net ? *But we ſtay* the leſs upon the *Compulſions of Experiments* becauſe commonly they fall not within the limits of literate experience ; but are rather referr'd to *Cauſes* ; and *Axioms* ; and the *New Organum.* For whereſoever there is a Negative ; Privative ; or excluſive faculty ; there is already ſome light given to the *Invention of Forms.* Thus far of the *Compulſion of Experiment.*

§ *Application of Experiment is nothing elſe than a witty Tranſlation of it to ſome other profitable Experiment.* Example may be this ; All Bodies have their own dimenſions, and their own weights: Gold is of greater weight, of leſs dimenſion, than Silver ; Water than Wine. From this is traduced a profitable Experiment ; that from a juſt weight and meaſure being taken, you may know how much Silver hath been mixt with Gold ; how much Water with Wine ; which was that celebrated Ε'υρηκα of *Archimedes.* So fleſh ſooner putrifies in ſome Cellars, than it doth in others. It will be of uſe to make application of this *Experiment* to the finding out of Airs, more or leſs healthful, for habitation ; namely, there where fleſh is longeſt preſerv'd from putrefaction. The ſame may be applied to the diſcovery of healthful, or peſtilential ſeaſons of the year. *But there* are innumerable examples of this Nature: Only let men awake, and perpetually fix their eyes, one while, on the nature of things ; another while, on the application of them to the uſe and ſervice of mankind. So much concerning the *Application of the Experiment.*

§ *Copulation of Experiment is the Links and Chain of Application ; when as things, ſingle, and ſeparate had been to little uſe, are, (connexed) of force and efficacy.* For example, you deſire to have late Roſes or fruit ; this is effected if you pull off the more early buds when they are newly knotted ; the ſame is done, if you lay the roots bare until the ſpring be well come on, and expoſe them unto the open Air ; but it will take the better, if you joyn both theſe practices of putting back germination. So Ice and Nitre do much conduce to refrigeration ;

tion; but commixt, together much more. But this experiment is clear of it self, notwithstanding here may covertly a fallacy lie hid, (as there may in all other effects, and conclusions where Axioms are wanting) if the *Copulation* be made of things which work after a different, and as it were, repugnant manner. And so much for *Copulation of Experiment.*

§ *There remain the Chances, or Fortunes of Experiment. This is altogether an irrational, and as it were, a passionate manner of experimenting, when you have a mind to try a conclusion not for that any reason, or other Experiment induceth you to it; but only because the like was never attempted before.* Yet I do not know whether or no, in this kind, there may not lie hid some secret of great use, if you try Nature every way. *For the* wonders of Nature commonly lie out of the high road, and beaten paths; so as the very absurdity of an attempt may sometimes be prosperous. But if reason go along with this practice; that is, that it is evident that such an Experiment was never yet tried; and yet there is great reason why it should be attempted; then it is a choice *Experiment*, and searcheth the very bosom of Nature. *For Example:* In the operation of Fire upon some Natural Body, one or other of these effects hitherto ever comes to pass; as that either something flies out, (as flame and fume in ordinary burning fewel) or at least there is made a local separation of Parts, and that for some distance; as in Distillation where the Lees settle, the vapours, after they have play'd about, are gathered into receptacles: But no man ever yet made trial of an imprison'd Distillation, for so we may call it: And it seems very probable, that if the force of heat immur'd with in the Cloisters of a Body, do so great matters, and work such alterations; and yet without loss, or manumission to the Body; that then this Proteus of Matter, fetter'd, as it were, with Manacles, may in time be forced to many transformations, if so be, that the heat be so temper'd; and intermutually chang'd, that the vessels be not broken. *For this* operation is like that of the womb, where the heat works without emission, or separation of any part of the Body, save that in the Matrix, there is conjoyn'd Alimentation; but for version, the thing is the same. These are the *fortunes, or adventures of Experiment. In the mean time,* we give this advice, touching Experiments of this Nature; that no man be discouraged, or confounded, if the *Experiments* which he puts in practice answer not his expectation; *For what succeeds pleaseth more; but what succeeds not, many times informs no less.* And this ought ever to be remembred (which we often press) *that Experimenta Lucifera Experiments of Light, and discovery, ought for a time to be much more enquired after, than Experimenta fructifera, Experiments of use and practice.* And thus much of *Literate Experience,* which (as we have said before) is rather a sagacity, and a hunting scent, than a Science.

§ *Now for the Novum Organum,* we say nothing, nor give any foretast thereof; being we have projected in our minds, by the assistance of the Divine favour, to make a perfect entire work of that subject; seeing it is a matter of higher consequence, than all the rest.

CHAP. III.

I The Partition *of the Inventive Art of Arguments, into Promptuary, or Places of Preparation; and Topick, or Places of Suggestion.* II. The Division *of Topick Art into General.* §. *And Particular Topicks.* III. In example *of Particular Topick in the Enquiry* De Gravi & Levi.

INvention *of Arguments is not properly an Invention; for to Invent is to discover things unknown, and not to recover, or recall that which is known already.* The Use *and Office of this kind of Invention seems to be no other, than out of the Mass of Knowledge, congested, and stored up in the Mind, readily to produce, that which may be pertinent to the Matter, and Question propounded.* For he that is little or nothing acquainted before hand with the Subject in question, *Topicks of Invention* will little advantage him : On the contrary he that hath Provision at home which may be applied to the purpose, even without *Art* and *Places of Invention,* will at length, (though not so readily and aptly) find out and produce Arguments. *So that this kind of Invention (as we have said) is not properly Invention, but only a Reduction into Memory, or Suggestion with Application.* But because custom and consent hath authoriz'd the word, it may in some sort be called *Invention :* For it may be as well accompted a chase, or finding of a. Deer, which is made within an inclosed Park; as that within a Forrest at large. But setting aside curiosity of words it may appear that the scope and end of this kind of *Invention,* is a certain promptitude, and expedite use of our Knowledge , rather than any encrease, or Amplification thereof.

I *To procure this ready Provision for discourse, there are two ways; either that it may be designed and pointed out, as it were, by an Index, under what Heads the matter is to be sought; and this is that we call* Topick*: Or else, that Arguments may be before hand framed, and stored up, about such things as are frequently incident, and come into disceptation; and this we will call promptuary Art, or of Preparation.* This later scarcely deserveth to be called a *Part of Knowledge,* seeing it rather consisteth in diligence, than any artificial erudition. And in this part *Aristotle* doth wittily indeed, but hurtfully deride the Sophists near his time, saying ; *They did as if one, that professed the Art of shoo-making, should not teach how to make up a shooe; but only exhibit in a readiness a number of shooes, of all fashions and sizes.* But yet a man might here reply, that if a Shoomaker should have no shooes in his shop, but only work as he is bespoken, he would be but a poor man, and weakly customed. But our Saviour speaking of Divine knowledge, saith far otherwise; *Every Scribe instructed for the Kingdom of heaven; is like a good housholder that bringeth forth both new and old store.* And we see the ancient Writers of Rhetorick do give it in Precept, *That Pleaders should have divers common Places prepared long before hand, and handled,* and illustrated both ways; for example, for the sence and equity of Law against the words, and letter of Law ; and on the contrary. And *Cicero* himself being broken

De Repr. Soph. lib. 2. c. 9. §. ult.

Mat. 13.

Cic. de Orat.

broken unto it by great experience, delivers it plainly; *That an Ora-* Ad Attic.
tor if he be diligent and sedulous, may have in effect premeditate, and Lib.XVI.
handled, whatsoever a man shall have occasion to speak of; so that in the EP.VI.
Pleading of the Cause it self he shall have no need to insert any new or
sudden matter, besides new names, and some individual Circumstances. *But* the pains and diligence of *Demosthenes* went so far, that in
regard of the great force that the entrance and access into a Cause hath
to make a good Impression upon the Minds of Auditors, he thought
it worth his labour to frame, and to have in readiness a number of *Pre-* Ejus &5
faces for Orations and Speeches. And these Presidents, and Authori- Exordia;
ties, may deservedly overweigh *Aristotle's* Opinion, that would advise si ejus.
us to change a Wardrope for a pair of Shears. Therefore this part of
knowledge touching *Promptuary Preparation,* was not to be omitted;
whereof for this place this is sufficient. And seeing it is common to
both *Logick* and *Rhetorick,* we thought good here amongst *Logicks,* only in Passage, to touch it; referring over a more ample handling of it
to *Rhetorick.*

II The other Part of *Invention, which is Topick, we will divide into
General and Particular Topick.* General *is that which is diligently and
copiously handled in Logick, or rational knowledge;* as it were needless to
stay upon the explication thereof. Yet thus much we thought meet to
admonish by the way; that this *Topick* is of use, not only in argumentations, when we come to dispute with another; but in meditations
also, when we reason and debate matters within our selves. Neither
do these places serve only for *suggestion,* or *admonition,* what we ought
to *affirm* or *assert;* but also what we ought to *enquire* and *demand.*
And a faculty of wise interrogating, is half a knowledge; for *Plato*
saith well, *Whosoever seeks, comprehends that he seeks for, in general no-* In Meno-
tion; else how shall he know it, when he hath found it? And therefore the ne.
*larger and more certain our anticipation is, the more direct and compendi-
ous is our search.* The same places therefore, which will conduce to
search the mind of our inward conceptions, and understanding; and to
draw forth the knowledge there stored up; will also help us to produce knowledge from without. So as if a man of Learning, and understanding be in presence, we might be able, aptly and wisely to propound a Question thereof; and likewise profitably select and peruse
Authors and Books, or parts of Books, which might teach and inform
us of those points we enquire.

§ *But particular Topicks do much more conduce to the purpose we speak*   *
of; and is to be accompted a thing of far greater use. There hath been TOPICÆ
PARTICU.
indeed some slight mention made hereof, by some Writers; but it hath LARES.
not yet been handled fully, and according to the dignity of the Subject.
But to let pass that humour and pride, which hath reigned too long in
Schools, which is, *to pursue with infinite subtilty, things that are within
their command; but never to touch at things any whit removed;* we do
receive and imbrace *particular Topick,* as a matter of great use, that is,
*places of enquiry and invention, appropriate to particular Subjects and Sci-
ences;* and these *places are certain mixtures of Logick, and the proper matter
of particular Sciences.* For he is but a weak man, and of narrow capacity, who conceives that the Art of *finding out Sciences* may be found
out, propounded and perfected at once, even in their first conception;

and

and presently be set down, and practised in some work. But let men know for certain, *That solid and true Arts of Invention do shoot up, and come to maturity with the Inventions themselves : So as when a man first enters upon the search of a knowledge, he may have many profitable Precepts of Invention ; but after he hath made farther progress in the knowledge it self, he may, and must excogitate new Precepts of Invention, which may, lead him more prosperously to further Discoveries.* For this kind of pursuit is like a going upon a plain and open Champion; for after we have gone a part of the way, we have not only gained this, that we are now nearer to our journeys end ; but we gain the better sight of that part of the way, which remains. So every degree of *proceeding in Sciences,* having past over that which is left behind, gives a better prospect to that which follows : And because we set down this part of Topick as *Deficient,* we will annex an example thereof.

III. *A particular Topick,* or the Articles of Enquiry de G R A V I *&* L E V I.

L ET it be *enquired* what Bodies those are which are susceptible of the *Motion of Gravity, what of Levity,* and whether there be any of a middle and indifferent Nature ?

2. *After an absolute Inquiry de Gravi & Levi ;* proceed to *comparative Inquiry;* as of *Ponderous Bodies,* which doth *weigh* more, which less, in the same demension ? so of *Light Bodies,* which are more speedily carried upward, which more slowly ?

3. *Let it be enquired,* what the *Quantum* of a Body may contribute, and effect towards the *Motion of Gravity.* But this, at first sight, may seem a superfluous *Inquiry,* because the computation of motion must follow the *computation of quantity :* But the matter is otherwise ; for although the *quantity* in the scales do compensate the *weight* of the Body it self, (the force of the Body every way meeting by repercussion, or by resistance, of the Basins, or of the Beam) yet where there is but small resistance (as in the falling down of a Body through the Air) the *quantity* of a Body little avails to the *incitation of the descent ;* seeing two Balls of Lead, one of *twenty, the other* of one *pound weight,* fall to the earth almost in an equal space of time.

4. *Let it be inquired,* whether the *Quantity* of a Body may be so increased, as that the *Motion of Gravity* may be utterly deposed and cast off; as in the Globe of the earth, which is pensil, and falls not ? Whether may there be other massive substances, so great, as may sustain _{V. DI-} themselves ? *For Local Descent to the Centre of the Earth, is a meer fiction;* and every great Mass abhorrs all Local Motion, unless it be overrul'd by another more predominant Appetite.

*V. DI-
ORES.*

5 *Let it be inquired,* what the *resistance* of a *Body interposing,* or *incountring* may do, or actuate towards the managing of the *Motion of Gravity :* For a Body descending, either *penetrates* and cutteth the Body occurrent ; or is arrested by it : If it *penetrates,* then there is *penetration ;* or with weaker resistence, as in Air, or with more strong, as in Water : If it be *staid,* it is staid either by a resistance *unequal,* where there is a *Pregravation ;* as if Wood should be put upon Wax ; or e-*qual,* as if Water should be put upon Water, or Wood upon Wood of the

the same kind : which the Schools, in a vain apprehension call the *non-Ponderation of a body within its own Sphere.* All these do vary the *Motion of Gravity* ; for *heavy substances* are otherways moved in scales, otherwise in falling down; nay,otherwise(which may seem strange) in Ballances hanging in the Air, otherwise in Ballances immersed in Water; otherwise in falling down through Water, otherwise in swimming, or transportation upon Water.

6. *Let it be inquired,* what the *Figure* of a body descending may, or doth work, to the moderating of the *Motion of Gravity,* as a broad *Figure* with tenuity ; a cubick *Figure*, long round, Pyramidal ; when they turn; when they remain in the same posture, wherein they were deliver'd.

7. *Let inquiry be made,* of that which the *Continuance* and *Progression* of a *Fall* or *Descent*, may, and doth work to this effect, that it may be carried with a greater incitation and force; and with what proportion, and how far that Incitation will carry ? For the Ancients, upon a slight contemplation, were of opinion, *that because that was a natural Motion, it would continually be augmented and improv'd.* **v. Di-CRES.**

8. *Let inquiry* be made of that which *Distance* and *Proximity of a Body descending from the earth,* may, and doth work to this end, that it may fall more speedily, more slowly, or else not at all, (if so be that it be without the Orb of Activity of the *terrene Globe,* which was *Gilbert's* opinion): as likewise what the *immersion of a Body descending more in the deep of the earth*; or the placing thereof *nearer to the superficies of the earth,* may produce ? For these kinds of Postures vary the Motion; as they experience that work in Mines. **De Magni**

9. *Let there be inquiry made* of that which the difference of Bodies; by which motion of Gravity is diffused, and communicated, can do and doth : And whether it may equally be communicated by Bodies soft, and porose; as by hard and solid : As if the Beam of the Ballance be on one side of the Tongue Wood, on the other side Silver, (though they be reduced to the same weight) whether doth it not beget a variation in the Scales ? In like manner, whether Metal put upon Wool, or upon a blown Bladder, weigh the same, it would do, if laid in the bottom of the Scale ?

10. *Let there be inquiry made* what the distance of a Body from the level-Poise; that is the quick, or late perception of the incumbent, or of depression, can do or doth : As in a Ballance where one part of the Beam is longer (though of the same weight) whether this doth sway the Ballance ? Or in the crooked Pipes, where certainly the longer part will draw the Water, although the shorter part, made more capacious, may contain a greater weight of Water.

11. *Let there be Enquiry made* of that which the intermixtion or copulation of a light Body with a weighty , may do to the raising of the *weight* of a Body, as in the poise of living Creatures; and Dead ?

12. *Let inquiry be made* of the secret ascensions , and descensions of the parts more light, and more weighty in one, and the same entire Body. Whereby there may be made oftentimes exact separations ; as in the separation of Wine and Water ; in the Ascension of the Flower of Milk, and the like.

13. *Let it be inquired* what is the line and direction of the Motion of Gravity ; and how far it may follow either the centre of the earth, that is,the mass of the Earth, or the centre of the Body it self; that is, the contention and driving on of the parts thereof; for those centres are profitable in demonstration, but of no use in Nature.

14. *Let it be inquired* touching the comparison of the Motion of Gravity, with other Motions ; what Motions it masters, to what it yields ? As in the Motion, which they call, *violent*, which is represt and bridled for a time; as when a far greater weight of Iron is drawn up by a small Load-stone, the Motion of *Gravity* gives place to the Motion of *Sympathy.*

15. *Let inquiry be made of the Motion of Air*, whether it be carried upwards, or be collateral and indifferent ? Which is a hard thing to find out, but by some exquisite Experiments : for the glittering apparition of Air in the bottom of Water, is rather by the Percussion of Water, than by the Motion of Air; being the same emication may be made in Wood. But Air mingled with Air discovers no *Experiment*; because Air in Air exhibits Levity no less , than Water in Water doth Gravity : But in a Bubble drawn over with the inclosure of a thin Skin, it stays for a time.

16. *Let it be inquired what is the Term of Levity*, for sure their meaning (who made the Centre of the Earth, the Centre of *Gravity*) is not, that the ultimate convexity of Heaven should be the stint and limits of *Levity :* Or rather, that as ponderous Bodies seem to be so far carried, that there they may cast Anchor as at a fixt Pillar ; so light Bodies are so far carried, that they may begin to wheel about, and come to a *motion without termination ?*

17. *Let inquiry be made*, why vapours and exhalations should be carried as high as the *middle Region* of the Air(as they call it);seeing they are somewhat a gross substance ; and the beams of the Sun by turns (as in the night) cease their Operation.

18. *Let inquiry be made of the conduct of the Motion of Flame upwards*; which is the more abstruse, because *Flame* exspires every moment ; save perchance in the imbracement of greater *Flames :* For *Flames* separated and broken off from their continuation, last not long.

19. *Let inquiry be made of the ascendant Motion of the Activity of Heat*, as when the Heat of red-hot Iron affecteth rather to mount upwards, than to move downwards ? *The example* therefore of *particular Topick* may be made in this manner; in the mean time, what we have begun to advise, we do again admonish, which is, that men vary their *particular Topicks* so, as after farther Progression made by *Inquiry*, they do substitute one, and after that another *Topick*, if ever they desire to reach the top of Sciences. As for us, we attribute so much to *particular Topicks*, as we do design to make a particular Work of them upon some Subjects in Nature, which are more observable, and more obscure , For *we are Commanders of Questions, not so of things.* And thus of *Invention.*

CHAP.

Chap. IV.

I. The Partition *of the Art of Judging, into Judgement by Induction.*
§ *And by Syllogism. Of the first a Collection is made in the New Organ.* § The first Partition *of Judgement by Syllogism into Reduction, Direct, and Inverst.* § The second Partition thereof, *into Analytick Art : and the Knowledge of Elenchs.* II. The Division of the *Knowledge of Elenchs, into Elenchs of Sophisms.* § *Into Elenchs of Interpretation of Terms.* § *And into Elenchs of Images, or Idolaes.* III. The Division of *Idolaes.* § *Into Impressions from the General Nature of Man, or* Idola Tribûs. § *Into Impressions from the Individual temper of particulars, or* Idola Specûs. § *Into Impressions by Words, aud Communicative Nature, or* Idola Fori. IV. An Appendix *of the Art of Judging, namely of the Analogic of* Demonstration *according to the Nature of the Subject.*

I. LET us now pass to *Judgement, or the Art of Judging, which handleth the Nature of Proofs, or Demonstrations.* And in this *Art of Judging* (as also generally it is accepted) *a Conclusion is inferred, either by* Induction ; *or else by Syllogism :* For *Enthymemes,* and *Examples* are only the abridgements of these two. *As for Judgement that it is by* Induction, we need nothing doubt. *For by one and the same Operation of the Mind, that which is sought, is both found and judged.* Neither is the thing perfected by any mean, but immediately after the same manner, for most part, as it is in *Sense :* For *Sense,* in her primary Objects, doth at once seize upon the species of an Object, and consent to the truth thereof. *But it is otherwise in Syllogism,* the Proof whereof is not *Immediate,* but perfected by a *Mean ;* and therefore *the Invention of the Medium is one thing ; and the Judgement of the consequence of Argument, is another : For the mind first discourseth, afterwards rests satisfied.* But a *Vitious Form of Induction* we utterly disclaim ; a *Legitimate Form* we refer over to the *New Organ.* Therefore enough in this place, of *Judgement by Induction.*

§ For that other *Judgement by Syllogism,* to what purpose is it to speak, seeing this is by the subtil files off mens wits amost worn away, and reduced into many minute pieces? And no marvel, being it is a thing hath such Sympathy with mans understanding. For *the mind of man doth wonderfully endeavour, and extremely covet this, that it may not be pensil ; but that it may light upon something fixt and immoveable, on which as on a firmament it may support it self, in its swift motions and disquisitions.* Surely, as *Aristotle* endeavoureth to prove, *That in all motion of Bodies there is some point quiescent ; and very elegantly expoundeth the Ancient Fable of* Atlas *that stood fixed, and bare up the Heavens from falling, to be meant of the Poles of the World, whereupon the Conversion is accomplisht. In like manner men do earnestly seek to have some* Atlas, *or Axeltree of their Cogitations within themselves, which may in*

De Animal. Motione.

some

some measure moderate the fluctuations, and wheelings of the understanding, fearing it may be, the falling of their Heaven. Therefore *men have haſtned too faſt to ſet down principles of Sciences, about which all the variety of Diſputations might turn without peril of ruine or ſubverſion. In truth not knowing that he who too early lays hold on certainties, will conclude in ambiguities; and he that ſeaſonably ſuſpends his Judgement, ſhall attain to Certainties.*

§ So then it is manifeſt, that this *Art of Judging by Syllogiſm* is nothing elſe, but the reduction of Propoſitions to Principles, by middle terms; and Principles are underſtood to be agreed of by all, and are exempt from Argument. But the invention of middle terms is permitted to the free ſagacity, and purſuit of mens wits. This *Reduction is of two kinds, Direct and Inverted.* *Direct* is, when the Propoſition is reduced to the Principle, which is call'd *Probation Oſtenſive.* *Inverſed* is, when the Contradictory of the Propoſition is reduced to the Contradictory of the Principle; which they term a *Probation from incongruity, or an abſurdity.* The number alſo of middle terms, or their ſcale is diminiſhed or increaſed, as they are remov'd from the Principle of the Propoſition.

§ *Theſe grounds laid, we will divide the Art of Judgement* (as for moſt part generally it is) *into Analytick Art; and the Doctrine of Elenchs;* the one giveth Direction, the other Caution. For *Analytick* ſetteth down the true Forms of Conſequences of Argument by a Variation, and Deflection, from which, the Concluſion is deprehended to be erroneous; and this part contains in it a kind of *Elench,* or Redargution.
V. Euclid. & Comment. For, as it is ſaid, *Rectum & ſui index eſt, & obliqui.* Notwithſtanding it is the ſafeſt way to ſet down *Elenchs* as Monitors, whereby *Fallacies,* which otherwiſe might inſnare the Judgement, may be more eaſily detected. *In the Analytick* Part we find nothing *Deficient,* which rather is loaden with ſuperfluities, than any way is wanting in acceſſions.

II. *The Knowledge of Elenchs* we divide into three Parts: *Elenchs of Sophiſms; Elenchs of Intepretation;* and *Elenchs of Images or Idolaes.* The Doctrine of *Elenchs of Sophiſms* is very uſeful; for although the the more groſs ſort of *Fallacies* is (as *Seneca* makes the compariſon ve-
Epiſt. 45. ry well) *But as the feats of Juglers, which though we know not how they are done; yet we know well it is not as it ſeems to be.* Yet the more ſubtil ſort of *Sophiſms* doth not only put a man beſides his anſwer, but doth in good earneſt abuſe his Judgement.

§ *This Part concerning the Elenchs of Sophiſms* is excellently handled by *Ariſtotle* in *Precept;* but more excellently by *Plato* in Example, not only in the Perſon of the Ancient Sophiſts, *Gorgias, Hippias, Protagoras* and *Euthidemus,* and the reſt; but even in the Perſon of *Socrates* him-
In Dial. ità inſcript. ſelf, who profeſſing to affirm nothing, but to infirm whatſoever others avouch, hath exactly expreſſed all the Forms of *Objections, Fallacies* and *Redargutions.* Wherefore in this Part we have nothing *Deficient.* But this, in the mean time, is to be noted, that though we make the ingenuous and principal uſe of this Knowledge to conſiſt in this, *That Sophiſms may be redargued; yet it is manifeſt, that the degenerate and corrupt uſe thereof is imploy'd to contrive, and impoſe Captions and Contradictions, by theſe Sophiſms; which paſſeth for a great Faculty,*

and

and no doubt is of great advantage. Though the difference was elegant-ly made by one betwixt an Orator, and a Sophist, *That the one is as the Grey-hound, which hath his advantage in the race ; the other as the Hare which hath her advantage in the turn.*

§ Now follow *Elenchi Hermeniæ,* for so we will call them, borrow-ing the Word, rather than the Sence, from *Aristotle.* And here let us call to mens memory what we have said before; (when we handled *Primitive Philosophy*) of *transcendent, and adventitious Conditions, or Adjuncts of Entity,* they be *Majority, Minority ; Much, Little ; Prio-rity, Posteriority; Identity, Diversity ; Power, Act; Habit, Privation ; Totality, Partiality ; Activity, Passivity ; Motion, Quietude ; Entity, Non-Entity,* and the like. But specially let men remember, and ob-serve the different Contemplations of these Properties, which is, that they may be enquired, either *Physically,* or *Logically.* The Physical handling of these adherent Qualities we have assigned to *Primitive Philosophy.* The *Logical* remaineth, and that is the very thing which we here stile *Doctrinam de Elenchis Hermeniæ,* the *Knowledge of the E-lenchs of Interpretation.* This indeed is a sound and material Portion of Knowledge: *For these Commune and general Notions have this Na-ture, that in all disputations they every where intervene, so as, if they be not by a careful Judgment accurately distinguisht at first ; they may won-derfully overcloud the whole light of Disputations ; and even bring the case to that pass, that the Disputations shall be resolved into a skirmish of words. For Æquivocations, and erronious acception of words* (specially of this Nature) *are the Sophism, of Sophisms.* Wherefore it seemeth better to constitute a Treatise of them apart, than to receive them into *Prime Philosophy,* I mean *Metaphysick;* or to annex them as a part of *Analy-ticks,* which Aristotle *very confusedly hath done.* And we have given it a name from the Nature and Use; *for the right use is plainly Redarguti-on, and Caution about the acception of words.* Nay that Part of *Predi-caments* touching Cautions, of not confounding, and transposing the terms of *Definitions,* and *Divisions,* if it were rightly instituted, would be of singular use, in our judgment, and might fitly be referred hither. And thus much of the *Elenchs of Interpretation.* Arist. Ana-lyt.

III *As for the Elenchs of Images or Idolaes ; certainly Idolaes are the profoundest Fallacies of the mind of man.* Nor do they deceive in *Parti-culars,* as the rest do ; casting a Cloud, and spreading snares over the Judgment; but apertly from a corrupt, and crookedly-set predispositi-on of the mind ; which doth, as it were, wrest and infect all the an-ticipations of the understanding. *For the mind of man* (drawn over, and clouded with the sable Pavillion of the Body) is so far from being like a smooth, equal, and clear Glass, which might sincerely take and reflect the beams of things, according to their true incidence ; that it is rather like an inchanted Glass, full of Superstitions; Apparitions, and Im-postures. ✷
FLENCHI
IDOLO-
RUM.

§ *Idolaes are imposed upon the understanding, either by the universal Na-ture of man in general ; or from the individual Nature of Particulars ; or by words, or nature Communicative.* The first sort of Images we wont to call *Idola Tribûs* ; the second, *Idola Specûs* ; the third, *Idola Fori:* There is also a fourth kind, which we call, *Idola Theatri ; and is intro-duced by depraved Theories or Philosophies, and perverse Laws of Demonstra-tions ;* NOV. OR.
Lib. i.
APH. LXI.
ad LXIX.

tions; but this kind may be denied and put off, wherefore we pass it over for the present. But the other do plainly besiege the mind, nor can they ever be quite removed, or extirpated. Therefore let none expect any Analytick Art in these; but the knowledge of *Elenchs* concerning these *Idolaes* is a Primary Knowledge. Nor (to speak truth) can this Knowledge of *Idolaes* be reduced into Art; but only by a contemplative wisdom, we may be instructed to beware of them. As for a just and more subtile Treatise thereof, we refer that to the *Novum Organum*, touching upon them in a generality in this place.

§ *Idola Tribûs* is thus exemplified, *The Nature of the mind of man is more affected with Affirmatives and Actives, than with Negatives and Privatives; whereas in a just and regular course it should present it self equal to both.* But the mind of man, if a thing have once been existent, and and held good, receives a deeper Impression thereof, than if the same thing, far more often fail'd and fell out otherwise; which is the root, as it were, of all superstition and vain credulity. *So that he* answered well to him that shewed him the great number of Pictures of such as had 'scaped Shipwrack, and had paid their vows; and being prest with this Interrogative, *Whether he did not now confess the Divinity of Neptune?* return'd this counter-question by way of answer; *yea, but where are they painted, that are drowned?* And there is the same reason of all such like Superstitions, as in Astrology; Dreams; Divinations, and the rest. An other *Instance* is this; *The Spirit of man being it self of an equal and uniform Substance, doth presuppose, and feign a greater equality, and uniformity in Nature, than in truth there is.* Hence that fiction of the Mathematicians, *that in the heavenly Bodies, all is moved by perfect Circles*; rejecting spiral Lines: so it comes to pass, that whereas there are many things in Nature, as it were *Monodica*, and full of imparity; yet the conceits of men still feign and frame unto themselves, *Relatives; Parallels, and Conjugates.* For upon this ground, *the Element of Fire and its Orb is brought in to keep square with the other three, Earth; Water; Air.* The *Chymicks* have set out a Phanatical Squadron of the word, feigning by a most vain conceit, in those their four Elements (*Heaven; Air; Water,* and *Earth,*) there are found to every one parallel and conform species. *The third Example* hath some affinity with the former, *That man is, as it were, the common measure and mirror, or glass of Nature*; for it is not credible (if all Particulars were scann'd and noted) what a troop of *Fictions* and *Idolaes* the reduction of the operations of Nature, to the similitude of humane Actions, hath brought into *Philosophy*; I say this very fancy, *that it should be thought that Nature doth the same things that man doth.* Neither are these much better than the Heresie of the *Anthropomorphites*, bred in the Cells and solitude of gross and ignorant Monks, or the Opinion of *Epicurus* answerable to the same in Heathenism, who supposed God to be of Humane shape. But *Velleius* the Epicurean needed not to have asked, why God should have adorned the heavens with stars and lights, as if he had been an *Ædilis*; one that should have set forth some magnificent shews or plays; for if that great Workman had conform'd himself to the imitation of an *Ædilis*, he would have cast the stars into some pleasant and beautiful works, and orders, like the curious roofs of Palaces, whereas one can scarce find in such an infinite number of stars a Posture in square, or Triangle,

or

Nov.or.
Lib.1.
Aph.
XLV.
ad LIII.
exclusive.

Cic.de N.
D.l.b.V.

V. T.I.
ORES.

Elem.Ig-
nis vide
Digrels.

Paracel.
Fludde
passim.

Epiphan.
lib.3. Ni-
ceph.Hist.
Eccl.lib.11

or right-Line. *So different a harmony there is between the Spirit of man, and the Spirit of the world.*

§ *Idola Speciûs are derived from the Individual Complexion of every Particular in respect of Mind, and of Body; as also, from Education; Custom, and Fortuitous Events,* which befall every man. For it is an excellent emblem that of *Plato's Cave*; for certainly (to let go the exquisite subtilty of that Parable) if a man were continued from his Childhood unto mature Age in a Grot, or a dark and subterraneous Cave, and then should come suddenly abroad, and should behold this stately canopy of heaven, and the Furniture of the World; without doubt he would have many strange and absurd imaginations come into his mind, and people his brain. So in like manner we live in the view of heaven; yet our Spirits are inclosed in the Caves of our Bodies; Complexions, and Customs, which must needs minister unto us infinite images of errors, and vain Opinions, if they do so seldom, and for so short a space appear above ground, out of their holes; and do not continually live under the Contemplation of Nature, as in the open Air. That Parable of *Heraclitus* doth well suit with this emblem of *Plato's Cave, that men seek Scienceees in their own proper World, and not in the greater World.*

§ But *Idola Fori are most troublesome, which out of a tacite stipulation amongst men, touching the imposition of words, and names, have insinuated themselves into the understanding.* Words commonly are imposed according to the capacity of the People; and distinguish things by such differences, as the Vulgar are capable of; and when a more prescissive conception, and a more diligent observation would discern, and separate things better; the noise of popular words confounds and interrupts them. And that which is the remedy to this inconvenience (namely *Definitions*) in many points is not a remedy sufficient for the disease; because the *Definitions* themselves consist of words, and words beget words. For although we presume that we are masters of our words, and expressions; and it is soon said, *loquendum ut vulgus, sentiendum ut sapientes,* and that words of Art, which are of Authority only with the Learn'd, may seem to give some satisfaction to this defect; and that the *Definitions* whereof we have spoken, premised, and presupposed in Arts according to the wisdom of the Mathematicians, may be of force to correct the depraved acceptations of words; yet all this secures us not from the cheating slights and charms of words, which many ways abuse us, and offer violence to the understanding; and after the manner of the Tartars Bow, do shoot back upon the judgment from whence they came. Wherefore this disease must have a new kind of remedy, and of more efficacy. But we do now touch these in passage briefly, in the mean time reporting this Knowledge which we will call, *the Great Elenchs,* or the Doctrine of *Idolaes, Native* and adventual of the mind of man, to be *Deficient.* But we refer a just Treatise thereof to the *Novum Organum.*

IV There remains one part of *Judgment* of great excellency, which likewise we set down as *Deficient.* For indeed *Aristotle* noteth the thing, but no where pursueth the manner of acquiring it. The Subject of this point is this. *The different kind of Demonstrations, and Proofs, to different kind of Matter and Subjects;* so that this Doctrine containeth the

Marginal notes:
NOV. OR. Lib. I. Aph. III. ad LIX.
Plat. de Rep. VII.
N. L.
NOV. OR. Lib. I. Aph. LIX; ad LXI.
Agell. N. H. alicubi.
*
DE ANALOGIA DEMONSTRATIONUM.

Indications of *Indications.* For *Aristotle* adviseth well, *That we may* Eth. lib. 1. *not require Demonstrations from Orators, or Perswasions from Mathematicians*; so that if you mistake in the kind of Proof, the judicature cannot be upright and perfect. And seeing there are four kinds of *Demonstrations* either by *immediate Consent, and commune Notions*; or by *Induction*; or by *Syllogism*; or by that which *Aristotle* calls *Demonstration in orb, or in Circle,* (that is not from the more known notions, but down right); every of these *Demonstrations* hath certain Subjects, and matter of Sciences, wherein respectively they have chiefest use; other Subjects from which respectively they ought to be excluded. *For a rigor and curiosity in requiring too severe proofs in some things; much more a facility and remission in resting satisfied in slighter Proofs, are to be numbred amongst those prejudices, which have been the greatest Causes of detriment, and impediment to Sciences.* Thus much concerning the *Art of Judging.*

C H A P. V.

I. The Partition *of Art Retentive, or of Memory into the Knowledge of the Helps of Memory.* §. *and the Knowledge of the Memory it self.* II. The Division *of the Doctrine of Memory into Prenotion.* §. *and Emblem.*

I **W**E *will divide the Art of Retaining, or of Custody, into two Knowledges; that is, into the knowledge of the Helps of Memory, and the Knowledge of the Memory it self.* Assistant to *Memory is writing*; and it must by all means be noted, that *Memory* of it self, without this support, would be too weak for prolix and accurate matters; wherein it could no way recover, or recall it self, but by Scripture. And this *subsidiary second* is also of most special use in *Inductive Philosophy, and the Interpretation of Nature.* For a man may as well perfect, and sum up the *Computations* of an *Ephemerides* by mere *Memory*; as comprehend the *Interpretation* of *Nature* by meditations, and the nude, and native strength of *Memory*; unless the same *Memory* be assisted by *Tables,* and *Indices* provided for that Purpose. But to let go the *Interpretation of Nature,* which is a new knowledge; there scarcely can be a thing more useful even to ancient, and popular Sciences, than a solid, and good *Aid* to *Memory*; that is, a substantial and Learned *Digest* of *Common places.* Neither am I ignorant, *that the referring of those things we read, or learn, into Common Places, is imputed by some as a Prejudice to Learning; as causing a retardation of Reading, and a slothful relaxation to Memory.* But because it is a Counterfeit thing in Knowledge, to be forward and pregnant, unless you be withal deep and full; I hold that the diligence, and pains in collecting *Common Places,* is of great use and certainty in studying; as that which Subministers Copy to *Invention*; and contracteth the sight of Judgment to a strength. *But this is true, that of the Methods and Syntagms of Common Places, which we have seen, there is none that is of any worth; for that in their Titles, they mere-*

ly

ly reprefent the face, rather of a School, than of the world; exhibiting Vulgar and Pedantical Divifions, and not fuch as any way penetrate the Marrow and Pith of things.

§ As for *Memory* it felf; that in my Judgement hitherto hath been loofely, and weakly inquired into. There is indeed an Art extant of it; but we are certain that there may be had both better Precepts for the confirming and increafing *Memory*, than that Art comprehendeth; and a better practice of that Art may be fet down, than that which is receiv'd. Neither do we doubt (if any man have a mind to abufe this Art to oftentation) but that many wonderful and prodigious Matters may be performed by it. But for ufe (as it is now managed) it is a barren thing. Yet this in the mean time we do not tax it withal, that it doth fupplant, or furcharge *Natural Memory* (as commonly is objected) but that it is not dexteroufly applied to lend affiftance to *Memory* in bufinefs, and ferious occafions. And we have learned this (it may be from our practifed Courfe in a civil Calling) that whatfoever makes oftentation of Art, and gives no affurance of ufe, we efteem as as nothing worth. For to repeat on the fudden a great number of names or words, upon once hearing, in the fame order they were delivered; or to pour forth a number of verfes upon any argument *extempore*; or to tax every thing that falls out in fome fatyrical fimile;or the turning of every thing to a Jeft; or the eluding of every thing by a contradiction or cavil, and the like; whereof in the faculties of the mind there is a great ftore; and fuch as by wit and practice may be exalted to a great degree of wonder. All thefe and the like, we make no more eftimation of, than we do of the agilities and tricks of Tumblers, Buffoons and Juglers: For they are almoft all one thing, feeing thefe abufe the Powers of the Body, thefe the Powers of the Mind; and perchance they may have fome ftrangenefs in them; but little or no worthinefs.

II. *This Art of Memory* is built upon two Intentions,*Prenotion* and *Emblem.*We call *Prenotion a Precifion of endlefs Inveftigation;*for when a man would recal any thing to *Memory*, if he have no *Prenotion* or *Preception* of that he feeketh, he fearcheth indeed,and taketh pains, rounding this way and that way, as in a maze of infinity. But if he have any certain *Prenotion*, prefently that which is infinite is difcharged and cut off; and the queftioning of the *Memory* is brought within a more narrow compafs; as in the hunting of a Fallow Deer within the Park. Therefore it is evident, *that the Method helps the Memory;* for *Prenotion* fuggefteth that it muft agree with order. So verfes are fooner gotten by heart than Profe; for if a man make a doubtful ftand at a word, *Prenotion* prompts him that the word which agrees with the verfe, muft be of fuch a Nature. And this *Prenotion* is the firft part of Artificial *Memory*. For in *Memory Artificial* we have places digefted and provided before hand : But we make *Images extempore*, according as the prefent fhall require. But *Prenotion* doth admonifh that the *Image* muft be fuch as hath fome refemblance with the *place*; this is that which awaketh, and in fome fort muniteth the *Memory* in the chafe of what we feek.

§ *Emblem deduceth conceptions intellectual to Images fenfible, and that which is fenfible, more forcibly ftrikes the Memory, and is more eafily imprinted, than that which is intellectual.* So we fee that even the *Memo-*

ry of Beasts is stirr'd up by a *sensible* object, not by an *intellectual.* So you will more easily *remember* the *Image* of a Hunts-man pursuing the Hare, or of an Apothecary setting in order his Boxes, or of a Pedant making a Speech, or of a Boy reciting Verses by heart, or of a Jester acting upon a Stage, than the *Notions of Invention, Disposition, Elocution, Memory, Action.* There are other things that pertain to the *help of Memory* (as we said even now) but the *Art* which now is in use consists of these two Inventions now set down. To pursue the *particular Defects* of Arts, would be to depart from our intended purpose. Wherefore let thus much suffice for the Art of *Retaining,* or of *Custody.* Now we descend in order to the fourth member of *Logick,* which handles *Tradition* and *Elocution.*

THE

THE

Sixth Book

OF

FRANCIS L. VERULAM

Vicount St *ALBAN,*

OF THE

Dignity and Advancement

OF

LEARNING.

To the KING.

CHAP. I.

I. The Partition *of the Art of Tradition into the Doctrine of the Organ of Speech. The Doctrine of the Method of Speech; And the Doctrine of the Illustration of Speech.* § The Partition *of the Doctrine of the Organ of Speech; into the Knowledge of the Notes of things; of Speaking; and of Writing; of which the two last constitute* Grammar, *and the Partitions thereof.* § The Partition *of the Knowledge of the Notes of things; into Hieroglyphicks; And into Characters Real.* **II.** *A* second Partition *of Grammar, into Literary and Philosophical.* **III.** *An Aggregation of Poesie, referring to Measure, unto the Knowledge of Speech. An Aggregation of the Knowledge of Cyphers to the Knowledge of Writing.*

Ertainly any man may assume the liberty (*Excellent King*) if he be so so humour'd, to jest and laugh at himself, or his own Projects. Who then knows whether this work of ours be not perchance a Transcript out of an Ancient Book found amongst the the Books of that famous Library of S. *Victor*, a Catalogue whereof *M. Fra. Rabelais* hath collected? For there a Book is found entitled *Formicarium Artium;* we have indeed accumulated a little heap of *small Dust;* and laid up many *Grains of Arts and Sciences* therein, whereto Ants may creep, and there repose a

while

Liv.2.c.7.
des faicts
& dicts de
Bon Pan-
tagr.

while, and ſo betake themſelves to new labours. Nay the wiſeſt of
Prov.6. Kings *ſends the ſlothful*, of what rank or quality ſoever, *unto the Ants;
whoſe only care is to live upon the main ſtock, but not to improve it by ſow-
ing the ground of Sciences over again, and reaping a new Harveſt.*

I. *Now let us come unto the Art of Delivery, or of Expreſſing, and Tranſ-
ferring thoſe things which are Invented, Judged, and laid up in Memory;
which, by a general name, we will term Tradition.* This comprehendeth
in it all Arts touching Words and Speeches ; for *though Reaſon be*, as it
were, *the Soul of Speech*, yet in the manner of handling, *Reaſon* and
Speech ſhould be ſeparate,even as the *Soul* and the *Body* are. We will
divide theſe *Traditive Sciences* into three Parts ; *into the Knowledge concerning the Organ of Speech; into the Knowledge concerning the Method of
Speech ; and into the Knowledge concerning the Illuſtration and Ornament of Speech.*

§ The Knowledge *concerning the Organ of Speech* generally receiv'd,
which is alſo called *Grammar*, hath two Parts ; the one of *Speech;* the
De Inter-   other of *Writing*. For *Ariſtotle* ſaith well, *Words are the Images of Cogi-
pret.   tations ; Letters are the Images of Words ;* we will aſſign both to *Grammar*. But to derive the Matter ſomewhat higher before we come to
Grammar, and the Parts thereof now ſet down ; we muſt ſpeak of the
Organ of Tradition in general. For there ſeems to be other *Traditive
Emanations* beſides *Words* and *Letters*. For this is certain whatſoever
may be diſtinguiſht into differences, ſufficient for number, to expreſs
the variety of Notions(ſo thoſe differences be perceptible to ſenſe)may
be the Convoy of the Cogitations from man to man. For we ſee Nations of different Language to trade one with the other, well enough
to ſerve their turn by *Geſtures*. Nay, in the practice of many, that
have been dumb and deaf from their birth, and otherwiſe were ingenious, we have ſeen ſtrange Dialogues held between them, and their
friends, who have learn'd their Geſtures. Moreover it is now generally
known that in *China*, and the Provinces of the high *Levant*, there are
at this day in uſe, certain *Real*, and not *Nominal Characters ;* that is,
ſuch as expreſs neither *Letters* nor *Words ;* but *Things* and *Notions :* in
ſo much, that many Countries that underſtand not one anothers Language, but conſenting in ſuch kind of *Characters* (which are more generally receiv'd amongſt them) can communicate one with another by
ſuch *Figures* written ; ſo as every Country can read and deliver in his
own native Tongue, the meaning of any Book written with theſe *Characters.*

§ *Notes* therefore of things, which without the help and mediation
＊   of *Words* ſignifie *Things*, are of two ſorts ; whereof the firſt ſort is ſig-
DE NOTIS   nificant of *Congruity ;* the other *ad placitum*. Of the former ſort are
RERUM.   *Hieroglyphicks* and *Geſtures ;* of the later are thoſe which we call *Characters Real*. The uſe of *Hieroglyphicks* is very ancient, and had in a
kind of Veneration ; eſpecially amongſt the Egyptians, one of the moſt
Ancient Nations : So that *Hieroglyphicks* ſeem to have been a *firſt-born
writing*, and elder than the *Elements* of *Letters ;* unleſs, it may be, the
Letters of the Hebrews. *As for Geſtures,*they are,as it were,Tranſitory
Hieroglyphicks. For as words pronounced vaniſh,*writings* remain ; ſo *Hieroglyphicks* expreſſed by *Geſtures,*are tranſient,but *painted,*permanent. As
when *Periander* being conſulted with, how to preſerve a Tyranny, bid
the

the Meſſenger ſtand ſtill, *and he walking in a Garden, topt all the higheſt* Herodot.
Flowers ; ſignifying the cutting off, and the keeping low of the Nobi-   Laeᵗ.
lity ; did as well make uſe of a *Hieroglyphick,* as if he had drawn the
ſame upon Paper.   This in the mean is plain, that *Hieroglyphicks* and
Geſtures ever have ſome ſimilitude with the thing ſignified, and are kind
of *Emblems* ;. wherefore we have named them the *Notes of things from
Congruity.*   But *Characters Real* have nothing of Emblem in them ; but
are plainly dumb and dead Figures, as the *Elements of Letters* are ; and
only deviſed *ad Placitum,* and, confirmed by Cuſtom, as by a tacit a-
greement.   And it is manifeſt alſo that there muſt needs be a vaſt number of them for writing ; at leaſt ſo many as there are Radical words.
Wherefore this portion of Knowledge *concerning the Organ of Speech,
which is of the Notes of Things, we report as Deficient.*   And though it
may ſeem of no great uſe,. conſidering that *Words* and *writings by Letters* are the moſt apt *Organs* of *Tradition* ; yet we thought good to make
mention of it here, as of a knowledge not to be deſpiſed.   For we here
handle, as it were, the *Coyns of things Intellectual* ; and it will not be
amiſs to know, that as Money may be made of other matter beſides
Gold and Silver ; ſo there may be ſtamped other *Notes* of things beſides *Words* and *Letters.*

II Let us proceed to *Grammar ; this doth bear the office as it were, of
an Uſher to other Sciences ; a place not very honourable, yet very neceſſary, eſpecially ſeeing that in our age Sciences are chiefly drawn from Learned
Languages, and not from Mother-tongues.*   Nor is the dignity thereof to
be eſteemed mean, ſeeing it ſupplies the place of an Antidote, againſt
that *Malediction* of the *Confuſion* of *Tongues.*   Surely the Induſtry of
man ſtriveth to reſtore, and redintegrate himſelf in thoſe Benedictions,
which by his guilt he forfeited ; and by all other Arts, arms and ſtrengthens himſelf againſt that firſt general Curſe of the *ſterility of the earth, and
the eating of his bread in the ſweat of his brows.*   But againſt that ſecond   Gen. 3.
Curſe, which was the *Confuſion of Tongues, he calls in the aſſiſtance of
Grammar.*   The uſe hereof in ſome Mother-tongues is indeed very ſmall ;
in forreign tongues more large ; but moſt ample in ſuch tongues, as
have ceaſed to be vulgar, and are perpetuated only in Books.

§ *We will divide Grammar into two ſorts, whereof the one is Literary,
the other Philoſophical.*   The one is merely applied to Languages, that
that they may be more ſpeedily learned ; or more correctedly and purely ſpoken.   *The other* in a ſort doth miniſter, and is ſubſervient to *Philoſophy.*   In this later part which is *Philoſophical,* we find *that Cæſar writ*   Suet in
Books De Analogia ; and it is a queſtion whether thoſe Books handled   ſul.
this Philoſophical Grammar whereof we ſpeak ?   Our opinion is, that
not any high and ſubtil matter in them, but only that they deliver'd   GRAM-
Precepts of a pure and perfect ſpeech, not depraved by popular Cu-   MATICA
ſtom ; nor corrupted and polluted by over-curious affectation ; in   PHILOSO-
which kind *Cæſar* excell'd.   *Notwithſtanding,* admoniſh'd by ſuch a   PHANS.
work, we have conceiv'd and comprehended in our mind, a kind of
Grammar, that may diligently enquire, not the *Analogy of words one*
with another, but the *Analogy* between Words and Things, or Reaſon ;
beſides that *Interpretation of Nature,* which is ſubordinate to *Logick.*
Surely *Words* are the *foot-ſteps of Reaſon* ; and foot-ſteps do give ſome
indications of the Body ; wherefore we will give ſome general deſcription

ption of this.   And firſt we do not allow that curious enquiry which
In Cratyl. *Plato* an excellent man purſued, touching the *impoſition* and *original E-*
tymology of names.   conceiving it, *as if words had not been impoſed at*
firſt, ad Placitum; but were ſignificantly derived and deduced from a cer-
tain reaſon and intendment.   Certainly an elegant and pliant ſpeculation, which might be aptly fain'd and made ſquare to the purpoſe: and
by reaſon it ſeemeth to ſearch the ſecrets of Antiquity, in ſome kind reverend.   But yet ſparingly mixt with truth, and without fruit.   *But*
without queſtion that would be a moſt excellent kind of *Grammar* (as
we ſuppoſe if ſome man throughly inſtructed in many *Languages*, as well
Learned, as *Mother-tongues*, ſhould write a Treatiſe of the divers Proprieties of *Languages*; ſhewing in what points every particular Language did excel; and in what points it was *Deficient*.   For ſo
Tongues might be enricht and perfected by mutual intertraffick one with
another; and a moſt fair Image of ſpeech (like the *Venus* of *Apelles*);
and a goodly pattern for the true expreſſion of the inward ſence of the
mind, might be drawn from every part which is excellent in every
Language.   *And withal* no ſlight Conjectures, but ſuch as were well
worth the obſervation, might be taken (which a man perchance would
little think) touching the natural diſpoſitions and cuſtoms of People, and
Nations, even from their Languages.   *For I willingly* give ear to *Cice-*
De Orat. *ro* noting that the Grecians have not a word which may expreſs this La-
lib.2. tine word, *Ineptum*; *becauſe* (ſaith he) *this vice was ſo familiar to the*
Grecians, that they did not ſo much as acknowledge themſelves guilty there-
of.   Certainly a Cenſure worthy a Roman gravity.   And what may
that infer, that the Grecians uſed ſuch a Liberty in compoſition of
words; contrarywiſe the Romans were in this point ſevere?   Surely a
man may plainly collect that the Grecians were more fit to ſtudy Arts;
the Romans to manage affairs of ſtate.   For diſtinctions of Arts, for
moſt part, require compoſition of words; but matters and buſineſs,
ſimple words.   *But the Hebrews ſo ſhun Compoſition, that they make choice*
rather to ſtrain a Metaphor too far, than to bring in a Compoſition.   Nay
they uſe ſo few words, and ſo unmingled, that a man may plainly perceive by their Tongue, that they were a Nazarite People, and ſeparate
from other Nations. *And is not that* worthy obſervation? (though it may
ſerve to abate our high conceit of our own times *)that ancient Languages*
were more full of Declenſions; Caſes; Conjugations; Tenſes, and the like;
the modern commonly deſtitute of theſe, do looſely deliver themſelves in
many expreſſions by Prepoſitions, and auxiliary verbs.   Certainly a man
may eaſily conjecture (however we may pleaſe our ſelves) that the wits
of former times were far more acute and ſubtil than ours are.   There
are an infinite number of obſervations of this kind which might make up
a juſt Volume.   Wherefore it will not be amiſs to diſtinguiſh *Gram-*
mar Philoſophical, from *mere and literary Grammar.* and to ſet it down
as *Deficient*,   Unto *Grammar* alſo belongs the conſideration of all *Acci-*
dents of words; ſuch as are *Meaſure; Sound; Accent*; but thoſe firſt
infancies of ſimple Letters (as, with what Percuſſion of the Tongue, with
what opening of the mouth; with what drawing of the lips, with what
ſtraining of the throat; the ſound of every Particular *Letter* is to be
made) belongs not unto *Grammar*; but is a Portion of the *knowledge of*
ſounds, to be handled *under ſenſe* and *ſenſibility*.   *Grammatical ſound*,
                                                              whereof

whereof we speak, belongs only to sweetness and harshness of sounds; of which some are common; for there is no Tongue but in some sort shuns the too much overture of concurrent Vowels, and the asperities of concurrent Consonants. There are other respective sounds which are pleasing, or unpleasing to the ear, according to the temper of divers Nations. *The Greek Tongue* is full of Diphthongs; the Latin is far more sparing; the Spanish Tongue hates small-sounding Letters, and presently changeth them into Letters of a middle tone; the Tongues derived from the *Goths* delight in Aspirates; there are innumerable of this nature; but perchance these are more than enough.

III. *But the measure of words* hath brought us forth an immense Body of Art, namely *Poesie*; not in respect of the Matter (of which we have spoken before) but in respect of stile, and the form of words, as *Metre* or *Verse*; touching which the Art is very small and brief, but the access of Examples large and infinite. Neither ought that Art (which the Grammarians call *Prosodia*) to be only restrain'd to the kinds and measures of *Verse*; for their are Precepts to be annext, what kind of *Verse* best fitteth every Matter or Subject. The Ancients applied *Heroical Verse* to *Histories* and *Laudatories*; *Elegies* to *Lamentations*; *Jambicks* to *Invectives*; *Lyricks* to *Songs* and *Hymns*. And this Wisdom of the Ancients is not wanting in the *Poets* of later Ages, in Mother-tongues; only this is to be reprehended, that some of them too studious of Antiquity have endeavoured to draw Modern Languages to Ancient Measures (as *Heroick, Elegiack, Saphick*, and the rest) which the Fabrick and composition of those Languages, will not bear; and withal is no less harsh unto the ear. In the Matters of this Nature the Judgement of Sense is to be preferr'd before Precepts of Art, as he saith,

> ————*Cænæ Fercula nostræ*
> *Mallem Convivis quam placuisse Coquis.*

Mart.
Ep. 9.

Nor is *this Art*, but the abuse of Art, seeing it doth not perfect, but perverts Nature. As for Poesie *(whether we speak of Fables, or Metre) it is, as we have said before, as a Luxuriant Herb brought forth without seed, and springs up from the strength and ranknes of the soyl. Wherefore it runs along every where, and is so amply spread, as it were a superfluous labour to be curious of any Deficients therein;* the care therefore for this is taken already.

§ *As for the Accents of Words,* there is no need, that we speak of so small a matter; unles, perchance, some may think it worth the noting, that there hath been exact observations made of the *Accents of Words*, but not of the *Accents of Sentences*; yet this, for most part, is the general Custom of all men, that in the close of a Period they let fall their voice, in a demand they raise it, and many such like usages.

§ *As for Writing*, that is perform'd either by the vulgar Alphabet, which is every where receiv'd; or by a secret and private Alphabet, which men agree upon between themselves, which they call *Cyphers*. But the *Vulgar Orthography* hath brought forth unto us a Controversie, and Question, namely, *Whether words should be written as they are spoken, or rather after the usual manner.* But this kind of writing, which seems to be reformed, which is, *that writing should be consonant to speaking,* is a branch of unprofitable subtilties; for *Pronunnciation* it self

Y   every

every day encreaſes and alters the faſhion ; and the derivation of
words, eſpecially from forreign Languages, are utterly defac'd and extinguiſht. In brief, ſeeing *writing*, according to the receiv'd Cuſtom,
doth no way prejudice the *manner of ſpeaking*, to what end ſhould this
innovation be brought in ?

§ *Wherefore let us come to Cyphers.* Their kinds are many, as *Cyphers
ſimple* ; *Cyphers intermixt with Nulloes*, or non-ſignificant Characters ;
Cyphers of double Letters under one Character ; *Wheel-Cyphers* ; *Kaye
Cyphers* ; *Cyphers of words* ; *Others*. But the virtues of them, whereby
they are to be preferr'd, are Three ; *That they be ready , and not laborious to write* ; *That they be ſure, and lie not open to Decyphering*: And
laſtly, *if it be poſſible, that they may be managed without ſuſpition*. For if
Letters Miſſive fall into their hands, that have ſome command and authority over thoſe that write ; or over thoſe to whom they were written ; though the Cypher it ſelf be ſure and impoſſible to be *decypher'd*
yet the Matter is liable to examination and queſtion ; unleſs the *Cypher*
be ſuch, as may be void of all ſuſpition, or may elude all examination.
As for the ſhifting off examination, there is ready prepared a new and
profitable invention to this purpoſe ; which, ſeeing it is eaſily procured,
to what end ſhould we report it, as *Deficient*. The invention is this :
That you have two ſorts of *Alphabets*, one of *true Letters*, the other of
Non-ſignificants ; and that you likewiſe fold up two *Letters* ; one
which may carry the ſecret , another ſuch as is probable the Writer
might ſend, yet without peril. Now if the Meſſenger be ſtrictly examined concerning the *Cypher*, let him preſent the *Alphabet of Non-ſigni-
cants* for true *Letters* , but the *Alphabet* of true *Letters* for *Non-ſignificants* : by this Art the Examiner falling upon the *exterior Letter*, and
finding it probable, ſhall ſuſpect nothing of the *interior Letter*. But
that jealouſies may be taken away , we will annex another invention ,
which, in truth, we deviſed in our youth, when we were at *Paris :* and is
a thing that yet ſeemeth to us not worthy to be loſt. It containeth the
higheſt degree of Cypher, which is to ſignifie *omnia per omnia*, yet ſo, as
the *writing infolding*, may bear a quintuple proportion to the *writing
infolded* ; no other condition or reſtriction whatſoever is required. It
ſhall be performed thus : Firſt, let all the *Letters* of the *Alphabet* , by
transpoſition, be reſolved into two *Letters* only ; for the transpoſition
of two *Letters* by five placings will be ſufficient for thirty two Differences, much more for twenty four, which is the number of the *Alphabet*. The example of ſuch an *Alphabet* is on this wiſe.

A aaaa. aaaab. aaaba. aaabb. aabaa. aabab.
aabba. aabbb. abaaa. abaab. ababa. ababb
abbaa. abbab. abbba. abbbb. baaaa. baaab
baaba. baabb. babaa. babab. babba. babbb.

Neither is it a ſmall matter theſe *Cypher-Characters* have, and may perform : For by this *Art* a way is opened, whereby a man may expreſs and ſignifie the intentions of his mind, at any diſtance of place, by objects which may be preſented to the eye, and accommodated to the ear : provided thoſe objects be capable of a two-fold difference only ; as by Bells, by Trumpets, by Lights and Torches, by the Reports of Muskets, and any Inſtruments of like nature. But to purſue our enterprise, when you addreſs your ſelf to write, reſolve your inward-infolded Letter into this *Bi-literary Alphabet.* Say the *interiour Letter* be

Fuge.

Example of Solution.

F. V. G. E.
Aabab. baabb. aabba. aabaa.

Together with this, you muſt have ready at hand a *Bi-formed Alphabet*, which may repreſent all the *Letters* of the *Common Alphabet.*

as well Capital Letters as the ſmaller Characters in a double form, as
may fit every mans occaſioh.

An Example of a Bi-formed Alphabet.

{ a. b. a. b. a. b. a. b. a. b. a b. a. b. a b.

{ A. A. a. a. B. B. b. b . C. C. c. c. D. D. d. d.

{ a. b. a. b. a. b. a b. a. b. a. b. a. b. a. b.

{ E. E. e. e. F. F. f. f. G. G. g. g. H. H. h. h

{ a. b. a. b. a. b. a. b. a. b. a. b. a. b. a. b

{ I. I. i. i. K. K. k. k. L. L. L. L. M. M. m. m

{ a. b. a. b. a. b. a. b. a. b. a. b. a. b. a. b. a

{ N. N. n. n. O. O. o. o. P. P. p. p. Q. Q. g. g. R.

{ b. a b. a b. a. b. a. b. a. b. a. b. a. b. a. b.

{ R. r. r. S. S. s. s. T. T. t. t. V. V. v. v.

{ a. b. a. b. a. b. a b. a. b. a. b. a. b. a. b. a

{ W. W. w. w. X. X. x. x. Y. Y. y. y. Z. Z. z. z

Now

Now to the interiour Letter, which is Bi-literate, you ſhall fit a Bi-formed exteriour Letter, which ſhall anſwer the other, Letter for Letter, and afterwards ſet it down.   Let the exteriour example be.

Manere te volo, donec venero.

An Example of Accommodation.

$$F \quad V \quad G \quad E$$

a abab̄b aab b.aa bb.a.aa ba.a.

Manere te volo donec venero

We have annext likewiſe a more ample Example of the Cypher of Writing *omnia per. omnia :* An interiour Letter, which to expreſs, we have made choice of a *Spartan* Letter ſent once in a *Scytale* or round Cypher'd-ſtaff.

Perditae Res Mindarus cecidit. Milites esuriunt. Neque hinc nos. extricare neque hic diutius. manere possumus

An exteriour Letter, taken out of the firſt Epiſtle of *Cicero*, wherein a *Spartan* Letter is involved.

Ego

*Ego, omni, officio, ae potius pietate erga te
exteris, satisfacio omnibus: Mihi. ipse nun=
quam satisfacio. Tanta est enim magni=
tudo. tuorum erga me meritorum. vt quoni=
am tu, nisi perfecta re, de me non conquies=
ti: ego, quia non. idem in tuâ causâ efficio,
vitam mihi esse acerbum putem. In cau=
sâ haec sunt: Ammonius Regis Legatus
aperte pecuniâ nos oppugnat: Res agitur
per eosdem creditores, per quos, cùm tu ode
rae, agebatur. Regis causâ, si qui sunt,
qui velint, qui pauci sunt, omnes ad Pompe=
ium rem deferri volunt. Senatus Reli=
gionis calumniam, non religione, sed ma=
leuolentia, et illius Regiae Largitionis
inuidiâ comprobat. &c.*

The knowledge of Cyphering, hath drawn on with it a knowledge relative unto it, which is the knowledge of *Discyphering,* or of Discreting *Cyphers* though a man were utterly ignorant of the *Alphabet* of the *Cypher,* and the Capitulations of secrecy past between the Parties. *Certainly* it is an Art which requires great pains and a good wit, and is (as the other was) consecrate to the Counsels of Princes: yet notwithstanding by diligent prevision it may be made unprofitable, though, as things are, it be of great use. For if good and faithful *Cyphers* were invented and practised, many of them would delude and forestal all the cunning of the *Decypherer,* which yet are very apt and easie to be read or written: but the rawness and unskilfulness of Secretaries, and Clerks in the Courts of Princes, is such, that many times the greatest Matters are committed to futile and weak Cyphers. But it may be, that in the enumeration, and, as it were, taxations of Arts, some may think that we go about to make a great Muster-rowl of Sciences, that the multiplication of them may be more admired; when their number perchance may be displayed, but their forces in so short a Treatise can hardly be tried. But for our parts we do faithfully pursue our purpose, and in making this *Globe of Sciences,* we would not omit the lesser and remoter Islands. *Neither* have we (in our opinion) touched these Arts perfunctorily, though cursorily; but with a piercing stile extracted the Marrow and Pith of them, out of a Mass of Matter. The judgement hereof we refer to those who are most able to judge of these *Arts. For seeing it is the fashion of many who would be thought to know much, that every where, making ostentation of words and outward terms of Arts, they become a wonder to the ignorant, but a derision to those that are Masters of those* Arts: *we hope that our Labours shall have a contrary success, which is, that they may arrest the judgement of every one who is best vers'd in every particular* Art; *and be undervalued by the rest.* As For those *Arts* which may seem to be of inferiour rank and order, if any man think we Attribute too much unto them; let him look about him; and he shall see that there be many of special note and great account in their own Country, who when they come to the chief City or Seat of the Estate, are but of mean rank, and scarcely regarded: so it is no marvail if these sleighter *Arts,* placed by the Principal and Supreme *Sciences,* seem petty things; yet to those that have chosen to spend their Labours and Studies in them, they seem great and excellent Matters. And thus much of the *Organ of Speech.*

CHAP.

CHAP. II.

I. The Doctrine touching *the Method of Speech is assigned a substantial and principal part of Traditive knowledge:* It is entituled, *The wisedom of Delivery.* 2. *The divers kinds of Methods are enumerated: their Profits and Disprofits are annexed.* 3. *The parts of Method two.*

I. *Et us now come to the doctrine concerning the Method of Speech:* This hath been handled as a part of *Logick*, so it hath found a place in *Rhetorick* by the name of *Disposition.* But the placing of *it* as a part of the Train of other *Arts*, hath been the cause that many things which refer unto *it*, and are useful to be known, are pretermiss'd : wherefore we thought good to constitute a *substantial and principal Doctrine*, touching *Method*, which by a general name we call the *wisedom of Tradition.* *The kinds of Method*, seeing they are divers, we will rather reckon them up, than divide them. *But for one onely* Method, *and continued Dichotomies we need not speak much of them; for it was a little Cloud of knowledge which was soon dispersed. Certainly a trivial invention, and an infinite prejudice to Sciences; for these Dichotomists, when they would wrest all things to the Laws of their Method, and whatsoever doth not aptly fall within those Dichotomies they would either omit or bow contrary to their natural inclination; they bring it so to pass, that the Kernels and Grains of Sciences leap out, and they clasp and inclose only the dry and empty husks: So this kind of Method brings forth fruitless Compends, destroys the substance of Sciences.*

II. Wherefore let the first difference of *Method* be set down, to be either *Magistral*, or *Initiative*: neither do we so understand the word *Initiative*, as if *this* should lay the ground-work, the *other* raise the perfect building of *Sciences*; but in a far different sence, (borrowing the word from sacred Ceremonies) we call that *Initiative Method*, which discloseth and unvails the Mysteries of Knowledges: For *Magistral teacheth, Initiative insinuateth: Magistral requires our belief to what is delivered, but Initiative that it may rather be submitted to examination.* The *one* delivers popular *Sciences* fit for Learners; the *other*, *Sciences* as to the *Sons of Science:* In sum, the one is referred to the use of *Sciences* as they now are; the other to their continuation, and further propagation. *The later of these*, seems to be a deserted and an inclosed path. For Knowledges are now delivered, as if both Teacher and Schollar sought to lay claim to error, as upon contract. *For he that teacheth, teacheth in such a manner as may best be believed, not as may be best examined: and he that learneth, desires rather present satisfaction, than to expect a just and stayed enquiry; and rather not to doubt, than not to err: So as both the Master, out of a desire of glory, is watchful, that he betray not the weakness of his knowledge; and the Scholar, out of an averse disposition to labour, will not try his own strength.* But Knowledge, which is delivered as a thread to be spun on, *ought to be intima-*

ted

ted (if it were poſſible) *into the mind of another, in the ſame Method wherein it was at firſt invented.* And ſurely this may be done in knowledge acquired by *Induction :* But in this ſame anticipated and prevented knowledge, which we uſe, a man cannot eaſily ſay, by what courſe of ſtudy he came to the knowledge he hath obtained. But yet certainly more or leſs a man may reviſit his own *Knowledge,* and meaſure over again the footſteps of his *Knowledge,* and of his conſent; and by this means ſo tranſplant *Science* into the mind of another, as it grew in his own. For it is in *Arts,* as it is in *Plants ;* if you mean to uſe the *Plant,* it is no matter for the Roots; but if you would remove into another ſoyl, than it is more aſſured to reſt upon roots than ſlips. So the *Delivery* of Knowledge, as it is now uſed, *doth preſent unto us fair Bodies indeed of Sciences, but without* the *Roots ;* good, doubtleſs for the Carpenter, *but not for the Planter.* But if you will have *Sciences* grow, you need not be ſo ſollicitous for the *Bodies ;* apply all your care that the *Roots* may be taken up ſound, and entire, with ſome little earth cleaving to them. Of which kind of *Delivery, the Method* of the *Mathematicks* in that ſubject, hath ſome ſhadow, but generally I ſee it neither put in ure, nor put in *Inquiſition ;* and therefore number it amongſt *Deficients,* and we will call it *Traditionem Lampadis, the Delivery of the Lamp, or the Method bequeathed to the ſons of Sapience.*

§ *Another diverſity of Method* followeth, in the intention like the former, but for moſt part contrary in the iſſue. In this both theſe *Methods* agree, that *they* ſeparate the vulgar *Auditors* from the *Select ;* here *they* differ, that the *former* introduceth a more open way of *Delivery* than is uſual ; the *other* (of which we ſhall now ſpeak) a more reſerved and ſecret. *Let therefore the diſtinction of them be this, that the one is an Exoterical or revealed ; the other an Acroamatical, or concealed Method.* For the ſame difference the Ancients 'ſpecially obſerved in publiſhing Books, the ſame we will transfer to the manner it ſelf of *Delivery.* So the *Acroamatick Method* was in uſe with the Writers of former Ages, and wiſely, and with judgement applied ; but that *Acroamatick* and Æenigmatick kind of expreſſion is diſgraced in theſe later times, by many who have made it as a dubious and falſe light, for the vent of their counterfeit merchandiſe. But the pretence thereof ſeemeth to be this, that by the intricate envelopings of *Delivery,* the Prophane Vulgar may be removed from the ſecrets of Sciences ; and they only admitted, which had either acquired the interpretation of Parables by Tradition from their Teachers ; or by the ſharpneſs and ſubtilty of their own wit, could pierce the veil.

§ *Another diverſity of Method* follows, of great conſequence to *Sciences;* which is, when Sciences are delivered by way of *Aphoriſm,* or *Methods.* For it is a thing worthy to be preciſely noted, that it hath been often taken into Cuſtom, that men out of a few Axioms and Obſervations upon any Subject, have made a compleat and ſolemn Art, filling it with ſome diſcourſes of wit, illuſtrating it with examples, and knitting it together by ſome *Method.* But that other way of *Delivery* by *Aphoriſms,* brings with it many advantages, whereto *Delivery by Method* doth not approach. For firſt it tryes the Writer whether he be ſuperficial or ſolid in knowledge. For *Aphoriſms* except they ſhould

Z   be be altogether ridiculous, cannot be made but out of the pyth and heart of Sciences: For Illustration and Excussion are cut off; variety of examples is cut off; Deduction and Connection are cut off; Description of Practice is cut off; so there remaineth nothing to fill the Aphorisms, but a good quantity of observations. And therefore no man can suffice, nor in reason will attempt to write *Aphorisms*, who is not copiously furnish'd and solidly grounded. But in *Methods*,

Horat.de Art.P.

———*Tantum series, juncturaque pollet;*
Tantum de medio sumptis accedit Honoris.

As oftentimes they make a great shew of (I know not what) singular Art; which if they were disjoynted, separated, and laid open, would come to little or nothing. Secondly, *Methodical Delivery* is more fit to win consent or belief; but less fit to point to Action; for *they* carry a shew of *Demonstration in Orb* or Circle, one part illuminating another; and therefore do more satisfie the understanding; but being that Actions in common course of life are disperst, and not orderly digested, they do best agree with dispersed Directions. Lastly, *Aphorisms* representing certain Portions only, and as it were fragments of Sciences, invite others to contribute, and add something; whereas *Methodical Delivery*, carrying shew of a total and perfect Knowledge, forthwith secureth men as if they were at the furthest.

§ Another diversity of Method follows, which is likewise of great weight, which is when *Sciences* are delivered either by *Assertions* with their *Proofs* annext; or by *Questions* together with their *Determinations*. The later kind whereof, if it be immoderately followed, is as prejudicious to the progression of Sciences, as it is to the fortunes and proceedings of an Army, to go about to besiege every little Fort or Hold. For if the field be kept, and the sum of the enterprize with diligence pursued, those smaller places will come in of themselves. Yet this I cannot deny, that it is not alway safe to leave any great and fortified town at his back. *In like manner the use of Confutations* in the Delivery of Sciences ought to be very sparing, and to serve only to remove and break strong Preoccupations and Prejudgements of mens minds, and not to excite and provoke *smaller Doubts*.

§ *Another diversity of Method* followeth, which is, that the *Method be accommodated to the purposed matter which is to be handled*, For there is a great difference in Delivery of the *Mathematicks*, which are of knowledges the most abstracted and most simple; and the *Politicks*, which are the most immersed and compounded: Neither can an *uniformity of Method* (as we have observ'd already) be fitly sorted with *multi-formity of Matter*; and therefore as we have allowed *Particular Topicks* for *Invention*; so we would likewise in some measure have *Particular Methods* for *Tradition*.

§ *Another diversity of Method* followeth, with judgement to be practis'd in the Delivery of Sciences; and it *is directed according to the light of Informations, and anticipations, of the Knowledge to be delivered, infused, and impressed in the minds of the Learners:* For that Knowledge which is new and foreign to mens minds, is to be delivered in another form than that which by long receiv'd, and imbibed opinions is naturalized

ralized and made familiar : And therefore *Aristotle* when he thinks to tax *Democritus* doth in truth commend him, where he saith, *If we shall indeed dispute, and not follow after similitudes, &c.* Charging it as a defect upon *Democritus* that he was too copious in *Comparisons. But those whose conceits are seated in popular opinions, have nothing else to do but to dispute and prove. Whereas on the contrary those whose conceits are beyond popular opinions, have a double labour; first, that what they produce may be conceiv'd ; then, that they be proved.* So that it is of necessity with them to have recourse to *Similitudes* and *Translations*, whereby they may insinuate themselves into mens capacities. Therefore we see in the infancy of Learning, in rude times, when those Comprehensions which are now Vulgar and Trivial, were then new and unheard of; the world was full of *Parables* and *Similitudes*; for otherwise men would have pass'd over without mark or due attention, or else rejected for Paradoxes, that which was propounded. For it is a rule of Traditive Art, *That whatsoever Science is not consonant to Anticipations or Presuppositions, must pray in aid of Similitudes and Comparisons.* And thus much of the divers sorts of Methods, namely such as have not heretofore been noted by others. As for those other *Methods, Analytick; Systatick ; Dieritick; Cryptick; Homerical,* and the like ; they have been well invented and distributed ; nor do we see any cause why we should dwell upon them.

III *But these are the kinds of Method; the Parts are two ;* the one of the *Disposition of a whole work ,* or of the *Argument of some Book;* the other of the *Limitations* of *Propositions.* For there belongs to *Architecture* not only the frame of the whole Building ; but likewise the form and figure of the Columns; Beams, and the like ; and *Method is as it were the Architecture of Sciences.* And herein *Ramus* merited better a great deal in reviving those excellent Rules Καθ᾽ ὅλυ πρῶτον, πάντος, καθ᾽ αὑτό, than in obtruding *one only Method* and *Dichotomie.* But it falls out I know not by what fate, *that of humane things (according as the Poets often feign) the most precious have the most pernicious Keepers.* Certainly diligent endeavours about the rank and file of Propositions, cast him upon those *Epitomes* and *shallows of Sciences* ; for he had need set out in a lucky hour, and to go on by the conduct of a happy Genius, that attempts to make *Axioms of Sciences Convertible* ; and yet withal not make them *Circular*, or returning into themselves ; notwithstanding we deny not, but that *Ramus's* intention in this kind is profitable. *There remains yet two Limitations of Propositions*, besides that they may be made *Convertible* ; the one touching the *Extension* ; the other touching the *Production* of them. Surely Knowledges have, if a man mark it well, two other dimensions besides *Profundity* ; namely *Latitude* and *Longitude.* For *Profundity* is referr'd to the Truth and Reality of them ; and these make them solid. As for the other two, *Latitude* may be taken and reckoned of Science into Science ; *Longitude* may be accepted and understood from the highest general Proposition, to the lowest particular in the same Science. The one comprehends the bounds and true limits of Sciences, that Propositions may be properly, not promiscuously handled ; and that all Repetition, Excursion, and Confusion may be avoided : the other gives rule how far, and to what degree of Particularity, Propositions of sciences may be deduced. Certainly

a Ramus.

there

Dion.In Anton.P.

there is no doubt but somewhat muſt be left to uſe and Practice; for for we ought to avoid the preciſe error of *Antonius Pius*, that we be not *Cumini ſectores in Scientiis, Mincers of Commin in ſciences*; nor that we multiply diviſions to the loweſt Particularity. Wherefore how we ſhould moderate our ſelves in this point is well worth the enquiry. For we ſee too remote Generalities, unleſs they be drawn down, do little inform, nay rather expoſe Knowledge to the ſcorn of Practical men; and are no more ayding to Practice, than an *Ortelius's Univerſal Mapp* is to direct the way between *London* and *Tork*. Surely the better ſort of Rules have not unfitly been compared to Glaſſes of ſteel, wherein you may ſee the Images of things, but firſt they muſt be filed and burniſht: ſo Rules and Precepts do then help, after they have been laboured and poliſht by Practice; but if thoſe Rules may be made clear and Chryſtalline aforehand, it would be the more excellent, becauſe they would leſs ſtand in need of diligence, labour and exerciſe after. *And thus much of the Knowledge of Method*, which we have named the *Wiſdom* of *Delivery*. Nor can we here pretermit that many more vain-glorious, than learned have laboured about a *Method*, which is not worthy the name of a lawful *Method*, ſeeing it is rather a *Method of Impoſture*; which yet to ſome vaporous, and vain-boaſting natures, without doubt hath been moſt acceptable. This *Method* doth ſo ſprinkle drops of any Knowledge, that any half-learned Clerk may with a little ſuperficiary Knowledge make a glorious ſhew. Such was the Art of *Lullius*; ſuch the *Typocoſmie* drawn by many; which were nothing elſe but a heap and maſs of words of all Arts, to give men countenance; that thoſe which have the terms of Art, might be thought to underſtand the Arts themſelves. Which kind of Collections are like a Fripper's or Broker's ſhop, that hath ends of every thing, but nothing of worth.

Lullius.

CHAP. III.

I The *Grounds and Duty of Rhetorick.* II. *Three Appendices of Rhetorick which appertain only to the Preparatory Part. The Colours of Good and Evil, as well ſimple as Compared.* III. *The Antitheta of things.* IV. *Leſſer ſtiles, or uſual forms of ſpeech.*

NOw come we to the Knowledge which concerneth the *Illuſtration of Speech*; it is that which is called *Rhetorick*, or Art of *Eloquence*; a Science certainly both excellent in it ſelf, and by Authors excellently well laboured. But *Eloquence*, if a man value things truly, is without doubt inferior to *Wiſdom*. For we ſee how far this leaves that behind, in thoſe words of *God* to *Moſes*, when he diſabled himſelf for that ſervice impoſed upon him, for want of this *Faculty*; *There is Aaron, he ſhall be thy Speaker, thou ſhalt be to him as God.* Yet in profit and popular eſteem, *Wiſdom* gives place to *Eloquence*; for ſo *Solomon, Sapiens corde appellatur prudens; ſed dulcis eloquio majora reperiet*; ſignifying not obſcurely *that profoundneſs of Wiſdom will help a man to fame and admiration; but that it is Eloquence which prevails in buſineſs and active Life.*

Exod.7.

Prov. XVI.

Life. And as to the labouring and culture of this Art, the Emulation of *Aristotle* with the *Rhetoricians* of his time, and the earnest and vehement diligence of *Cicero*, labouring with all might to raise and ennoble that *Art*, joyned with long Experience, hath made them in their Books written of this *Art* to exceed themselves. Again, the excellent example of *Eloquence* in the *Orations* of *Demosthenes*, and *Cicero*, added to the subtilty and diligence of Precepts, have doubled the Progression in this *Art*. Wherefore the *Deficients* which we find in this *Art*, will be rather in some Collections, which may as Hand-maids attend the *Art*; than in the Rules and the use of the *Art it self.* For even then when we made mention of a *Promptuary Knowledge* in *Logick*, we engaged our selves by Promise, to exhibit Examples at large thereof in *Rhetorick.*

Notwithstanding that we may stir up and subdue the earth a little, about the Roots of this *Science*, as our manner is to do in the rest; surely *Rhetorick* is *sub-servient* to the *imagination*, as *Logick* is to the *Understanding.* And the office and duty of *Rhetorick* (if a man well weigh the matter) is no other, than *to apply and command the Dictates of Reason to the Imagination, for the better moving of the Appetite and Will.* For we see the government of Reason is disquieted, and assailed three ways; either by *Illaqueation* of *Sophisms*, which pertains to *Logick*; or by the *deceits of words*, which pertains to *Rhetorick*; or by the *violence of Passions*, which pertains to *Morality*: And as in negociation with others, a man may be wrought and overcome either by *Cunning*, or by *Importunity*, or by *Vehemency*, so in that inward negociation which we practise within our selves, either we are undermined *by the Fallacies of Arguments*; or sollicited and disquieted by the *assiduity of impressions and observations*; or shaken and transported *by the assault of affections and passions.* But yet the state of man's nature is not so unfortunate, as that those *Powers* and *Arts* should have force to disturb *Reason*, and not to establish and advance it; nay, rather much more do they conduce to this effect, than to the contrary. For the end of *Logick*, is to teach a form of Arguments, to secure Reason, and not to entrap it; so the end of Morality is to compose the *Affections*, that they may fight for Reason, and not that they may invade it; the end likewise of *Rhetorick*, is to fill the *Imagination* with observations and resemblances, which may second Reason, and not oppress and betray it : for these abuses of *Arts* come in but *ex obliquo* for prevention, not for practice. And therefore it was great injustice in *Plato* (though springing out of a just hatred to the *Rhetoricians* of his time) to place *Rhetorick* amongst *Arts voluptuary*, resembling it to *Cookery*, that did marr wholesome meats, and help unwholesome by the the abuse of of variety of sawces and seasonings, to the pleasure of the taste. But be it far away, that speech should not be much more conversant in a-doring that which is fair and honest, than in colouring that which is foul and evil : for this is every where at hand; and there is no man but speaks more honestly than he can do or think. Indeed it was excellently noted by *Thucydides*, that some such thing as this, used to be objected to *Cleon*, that because he used to hold the bad side in causes he pleaded, therefore he was ever inveighing against *Eloquence*, and *good speech*, for he knew no man could speak fair of things sordid and base

In Gorg.

In Menon.

Tufc. Q.
lib.

bafe, but in things honeſt it was an eaſie matter to be *eloquent.* *Plato* ſaith elegantly (though the ſaying be now popular) *That vertue, if ſhe could be ſeen, would move great love and affeltion :* but Rhetorick paints our vertue and goodneſs to the life, and makes them in a ſort conſpicuous : For ſeeing they cannot be ſhewed to ſenſe in corporal ſhape, the next degree is by the fair attire of words, to ſhew them to the Imagination, ſo far as may be in a lively repreſentation : for the cuſtom of the Stoicks was deſervedly derided by *Cicero,* who labour'd to thruſt vertue upon men, by conciſe and ſharp ſentences and concluſions , which have no ſympathy with the Imagination and Will. Again, if the *Affeltions* themſelves were brought into order, and ſo reclaim'd from exorbitant courſes, as to be pliant and obedient to *Reaſon,* it were true, there ſhould be no great uſe of perſwaſions and inſinuations, which might give acceſs to the mind ; but it would be enough if things were nakedly and ſimply propoſed and proved : but on the contrary, the *Affeltions* make ſuch revolts ; and raiſe up ſuch mutinies and ſeditions (according to that

Ovid.
Met.7.

———*video meliora Proboque*
Deteriora ſequor)———

That *Reaſon* would be forcibly led away into ſervitude and captivity, if the perſwaſion of *Eloquence* did not practiſe, and win the Imagination from the Affeltions part, and contract a league between *Reaſon* and *Imagination* againſt *Affeltions.* For it muſt be noted that the *Affeltions* themſelves are ever carried to a good Apparent, and, in this reſpect, have ſomewhat common with *Reaſon :* but herein they differ ; *that the affeltions behold principally good in preſent* ; *Reaſon beholds a far off, even that which is future, and in ſumm.* And therefore ſeeing things in preſent ſight do more ſtrongly fill the *Imagination* ; Reaſon commonly yields and is vanquiſht : but after that by *Eloquence,* and the force of perſwaſion, things *future* and *remote* are propoſed, and beheld , as if they were actually preſent ; then upon the falling off of the *Imagination,* to take part with *Reaſon, Reaſon* prevails. *Let us* conclude therefore, that *Rhetorick,* can no more be charged with the colouring and adorning of the worſe part than *Logick,* with the ſetting out and ſuborning of Sophiſms : for who knows not that the doctrine of contraries are the ſame, though they be oppoſite in uſe. Again, *Logick* differs from *Rhetorick* ; not only in this, that the one (as commonly is ſaid) *is like the Fiſt, the other like the Palm* ; that is, one handleth things cloſely, the other at large : but much more in this, that *Logick* conſidereth Reaſon in its Naturals ; *Rhetorick,* as it is planted in vulgar opinion. Therefore *Ariſtotle* doth wiſely place *Rhetorick* between *Logick* on the one ſide, and *Ethick* with *Civil Knowledge* on the other : as participating of both. For the Proofs and Demonſtrations of *Logick,* are to all men indifferent and the ſame ; but the Proofs and Perſwaſions of *Rhetorick,* muſt be varied according to the Auditors, that a man , like a skilful Muſician accommodating himſelf to different ears, may become ———

Orpheus in ſylvis, inter Delphinas Arion.

Which

Which *Application and variance of speech* (if a man defire indeed the perfection and height thereof) ought to be fo far extended, *that if the fame things fhould be fpoken to feveral perfons, he fhould fpeak to them all refpectively, and feveral ways.* Though it is certain that the greateft Orators many times may want *this politick and active part of Eloquence in private Speech*; whilft by the obferving the Grace, and Elegant forms of Expreffion, they loofe that *voluble application*; and *characters of speech*, which in difcretion they fhould have ufed towards particular perfons. Surely it will not be amifs to recommend this whereof we now fpeak, to a new *Inquiry*, and to call it by name, *The Wifdom of private Speech*, and to refer it to *Deficients*; a thing certainly which the more ferioufly a man fhall think on, the more highly he fhall value; and whether this kind of *Prudence* fhould be placed between *Rhetorick* and the *Politicks*, is a matter of no great confequence.

§ Now let us defcend to the *Deficients* in this Art, which (as we have faid before) are of fuch nature as may be efteemed rather *Appendices*, than *portions of the Art* it felf; and pertain all to the *Promptuary* part of *Rhetorick*.

II. Firft, we do not find that any man hath well purfued or fupplied the wifdom and the diligence alfo of *Ariftotle*: for he began to make a collection of the *Popular Signs and Colours of Good and Evil in appearance, both fimple and comparative,* which are, indeed, the *Sophifms of Rhetorick*: they are of excellent ufe, fpecially referred to bufinefs, and the *wifdom of private fpeech*. But the labours of *Ariftotle* concerning thefe Colours, is three ways *defective*; *Firft,* that there being many; he recites very few. *Secondly,* becaufe their *Elenchs* or *Reprehenfions* are not annext. *Thirdly,* that he conceiv'd but in part the ufe of them, for their ufe is not more for Probation, than for impreffion and raifing the affections. For many *Forms of fpeaking* are equal in *fignification,* which are different in *impreffion*: for that which is fharp pierceth more forcibly, than that which is flat, though the ftrength of the percuffion be the fame. Surely there is no man but will be a little more raifed by hearing it faid, *Your enemies will triumph in this,*

Hoc Ithacus velit & magno mercentur Atridæ,

Then if it fhould be merely thus rendred, *This will be to your difadvantage*; wherefore the *fharp-edged*, and *quick-pointed fpeeches* are not to be defpifed. And being we report this part as *Deficient*, we will, according to our cuftom, confirm it by Examples, for Precepts have not fufficiently illuftrated the Point.

PRUDEN-TIA SER-MONIS PRIVATI.

COLORES BONI ET MALI. In Trop.

Virg. Æn. 2.

Examples

Examples of the Colours of Good and Evil, both Simple and Comparative.

The Colour.

1. *What men Praise and Celebrate, is Good ; what they Dispraise, and Reprehend is Evil.*

The Reprehension.

Plutar. in vita.

THis *Colour* deceives four ways ; either through *Ignorance*, or through *Fraud*, or out of *Partialities* and *Faction* ; or out of the *natural disposition* of such as *Praise* or *Dispraise*. Out of *Ignorance* ; for what's the judgement of the common People to the trial and definition of *Good* and *Evil? Phocion* discern'd better, who when the People gave him an unusual applause, demanded *whether he had not perchance some way or other done amiss ?* Out of *Fraud* and Circumventive *cunning*, for Praisers and Dispraisers many times do but aim at their own ends, and do not think all they say

Horat.lib. 2. Epl.

Laudat venaleis qui vult extrudere merces,

Prov. 20. So, *It is naught , it is naught saith the Buyer, and when he is gone he vaunteth.* —— Through *Factions* ; for it is plain that men are wont to extol their own side, beyond the modest bounds of desert, but to depress those of the contrary part below their demerit. *Through an inbred disposition* ; for some men are by nature made and moulded to servile Flattery ; others on the other side are by nature Sowre and Censorious ; so as in their commendations, or vituperations they are only indulgent to their own humours, little or nothing sollicitous of truth.

The Colour.

2. *What draws Commendation even from an Enemy , is a great Good, What moves Reprehension even from a Friend, is a great Evil.*

The *Colour* seems to be built upon this foundation ; that whatsoever we speak against our will, and contrary to the affection and propension of our own mind, it is easily believed, that the force of truth wrested the same from us.

The Reprehension.

THis *Colour deceives* through the Art and Subtilty both of Enemies and Friends : for Enemies do sometimes ascribe *Praises*, not unwillingly, nor as urg'd from the force of Truth : but yet selecting such
points

points of *Praife*, as may create envie and danger to their Enemies. wherefore a fuperftitious conceit went currant amongft the Grecians as they believed, *that he who was praifed by another malicioufly, and to his hurt, fhould have a pufh rife upon his nofe.* Again it *deceives*, becaufe e-nemies fometimes attribute *Praifes*, as certain brief Prefaces, that fo they may more freely and fpitefully traduce afterwards. On the other fide, this *Colour* deceives through the flight and cunning of Friends; for their cuftom is fometimes to acknowledge and lay open the infirmities of their Friends, not out of a tender Confcience from the impreffion of Truth, but making choice of fuch imperfections, as may leaft prejudice the reputation, or provoke the indignation of their Friends; as if in all other points they were excellent men. *Again it deceives*, becaufe Friends ufe their Reprehenfions (as we have obferved Enemies do their Praifes) as certain fhort Introductions, that they may expatiate more amply in their commendations aftewards.

The Colour.

3 *Whofe Privation is Good, that fame is Evil; Whofe Privation is Evil, that fame is Good.*

The Reprehenfion

THis *Colour* deceives two ways; either by reafon of the *Comparifon* of *Good* and *Evil*; or by reafon of the *Succeffion* of *Good* to *Good*, or of *Evil* to *Evil*. By reafon of *Comparifon*; if it were *Good* for mankind to be *deprived* of the eating of Acorns, it follows not that fuch food was *Evil*, but that Maft was *Good*, Corn *Better*. Neither if it were *Evil* for the State of *Sicily* to be deprived of *Dionyfius* the Elder; doth it follow that the fame *Dionyfius* was a *Good* Prince; but that he was *lefs Evil* than *Dionyfius* the younger. By reafon of *Succeffion*; for the *Privation* of fome *Good*, doth not always give place to *Evil*; but fometimes to a *greater Good*; as when the *Flower* falleth, Fruit *fucceedeth*. Nor doth the *Privation* of fome *Evil* always yield place to *Good*, but fometimes to a *greater Evil*; for *Clodius* an enemy being taken away, *Milo* withal forfeited a fair harveft of Glory.

The Colour.

4 *That which draws neer to Good or Evil, the fame is likewife Good or Evil: But that which is remov'd from Good is Evil; from Evil, is Good.*

Such commonly is the internal condition of things, that things of like Quality, and confenting in Nature, confent likewife in place, and are, as it were, qnartered together, but fuch things as are contrary and diftant in Nature, are alfo fevered and disjoyned inplace; in regard that all things defire to approach things fymbolizing with them; to exterminate and chafe away their contraries.

The

The Reprehenſion.

BUt the *Colour* deceives three ways: Firſt, in reſpect of *Deſtitution :* Secondly, in reſpect of *Obſcuration :* Thirdly, in reſpect of *Protection.*. In regard of *Deſtitution,* it comes to paſs that thoſe things, which in their kind are moſt ample, and do moſt excel, do (as much as may be) ingroſs all to themſelves, and leave that which is next them deſtitute and pined ; wherefore you ſhall never find thriving Shoots or Under-wood near great ſpread Trees : ſo he ſaid well——

——*Divitis ſervi máximè ſervi ;* ——

and the deriſion was pleaſant of him that compared the lower Train of Attendants in the Courts of Princes, to *Faſting-days* which were next to Holy-days, but otherways were the leaneſt days in all the week. In regard of *Obſcuration,* for this is the quality of things in their nature excellent and predominant, that though they do not extenuate and impoveriſh the ſubſtance of things adjoyning to them, yet they darken and ſhadow them : And this the Aſtronomers obſerve of the the Sun, that it is good by Aſpect, but evil by Conjunction and Approximation. In regard of *Protection ;* for things approach and congregate not only for conſort and ſimilitude of Nature ; but even that which is evil (eſpecially in Civil Matters) approacheth to good for Concealment and *Protection ;* ſo wicked perſons betake themſelves to the ſanctuary of the Gods, and Vice it ſelf aſſumes the ſhape and ſhadow of Virtue.

Sæpe latet vitium proximitate boni.

So on the other ſide, *Good* draws near to *Evil*, not for ſociety, but for converſion and reformation of it into *Good ;* and therefore Phyſicians are more converſant with the ſick than the ſound ; and it was objected to our Saviour *that he converſed with Publicans and Sinners.*

Mat. 9.

The Colour.

5 *That ſide, to which all other Parties and Sects unanimouſly confer ſecond voices, after every particular hath aſſerted a Primacy to it ſelf, ſeems to be juſtly preferr'd before the reſt : for every Sect may be preſum'd to uſurp the firſt place, out of Paſſion and Partiality ; but to yield the ſecond place, out of Truth and Merit.*

So *Cicero* went about to prove the *Sect* of *Academicks,* which ſuſpended all aſſeveration, for to be the beſt of all Phiſoſophies ; for (ſaith he) ask a *Stoick* which *Sect* is better than other, he will prefer his own before the reſt : Then ask him which approacheth next in dignity, he will confeſs the *Academick,* ſo deal with an *Epicure* that will ſcant endure the *Stoick* to be in the ſight of him, ſo ſoon as he hath placed himſelf in the chief room, he will place the *Academick* next him. So if a place were void, and a Prince ſhould examine Competitors ſeverally, whom next themſelves
they

Cicero.
Q. A.

they would 'specially commend, it were like that the moſt ſecond voices would concurr upon the ableſt men.

The Reprehenſion.

THe fallax of this *Colour* is in reſpect of *Envy :* for men are accuſtomed after themſelves, and their own faction, to incline and bend unto them, which of all the reſt are the ſofteſt and weakeſt, and are leaſt in their way in deſpight and derogation of them who have moſt inſulted over them, and have held them hardeſt to it.

The Colour.

6 *That whoſe excellency, and ſupereminency is better, the ſame is every way better.*

Appertaining to this are the uſual *forms ; Let us not wander in gene-ralities, let us compare particular with particular.*

The Reprehenſion.

THis *Apparence* ſeems to be of ſtrength, and rather *Logical,* than *Rhe-torical :* yet is it very often a *fallax.* Firſt, becauſe many things are caſual, which if they eſcape, prove excellent ; ſo that in kind they are inferiour, becauſe they are ſo ſubject to peril, and to periſh before they come to perfection ; but in the *Individual* more noble. Of this ſort is the *Bloſſom of March,* whereof the French Proverb goes

> *Burgeon de Mars , Enfans de Paris,*
> *Si un eſchappe bien vaut dix.*

So that the *Bloſſom of May* generally is better than the *Bloſſom of March,* and yet in particular the beſt *Bloſſom of March,* is better than the beſt *Bloſſom of May.* Secondly it deceives, becauſe the nature of things, in *ſome kinds, or ſpecies,* is to be more *equal,* in ſome kinds more *inequal :* as it hath been obſerved that warmer climates produce generally more acute wits; but in Northern climates the wits of chief ſur-paſs the acuteſt wits of hotter Regions. So in many Armies, if the Matter ſhould be tried by Duel between particular champions ſingled out, perchance the victory ſhould go on the one ſide ; if it be tried by the groſs, it would go on the other ſide: for *excellencies,* and *eminencies* go, as it were, by chance, but kinds are governed by Nature and Art. So likewiſe generally Metal is more precious than Stone; and yet a *Diamond* is more precious than *Gold.*

The Colour.

7 *That which keeps the Matter entire in our own hands, is Good; that which leaves no paſſage open for retrait, is Evil : for not to be able to come off is a kind of impotency, but the Power of diſengaging our ſelves is good.*

⸺reof

Æsop.

Hereof *Æsop* framed the Fable of the two Froggs, that consulted together in the time of drouth (when many plashes, they had repaired to, were dry) what was now at last to be done; the first said *let us go down into a deep well, for it is not like the water would fail there,* to whom the other replied, *yea, but if it do fail; how shall we get up again?* The ground of this *colour* is, that humane actions are so uncertain and exposed to perils, *as that seemeth to be the best course, which hath most passages out of it.* Appertaining to this perswasion the *Forms* are; *you shall wholly engage and oblige your self, non tantum, quantum voles, sumes ex fortuna, you shall not be your own carver, nor keep the matter in your own hand,* &c.

The Reprehension.

THe *Fallax* of this *Colour* is first, because in Humane Actions Fortune urgeth us at length to decree, and to resolve upon somewhat: for as he saith elegantly, *not to resolve, is to resolve;* so that many times a suspension of a final decision engageth and implicates us in more necessities, than if we had determin'd of somewhat. And this disease of the mind is like that of covetous men translated from the desire of retaining wealth, to the desire of retaining Free-will and Power: for the covetous man will enjoy nothing, lest he should substract from the total; and this kind of *Sceptick* will execute nothing, that all things may be entire and indifferent to him. *Secondly,* it *deceives* because necessity, and this same *jacta est alea,* awakens the powers of the Mind and puts the spurs to any enterprise; as he saith, *Cæteris pares, necessitate certè superiores estis.*

The Colour.

8 *What a man hath contracted through his own Default, is a greater Evil; what is imposed from without, is a less Evil.*

The reason hereof, is, *because the sting and remorse of the Mind accusing it self, doubles all adversity; contrariwise the recording inwardly that a man is clear and free from fault, and just imputation, doth much attemper outward calamities.* Wherefore the *Poets* do exceedingly aggravate those passionate Lamentations, as fore-runners to desperation; when a man accuseth and tortures himself.

Virg. Æn.
12.

> *Se causam clamat, crimenq; caputq; malorum.*

Contrariwise the *conscience of Innocence* and good deserving, do mollifie and mitigate the calamities of worthy persons. *Besides* when the evil comes from without, cast upon us by others, a man hath whereof he may justly and freely complain, whereby his griefs may evaporate and not stifle the heart: for what comes from the injuries of men, we are wont to take indignation at, and meditate revenge; or else to implore, or expect, that the divine Nemesis, and Retribution, may take hold on the Authors of our hurt; or if it be inflicted from *Fortune* , yet their is left a kind of expostulation against the Divine Powers,

Atq;

Atque Deos atque Aſtra vocat Crudelia Mater.

But on the other ſide, where the evil is derived from a man's own fault, there the grief ſtrikes inward, and does more deeply wound and pierce the heart.

The Reprehenſion.

THe *Fallax* of this *Colour* is, firſt in reſpect of *Hope*, which is a great Antidote againſt *Evils :* for the reformation of a fault is many times in our own power, but the amendment of fortune is not. Wherefore in many of his Orations *Demoſthenes* ſaith thus to the People of *Athens :* Demoſ. *That which having regard to the time paſt, is the worſt Point and Circum-* orat. *ſtance of all the reſt; that as to the time to come, is the beſt : what is that ? Even this, that by your ſloth, irreſolution, and miſgovernment, your affairs are grown to this declination and Decay; for had you uſed and ordered your means and forces to the beſt, and done your parts every way to the full, and notwithſtanding your matters ſhould have gone backward in this point as they do, there had been no hope left of recovery or reputation for hereafter; but ſince it hath been only by your own errors chiefly, you may have good aſſurance, that thoſe errors amended, you may again recover the honour of your former ſtate.* So *Epictetus* ſpeaking of the Degrees of Epictet. the Tranquillity of mind, ſaith *the worſt ſtate of man is to accuſe extern things; better then that, to accuſe a mans ſelf; and beſt of all to accuſe neither.* Secondly this colour deceivs in reſpect of that *pride* which is implanted in the minds of men, whereby they are with much ado induced to an acknowledgement of their own perſonal errors; but that they may ſhift off this acknowledgement, they can ſuffer with far greater patience ſuch *evils,* as they have by their own overſights drawn upon themſelves. For as we ſee it comes to paſs that when a fault is committed, and it is not yet known who is the delinquent, men make much ado; grow hot and impatient above meaſure upon the matter : but after, if it appear to be done by a ſon; or by a wife, or by a near friend, then it is light made of, and preſently all is quiet : ſo it is when any thing falls out ill, the blame whereof muſt needs lite upon our ſelves. And this is commonly ſeen to come to paſs in women, who if they have done any thing unfortunately againſt their Parents or Friends conſents, what ill ſoever betide them upon it, yet you ſhall ſee them ſeldom complain, but ſet a good face on it.

The Colour.

9 *The Degree of Privation ſeems greater than the Degree of Diminution; and again, the Degree of Inception, ſeems greater than the Degree of Increaſe.*

It is a poſition in the Mathematicks; *that there is no proportion between ſomewhat and nothing : therefore the Degrees of Nullity and Quiddity ſeems larger, than the Degrees of Increaſe and Decreaſe.* As to a Monoculus, it is is more to loose one eye, than to a man that hath two eyes: so if one have divers children, it is more grief to him to loose the last surviving son, than all the rest. And therefore *Sibylla* when she had burnt her two first *Books*, doubled the price of the *Third*, because the loss of that had been *gradus Privationis*, and not *Diminutionis*.

Agell lib.
1 No. At.

The Reprehension.

THe *Fallax* of this *Colour* is reprehended; *first in those things, the use and service whereof resteth in sufficiency, or competency, that is in a determinate Quantity.* As if a man be bound upon penalty to pay a sum of money at an appointed day, it would be more to him to want one *Noble*, than if, (supposing he could not tell where to be furnisht with this one Noble) ten Nobles more were wanting. So in the decay of a man's estate, the degree of Debt which first breaks the stock, and casts him behind, seems a greater damage, than the last Degree, when he proves nothing worth. And hereof the common *Forms* are, *Sera in*

Hesiod.

fundo Parsimonia: and as good never a whit, as never the better, &c. Secondly this Colour deceives in respect of that Principle in Nature; Corruptio unius, Generatio alterius: so that the *degree of ultimate Privation,*

Arist.1.de
Gen.&
Cor.

doth many times less disadvantage, because it gives the cause, and sets the wits a-work to some new course. Which is the cause that *Demosthenes*

Orat.1. in
Philip.

often complains before the people of Athens. *That the conditions imposed by Philip, and accepted by them, being neither profitable, nor honourable, were but aliments of their sloth and weakness, that it were much better they were taken away; for by this means their industries might be awaked to find out better remedies and stronger resolutions.* We knew a Physician was wont to say pleasantly and yet sharply to delicate Dames, when they complained they were they could not tell how, but yet they could not endure to take any Physick; he would tell them, *your only way is to be sick indeed, for then you will be glad to take any medicine.* So further, this *Degree of Privation,* or of the highest period of want, serveth not only to stir up industry, but also to command patience. As for the *second* branch of this *Colour,* it depends upon the same reason, which is the degrees of *Quiddity and Nullity;* hence grew the common Place of extolling the *beginning* of every thing.

Dimidium facti qui bene cæpit habet.

This made the Astrologers so idle as to make a judgement upon a man's nature and Destiny, from the moment or point of constellation in his Nativity, or Conception.

The Reprehension.

THis *Colour first deceives, because in many things, the first inceptions are nothing else than what Epicurus terms them in his Philosophy, Tentamenta, that is imperfect Offers, and Essays, which vanish and come to no substance without iteration and improvement.* Wherefore in this case the *second degree* seems the worthier, and more potent than the *First:* as the Body-horse in the Cart that draws more than the formost. And

it

it is a common saying, and not without good sence, *The second blow is that which makes the fray:* for the first, it may be, would have vanisht without farther harm : and therefore *Prius Malo Principium dedit, sed posterius modum abstulit.* Secondly this colour deceives in respect of the dignity of *Perseverance, which consists in the Progression, and not in the Aggression.* For chance, or instinct of Nature, may cause inception ; but setled affection and judgement makes the continuance. *Thirdly, this Colour deceives in such things which have a natural course and inclination contrary to an Inception ; so that the first Inception is perpetually evacuated, unless the force and faculty be continued.* As in those common forms it is said *Non progredi est Regredi* ; and *Qui non proficit deficit,* as in running against the hill ; rowing against the stream ; for if it be with the hill or with the stream , then the *degree of Inception* is more than all the rest. Again this Colour is not only extended to the *Degree of Inception, which is from Power to Act, compar'd with the Degree, which is from Act to increment ; but also is to be understood of the degree which is from Impotency to power, compared with the Degree which is from power to Act :* for the *Degree, from Impotency to Potency, seems greater, than from Power to Act.*

The Colour.

10 *That which is referred to Truth, is more than that which is referred to opinion. The manner and Proof of that which pertains to Opinion, is this ; that a man would never have done it, if he thought it should be sepulchred in secrecy and oblivion.*

So the Epicures say to the Stoicks, *Felicity placed in virtue,* that it is like the *Felicity* of a Player, who if he were left of his Auditors, and their applause, he would streight be out of heart and countenance ; therefore they call virtue, out of a spiteful emulation, *Bonum Theatrale.* But it is otherwise of Riches, whereof the Poet saith

―――*Populus me sibilat : at mihi plaudo*   Horat.

Likewise of *Pleasure* ;

―――*Grata sub imo*
Gaudia Corde premens, vultu similante pudorem.

The Reprehension.

THe *Fallax* of this *Colour* is somewhat subtil ; though the answer to the exemple alledged be ready ; for neither is virtue chosen *propter Auram Popularem* ; seeing that also is given in Precept, *That a man should above all things, and persons, revere himself* ; so that a *Good* man is the *same* in *solitude* which he is in the *Theatre* ; though perchance virtue will be more strong by glory and fame, as heat is encreased by reflection : But this denyes the supposition, but doth not redargue the *Fallax.* The Reprehension is this, be it granted that virtue (especially such as is joyned with labour and conflict) would not be chosen but for her concomitants, *Fame* and *Opinion* ; yet it follows not that an appetite and chief Motive to virtue, should not be real, and for it self ;

felf; for Fame may be only *caufa impulfiva*, or *fine qua non*, and not a caufe *Conftituent* or *Efficient*.   For example, if there were two Horfes, whereof the one would perform with good fpeed, without the fpur ; but the other with the fpur would far exceed the performance of the former; this latter (I fuppofe) will bear away the prize, and be judg'd to be the better *Horfe*; and it will not move any man of found judgement to fay, *Tufh the life of this Horfe, is but in the fpur :* for feeing the ordinary inftrument of Horfemanfhip is the *fpur*, and that it is no matter of impediment or burden ; the *Horfe* is not to be lefs accounted of, which will not do well without the fpur: nor is that other which without the fpur will do great matters, therefore to be reckoned the better, but the more delicate.   So in like manner, *Glory and Honour are the Goads and fpurs to virtue;* and though virtue would fomewhat languifh without them, yet fince they be always at hand to attend virtue, even when they are not invited ; there is no impeachment but that virtue may be defired for it felf; and therefore the Pofition, *That the note of a thing chofen for Opinion and not for Truth, is this; That if a man thought that what he doth, fhould never come to light, he would never have done it ;* is reprehended.

The Colour.

11 *What is purchafed by our own induftry and virtue, is a greater Good ; what is derived upon us, from the benefit of others, or from the indulgence of Fortune, is a leffer Good.*

The reafons are thefe ? *Firft in refpect of future Hope; becaufe in the favour of others, or the good winds of fortune, we have no ftate or certainty; in our own endeavours or abilities we have.*   So when they have procured us one good fortune, we have the fame inftruments ready for a new purchafe; nay by cuftom and fuccefs, ftronger than before.   *Secondly becaufe thefe Properties which we enjoy by the benefit of others, we are debtors to others for them; whereas what we derive from our felves, brings no burden with it, nor draws upon us an obligation to another.*   Again, if the Divine Providence confer a favour upon us, it importunes a kind of Retribution towards the goodnefs of God, which ftings ungracious and wicked men; whereas in that other kind of happinefs,

Hab.1. that of the Prophet commonly falls out, *They rejoyce and triumph; they facrifice unto their net, and burn incenfe unto their drag.   Thirdly becaufe,* that which cometh unto us without our own abilities, yieldeth not that commendation and reputation.   For Actions of great Felicity draw

Pro.M.
Marcel. wonder, not praife; as *Cicero* faid to *Cæfar. Quæ miremur habemus, quæ laudemus expectamus.   Fourthly.* becaufe the purchafes of our own induftry are joyned commonly with labour and ftrife, which makes the fruition of our defires more pleafant, as faith *Solomon, Suavis cibus à venatu:*

The Reprehenfion.

B*Ut there are four Contre-Colours which encline the cafe to the contrary Part, and may be as Reprehenfions to the former Colours,*
Firft

First because Felicity seems to be a seal and character of Divine favour; *and accordingly begets both confidence and alacrity in our selves ; and respect and authority from others :* And this Felicity comprehends many casualties, whereunto the power and providence of a man cannot aspire.   As when *Cæsar* encouraging the Sayler, said *Cæsarem portas & fortunam ejus;* but if he had said, *Cæsarem portas & virtutem ejus,* it had been a cold comfort against a tempest.   *Secondly because that such things as proceed from virtue and industry, are imitable, and feasable by others to be practised ; whereas Felicity is a thing inimitable, and a Prerogative of some few singular persons.*   Wherefore we generally see, that things of Nature are preferr'd before things of Art, because they be inimitable: for what is imitable is in effect Prostitute and common.   *Thirdly the Revenues of Felicity, seem to be no purchase of our own, but a Donative from others : but what is acquired by our own proper virtue is, as it were, bought at a price.*   Whereupon *Plutarch* saith elegantly of the Arts of *Timoleon,* a man of all men most fortunate, compared with the Acts of *Agesilaus* and *Epaminondas* who lived in the same Age, *That they were like Homer's verses, which as they excell'd in other points, so they seem'd to have an easie native slide in them and to be conducted by a happy Genius.*   Fourthly *because what falls out beyond hope and expectation, insinuates it self more sweetly, and with greater delight, into the minds of men;* but this cannot be incident to those things, which proceed from our own care and compass.

In margin: Suet. in Jul.

In margin: In Timol.

The Colour.

12 " *What consists of many and divided parts, is greater than that which* " *consists of few Parts, and is more entire ; for all things considered by* " *parts seem greater : wherefore both plurality of parts hath a shew of* " *Magnitude ; and the same Plurality works more strongly, if it be pre-* " *sented unto us without order ; for it induceth a resemblance of* Infinity, " *and hinders Comprehension.*

This *Colour* seems a *Fallax,* at first sight very palpable : for not the *Plurality of Parts* alone, but the *Majority,* may make the total Greater ; yet nevertheless the *Colour* many times carryes the imagination away ; yea, it deceives sense.   For it seems to the eye, a shorter distance of way, if it be all dead and continued, so as nothing intercurr which may break the sight ; than in such a coast or quarter, where there are Trees and Buildings, and other marks, which may measure and Divide the space. So when a great Monied-man hath divided and distributed his chests and bags into several and distinct rooms, he seemeth to himself richer than he was.   Therefore a way to *Amplify* any thing, is to *break* it into *many Parts,* and to handle every part severally by it self.   And this again will more fill the imagination, if it be done promiscuously and without order ; for *confusion* raiseth an opinion of multitude ; so what are presented and propounded in *order,* both seem to be more finite, and demonstrate that nothing is left out, but all is there : whereas on the contrary, whatsoever things are represented confusedly, are not only thought to be more numerous in themselves ; but they leave a suspicion that more might be said than is expressed.

B b

The

The Reprehenfion.

THe Fallax of this Colour is. *Firft when a man doth over-conceive, or prejudicate of the greatneſs of any thing, comprehending it beyond the true limits of Magnitude ; for then the breaking of it will make it ſeem leſs, and rectifie that falſe opinion, and preſent the object in its native verity, and not with amplification.* Wherefore if a man be in ſickneſs or in pain, the time will ſeem longer to him without a Clock or an Hour-glaſs, than if it were meaſured with them : for if the wearyſomeneſs, and vexation of a diſeaſe, make the time ſeem longer than in truth it is ; yet the computation of time reforms that miſtake, and makes it ſhorter than that erroneous opinion conceived it to be. So in a dead Plain (whereof even now we gave a contrary inſtance) it ſometimes falls out ; for though at firſt the eye preconceiv'd the way ſhorter, becauſe it was undivided, yet if upon this ſuppoſition, an opinion poſſeſs the imagination of a far ſhorter ſpace of ground than it proves to be, the fruſtrating of that vain conceit, makes it ſeem longer than the truth. Therefore if any man deſire to humour and ſecond the falſe opinion of another, touching the *greatneſs* of any thing, let him beware of diſtributions, and breaking it in ſeveral conſiderations, but let him out of hand extol the matter entire, and in the groſs. *Secondly this Colour deceives when the Diſtribution is diſtracted or ſcattered, or is not preſented entire, or doth not at once object it ſelf to the ſight.* Therefore if flowers in a Garden be divided into ſeveral beds, they will ſhew more than if they were all growing in one bed ; ſo the Beds be within a plot that they be the object of view at once ; otherwiſe, union is of more force in this caſe than ſcattered diſtribution. Therefore their Revenues ſeem greater, whoſe Lands and Livings lie together in one ſhire ; for if they were diſperſed, they would not fall ſo eaſily within notice and comprehenſion. *Thirdly this Colour deceives in reſpect of the dignity of unity above multitude ; for all compoſition is a ſure mark of deficiency, in particularities ſeverally conſidered, which thus pieces out one thing with the addition of another.*

Et quæ non proſunt ſingula, multa juvant.

Luk. 10.
Æſop. And therefore *Mary* had choſen the better part ; *Martha, Martha, attendis ad plurima, unum ſufficit.* Hereupon *Æſop,* framed the fable of the *Fox* and the *Cat.* *The Fox bragged what a number of ſhifts and devices he had to get from the Hounds ; the Cat ſaid ſhe had but one only way to truſt to, which was this ; ſhe had a poor ſlender faculty in climbing up a tree:* which yet in proof was a ſurer guard then all Vulpone's policies and ſtratagems: whereof the proverb grew, *multa novit Vulpes, ſed Felis unum magnum,* the Fox knows many practices, but the Cat one ſpecial ; one that will help at a dead lift. And in the Moral of this Fable it it comes likewiſe to paſs , *that a potent and faithful Friend, is a ſurer Card at a pinch than all the Plots and Policies of a man's own wit.*

And theſe ſhall ſuffice for example : we have an infinite number more of *Colours,* of this nature, which we collected in our youth ; but
without

without their *Illuftrations* and *Reprehenfions*, which at this time we have now leifure to perfect and digeft; wherefore we thought it incongruous to expofe thofe *Colours* naked, without their *Illuftrations*; feeing thefe other come abroad attired. Yet thns much in the mean time we admonifh, that this branch of knowledge, in our judgement, whatfoever it may feem, is of no contemptible confequence, but a matter of high price and ufe, as that which participates both of *Primitive, Philofophy*, of *Policy*, and of *Rhethorick*. Thus much of popular marks, or of the *Colours of Good and Evil in apparence*, as well *fimple as comparative.*

III. A fecond collection, which appertains to a ready *provifion*, or preparatory *ftore*, is that which *Cicero* intimates (as we have noted before in *Logick*) where he gives it in Precept, that we have *Common-places* in ready preparation argued and handled *Pro* and *Contra*; fuch as are, *For the words and letters of Law, for the fence and mind of Law*, and the like. And we extend this Precept to other things alfo; as that it may be applied, not only to *Judicial* Forms; but to *Deliberative* and *Demonftrative* alfo. Generally this is it we would have done; namely, that we have all *places*, whereof there is more frequent ufe (*whether we refpect Probations and Confutations, or Perfwafions and Diffwafions, or Praifes and Vituperations;*) ftudied and meditated beforehand, and the fame extoll'd and depreffed by the higheft ftrains of Wit and Invention; and perverfely wrefted, as it were, of purpofe utterly beyond Truth. And in our opinion the manner of this *Collection*, as well for ufe as for brevity, would be the beft, if fuch common-places, and feeds of feveral Arguments were abridg'd and caft up into fome brief and acute fentences, as into Skains or Bottoms of Thread to be drawn out, and unwinded into larger Difcourfes as occafion fhould be prefented. A *Collection in this nature* we find in *Seneca*, but in fuppofitions only, or Cafes. Of this fort (in regard we have many ready prepared) we thought good to fet down fome of them for example: Thefe we call *Antitheta Rerum.*

* ANTI-THETA RERUM. Cicero.

Sen. Contro.

Examples of the *Antitheta.*

NOBILITY. I.

Pro.	Contra.

THey *whofe vertue is altogether deriv'd from the ftock; thefe not only have not a will, but want a power to be wicked.*

Nobility is a Garland of Bays, wherewith time Crowns men.

We reverence Antiquity even in dead Monuments, how much more in living.

NObility *feldom fprings from Vertue; Vertue more feldom from Nobility.*

Nobles by birth more often ufe the interceffion of their Anceftors for Pardon, than their fuffrage for Honours.

The induftry of new rifing men is oftentimes fuch, as Nobles compar'd with them are but Statues.

*If you regard not the Honour of an
ancient House : Then what difference
will there be between the Race of
Men, and the Race of Beasts?*

*Nobility removes Vertue from En-
vy; recommends it to Grace and
Favour.*

*Nobles by blood, look too often back
in the course; which is the quality
of an ill Racer.*

BEAUTY. II.

Pro.

*Deformed persons commonly have
their revenge of Nature.*

*Vertue is nothing else but inward
Beauty; and Beauty nothing else but
an outward Vertue.*

*Deformed persons seek to rescue
themselves from scorn, by malice and
boldness.*

*Beauty makes Vertues shine, vices
blush.*

Contra.

*Vertue is like a rich Stone, best
plain set.*

*What a fair vestment is to a de-
formed Body, the same is a comely Body to a deformed Mind.*

*They usually are of no great parts,
whom Beauty commendeth or mo-
veth.*

YOUTH. III.

Pro.

*Our first cogitations, and the coun-
sels of Youth stream more divinely.*

*Old men are more wise for them-
selves, than they are for others and
the Repub.*

*If it could be made visible, Old
age doth more deform the mind than
the body.*

*Old men fear all things save the
Gods.*

Contra.

Youth is the field of Repentance.

*There is in Youth an inbred dis-
esteem of the Authority of Age, that
every one may grow wise at his own
peril.*

*Those Counsels to which Time was
not call'd, Time will not ratifie.*

In old men Venus *is changed into the* Graces.

HEALTH. IV.

Pro.

*The regard of Health makes the
Mind humble, and obsequious to the
Body.*

*A sound Body is the Souls Host,
but a sickly her Jaylor.*

*Nothing so promotes the summ of
Business, as a prosperous state of Body; but on the contrary, a sickly constitution makes too many Holy-days.*

Contra.

*Often to recover health, is often to
grow young again.*

Indisposition of Health *is a common excuse, hither we fly even when
we are well.*

*Health unites the Soul and the
Body in too strict a league.*

*The Conch hath govern'd mighty
Empires; and Litter mighty Armies*

WIFE

WIFE and CHILDREN.

Pro.	Contra.

Charity to the Common-wealth, begins at a private Family.

Wife and Children are a kind of Discipline of Humanity; but unmarried men are cruel and hardhearted.

Single life and a Childless state, are good for nothing but for flight.

He that procreates no Children, sacrificeth to Death.

They that are happy in all other things, are commonly unfortunate in their Children : lest being men they should approach too near to a condition Divine. *

He that hath Wife and Children, hath given Hostages to Fortune.

Generation and Issue are Humane Acts; Creation and its Works are Acts Divine.

Issue is the Eternity of Beasts, Fame, Merit, and wholesome Precepts, the Eternity of Men.

Oeconomical respects many times supplant Political Duties.

To some Natures the Fortune of Priamus is acceptable, who surviv'd his whole Posterity.

RICHES. VI.

Pro.	Contra.

They despise Riches, that dispair of them.

An envy conceiv'd against Riches, hath extoned Vertue to a Deity.

Whilst Philosophers call in doubt whether all things are to be referr'd to Vertue or Pleasure; survey the instruments of them both.

Vertue, by means of Riches, is converted into a common good. • •

All other kinds of Good have a provincial command, only Riches a general.

Of great Riches, there is either a custody, or a dispensation, or a fame; but no solid use.

Do you not see what feigned prises are set upon little Stones, and such kind of Rarities, that there may be some use made of great Riches ?

Many, whilst they have entertain'd an opinion that all things might be bought with their money; have in this conceit, first sold themselves.

I cannot call Riches better than the Baggage of Vertue; for they are both necessary to Vertue, and yet combersome, hindring the March.

Riches are a good Hand-maid, but the worst Mistress.

HONOURS. VII.

Pro.	Contra.

Honours are not suffrages of Tyrants, but of Divine Providence.

Honours make both Vertues and Vices conspicuous; therefore those

Whilst we seek Honours, we loose liberty.

Honours commonly give men a power over those things, wherein they

they excite, these they repress.

No man can tell what proficience he hath made in the Race of Vertue, unless Honours afford him an open Field.

The motion of Vertue as of other things, is violent to its place, calm in its place; and the place of Vertue is Honour.

the best condition is, not to will; the next not to can.

The stairs to Honours are steep, the standing slippery, the regress a downfal.

They that are in great place had need to borrow other mens opinions, to think themselves happy.

EMPIRE. VIII.

Pro.

It is a great blessing to enjoy Happiness; but to have the power to confer it on others, is far greater.

Kings are rather like stars than men; for they have a powerful influx upon all men, and upon times themselves.

To resist God's vicegerents, is not only the guilt of Treason, but a kind of Theomachie.

Contra.

What a miserable state is it, to have a few things to desire, infinite things to fear!

Princes are like heavenly bodies which have much veneration, but no rest.

None of Humane condition is admitted to the Banquet of the Gods, but to his reproach.

PRAISE, REPUTATION. IX.

Pro.

Praises are the reflexed Beams of Vertue.

That praise is an Honour which comes from voices freely conferr'd.

Many States confer Honours; but Praises are every where the Attributes of Liberty.

The voice of the people hath some divineness in it; else how should so many men agree to be of one mind?

You need not wonder if the communalty speak more truly than the Nobility; for they speak more safely.

Pro.

Fame is a better Nurse than a Judge.

What hath a good man to do with the dull approbation of the vulgar?

Fame like a River bears up things light and swoln; drowns things weighty and solid.

The lowest vertues draw praise from the common people; the middle vertues work in them Astonishment or Admiration; but of the highest Vertues they have no sence or perceiving at all.

Praise proceeds more out of a bravery than out of merit; and happens rather to vain and windy persons, than to persons substantial and solid.

NATURE. X.

Pro.

The Progress of Custom is Arithmetical; of Nature Geometrical.

Contra.

Mens thoughts are according to Nature; their words according to

As

As *Laws* are to *Custom* in *Civil States,* *so is* Nature *to* Custom *in* every particular person.

Custom against *Nature* is a kind of *Tyranny,* and is quickly and upon light occasion oppressed.

Precept ; but their deeds according to custom.

Nature is a kind of *Pedant ;* Custom a *Magistrate.*

FORTUNE. XI.

Pro.

Ouvert and apparent vertues bring forth praise ; secret and hidden vertues bring forth fortune.

Vertues of duty bring forth praise; vertues of ability bring forth fortune.

The way of *Fortune* is like the milken way in the skie ; which is a meeting or knot of certain small obscure vertues without a name.

Fortune is to be honour'd and respected, and it be but for her daughters confidence and reputation.

Contra.

The folly of one man, is the fortune of another.

In Fortune this I may chiefly commend, that being she makes no election, she gives no protection.

Men of place and quality while they decline the envy of their own vertues; have been found among the worshippers of Fortune.

LIFE. XII.

Pro.

It is a foolish and preposterous affection, to love the Accessories of life, more than life it self.

A full course is better than a short ; a fair advantage to all things, yea even to vertue.

Without a good spacious compass of life, we can neither fully perfect, nor learn, nor repent.

Contra.

The Philosophers, whilst they raise so great preparations against Death, have made it but appear more terrible.

Men fear Death because they know it not ; as Children fear the dark.

You can find no passion in the mind of man so weak; which if it be but a little prest, masters not the fear of death.

To be willing to die, not only a valiant man, or a miserable man may, or a wise ; but even a fastidious man , and a coward may do as much.

SUPER-

SUPERSTITION. XIII.

Pro.	Contra.
They that err out of a well meant zeal, may not be approved, but yet may be beloved.	*As it adds deformity unto an Ape, to be so like a man; so the similitude of superstition to Religion, makes it more deform'd.*
Mediocrities are due to Moral vertues; extremities to divine.	*Look how odious Affectation is in matters Civil; so hateful is superstition, in matters Divine.*
A superstitious man is a religious Formalist.	*It were better to have no opinion of God at all, than such an opinion as is reproachful unto him.*
I should sooner believe all the Fabulous wonders of any Religon, than that this univerfal Frame was built without a Deity.	*It is not the School of* Epicurus, *but the Porch of the Stoicks that hath perturbed ancient States.*
	It cannot come into the mind of man to be a mere Atheist in Opinion; but your great Hypocrites are the true Atheists, who are ever handling holy things, but never revere them.

PRIDE. XIV.

Pro.	Contra.
Pride is even with vices incompetible: And as poyson is expelled by poyson, so many vices are by pride.	*Pride is the insinuating Ivie to Vertues, and all good Qualities.*
A soft nature becomes guilty of the crimes of others; but a proud spirit only of his own.	*All other vices are only contrary to vertues, pride alone is contagious.*
Pride if it ascend from contempt of others to a contempt of itself, at last is chang'd into Philosophy.	*Pride wants the best condition of vice, that is, concealment.*
	A proud man while he despiseth others prejudiceth himself.

INGRATITUDE. XV.

Pro.	Contra.
The guilt of ingratitude is nothing else ;but a too precise consideration and inquisition into the cause of a benefit conferr'd.	*The crime of Ingratitude is not to be repressed by punishments, but to referred over to the Furies.*
Whilst we endeavour to be grateful to others, we neither perform	*The obligations of benefits are more strict than of Duties, where-justice*

justice to others, nor reserve liberty to our selves.

Where the valuation of a Benefit is uncertain, there the less thank is due.

fore he that is unthankfull is unjust, and any thing.

Such is man's condition; no man is born to so high a fortune, but that he is a debtor to the retribution both of Private thanks, and personal revenge.

ENVY. XVI.

Pro.	Contra.
It is natural for a man to hate the reproach of his Fortune.	Envy never makes Holyday.
Envy in a state is a wholsome Ostracism.	Nothing but death reconciles Envy to virtue.
	Envy doth put vertue to it, as Juno did Hercules.

INCONTINENCE. XVII.

Pro.	Contra.
Chastity may thank Jealousie that she is become a virtue.	Incontinence is one of Circes her worst transformations.
He had need be endued with much Gravity, that makes the sports of Venus any matter of Earnest.	An unchast liver hath utterly lost a reverence to himself, which is the bridle of all vice.
Why do you place either a spare diet, or a shew of Honesty, or the Daughter of Pride, amongst the virtues?	They that with Paris, make beauty their wish, lose, as he did, Wisdom and Honour.
Of loves, as of wild fowl, there is no property; but the right is past over with the possession.	Alexander fell upon no popular truth, when he said, that sleep and lust were the earnests of Death.

CRUELTY. XVIII.

Pro.	Contra.
No virtue is so often guilty as clemency.	He that delights in blood, is either a wild beast or a Fury.
Cruelty if it proceed from revenge, it is justice; if from Peril it is wisdom.	Cruelty to a Good man, seems to be but a Fable, and some Tragical fiction.
He that shews mercy to his enemy, denyes it to himself.	
Phlebotomy is not more necessary in the Body Natural, than it is in the body Politick.	

VAIN.

Pro.

He that seeks his own praise, withal seeks the profit of others.

He that is so reserv'd, as to regard nothing that is forreign; it may be suspected, that he will account publick affairs, forreign impertinencies.

Such Dispositions as have a commixture of Levity in them, more easily undertake a publick charge.

Contra.

Vain-glorious persons are always factious, lyers, inconstant, over-doing.

Thraso *is* Gnatho's *prey.*

It is a shame for a Lover to make suit to the hand-maid; but Praise is vertues hand-maid.

JUSTICE. XX.

Pro.

Kingdoms and States are only the Appendices of Justice: for if Justice otherwise could be executed, there would be no need of them.

It is the effect of Justice, that man is to man a God, and not a Wolf.

Though Justice cannot extirpate Vice; yet it represseth it from doing hurt.

Contra.

If this be to be just, not to do to another what you would not have done to your self; then is mercy Justice.

If we must give every one his due, then surely pardon to Humanity.

What tell you me of equity when to a wise man all things are unequal?

Do but consider what the condition of the guilty was in the Roman State; and then say Justice is not for the Republick.

The common Justice of States is as a Philosopher in Court; that is, it makes only for a reverential respect of such as bear Rule.

FORTITUDE. XXI.

Pro.

Nothing but fear is terrible. There is nothing solid in pleasure, nor assur'd in vertue, where fear disquiets.

Contra.

That's a goodly vertue to be willing to dye, so you may be sure to kill.

He that confronts dangers with open eyes, that he may receive the charge; marketh how to avoid the same.

All other vertues; free us from the Dominion of Vice; only Fortitude from the Dominion of Fortune.

That's a goodly vertue sure, which even drunkenness may induce.

He that is prodigal of his own life, will not spare the life of another.

Fortitude is a vertue of the Iron Age.

TEMPERANCE. XXII.

Pro.

To abstain and to sustain, are vertues proceeding commonly from the same habit.

Uniformities, concords, and measures of motions, are things celestial, and the characters of Eternity.

Temperance as wholesome colds, concentrate and strengthen the forces of the Mind.

Too exquisite and wandring senses, had need of Narcoticks; and so likewise wandring affections.

Contra.

I like not these negative vertues; for they argue Innocence not Merit.

That mind languisheth which is not sometimes spirited by excess.

I like those vertues which induce the vivacity of Action, and not the dulness of Passion.

When you set down the equal tempers of the mind, you set down but few; nam pauperis est numerare pecus.

These Stoicisms (not to use that so you may not desire; not to desire that so you may not fear) are the resolutions of pusillanimous, and distrustful natures.

CONSTANCY. XXIII.

Pro.

Constancy is the foundation of vertue.

He is a miserable man that hath no perception of his future state, what it shall or may be.

Seeing man's judgement is so weak, as that he cannot be constant to things; let him at least be true to himself, and to his own designs.

Constancy gives reputation even to vice.

If to the Inconstancy of Fortune we add also the inconstancy of mind, in what mazes of darkness do we live.

Contra.

Constancy like a sullen-self-will'd Porteress, drives away many fruitful informations.

There is good reason that Constancy should patiently endure crosses, for commonly she causeth them.

The shortest folly is the best.

Fortune is like Proteus, *if you perfift, fhe returns to her true fhape.*

MAGNANIMITY. XXIV.

Pro.

When once the mind hath propounded to it felf honourable ends; then not only vertues, but even the Divine powers are ready to fecond.

Vertues fpringing from Habit or Precept, are vulgar; but from the end heroical.

Contra.

Magnanimity is a vertue Poetical.

KNOWLEDGE, CONTEMPLATION. XXV.

Pro.

That delight only is according to Nature, whereof there is no fatiety.

The fweetest prospect is that, which looks into the errors of others, in the vale below.

How pleafing and profitable a thing is it, to have the orbs of the mind concentrick, with the orbs of the World.

All depraved affections are falfe valuations; but goodnefs and truth are ever the fame.

Contra.

A contemplative life is a fpecious floth.

To think well is little better than to dream well.

The divine providence regards the world; thou thy country.

A right Politick procreates Contemplations.

LEARNING. XXVI.

Pro.

Reading is a converfe with the wife; Action, for the moft part, a commerce with fools.

Thofe Sciences are not to be reputed altogether unprofitable, that are of no ufe; if they fharpen the wits, and marfhal our conceptions.

Contra.

To be wife from Precept and from Experience, are two contrary habits; fo as he that is accuftomed to the one, is inept for the other.

There is many times a vain ufe of Art, left there fhould be no ufe.

This commonly is the humour of all Scholars, that they are wont to acknowledge all they know; but not to learn what they know not.

PROMPTITUDE. XXVII.

Pro.

That is not seasonable wisdom, which is not quick and nimble.

He that quickly errs, quickly reforms his error.

He that is wise upon deliberation, and not upon present occasion; performs no great matter.

Contra.

That wisdom is not far fetcht, nor deeply grounded, which is ready at hand.

Wisdom is as a Vestment, that is lightest, which is readiest.

Age doth not ripen their wisdom, whose counsels deliberation doth not ripen.

What is suddenly invented, suddenly vanisheth; soon ripe soon rotten.

Silence in matters of Secrecy. XXVIII.

Pro.

From a silent man, nothing is conceal'd; for all is there safely laid up.

He that easily talks what he knows, will also talk what he knows not.

Mysteries are due to secrecies.

Contra.

Alteration of Customs placeth the mind in the dark; and makes men go invisible.

Secrecy is the vertue of a Confessor.

From a silent man all things are conceal'd, because all is repai'd with silence.

A close man is next to an unknown man.

FACILITY. XXIX.

Pro.

I like the man that is pliant to another's inclination, but yet reserves his judgement from flattery.

He that is flexible comes nearest to the nature of Gold.

Contra.

Facility is a weak privation of judgement.

The good offices of facile natures seem debts; their denials, injuries.

He owes the thanks to himself, that obtains any thing of a facile-natur'd man.

All difficulties press upon a too accessible and yielding nature; for he ingages himself in all.

Facile natures seldom come off with credit.

POPULARITY. XXX.

Pro.

The same things commonly please wise men, but it is also a point of wisdom; to humour the changeable disposition of fools.

To honour the people is to be honoured.

Men in place usually stand in awe, not of one man, but the multitude.

Contra.

He whose nature rightly sorts with fools, may himself be suspected.

He that hath the Art to please the people; commonly hath the power to raise the people.

No terms of moderation takes place with the vulgar.

To fawn on the people, is the lowest degree of Flattery.

LOQUACITY. XXXI.

Pro.

Silence argues a man to be jealous, either of others, or of himself.

Restraint of liberty in what kind soever is an unhappy case, but the worst of all is that of silence.

Silence is the vertue of fools; where he said truly to a silent man, If you be wise you are a Fool; if you be a Fool you are wise.

Silence like night is fit for Treacheries.

Cogitations are like waters, most wholesome in the running stream.

Silence is a kind of solitude.

He that is silent prostitutes himself to censure.

Silence neither dischargeth it self of Evil thoughts, nor contributes any good.

Contra.

Silence adds grace and authority to a man's words.

Silence like a kindly sleep refresheth wisdom, and settles the judgement.

Silence is the Fermentation of our thoughts.

Silence is the stile of wisdom.

Silence is a candidate for Truth.

Pro.

Dissimulation is a compendious wisdom.

We are not tied to say the same, but to intend the same.

Nakedness even in the Mind is uncomely.

Dissimulation is both a Grace and a Guard.

Dissimulation is the fence of counsels.

Some through their too apert fair dealing become a prey.

He that carries all things with an open frankness deceives, as he that somewhat dissembles: for many either do not comprehend him, or do not believe him.

Open dealing is nothing else but a weakness of mind.

Contra.

When we cannot think according to the verity of things, yet at least let us speak according as we think.

Whose shallow capacities comprehend not the Arts of State; in them, a habit of dissimulation goes for wisdom.

He that Dissembles, deprives himself of one of the most principal instruments for Action, which is belief.

Dissimulation invites Dissimulation.

A dissembler is not exempt from bondage.

BOLDNESS XXXIII.

Pro.

A shamefac'd suitor teaches the way how to be denied.

What Action is to an Orator, the same is boldness to a Politick; the first, the second, the third vertue.

I love him that confesseth his modesty, but I cannot endure him that accuseth it.

A confidence in carriage soonest unites affections.

I like a reserved countenance, and an open speech.

Contra.

Boldness is the Verger to folly.

Impudence is good for nothing but for Imposture.

Confidence is the fool's Empress, and the wise man's buffoon.

Boldness is a kind of Dulness of sense, together with a perverseness of will.

Ceremonies, Puntoes, Affectation. XXXIV.

Pro.

A comely moderation of Countenance and Gesture, is the true seasoning vertue.

Contra.

What can be a more deformed spectacle, than to transfer the sense into to our common course of life?

Is

If we observe the vulgar in the use of Words, why not in Habit and Gesture?

He that keeps not a decorum in smaller matters, and in his daily customs, though he be a great man, yet set it down for truth; that such a personage is wise, but at certain seasons.

Vertue and wisdom, without all points of respect and complement, are like forreign languages, they are not understood by the common people.

He that apprehends not the meaning of the common people, neither by a congruous application, nor yet by observation, is of all men most senseless.

Puntoes and ceremonies are the translation of vertue into a mother-tongue.

Fair ingenious behaviour wins grace and favour; but affectation and art procures hatred.

Better a painted face and crisped hair; than painted and crisped manners.

He cannot comprehend great matters, who breaks his mind to small observations.

Affectation is the shining Putrefaction of ingenuity.

JESTS. XXXV.

Pro.

A conceit is the altar of an Orator.

He that mingles modest mirth in all his commerce with others, reserves a freedom of mind.

It is a matter more politick, than a man would think, smoothly to pass from jest to earnest, and from earnest to jest.

A witty conceit is oftentimes a convoy of a Truth, which otherwise could not so handsomely have been ferried over.

Contra.

What man despiseth not those that hunt after these deformities and concinnities?

To put off the importance of business with a jest, is a base flight of wit.

Then judge of a jest, when you have done laughing.

Merrily conceited men, seldom penetrate farther than the superficies of things, which is the point where the jest lies.

To put a jest, as a matter of moment upon serious affairs, is a childish Levity.

LOVE. XXXVI.

Pro.

Do you not see how all men seek themselves, but a lover only finds himself.

Contra.

The stage is much beholding to love; the life of man nothing.

Ther

There is no better government of the mind, than from the command of some powerful affection.

He that is wise, let him pursue some desire or other; for he that doth not affect some one thing in chief, unto him all things are distastful and tedious.

Why should not that which is one, rest in unity?

There is nothing hath so many names as Love; for it is a thing either so foolish, that it knows not it self, or so base that it must needs disguise it self under a counterfeit habit.

I like not such natures as are only intent upon one thing.

Love is a poor narrow contemplation.

FRIENDSHIP. XXXVII.

Pro.

Friendship accomplisheth the same things that Fortitude doth, but more sweetly.

Friendship is a pleasant sauce to any temporal happiness.

The worst solitude is to be destitute of sincere friendship.

It is a just punishment for false-hearted dispositions, to be deprived of friendship.

Contra.

Who contracts strict leagues of Amity, draws upon himself new engagements.

It is a note of a weak spirit to divide fortune.

FLATTERY. XXXVIII.

Pro.

Flattery proceeds more out of custom than out of Malice.

It was ever a form of civility due to Great Persons, by praising them to instruct them.

Contra.

Flattery is the stile of Servants.

Flattery is the cement of vice.

Flattery is that kind of fowling, which deceives Birds, by resemblance of voice.

The deformity of flattery is Comical, but the dammage Tragical.

To give wholesome counsel, is a task most difficult.

REVENGE. XXXIX.

Pro.

Private Revenge is a kind of wild Justice.

He that returns wrong for wrong, violates the Law, not the Person.

Contra.

He that does a wrong is the beginner of a quarrel, but he that retaliates, takes away all means of ending it.

Revenge by how much the more natural, by so much the more to be repressed.

D d   *The*

The fear of Private revenge is a profitable reſtraint, for laws are too often aſleep.

He that is inclinable to retribute a wrong, is behind-hand perchance in time, but not in will.

INNOVATION. XL:

Pro.

Every medicine is an innovation.

He that will not apply new remedies, muſt expect new diſeaſes.

Time is the greateſt innovator; why then may we not imitate time.

Ancient preſidents are inconformable, recent, corrupt, and degenerate.

Let ſimple and contentious perſons, ſquare their actions, according to examples.

As thoſe that firſt bring honour into their Family, are commonly more worthy than moſt that ſucceed: So the Innovation of things for the moſt part excells thoſe things which are done out of Imitation.

A froward retention of Cuſtoms, is as turbulent a thing as Innovation.

Seeing that things of their own courſe alter to the worſe, if they be not by counſel altered to the better, what ſhall be the end of Evil.

The ſervants of cuſtom, are the ſcorn of Time.

Contra.

New Births are deformed things.

No author is accepted, until time have authoriz'd him.

All novelty is with injury, for it defaceth the preſent ſtate of things.

Thoſe things which cuſtom hath confirmed, if they be not profitable, yet they are conformable and piece well together.

What Novator follows the example of time, which inſinuates innovations ſo quietly, as is ſcarce perceptible to ſenſe.

Whatſoever comes unlooked for, is the leſs acceptable to him whom it helps; and the more troubleſome to him whom it hurts.

DELAY. XLI.

Pro.

Fortune ſelleth many things to the haſty; which ſhe gives to the ſlow and deliberate.

Whilſt we make too much haſt to ſurprize the beginnings and onſets of things, we claſp ſhadows.

Whilſt things are at a doubtful ſtand, we muſt weigh them; when they incline we may fall awork.

It is good to commit the beginning of Actions to Argus, with his hundred eyes; the ends to Briareus, with his hundred hands.

Contra.

Occaſion turns the handle of the Bottle firſt, to be received; and after the belly.

Occaſion, like Sybilla, diminiſheth the commodity, but enhanceth the Price.

Celerity is the helmet of Pluto.

Thoſe things which are ſeaſonably undertaken, are performed with judgement; but what are put off too long, are compaſs'd with trouble and by ambages.

PRE-

Pro.

He that attempts a great matter with small means ; fancies to himself the advantage of opportunity, that he may not despair.

With slender provision we buy wit not fortune.

Contra.

The first occasion of action, is the best point of preparation.

Let no man think to fetter fortune, with the chains of his preparation.

The alteration of preparation, and action, are politick Arts ; but the seperation of them is a vaporous conceit, and unprosperous.

Great preparation is a prodigal both of time and business.

To Encounter first Assaults. XLIII.

Pro.

More dangers deceive us by fraud, than overcome us by force.

It is less trouble to meet danger by early remedies, than to watch and ward the approaches and progress thereof.

A danger is no more light, if it once seem light.

Contra.

He teacheth danger to come on, who over-early addresseth himself against danger ; and fixeth it by application of a remedy.

In the redress of dangers, lighter dangers fall off of themselves

It is better to deal with a few authentick and approv'd remedies ; than to venture upon a world of unexperienc'd particular receipts.

VIOLENT COUNSELS. XLIV.

Pro.

Those that affect a mild and gentle kind of Prudence ; to them the augmentation of an evil is a wholesome remedy.

That necessity which resolves upon desperate courses ; commonly goes through with them.

Contra.

Every violent remedy is pregnant of a new evil.

No man gives violent advice, but out of fury or fear.

SUSPI-

SUSPICION. XLV.

Pro.

Diffidence is the nerves of wisdom ; but suspicion a remedy for the joynts.

That sincerity is justly suspected, which suspicion weakens or overthrows.

Suspicion defeats an inconstant integrity ; but confirms a strong and resolute.

Contra.

Suspition breaks the bond of faith.

The distemper of suspicion, is a kind of Civil Madness.

The words of Law. XLVI.

Pro.

It is no exposition , but a divination , which departs from the letter.

When there is made a departure from the Letter of Law ; the Judge, of an Interpreter, becomes a Lawgiver.

Contra.

Out of all the words in the generality, such a sence must be extracted, as may expound the mind of every particular passage.

The worst tyranny , is Law upon the rack.

For Witnesses against Arguments. XLVII.

Pro.

He that relies upon Arguments , defines according to the pleader, not according to the cause.

He that gives credit rather to Arguments than Witness, must withall trust more to Wit than sense.

It were a safe way to believe Arguments of Reason , if men were not guilty of Absurdities against Reason.

Arguments brought against Testimonies accomplish thus much ; that the case seems strange, but not that it seems true.

Contra.

If proofs by witness, are to be preferr'd before Proofs from Reason. then there needs no more ado, but that the Judge be not deaf.

Arguments are an Antidote against the Poyson of Testimonies.

Those kind of Proofs are most safely believed, which do most seldom lye.

Now

Now thefe *Antitheta* which we have propounded, are not perchance fo much worth ; but being they were prepared and collected by us long ago, we were loath the diligence of our youth fhould perifh : fpecially feeing they are (if one exactly confider them) *Seeds, and not Flowers.* But herein they do plainly breath a youthly heat, in that they are fo plentiful in the *Moral* or *Demonstrative* kind, fo thin and fparing in the *Deliberative* and *Judicial.*

IV. A third Collection which pertains to *preparatory ftore* or *Provifion,* and is *Deficient,* is that which we think fit to call *Formulæ Minores, Leffer Forms or Stiles of Speech.* And thefe are (as it were) the Portals, Poftern-doors, outer-Rooms, back-Rooms, Paffages of Speech, and the like ; which indifferently may ferve for all Subjects.   Such are *Prefaces, Conclufions, Digreffions, Tranfitions, Promifes, Excufations,* and many of like nature.   *For as in Building* there is great pleafure and ufe in the well-cafting of the Frontifpieces, Stair-cafes, Doors, Windows, Entries, Paffages, and the like : fo in fpeech if the acceffory conveyances and interpofures be decently and skilfully contrived and placed , they are of fpecial ornament and effect, to the whole ftructure of the fpeech. Of thefe *Formulæ,* we will propofe an example or two, and ftay no longer upon them.   For although they be Matters of no fmall ufe, yet becaufe we add nothing here of our own, but defcribe the naked *Forms* only, out of *Demofthenes* or *Cicero,* or fome other felect Author, they may feem a more trivial and common obfervation, than that we fhould wafte much time therein.

* FORMU-
LÆ MI-
NORES.

Examples of Minor Forms.

A Conclufion of a Speech Deliberative.

" *So we may both redeem the fault which is paffed, and with the fame di-*
" *ligence provide againft future inconveniences.*

The Corollary of an accurate Partition.

" *That every one may underftand that I feek not to balk any thing by*
" *filence, or to cloud any thing by words.*

A Tranfition with a Caveat.

But let us fo pafs by thefe, that reflecting upon them, and keeping them within view, we may leave them.

A preoccupation againft an inveterate opinion.

I fhall fo open the matter as you may underftand in the whole manage of the bufinefs, what the cafe it felf hath brought forth ; what error hath faftned upon it ; what envy hath rais'd.   And let thefe fuffice for example, wherewith (annexing two *Rhetorical Appendices*) which refpect the *Promptuary Part* we conclude.

CHAP.

Chap. IV.

I. *Two General Appendices of the Art of Delivery, Art* Critical.
And Pedantical.

There remains two *Appendices* in general, *touching the Tradition of Knowledge*; *the one* Critical; *the other* Pedantical. For as the principal part of *Tradition of Knowledge* confifteth in writing of Books; fo the relative part thereof confifts in reading of Books: but reading is governed and directed, either by the help of Preceptors and Tutors; or perfected by every man's particular and proper endeavour and induftry: and to this purpofe conduce thofe two knowledges, whereof we have fpoken. *To the* Critical *part appertains*; *firft, an immaculate correction and amended edition of approved Authors:* Whereby both the honour of Authors themfelves is vindicated, and a light given to the ftudious Readers. Wherein neverthelefs, the rafh diligence of fome Writers hath done great prejudice to Studies. For it is the manner of many Criticks, when they fall upon a paffage which they do not underftand, prefently to prefume a fault in the Copy. As in that place in *Tacitus*, when a certain Colony in the open Senate, claimed the priviledge of an *Afylum*, *Tacitus* reports that the reafons they preferr'd were not much favour'd by the Emperour and the Lords of the Senate; wherefore the Embaffadors miftrufting the iffue of the bufinefs, gave a round fumm of mony to *Titus Vinius*, that he would mediate their caufe, and take upon him the protection of their liberties; by this means their petition was heard and granted; *Tum dignitas & antiquitas Coloniæ valuit*, faith *Tacitus*, as if the arguments that feemed light before, were now made weighty through bribes and corruption. But one of the Criticks, a man of no obfcure note, hath expunged the word *Tum*, and in ftead thereof, put in *Tantum*. And by this perverfe cuftom of *Criticks*, it comes to pafs (as one wifely noteth) *that the moft corrected copies are commonly the leaft correct.* Nay, (to fpeak truth) unlefs the *Criticks* be well skill'd in the knowledges handled in the Books which they fet forth, their diligence is with peril and prejudice. *Secondly, their appertains to the* Critick Art, *the Expofition, and Explication of Authors, by Commentaries, Scholies, Notes, Spicilegies, and the like.* In labours of this kind, that worft difeafe of *Criticks* hath feis'd on many; that they blanch and wave many obfcurer paffages; and fuch as are plain and perfpicuous, thofe they dwell and expatiate upon, even to a faftidious tedioufnefs; and it is not fo much intended, that the Author may be illuminated, as that the *Critick* may take occafion hereby to glorifie himfelf, in his multiplicious and various learning. It could be efpecially wifhed (although this point belongs to *Tradition* in chief, and not to *Appendices*) that the Writer which handles obfcure and noble Arguments, fhould annex his own *explications*; that neither the Text it felf may be broken off, by *Digreffions* and *Explications*; and that the Annotations may not depart from the mind and intention of the Writer. Some fuch thing we conceive of *Theon* upon *Euclid*.

Thirdly

Thirdly it belongs to Critick Art *(from whence it derives the name) to in-*
terpose a brief censure and judgement of the Authors which they publish, and
to compare and value them with other Authors upon the same subject : That
by such a censure the Learned and Studious, may be both advertis'd of
the choice of Books ; and come better provided to the perusing of them.
This last duty is, as it were, *the* Chair of the Criticks, which many
great and famous men in our age have ennobled ; greater surely in our
judgement, than for the model of *Criticks.*

II. *For* Pedantical knowledge, it were soon said, *consult the Schools of*
the Jesuites, *for there is nothing for the use and practice better than their Pre-*
cepts : but we will according to our manner, as it were, gleaning a
few ears, give some few advertisements. *We do by all means approve a*
Collegiat *education and institution of Childhood and Youth* ; not in private
houses, nor only under Schoolmasters.   There is in Colledges a greater emulation of Youth towards their equals ; besides, there is the sight
and countenance of Grave men, which seems to command modesty ;
and fashions and moulds tender minds, even from their first growth to
the same Pattern : in some there are many other utilities of Collegiat *E-*
ducation.

§ *For the order* and manner of Discipline, this I would principally
advise, *that Youth beware of compends and abridgements, and too for-*
ward maturation of knowledge, which makes men bold and confident ; and
rather wants great proceeding, than causeth it.

§ *Further there is an indulgence to be given to the liberty and vent of*
nature in particulars; as if there be any which performs such tasks as the
discipline of the place requires ; and yet withal steals some hours to bestow on other studies, to which he hath a natural propensity ; such a
disposition by no means should be checkt or restrain'd.

§ *Again,* it will be worth the pains diligently to observe (which
perchance hitherto hath not been noted) that there are two ways, and
they, as it were, reflexively opposite, of *training* up of wits, and of *exer-*
cising and *prepairng* them. The one *begins with the more easie precepts,*
and by degrees leads us to the more difficult ; the other at first commands
and presseth more difficult practices, which when they are conquered, the o-
ther sweetly yield and are won with ease. For it is one *Method* to practise swimming by bladders which lift up, and another *Method* to practise dancing with heavy shooes, which press down the Body ; and it
is not easie to express, how much a wise intermixtion of these *Methods,*
conduceth to the advancing of the faculties, both of the Mind and of the
Body.

§ *So the Application and Election of studies according to the propriety*
of wits, which are instructed, is a matter of singular use and judgement ;
a true and perfect discovery whereof, Schoolmasters *and* Tutors *owe to the*
Parents of Children, *from whom they may expect such informations, that*
so they may the better advise upon the particular course of life, unto which
they would design and dedicate their sons. But this also is to be exactly observed that not only exceeding great progression may be made in those studies, to which a man is swayed by a natural proclivity; but also that there,
may be found, in *studies* properly selected for that purpose, cures and
remedies to promote such kind of knowledge, to the impressions whereof, a man may, by some imperfection of nature, be most unapt and in-
sufficient :

sufficient. *As for example*, if a man may be *Bird-witted*, that is quickly carried away, and hath not the patient faculty of attention; the *Mathematicks* give a remedy thereunto, wherein, if the wit be caught away but for a moment, the demonstration is new to begin.

§ *So of exercises in course of teaching, there is matter of great consequence: but there is a point here that hath been noted of few, that there should be of exercises, not only a wise institution, but also a wise intermission.* It hath been excellently observed by *Cicero*, *That in exercises it often falls out, that men practise as well their faults, as their faculties;* so that an *ill habit* is sometimes gotten, and insinuates it self together with a *Good*; wherefore it is a safer way to break exercises, and after to fall to them again, than incessantly to pursue and press them. *But of these enough.* Certainly these things at first view seem no such solemn and grave matters, yet are they in the issue found efficacious and useful. *For as in Plants*, the wronging or cherishing of them while they are Young, is that, that is most important to their thriving or miscarrying: or as the immense greatness of the state of Rome, is by some deservedly attributed to the virtue and wisdom of those *six Kings*, which were as Tutors and Foster-fathers of that state in the Infancy thereof: so surely the culture and manurance of minds in young and tender years, hath such a forcible operation (though unseen and not obvious to every mans observation) which neither length of time, or assiduity and contention of Labour in riper age afterwards, can any way countervail. And it is not amiss to observe how small and mean faculties, if they fall into Great men, or upon Great matters, do sometimes work Great and important effects. *Hereof we* will set down a memorable example, which we the rather note, because the Jesuites themselves seem not to despise this kind of Discipline; in our opinion upon sound judgement, and it is a matter, which if it be made professory, is ignominious, if disciplinary, one of the best qualities: *We mean Action upon the stage; as that which strengthens memory, moderates the tone and emphasis of voice, and Pronunciation; composes the countenance and gesture to a Decorum, procures a good assurance, and likewise inureth Youth to the faces of men.* The example shall be taken out of *Tacitus*, of one *Vibulenus*, who had been sometimes an Actor upon the stage, but at that time a common souldier in the Pannonian Garrisons. This fellow upon the death of *Augustus* had rais'd a mutiny, so that *Blæsus* the Lievtenant, committed some of the mutiners to Prison; but the souldiers by violent impression brake open the Prisons, and set them at liberty; and *Vibulenus* about to make a Tribunitial speech before the Souldiers, began in this manner. "You

Annal, 1. "have given light and life to these poor innocent wretches; but who "restores my brother to me, or life unto my brother, that was sent hi-"ther in message from the Legions of Germany, to treat of the com-"mon cause, and he hath murthered him this last night by some of his "Fencers, that he hath about him for his executioners upon souldiers. "Answer *Blæsus*, where hast thou thrown his body? the most mortal "enemies, do not deny burial: when I have performed my last duties "unto the corps with kisses, with tears, command me to be slain be-"sides him; so that these my fellows for our good meaning, and our "true hearts to the Legions, may have leave to bury us. With which speech he put the Army into such an infinite fury and amaze, that if it

had

had not incontinently appeared, that there was no such matter, and that he never had any brother ; the Soldiers would hardly have spared the Lieutenant's life ; for he played it merely, as if it had been some interlude upon the Stage.

§ Now we are come to a period of our Treatise concerning *Ratio-nal knowledges* ; wherein if we have sometimes departed from the *re-ceiv'd partitions*, yet let no man think that we disallow all those *parti-tions* which we have not used: for there is a double necessity imposed up-on us, of altering the *Divisions* ; The one *because these two, namely to sort together those things which are next in nature, and to cast into one pile those things which are next in use*; *are in their end and purpose altogether differing.* For example : A Secretary of a Prince, or of Estate, so di-gests his Papers, without doubt, in his Study , as he may sort together things of like nature , as Treaties apart , Instructions apart , Forreign Letters, Domestick letters, all apart by themselves ; on the contrary in some particular Cabinet, he sorts together those that he were like to use together, though of several nature: so in this general *Cabinet of Knowledge,* we were to set down *partitions* according to the nature of things themselves : whereas, if any particular Science were to be handled, we should have respected the divisions fittest for use and pra-ctice. *The other reason for changing the Division is, because the adjection of Deficients to Sciences* ; *and the reduction of them into an intire Body did by consequence alter the partition of the Sciences themselves.* For say, the Arts which are extant (for demonstration sake) be in number 15, and the Deficients superadded make up the number 20 : I say that the parts of 15 are not the parts of 20, for the parts of 15 are 3 and 5, but the parts of 20, are 2, 4, 5 and 10, so is it plain these could not o-therwise be. And so much of *Logical Sciences.*

E e   THE

Seventh Book

OF

FRANCIS L. VERULAM

VICOUNT St. *ALBAN,*

OF THE

Dignity and Advancement

OF

LEARNING.

To the KING.

CHAP. I.

I. The Partition *of Moral Knowledge, into the Doctrine of Exemplar, or Platform ; and into the Georgicks or Culture of the Mind.* §. The Division of the Platform *of Good, into Good Simple, and Good compar'd.* II. *The Division of Good Simple, into Individual Good, and Good of Communion.*

 E are now come (Excellent *King*) *unto Moral Knowledge, which respecteth and handleth the will of Man : Right Reason governs the Will, Good Apparent seduceth it ; the Incentives of the Will are the Affections, the Organs and voluntary Motions are her Ministers ;* of this faculty *Salomon* faith, *Above all keepings, keep thy Heart ; for out of it issue* Prov.4; *the affections of life.* In handling of this Science, those which have written thereof, seem to me to have done, as if a man that professed the Art of writing, should only exhibit fair Copies of *Alphabets* and Letters joyned, without giving any precepts for the carriage of the hand, and framing of the Characters : so have they propounded unto us good and fair examples and draughts, or accurate protraitures of

Good

Good, *Vertue*, *Duties*, *Felicity*, as the true objects and scopes of *man's Will* and *Desires :* but how to take a just level at *these marks* (excellent indeed, and by them well set down) that is, by what precepts and directions, the *Mind* may be subdued and framed, to pursue and attain *them ;* either they pass it over altogether, or perform it slightly and unprofitably. It is not the disputing that *Moral Vertues are in the mind of Man by habit, and not by Nature ;* or formally distinguishing between *generous spirits, and the obscure vulgar ; that those are won by*

Ariftot.
Et. lib.2.

the weight of Reasons ; these by reward and punishment ; or the witty Precept, *that to rectifie the mind of man, it must like a staff be bowed the contrary way to its inclination ;* and the like glances scattered here and there. These and the like are far short of being a just excuse of the deficience of that thing, which now we seek: *The reason of this neglect, I suppose to be, that hidden Rock, whereupon so many Barks of Knowledges have run and been cast away ; which is,that writers despise to be conversant in ordinary and common matters ; which,are neither subtile enough for Disputation, nor flourishing enough for Ornament.* Verily it cannot easily be expressed, what calamity this thing we now speak of hath brought upon Sciences ; *that out of an inbred pride and vain-glory, men have made choice of such subjects of Discourse, and of such a manner and method of handling, as may commend rather their own wit, than consult*

In Epift.

the Readers profit. Seneca saith excellently, *Nocet illis eloquentia, quibus non rerum facit cupiditatem, sed sui ;* For Writings should be such as should make men in love with the *Lessons* , and not with the *Teachers.* Therefore they take a right course, which can openly avouch the same of their Counsels, which *Demosthenes* once did, and can conclude

Demoft.

with this clause, *which if you put in execution, you shall not only commend the Orator for the instant, but your selves likewise, not long after, in a more prosperous state of your affairs. As for my self* (Excellent King) *to speak the truth of my self, I have often wittingly and willingly neglected the glory of mine own Name, and Learning (if any such thing be) both in the works I now publish, and in those I contrive for hereafter ; whilst I study to advance the good and profit of mankind. And I, that have deserv'd, perchance, to be an Architect in Philosophy and Sciences, am made a Work-man and a Labourer, and at length any thing else whatsoever ; seeing I sustain and work out my self many things that must needs be done ; and others out of a natural disdain shift of and refuse to do.* But, (to return to the matter) which we were about to say , *Philosophers in Moral Science, have chosen to themselves a resplendent and lustrous mass of matter ; wherein they may most glorifie themselves, for sharpness of Wit, or strength of Eloquence : but such precepts as specially conduce to practice, because they cannot be so set out, and invested with the ornaments of speech ; they have in a manner pass'd over in silence.* Neither needed men of so excellent parts, to have despaired of a Fortune like that, which the Poet *Virgil*, had the confidence to promise to himself, and indeed obtain'd ; who got as much glory of Eloquence, Wit and Learning, in the expressing of the observations of husbandry ; as in describing the Heroical Acts of *Æneas.*

Nec sum animi dubius, verbis ea vincere, magnum‡
Quam sit, & angustis his addere rebus honorem.

Geor.3.

And surely if the purpose be good in earnest, not to write at leisure, that which men may read at leisure; but really to instruct and be a subsidiary to Active life; these *Georgicks of Man's Mind*, ought to be had in as great esteem with men, as those heroical portraitures of Virtue, Goodness, and Felicity, wherein so much labour and cost hath been bestowed.

I. We will therefore divide *Moral Philosophy*, into two main and Principal *Knowledges*; *the one concerning the Exemplar or Image of Good*; *the other concerning, the Regiment and Culture of the Mind*, which we are wont to call the *Georgicks of the Mind:* that describes the *Nature of Good*; this prescribes rules, how to subdue and accommodate the mind of Man thereunto.

§ The *Doctrine touching the Platform*, which respects and describes the *Nature of Good*, considers *Good* either *Simple* or *Compared*, I say either the *kinds* of Good, or the *Degrees of Good*. In the later of *these*, those infinite Disputations and Speculations *touching the supreme degree of Good*, which they term *Felicity*; *Beatitude*, the *highest good*, (the Doctrines of which were the Heathens Divinity) are by the Christian Faith, taken away and discharged. For as *Aristotle* saith, *That Young men may be happy, but not otherwise but by hope*; so must we all, being so taught by Christian Faith, acknowledge our selves to be but children and in our Minority; and think of no other felicity, than that which is in hope of the future world. Freed therefore by happy fate from this doctrine, which was the *Heathens Heaven* (wherein without doubt, they attributed a higher elevation of man's Nature, than it was capable of; for we see in what a height of stile *Seneca* writes, *verè Magnum habere fragilitatem hominis, securitatem Dei*) we may certainly with less loss of Sobriety and Truth, receive for most part the rest of their enquiries concerning the doctrine of the *Platform*. As concerning the *Nature of Good Positive and Simple*, surely they have set it out in beautiful colours and drawn it to the life, upon excellent Tables; representing with exact diligence to the eye, *the Forms, Postures, Kinds, Affinities, Parts, Subjects, Provinces, Actions, Administrations of Virtues and Duties*. Nor do they so leave the pursuit; for they have commended and insinuated all these into the spirit of man, with great quickness and vivacity of Arguments, and sweetness, and beauty of Perswasions; yea and fortified and intrenched the same (as much as discourse can do) against corrupt and popular opinions and invasions. *As touching the nature of comparative good*, they have also well handled that, in setting down that *triplicite Order of Good*, in *comparing contemplative life with Active*; *in distinguishing between virtue with reluctation, and virtue setled by security and confirmed: in the conflict and encounter between honesty and profit*; *in the ballancing of virtue with virtue, to see which preponderates other*; and the like. So as this part touching the *Platform*; I find excellently laboured, and that the ancients herein have shewed themselves admirable men: yet so as the pious and painful diligence

Rhet.lib. 2.

In Epist.

ligence of Divines, being practis'd in *Duties, Moral virtues, Cases of Conscience, and circumscriptions of sin,* have far outgone the Philosophers. *Notwithstanding* (to return to the Philosophers) if before they had addrest themselves to the popular and receiv'd notions of *Virtue, Vice, Pain, Pleasure,* and the rest; they had staid a little longer and had searched the *Roots of Good and Evil, and the strings of those Roots;* they had given in my judgement a great light unto all which might fall into enquiry afterwards: especially if they had consulted as well with the *Nature of things, as with the Axioms of Morality,* they had made their Doctrines less prolix, and more profound: which being by them either altogether omitted, or very confusedly handled, we will briefly re-examine and endeavour to open and clear the springs of *Moral habits,* before we come unto the doctrine of the *Culture or Manurance of the Mind,* which we set down as *Deficient.*

II. There is inbred and imprinted in every thing an appetite to a *duple Nature of Good; the One as every thing is a Total or Substantive in it self; the other as it is a part or member of some greater Total:* and this *latter* is more excellent and potent than the *other:* because it tendeth to the conservation of a more *ample form. The first may be called Individual or self-Good; the latter the Good of Communion: Iron* in a particular Sympathy moves to the *Loadstone,* but yet if it exceed a certain Quantity it forsakes those affections, and like a good Citizen and a true Patriot moves to the Earth, which is the Region and Country of its connaturals. To proceed a little further; *Dense* and *Massie Bodies* move to the Earth, to the great Congregation of *close-compacted Bodies;* yet rather than to suffer a divulsion in the continuance of nature, and that there should be, as they call it, a *Vacuum,* these Bodies will move upwards, forsaking their duty to the *Earth* that they may perform the general duty they owe unto the *World:* so it is ever seen *that the Conservation of the more general and publick form, commands and governs the lesser and more particular Appetites and Inclinations.* But this Prerogative of the *Good of Communion,* is especially engraven upon Man, if he degenerate not, according to that memorable speech of *Pompeius Magnus,* who being in Commission for purveyance for a Famine at Rome, and being disswaded with great vehemence and instance by his friends that he would not hazard himself to Sea in an extremity of weather, he answered only this, *Necesse est ut eam, non ut vivam.* So as the love of life which in every Individual Creature is so predominant an affection, could not out-ballance his love and loyalty to the state. But why do we dwell upon this Point? There was never extant in any age of the world, either Philosophy, or Sect, or Religion, or Law, or Discipline, which hath so highly exalted the *Good of Communion* and deprest'd *Good private and particular,* as the *Holy Christian Faith,* whereby it clearly appears, that it was one and the same *God* that gave the Christian Law to Men, who gave those Laws of Nature to Creatures of inferior order. Wherefore we read that many of the elect Saints of God have rather wished themselves anathematiz'd and raz'd out of the *Book of Life,* than that their brethren should not attain salvation; provoked through an extasie of Charity and an infinite feeling of the *Good of Communion.* This being set down and strongly planted, doth judge and

St. Paul. Rom. IX.

and determine many of the profoundeſt Controverſies in *Moral Philoſophy*. For firſt, it decideth the Queſtion *touching the preferment of the Contemplative or Active life*; and that againſt the opinion of *Ariſtotle* : for all the reaſons which he brings for the *Contemplative*, reſpect a *private Good*, and the pleaſure and dignity of an Individual only; in which reſpects (no queſtion) a *Contemplative life* hath the preheminence. For the *Contemplative life* is not much unlike to that comparison which *Pythagoras* made for the gracing and magnifying of *Philoſophy* and *Contemplation*; who being askt by *Hiero* what he was, anſwered; "*That* "*if Hiero were ever at the Olympian Games, he knew the manner that ſome* "*came to try their fortunes for the prizes; and ſome came as Merchants to* "*utter their commodities; and ſome came to make good cheer, to be merry,* "*and to meet with their friends; and ſome came to look on, and that he* "*was one of them that came to look on.* But men muſt know that in this Theatre of Man's life, it is reſerved only for God and Angels, to be Lookers on. Neither ſurely could it have been that any doubt, touching this point, ſhould ever have been rais'd in the Church (notwithſtanding that ſaying was frequent in many mens mouths, *Pretioſa in oculis Domini mors ſanctorum ejus* : by which place they uſe to exalt their *Civil Death* and the Laws of a Monaſtick and Regular courſe of life;) but upon this defence, *that the Monaſtical life is not ſimply Contemplative*; but is altogether converſant in *Eccleſiaſtick Duties*, ſuch as are inceſſant Prayer; Sacrifices of Vows performed to God; the writing alſo, in ſuch great leiſure, Theological Books for the propagation of the knowledge of the *Divine Law*, as *Moſes* did when he abode ſo many days in the *retir'd ſecrecy of the Mount*. And ſo we ſee *Enoch* the ſeventh from *Adam*, who ſeems to be the firſt founder of a *Contemplative life*, (for he is ſaid to *have walked with God*) yet endowed the Church with a Book of Prophecie, which is alſo cited by St. *Jude*. But as for a *mere Contemplative life*, and terminated in it ſelf, which caſteth no Beams of heat or light upon humane ſociety; aſſuredly Divinity knows it not. It decides alſo the Queſtion controverted with ſuch heat between the Schools of *Zeno* and *Socrates*, on the one ſide, who placed Felicity in Virtue ſimple or attended, which hath a great ſhare in the *Duties of life* : and on the other ſide other Sects and Profeſſions, as the Schools of the *Cyrenaicks* and *Epicureans*, who placed it in pleaſure; and made Virtue, (as it is uſed in ſome Comedies, where the Miſtreſs and the Maid change habits) to be but as a hand-maid, without which Pleaſure cannot be well waited and attended upon; as alſo that other, as it were, reformed School of *Epicurus*, which aſſerted *Felicity* to be nothing elſe than a Tranquillity and Serenity of Mind free and void of all Perturbations; as if they would have depoſed *Jupiter* from his Throne and reſtored *Saturn* with the Golden Age, when there was no Summer nor Winter, nor Spring nor Autumn, but all after one Air and Seaſon. Laſtly, the exploded School of *Pyrrho* and *Herillus*, which placed Felicity in the utter exſtinction and extirpation of all the ſcruples and diſputes of the mind, making no fixt and conſtant nature of Good, and Evil, but eſteeming Actions Good or Evil, as they proceed from the Mind in a clear and reſolute motion; or contrary-wiſe with averſation and reluctance. Which opinion notwithſtanding hath revived in the

Iamb. in vita.

Pſal. CXVI.

Exod. XXIII.

Gen. V.

In Epiſt.

Laert. vi- ta.

Hereſy

Herefy of the *Anabaptifts, who meafur'd all things according to the Motions and Inftinets of the fpirit, and the conftancy, or wavering of Belief.* But it is manifeft that all this we have recited, tends to private repofe and complacency of Mind, and no way to the Point of *Society,* and the Epict. En- *Good of Communion.* Again, it cenfures alfo the Philofophy of *Epicte-* chir. Arri- *tus,* who layes down this prefuppofition ; *That Felicity muft be placed in* rian. Lib. *thofe things which are in our power, left we be liable to fortune and di-* 1. *fturbance :* as if it were not a thing much more happy, to be difturbed and fruftrated of a good fuccefs in worthy and generous intentions and ends, which concern the *Publick Good,* than to obtain all that we can wifh to our felves, in thofe things which refer to our *Private Fortune.* As *Confalvo* fhewing his Souldiers *Naples,* bravely protefted, *That he had rather run himfelf upon certain ruine with one foot forward, than to have his life fecur'd for long, by one foot of retreat.* Whereunto the wifdom of that heavenly leader and commander hath fign'd, who affirm'd, Prov. xv. *That a good confcience is a continual Feaft ;* by which words is plainly fignified, that a *Mind Confcious of good Intentions, however fucceeding, affords more folid and fincere joy, and to nature more agreeable, than all that provifion wherewith man may be furnifht either for the fruition of his defires, or the repofe of his Mind.* It cenfureth likewife that abufe of Philofophy, which grew general about the time of *Epictetus,* which was, that *Philofophy* was converted into a profeffory kind of life, and, as it were, into an Occupation or Art; as if the purpofe of Philofophy, was not to reprefs and extinguifh perturbations, but to fly and avoid the caufes and occafions of them ; and therefore to fhape a particular kind and courfe of life to that end ; introducing indeed fuch a kind of health of mind, as was that of *Herodicus* in body, whereof *Ariftotle* makes mention, which was, *that he did nothing all his life long but intend his health,* and therefore abftain'd from infinite number of things, being amerc'd by the fruition of his body : whereas if men refer themfelves to duties of fociety, that health of Body is principally to be defired, which may beft endure and overcome all alterations and extremities : fo likewife that mind is properly found and ftrong, which can break through the moft and greateft temptations and perturbations. So as *Diogenes* feems to have fpoken well, who commends thofe powers of the Mind, *which* Αὐτὴ *were able not warily to abftain but valiantly to fuftain,* and which could Αντίχη refrain the violent encounter of the Mind, even in the fteepeft Preci- Summa pices, and which could give unto the Mind (which is commended in Stoic. well-broken horfes) the fhorteft ftop and turn. Laftly, it cenfures the Philof. tendernefs and the want of Morigerous application, noted in fome of the moft ancient and reverend Philofophers, that did retire too eafily from Civil bufinefs, that they might difcharge themfelves of all indignities and perturbations, and fo might live, in their opinion, more unftained, and, as it were, fanctified perfons ; whereas the refolution of a man truly moral, ought to be fuch, as the fame *Confalvo* required in a fouldier, which is that his Honour fhould be woven *è Tela Craffiore,* and not fo fine as that every thing fhould catch in it, and tear it.

CHAP.

CHAP. II.

I. The Partition of *particular or private Good, into Good Active, and Good Passive.* II. The Division *of Good Passive, into Conservative Good, and Perfective Good.* III. The Division *of the Good of Communion, into General and Respective Duties.*

I. **W**Herefore let us now resume and prosecute, first *private or particular Good,* we will divide it into *Good Active* and *Good Passive,* for this difference of *Good* (not unlike surely to those Appellations, which, amongst the Romans, were familiar in their Houshold Terms of *Promus* and *Condus*) is found impress'd in the whole course of Nature : but chiefly discloseth it self in the two several Appetites of Creatures; the one of *conserving and fortifying* themselves; the other of *multiplying and dilating* themselves; and this latter which is *Active,* and as it were, the *Promus,* seems to be the more powerful, and the more worthy; but the former which is *Passive,* and, as it were, the *Condus,* may be taken as inferiour and less worthy. For in the universal frame of Nature, the Heavenly Nature is chiefly the *Agent;* the Terrestial Nature the *Patient :* so in the pleasures of living Creatures, the pleasure of Generation is greater than that of Nutrition:and in the divine Oracles it is pronounced, *Beatius esse dare quam accipere.* Nay farther, in the common course of life, there is no mans spirit so soft and effeminate, but esteems the effecting, and bringing to some issue that which he hath fixt in his desire , more than any sensuality or pleasure. And certainly this preheminence of *Active Good,* is infinitely exalted from the consideration of our humane condition, that it is mortal, and also exposed to the stroak of Fortune : for if there could be obtained a license of perpetuity and certainty in humane Pleasures, their price would be advanced, for their security and continuance. And in as much as we see, that the summ of all comes to this, *Magni æstimamus mori tardus; Et ne glorieris de crastino, nescis partum Diei :* it is no wonder, if with all contention of spirit , we pursue those things , which are secur'd and exempt from the injuries and affronts of time : and these things can be nothing else but only our *deeds,* as it is said, *opera eorum sequuntur eos.*   Apoc xiv.

§ There is likewise another preheminence of *Good Active* of import, implanted in, and supported by that affection, which cleaves close to man's nature, as an individuate companion; which is the *love of Novelty and Variety.* And this *Affection* in the pleasures of senses (which are the very principal part of *Passive Good*) is exceeding narrow, and hath no great latitude : *Do but think* (saith *Seneca*) *how often you have acted over the same things, Meat, Sleep, Mirth; we*   Sen alicubi. *run round in this circle, to be willing to dye, not only a valiant, or a wretched, or a wise man may, but even a fastidious and nice nature may.* But in the Enterprises, Purposes and Pursuits of our life, there is much variety, whereof we are sensible in our inceptions, progres-

sions

Act. 20.

Sen. in Ep.

Prov.

sions, rests, recoils, to redintegrate our forces, approaches, attainings, and the like; so as it was very well said, *vita sine Proposito languida & vaga est :* which indifferently befals both to the wise and unwise, as saith *Solomon, A light-brain'd man seeks to satisfie his fancy, and intermixeth himself in all things.* Nay, we see likewise, that many great Princes, who may have at command whatsoever can delight the Senses, notwithstanding many times, have procured to themselves poor desires, and set their hearts upon toys; (as Nero, *in playing upon the Harp ;* Commodus *in playing at Fence ;* Antoninus *in driving Chariots,* and others taken up with other delights) which to them were more acceptable than all the affluence of sensual pleasures : *so much greater refreshing and contentment it is, to go forward in Action, than to stand at a stay in fruition.* This, in the mean time, is to be somewhat more diligently noted ; that this *Active individual Good,* altogether differs from the *good of Society,* though oftentimes they are coincident; for although that *particular active Good* doth many times breed, and bring forth *Acts of Beneficence,* which is a *Vertue of Communion;* yet here's the difference, that those Acts are by most men performed, not with intention to benefit and make happy others, but merely in a private respect to themselves, and their own power and amplification. This best appears when *Good Active* lites upon a subject which is contrary to the *Good of Communion :* for that Gigantive State of mind which posseffeth the troublers of the world (such as was *L. Sylla,* and infinite others, though in a far smaller Model) who seem to endeavour this, to have all men happy or unhappy, as they were their Friends or Enemies, and that the world might bear their stamp, and be formed to their humours (which is the true *Theomachie*) this, I say, aspires to *active particular Good* at least in appearance, although it doth most of all recede from the *Good of Society.*

II. But we will divide *Passive Good* into *Good Conservative* and *Good Perfective :* For there is implanted in every thing a triple Appetite in respect of *private* or *particular Good ; the first of preserving or continuing it self ; the second of advancing and perfecting it self ; the third of multiplying and extending it self :* but this last Appetite is referr'd to *Active Good,* whereof we speak even now. There remain therefore the two other kinds of *Good,* of which the *Perfective* excels ; for it is less to conserve a thing in its natural state, but greater to advance the same thing to a higher nature ; for there are found through all Essences some nobler natures to the dignity and excellency whereof inferiour natures do aspire, as to their Originals and Springs. So concerning Men, the Poet doth not impertinently describe,

Virg. Æn. 6.

Igneus est Ollis vigor & Cœlestis Origo ;

Man's assumption or approach to a Divine or Angelical Nature is the perfection of his Form ; a depraved and preposterous imitation of which *Perfective Good* is the destruction of humane life, and a violent tempest which bears down and ruines all, that is, while men

instead

inftead of a formal and effential advancement are carried in a blinde ambition to an advancement only Local. *For as thofe which are* fick and find no Remedy, do tumble up and down, and change place, as if by a remove Local, they could obtain a remove Internal, and fhift of their difeafe: fo it is in Ambition that men being poffefs'd and led away with a falfe refemblance of exalting their nature, purchafe nothing elfe but an eminence and celfitude of *Place.*

§. But *Good Confervative* is no other than *the reception and fruition of things agreable to our Nature*; and this *Good* though it be moft fimple and native; yet feems it to be of all other kinds of *Good* the fofteft and loweft. And this *Good* alfo admits a difference, which hath neither been well judg'd of, nor well inquired; for the *Good of Fruition*, or (as it is commonly call'd) the dignity and commendation *of delightful Good*, is placed either in the *Sincerity of the Fruition*, or in the *quicknefs and vigor* of it; whereof the one is fuperinduced by *Equality*; the other by *Variety* and *Viciffitude*: the one having a lefs mixture of *Evil*; the other a more ftrong and lively impreffion of *Good*. But of thefe, *whether is the greater Good*, is a queftion controverted: But *whether a man's nature may be capable of both at once, is a queftion not inquired.*

§ As touching that whereof a Queftion is rais'd: a Controverfie began to be debated between *Socrates* and a *Sophift*; *Socrates* affirm'd, *That Felicity was placed in a conftant Peace and Tranquility of mind*; but the *Sophift* in this, *That a man defire much and enjoy much.* And *so* they fell from Arguments to ill words; the *Sophift* faying that *Socrates's Felicity was the Felicity of a block or ftone:* *Socrates* on the other fide, *That the* Sophift's *Felicity was the Felicity of one that had the Itch, who did nothing but itch and fcratch.* And both thefe opinions do not want their fupports; for to *Socrates's* opinion affents even the School of *Epicurus*, which deems not but that Vertue beareth a great part in Felicity; and if fo, *Certain it is, that Vertue hath more ufe in clearing Perturbations, than in compaffing defires.* The *Sophift's* opinion is much favour'd by the affertion we laft fpake of; namely that *Good Perfective is greater than Good Prefervative, becaufe the obtaining of things defired, feems by degrees to perfect nature; which though it do not do it indeed, yet the very motion it felf in circle hath a fhew of Progreffive Motion.* [margin: Plato in Gorg.]

But the fecond Queftion, (*whether humane nature may not at once retaine, both the tranquility of mind, and the active vigor of fruition.*) decided, the true way makes the former idle and fuperfluous. For do we not often fee that fome men are fo fram'd and compofed by Nature, as they are extremely affected with pleafures while they are prefent; and yet are not greatly troubled at the leaving or lofs of them. So as the Philofophical confequence, *Non uti, ut non appetas, non appetere, ut non metuas,* feems to be the refolution of a poor and diffident fpirit. Surely moft of the Doctrines of Philofophers feem to be fomewhat more fearful and cautionary, than the nature of things requireth; as when they encreafe the fear of death by curing it: for when they would have a man's whole life to be but a difcipline or preparation to dye, how can it be, that that enemy fhould not feem

wonderful

wonderful terrible, againſt whom there is no end of preparing ? bet﹅ter ſaith the Poet though a Heathen,

Juven.Satyr.
10.

     *Qui ſpacinm vitæ extremum, inter munera ponat
     Naturæ.——*

So have the Philoſophers ſought to make the Mind in all things uni-form and Harmonical ; by not breaking them to contrary Motions and Extremes.   The reaſon whereof I ſuppoſe to have been, becauſe they dedicated themſelves to a private courſe of life ; exempt and free from active imployments and obſervances to others.   But let men rather imitate the wiſdom of Jewellers, who, if perchance, there be in the Gemm a Cloud or an Ice, which may ſo be grownd forth, as it abate not the ſtone too much, they help it, otherwiſe they will not meddle with it : ſo ought men ſo to procure *Serenity* of mind as they deſtroy not *Magnanimity*.   Thus much of *Particular Good*.

III.   Now therefore after we have ſpoken of *Self-good* (which alſo we uſe to call *Good Particular, Private, Individual*, let us reſume the *Good of Communion*, which reſpecteth *Society*, this is commonly termed by the name of *Duty*, becauſe the term of *Duty*, is more pro-per to a mind well fram'd and diſpos'd towards others ; the term of *Virtue*, to a mind well form'd and compos'd in it ſelf.   But this part at firſt ſight may ſeem to pertain to *Science Civil*, or *Politick*, but not if it be well obſerved ; for it concerns the Regiment and Go-vernment of every man over himſelf, and not over others. *And as in Architecture*, it is one thing, to to frame the Poſts, Beams, and other parts of an Edifice, and to prepare them for the uſe of building ; and another thing, to fit and joyn the ſame parts together : and as in Mechanicals, the direction how to frame, and make an inſtrument or engine, is not the ſame with the manner of erecting, moving, and ſetting it on work : So the doctrine of the conjugation of men, in a *City or Society*, differs from that which makes them conformed, and well affected to the weal of ſuch a *So-ciety*.

§   This Part of Duties is likewiſe diſtributed into two portions, whereof the one reſpects the *common duty of every man*, the other *the ſpecial and reſpective Duties* of every man in his profeſſion, vocati-on ſtate, perſon, and place.   The firſt of theſe, hath been well la-boured, and diligently explicated by the Ancients and others, as hath been ſaid : the other we find to have been ſparſedly handled, al-though not digeſted into an entire body of a *Science* ; which man-ner of diſperſed kind of writing, we do not diſlike ; howbeit in our judgement, to have written of this Argument by parts, were far bet-ter.   For who is endewed with ſo much perſpicacity and confidence, as that he can take upon him to diſcourſe, and make a judgement skilfully, and to the life, of the *peculiar and reſpective duties* of eve-ry particular order, condition and Profeſſion? *And the treatiſes which are not ſeaſon'd with experience, but are drawn only from a general and Scholaſtical notion of things, are touching ſuch matters, for moſt part, i-dle and fruitleſſ diſcourſes.*   For although ſometimes a looker on

may

may fee more than a Gamefter; and there be a common proverb, more arrogant than found, proceeding from the cenfure of the vulgar, touching the actions of Princes, *That the vale beft difcovereth the Hills*; yet it could be efpecially wifhed, that none would intermeddle or engage themfelves in fubjects of this nature, but only fuch as are well experienc'd and and practis'd in the particular cuftoms of men. *For the labours and vigilancies of fpeculative men, in Active Matters, do feem to men of experience, little better, than the difcourfes of Phormio of the wars, feemed to Hannibal, which efteemed them but dreams and dotage.* Only there is one vice which accompanies them, which write books of matters pertaining to their own profeffion, and Art, which is, that they magnifie and extol them in excefs.

Cic. Lib. 2. de Oratore.

§ *In which kind of Books, it were a crime Piacular, not to mention,* Honoris caufa, *Your Majeftie's excellent work* touching the duty of a King: *for this writing hath accumulated and congefted within it many treafures as well open as fecret of* Divinity, Morality, *and* Policy, *with great afperfion of all other Arts; and it is in my opinion one of the moft found and healthful writings that I have read. It doth not float with the heat of Invention; nor freez and fleep with the coldneff of negligence: it is not now and then taken with a wheeling dizzineff, fo to confound and lofe it felf in its order; nor is it diftracted and difcontinued by digreffions, as thofe difcourfes are; which by a winding expatiation, fetch in and enclofe matter that fpeaks nothing to the purpofe; nor is it corrupted, with the cheating Arts of Rhetorical perfumes and paintings, who chufe rather to pleafe the Reader, than to fatisfie the nature of the Argument. But chiefly that work hath life and fpirit, as Body and Bulk, as excellently agreeing with truth, and moft apt for ufe and action: and likewife clearly exempt from that vice noted even now, (which if it were tolerable in any, certainly, it were fo in Kings, and in a writing concerning Regal Majefty) namely, that it doth not exceffively and invidioufly exalt the Crown and Dignity of Kings.* For Your Majefty *hath not defcribed a King of Perfia or Affyria, radiant, and fhining in extreme Pomp and Glory; but really, a* Mofes *or a* David, *Paftors of the People. Neither can I ever lofe out of my remembrance, a Speech,* which Your Majefty, *in the facred Spirit, wherewith you are endowed to govern Your people, delivered in a great caufe of Indicature, which was,* That Kings rul'd by the Laws of their Kingdoms, as God did by the Laws of Nature; and ought as rarely to put in ufe that their prerogative, which tranfcends Laws, as we fee God put in ufe his power of working Miracles. *And yet notwithftanding in that other book, written by* Your Majefty, *of a free Monarchy, You give all men to underftand, that* Your Majefty, *knows and comprehends the Plenitude of the Power of Kings, and the Ultimities (as the Schools fpeak of Regal Rights; as well as the circle and bounds of their Office, and Royal Duty.* Wherefore I have prefumed, to alledge *that book* written by Your Majefty, as a prime and moft eminent example of Tractates, concerning *fpecial and refpective Duties.* Of which Book, what I have now faid, I fhould in truth have faid as much, if it had been written by any King a thoufand years fince. Neither doth that kind of nice Decency move me, whereby commonly it is prefcribed

K. IAMES, DORON. BASIL.

JACOB. R. dictum memorab.

DE LIB. MONAR.

nos

not to praise in presence, so those Praises exceed not measure; or be

Cicero.
attributed unseasonably or upon no occasion presented. Surely *Cicero,* in that excellent oration *Pro M. Marcello,* studies nothing else, but to exhibit a fair Table drawn by singular Art, of *Cæsar's virtues,* though

Plin. Jun.
that Oration was made to his face; which likewise *Plinius secundus* did to *Trajan.* Now let us resume our intended purpose.

SATYRA
SERIA,
sive de Interi-
oribus rerum.
§ There belongs farther to this part, touching the *Respective Duties of vocations and particular Professions,* and other *knowledge,* as it were, Relative and opposite unto the former, concerning the *Frauds, Cautels, Impostures,* and *Vices of every Profession :* For Corruptions and Vices, are opposed to Duties and Virtues. Nor are these *Depravations* altogether silenced in many Writings and Tractates; but for most part, these are noted only upon the by, and that by way of Digression: but how? rather in a Satyr and Cynically after *Lucian's* manner, than seriously and gravely, for men have rather sought by wit to traduce, and to expose to scorn that which is useful and sound, in Arts and Professions; than to sever that which is good and wholsome, from that which is corrupt and vitious. But

Prov. XIV.
Solomon saith excellently; *A scorner seeks wisdom and finds it not; but knowledge is easie unto him that understands :* for he that comes to seek after knowledge, with a mind to scorn, and censure; shall be sure to find matter for his humour, but no matter for his instruction. And certainly a grave and wise Treatise of this argument, whereof we now speak, and that with sincerity and integrity, seemeth worthy to be reckoned one of the best fortifications of virtue and honesty, that can be planted. *For as the Fable goes* of the Basilisk, that if he see a man first, the man dyes; but if a man see him first, the Basilisk dyes; so it is with Frauds, Impostures, and evil Arts; if a man discover them first, they lose their power of doing hurt; but if they prevent, then, and not otherwise they endanger. So that we are much beholding to *Machiavil,* and such writers, who discover apertly and plainly, what men use to do, not what men ought to do: for it is not possible to joyn the *wisdom of the Serpent, with the Innocency of the Dove,* except a man know exactly the nature of evil it self; for without this skill, virtue lyes open and unfenc'd; nay a sincere and honest man can do no good upon those that are wicked, to reclaim them, unless he know all the coverts and profundities of Malice. For men of corrupt minds and deprav'd judgements presuppose, that honesty grows out of the weakness of Nature, and simplicity of Manners, and only out of a belief given to Preachers and School-Masters; as likewise to Books; Moral Precepts; and popular opinions : so that unless you can make them plainly to perceive, that their deprav'd and corrupt Principles, and crooked Rules, are as deeply founded, and as plainly discovered by those who exhort and admonish them, as they are to themselves, they despise all the integrity of Moral Practices or Precepts; according to that admirable Oracle of *Solomon, Non recipit stultus verba prudentiæ, nisi ea di-*

Prov. 18.
xeris, quæ versantur in corde ejus. But this part concerning *Respective Cantels and vices,* we place in the number of *Deficients,* and will call it by the name of *Satyra Seria,* or of a Treatise *De interioribus Rerum.*

So

So to this kind of knowledge, touching *Respective Duties*, do also appertain the *Natural Duties* between Husband and Wife; Parents and Children, Master and Servant: so likewise the laws of Friendship and Gratitude; as also the Civil bonds of Corporations, Companies, Colledges, Neighbour-hood and the like. But it must ever be presuppofed, that they are here handled, not as parts of *Civil society* (for that is referr'd to the Politicks) but as to the framing and predispofing of the minds of Particular perfons, to the maintaining of thofe *Bonds of Society.*

§ But the *Knowledge concerning the Good of Communion or of Society,* even as that of *Good Individual,* doth handle *Good* not *simple alone,* but also *comparatively;* whereunto belongs the weighing of Duties between Perfon and Perfon; Cafe and Cafe; Private and Publick; between time Prefent and Future: as we may fee in the fevere and cruel proceeding of L. *Brutus* againft his own Sons, which by the moft was extoll'd to the heavens; yet another faid

Infœlix utcunque ferent ea fata Minores.

Liv. Hift. lib.2.
Florus Hift. lib.1.
Plutar. in M.Bruto.

The fame we may fee in that fupper unto which *M. Brutus,* and *C. Cassius* were invited, for there, when there was a queftion fhrewdly caft forth, *Whether it was lawful to kill a Tyrant?* on purpofe to feel the minds of the company, touching a confpiracy intended againft *Cæsar's* life; the guefts were divided in opinion; fome faid it was directly lawful, *for that fervitude was the extreme of Evils;* others were of a contrary mind, *for that Tyranny was not fo great a mifery as Civil war;* a third fort, as if they had iffued out of the School of *Epicurus,* avouched; *That it was an unworthy thing, that wife men fhould hazard their lives and ftates for Fools.* But there are many Cafes touching *comparative Duties,* amongft which, that of all other is the moft frequent; *Whether a man ought to fwerve from the rule of Juftice, for the fafety of his Country, or fomefuch notable Good to enfue afterward?* Touching which cafe *Jafon* of *Theffaly* was wont to fay, *Aliqua funt injuftè facienda ut multa juftè fieri poffint,* but the Reply is ready, *Authorem prefentis juftitiæ habes, fponforem futuræ non habes:* Men muft pursue things which are juft in prefent, and leave the future to the Divine Providence. And thus touching the *Exemplar,* or of the defcription of *Good.*

Plut.Moral. Præc.gerend. Reip.

Cʜᴀᴘ. III.

I. *The Partition of the Doctrine of the Culture of the Mind, into the Knowledge of the Characters of the Mind.* II. *Of the Affections or Passions.* III. *And of the Remedies or Cures.* IV. *An Append of the same Doctrine, touching the Congruity between the Good of the Mind, and the Good of the Body.*

Now that we have spoken in a Philosophical sence of the *fruit of Life*, it remains that we speak of the *Culture of the Mind*, which is due unto it, without which the former part seems nothing else, than an Image or Statue, beautiful to contemplate, but destitute of Life and Motion; to which opinion, *Aristotle* himself subscribes in these plain words, *Wherefore it is necessary to speak of virtue, both what it is, and from what it proceeds: for it would be to little purpose, to know virtue, and to be ignorant of the manner and means how to compass it. Concerning virtue therefore inquiry must be made, not only of what kind it is but by what ways it may be acquired: for we desire both these, the knowledge of the thing it self, and the fruition thereof; but this cannot be effected, unless we know of what materials it is compounded, and how to procure the same:* In such full words, and with such iteration doth he inculcate this Part; which yet notwithstanding himself pursues not. This likewise is the very same which *Cicero* attributes to *Cato* the Younger, as a great commendation, which was, that he had applyed himself to Philosophy, *Non disputandi causa, ut magna pars, sed ita vivendi.* And although, through the negligence of the times wherein we live, few hold any consultation diligently, to manure and till the Mind, and frame their course of life (according to some Rule; according to that of *Seneca, De partibus vitæ quisque deliberat, de summâ nemo*; so as this part may seem superfluous,) yet this moves us not, so as to leave it untouched, but rather we conclude, with that Aphorism of *Hippocrates, They who are sick of a dangerous disease, and feel no pain, are distempered in their understanding:* Such men need medicine, not only to assuage the disease, but to awake the sense. And if it be said that the *Cure of mens minds*, belongs to sacred Divinity, it is most truly said; but yet why may not *Moral Philosophy* be accepted into the train of *Theology*, as a wise servant and a faithful handmaid, ready at all commands to do her service? For as it is in the Psalm, *That the eyes of the Handmaid, look perpetually towards the Mistress*; and yet no doubt many things are left to the discretion and care of the Hand-maid; so ought *Moral Philosophy* to give all due observance to Divinity, and to be obsequious to her Precepts; yet so, as it may yield of it self, within its own limits, many sound and profitable directions. *This Part therefore*, when I seriously consider, the excellency thereof, I cannot but find exceeding strange, that it is not yet reduced into a *Body of Knowledge.* Wherefore seeing we have reported it as *Deficient*, we will after our manner give some Adumbrations thereof.   I. *First*

Mag. Moral. lib. 1.

Pro. L. Muræn.

De Brev. vitæ.

Aphof. l. 2.

Pſal. 123.

I. *Firſt therefore*, in this as in all things which are Practical, we ought to caſt up our account, *what is in our power, and what not :* for the one may be dealt *with by way of Alteration; the other by way of Application only.* The Husband-man cannot command either the nature of the Earth, or the ſeaſons of the weather; no more can the Phyſician the natural temper or conſtitution of the Patient or the variety of Accidents. Now in the *Culture of the mind of Man,* and the cure of the Diſeaſes thereof; three things fall into conſideration : *The divers Characters of Diſpoſitions ; the Affections ; and the Remedies.* As in curing the Body three things are propounded, the *Complection or Conſtitution of the Patient ; the Diſeaſe ; and the Cure ;* and of theſe three, the laſt only is in our power, the two former are not. Yet even in thoſe things which are not in our power, no leſs diligent inquiry is to be made thereof, than in thoſe which are ſubject to our power; for a diſtinct and exact knowledge of them is to be laid as a ground-work to the *knowledge of the Remedies ;* that they may be more aptly and ſucceſsfully applied; for neither can a garment be well fitted to the Body, unleſs you firſt take the meaſure of the Body.

§ *Wherefore* the firſt article of this knowledge *of the Culture of the Mind,* ſhall be converſant about the *divers Characters of mens natures or diſpoſitions.* Neither do we here ſpeak of thoſe common Proclivities to virtues and vices; or Perturbations and Paſſions : but of thoſe which are more intrinſick and radical. Surely for this part of knowledge, I do much wonder that it ſhould be, for moſt part, ſo neglected or ſlightly paſt over, by writers Moral and Political ; conſidering it caſts ſuch reſplendent Beams upon both thoſe kinds of knowledges. In the Traditions of *Aſtrology,* the natures and diſpoſitions of men, are not without ſome colour of truth, diſtinguiſht from the Prædominancies of Planets ; as that ſome are by nature made and proportioned for *contemplation ;* others for *matters Civil ;* others for *War ;* others for *Advancement ;* others for *Pleaſure ; others* for *Arts ;* others for changeable courſe of life. So among the Poets, Heroical, Satyrical, Tragedians, Comedians, you ſhall find every where, the Images of wits, although commonly with exceſs and beyond the bounds of Truth. Nay this ſame Argument of the *divers Characters of Nature,* is one of thoſe Subjects, wherein the common diſcourſes of men, (which very ſeldom, yet ſometimes falls out) are more wiſe than Books. But the beſt proviſion and collection for ſuch a treatiſe, ought to be fetcht from the obſervations of the wiſeſt ſort of Hiſtorians ; not only from Elogies and Panegyricks, which commonly follow the death of a Perſon ; but much more from the entire body of a Hiſtory, ſo often as ſuch a perſonage doth, as it were, enter upon the ſtage. For this inter-woven Image, ſeems to be a more lively deſcription, than the cenſure of an Elogy ; ſuch as is that in *T. Livius,* of *Africanus,* and of *Cato the Elder ; in Tacitus* of *Tiberius, Claudius and Nero ; in Herodian,* of *Septimius Severus ; in Philip de Commines,* of *Lewis the XI. King* of France ; *in Fra. Guicciardine, of Ferdinand King of Spain ; Maximilian the Emperor ; Leo and Clemens, Biſhops of Rome.* For thoſe writers fixing their eyes continually on the Images of theſe Perſons, whom they made choice of to decipher,

GEORGICA A-NIMI, ſive de cultu-ra Morum.

and pourtrait, feldom mention their Acts and Atchievements, but
withal, infert fomething touching their nature and difpofitions; fo
likewife many *Relations, touching the Conclaves of Popes,* which we
have met withal, reprefent *good Characters, and lively Impreffions,*
of the natural difpofitions of *Cardinals*; as the letters of Ambaffadors,
fet forth the nature and manners of Counfellors to Princes. Wherefore let there be a full, and perfect collection made of this argument,
whereof we have fpoken, which certainly is fertil and copious. *Neither would we,* that thofe *Characters* in the *Ethicks* (as it is with Hifto-
rians, Poets, and in common fpeech,) fhould be accepted as perfect
politick Images; which compounded and commixt conftitute any
refemblances whatfoever; how many and of what fort they may be;
and how they are connext and fubordinate one with another: that
there may be made, as it were, an artificial and accurate diffection of
natures and difpofitions; and a difcovery of the fecret inclinations
of Individual tempers; and that from a knowledge thereof, precepts
of cure may be more pertinently prefcribed.

§ And not only the *Characters of difpofitions,* impreffed by nature,
fhould be received into this Tractate; but thofe alfo which are impo-
fed upon the mind, from Sex, Age, Region, Health, Beauty, and
the like: as alfo thofe from extern fortune, as of Princes, Nobles,
obfcure Perfons; Rich, Poor, Private perfons, Profperous, Mifera-
ble and the like.   For we fee *Plautus* makes it a wonder to fee an old
man Beneficent, *Benignitas quidem hujus, oppidò ut adolefcentuli eft;*
and St. *Paul,* commanding that the feverity of difcipline, fhould be
ufed to the *Cretans,* (*rebuke them fharply*) accufeth the nature of that
Nation from a Poet; *Cretenfes femper mendaces, malæ beftiæ, ventres
pigri.   Saluft* notes this in the nature of Kings, that it is ufual with
them to defire contradictories; *Plerunq; Regiæ voluntates ut vehemen-
tes funt;   fic mobiles, fæpeq; ipfæ fibi adverfæ,   Tacitus* obferves that
Honours and Advancements, oftner change mens natures to the worfe,
than to the better, *Solus Vefpafianus mutatus in melius. Pindarus* makes
an obfervation, that great and *Sodoms* fortune, for moft part, loofens
and diffinews mens minds; *funt, qui magnam felicitatem concoquere
non poffunt:* fo the Pfalm fheweth, that it is more eafie to keep a
meafure and temperament, in a modeft confiftency; than in the increafe of Fortune, *If Riches increafe, fet not your heart upon them.*
Thefe obfervatioms and the like, I deny not, but are touched a little by *Ariftotle,* as in paffage, in his Rhetoricks; as likewife in the
writings of others difperfedly by the way; but they were never yet
incorporated into *Moral Philofophy,* to which they do principally appertain; no lefs certainly, than the handling of the diverfity of grounds
and moulds, doth to *Agriculture;* or the handling of the diverfity of
complections and conftitutions of the body, doth to *Medicine.* The
fame muft be obferved here, except we mean to follow the indifcre-
tion of Empiricks, which minifter the fame medicines to all Patients,
of what conftitution foever.

II. *After the knowledge of Characters* follows the *knowledge of Affections* and *Paffions,* which are as the *Difeafes of the Mind,* as hath
been faid.   For as the Ancient Politicks in Popular States were wont

Mil. Glo.
Ad Tit.c.1 ex
Epimen.

In Jugurth.

Hift.lib.1.

Pindar.

Pfal.62.

to fay, *That the people were like the Sea, and the Orators like the winds*; becaufe as the *Sea* would of it felf be calm and quiet, if the *winds* did not move and trouble it; fo the *People* of their own nature would be peaceable and tractable, if the *feditious Orators* did not fet them in working and agitation.   So it may be truly affirmed, that *mans mind* in the nature thereof, would be temperate and ftaid, if the *affections,* as winds, did not put it into tumult and perturbation.   And here again I find it ftrange, that *Aristotle,* who writ fo many books of *Ethicks,* fhould never in them handle the *Affections,* as an effential member of *Ethicks*; and yet in the *Rhetoricks,* where they are confidered but Collaterally, and in a fecond degree (that is, fo far as they may be rais'd and moved by fpeech) he finds place for them, (in which place notwithftanding, for fuch an abridgement, he difcourfeth acutely and well:) for his difputations about *pleafure and pain,* no way fatisfieth this inquiry; no more than he that fhould write only of *light* and *lightning,* could be faid, to have written of the nature of *particular Colours*; for *Pleafure* and *Pain,* are to the particular affections, as *light* is to *Colours.*   Better travels the Stoicks have taken in this argument, as far as may be conjectured from fuch Remains as are extant; but yet fuch as confifted rather in curiofity of Definitions, than any full and ample defcriptions.   So likewife I find fome elegant Books of fome *affections,* as of *Anger,* of *Tenderneß,* of *Countenance,* and fome few other.   But to fpeak the truth, the beft Doctors of *this knowledge* are the Poets, and writers of Hiftories, where we may find painted and diffected to the life, how affections are to be ftirred up and kindled; how ftill'd and laid afleep; how again contain'd and refrain'd, that they break not forth into Act; likewife how they difclofe themfelves, though repreffed and fecreted; what operations they produce; what turns they take; how they are enwrapt one within another; how they fight and encounter one with another; and other the like Particularities.   Amongft the which, this laft is of fpecial ufe in Moral and Civil matters, *How, I fay, to fet Affection againft Affection; and by the help of one to mafter and reclaim another?* After the manner of Hunters and Fowlers, who hunt Beaft with Beaft; and fly Bird with Bird; which percafe of themfelves without the affiftance of Bruit Creatures, a man could not fo eafily recover.   Nay farther, upon this foundation, is erected, that excellent and univerfal ufe in matters Civil of *Præmium* and *Pæna,* which are the *Pillars of Civil States*; feeing thofe *predominant Affections* of *Fear* and *Hope* do bridle and fuppreſs all other exorbitant *Affections.*   Again, as in government of States, it is fometimes neceffary to confront and bridle one Faction with another; fo it is in the inward *Gavernment of the Mind.*

III. Now come we to thofe Points which are *within our own command,* and have force and operation upon the mind, and alfo affect, difpofe, and manage the *Will* and *Appetite*; and therefore are of great force to alter the manners.   In which part the Philofophers ought to have made a painful and diligent *Inquiry* touching the *Power and Energy of Cuftom, Exercife, Habit, Education, Converfation, Friendfhip, Praife, Reprehenfion, Exhortation, Fame, Laws, Books, Studies,*

dies, and other points of like nature. *These* are *they* which have the sway and dominion in *Morality*, from these Agents the mind suffereth and is disposed; of these, as of Ingredients, receits are compounded, which conduce to the conservation and recovery of the Health and good Estate of the Mind, as far as may be performed by Humane Remedies. Of which number we will select one or two whereupon we will a little insist as an example to the rest. We will therefore insinuate a few points *touching Custom* and *Habit*.

Moral Nicom. lib. 2.

That opinion of *Aristotle* seemeth to me to favour of negligence and a narrow Contemplation, where he asserts— *that those Actions which are natural cannot be changed by custom;* using for example— *that if a stone be thrown a thousand times up, it will not learn to ascend of its own accord: Moreover, that by often seeing or hearing, we do not learn to hear or see the better:* for though this principle be true in some things wherein Nature is Peremptory (the reasons whereof we cannot now stand to discuss) yet it is otherwise in things wherein Nature, according to a *Latitude*, admits *intention* and *remission*. He might see that a strait glove by often drawing on, is made wider; and that a wand by use and continuance is bowed contrary to its natural bent in the growth, and soon after stays in the same posture; that the voice by exercising it becomes louder and stronger; that heat and cold are better endur'd by custom; and many instances of like kind. Which two latter examples have a neerer resemblance and come neerer to the point, than those he there alledgeth. But however this case be determin'd, by how much the more true it is; *that both Virtues and Vices consist in habit;* he ought, by so much the more, to have endeavour'd, to have so prescrib'd rules *how such habits might be acquired, or remov'd:* for there may be many Precepts made of the wise ordering of the *Exercises of the Mind*, no less than of the *Exercises of the Body;* whereof we will recite a few.

§ *The first shall be; that we beware even at first of higher or smaller tasks, than the nature of the business requires, or our leasure or abilities permit:* For if too great a task be impos'd, in a mean diffident nature, you blunt the edge of chearfulness and blast their hopes; in a nature full of Confidence, you breed an opinion whereby a man promiseth to himself more than he is able to perform, which draws on sloth and security; and in both those temperatures, it will come to pass that the experiment doth not satisfie the expectation; which ever discourageth and confounds the mind: but if the Task be too weak and easie, in the summ of proceeding there is a loss and prejudice.

§ *A second shall be; that to the practising of any faculty, whereby a habit may be superinduced, two Seasons are chiefly to be observed, the one when the mind is best disposed to a business; the other when it is worst:* that by the one, we may be well forwards on our way; by the latter, we may by a strenuous contention work out the knots and stonds of the mind; which makes middle times to pass with more ease and pleasure.

Moral. Nicom. lib. 2.

§ *A third Precept shall be that which Aristotle mentions by the way, which is to bear ever towards the contrary extreme of that whereunto we*
are

are by nature inclin'd, so it be without vice. Like as when we row against the stream; or when we make a crooked wand straight by bending it the contrary way,

§ *The fourth Precept is grounded upon that Axiom which is most true. That the mind is brought to any thing with more sweetness and happiness, if that, whereunto we pretend, be not principal in the intention of the Doer; but be overcome, as it were, doing somewhat else; because the instinct of Nature is such a freedom as hates necessity and compulsive commands.* Many other rules there are which might profitably be prescribed touching the *Direction of Custom:* for *Custom,* if it be wisely and skilfully induced, *proves* (as it is commonly said) *another Nature;* but being conducted absurdly and by chance, *it is only the Ape of Nature;* which imitates nothing to the life, but in a foolish deformity only.

§ *So if we should speak of Books and Studies,* and of their power and influence upon Manners; are there not divers Precepts, and fruitful Directions appertaining thereunto? Hath not one of the Fathers in great indignation called *Poesie, vinum Dæmonum;* being indeed it begets many Temptations, Lusts, and vain Opinions? It is not a wise opinion of *Aristotle,* and worthy to be regarded: *That young men are no fit auditors of Moral Philosophy, because the boyling heat of their affections, is not yet setled, nor attemper'd with Time and Experience.* And to speak truth, doth it not hereof come that those excellent Books and Discourses of ancient Writers (whereby they have perswaded unto vertue most effectually, representing as well her stately Majesty to the eyes of the world, as exposing to Scorn, popular Opinions in disgrace of Vertue, attired, as it were, in their *Parasite Coats*) are of so little effect towards honesty of Life, and the reformation of corrupt Manners; because they use not to be read and revolv'd by men mature in years and judgement; but are left and confin'd only to Boys and Beginners. *But is it not true also, that young men are much less fit Auditors of Policy than Morality,* till they have been throughly season'd with *Religion,* and the knowledge of Manners and Duties; lest their judgements be corrupted and made apt to think, that there are no *Moral* differences true and solid of things; but that all is to be valued according to utility and fortune. As the Poet saith,

Moral. Ni-com. Lib.

Prosperum & felix scelus virtus vocatur.

Juvenal. Sat. 13.

And again,

Ille crucem pretium sceleris tulit, hic Diadema.

But the Poets seem to speak this Satyrically, and in indignation; be it so, yet many Books of Policy do suppose the same seriously and positively: for so it pleased *Machiavel* to say, *That if* Cæsar *had been overthrown, he would have been more odious than ever was* Cataline;

as

as if there had been no difference but in *fortune* only, between a very fury compofed of Luft and Blood; and the moft excellent fpirit (his ambition referved) in the world. By this we fee how neceffary it is, for men to drink deeply *Pious and Moral Knowledges*, before they tafte *Politick*; for that they who are bred up in the Courts of Princes from tender years, and in affairs of State, commonly never attain an inward and fincere Probity of Manners; how much farther off from honefty, if to this fire of corrupt education there be admiftred the fewel of corrupt Books? *Again*, even in Moral inftructions themfelves, or at leaft in fome of them, is there not a Caution likewife to be given, left they make men too precife, arrogant and incompatible? according to that of *Cicero*, touching *M. Cato*, *Thefe Divine and excellent qualities which we fee, are his own proper endowments, but fuch as are fometimes deficient in him, are all deriv'd from Teachers, and not from Nature.* There are many other Axioms touching thofe properties and effects which Studies and Books do inftill into the minds of men: for it is true that he faith, *abeunt ftudia in mores*; which may likewife be affirm'd of thofe other points touching *Company*, *Fame*, the *Laws of our Country*, and the reft, which a little before we recited. But there is a kind of *Culture of the Mind* which feems yet more acurate and elaborate than the reft, and is built upon this ground, *That the minds of all Mortals are at fome certain times in a more perfect ftate*; *at other times in a more depraved ftate.* The purpofe therefore, and direction of this *Culture* is, that thofe good feafons may be cherifht, and the evil croft, and expunged out of the Calender. The *fixation of good Times* is procured by two means, by *vows, or at leaft moft conftant Refolution* of the Mind, and by *Obfervances and Exercifes*, which are not to be regarded fo much in themfelves, as becaufe they keep the mind in her devoir and continual obedience. The *obliteration of evil Times* may be in like manner perfected two ways; by fome *kind of Redemption, or expiation of that which is paft*; and by a *new courfe of life*, as it were, *turning over a clean leaf.* But this part feems wholly to appertain to Religion, and juftly confidering that true and genuine *Moral Philofophy*, as was faid, fupplies the place of a Hand-maid only to *Divinity*. Wherefore we will conclude this part of the *Culture of the Mind*, with that remedy, which of all other means is the moft compendious and fummary: And again, the moft noble and effectual, to the reducing of the mind to vertue, and the placing of it in a ftate next to perfection, and this is, *That we make choice of, and propound to our felves, right ends of life and actions, and agreeing to vertue; which yet muft be fuch as may be in a reafonable fort within our compafs to attain.* For if thefe two things be fuppos'd, *that the ends of actions be honeft and good*; and *that the refolution of the mind, for the purfuing and obtaining them, be fixt, conftant, and true unto fuch ends*; it will follow that the mind fhall forthwith transform and mould it felf into all vertues at once. And this indeed is an operation, which refembleth the *work of nature*, whereas other courfes, whereof we have fpoken, are like the *work of the hand.* For as when a Carver cuts and carves an Image, he fhapes only that part whereupon he works, and not the reft ; as if he be fafhioning the Face, the reft of the body is a rude and formlefs ftone ftill, till fuch time as he come to it : but contrariwife, when *Nature* makes a Flower or *Living Creature,* fhe ingenders and brings forth rudiments of all the parts at one time. So in obtaining vertues by *habit,* while a man practifeth *Temperance,* he doth not profit much to *Fortitude,* and the like; but when we wholly dedicate and devote our felves to good and honeft ends ; look what vertue foever *fuch ends* commends and commands our mind unto, we fhall find our felves already invefted and predifpofited with a kind of hability and propenfion to purfue and exprefs the fame. And this may be that *State of Mind,* which is excellently defcribed by *Ariftotle,* and expreffed with the Character, not of *vertue,* but a kind of *Divinity,* his words are thefe ; *And with Immanity, we may not unaptly countre-ballance, that ability which is above humanity ; Heroick or Divine Vertue :* and a little after, *for as Savage Creatures are incapable of Vice or Vertue ; fo is the Deity : but this ftate is a thing higher than vertue ; that, fomewhat elfe than vice.* Indeed *Plinius Secundus,* from the licenfe of Heathen magniloquence, fet forth the vertue of *Trajan,* not as an imitation, but as a pattern too Divine, when he faith, *That men need to make no other prayers to the Gods, but that they would continue as good and as gracious Lords to them, as* Trajan *had been.* But thefe are the prophane and unhallowed Airs of Heathens, who apprehend fhadows greater than the body : but true Religion, and the Holy Chriftian Faith, lays hold on fubftance it felf, imprinting upon mens Minds *Charity,* which is moft properly called, *The bond of perfection ;* becaufe it comprehends and faftens all vertues together. Surely it is elegantly faid by *Menander* of *vain Love,* which is but a counterfeit imitation of *Divine Love; Amor melior fophiftâ lævo, ad humanam vitam ;* by which words he infinuates, *that good and decent carriage, is better learnt from* Love, *than from a Sophift, or an inept Tutor ;* whom he calls *Lefthanded,* becaufe with all his tedious Rules and Preceps, he cannot form a man fo dexteroufly, and with that facility to value himfelf, and govern himfelf, as *Love* can do. So certainly, if a mans mind be truly inflamed with the *heat of Charity,* he fhall be exalted to a greater degree of Perfection, than by all the *Doctrine of Morality,* which, indeed, is but a *Sophift* in comparifon of the other. Nay farther, as *Xenophon* obferved truly, *That all other affections, though they raife the Mind, yet they diftort and diforder it by their extafes and exceffes ; but only love doth at the fame inftant, dilate and compofe the Mind.* So all other humane excellencies, which we admire; though they advance Nature, yet they are fubject to *excefs ;* only *Charity* admits no excefs. So we fee the Angels, while they afpired to be like God in Power, prevaricated and fell, *I will afcend above the altitude of the clouds, I will be like the moft high.* So man, while he afpired to be like God in Knowledge, digreffed and fell : *ye fhall be like Gods knowing Good and Evil :* but by afpiring to a fimilitude of God's *Goodnefs* or *Love,* neither Man nor Angel ever was endangered, nor fhall

Moral. Ni-com. lib.7.

Paneg.

Colof. 3.

De Inft. Cyri.

Efa.14.

Gen. 3.

Mat.5.

shall be endangered. Nay, we are invited to this imitation, *Bless them that curse you, and pray for them that despitefully use you, and perse-cute you; that you may be the sons of your father which is in Heaven: for he makes his Sun to rise on the Evil, and on the Good; and sends rain up-on the just, and upon the unjust.* So in the first Platform of the Di-vine Nature, the Heathen Religion placeth Gods Attributes thus,

Psal.145.

Optimus Maximus; and sacred Scripture speaks thus, *Misericordia e-jus, supra omnia opera ejus.*

§ Wherefore we have now concluded this part of *Moral Know-ledge* concerning the *Culture and Regiment of the Mind;* wherein if any from a contemplation of the Portions thereof, which we have strictly enumerated, doth judge that our labour is only this, *to Collect and Digest, into an Art or Science, that which hath been pretermitted by other writers, as matters of common sense and experience, and of themselves clear and perspicuous;* let him freely enjoy his judgement: yet in the mean time let him be pleased to remember what we pre-monisht at first; that our purpose was not to pursue the flourish and beauty of things; but their use and verity. Likewise let him a while ponder in his mind that invention of the Ancient Parable, touching the *two gates of sleep.*

Virg. Æn.6.

> *Sunt geminæ somni Portæ, quarum altera fertur*
> *Cornea, qua veris facilis datur exitus umbris.*
> *Altera candenti perfecta nitens Elephanto*
> *Sed falsa ad Cælum mittunt insomnia Manes.*

A gate of *Ivory* is indeed very stately, but true Dreams pass through the *gate of Horn.*

IV. By way of suppliment, that observation about *Moral Know-ledge,* may be set down, which is, *that there is a kind of relation and conformity between the Good of the Mind, and the Good of the Body.* For as the *Good of the Body* consists, as hath been said, of *Health, Beauty, Strength* and *Pleasure :* So the *Good of the Mind,* if we con-sider it according to the Axioms and Precepts of *Moral Knowledge,* we shall perceive tend to this point, *to make the mind sound, and dis-charg'd from perturbation; beautiful and graced with the ornaments of true decency; strong to all duties of life: Lastly, not stupid, but retaining an active and lively sense of pleasure, and honest recreation.* But these four, as in the body, so in the mind, seldom meet altogether. *For it is easie to observe,* that many have strength of wit and courage; who yet notwithstanding are infested with perturbations, and whose man-ners are little season'd with Elegancy and Beauty of Behaviour, in their doings: *Some again,* have an Elegancy and Fineness of Car-riage, which have neither Soundness of Honesty, nor Substance of Sufficiency in their doings: *some have* honest Minds, purified from the stain of Guilt, which yet can neither become themselves, nor manage business : *Others* which perchance are capable of all these three Qualities; but possest a with sullen humour of Stoical sadness,

and

and ſtupidity, they practiſe virtuous Actions, but enjoy neither themſelves, nor the the fruit of their good Parts : and if it chance that of theſe four *two* or *three* ſometimes meet, yet a concurrence of all *four* very ſeldom falls out. And now we have concluded that Principal Member of *Humane Philoſophy*, which conſiders *Man*, *as he conſiſts of Body and Soul; but yet, as he is ſegregate and ſeparate from ſociety.*

H h   THE

THE
Eighth Book
OF
FRANCIS L. VERULAM
Vicount S. *ALBAN*,

OF THE

Dignity and Advancement

OF

LEARNING.

To the KING.

Chap. I.

I. *The* Partition *of* Civil Knowledge *into the* Knowledge *of* Conver-
sation ; *the* Knowledge *of* Negociation ; *and the* Knowledge *of*
Empire, *or of State Goverment.*

HERE is an ancient Relation (Excellent *King*) of a
solemn Convention of many Philosophers before the
Ambassador of a forreign Prince, and how that every one according to their several abilities made demonstration of their Wisdom; that so the Ambassador
might have matter of report touching the admired
wisdom of the Grecians: But amongst these, one there was, as the
story goes, that stood still and utter'd nothing in the assembly, info-
much as the Ambassador turning to him should say : *And what is* Plutar. in
your gift, that I may report it ? To whom the Philosopher, *Report* Moral.
(saith he) *unto your King, that you found one amongst the Grecians
that knew how to hold his peace :* and indeed, I had forgotten in this
compend of Arts to interfert the *Art of silence* ; which notwithstanding
(because it is *Deficient*) I will teach by mine own Example. For

H h 2   seeing

feeing the order and contexture of matter hath brought me at length
to this point; that I muft now a little after handle the *Art of Empire*;
and being I write to fo *Great a King*, which is fo perfect a Mafter in
this Science, wherein he hath been trained up even from his infancy;
nor can I be altogether unmindful, what place I hold under your Majefty; I thought it would beft become me in this point to approve
my felf unto your Majefty, by *Silence*, rather than by *Writing*. *Ci-*
cero makes mention not only of an *Art*, but of a kind of *Eloquence*
found in *Silence* : for after he had commemorated in an *Epiftle to*
Atticus, many conferences which had interchangeably paft between

Ad Atticum.

him and another, he writeth thus; *In this place I have borrowed fome-*
what from your Eloquence, for I have held my peace. And *Pindar* to
whom it is peculiar fuddenly to ftrike, as it were, with a Divine
Scepter, the minds of men by rare fhort fentence, darts forth fome

Pindar.

fuch faying as this, *Interdum, magis afficiunt non dicta quam dicta*:
wherefore I have refolv'd in this part to be *Silent*, or which is next to
Silence, to be very brief. But before I come to the *Arts of Empire*,
fome things by way of Preoccupation are to be fet down concerning
other *Portions of Civil Doctrine*.

§ *Civil Science* is converfant about a fubject, which of all other is
moft immers'd in matter, and therefore very difficultly reduced unto
Axioms : yet there are many circumftances which help this difficulty :
for firft, *Cato* the Cenfor was wont to fay of his Romans: *That they*

Plutar. in M.
Catone.

were like Sheep, a man were better drive a Flock of them, than one of
them; for in a Flock, if you could get but fome few to go right, you fhall
have all the reft follow of their own accord: So in this refpect indeed,
the *Duty of Morality* is fomewhat more difficult than that of Policy.
Secondly, *Morality* propounds to it felf that the Mind be imbued and
furnifht with *Internal Goodnefs*; but *Civil Knowledge* requires no more
but *Goodnefs External* only, for this, as refpecting fociety, fufficeth.
Wherefore it often comes to pafs that the Government is Good, the
Times Bad : for in Sacred Story the faying is often repeated, fpeaking of Good and Godly Kings, *And yet the People directed not their*
hearts to the Lord God of their Fathers; wherefore in this refpect alfo,
the parts of Ethick are more auftere and difficult. *Thirdly*, *States*
have this nature, that like great Engines they are flowly moved, and
not without great pains; whence it comes, that they are not fo eafily
put out of frame : *For as in Ægypt* the feven good years upheld the
feven bad; fo in States, the good Government and Laws of the
Precedent times caufe, that the errors of fucceeding times, do not
quickly fupplant and ruine : But the Decrees and Cuftoms of particular perfons, are more fuddenly fubverted : And this likewife doth
charge Morality, but eafeth Policy.

I *Civil Knowledge* hath three parts, according to the three fummary Actions of Society; *The Doctrine of Converfation*; *The Do-*
ctrine of Negociation; *and the Doctrine of Empire or Republicks*. For
there are three forts of Good, which men feek to procure to themfelves from civil Society; *Comfort againft Solitude, Affiftance in Bufi-*
nefs, *and Protection* againft Injuries : and thefe be three wifdoms diftinct one from the other, and often times disjoyn'd;

Wifdom

Wisdom in Conversation; Wisdom in Negotiation, and Wisdom in Guber-nation.

§ As for *Conversation*, certainly it ought not to be affected, but much less despised; seeing a wise moderation thereof, hath both an honour, and grace of Manners in it self; and a powerful influence for the apt manage of Business; as well Publick, as Private. *For as A-ction in an Orator* is so much respected, (though it be but an out-ward quality) that it is prefer'd before those other Parts which seem more grave and intrinsick; so *Conversation* and the government there-of, in a man of a Civil Practick life (however it consisteth in outward ceremonies) finds, if not the chiefest, yet certainly a very eminent place. Of what special importment the very *Countenance* is, and the composure thereof, the Poet insinuates where he saith,

> *Nec vultu destrue verba tuo.*

A man may cancel and utterly betray the force of his words, with his *Countenance.* Nay the *Deeds* as well as *Words* may likewise be de-stroyed by the *Countenance,* if we may believe *Cicero,* who when he would commend to his Brother *Affability* towards the Provincials said, that *it* did not chiefly consist in this, to give easie access unto his Per-son, unless likewise he received them courteously even with his *Coun-tenance; Nil interest habere ostium apertum, vultum clausum: It is nothing won, to admit men with an open door, and to receive them with a shut and reserved countenance.* So we see *Atticus,* before the first inter-view between *Cæsar* and *Cicero* the war depending, did diligently and seriously advise *Cicero* by a letter touching the composing and or-dering of his *countenance* and *gesture.* And if the government of the *Face* and *Countenance* alone be of such effect, how much more is that of familiar *speech* and other *carriage* appertaining to *Conversation.* And indeed the summ and abridgement of the Grace and Elegancy of Be-haviour, is for most part comprized in this, *that we measure in a just ballance and maintain both onr own Honour and the Reputation of others.* The true Model whereof *T. Livius* hath well ascribed (though inten-ded to another purpose) in the Character of a Person, *Lest* (saith he) *I should seem either arrogant or obnoxious; whereof the one is the hu-mour of a man that forgets the liberty of another; the other of a man that forgets the liberty of himself.* But on the other side if *Urbanity and out-ward Elegancy of Behaviour* be intended too much, they pass into a de-formed and counterfeit *Affectation. Quid enim deformius quam sce-nam in vitam transferre. To Act a mans life.* But though they fall not by insensible degrees into that vitious extreme; yet too much time is consumed in these small matters; and the mind by studying them is too much depress'd and broken. And therefore as Tutors and Pre-ceptors use to advise young Students in Universities, too much addi-cted to keep company; by saying, *Amicos esse fures temporis:* so cer-tainly this same continual intention of the mind upon the *comeliness of Behaviour,* is a great thief to more solemn Meditations. *Again,* such as are so exactly accomplisht *in Urbanity,* and seem, as it were, form'd by nature for this quality alone, are commonly of such a disposition,

De Petit. Con-sulatus.

Lib XII. Epist ad Att.

Livius.

a S

as pleafe themfelves in this one habit only, and feldom afpire to high-er and more folid virtues: whereas on the contrary, thofe that are confcious to themfelves of a Defect this way, feek *Comelinefs* by *Repu-tation*; for where *Reputation* is, almoft every thing becometh; but where *that* is not, it muft be fupplied by *Puntoes* and *Complements.* *Again*, there is no greater or more frequent impediment of Action than an overcurious obfervance of *Decency* and of that other ceremo-ny attending on it, which is a too fcrupulous *Election of time* and op-portunities : for *Solomon* faith excellently, *qui obfervat ventum non feminat, & qui confiderat nubes nunquam metet :* We muft make op-portunity oftner than find it. To conclude, this *comely grace of Behaviour* is, as it were, the Garment of the Mind, and therefore muft have the conditions of a Garment : for firft, it ought to be fuch as is in fafhion; again, it ought not to be too curious or coftly ; then it ought to be fo fhaped as to fet forth any good making of the mind, and to fupply and hide any deformity ; laftly and above all, it ought not to be too ftrait, or fo to reftrain the fpirit, as to reprefs and hin-der the motion thereof in bufinefs. But this part of *Civil knowledge* touching *Converfation*, hath been indeed elegantly handled, nor can it any way be reported as *Deficient.*

C H A P.   II.

I. The Partition *of the Doctrine of Negotiation into the knowledge of* difperfed Occafions.   II. And into *the Knowledge of the Advance-ment of life.* § Examples *of the knowledge of Scatter'd Occafions from fome of* Solomon's *Parables.* § Precepts *touching the Ad-vancememt of fortune.*

THe knowledge touching *Negotiation*, we will divide into a knowledge concerning *Scatter'd Occafions*; and the Knowledge concerning the *Advancement of Life*; whereof the one comprehends all the variety of *Bufinefs*, and is, as it were, the *Secretary* of a Pra-ctick courfe of life; the other only felects and fuggefts fuch obferva-tions as appertain to the *advancing of a mans proper fortune*, which may be to every man as intimate and referved *Table-Books*, and *Me-morials* of their Affairs.

§ But before we defcend to the Particular kinds, we will fpeak fomething by way of Preface, in general, touching the *knowledge of Negotiation. The knowledge of Negotiation* no man hath handled hither-to according to the dignity of the Subject ; to the great derogation of Learning, and the Profeffors of Learning : for from this root fprin-geth that note of *Dulnefs* which hath defamed the Learned, which is ; *That there is no great concurrence between Learning and Practick wifdom.* For, if a man obferve it well, of the three *wifdoms* which we have fet down to pertain to Civil life, that of *Converfation* is by learned men for the moft part defpifed as a fervile thing and an enemy to Me-ditation. As for that *wifdom* concerning *Government*: Learned men

ac-

acquit themselves well, when they are called to the manage of Civil Affairs in ſtate; but that is a Promotion which happeneth to
few. Concerning the *Wiſdom of Buſineſs* (whereof we now ſpeak)
wherein man's life is moſt converſant; there be no Books at all written of it except, a handful or two of ſome few *Civil Advertiſements,*
that have no proportion to the magnitude of this Subject. For if there
were Books extant of this Argument, as of other, I doubt not, but
Learned men with mean experience would far excel men of long experience without Learning; and *out-ſhoot them* (as they ſay) *in their
own Bow.* Neither is there any cauſe why we ſhould fear leſt the Matter of this *Knowledge* ſhould be ſo various, that it could not fall under Precepts, for it is much narrower than the *Science of Government,*
which notwithſtanding we ſee is exactly labour'd, and ſubdued. Of
this kind of *Wiſdom,* it ſeems there have been ſome Profeſſors amongſt
the *Romans* in their beſt and wiſeſt times. For *Cicero* reports that it   Cicero.
was in uſe a little before his time for Senators, that had the name and
opinion for wiſe and experienced men (the *Coruncanii, Curii, Lælii,*
and others) to walk at certain hours in the *Forum,* where they might
give acceſs and audience to the Citizens, and might be conſulted
withall; not only touching *point of Law,* but of all *ſorts of Buſineſs*;
as of the *Marriage of a Daughter*; or of the *bringing up of a Son*; or
of a Purchaſe, of a Bargain, of an Accuſation, Defence; and every o-
ther occaſion incident to man's life. By this it plainly appears, that
there is *a Wiſdom of giving Counſel and Advice* even in Private Buſineſs; ariſing out of an univerſal inſight into the Affairs of the World;
which is uſed indeed upon Particular Cauſes, but is gathered by general obſervation of Cauſes of like nature. For ſo we ſee in the Book
which *Q. Cicero* writeth unto his Brother, *De Petitione Conſulatus,*   Q. Cicero de
(being the only Book of Particular Buſineſs, that I know written by   Petitione
the Ancients) although it concerned ſpecially an Action then on   Conſul.
foot, yet it contains in it many Politick Axioms, which preſcribe not
only temporary uſe, but a perpetual direction in the caſe of Popular
Elections. *And in this kind* nothing is extant which may any way be
compar'd with thoſe Aphoriſms which *Solomon the King* ſet forth, of
whom the Scriptures teſtifie, *That his Heart was as the Sands of the Sea*:
For as the Sands of the Sea do incompaſs all the utmoſt bounds of the   1. Reg. iv.
world; ſo his wiſdom comprehended all matters, as well humane as divine. In theſe *Aphoriſms* you ſhall clearly diſcover, beſides thoſe precepts which are more divine, many moſt excellent Civil precepts and
advertiſements, ſpringing out of the profound ſecrets of *wiſdom,* and
flowing over into a large field of variety. Now becauſe we report
as *Deficient, the Doctrine touching diſperſed occaſions,* (which is a firſt
portion of the *knowledge of Buſineſs*) we will, after our manner, ſtay
a while upon it, and propound an example thereof, taken out of thoſe
Aphoriſms, or *Parables* of *Solomon.* Neither is there, in our judgement, any cauſe of juſt reprehenſion, for that we draw from writers
of ſacred Scripture, ſomething to a Politicall ſence; for I am verily
of opinion, that if thoſe *Commentaries of the ſame Solomon were now ex-*   1. Reg. iv.
tant concerning Nature (wherein he hath written of all *Vegetables, From
the Moſs upon the wall, to the Cedar of Libanus*; and of living creatures)
it

it were not unlawful to expound them according to a natural fence; the same liberty we may take in the *Politicks.*

* AMANUEN-SIS VITÆ, five de occafi-onibus Spar-fis.

An Example of a Portion of the Doctrine concerning Difperfed Occafions, from fome *Parables of Solomon.*

THE PARABLE.

Prov. XV.

I. *A foft Anfwer appeafeth Wrath.*

THE EXPLICATION.

If the wrath of a Prince or of a great Perfon be kindled againft thee, and it be now thy turn to fpeak, *Solomon* gives in precept two points; one is, *that an anfwer be made;* the other, *that the fame be foft:* The Firft contains three precepts; *Firft that you beware of a fad, and fullen filence:* for that either charges the fault wholly upon your felf, as if you had nothing to fay for your felf; or clofely appeacheth your Mafter of fome injuftice, as if his ears were not open to a juft Defence. *Secondly that you beware of delaying and putting off a Bufinefs,* and that you crave not a longer day to give in your defence: for this procraftination, either infinuates the fame prejudice the former did, (which is that your Lord and Mafter is led away with too much paffion and partiality) and plainly betrays, that you are in divifing fome cunning and counterfeit Apology, feeing you have no prefent anfwer ready. Wherefore it is ever the beft courfe to fay fomething inftantly in your own defence, according as the occafion of the prefent bufinefs fhall adminifter. *Thirdly that by all means an anfwer be made;* an anfwer (I fay) not a meer confeffion or a meer fubmiffion, but yet not without fome fprinklings of an Apology and excufe let fall here and there; nor is it fafe to bear your felf otherwife, unlefs you have to deal with very generous and noble difpofitions; which are very rare. *It follows in the fecond place,* that the anfwer made be foft and temperate; and not harfh and peremptory.

THE PARABLE.

Prov. XVII.

II. *A wife Servant fhall have command over a reproachful Son, and fhall divide the Inheritance among the brethren.*

The

THE EXPLICATION.

IN all troubled and difagreeing Families, there ever arifeth up fome fervant, or gentle friend, powerful with both fides; which may moderate, and compound the differences of the Family; to whom, in that refpect, the whole Houfe, and the Mafter himfelf are engag'd and beholding. *This Servant,* if he aim only, at his own ends, cherifhes and aggravates the Divifions of a Family; but if he be fincerely faithful, and upright, certainly he deferves much; fo, as to be reckoned as one of the brethren; or at leaft, to receive a Fiduciary Adminiftration of the Inheritance.

THE PARABLE.

III. *If a wife man contefts with a Fool, whether he* Prov. xxix, *be in anger, or in jeft, there is no quiet.*

THE EXPLICATION.

WE are often admonifht to *avoid unequal commerce*; in this fence, *not to contend with our Betters:* but it is a no lefs profitable inftruction, which *Solomon* here fets down, *Not to undertake a worthlefs perfon*; for fuch a bufinefs is ufually concluded upon terms of difadvantage; for to overcome is no victory, but to be conquer'd a foul difgrace: and it is all one in the heat of this engagement, whether we deal by way of jefting, or by way of difdain and fcorn; for howfoever we change Copy, we are embafed and made the lighter thereby; nor fhall we handfomely come off with credit. *But* the worft inconvenience of all is, when the Perfon with whom we contend (as *Solomon* fpeaks) hath fomewhat of the *Fool* in him; that is, if he be witlefs and wilful; have fome heart, no brain.

THE PARABLE.

IV. *Lend not an Ear to all words that are fpoken, left* Ecclef. vii; *perchance thou heareft thy fervant curfe thee.*

THE EXPLICATION.

IT is a matter almoft beyond belief, what difturbance is created by *unprofitable curiofity,* about thofe things which concern our perfonal intereft: that is, when we make a too fcrupulous enquiry after fuch fecrets; which once difclofed and found out, do but caufe moleftation of mind, and nothing conduce to the advancing of our

designs.

deſigns.   *For firſt there follows vexation and diſquietneſs of Mind* ; being that all humane affairs are full of faithleſneſs and ingratitude ; ſo as if there could be procured ſome enchanted glaſs, wherein we might behold the hatred, and whatſoever malice is any way raiſed up againſt us ; it were better for us that ſuch a Glaſs, were forthwith thrown away and broken.   *For ſlanders* of this nature, are like the impotent murmures of Leaves on Trees, and in ſhort time vaniſh. *Secondly, this Curioſity fills the mind with ungrounded jealouſies,* which is a capital enemy to Counſels, and renders them inconſtant and involv'd.   *Thirdly, the ſame curioſity doth oftentimes fix evils, which of themſelves would fly away.*   For it is a dangerous matter for to provoke mens conſciences, who if they think themſelves undiſcover'd are eaſily chang'd to the better ; but if once they perceive themſelves diſmaskt, they drive out one miſchief with an other.   Wherefore it was deſervedly judg'd, a point of great wiſdom in *Pompeius Magnus,* that he inſtantly burnt all *Sertorius*'s papers unperus'd by himſelf ; or permitted to be ſo by others.

Plutar. in
Pomp.

THE PARABLE.

Prov. vi.

V. *Thy Poverty ſhall come as a Traveller, and thy Want as an armed Man.*

THE EXPLICATION.

IN this Parable, it is elegantly deſcribed how the ſhipwrack of Fortunes falls upon Prodigals, and on ſuch as are careleſs of their Eſtates ; for Debt and Diminution of Stock comes upon them at firſt by inſenſible degrees, with ſoft-ſilent paces, like a Traveller, and is hardly perceived ; but ſoon after *neceſſity invades him like an armed man,* that is, with ſo ſtrong and potent an arm, as there is no more reſiſtance to be made ; ſo it was ſaid by the Ancients, *that of all things neceſſity was the ſtrongeſt.*   Wherefore we muſt prevent the Traveller ; and be well provided againſt the armed Man.

THE PARABLE.

Prov. ix.

VI. *He that inſtructs a ſcorner, procures to himſelf a reproach ; and he that reprehends a wicked man, procures to himſelf a ſtain.*

THE EXPLICATION.

Mat. ⸪

THis Parable agrees with our Saviours Precept, *That we caſt not our Pearls before ſwine.*   In this Parable the Actions of *Inſtruction,* and of *Reprehenſion* are diſtinguiſht ; as alſo the Actions of a
ſcorner

fcorner, and of a *wicked perſon*. Laſtly that which is retaliated, is differenced. For in the former part, loſt labour is return'd ; in the latter, a ſtain and diſhonour is repaid. For when a man teacheth and inſtructeth a *fcorner*, firſt, the time thus imployed is caſt away ; and then others alſo deride his pains, as a fruitleſs deſign, and a labour ill placed : Laſt of all, the fcorner himſelf deſpiſeth the knowledge, which he hath learned. But the matter is tranſacted with greater danger in the *reprehenſion of the wicked* ; becauſe a wicked nature, not only gives no ear to advice, but turns head againſt his *Reprehender*, now made odious unto him ; whom he either wounds preſently with contumelies ; or traduces afterwards to others.

THE PARABLE.

VII. *A wiſe Son is the gladneſs of his Father ; but* Prov.x. *a fooliſh Son is the ſadneſs of his Mother.*

THE EXPLICATION.

THe *joys* and *griefs domeſtical* of *Father* and *Mother* touching their Children, are here diſtinguiſht : for a wiſe and well-govern'd Son, is chiefly a comfort, to the Father, who knows the value of virtue, better than the Mother, and therefore more rejoyceth at the towardlineſs of his Son inclinable to goodneſs : yea, and it may be his education of him, that he hath brought him up ſo well ; and implanted in his tender years the Civility of manners, by precepts and example, is a joy unto him. *On the other ſide*, the Mother is more griev'd, and diſcomforted at the calamity of a Son, both becauſe the affection of a Mother is more ſoft and tender ; as alſo perchance, being conſcious of her too much indulgence, ſhe hath tainted and corrupted his tender years.

THE PARABLE.

VIII. *The memory of the Juſt is bleſt ; but the name* Prov.x. *of the wicked ſhall putrifie.*

THE EXPLICATION.

HEre is diſtinguiſht the *Fame* of good men and of evil, ſuch as commonly falls out after Death : for the *Name* of good men, after envy is extinguiſht, (which cropt the bloſſom of their *Fame*, while they were alive) preſently ſhoots up and flouriſheth ; and their *Praiſes* dayly encreaſe in ſtrength and vigor : but for wicked men (though their Fame through the partial favour of Friends, and of men of their own faction laft for a fhort time) a deteftation of their *Name* fprings up, and at laft their tranfient glory exhales in infamy, and expires in a filthy and noifom odour.

THE PARABLE.

Prov. xi. **IX.** *He that troubles his own houfe fhall inherit the wind.*

THE EXPLICATION.

A Very profitable admonition touching *Difcord and Domeftick breaches.* Many promife to themfelves great matters, *by the diffentions of Wives;* or the *Dif-inheriting of Sons; or the* often *changing of Servants;* as if the Tranquillity of mind; or the adminiftration of their affairs were by this means advanced, and fhould become more profperous unto them. But commonly *their hopes turn to wind;* for thofe alterations, for moft part, fucceed ill, and thofe *Perturbers of their own houfe* oftentimes meet with many vexations, and ingratitudes from *them,* whom (paffing by others) they adopted and loved: Nay, by this means they draw upon their Perfons ill Reports, De Pet. Conful. and doubtful rumours. For it is well noted of *Cicero, Omnem famam à Domefticis emanare.* Both thefe evils *Solomon* excellently expreffes by the *inheritance of Winds:* For the *Fruftrating of Expectation,* and the *raifing of Rumours,* are rightly compared to *Winds.*

THE PARABLE.

Ecclef. vii. **X.** *Better is the end of a Speech, than the beginning thereof.*

THE EXPLICATION.

THis Parable taxeth, and reforms a frequent error committed, not only by them which chiefly *ftudy words;* but even by the more wife and grave. The error is this, *that men are more follicitous of the ingrefs and entrance of their fpeech; than of the clofe and iffue: and more exactly meditate the Exordiums and Prefaces; than the conclufions of Speeches.* But they fhould neither neglect thofe, and yet have thefe about them, as the more material parts, ready prepar'd and digefted; confidering with themfelves, and, fo far as may be, fore-cafting in their minds, what may be the iffue of fpeech and conference at laft; and bufineffes thereby may be promoted and matured. Yet this is not all; for you muft not only *ftudy Epilogues, and conclufions of Speeches, which may be pertinent to bufinefs; but alfo regard muft be taken of fuch Speeches, as may aptly and pleafantly be caft in, at the very inftant of your departure, although they have no reference at all to the bufinefs in hand.* I knew two Counfellors,

Perfonages

Perſonages of high rank, and wiſe men; and on whom the charge of State affairs did then principally depend ; whoſe common, and, to them, peculiar cuſtom it was , that ſo often as they were to nego- ciate with their Princes about their own affairs ; never to cloſe their conference with any matter referring to that buſineſs ; but ever ſeek diverſions, either by way of jeſt ; or by ſomewhat that was delight- ful to hear ; and ſo, as the Adages render it, *waſh over at the concluſion of all, their Sea-water diſcourſes, with freſh fountain water.*   And this uſage was one of their chief Arts.

THE PARABLE

XI. *As dead Flies. cauſe the beſt oyntment to ſend* Ecclef.x:
*forth an ill Odour ; ſo doth a little folly him that is in
reputation for wiſdom and honour.*

THE EXPLICATION.

THe caſe of Men remarkable *for eminent gifts ,* is very unhap- py and miſerable (as the *Parable* excellently notes,) becauſe their errors, be they never ſo ſmall find no remiſſion.   *But as in a pure Diamond* every leaſt grain, or little cloud ſtrikes the eye, and af- fects it with a kind of trouble ; which upon a more groſs Diamond would hardly be diſcerned : even ſo in men of eminent parts, the leaſt infirmities are preſently ſpied, talked of, and more deeply cen- ſur'd ; which in men of more mean and obſcure gifts, and rank , would either altogether paſs without notice, or eaſily procure par- don.   *Therefore a little Folly in a very wiſe man ; and a ſmall offence in a very honeſt man ; and a ſlight indecency of manners, in a man of Courtly and Elegant behaviour ; much derogates from their fame and re- putation.*   So that it is not the worſt courſe for eminent perſons, *to mingle ſome abſurdities* (ſo it may be done without guilt) *in their A- ctions ;* that they may retain a kind of liberty to themſelves, and con- found the characters of ſmaller defects.

THE PARABLE.

XII. *Scornful men inſnare a City , but wiſe men di-* Prov.xx.12.
vert Wrath.

THE EXPLICATION.

IT may ſeem ſtrange, that *Solomon* in the deſcription of men made, as it were, and by nature fram'd to the ruine and deſtruction of a ſtate, hath choſen the character ; *not of* a proud and inſolent man ; *not of* a tyrannical and cruel nature, *not of* a raſh and violent man ;

not of an impious and wicked perſon; *not of* a ſeditious and turbulent ſpirit; *not of* an incontinent and ſenſual inclination; *not of* a
fooliſh and and unhabile Perſon; *but of a Scorner.* But this is a
judgement worthy the wiſdom of that King, who beſt knew the
grounds of the conſervation, or everſion of a State. For there is
not commonly a like Plague to Kingdoms and Common-wealths,
than if Counſellors of Princes, or Senators, and ſuch as ſit at the helm
of Government, are by nature *Scorners.* For ſuch perſons, that they
may win the reputation of undanted States-men, do ever extenuate
the greatneſs of dangers, and inſult over thoſe that value dangers,
according to the true weight; as timorous and faint-hearted natures.
They *ſcoff* at all mature delays, and meditated debatings of matters
by conſultation, and deliberation; as a thing too much taſting of
an oratory-vein; and full of tediouſneſs; and nothing conducing
to the ſum and iſſues of Buſineſs. *As for Fame,* at which the counſels of Princes ſhould eſpecially level, they contemn it, *as the ſpirit
of the vulgar,* and a thing will be quickly blown over. *The Power*
and Authority of Laws, they reſpect no more, than as cobwebs, which
ſhould not inſnare matters of greater conſequence: *Counſels* and Pre-
cautions, foreſeeing events a far off, they reject, as meer dreams and
melancholy apprehenſions: *men ſeriouſly* wiſe, and well ſeen in the
world, and of great reſolution and counſel, they defame with gibes
and jeſts: *in a word,* they do at once prejudice and weaken the whole
foundation of Civil Goverument; which is the more to be looked
into, becauſe the Action is performed by ſecret fraud, and not open
force; and is a practice not ſo ſuſpected, as it demerits.

THE PARABLE.

Prov. XXIX. **XIII.** *A Prince that lends a willing ear to lies, his
ſervants are all wicked.*

THE EXPLICATION.

WHen a *Prince,* is of ſuch a temper, as to *lend an eaſie and credulous ear, without due examination, to Detractors and Sy-
cophants,* there breaths a peſtilential Air from the *Kings* ſide; which
corrupts and infects all his ſervants. Some feel out the fears and jealouſies of a *Prince;* and aggravate the ſame with feign'd reports. *O-
thers* awake the furies of envy, eſpecially againſt the beſt deſerving
in the ſtate: *Others* ſeek to waſh away their own guilt, and the
ſtains of a foul conſcience, by defaming others: *Others* give ſail to
the Honours and wiſhes of their friends, by traducing, and debaſing
the merit of their competitors: *Others* compoſe Fabulous enter-
ludes againſt their enemies, and concurrents, as if they were upon
the ſtage; *and* infinite ſuchlike. And theſe are the Arts of ſuch ſervants to Princes, as are of a vile and baſe nature. But they that are
of a more honeſt diſpoſition, and better civiliz'd, when they perceive
their

their innocence to be no safe sanctuary (in that their Prince knows not how to distinguish between truth and falshood) they put off moral honesty, and gather in the Court-winds ; and are therewith carried about in a servile manner.   For as *Tacitus* saith of *Claudius. There is no safety with that Prince , into whose head all things are conveyed, as it were, by infusion and direction from others.*   And *Commines* very well, *It is better to be servant to a Prince, whose jealousies have no end, than to a Prince, whose Credulity hath no mean.*

THE PARABLE.

XIV. *A Just man is merciful to the life of his Beast ;* Prov. xii.
but the mercies of the wicked are cruel.

THE EXPLICATION.

THere is implanted in man by nature , a noble and excellent affection of *Piety and Compassion,* which extends it self even to brute creatures, that are by divine ordination subject to *his* command : and this *Compassion* hath some Analogy with that of a Prince towards his subjects.   Nay farther, it is most certain, that the more noble the mind is , the more compassionate it is ; for contracted and degenerate minds think these things nothing to pertain to them ; but the Mind, which is a nobler portion of the world, is affected in the gross out of community.   Wherefore we see that there were under the old Law, many Precepts, not so merely *Ceremonial,* as *Institutions of Mercy* ; such as was that *of not eating flesh with the blood thereof,* and the like : even in the sect of the *Esseans* and *Pythagoreans,* they altogether abstain'd from *eating Flesh* ; which to this day is observed by an inviolate superstition, by many of the Eastern people under the *Mogol.*   Nay the Turks, (both by Descent and Discipline a cruel and bloody Nation) yet bestow alms upon brute Creatures ; and cannot endure to see the vexation and torture of any live thing.   But lest, what we have said, should perchance seem to maintain all kinds of *Mercy* ; *Solomon* upon sound advice annexeth, *That the mercies of the wicked are cruel* : These *Mercies,* are, when lewd and wicked persons are spar'd from being cut off by the sword of justice ; this kind of *Mercy* is more *Cruel,* than *Cruelty* it self : for *Cruelty* is extended in practice on particulars ; but this kind of *Mercy,* by a grant of impunity, arms and suborns the whole band of impious men against the innocent.

THE PARABLE.

Prov.xxıx. XV. *A Fool utters all his mind; but a wise man re-*
ferves fomewhat for hereafter.

THE EXPLICATION.

THe Parable (it feems) efpecially corrects; *not the futility* of vain
Perfons, which eafily utter, as well what may be fpoken, as
what fhould be fecreted: *not the bold roving language* of fuch as without all difcretion and judgement fly upon all men and matters: *Not*
Garrulity, whereby they fill others even to a furfeit: *but another vice,*
more clofe and retired; namely *the Government of fpeech,* of all adventures the leaft prudent and politick, which is, *when a man fo ma-*
nages his fpeech in private conference, as whatfoever is in his mind,
which he conceives any way pertinent to the purpofe and matter in hand,
out it muft at once,as it were,in one breath,and in a fet continued difcourfe:
this is that which doth much prejudice Bufinefs. *For firft, a difconti-*
nued fpeech, broken off by interlocutions, and inftill'd by parts, penetrates deeper, than a *fetled continued fpeech;* becaufe that in a continued Difcourfe, the weight of Matters is not precifely and diftinctly taken, nor by fome convenient refts fuffer'd to fix; but Reafon
drives out Reafon before it be fully fetled in the Comprehenfion of
the Hearers. *Secondly* there is no man of fo powerful and happy a
Delivery of himfelf, as at the firft onfet and encounter of his fpeech,
he is able fo to ftrike him dumb and fpeechlefs, with whom he difcourfeth; but that the other will make fome interchangeable reply,
and peradventure object fomething, and then it may fall out, that
what fhould have been referv'd for refutation and replication, by this
unadvifed anticipation being difclofed and tafted before-hand, loof-
eth its ftrength and grace. *Thirdly* if a man difcharge not all at once
what might be faid, but deliver himfelf by *Parcels,* now one thing,
anon cafting in another, he fhall gather from the looks and anfwers
of him with whom he difcourfes, how every particular Paffage affects
him, and in what fort they find acceptation; fo as what is yet remaining to be fpoken, he may with greater Caution either felect, or
filence.

THE PARABLE.

Ecclef.x. XVI. *If the difpleafure of a Great Man rife up againft*
thee, forfake not thy Place ; for pliant demeanure
pacifies great Offences.

THE

THE EXPLICATION.

THe Parable gives in Precept, how a man ought to demean himself, having incurr'd the wrath and displeasure of his Prince. The Precept hath two branches. First *that he relinquish not his place*; Secondly, *that with caution and diligence he attend the Cure, as in case of some dangerous disease.* For men are wont after they perceive their Princes displeasure against them, to retire themselves from the execution of their charge and office; *partly* out of an impatience of disgrace; *partly* lest they should revive the wound by being in the Presence; *partly* that Princes may see their sorrow and humility; *nay sometimes* to resign up the Places and Dignities they held, into the hands of the Prince. But *Solomon* censures this way of *Cure*, as prejudicious and hurtful; and that upon a very good ground. *For first this course doth too much noise abroad the disgrace it self*; so as enemies and enviers become more confident to hurt, and friends more fearful to help him. *Secondly it comes to pass that the wrath of the Prince*, which perchance, if it had not been publisht, would have died of it self, is now become more fixt; and having once made way to his ruine, is carried on to his utter subversion. *Lastly, this retiring tasts somewhat of a malignant humour, and of one fallen out with the times*; *which cumulates the evil of* Indignation, *to the evil of suspicion :* Now the precepts for cure are these. *First, above all things let him take heed that he seem not insensible, or not so affected, as in duty he ought to be, for the Prince's displeasure, through a stupidity or stubborness of mind :* that is, that he compose his countenance, not to a sullen and contumacious sadness; but to a grave and modest pensiveness; and in all matters of imployment, that he shew himself less pleasant, and chearful than he was wont to be; and it will promote his case to use the assistance and mediation of some friend, unto the Prince, which may seasonably insinuate, with what feeling grief he is inwardly afflicted. *Secondly let him carefully avoid all, even the least occasions whereby the matter, that gave the first cause to the indignation, might be reviv'd*; or the Prince take occasion to be again displeased with him, or to rebuke him for any thing, before others. *Thirdly, let him with all diligence seek out all occasions wherein his service may be acceptable to his Prince*; that he may shew both a prompt affection to redeem his fore-past offence; and *that his Prince may understand what a good servant he may chance to be deprived of*, if he thus cast him off. *Fourthly, that by a wise art of Policy, he either lay the fault it self upon others*; *or insinuate, that it was committed with no ill intention*; *or make remonstrance of their Malice, who accused him to the King, and aggravated the matter above demerit. Last of all, let him be every way circumspect and intent upon the Cure.*

THE PARABLE.

XVII. *The First in his own cause is Just ; than* [Prov. xviii.]
comes the other Party and enquires into him.

K k   THE

THE EXPLICATION.

THe firſt information in any cauſe, if it a little fix it ſelf in the mind of the Judge, takes deep root, and wholly ſeaſons and prepoſſeſſeth it ; ſo as it can hardly be taken out, unleſs ſome manifeſt falſhood be found in the matter of Information ; or ſome cunning dealing, in exhibiting and laying open the ſame. For a bare and ſimple defence, though it be juſt and more weighty, hardly compenſates the prejudice of the firſt information ; or is of force of it ſelf to reduce the ſcales of Juſtice, once ſway'd down, to an equal weight. *Wherefore* it is the ſafeſt courſe both for the Judge, that nothing touching the proofs and merit of the cauſe, be intimated before-hand until both parties be heard together ; and the beſt for the Defendant, if he perceive the Judge preoccupated ; to labour principally in this (ſo far as the quality of the cauſe will admit) to diſcover ſome cunning ſhift and fraudulent dealing practiſed by the adverſe party to the abuſe o the Ju d ge.

Prov. xxix.

THE PARABLE.

XVIII. *He that delicately brings up his ſervant from a child, ſhall find him contumacious in the end.*

THE EXPLICATION.

Machia. Diſcorſo ſopra. Liv.

*P*Rinces *and* Maſters, from the Counſel of *Solomon, muſt keep a mean in the diſpenſation of their Grace and Favour towards Servants.* The mean is three-fold ; *Firſt that Servants be promoted by degrees and not by faults.* Secondly, *that they be now and then accuſtomed to repulſes :* Thirdly, (which Machiavel well adviſeth) *that they have ever in ſight before them ſomething whither to they may farther aſpire.* For unleſs theſe courſes be taken in the raiſing of ſervants, Princes ſhall bear away from their ſervants, inſtead of a thankful acknowledgement and dutiful obſervances, nothing but *diſreſpect and contumacy :* for from ſudden promotion ariſeth inſolency ; from a continued atchievement of their deſires, an impatience of Repulſe : if the accompliſhment of wiſhes be wanting ; alacrity and induſtry will likewiſe be wanting.

THE PARABLE.

Prov. xxii.

XIX. *Seeſt thou a man of Diſpatch in his Buſineſs ; he ſhall ſtand before Kings, he ſhall not be ranked amongſt mean men.*

THE EXPLICATION.

Amongſt the qualities which Princes do chiefly reſpect and require in the choice of their ſervants, *celerity and alacrity in the Diſpatch of Buſineſs, is above all the reſt, moſt acceptable.* Men of *profound Wiſdom* are ſuſpected by Kings, as men too ſpeculative and penetrating, and ſuch as are able by the ſtrength of wit, as with an engine, to turn and wind their Maſters, beyond their comprehenſion and againſt their inclination. *Popular natures* are ſpighted as thoſe that ſtand in the light of Kings, and draw the eyes of the people upon themſelves. *Men of courage,* are commonly taken for turbulent ſpirits, and daring, more than is meet. *Honeſt men* and of an impartial upright converſation, are eſteemed too ſtiff and Stoical; nor ſo pliable as they ſhould be to the whole pleaſure of thoſe on whom they depend. *To conclude,* there is not any other good quality which preſents not ſome ſhadow, wherewith the minds of Kings may not be offended; *only quickneſs of Diſpatch in the execution of command, hath nothing in it which may not pleaſe.* 'Again, the motions of the minds of Kings are ſwift and impatient of delay; for they think they can do all things; only this is wanting, *that it be done out of hand;* wherefore above all other qualities, *celerity is to them moſt acceptable.*

THE PARABLE.

XX. *I ſaw all the living which walk under the ſun, with the ſucceeding young Prince, that ſhall riſe up in his ſtead.* Eccleſ.IV.

THE EXPLICATION.

THe parable notes *the vanity of men who are wont to preſs and flock about the deſigned ſucceſſors of Princes:* The root of this vanity is that Frenzie, implanted by nature in the minds of men, which is, that they too extremely affect their own projected hopes. *For the man is rarely found that is not more delighted with the contemplation of his future Hopes, than with the fruition of what he poſſeſſeth.* So further, *Novelty is pleaſing to mans nature, and earneſtly deſired.* Now in a ſucceſſour to a Prince theſe two concur, *Hope and Novity.* The Parable expreſſeth the ſame which was long ago utter'd firſt by *Pompeius* to *Sylla,* after by *Tiberius* touching *Macro; Plures adorare ſolem Orientem quam Occidentem.* Yet notwithſtanding Princes in preſent poſſeſſion, are not much mov'd with this fond humour; nor make any great matter of it, as neither *Sylla* nor *Tiberius* did, but rather ſmile at the levity of men, and do not ſtand to fight with *Dreams;* for *Hope* (as he ſaid) *is but the Dream of a man awake.* Tacit. Annal.5. Plutar.in Pomp.

THE PARABLE.

Ecclef. 1x.   XXI. *There was a little City, and mann'd but by a few; and there was a mighty King that drew his army to it, and erected bulwarks against it, and intrench'd it round. Now there was found within the walls a poor wise man, and he by his wisdom rais'd the siege, but none remembred that same poor man.*

THE EXPLICATION.

THis *Parable* describeth the depraved and malignant nature of Men : In extremity and straits they commonly flie for sanctuary to men of wisdom and power, whom before they despis'd ; but so soon as the storm is gone, they become unthankful creatures to their Discorso fopra Liv. Lib. 1. confervers. *Machiavel* not without reason propounds a Question, *whether should be more ingrateful to well deserving Persons, the Prince or the People ?* But in the mean time, he taxeth them both of Ingratitude. Notwithstanding, this vile dealing ariseth not from the ingratitude of the Prince or People alone ; but oft-times there is added to these *the envy of the Nobility*, who in secret repine at the event, though happy and prosperous ; because it proceeded not from themselves ; wherefore they extenuate the merit of the Act, and depress the Author.

THE PARABLE.

Prov. 15.   XXII. *The way of the slothful is a Hedge of Thorns.*

THE EXPLICATION.

THe Parable expresseth most elegantly, *that sloth proves laborious in the end:* For a diligent and sedulous preparation effects this, that the foot doth not strike it self against any impediment, but that the way is levell'd before it be gone. But he that is slothful and puts off all to the last point of Execution, it must needs follow, that continually, and at every step he passes, as it were, through Briars and Brambles, which ever and anon entangle and detain him. The same observation may be made upon the governing of a Family, wherein if there be a care and providence taken, all goes on cheerfully, and with a willing alacrity, without noise or tumult : but if these fore-casts be wanting, when some greater occasions unexpectedly

ly

ly fall out, all matters throng in to be difpatched at once; the fervants brawl; the whole houfe rings.

THE PARABLE.

XXIII. *He that refpects Perfons in judgement doth* Prov.xxviii.
*not well; for that man will forfake the truth even
for a piece of Bread.*

THE EXPLICATION.

THe Parable moft wifely noteth that in a Judge, *Facility of Deport-
ment is more pernicious than the corruption of Bribes:* for all perfons do not give Bribes; but there is hardly any caufe wherein
fomewhat may not be found, that may incline the mind of the
Judge, if *Refpect of Perfons* lead him. For one fhall be refpected as
a Country-man; another as an ill-tongu'd man; another as a Rich
man; another as a Favourite; another as commended by a Friend;
and to conclude, all is full of iniquity, where *Refpect of Perfons
bears rule*; and for a very flight matter, as it were, *for a piece of
Bread,* Judgement is perverted.

THE PARABLE.

XXIV. *A poor man that by extortion oppreffeth the* Prov.xxviii.
poor, is like a land-floud that caufes famine.

THE EXPLICATION.

THis Parable was by the Ancients expreft and fhadowed forth, under the Fable of the *two Horfe-leeches,* the Full and the Hungry:
for *Oppreffion coming from the Poor and neceffitous perfons, is far more
heavy than the Oppreffion caufed by the Full and Rich; becaufe it is fuch
as feeks out all Arts of Exaction, and all Angles for Money.* This kind
of Oppreffion was wont alfo to be refembled to *fpunges,* which being
dry, fuck in ftrongly; not fo, being moift. The *Parable* comprehends in it a fruitful Inftruction, both to Princes, that they commit
not the government of Provinces, or offices of charge to indigent
and indebted perfons; as alfo to people that they fuffer not their
Kings to be diftreffed with too much want.

THE

THE PARABLE.

PROV. XXV.   **XXV.** *A just man falling before the wicked, is a troubled fountain, and a corrupted spring.*

THE EXPLICATION.

THE Parable gives it in Precept, *that States and Republicks must above all things beware of an unjust and infamous sentence, in any cause of grave importance, and exemplar in the face of the world; specially where the guilty is not quitted, but the innocent is condemned.* For Injuries ravaging among private Persons, do indeed *trouble,* and *pollute the waters of Justice,* yet as in the *smaller streams;* but *unjust Judgements,* such as we have spoken of, from which examples are derived, infect and distain the very *Fountains of Justice:* for when the *Courts of Justice* side with *Injustice,* the state of things is turned, as into a *publick Robbery,* and it manifestly comes to pass, *ut Homo Homini sit Lupus.*

THE PARABLE

PROV. XXVI.   **XXVI.** *Make no friendship with any angry man; nor walk thou with a furious man.*

THE EXPLICATION.

BY how much the more devoutly the Laws of Friendship amongst good men, are to be kept and observed, by so much the more it stands us upon to use all Caution, even at first in a prudent election of Friends. *In like manner the disposition and humours of Friends, so far as concerns our personal interest, should by all means be dispensed withall: but when they impose a necessity upon us, what quality of persons we must put on, and sustain; it is a very hard case, and an unreasonable condition of Friendship.* Wherefore according to *Solomon's* Precept, it principally conduceth to Peace, and Safety in the course of this world, *that we intermingle not our affairs with Cholerick natures,* and such as easily provoke and undertake Quarrels and Debates; for such kind of Friends will daily espouse us to Factions and Contentions; that we must of necessity be forced to break off all terms of Friendship; or else be wanting to our own personal safety.

THE PARABLE.

XXVII. *He that conceals a fault seeks friendship;* Prov. xvii.
*but he that repeats a matter, separates united
friends.*

THE EXPLICATION.

THe way to arbitrate differences, and to reconcile affections is of
two forts. The one begins by an *Amnesty*, and passing over that
which is past. The other, *from a Repetition of wrongs, interlacing A-
pologies and Excusations.* For I remember the speech of a very wife
Person, and a great States-man, which was to this effect; *He that
deals about a Treaty of Peace, without any recapitulation of the terms
of Difference, and falling out, he rather deludes mens minds with the
sweetness of an Agreement, than compounds the differences, by equity
and moderation of Right.* But *Solomon,* a wifer man than he; is of a
contrary opinon, approves *Amnesty,* and prohibites *Repetition,* for in
Repetition, there are thefe inconveniences, for that it is, as it were,
unguis in ulcere, the nail in the ulcer; as alfo, *there is a danger of breeding a new Quarrel,* for the Parties at difference will never accord
upon the terms of their falling out. And laftly, *for that in the issue,
it brings the matter to Apologies:* but both the one and the other
Party, would feem rather to remit an offence, than to admit of an ex-
cufation.

THE PARABLE.

XXVIII. *In every good work there shall be abun-* Prov. xiv.
*dance; but where words do abound, there com-
monly is want.*

THE EXPLICATION.

IN this Parable *Solomon separates the the fruit of the Labour of the
Tongue, and of the Labour of the Hands; as if Wealth were the Revenues of the one, want the Revenues of the other.* For it commonly
comes to pafs, that they that talk much, boaft many things, and promife great matters; receive no emolument from the things whereof
they difcourfe: nay, rather fuch natures for moft part are no way
induftrious, and diligent at work; but only feed and fill themfelves
with words, as with wind. Certainly, as faith the Poet,

——— *Qui silet est firmus* ———

for he that is conscious to himself of proficiency in his indeavours, applauds himself inwardly, and holds his peace; but on the contrary, he that is guilty to himself of hunting after vain glory, talks many things, and reports wonders to others.

THE PARABLE.

Prov. xxvii. **XXIX.** *Open Reprehension is better than secret Affection.*

THE EXPLICATION.

THe Parable reprehends the soft nature of Friends, which will not use the priviledge of friendship, in admonishing their Friends with freedom and confidence, as well of their errors as of their dangers. *For what shall I do?* (will such a tender hearted friend say) *or which way shall I turn my self? I love him as dearly as any man can do; and if any misfortune should befall him, I could willing impawn my own person for his redemption; but I know his disposition, if I deal freely with him, I shall offend him, at least make him sad, and yet do no good; and I shall sooner estrange him from my friendship, than reclaim him, or withdraw him from those courses, which he hath fixt and resolved upon in his mind.* Such a friend as this, *Solomon* here reprehends, as weak and worthless; and that a man may reap more profit from a manifest Enemy, than from such an effeminate Friend: for he may perchance hear that by way of reproach from an Enemy, which through too much indulgence was but faintly whisper'd by a friend.

THE PARABLE.

XXX. *A wise man is wary of his ways; a cunning Fool seeks evasions.*

THE EXPLICATION.

THere be two sorts of wisdom; *the one true and sound, the other counterfeit and false,* which Solomon *doubts not to entitle by the name of* Folly. He that applies himself to the former, *takes heed to his way and footing, fore-seeing dangers, and studying remedies; using the assistance of good men, muniting himself against the invasions of the wicked; wary in his entrance and engagement upon a business, not unprepar'd of a retreat, and how to come off; attent upon advantages, couragious against encounters; with infinite other circumstances, which respect the government of his ways and actions.* But that other kind wisdom *is altogether made up of fallacies and cunning devices, and wholly relies upon circumventing of others, and casting them according to the form of their own mould.* This wisdom the Parable deservedly rejects, not only as *Wicked, but also as foolish. For first* it is not in the number of those things, which are in our own power; nor is

it

it directed by any constant Rule; but new stratagems must every day be contrived, the old failing and growing out of use. *Secondly*, he that is once attainted with the same and opinion of a *cunning crafty Companion*, hath deprived himself of a principal Instrument for the manage of his affairs, and a practical life, that is, *Trust*; and so he shall find by experience all things to go *Cross* to his desires. *To conclude*, these Arts and Shifts, howsoever they promise fair, and much please such as practise them; yet are they many times frustrated. Which *Tacitus* hath well observed, *Consilia Callida & audacia, expectatione læta; tractatu dura; eventu tristia.*   Tacit.

THE PARABLE.

XXXI. *Be not too precisely Righteous; nor make thy self too excessively wise; why should'st thou unseasonably sacrifice thy safety?*   Eccl.vi 2,

THE EXPLICATION.

THere are *Times* (saith *Tacitus*) *wherein too great vertues are exposed to certain ruine*. And this fate befals men eminent for Vertue or Justice, sometimes suddenly, sometimes fore-seen a far off: and if these excellent parts be seconded by the access of *wisdom*, that is, that they are wary and watchful over their own safety, then they gain thus much, that their ruine comes suddenly, altogether by secret and obscure counsels; whereby both envy may be avoided, and destruction assail them unprovided. As for that *Nimium*, which is set down in the Parable, (in as much as they are not the words of some *Periander*, but of *Solomon*, who now and then notes the evils in man's life, but never commands them)it must be understood, not of vertue it self, in which there is no *Nimium* or excessive extremity, but of a vain and invidious Affectation and Ostentation *thereof*. A point somewhat resembling this, *Tacitus* insinuates in a passage touching *Lepidus*, setting it down as a Miracle, that he had never been the Author of any servile sentence, and yet had stood safe in so cruel and bloody times. *This thought* (saith he) *many times comes into my mind, whether these things are governed by Fate; or it lies also in our own Power to steer an even course void of Danger and Indignity, between servile Flattery and sullen Contumacy.*   Annal. iv.

THE PARABLE.

XXXII. *Give occasion to a wiseman and his wisdom will be increased.*   Prov.ix.

THE EXPLICATION.

THe Parable distinguishes between that *wisdom which is grown, and ripened into true Habit; and that which swims only in the Brain and conceit, or is boasted in speech, but hath not taken deep root.* For the one upon occasion presented, wherein it may be exercis'd, is instantly quickned, prepared, and dilated, so as it seems greater than it self: but the other which before occasion was quick and active, now occasion is given, becomes amaz'd and confused, that even he who presumed the possession thereof, begins to call into doubt whether the preconceptions of *such wisdom* were not meer Dreams, and empty speculations.

THE PARABLE.

Prov. xxvii. **XXXIII.** *He that praiseth his friend aloud, rising early, it shall be to him no better than a curse.*

THE EXPLICATION.

Oderate and seasonable *Praises*, and utter'd upon occasion, *much* conduce both to mens *Fame* and *Fortunes* ; *but immoderate, streporous, and unseasonably pour'd out, profit nothing, nay rather from the sence of this Parable they do much prejudice.* For *first,* they manifestly betray themselves to proceed either from too extreme *Affection,* or from a too studied *Affectation,* to the end that him whom they have thus praised, they may by false acclamations demerit rather to themselves ; than by just attributes adorn his person. *Secondly,* sparing and modest *Praises,* commonly invite such as are present to add something of their own to the commendations ; Contrarywise profuse and immodest Praises, invite the hearers to detract and take away something. *Thirdly,* (which is the principal point) *too much magnifying a man* stirs up envy towards him ; seeing all *immoderate Praises* seem to be a Reproach to others, who merit no less,

THE PARABLE.

Prov. xxvi. **XXXIV.** *As Faces shine in waters, so mens hearts are manifest to the wise.*

THE EXPLICATION.

He *Parable distinguisheth between the Hearts of wise men and of other Men* ; comparing those to waters or glasses, which receive and represent the forms and Images of things ; whereas the other are like to Earth, or rude stone, wherein nothing is reflected. And the more aptly is the mind of a wise-man compar'd to a *Glass* or Mirror ; because in a *Glass* his own *Image* may be seen together with the *Images* of others ; which the eyes cannot do of themselves without a *Glass.* Now if the mind of a wise man be so capable, as to observe and comprehend such an infinite diversity of Natures and Customs, it remains

to

to be endeavour'd, that it may become no less various in the Application, than it is in the Representation,

> *Qui sapit, innumeris Moribus aptus erit.*   Ovid.de A.A.

THus have we staid perchance somewhat longer upon these *Parables of Solomon,* than is agreeable to the proportion of an example, being carried away thus far for the Dignity both of the matter it self, and of the Author.   Neither was this in use only with the Hebrews, but it is generally to be found in the wise men of ancient times; that if any mans observation lite upon any thing that was good and beneficial to the common practick course of life, he would reduce and contract it into some *short sentence* or *Parable,* or else *some Fable.* But for *Fables* (as we have noted elsewhere) they were in times Lib.2.cap. 12. past *Vicegerents,* and *supplements of Examples*; now that the times abound with *History,* the aim is more right and Active, when the Mark is alive.   But the form of writing which best agrees with so variable and universal an Argument (as is the handling of *negotiations and scatter'd Occasions*) that would be of all other the fittest which *Machiavel* made choice of, for the handling of matters of *Policy and Government*; Discorso la namely by *Observations or Discourses,* as they term them, upon *History* and *Examples.*   For knowledge drawn freshly, and, as it were in our view, out of *Particulars,* knows the way best to *Particulars* again; and it hath much greater life for Practice, when the *Discourse* or *Disceptation* attends upon the *Example,* than when the *Example* attends upon the *Disceptation :* for here not only *Order* but *Substance* is respected.   For when the *Example* is set down as the Ground of the *Disputation,* it useth to be propounded with the preparation of circumstances, which may sometimes controul the *discourse* thereupon made; sometimes supply it; so it may be in place of a pattern for imitation and practice : whereas on the contrary, *examples* alledged for the *Disputations* sake, are cited succinctly and simply, and as bondmen wait, in a servil aspect, upon the commands of the *Discourse.* But this difference is not amiss to be observed, *that as Histories of Times afford the best matter for Discourses upon Politicks,* such as are those of Machiavel; *So the Histories of lives, are the best Instructions for discourse of Business;* because they comprize all variety of *Occasions and Negotiations,* as well great as small.

§ *Nay there is* a ground of Discourse for *Precepts touching Business,* more accommodate than both those *sorts of History*; which is, *when Discourses are made upon Letters, but such as are wise and serious,* as those of *Cicero ad Atticum,* and others.   For letters usually represent Business more particularly, and more to the life ; than either *Chronicles or Lives.*   Thus have we spoken both of the Matter and Form of the first portion of the *Knowledge of Negotiation,* which handles *dispersed Occasions,* which we deliver up upon the accompts of *Deficients.*

II. There is also another portion of the *same Knowledge,* which dif- FABER. fereth as much from that other, whereof we have spoken as *sapere,* and FORTU- *sibi sapere : for the one seems to move as it were, from the centre to the* Ambitu vitæ. NÆ. sive de *circumference ; the other as it were , from the circumference to the centre.* For there is a wisdom of giving *Counsel* unto others ; and there is a wisdom of forecasting for his own *fortunes* ; and these do sometimes meet, but more often sever, For many are exceeding wise in their own ways, which yet are weak for administration of civil affairs, or giving of Counsel, like the *Ant, which is a wise creature for it self, but very hurtful for the Garden.* This wisdom the Romans those excellent Patriots, did take much knowledge of ; whereupon the Comical Poet saith, *Certainly the Mould of a wise mans Fortune is in his own hands ;* yea it grew into an Adage among them,

Plaut.in Trin.
Cic.in Par.
Saluft.ad
Cæf.Lib.1.
Dec. iv.

Faber quisque Fortunæ propriæ—— ;

And *Livy* attributes the same virtue to *Cato Major : In this man there were such great abilities of wit and understanding, that into what climate soever his nativity had cast him, he seem'd to be able to command a fortune.* This kind of wisdom, if it be profest and openly declar'd, hath ever been thought not only impolitick, but an unlucky and ominous thing : as it was observed in *Timotheus* the *Athenian,* who after he had done many excellent services to the honour and utility of the state, and was to give an account of his government to the people, as the manner was, concluded every particular with this clause, *and in this, Fortune had no part :* but it fell out that he never prosper'd in any thing he took in hand afterwards. *This is in truth* too high and savouring of extreme arrogance, aspiring to the same point of Pride which *Ezekiel* records of *Pharaoh, Dicis fluvius est meus, & ego feci meipsum* ; or of that which another Prophet speaks, *They exult and offer sacrifices to their net, and burn incense to their snare.* or of that which the Poet expresseth of *Mezentius* a Despiser of the *Gods.*

Plutar.in Sylla.

Ezech 29.

Habac.1.

Virg.Æn. 10.

Dextra mihi Deus, & telum quod missile libro,
Nunc adsint.——

Finally Julius Cesar, never to my remembrance, betrayed the impotency of his hidden thoughts so much, as in a speech of like nature ; for when the *Augur* gave him information *that the entrails were not prosperous,* he closely murmur'd to himself *Erunt lætiora cum volo,* which saying of his preceded not long before the misfortune of his death. *But this extremity of Confidence,* (as we have said) as it is an unhallowed thing, so was it ever unblest. And therefore they that were great Politicks indeed, and truly wise, thought it their safest course, ever to ascribe their successes to their Felicity ; and not to their skill and virtue. So *Sylla* sirnam'd himself *Felix,* not *Magnus* ; and Cæsar (more advisedly than before) saith to the *Pilot, Cæsarem vehis, & fortunam ejus.* But yet nevertheless these Positions ; *Faber Quisque Fortunæ suæ. Sapiens dominabitur Astris. Invia virtuti nulla est via,* and the like ; if they be understood and applied rather as spurs to industry, than as stirrops to insolency ; and rather to beget in men courage and constancy of Resolutions, than Arrogancy and Ostentation ; are deservedly accounted sound and healthful ; and (no question) have been

Suet.in Julio.

Plut.in J.
Cæf.

ever imprinted in the greateſt Minds, ſo ſenſibly, as ſometimes they can ſcarce diſſemble ſuch cogitations. *For we ſee Auguſtus Cæſar* (who compared with his uncle, was rather diverſe, than inferiour, but certainly a perſon more ſtaid and ſolemn) when he died, deſired of his friends that ſtood about his Bed, *that when he expired they would give him a Plaudite* ; as if he were conſcient to himſelf, that he had plaid his part well upon the ſtage. *This portion* alſo of knowledge is to be ſumm'd up amongſt *Deficients* ; not but that it hath been uſurped and frequented in Practice, far more exceſſively than is fittting ; but becauſe books concerning *this Argument* are ſilent. *Wherefore* according to our cuſtom, as we did in the former ; we will ſet down ſome heads or paſſages of it ; and we will call it *Fabrum Fortunæ*, or as we have ſaid; ——*Doctrinam de Ambitu vitæ.*——Wherein, at the firſt view, I may ſeem to handle a new and ſtrange Argument, in teaching men how they may be *raiſers and makers of their own fortune* ; a doctrine certainly to which every man will willingly yield himſelf a Diſciple, till he throughly conceives the difficulty thereof. *For* the conditions are neither lighter, or fewer, or leſs difficult to the Purchaſe of Fortune, than to the purchaſe of virtue ; and it is as hard and ſevere a Thing to be a true *Politick*, as to be truly *Moral.* But the handling hereof concerns learning greatly, both in *Honour* and in *Subſtance.* For it is a principal point which nearly concerns the *Honour of Learning*, that Pragmatick men may know, *that Learning is not like ſome ſmall Bird, as the Lark, that can mount and ſing, and pleaſe her ſelf, and nothing elſe ; but that ſhe holds as well of the Hawk, that can ſoar aloft, and after that when ſhe ſees her time, can ſtoop and ſeize upon her prey.* Again this kind of *wiſdom* much reſpects the *Perfection of Learning* ; becauſe it is the right rule of a perfect enquiry, *that nothing be found in the Globe of Matter, that hath not a Parallel in the Chriſtalline Globe, or the Intellect :* That is, that there be not any thing in Being and Action, that ſhould not be drawn and collected into contemplation and Doctrine. Neither doth learning otherwiſe admire or eſteem *this Architecture of Fortune*, than as a work of an inferiour kind : for no mans proper fortune can be a retribution any way worthy the donation of his Eſſence and Being granted him from God ; nay it often comes to paſs, that men of excellent gifts abandon their Fortunes willingly, that their minds may be vacant for more ſublime reſpects : yet nevertheleſs *Fortune*, as an Organ of virtue and merit, deſerves likewiſe her ſpeculation and Doctrine.

§ *Unto this knowledge* appertain precepts, ſome *ſummary* and Principal ; ſome *ſpars'd* and *various.* Precepts *Summary* are converſant about the true knowledge *both of others ; and of himſelf.* The *firſt Precept*, wherein the principal point of the *knowledge of others* doth conſiſt, may be determined this ; that we procure to our ſelves, ſo far as may be, *that window* which *Momus* once required. He, when he ſaw in the frame of Mans heart, ſo many Angles and Receſſes, *found fault that there was not a window, through which a man might look into thoſe obſcure and crooked windings.* This *window* we ſhall obtain, if with all diligent circumſpection we purchaſe and procure unto our ſelves good information touching particular Perſons, with whom we negotiate and have

to

Suet. in Auguſt,

Plato de Rep.

to deal; as alfo of their natures, their defires, their ends, their cuftoms, their Helps and Advantages, whereby they are chiefly fupported and are powerful; and again, of their weakneffes and difadvantages, and where they lie moft open and are obnoxious; of their
Friends, Factions, Patrons and Dependancies; and again of their
Oppofites, Enviers, Competitors; as alfo their Modes, Times, and
Critical feafons of eafie Accefs.

Virg. Æn. iv.
Sola viri molles Aditus, & tempora noris.

Laftly the Principles and Rules which they have fet down to themfelves; and the like.   And this information muft be taken not only
of *Perfons*, but of Particular Actions alfo which are on Foot, from time
to time, and as it were hot upon the Anvil; how they are conducted
and fucceed; by whofe furtherances they are favour'd, by whom op-
pos'd, of what weight and moment they are, and what confequence
they infer; and the like.   *For the knowledge of prefent Actions* is not
only material in it felf, but hath this advantage alfo, as without it the
knowledge of Perfons will be very deceitful and erroneous: for *Men*
change with the *Actions*; and while they are implicated in Actions, engaged and and environed with bufinefs, they are one; when they return to their Nature, they are another.   Thefe *Informations* touching *Particulars*, respecting as well *Perfons* as *Actions*, are as the *Minor
Propofitions* in every *Active Syllogifm:* for no verity or excellency of
Obfervations or *Axioms* (whereof the *Major Propofitions Politick* are
made) can fuffice to ground a conclufion, if there be error and miftaking in the *Minor Propofition*.   And that fuch knowledge may be com-
Prov. xx.
paffed, *Solomon* is our furety, who faith—*Counfel in the Heart of a Man
is like a deep water, but a wife man will draw it out.*—And although the
knowledge it felf fall not under Precept, becaufe it is of Individuals,
yet inftructions for the deducing of it may with profit be fet down.
§ The *knowledge of Men* fix ways may be difclofed and drawn out;
by their *Faces* and *Countenances*, by *Words*, by *Deeds*, by their *Nature*, by their *Ends*, and by the *Relations* of others.   As for the *Vifage*
and *Countenance*, let not the ancient Adage move us,

Juv. Sat. II.
Fronti nulla fides——

For though this faying may not amifs be meant of the outward and general compofure of the *Countenance* and *Gefture*, yet there are certain
fubtil motions and labours of the *Eyes*, *Face*, *Looks*, and *Gefture*,
whereby, as *Q. Cicero* elegantly faith, is unlockt and open'd—*Ianua
quædam animi*——*the gate of the mind.* Who more clofe than *Tiberius*
De Pet. Conf. *Cæfar?* But *Tacitus*, noting the Character and different manner of fpeaking, which *Tiberius* us'd in commending in the Senate the great fervices
done by *Germanicus* and *Drufus*; of the commendations given of *Germa-
Annal. i. nicus* he faith thus—*Magis in fpeciem verbis adornata, quam ut penitùs
fentire crederetur*, of the commendations given of *Drufus* thus,—*Paucio-
Annal. iv. ribus; fed intentior, & fidâ oratione.*   Again *Tacitus* noting the fame
Tiberius at other times fomewhat more clear and legible faith—*Quin
ipfe*

ipse compositus aliâs & velut ª *eluctantium verborum; solutiús prompti-*
usq; loquebatur quoties subveniret. Certainly there can hardly be
found any Artificer of *Diſſimulation* ſo cunning and excellent, or a
Countenance ſo forced, or as he ſaith — *vultus juſſus* — ſo commanded, that can ſever from an artificious and feigned ſpeech, theſe Notes ;
but that the ſpeech is either more *ſlight* and *careleſſ,* or more *ſet* and
formal, or more *tedious* and *wandring,* or more *dry* and *reluctant,*
than uſual.

Orl. & velut elector anxi-us.

§ As for Mens *words* they are (as Phyſicians ſay of *Waters*) full
of flattery and uncertainty ; yet theſe counterfeit colours are two
ways excellently diſcover'd ; namely when *words* are uttered either
upon the *ſudden,* or elſe in *paſſion.* So *Tiberius* being ſuddenly moved,
and ſomewhat incens'd upon a ſtinging ſpeech of *Agrippina,* came a
ſtep forth of his inbred diſſimulation. —— *Theſe words* ſaith Tacitus
heard by Tiberius, *drew from his dark covert Breaſt ſuch words*
as he us'd ſeldom to let fall ; and taking her up ſharply, told her her
own in a Greek verſe. *That ſhe was therefore hurt becauſe ſhe did not*
reign. Therefore the Poet doth not improperly call ſuch *Paſſions* ——
Tortures — becauſe they urge men to confeſs and betray their
ſecrets,

Annal. iv;

Vino tortus & Ira ——

Hor. Ep. l. 1,

Experience indeed ſhews that there are few men ſo true to themſelves, and ſo ſetled in their reſolves, but that ſometimes upon heat,
ſometimes upon bravery, ſometimes upon intimate good will to a
Friend, ſometimes upon weakneſs and trouble of mind, that can no
longer hold out under the weight of griefs ; ſometimes from ſome o-
ther Affection or Paſſion, they reveal and communicate their inward
Thoughts : but above all, it ſounds the mind to the bottom, and ſearch-
eth it to the quick, when Simulation is put to it by a counter-Diſſi-
mulation according to the proverb of *Spain,* Di *Mentira, y ſacaras*
verdad, Tell a lye and find a Truth.

§ Neither are *Deeds,* though they be the ſureſt pledges of mens
minds, altogether to be truſted without a diligent and judicious
conſideration of their *Magnitude* and *Nature :* For the ſaying is moſt
true, *That fraud erects it ſelf a countermure of credit in ſmaller matters,*
that it may cheat with better advantage afterwards. The *Italian* thinks
himſelf *upon the Croſs with the Cryer,* and upon the point to be
bought and ſold, when he is better uſed than he was wont to be,
without manifeſt cauſe : for ſmall favours, they do but lull men a
ſleep, both as to *caution,* and as to Induſtry, and are rightly called
by *Demoſthenes Alimenta ſocordiæ.* Again, we may plainly ſee the
falſe and inconſtant propriety and nature of ſome *Deeds,* even of
ſuch as are accounted *Benefits,* from that particular which *Mutianus*
practis'd upon *Antonius primus, who* upon that hollow and unfaithful
reconcilement made between them, advanced many of the Friends
of *Antonius,* and beſtowed *upon them Tribuneſhips, and Captainſhips*
liberally : by this ſubtile pretence of demerit, he did not ſtrengthen,
but altogether diſarm and deſolate *Antonius,* and win from him his
Dependances, and made them his own creatures.

Demoſt;

Tacitns H. ſt. iv.

§ But

§ But the fureſt key, to unlock the minds of Men, *conſiſts in ſearch-ing and diſcloſing either their Natures and diſpoſitions, or their ends and intentions.* And certainly the weakeſt and ſimpleſt ſort of men are beſt interpreted by their *Natures*; but the wiſeſt and more re-ſerved are beſt expounded by their *Ends.* For it was wiſely and pleaſantly ſaid (though in my judgement very untruly) by a *Nun-tio* of the Popes, returning from a certain Nation, where he ſerved as *Leidger*, whoſe opinion being askt, touching the appointment of one to go in his place, gave counſel, *that in any caſe his Hol. would not ſend one too wiſe, becauſe, ſaid he, no wiſe man would ever imagine, what they in that country were like to do.* Certainly it is a frequent error, and very familiar with wiſe men, to meaſure other men, by the Module of their own abilities; and therefore often ſhoot over the mark, ſuppoſing men to project and deſign to themſelves deeper ends, and to practiſe more ſubtil Arts, and compaſt reaches, than indeed ever came into their heads, which the *Italian* Proverb ele-gantly noteth, ſaying,

> Dì Denári, dì Sénno, e dì Féde
> C'n'è Mánco ché non Créde.

There is commonly leſſ Mony, leſſ Wiſdom, and leſſ good Faith than men do accompt. Wherefore if we be to deal with men of a mean and ſhallow capacity, becauſe they do many things abſurdly, the con-jecture muſt be taken rather from the proclivity of their *Natures*, than the deſigns of their *ends.* Furthermore, *Princes* (but upon a far o-ther reaſon) are beſt interpreted by their *Natures*; and *private per-ſons by their ends.* For *Princes* being at the top of humane Deſires, they have, for the moſt part, no particular ends propounded to them-

Prov. 25.

ſelves, whereto they aſpire, ſpecially with vehemency and perſe-verance; *by the ſite and diſtance of which ends*, a man might take mea-ſure and ſcale of the reſt of their *Actions*, and *Deſires*; which is one of the chief cauſes *that their Hearts* (as the Scripture pronounceth) *are inſcrutable.* But private perſons are like Travellers which intentive-ly go on aiming at ſome *end* in their journey, where they may ſtay and reſt; ſo that a man may make a probable conjecture and pre-ſage upon them, what they would, or would not *Do*: for if any thing conduce unto their ends, it is probable they will put the ſame in execution; but if it croſſ their deſigns, they will not. *Neither* is the information touching the diverſity of mens *ends* and *natures*, to be taken only *ſimply*, but *comparatively* alſo; as namely *what affecti-on and humor have the predominancy and command of the reſt?* So we ſee, when *Tigellinus* ſaw himſelf outſtript by *Petronius Turpilianus* in adminiſtring and ſuggeſting pleaſures to *Neroes* humor, —*Metus e-*

Annal. xiv.

jus rimatur— ſaith *Tácitus*, he wrought upon *Neroes Fears*, and by this means brake the neck of his Concurrent.

§ *As for the knowing of mens minds at ſecond hand from Reports of others,* it ſhall ſuffice to touch it briefly. *Weakneſſes and faults you ſhall beſt learn from enemies; vertues and abilities, from friends; cu-ſtoms and times, from ſervants; cogitations and opinions, from inti-mate*

mate confidents, with whom you frequently and familiarly discourse. Popular fame is light, and the judgement of superiours uncertain; for before such, men are more maskt;

Q. Cic. de
Pet. Con.

————Verior Fama è Domesticis emanat——

But to all this part of enquiry, the most compendious way resteth in three things. *First*, to have general acquaintance and inwardness with those which have most lookt into the world, and are well verst both in men and matters; but especially to endeavour to have privacy and conversation with some particular friends, who according to the diversity of Business and Persons, are able to give us solid information, and good intelligence of all passages. *Secondly*, to keep a *discreet temper* and *mediocrity*, both in liberty of speech and *Taciturnity*; more frequently using *liberty*, but *secrecy* where it imports. *For liberty of speech invites and provokes others to use the same liberty to us again; and so brings much to a mans knowledge; but silence induceth trust and inwardness, so as men love to lay up their secrets with us as in a closet.* *Thirdly*, we must by degrees acquire the *Habit of a watchful and present wit*, so as in every conference and action we may both *promote the main matter in hand, and yet observe other circumstances that may be incident upon the Bye.* For as *Epictetus* gives it in Precept, a Philosopher in every particular action, should say thus to himself, *I will do this also, and yet go on in my course.* So a *Politick* in every particular occurrence should make this account and resolution with himself; *And I will do this likewise, and yet learn something that may be of use hereafter.* And therefore they who are of such a heavy wit and narrow comprehension, as to overdo one particular, and are wholly taken up with the business in hand; and do not so much as think of any matters which intervene (a weakness that *Montaigne* confesses in himself) such indeed are the best instruments of Princes and of State; but fail in point of their own *Fortune*. But in the mean time, above all things caution must be taken, *that we have a good stay, and hold of our selves, by repressing a too active forwardness of disposition;* lest that this knowing much, do not draw us on to much meddling; for nothing is more unfortunate, than light and rash intermeddling in many matters. So that this *variety of knowledge of Persons and Actions*, which we give in Precept to be procured, tends in conclusion to this; to make a judicious choice both of those *Actions* we undertake, and of those *Persons* whose advice and assistance we use, that so we may know how to conduct our affairs with more dexterity and safety.

Epict. Enchir.

Essays.

§ *After the knowledge of others* follows the *knowledge of our selves*; for no less diligence, rather more, is to be taken in a true and exact understanding of *our own Persons*; *than of the Persons of others*, for the Oracle, *Nosce Teipsum*, is not only a rule of universal Prudence, but hath a special place in *Politicks*; for as St. *James* excellently puts us in mind, *that he that views his Face in a Glass, yet instantly forgets what one he was;* so that there is need of a very frequent inspection. The same holds also in Civil Affairs; but there are indeed

Jacob.1.

divers *Glaſſes* ; for the *Divine Glaſs* in which we muſt look our ſelves, is the Word of God ; but the *Politick Glaſs* is nothing elſe but the State of the World and times wherein we live. *Wherefore* a man ought to take an exact examination, and an impartial view (not ſuch as uſeth to be taken by one too much in love with himſelf) of his own abilities, vertues and ſupports ; as likewiſe of his own defects, Inabilities, and Impediments ; ſo making his accounts, that he ever eſtimate *theſe* with the moſt, *thoſe* rather with the leaſt ; and from this view and examination, theſe points following come into conſideration.

§ *The firſt Conſideration ſhould be, how a man's individual conſtitution and moral temper ſorts with the general ſtate of the times ; which if they be found agreeable, then he may give himſelf more ſcope and liberty, and uſe his own nature ; but if there be any antipathy and diſſonancy, then, in the whole courſe of his life, he ſhould carry himſelf more cloſe retired, and reſerved.* So did *Tiberius,* who being conſcient of his own temper, not well ſorting with his times, was never ſeen at publick Plays: and came not into the Senate in twelve of his laſt years: whereas on the contrary *Auguſtus* lived ever in mens eyes, which alſo *Tacitus* obſerved : *Alia Tiberio Morum via* ; the ſame reaſon too was to ſecure his perſon from danger.

Annal.1.

§ *The ſecond Conſideration ſhould be how a man's nature ſorts with the profeſſions and courſes of life, which are in uſe and eſteem, and whereof he is to make his choice ; that ſo if he have not yet determined what race to run, or what courſe of life to take, he may chuſe that which is moſt fit and agreeable to his natural diſpoſition ; but if it he be engaged already in a condition of life, to which by nature he is not ſo fitted, let him make a departure at the firſt opportunity, and take another Profeſſion:* This we ſee was done by *Valentine Borgia,* that was deſign'd by his father to a Sacerdotal profeſſion, which, obeying the bent of his own nature, he quitted ſoon after, and applied himſelf to a Military courſe of life ; though as equally unworthy the dignity of a Prince as of a Prieſt, ſeeing the peſtilent Man hath diſhonoured both.

§ *The third Conſideration ſhould be how a man may be valued, and may deport himſelf as he is compar'd with his Equals and Rivals, whom it is likely he may have Competitors and Concurrents in his Fortune, and that he take that courſe of life wherein there is the greateſt ſolitude of able men ; and himſelf like to be moſt eminent.* Thus *Julius Cæſar* did, who at firſt was an Orator or Pleader, and was chief converſant in Gown-Arts of Peace ; but when he ſaw *Cicero, Hortenſius* and *Catulus* to excel in the glory of Eloquence, and no man eminent for the Wars but *Pompeius,* he forſook his courſe, and bidding a long farewell to a civil and popular Greatneſs, transfer'd his deſigns to the Wars, and to the Martial Greatneſs ; by which mean he aſcended to the top of Sovereignty.

The fourth Conſideration may be, that in the choice of friends and inward dependances, a man conſult his own nature and diſpoſition, and proceed according to the compoſition of his own temper ; for different conſtitutions require different kinds of friends to comply withall ; to ſome men,

men, *folemn and filent natures,* to others *bold and boafting humours are acceptable*; *and many of the like fort.* Certainly it is worth the ob-fervation, to fee of what difpofition the friends and followers of *Ju-lius Cæfar* were, (as *Antonius, Hirtius, Panfa, Oppius, Balbus, Dolabella, Pollio,* the reft) thefe were wont to fwear, *ità vivente* Cæfare *moriar* ; bearing an infinite affection to *Cæfar,* but towards all others difdain-ful and arrogant, and they were men in publick Bufinefs active and effectual ; in fame and reputation, not folemn and celebrated.

The fifth Confideration may be that a man take heed how he guide him-felf by Examples, and that he do not fondly affect the Imitation of o-thers ; *as if that which is pervious to others, muft needs be as patent to him, never confidering with himfelf what difference perhaps there is be-twixt his and their natures and carriages, whom he hath chofen for his pattern and example.* This was manifeftly *Pompeius*'s error, who, as *Cicero* reports it, was wont often to fay, *Sylla potuit, Ego non potero ?* wherein he was much abufed, the nature and proceedings of him-felf and *Sylla,* being the unlikelieft in the world ; the one being fierce, violent, and preffing the fact ; the other folemn, reverencing Laws, directing all to Majefty and Fame ; and therefore the lefs effectual and powerful to go thorough with his defigns. There are more Precepts of this nature, but thefe fhall fuffice for Example to the reft.

§ *Nor is the well underftanding, and difcerning of a man's felf fuf-ficient, but he muft confult with himfelf upon a way how he may aptly and wifely open and reveal himfelf, and in fumm, become flexible and moulded to the feveral forms and impreffions of occafions.* As for the *Revealing of a man's felf,* we fee nothing more ufual, than for the lefs able man to make the greater fhew. Wherefore it is a great advan-tage to good parts, if a man can by a kind of Art and Grace *fet forth himfelf to others,* by aptly *revealing* (fo it be done without diftafte or arrogance) his Vertues, Merits and Fortune ; and on the contra-ry by covering artificially his weakneffes, defects, misfortunes and difgraces ; ftaying upon thofe, and as it were, turning them to the light ; fliding from thefe, and leffening them by an apt ex-pofition, and the like. *Wherefore Tacitus* faith of *Mucianus,* who was the wifeft man and the greateft Politick of his time, *Omnia quæ dixerat feceràtq; Arte quâdam oftentator. This fetting forth of a* Hift. *man's felf* requires indeed fome Art, left it turn tedious and arrogant ; but yet fo, as fome kind of *Oftentation,* though it be to the firft de-gree of vanity, feems rather a vice in the *Ethicks,* than in the *Poli-ticks.* For as it is ufually faid of *Slander, Audacter caluminare, femper aliquid hæret.* So it may be faid of *Oftentation* (unlefs it be in a grofs manner deform'd and ridiculous) *Audacter te vendita, femper aliquid hæret* ; it will ftick certainly with the more ignorant and inferiour fort of men, though the more wife and folemn fmile at it, and de-fpife. *Therefore the Eftimation won with many, fhall countervail the dif-dain of a few.* But if this *Oftentation of a man's felf,* whereof we fpeak, be carried with decency and difcretion ; for example, if it make fhew of a native candor and inbred ingenuity ; or if it be affum'd at times, when other Perils approach (as in Military perfons in time of War)

or at times when others are moſt envied, or if words which reſpect a
mans *own Praiſe,* ſeem to fall from him in a careleſs paſſage, as intend-
ing ſomething elſe, without dwelling too long upon them, or being
too ſerious; or if a man ſo *grace himſelf,* as with equal freedom, he
forbears not to tax and jeſt at himſelf; or in ſum,if he do this not of his
own accord, but as urg'd and provokt by the inſolencies and contumelies of others, it doth greatly add to a mans Reputation. *And ſurely* not a few (more ſolid than windy natures, and therefore want the
Art of bearing up ſayl in the height of the winds;) ſuffer for their moderation, not without ſome prejudice, and diſadvantage to their reputation and merit.   But for *theſe* Flouriſhes and enhancements of vertue,
howſoever ſome of weak judgement, and perchance too ſeverely Moral, may diſallow, no man will deny this, but that we ſhould endeavour at leaſt, that vertue thorow careleſs negligence be not diſvalued,
and imbaſed under the juſt price. *This diminution* of the value, and
abating the price in eſtimating Virtue, is wont to fall out three wayes.
Firſt when a man offers and obtrudes himſelf and ſervice in matters of
imployment not call'd nor ſent for; ſuch prompt offices as theſe are reputed well rewarded, if they be not refuſed. *Secondly when* a man in
the beginning and firſt on-ſet of an imployment, too much abuſeth his
own forces and abilities, when that which ſhould have been performed
by degrees, he laviſheth out all at once; which in matters well managed, wins early grace and commendation, but in the end induceth
ſatiety. *Thirdly when* a man is too ſuddenly ſenſible, and too incon-
ſiderately tranſported with the fruit of his vertue, in commendation,
applauſe, honour, favour confer'd upon him; and is too much affected and delighted therewith : of this point there is a wiſe Aviſo. *Beware leſt you ſeem unacquainted with great matters, that are thus pleas'd
with ſmall, as if they were great.*

§ But the covering of *Defects is* of no leſs importance than a wiſe and
dexterous oſtentation of vertues. Defects are conceal'd and *ſecreted by a
three-fold induſtry, and as it were under three coverts, Caution, Colour, and Confidence. Caution* is that, when we do wiſely avoid to be
put upon thoſe things for which we are not proper; whereas contrariwiſe bold and unſtaid ſpirits will eaſily engage themſelves without
judgement, in matters wherein they are not ſeen, and ſo publiſh and
proclaim all their imperfections. *Colour* is when we do warily and
wiſely prepare and make way, to have a favourable and commodious
conſtruction made of our faults and wants; as proceeding from a better cauſe, or intended for ſome other purpoſe than is generally conceiv'd : for of the Covert of Faults the Poet ſaith well,

Ovid,   *Sæpe latet vitium proximitate Boni.*

Wherefore if we perceive a *Defect* in our ſelves, our endeavour muſt
be to borrow and put on the *Perſon* and *Colour* of the next bordering
Vertue, wherewith it may be ſhadowed and ſecreted.   For inſtance,
he that is *Dull,* muſt pretend *Gravity;* he that is a *Coward, Mildneſs,*
and ſo the reſt.   And it will advantage, to frame ſome probable cauſe,
and to give it out and ſpread it abroad, that induced us to diſſemble

our

our abilities and not do our beſt; that ſo *making a Vertue of Neceſſity,*
what was not in our *power,* may ſeem not to have been in our *will* to
do. *As for Confidence,* it is indeed an impudent, but the ſureſt and
moſt effectual remedy; namely that a man profeſs himſelf to deſpiſe
and ſet at naught, what in truth he cannot attain; according to the
Principle of wiſe Merchants, with whom it is familiar to raiſe the price
of their own Commodities, and to beat down the price of others. *But
there* is another kind of *Confidence* far more impudent than this, which
is to *face ont a mans own Defects,* to boaſt them and obtrude them upon Opinion; as if he conceiv'd that he was beſt in thoſe things, wherein he moſt fails; and to help that again, that the Deception put upon others may come off more roundly, he may feign, that he hath
leaſt opinion of himſelf in thoſe things, wherein he is beſt. *Like* as
we ſee it commonly in Poets; for a Poet reciting his verſes, if you
except againſt any verſe, you ſhall preſently hear him reply, *And
for this verſe it coſt me more labour than the reſt;* and then he will bring
you ſome other verſe, and ſeem to diſable and ſuſpect that rather, and
ask your judgement of it, which yet he knows to be the beſt in the number, and not liable to exception. *But above* all, in this *Helping a mans
ſelf in his carriage,* namely, that a man may ſet the faireſt gloſs upon
himſelf before others, and right himſelf in all points, nothing, in my
opinion, avails more, *than that a man do not diſmantle himſelf and expoſe his perſon to ſcorn and injury by his too much Goodneſs and Facility of
Nature; but rather in all things ſhew ſome ſparkles and edge of a free and
generous ſpirit, that carries with it as well a ſting, as Hony.* Which
kind of fortified carriage, together with a prompt and prepared reſolution to vindicate a mans ſelf from ſcorn, is impoſed upon ſome by accident and a kind of an invitable neceſſity, for ſomewhat inherent in
their perſon or fortune; as we ſee it in Deformed Perſons and Ba-
ſtards, and in Perſons any way diſgrac'd; ſo that ſuch natures, if they
have any good parts, commonly they ſucceed with good felicity.

§ *As for the declaring of a Mans ſelf,* that is a far different thing from
Oſtentation, or the *Revealing of a mans ſelf,* whereof we ſpake even now;
for it refers not to Mens *abilities* or *weakneſſes,* but to the *Particular
Actions* of life; in which point, *nothing is more Politick, than to obſerve
a wiſe and diſcreet mediocrity in the diſcloſing or ſecreting the inward intentions and meanings of the mind touching particular Actions.* For although depth of ſecrecy and concealing of Counſels, and that manner
of managing Buſineſs, when men ſet things awork by dark, and as the
French ſtiles it, *Sourdes Menées, ſourd Arts, cloſe Carriages,* be
a thing both proſperous and admirable; yet many times it comes to
paſs, as the ſaying is, *That Diſſimulation begets errors, and illaqueates
Diſſembler himſelf.* For we ſee the ableſt men, and greateſt *Poli-
ti*s that ever were, have made no ſcruple of it, openly to profeſs,
freely and without diſſimulation, the ends they aim at: ſo *L. Sylla* ^{Plutar.in Syl.
la.}
made a kind of profeſſion, *That he wiſht all men happy or unhappy as they* ^{Plutar.in J.}
ſtood his friends or enemies: So *Cæſar* when he went firſt into *Gaul* con- ^{Cæſ.}
ſidently profeſt, *That he had rather be firſt in an obſcure village, than ſecond at Rome:* the ſame *Cæſar* when the war was now begun did not

play

play the diffembler, if we obferve what *Cicero* reports of him ; *the o-*
ther (meaning of *Cæfar*) *refufeth not, nay in a fort defires, that, as mat-*
ters ftand, he may fo be called Tyrant. So we may fee in a letter of *Ci-*
cero's to *Atticus,* how far from a *Diffembler Auguftus Cæfar* was, who
in his very entrance into Affairs, while he was a darling to the Senate,
yet in his Harangues and fpeeches to the People was wont to fwear after this manner, *Ità parentis honores confequi liceat,* which was no lefs
than the Tyranny; fave that, to help the matter a little, he would
withal ftretch forth his hand to a ftatue of *Iulius Cæfars,* which was e-
rected in the *Roftra :* and men laught and applauded, and wondred
and difcourfed thus amongft themfelves, *what means this ? What a*
young man have wé here ? and yet thought he meant no hurt, he did
fo candidly and ingenuoufly fpeak what he meant. *And all thefe,* we
have nam'd, were profperous: Whereas on the other fide, *Pompeius,*
who tended to the fame ends, but by more umbragious and obfcure
ways (as *Tacitus* faith of him, *Occultor non melior;* a cenfure wherein
Saluft concurrs, *Ore probo, Animo inverecundo,*) made it his defign,and
endeavoured by infinite engines, that deeply hiding his boundlefs defires and ambition, he might in the mean fpace caft the ftate into an
Anarchy and Confufion, whereby the ftate muft neceffarily caft it felf
into his arms for protection, and fo the fovereign Power be put upon
him, and he never feen in it : and when he had brought it, (as he
thought,) to that point, when he was chofen *Conful* alone, as never
any was; yet he could make no great matter of it; becaufe thofe,that
without queftion would have cooperated with him, underftood him
not; fo that he was fain in the end, to go the beaten and common
track of getting Arms into his hands, by colour of oppofing himfelf a-
gainft Cæfar : fo tedious, cafual, and unfortunate are thofe Counfels which are cover'd with *deep Diffimulation;* whereof it feems *Taci-*
tus made the fame judgement, when he makes the *Arts of Simulation,*
a prudence of an inferior form, in regard of *true Policy,* attributing
the one to *Auguftus,* the other to *Tiberius ;* for fpeaking of *Livia* he
faith thus, *That fhe forted well with the Arts of her husband, and Diffi-*
mulation of her fon.

§ *As touching the bending and moulding of the Mind ; it muft indeed*
by all poffible means be endeavoured, that the mind be made pliant and
obedient to occafions and opportunities, and that it be not any way ftiff and
renitent to them : for nothing hinders the *effecting of Bufinefs, and the*
making of mens fortunes fo much as this : Idem manebat neque idem de-
cebat, that is, when men are where they were, and follow their own bent
when occafions are turn'd. Therefore *Livy,* when he brings in *Cato Ma-*
jor, as the experteft Architect of his fortune, very well annexes this,
that he had, *verfatile ingenium,* and thereof it comes, that thefe grave
folemn wits, which muft be like themfelves, and cannot make de▉
ture, have for moft part more dignity than felicity. But in fome ▉s
nature to be vifcuous and inwrapt and not eafie to turn: in others it
is cuftom, that is almoft a nature, and a conceit, which eafily fteals into mens minds, which is, that men can hardly make themfelves believe, that they ought to change fuch courfes, as they have found good
and profperous by farther experience. For *Machiavel* notes wifely in

Fabius Maximus, How *he would have been temporizing still according to his old biass, when the nature of the war was altered and required hot pur-* suit. In some others the same weaknefs proceeds from want of penetration in their judgement, when men do not in time difcern the Periods of things and Actions, but come in too late after the occafion is efcaped.   Such an overfight as this, *Demofthenes* reprehends in the People of Athens, faying, *they were like countrey-fellows playing in a Fence-fchool, that if they have a blow, then they remove ther weapons to that ward and not before.*   Again in others this comes to pafs, becaufe they are loth to lofe the labour, in that way, they have enter'd into, nor do they know how to make a retrait; but rather entertain a conceit, that by perfeverance they fhall bring about occafions to their own ply. But from what root or caufe foever this vifcofity and reftivenefs of mind proceeds, it is a thing moft prejudicial both to a mans affairs and fortunes; *and nothing is more politick, than to make the wheel of our mind concentrick and voluble with the wheels of Fortune.*   Thus much of the two fummary precepts touching the *Architecture of Fortune.   Precepts fcatter'd* are many, but we will only felect a few to ferve as examples to the reft.

§ *The firft Precept is,* that this *Architect of his own fortune rightly ufe his Rule, that is, that he inure his mind to judge of the Proportion and valure of things, as they conduce more or lefs to his own fortune and ends; and that he intend the fame fubftantially, and not fuperficially.*   For it is ftrange, but moft true, that there are many, whofe *Logical part of Mind* (if I may fo term it) is good, but the *Mathematical part* nothing worth; that is, who can well and foundly judge of the confequences, but very unskilfully of the prizes of things.   Hence it comes to pafs, that fome fall in love and into admiration with the private and fecret accefs to Princes; *others* with popular fame and applaufe, fuppofing they are things of great purchafe, when in many cafes they are but matters of envy, peril, and impediment: *others* meafure things, according to the labour and difficulty fpent about them, thinking that if they be ever moving, they muft needs advance and proceed; as *Cæfar* faid in a defpifing manner of *Cato Uticenfis,* when he defcribes how laborious, affiduous and indefatigable he was to no great purpofe, *Omnia* (faith he) *magno ftudio agebat.   Hence* likewife it comes to pafs, that men often abufe themfelves, who if they ufe the favour and furtherance of fome great and honourable Perfon, they promife themfelves all profperous fuccefs; whereas the truth is, that not the greateft, but the apteft inftruments, fooneft, and more happily accomplifh a work.   *And for* the true direction of the *Mathematical fquare of the Mind;* it is worth the pains efpecially to know, and have it fet down. what ought *firft* to be refolved upon for the *building and advancing of a mans fortune;* what *next,* and fo forward.

§ *In the firft place I fet down, the Amendment of the mind;* for by taking away and fmoothing the impediments, and rubs of the Mind, you fhall fooner open a way to fortune, than by the affiftance of Fortune, take away the impediments of the Mind. *In the fecond place I fet down wealth and Means,* which perchance moft men would have placed firft, becaufe of the general ufe it bears towards all va-

riety

Difcors fupra Liv.

Orat.in Phi. lip.1,

riety of occasions; but that opinion I may condemn with like reason, as *Machiavel* in another case not much unlike; for whereas the old saying was, that *Monies were the sinews of war*, he on the contrary affirmed, *that there were no other sinews of wars, save the sinews of valiant mens arms*. In like manner it may be truly affirmed, *that it is not Monies that is the sinews of Fortune*, but the sinews rather and abilities of the Mind, Wit, Courage, Audacity, Resolution, Moderation, Industry, and the like. *In the third place, I set down Fame and Reputation*, and the rather because they have certain tides and times, which if you do not take in their due season, are seldom recovered; *it being a very hard matter to play an after-game of Reputation*. *In the last place I set down Honours*, to which certainly there is a more easie access made by any of the other three, much more by all united; than if you begin with *Honours* and so proceed to the rest. But as it is of special consequence, to observe the order and priority of *things*; so is it of less import, to observe the order and priority of *Time*; the preposterous placing whereof, is one of the commonest errors; while men fly unto their ends, when they should intend their beginnings; and whilst we suddenly seize upon the highest matters, we rashly pass over what lies in the midst; but it is a good precept, *Quod nunc instat agamus.*

The *second precept is, that upon a greatness and Confidence of Mind, we do not engage our forces in too arduous matters, which we cannot so well conquer; nor that we row against the stream.* For as touching mens Fortune, the counsel is excellent,

——*Fatis accede Deisque.*

Let us look about us on every side, and observe where things are open, where shut and obstructed; where easie, where difficile, to be compassed; and that we do not overstrain and misemploy our strength where the way is not passible, for this will preserve us from foil; not occupy us too much about one matter; we shall win an opinion of Moderation; offend few; and lastly, make a shew of a perpetual felicity in all we undertake; whilst those things which peradventure would of their own accord have come to pass, shall be attributed to our providence and industry.

The *third Precept* may seem to have some repugnancy with that former immediately going before; though if it be well understood, there is none at all. *The Precept is this; that we do not always expect occasions, but sometimes provoke them, and lead the way unto them;* which is that which *Demosthenes* intimates in high terms. *For as it is a received principle that a General should lead the Army; so wise and understanding men should conduct and command matters, and such things should be done as they saw fit to be done; and that they should not be forc'd to pursue and build only upon events.* For if we diligently consider it, we shall observe *two* differing kinds of sufficiency in managing affairs and handling business; for some can make use of occasions aptly and dexterously, but plot and excogitate nothing; some are all for Plots, which they can well urge and pursue, but cannot accommo-

date

Orat. in Phil. 1.

date and take in: Either of which abilities is maimed, and imperfect
without the other.

*A fourth Precept is, not to embrace any matters which do occupy too
great a quantity of time; but to have that verse ever sounding in our ears.*

Sed fugit intereà, fugit irreparàbile tempùs.

*And the cause why those who addict themselves to professions of burden and
the like, as Lawyers, Orators, painful Divines, writers of Books, and
the like, are not commonly so politick in contriving and promoting their
own fortunes, is no other than this; that they want time, which is otherwise imployed, to inform themselves of Particulars; and to wait upon
occasions, and to devise and project designs which may conduce to
the making of their fortune.* Nay farther, in the Courts of Princes
and in States, you shall have those that are exceeding powerful
and expert how to advance their own Fortune, and to invade the
Fortune of others, which undergo no publick charge, but are continually practised in that whereof we speak. *The Advancement of
Life.*

A Fifth Precept is, to imitate nature which doth nothing in vain.
Which certainly we may do, if we discreetly mingle and interlace
our businesses of all sorts. For the mind should in every particular a-
ction be so disposed and prepared; and our intentions so subdued, and
subordinated one under another; as if we cannot have that we seek
in the best degree, yet we may have it in a second, or at least in a
third: but if we can get no footing nor any consistency at all in any
part of a thing we desire; then we may turn the pains we have taken
upon some other end, than that whereto it was designed: but if we
cannot make any thing of it for the present, at least we may extract
something out of it that may stand us in stead for the time to come;
but if we can derive no solid effect or substance from it, neither for
the present nor for the future; let us yet endeavour to win some good
opinion and reputation by it; and the like: ever exacting accounts
of our selves, whereby it may appear that we have reapt somewhat
more or less from every particular Action and Counsel; never suffe-
ring our selves to be cast down and dispirited, like men amaz'd and
confused, if perchance we fail in the principal scope of our intentions. For nothing is more prejudicious to a Politick, than to be
wholly and solely taken up with one thing; for he that doth so, los-
eth infinite occasions which do intervene upon the by; and which
perhaps are more proper and propitious for somewhat may be of use
hereafter; than for those things we urge for the present: and therefore we must be perfect in that Rule; *Hæc oportet facere & illa non o-* Epist. Ench.
mittere.

*A sixth Precept is, that we engage not our selves too peremptorily in any
thing though it seem not at first sight, liable to accident; but that we ever
have either an open window to fly out at, or a secret postern-way to retire
by.*

A seventh Precept is, that ancient Rule of *Bias*; so it be construed
not to any point of Perfidiousness; but to caution and moderation.

So love a man as yet thou maiſt become an enemy, ſo hate a man as yet thou maiſt become his Friend; for it utterly betrays and fruſtrates all utility, for a man to embark himſelf too far in unfortunate friendſhips, unquiet and troubleſome ſpleens, or childiſh and humorous Æmulations.

Theſe ſhall ſuffice for examples touching the knowledge *of the Advancement of Life:* yet I would have it remembred, that theſe adumbrations which we have drawn and ſet down as *Deficients*, are far from compleat Tractates of them, but only that they are as little pieces and edgings for patterns, whereby a judgement may be made of the whole web. Again we are not ſo weak and fooliſh as to avouch that *Fortunes* are not to be obtained without all this ado ; for we know well they come tumbling into ſome mens laps, and a number obtain good *fortunes* only with diligence and aſſiduity (with ſome little caution intermingled) in a plain way, without any great or painful Art. But as *Cicero,* when he ſets down the Idea of a perfect Orator, doth not mean that every Pleader ſhould be or can be ſuch : and again as in the deſcription of a Prince or a Courtier, by ſuch as have handled thoſe ſubjects ; the Mould is made according to the perfection of the Art, and not according to common practice : the ſame we have performed in the inſtruction of a *Politick* man ; I mean *Politick for his own Fortune.* And likewiſe take this advertiſement along with you, That the Precepts which we have choſen and ſet down, are all of that kind which may be counted and called *Bonæ Artes.* As for

Evil Arts, if a man would yield himſelf a diſciple to *Machiavel* who gives it in precept, *That a man needs not much care for vertue it ſelf, but for the appearance only thereof in the eyes of the world, becauſe the ſame and credit of vertue, is a help, but the uſe of it a cumber;* who in another place gives this rule : That a Politick man lay this as a foundation of his practick wiſdom, *that he preſuppoſe, that men are not rightly and ſafely to be wrought upon and bowed to the bent of our wills, otherwiſe than by fear;* and therefore let him endeavour by all means poſſible to have *every man obnoxious, low and in ſtreights.* So as Machiavel's Politician ſeems to be what the Italians call *il ſeminatore délle ſpine;* or if any would embrace that Principle which *Cicero* cites, *Cadant amici, dummodo inimici intercidant;* as the *Trinmviri* ſold the lives of their friends, for the deaths of their enemies. Or if a man would be an imitator of *L. Catilina* to become an incendiary and a perturber of ſtates, to the end he may better fiſh in droumy waters, and unwrap his fortune's; *I* (ſaith he) *if once a fire ſeize upon my Fortune, will extinguiſh it not with water but with ruine;* or if any one would convert to his uſe that of *Lyſander,* who was wont to ſay, *That children are to be deceived with Comfits, and men with Oaths.* With other ſuch corrupt and pernicious Poſitions of the ſame impreſſion, whereof (as in all other things,) there are more in number, than of the good and ſound. If any (I ſay) be delighted with ſuch contagious and polluted wiſdom, I deny not but with theſe diſpenſations from all the laws of charity and integrity, wholly enſlaved to the preſſing of his own *Fortunes,* he may be more ſpeedy and compendious *in the promoting of his Fortune:* but it is in life, as it is in ways, the ſhorteſt way is commonly the fouleſt ; and ſurely the fairer way is not much about.

about. *But it is so* far from the mind and purpose of this Difcourfe that men fhould apply themfelves to thefe corrupt and crooked Arts, that rather indeed (if they be in their own power, and are able to bear and fuftain themfelves, and be not carried away with the whirl-wind and tempeft of Ambition) they ought in the purfuit of Fortune to fet before their eyes, not only that general Map of the world, *That all things are vanity and vexation of fpirit* ; but alfo that more particular card and direction, *That Being, without well-Being, is a curfe, and the greater Being, the greater curfe* ; and that all vertue is moft rewarded, and all wickednefs moft punifht in it felf: according as the Poet faith excellently,

Virg. Æn. 9;

> *Quæ vobis, quæ digna, viri, pro talibus aufis*
> *Præmia poffe reor folvi ? Pulcherrima primùm*
> *Dii Morefq; dabunt veftri.———*

And fo on the contrary he fpeaks as truly of the wicked— *atq; eum ulcifcentur mores fui.———* Nay further, the race of Mortality, whilft their working heads every way tofs and diffufe their thoughts how they may beft fore-caft and confult *their advancement in the world*, ought, in the midft of thefe heats, and eager purfuits, to look up to the Divine Judgement, and the Eternal Providence, which oftentimes fubverts and brings to nothing the plots of the wicked, and their evil counfels, though never fo profound ; according to that of facred Scripture, *He conceived wicked thoughts, travel'd great with mifchief, and fhall bring forth delufive vanity.* Nay, though men fhould refrain themfelves from injuries and evil arts ; *yet this inceffant and Sabbathlefs afpiring to the fteep height of Fortune, pays not the tribute of our time due unto God, who (as we may fee) demands and fets apart for himfelf a Tenth of our fubftance, and a Seventh of our time.* For it is to fmall purpofe to have an erected face towards heaven, and a groveling fpirit upon earth, eating duft as doth the ferpent ; an oppofition which even Heathens could fee and cenfure.

Pfal. v. 11

Horat. fer. 2;

> *Atq; affigit humo divinæ particulam Auræ.*

And if any man fhould herein flatter himfelf, that he refolves to imploy his Fortune well, though he fhould obtain it ill ; as was wont to be faid of *Auguftus Cæfar* and *Septimius Severus*, *That either they fhould never have been born, or elfe they fhould never have dyed*, they did fo much mifchief in the purfuit and afcent of their greatnefs ; and fo much good, when they were eftablifh'd ; let him take this with him, that fuch compenfation of evil by good, may be allowed after the Fact, but is defervedly condemn'd in the purpofe. *Laftly*, it will not be amifs for us, in that fwift and hot race towards our fortune, to cool our felves a little, with that elegant conceit of the Emperour *Charls* the Fifth, in his inftructions to his Son, *That Fortune hath fomewhat of the nature of a woman, that if fhe be too much wooed, fhe is the farther off* : but this laft remedy is for thofe whofe tafte, from fome diftemper of the mind, is corrupted : let men rather build upon that foundation, which is as a corner-ftone of Divinity and Philofophy

Scrip. Getm. A.C. 1519.

lofophy, wherein they almoft joyn clofe by the fame affertion of *what
fhould be firft fought* ; for *Divinty* commands, *Firft feek the Kingdom
of God, and all thefe things fhall be fuperadded unto you* ; and Philo-
fophy commands fomewhat like this; *Seek firft the goods of the mind,
and the reft fhall be fupplied, or no way prejudiced by their abfence.*
And although this foundation laid by man, is fometimes placed upon
the fands, as we may fee in *M. Brutus,* who in the laft fcene of his
life, brake forth into that fpeech,

      Te Colui virtus ut Rem, aft Tu Nomen inane es:

Yet the fame foundation laid by the hand of heaven, is firmly fettled
upon a Rock. *And here* we conclude the knowledge of *Advancement of Life* ; and withall the general knowledge of *Negotiations.*

C H A P.   III.

The Partitions *of the Art of Empire or Government* are omitted;
    only accefs is made to two *Deficients.* I. *The knowledge of en-
larging the* Bounds of Empire. II. *And the knowledge of* univerfal Juftice; *or of the Fountains of Law.*

I.   **I** Come now to the *Art of Empire,* or the *the knowledge of Civil
       Government* ; under which *Houfe-hold Government* is compre-
hended, as a *Family* is under a *City.* " In this part, as I faid before, I
" have commanded my felf filence: yet notwithftanding I may not
" fo difable my felf ; but that I could difcourfe of this part alfo, per-
" chance not impertinently, nor unprofitably; as one practifed by
" long experience; and by *your Majefty's* moft indulgent favours, and
" no merit of mine own, raifed by the degrees of office and honours,
" to the higheft Dignity in the State; and have born that office for
" four years; and which is more, have been accuftomed to *your
" Majefties* commands and conferences, for the continued fpace of
" eighteen years together, (which even of the dulleft mould might
" fafhion and produce a State-man) who have fpent much time, a-
" mongft other knowledges, in Hiftories and Laws. *All which I report to Pofterity, not out of any arrogant oftentation ; but becaufe I
prefume it makes fomething to the honour and dignity of Learning ; that
a man born for Letters more than any thing elfe, and forcibly carried a-
way, I know not by what fate, againft the bent of his own Genius, to a
Civil active courfe of life, fhould yet be advanc'd to fo high and honourable charges in the State, and that under fo wife a King.* But if my
times of leifure fhall bring forth hereafter any thing touching the
wifdom of Government, and ftate-matters, it will be perchance an
Abortive, or an After-birth. In the mean fpace, now that all Sciences
are diftributed and ranged, as it were, into their true Forms, left
                                             fuch

such an eminent place as this should remain empty, I have judg'd it fit to note as *Deficients* two Portions only of *Civil Knowledge*, which pertain, not to the *Secrets of Empire*, but are of a more open and publick nature ; and, according to our custom, to propound examples thereof. *Seeing the Arts of Government*, comprehend three sorts of *Politick Duties : First*, that a Kingdom or State be conserved : *Secondly*, that it may become happy and flourishing : *Thirdly*, that it may be amplified, and the bounds thereof propagated and extended. Of these duties the *two first* are, for the most, by many, excellently well handled ; but the *third* is past over in silence ; wherefore we will set this down in the number of *Deficients*, and according to our manner propose examples thereof ; calling this part of Civil Know-ledge *Consulem Paludatum*, or a *knowledge of the enlarging the Bounds of Empire.*

EXAMPLE

Of a Summary Treatise touching the enlarging of the Bounds *of Empire.*

CONSUL PALUDA-TUS, sive de proferendis Imperii fini-bus.

THe speech of *Themistocles*, taken to himself, was indeed some-what uncivil and haughty ; but if it had been applied to others, and at large, certainly it may seem to comprehend in it a wise ob-servation, and a grave censure.   Desired at a Feast to touch a Lute, he said, *He could not Fidle, but yet he could make a small Town a great City :* These words drawn to a Politick sence, do excellently ex-press and distinguish two differing Abilities, in those that deal in bu-siness of Estate.   *For if a* true survey be taken of all Counsellors and States-men that ever were, and others promoted to publick charge, there will be found (though very rarely) those which can make a *small State great, and yet cannot fidle ;* as on the other side there will be found a great many, *that are very cunning upon the Cittern or Lute,* (*that is in Court-Trifles*) but yet are so far from being able to make a *small State, great ;* as their gift lies another way, *to bring a great and flourishing Estate to ruine and decay.*   And certainly those degenerate Arts and Shifts, whereby many Counsellors and Governours gain both favour with their Masters, and estimation with the vulgar, deserve no better name than *Fidling ;* being things rather pleasing for the time, and graceful to the Professors themselves ; than tending to the *weal and advancement of the State,* which they serve.   There are also (no doubt) *Counsellors* and *Governours*, not to be despised, which may be held sufficient men, and equal to their charge ; able to manage Affairs, and to *keep them from precipices, and manifest inconveniencies,* which nevertheless are far from the Ability *to raise and amplifie an Estate.*   But be the work-men what they may be, let us cast our eyes upon the work, that is, *what is the true greatness of Kingdoms and States, and by what means it may be obtained ?*   An argument fit for great Princes to have perpetually in their hand, and diligently to meditate ; to the end that neither by overmeasuring their Forces,

Plutar. in Them.

they

they lose themselves in vain, and too difficile enterprises; nor on the other side undervaluing them, they descend to fearful and pusillanimous Counsels. *The Greatness of an Estate in Bulk and Territory, doth fall under measure; the Greatness of Financies and Revenue doth fall under computation.* The number of Citizens and the Pole may be taken by Musters; and the multitude and greatness of Cities and Towns, by Cards and Mapps. But yet there is not any thing amongst Civil Affairs, more subject to error, than a true and intrensick valuation, concerning the Power and Forces of an Estate. *The Kingdom of Heaven is compar'd not to an* Acorn *or Nut; but to a* Grain *of* Mustard-seed, *which is one of the least Grains, but hath in it a property and spirit hastily to get up and spread.* So are there *Kingdoms and States* in compass and territory very great, and yet not so apt to *enlarge their Bounds or Command*; and some on the other side that have but a small dimension of stemm, and yet apt to be the Foundations of great Monarchies.

I. *Walled Towns*, stored Arcenals and Armories, goodly Races of Horse, Chariots of war, Elephants, Ordinance, Artillery, and the like; *all this is but a sheep in a Lions skin, except the Breed and Disposition of the people be stout and war-like.* Nay, number it self in Armies imports not much, where the people is of a faint and weak courage: for, as *Virgil* saith, *It never troubles a Wolf, how many the sheep be.* The Army of the Persians in the Plains of *Arbela*, was such a vast sea of people, as it did somewhat astonish the *Commanders in Alexander's Army*; who came to him therefore, and wisht him to set upon them by Night, but he answered, *I will not Pilfer the victory*; and the Defeat by that couragious assurance was the more easie. When *Tigranes* the *Armenian*, being encamped upon a hill with an Army of 400000 Men, discovered the Army of the *Romans* being not above 14000 marching towards him, he made himself merry with it, and said; *yonder men are too many for an Ambassage, and too few for a Fight*: but before the sun set he found them enow to give him the chase with infinite slaughter. Many are the examples of the great odds between number and courage. *First* then a man may rightly make a judgement and set it down for a sure and certain truth, That the principal point of all other which respects the *Greatness of any Kingdom or State, is to have a Race of Military men.* And that is a more trite than true saying, *That Money is the Sinews of War*, where the sinews of mens arms in base and effeminate people are failing: for *Solon* said well to *Crœsus* (when in ostentation he shewed him his gold) *Sir, if any other come that hath any better Iron than you, he will be master of all this Gold.* Therefore let any *Prince* or *State* think soberly of their Forces, except their *Militia* of Natives be of Good and Valiant Souldiers: and let Princes on the other side that have Subjects of stout and martial disposition, know their own strength, unless they be otherwise wanting to themselves. As for Mercenary Forces (which is the help in this case where native forces fail) all times are full of examples, whereby it manifestly appears, that whatsoever State or Prince doth rest upon them, *he may spread his Feathers for a time beyond the compass of his nest; but he will mew them soon after.*

Margin notes:
B Ecl 7.
Plutar in Alex.
Plut. in Lucul.
Mach. Disc. orss. sopra Livio lib. 2.
Plut. in Solone,

2. *The*

2 *The bleſſing of Judah and Iſſachar* will never meet. *That the ſame Tribe or Nation ſhould be both the Lions whelp, and the Aſs between Burdens*; neither will it be *that a people overlaid with Taxes, ſhould ever become Valiant, and Martial.* It is true that *Taxes* levied by publick conſent of the eſtate do depreſs and abate mens courage leſs; as a man may plainly ſee in the Tributes of the Low-countries, which they call *Exciſes*; and in ſome degree in thoſe contributions which they call *Subſidies* in England. For you muſt note that we ſpeak now of the Heart and not of the Purſe; ſo that although the ſame Tribute conferr'd by conſent or impoſed by command, be all one to the purſe, yet it works diverſly upon the courage: Therefore ſet down this too as a Principle, *That no People overcharg'd with Tribute, is fit for Empire.*

Gen. XLIX.

3 *Let ſtates* and *kingdoms* that aim at *Greatneſs* by all means take heed how the *Nobility,* and *Grandees,* and that thoſe which we call *Gentle-men,* multiply too faſt; for that makes the common ſubject grow to be a Peaſant and Baſe ſwain driven out of heart, and in effect nothing elſe but the Noble mans Bond-ſlaves and Labourers. Even as you may ſee in Coppice-wood, *If you leave your ſtuddles too thick, you ſhall never have clean underwood, but ſhrubs and buſhes*: So in a countrey, if the *Nobility* be too many, the *Commons* will be baſe and heartleſs, and you will bring it to that, that not the hundredth Pole will be fit for an Helmet; eſpecially as to the *Infantry,* which is the nerve of an Army; and ſo there will be great Population and little ſtrength. This which I ſpeak of, hath been in no Nation more clearly confirm'd than in the examples of *England* and *France,* whereof *England,* though far inferiour in Territory and Population, hath been nevertheleſs always an overmatch in Arms; in regard the middle-people of *England* make good Souldiers, which the Peaſants of *France* do not. And herein the deviſe of *Henry the Seventh King of England* (whereof I have ſpoken largely in the Hiſtory of his life) was profound and admirable, in making Farms and Houſes of Husbandry of a ſtandard; that is, maintain'd with ſuch a Proportion of land unto them, as may breed a ſubject to live in convenient plenty, and to keep the Plough in the hands of the Owners, or at leaſt uſu-fructuary, and not hirelings and Mercenaries; and thus a Countrey ſhall merit that Character whereby *Virgil* expreſſes ancient *Italy,*

Hiſtor. Hen. VII.

Terra potens Armis, atque ubere Glebâ.

Æn. 1.

Neither is that ſtate which is almoſt peculiar to *England,* (and for any thing I know, hardly to be found any where elſe, except it be perhaps in *Poland*) to be paſſed over; I mean the ſtate of Free-ſervants and Attendants upon Noble men and Gentle-men; of which ſort, even they of inferiour condition, do no ways yield unto the *Yeomanry,* for *Infantry.* And therefore out of all queſtion the Magnificence and that Hoſpitable ſplendor, the Houſhold ſervants, and great Retinues of Noble men and Gentle-men, receiv'd into cuſtom in *England,* doth much conduce unto *Martial Greatneſs*: whereas on the other ſide, the cloſe, reſerved and contracted living of Noble men, cauſeth a Penury of *Military Forces*:

4 *By all means it is to be procured, that the Trunk of Nebuchadnez-zar's Tree of Monarchy, be great enough to bear the Branches and the Boughs ;* that is, that the number of *Natural Subjects* to the Crown or State, bear a sufficient proportion for the over-topping the *stronger Subjects.* Therefore all States that are liberal of *Naturalization* towards *strangers,* are fit for the *Greatness of Empire.* For it is a vain opinion to think that a handful of people, can with the greatest courage and Policy in the world, keep and repress under the laws of Empire, too large and spacious extent of *Dominion ;* this may hold for a time, but it will fail suddenly. The *Spartans* were a sparing and nice People in point of *Naturalization,* whereby while they kept their compass, they stood firm and assured ; but when they began to spread and enlarge their Dominion, and that their boughs, multiplied by strangers, were becoming too great for the stemm of the *Spartans,*they became a wind-fal upon the sudden. Never any State was in this point so open to receive strangers into their Body, as were the Romans ; therefore their Fortune seconded their wise institution, for they grew to the greatest

Exempla a-pud Cic. pro L. C. Bal. Monarchy in the world. Their manner was to grant *Naturalization* (which they called *Jus Civitatis*) and to grant it in the highest degree; that is, not only *Jus Commercii, Jus Connubii, Jus Hæreditatis;* but also *Jus Suffragii,*and *Jus Petitionis sive Honorum ;* and this not to singular persons alone, but likewise to whole families, yea to Cities, and sometimes to whole Nations. Add to this, their custom of *Plantation of Colonies,* whereby the *Roman Plants* were removed into the soil of other Nations : and putting both constitutions together, you will say, *that it was not the Romans that spread upon the world ; but it was the world that spread upon the Romans ;* which was the securest way of *Enlarging the Bounds of Empire.* I have marvelled sometimes at *Spain,* how they clasp and govern so large Dominions, with so few natural *Spaniards :* but surely the whole compass of Spain, is a very great body of a Tree ; being it contains far more ample Territories, than *Rome* or *Sparta* at their first risings. And besides, though the Spaniards have not had that usage to *Naturalize* liberally ; yet they have that which is next to it, that is, *To employ, almost indifferently, all Nations in their Militia of Ordinary souldiers ;* yea and sometimes they confer their highest commands of war, upon Captains that are no natural Spaniards : nay it seems, not long ago, they have begun to grow sensible of this want of Natives, and to seek a Remedy, as appears by the *Pragmatical Sanction* publisht this year.

5 *It is most Certain that sedentary and within door Mechanical Arts ; and Delicate Manufactures* (that require rather the Finger, than the Arm,) *have in their nature a contrariety to a military Disposition.* And generally all warlike People are a little idle ; and love danger better than travail : neither must they be too much Broken of it, if we will have their spirits preserv'd in vigor. Therefore it was great advantage in the ancient states of *Sparta, Athens, Rome,* and others, that they had the use, not of *Free-men,* but of *Slaves,* which commonly did rid those *Manufactures :* but the use of *Slaves* since the receiving of the *Christian Law,*is, in greatest part abolisht. That which comes neerest to this custom, is to leave those Arts chiefly to strangers,
which

which for that purpose are to be allured, or at least the more easily to be received. The *vulgar Natives* should consist of three sorts of men; that is, of *Tillers of Ground*; *Free-servants*; and *Handy-crafts-men* of strong and *Manly Arts*, as Smiths, Masons, Carpenters, &c. not reckoning professed Souldiers,

6 But above all, *for the Greatness of Empire*, it imports most; *that a Nation do profess Arms as their glory*, Principal study, and chiefest Honour. For the things which we formerly have spoken of, are but *Habilitations* towards Arms; and to what purpose is *Habilitation* without endeavour to produce it into *Act? Romulus, after his death*, (as they report or feign) *sent a present to the* Romans, *that above all they should intend* Arms, *and then they should prove the greatest* Empire *of the World*. The whole Fabrick of the *State of Sparta*, was, industriously (though not so wisely) compos'd and built to that scope and end. The *Persians* and *Maccdonians* had the same usage, but not so constant and lasting. The *Britans, Galls, Germans, Goths, Saxons, Normans*, (for a flash of time) gave themselves chiefly to *Arms*. The *Turks* not a little instigated thereto by their Law, retain the same *discipline* at this day, (though as it is now practised) with great declination of their *Militia*. Of Christian *Europe* they that retain and profess it, are in effect only the *Spaniards*. But it is so liquid and manifest, *that every man profiteth most, in that he most intendeth*, that it needs not to be stood upon. It is enough to point at it; *That no Nation which doth not profess Arms, and practise Military Arts, making it their principal study and occupation, may ever hope to have any notable greatness of Empire, fall into their mouths :* and on the other side, it is a most certain Oracle of time, *That those Nations that have continued long in the profession and study of Arms (as the Romans and Turks principally have done, for the propagation of Empire,) work wonders*. Nay those that have flourisht for the glory of Arms, but for the space only of one age; have commonly attain'd *that Greatness of Dominion*, in that one age, which maintained them long after, when their profession and exercise of Arms hath grown to decay.

7 Incident to this Precept is; *for a state to have such laws and customs which may readily reach forth unto them just occasions, or at least pretences of taking Arms*. For there is that apprehension of Justice imprinted in the nature of men, that they enter not upon *wars* (whereof so many calamities do ensue) but upon some, at the least specious grounds and Quarrels. The Turk hath at hand for cause of war the Propagation of his law and sect; a quarrel that he may always command. The *Romans* though they esteemed the *extending of the Limits of their Empire*, to be great honour to their Generals, when it was done; yet for that cause alone, to *Propagate their bounds*, they never undertook a war. Therefore let a nation that pretends to *Greatness*, and aspires to *Empire*, have this condition, that they have a quick and lively sense of any wrongs either upon Borderers, Merchants, or publick Ministers; and that they sit not too long upon the first provocation. *Again*, Let them be prest, and Active to send Aids and Succours to their Allies and confederates; as it ever was with the *Romans :* insomuch

Liv.lib.1.v.c 37.

as if a hoftile invafion were made upon a confederate, which alfo had
leagues Defenfive with other ftates,and the fame implored their ayds
feverally; the Romans would ever be the formoft; and leave it to
no other to have the Honour of the Affiftance. *As for* the wars which
were anciently made for a kind of conformity,or tacite corresponden-
cy of Eftates, I do not fee upon what Law they are grounded. Such
were the wars undertaken by the Romans, for the liberty of *Grecia :*
fuch were thofe of the *Lacedæmonians* and *Athenians,* to fet up or pull
down *Democracies* and *Oligarchies :* fuch are the wars made fometimes
by States, and Princes, under pretence of protecting Forreign fubjects, and freeing them from Tyranny and oppreffion, and the like.
Let it fuffice for the prefent point that it be concluded, *That no eftate
expect to be Great, that is not inftantly awake, upon any juft occafion of
Arming.*

8 *No body can be healthful without exercife, neither Natural Body nor
Politick : and certainly to a Kingdom or Eftate a juft and honourable war
is in place of a wholfome exercife.* A Civil war indeed, *is like the heat
of a Fever;* but a Forreign *is like the heat of Exercife,*and ferves to keep
the body in health : for in a floathful and drowfle Peace, both cou-
rages will effeminate, and Manners corrupt But howfoever it be for
the *Happineſs* of any *Eftate,* without all queftion, for *Greatneſs,* it
maketh, to be ftill for the moft part in Arms : and a *veteran* Army
(though it be a chargeable Bufineſs) always on foot, is that which
commonly gives the Law, or at leaft the Reputation amongft all *neigh-
bour-ftates.* This is notably to be feen in *Spain,* which had in one
part or other a *veterane Army* almoft continually, now by the fpace of
fix-fcore years.

9 *To be Mafter of the Sea, is an Abridgement of a Monarchy, Cicero*
writing to *Atticus* of *Pompeius* his preparation againft *Cæfar,*faith; *Con-
filium Pompeii, plane Themiftocleum eſt; putat enim, qui mari Potitur,
eum Rerum potiri.* And without doubt *Pompey* had tyred out and
broken *Cæfar,* if upon a vain confidence he had not left that way.We
fee from many examples the great effects of *Battels by Sea :* The Battel of *Actium* decided the Empire of the world : the Battel of *Lepan-
to* put a ring in the nofe of the Turk : *Certainly* it hath often fallen
out that *Sea-fights* have been final to the war; but this is when Princes or States have fet up their Reft upon thofe Battels. Thus much
is without all doubt, *that he that commands the Sea, is at great liberty; and may take as much and as little of the war as he will : whereas
on the Contrary, thofe that be ftrongeft by Land, are many times neverthelefs in great ftraits.* But at this day and with us of *Europe,* the van-
tage of ftrength at Sea (which is indeed one of the principal *Dowries of
this Kingdom of Great Brittain*) is in the fum of Affairs of great
import : both becaufe moft of the Kindoms of *Europe,* are not
merely Inland, but girt with the Sea moft part of their compafs, and becaufe the Treafures and Wealth of both Indies, feems
in great part but an Acceffary to the *command of the Seas.*

10. *The wars of latter Ages seem to be made in the dark, in respect of the Glory and Honour which reflected upon Military men from the wars in ancient times.* We have now perchance, for Martial encouragement, some degrees and orders of Chivalry, which neverthelefs are conferred promifcuoufly upon Soldiers, and no Soldiers; and fome Pedegrees of Families perhaps upon Scutchions; and fome publick Hofpitals for emerited and maim'd Soldiers, and fuch like things. But in ancient times, the *Trophy* erected upon the place of the Victory; the Funeral Laudatives and ftately Monuments for thofe that died in the Wars; Civick Crowns, and Military Garlands awarded to particular perfons; the ftile of Emperor, which the greateft Kings of the World after, borrowed from Commanders in War; the folemn Triumphs of the Generals upon their return, after the Wars were profperoufly ended; the great Donatives and Largeffes upon the disbanding of the Armies: thefe, I fay, were matters fo many and great, and of fuch glorious luftre and blaze in eyes of the world, as were able to create a Fire in the moft frozen breafts, and to inflame them to War. *But above all,* that of the *Triumph* amongft the Romans, was not a matter of mere pomp, or fome vain fpectacle or pageants; but one of the wifeft and nobleft inftitutions that ever was: for it contain'd in it three things, *Honor and Glory to the Generals; Riches to the Treafury out of the Spoils; and Donatives to the Army.* But the *Honours of Triumph* perhaps were not fit for Monarchies, except it be in the perfon of the King himfelf, or of the Kings Sons; as it came to pafs in the times of the *Roman Emperors;* who did impropriate the *Honor of Triumph* to themfelves, and their Sons; for fuch Wars as they did atchieve in Perfon, and left only by way of indulgence, *Garments* and *Triumphal* Enfigns to the Generals.

§ But to conclude thefe difcourfes, (*There is no man* (as facred Mat. vi. Scripture teftifies) *that by-care taking can add a cubit to his ftature,* in this little Model of Man's body; but in the great Frame of *Kingdoms* and *Common-wealths,* it is in the Power of Princes and Eftates, to add Amplitude and Greatnefs to their *Kingdoms.* For by introducing fuch ordinances, conftitutions and cuftoms, as we have now propounded, and others of like nature with thefe, they may fow greatnefs to Pofterity and Future Ages. But thefe counfels are feldom taken into confideration by Princes; but the Matter is commonly left to fortune to take its chance.

§ And thus much for the points that, for the prefent, have offered themfelves to our confideration touching *the Enlarging of the Limits of a State or Kingdom.* But to what end is this comtemplation, feeing of all Imperial Soveraignties in this World, the Roman Monarchy (as it is believed) was to be the laft? but that, being true to our own Defign, nor any where declining out of the way (in as much as *the Amplification of a Kingdom* was, amongft the three Politick Duties, the third) we could not altogether pafs it over untouch't. *There remains* now another *Deficient* of the two we have fet down; that is, of *Univerfal Juftice, or the Fountains of Law.*

11. All they which have written of Laws, have handled that Argument either as Philosophers, or as Lawyers, and none as Statesmen. *As for Philosophers*, they propound many things goodly for discourse, but remote from use. *For the Lawyers*, they are mancipated and wholly devoted every one to the Laws of the State where they live, or to the Placits of the *Emperial or Pontifical Laws*, and cannot use impartial and sincere judgement; but discourse as out of Gives and Fetters. *Certainly* this kind of knowledge pertains properly to *States-men*; who can best discern what humane society is capable of; what makes for the weal of the publick; what natural equity is; what the law of Nations, the custom of Countries, the divers and different forms of States and Republicks; and therefore are able to discern and judge of Laws, from the Principles, both of natural Equity and Policy. *Wherefore* the business in hand is, to have recourse unto, and make enquiry of the *Fountains* of *Justice*, and of *Publick utility*, and in every part of Law to represent a *pair of Character and Idea of that which is just*; by which general mark and direction he that shall intend his mind and studies that way, may try and examine the *several laws of particular Kingdoms and Estates*; and from thence endeavour an emendation. *Wherefore* after our accustom'd manner we will, in *one Title* propound an example thereof.

EXAMPLE

*
IDEA JUSTI-
TIÆ UNI-
VERSALIS
sive de Fon-
tibus Juris.

Of a Treatise touching *Universal Justice*, or the *Fountains of Law* in one Title by way of *Aphorism*.

THE PROEM.

APHORISM I.

IN Civil society either *Law* or *Power* prevails; for there is a *Power* which pretends *Law*, and some Law tastes rather of *Might* than *Right*. Wherefore there is a threefold *Fountain of Injustice*; Mere *Power*; Cunning *Illaqueation* under colour of Law; and the *Harshness of Law it self*.

APHORISM II.

The force and efficacy of *Private Right* is this. He that doth a wrong, by the *Fact*, receives *Profit* or *Pleasure*; by the *Example*, incurs *Prejudice* and *Peril*: others are not Partners with him in his *Profit* or *Pleasure*; but they take themselves interressed in the *Example*; and therefore easily combine and accord together, to secure themselves by Laws, lest injuries by turns seise upon every particular. But if thorough the corrupt humour of the times, and the generality of guilt, it fall out, that to the greater number and the more Potent, danger is rather created than avoided, by such a *Law*; Faction disanuls that *Law*, which often comes to pass.

APHORISM III.

Private Right is under the Protection of *Publick Law* : for *Laws* are for the *People* ; *Magistrates for Laws* ; and the authority of Magistrates depends upon the Majesty of Empire, and the form of Policy ; and upon Laws Fundamental : wherefore if this Part be sound and healthful, Laws will be to good purpose ; if otherwise, there will be little security in them.

APHORISM IV.

Yet notwithstanding, the end of *Publick Law* is not only to be a Guardian to *Private Right*, lest that should any way be violated ; or to repress Injuries : but it is extended also unto Religion, and Arms and Discipline, and Ornaments, and Wealth, and finally to all things which any way conduce unto the prosperous Estate of a Commonwealth.

APHORISM V.

For the End and Aim at which *Laws* should level, and whereto they should direct their Decrees and Sanctions, is no other than this *That the People may live happily :* This will be brought to pass, if they be rightly train'd up in *Piety* and *Religion*, if they be *Honest* for Moral conversation ; *secur'd by Arms* against foreign enemies ; *munited by Laws*, against seditions, and private wrongs ; *Obedient* to Government and Magistrates ; *Rich and flourishing* in Forces and wealth : but the Instruments and sinews of all Blessings are *Laws*.

APHORISM VI.

And this end the best *Laws* attain ; but many Laws miss this mark : for there is a great difference, and a wide distance in the comparative valure and virtue of *Laws* ; for *some Laws* are excellent, *some* of a middle temper; *others* altogether corrupt. We will exhibite according to the measure of our judgement, some certain *Laws* (as it were) of *Laws*, whereby information may be taken, what in all *Laws* is well or ill set down, and Establisht.

APHORISM VII.

But before we descend to the Body of *Laws in particular* ; we will briefly touch the Merit and Dignities of *Laws in general*. A *Law* may be held good, that is, *Certain in the intimation*, *Just in the Precept*, *Profitable in the Execution*, *Agreeing with the Form of Government in the present State* ; and begetting vertue in those that live under them.

TITLE

TITLE. I.

Of the first Dignity of Laws, that they be Certain.

A P H O R I S M   VIII.

CErtainty is so Essential to a *Law,* as without it a *Law* cannot be
    Just ; Si enim incertam vocem det Tuba, quis se parabit ad Bellum?
So if the Law give an *uncertain sound,* who shall prepare himself to o-
bey ? A Law then ought to give warning before it strike : and it is
a good Rule, *That is the best Law which gives least liberty to the Arbi-
trage of the Judge,* which is that, the *Certainty* thereof affecteth.

A P H O R I S M.   IX.

Incertainty *of Laws* is of two sorts ; one where *no Law is prescribed ;* the other, *when a Law is difficile and dark :* we must therefore
first speak of *Causes omitted* in the *Law ;* that in these likewise there
may be found some Rule of *Certainty.*

Of Cases omitted in Law.

A P H O R I S M   X.

THe narrow compass of man's wisdom, cannot comprehend all
    cases which time hath found out ; and therefore *Cases omitted,*
and new do often present themselves.   In these cases there is applied
a threefold remedy, or supplement ; either by a proceeding upon *like
Cases,* or by the use of *Examples,* though they be not grown up into Law ; or by *Jurisdictions,* which award according to the Arbitrement of some Good Man, and according to sound judgement ; whether they be *Courts Pretorian , or of Equity , or Courts Censorian or
of Penalty.*

Of Proceeding upon like Presidents ; *and of the*
Extensions of L A W S.

A P H O R I S M   XI

IN *Cases omitted,* the Rule of Law is to be deduced from *Cases of
    like nature ;* but with Caution and Judgement.   Touching
which these Rules following are to be observed. *Let Reason be fruitful ; Custom be barren, and not breed Cases.*   Wherefore whatsoever
is accepted against the *Sence* and *Reason* of a Law ; or else where
the *Reason* thereof is not apparent, the same must not be drawn into
consequence.

APHO.

APHORISM XII.

A fingular Publick Good doth neceffarily introduce *Cafes pretermitted.* Wherefore when a Law doth notably and extraordinarily refpect, and procure the profit and advantage of a State, *Let the interpretation be ample and extenfive.*

APHORISM XIII.

· *It is a hard Cafe to torture Laws, that they may torture Men.* We would not therefore *that Laws Penal, much lefs Capital, fhould be extended to new Offences :* yet if it be an old Grime, and known to the Laws, but the Profecution thereof falls upon a new Cafe, not forefeen by the Laws; we muft by all means depart from the *Placits of Law,* rather than that offences pafs unpunifht.

APHORISM XIV.

In thofe ftatutes, which the *Common Law* (fpecially concerning cafes frequently incident, and are of long continuance) doth abfolutely repeal; *We like not the proceeding by fimilitude, unto cafes omitted :* for when a *State* hath for a long time wanted a *whole Law,* and that, in *Cafes expreft*; there is no great danger if the *cafes omitted* expect a remedy by a *new ftatute.*

APHORISM XV.

Such conftitutions as were manifeftly, *the Laws of Time,* and fprung up from emergent Occafion , then prevailing in the *Common-wealth*; the ftate of times once changed, they are reverenc'd enough, if they may conferve their authority within the limits of their own proper cafes: and it were prepofterous any way to extend and apply them to *Cafes omitted.*

APHORISM XVI.

There can be no *Sequel of a Sequel,* but the extention muft be arrefted within the limits of *immediate Cafes :* otherwife we fall by degrees upon *unrefembling Cafes*; and the fubtilty of wit will be of more force, than the Authority of Law.

APHORISM XVII.

In Laws and Statutes of a *compendious ftile,* extention may be made more freely ; but in thofe *Laws* which are punctual in the *enumeration of Cafes* Particular, more verily : for as *exception* ftrengthens the force of a *Law,* in *Cafes not excepted*; fo *enumeration* weakens it, in Cafes not *enumerated.*

A P H O R I S M XVIII.

An *Explanatory Statute* dams up the ſtreams of a *Former Statute* ; neither is the extenſion received afterwards, in the one or the other : for their is no *ſuper-extenſion* can be made by a *Judge*, where once an *extenſion* hath begun to be made by a *Law*.

A P H O R I S M XIX.

The *Form* of Words, and Acts of Courts, doth not admit an *Extenſion* upon like Caſes ; for that looſeth the nature of *Formality*, which departs from Cuſtom to Arbitrement : and the introduction of *new Caſes* imbaſeth the Majeſty of the *old*.

A P H O R I S M XX.

Extenſion of Law is aptly applied unto *Caſes Poſt-nate*, which were not exiſtent in nature, when the Law was enacted : for where the Caſe could not be expreſt, becauſe there were none ſuch extant ; a *Caſe omitted* is accepted for a *Caſe expreſt*, if the reaſon be the ſame. So for *Extenſion of Laws in Caſes omiſt*, let theſe Rules ſuffice. *Now we muſt ſpeak of the uſe of Examples*.

Of Preſidents, and the uſe thereof.

A P H O R I S M XXI.

NOw it follows we ſpeak of *Examples*, from which *Right* is inferr'd, where *Law* is deficient : as for *Cuſtom*, which is a kind of *Law* ; and for *Preſidents* which by frequent Practice are grown into Cuſtom, as into a *Tacite Law* ; we will ſpeak in due place. But now we ſpeak of *Examples* or *Preſidents*, which rarely and ſparſedly fall out ; and are not yet grown up to the ſtrength of a *Law* ; namely when, and with what caution a *Rule* of *Law* is to be derived from them, where *Law is Deficient*.

A P H O R I S M XXII.

Preſidents muſt be derived from *Good* and *Moderate* ; and not from *Bloudy, Factious*, or *Diſſolute Times* : for *Examples* fetch from ſuch times, are a Baſtard iſſue, and do rather Corrupt, than Inſtruct.

A P H O R I S M XXIII.

In *Examples* the more *Modern*, are to be reputed the *more ſafe* : for that which was but lately done, and no inconvenience enſued thereon, why may it not be done again ? Yet nevertheleſs *Recent Examples* are of leſs Authority : and if perchance it ſo fall out, that
a Re-

a Reformation muſt be made, *Modern Preſidents* taſte more of their own *Times*, than of right *Reaſon*.

APHORISM XXIV.

But *more Ancient Preſidents* muſt be received with caution, and choice: for the Revolution of an Age altereth many things; ſo as what might ſeem *Ancient* for Time, the ſame through perturbation, and inconformity to the preſent Age, may be altogether *New*. Wherefore the *examples* of a *middle time* are beſt ; or of ſuch *an Age*, as beſt ſorts with the *Preſent Times*; which now and then the Time further off better repreſents, than the *Time cloſe at hand*.

APHORISM XXV.

Keep your ſelf within, or rather on this ſide the *limits of an Example*, and by no means ſurpaſs thoſe bounds: for where there is no *Rule of Law*, all ought to be entertain'd with jealouſie : wherefore here, as in obſcure Caſes, *follow that which is leaſt doubtful*.

APHORISM XXVI.

Beware of *Fragments* and *Compends* of *Examples* ; and view the *Examples* entire, and every particular paſſage thereof: for if it be inequitable and unreaſonable *before a perfect comprehenſion of the whole Law, to make a judgement upon a Part, or Paragraph thereof*; much more ſhould this Rule hold in *Examples*, which unleſs they be very ſquare and proper, are of doubtful uſe and application.

APHORISM XXVII.

In *Examples* it imports very much thorough what hands they have paſt, and have been tranſacted ; for if they have gone current with *Clerks* only and *Miniſters* of *Juſtice*, from the *courſe of ſome Courts*, without any notice taken thereof by *ſuperiour Counſellors* ; or with the *Maſter of Errors, the People*; they are to be rejected and little eſteemed of : but if they have been ſuch preciſe *Preſidents* to Counſellors of Eſtate, Judges or Principal Courts, as that it muſt needs be, that they have been ſtrengthened by the tacite approbation, at leaſt, of Judges ; they carry the more Reverence with them.

APHORSIM XXVIII.

Preſidents that have been publiſht, however leſs practiſed, which being debated and ventilated by mens diſcourſes and diſceptations have yet ſtood out unargued, are of greater Authority : but ſuch as have remained buried, as it were, in Cloſets and Archives, are of leſs : for, *Examples like waters are moſt wholſome in the running ſtream*.

A P H O R I S M XXIX.

Examples that refer to *Laws,* we would not have them drawn from writers of *History,* but from publick *Acts,* and more *diligent Traditions:* for it is an infelicity familiar even with the best Historians, that they pass over *Laws and Judicial proceedings* too slightly : and if perhaps they have used some diligence therein, yet they vary much from *Authentick Constitutions.*

A P H O R I S M XXX.

An *Example,* which a contemporary Age, or a time neerest unto it hath repeal'd, should not easily be taken up again, though the like case should afterwards ensue : nor makes it so much for an *Example,* that men have sometimes used it ; as it makes against an *example,* that upon experience, they have now relinquisht *it.*

A P H O R I S M XXXI.

Examples are admitted into Counsils ; but do in like manner prescribe or command ; therefore let *them* be so moderated, that the Authority of the time past, may be bowed and plied to the practice of the time present. And thus much concerning information from *Presidents* where *Law* is Deficient. Now follows that we speak of *Courts Prætorian* and *Censorian* ; Courts of Equity, and of Penalty.

Of Courts Prætorian and Censorian.

A P H O R I S M XXXII.

LEt there be *Courts* and *Jurisdictions,* which may define according to the Arbitrement of some Good man, and according to sound judgement : for the *Law* (as is observ'd before) cannot provide for *all Cases* ; but is fitted to such occurrences as commonly fall out ; and Time (as was said by the Ancients) *is a most wise Thing, and daily the Author and Inventor of new Cases.*

A P H O R I S M XXXIII.

New cases fall out both in *Matters Criminal,* which have need of Penalty, and in *Matters Civil,* which have need of Relief : the *Courts* which respect the Former, we call *Censorian* ; which respect the latter, *Prætorian.*

A P H O R I S M XXIV,

Let the *Censorian Courts of Justice,* have jurisdiction and Power not only of *punishing new offences* ; but also of *increasing Penalties* assigned

by

by the Laws for *old crimes*, if the cases be hainous and enormous, so they be not *Capital*: for a Notorious guilt, as it were, a new Case.

APHORISM XXXV.

In like manner, let *Prætorian Courts of Equity*, have power to *qua-life the Rigor of Law*; as also of *supplying the Defects of Law*: for if a Remedy ought to be extended to him whom *the Law hath past by*; much more to him whom *it hath wounded*.

APHORISM XXXVI.

Let these *Censorian* and *Prætorian Courts* be by all means limited within *Cases Hainous* and extraordinary; and not invade ordinary Jurisdictions; left peradventure the matter extend to the *supplantation*, rather than the *supplement* of Law.

APHORISM XXXVII.

Let these *Jurisdictions* reside only in the *Highest Courts of Judicature*, and not be communicated to *Courts inferior*: For the Power of *extending*, or *supplying*, or *Moderating Laws*, little differs from the Power of *Making* them.

APHORISM XXXVIII.

But let not these *Courts* be assigned over to *one man*, but consist of *Many*: Nor let the Decrees thereof issue forth with silence, but let the Judges alleage Reasons of their sentence, and that openly in the Audience of the Court; that what is free in the Power, may yet in the same and reputation be confined.

APHORISM XXXIX.

Let there be no *Rubrics of Bloud*; neither Define of *Capital crimes* in what Court soever, but from a known and certain Law; for God himself first denounced Death, afterwards inflicted it. Nor is any man to be put to death, but he that knew before-hand, *that he sinned against his own life*.

APHORISM XL.

In *Courts of Censure*, give way to a third Trial, that a necessity be not imposed upon Judges of absolving or of condemning, but that they may pronounce a *Non liquet*; so in like manner, let *Laws Censorian*, not only be a *Penalty*, but an *Infamy*, that is, which may not inflict a punishment, but either end in admonition; or else chastise the delinquent with some light touch of Ignominy, and as it were, a blushing shame.

APHORISM XLI.

In *Cenforian Courts* let the *first aggreffions*, and the middle Acts of Great offences, and wicked attempts be punifht; yea although they were never perfectly accomplifht : and let that be the chiefeft ufe of *thofe Courts*; feeing it appertains to *feverity*, to punifh the firft approaches of wicked enterprizes; and to *Mercy* to intercept the perpetration of them by correcting middle Acts.

APHORISM XLII.

Special regard muft be taken, that in *Prætorian Courts*, fuch Cafes be not countenanc'd, which the Law hath not fo much pretermitted, as flighted as Frivolous; or, as odious, judg'd unworthy redrefs.

APHORISM XXLIII.

Above all it moft imports the *Certainty of Laws*, that Courts of *Equity* do not fo fwell and overflow their banks, as under pretence of *mitigating the Rigor of Laws*, they do diffect or relax the ftrength and finews thereof, by drawing all to *Arbitrement*.

APHORISM XLIV.

Let not *Prætorian Courts* have Power to Decree againft *exprefs ftatute*, under any pretence of equity : for if this fhould be permitted, a *Law-interpreter*, would become a *Law-maker*; and all matters fhould depend upon *Arbitrement*.

APHORISM XLV.

Some are of opinion, that the Jurisdiction of Defining according to *Equity and Confcience*; and that other, which proceeds according to *ftrict Law*; fhould be deputed to the *fame Courts*; but others fay to *feveral* : by all means let there be a *feparation of Courts*; for there will be no *diftinction of Cafes, where there is commixtion or Jurisdictions*; but you fhall have *Arbitrement* incroach upon, and at laft, fwallow up *Law*.

APHORISM XLVI.

The *Tables of the Pretors* amongft the Romans came in ufe upon good ground : in thefe the *Pretor* fet down and publifht afore-hand, by what form of Law he would execute Judicature. After the fame example, Judges in *Prætorian Courts*, fhould propound *certain Rules* to themfelves (fo far as may be) and openly publifh them : *for that is the beft Law, which gives leaft liberty to the Judge; he the beft Judge that takes leaft liberty to himfelf.* But of thefe *Courts* we fhall fpeak more at large, when we come to the Title *De Judiciis*; we now fpeak of them

in

in paſſage only, ſo far as they clear and ſupply that which is omitted by the Law.

Of the Reflective Aſpect, or Reference of Laws one to another.

APHORISM XLVII.

THere is likewiſe another kind of *ſupplement of Caſes omitted*; when one Law falleth upon another, and withall draws with it *Caſes pretermitted*. This comes to paſs in *Laws or Statutes*, which (as the uſual expreſſion is) look back or *reflect* one upon another. *Laws* of this nature, are rarely and with great Caution to be alleag'd: for we like it not, to ſee a *two Fac'd* Janus *in Laws*.

APHORISM XLVIII.

He that goes about to elude and circumvent the words and ſentence of Law by *Fraud*, and *captious Fallacies*, deſerves in like manner to be himſelf inſnar'd by a ſucceeding Law : wherefore in caſe of *ſubtil ſhifts* and *ſiniſter deviſes*, it is very meet that laws ſhould *look back* upon and *mutually ſupport* one another, that he who ſtudies evaſions, and everſion of *Laws Preſent*, may yet ſtand in awe of *future Laws*.

APHORISM XLIX.

Laws which ſtrengthen and eſtabliſh the true *intentions of Records and Inſtruments*, againſt the *Defects of Forms and Solennities*, do rightly comprehend matters paſt : for the greateſt inconvenience in a law that *refers back*, is, that it diſturbeth : But theſe *confirmatory Laws*, reſpect the peace and ſetling of thoſe caſes, which are tranſacted and determin'd ; yet we muſt take heed that *caſes already adjudg'd*, be not *reverſt or violated*.

APHORISM L.

We muſt be very careful that, not thoſe *Laws* alone, be thought to *reſpect things paſt*, which invalid *caſes already decided*; but thoſe alſo which *prohibite* and *reſtrain future caſes* neceſſarily connext with *matters paſt*. As for example, if a Law ſhould interdict ſome kind of Trades-men the vent of their commodities for *hereafter* : the Letter of this Law is for the *future* ; but the ſence and meaning takes hold of the *time paſt* ; for now it is not warrantable for ſuch perſons to get their living *this* way.

APHORISM LI.

Every *Declaratory Law*, although there be no mention of *time paſt*; yet by the force of the Declaration, it is by all means to be extended

tended to *matters paſt.*: for the *Interpretation* doth not then begin to
be in force, when it is *declared*; but is made *contemporary* with the
Law it ſelf. Wherefore never enact *declaratory Laws*; but in caſe
where Laws may in equity refer and *look back* one upon another.
And here we have done with that part which handles the Incertitude *of*
Laws, *where no Law is found.* It remains, we now ſpeak of that other
part, namely where there is a Law extant, but ſuch a one as is Perplext
and Obſcure.

Of the Obſcurity of Laws.

A P H O R I S M LII.

OBſcurity of Laws ſprings from four cauſes: either from the exceſſive *accumulation of Laws*, ſpecially where there is a mixture of Obſolete Laws : Or from an *ambiguous*, or not perſpicuous
and *delucid deſcription of Laws :* or from the *manner of expounding
Law*, either altogether neglected, or not rightly purſued : or laſtly,
contradiction and *incertainty of judgments*.

Of the Ecceſſive Accumulation of Laws.

A P H O R I S M LIII.

THe Prophet ſaith, *Pluet ſuper eos Laqueos* ; now there are no worſe
ſnares than the ſnares of Laws, ſpecially Penal ; if they be *im-
menſe for number* ; and through the alterations of times *unprofitable* ;
they do not *preſent a torch, but ſpread a net to our feet.*

A P H O R I S M LIV.

There are two ways in uſe of making *a new Statute*; the one eſtabli-
ſheth and ſtrengthens the *Former Statute* about the ſame ſubject; and
then adds and changes ſome things : *the other* abrogates and cancels
what was Decreed before, and ſubſtitutes *de integro, a new and uni-
form Law.* The *latter way* we approve : for by the *former way* Decrees become complicate and perplext ; yet what is undertaken is
indeed purſued , but the Body of Law is in the mean time corrupted. But certainly the more diligence is required in the *latter*,
where the Deliberation is of the *Law it ſelf* ; that is , the Decrees
heretofore made, are to be ſearched into, and duely weighed and
examin'd, before the Law be publiſht : but the chief point is, that
by this means the *Harmony of Laws* is notably advanced for the
future.

A P H O R I S M LV.

It was a cuſtom in the State of *Athens*, to delegate ſix perſons, for
to reviſe and examine every year the *contrary Titles of Law*, which
                                                                  they

they called *Anti-nomies* ; and such as could not be reconciled, were propounded to the people , that some *certainty* might be defined touching them.   After this example, let such in every State, as have the Power of making Laws, review *Anti-nomies* every third or fifth year, or as they see cause.   And these may be first searcht into, and prepar'd by Committees assign'd thereto, and after that exhibited to Assemblies ; that so what shall be approv'd, may by suffrages be established and setled.

A P H O R I S M LVI.

And let there not be too scrupulous and anxious pains taken in reconciling *Contrary Titles of Law*, and of Salving (as they term it) all points by subtil and studied Distinctions.   For this is the Web of Wit ; and however it may carry a shew of Modesty and Reverence, yet it is to be reckoned in the number of things Prejudicial ; as being that which makes the whole body of Law ill-sorted, and incoherent.   It were far better that the worst *Titles* were cancel'd, and the rest stand in force.

A P H O R I S M LVII.

Obsolete Laws, and such as are grown out of use, as well as *Anti-nomies*, should be propounded by delegates, as a part of their charge to be repeal'd : for seeing express Statute cannot regularly be voided by *Disuse* ; it falls out that through a Disestimation of *Obsolete Laws*, the authority of the rest is somewhat embased ; and *Mezentius* Torture ensues ; *that Laws alive are killed with the embracements of Laws dead : but above all beware of a* Gangreen in Laws.

A P H O R I S M LVIII.

So likewise for *Obsolete Laws* and Statutes, and such as are not lately publisht ; let the *Pretorian Courts* have power : in the mean space, to define contrary to them : for although it hath been said not impertinently, *no man ought to make himself wiser than the Laws* ; yet this may be understood of Laws, when they are awake, not when they are asleep.   On the other side, let not the more recent *Statutes*, which are found prejudicial to the *Law-publick*, be in the Power of the Judges ; but in the Power of Kings and Counsellors of Estate, and supreme Authorities for Redress, by suspending their execution through Edicts and Acts ; until Parliamentary Courts, and such High Assemblies meet again, which have power to abrogate them ; lest the safety of the Common-wealth should in the mean while be endanger'd.

Of

Of New Digests of Laws.

A P H O R I S M LIX.

BUt if *Laws accumulated upon Laws*, swell into such vast volumes, or be obnoxious to such confusion, that it is expedient to revise them anew, and to reduce them into a sound and solid body; intend it by all means; and let such a work be reputed an Heroical noble work; and let the Authors of such a work, be rightly and deservedly ranckt in the number of the *Founders* and *Restorers of Laws.*

A P H O R I S M LX.

This *Purging of Laws*, and the contriving of a new Digest is five ways accomplisht. *First*, let *Obsolete Laws*, which *Justinian* terms *old Fables* be left out. *Secondly*, let the most approved of *Antinomies* be received; the contrary abolisht. *Thirdly*, let all *Coincident Laws*, or *Laws* which import the same, and are nothing else but repetitions of the same thing, be expung'd; and some one, the most perfect among them, retain'd instead of all the rest. *Fourthly*, if there be any *Laws which determine nothing*, but only propound Questions, and so leave them undecided, let these likewise be casher'd. *Lastly*, let *Laws too wordy* and too prolix be abridged into a more narrow compass.

A P H O R I S M LXI.

And it will import very much for use, to compose and sort apart in a new *Digest of Laws*, Law recepted for *Common Law*, which in regard of their beginning are time out of mind; and on the other side *Statutes* superadded from time to time: seeing in the delivery of a Juridical sentence, the interpretation of *Common Law*, and *Statute-Laws* in many points is not the same. This *Trebonianus* did in the Digests and Code.

A P H O R I S M LXII.

But in this *Regeneration* and *new structure of Laws*, retain precisely the *Words and the Text of the Ancient Laws*, and of the Books of Law; though it must needs fall out that such a collection must be made by centoes and smaller portions: then sort them in order. For although this might have been performed more aptly, and (if you respect right reason) more truly, by a *New Text*, than by such a consarcination; yet in Laws, not so much the *stile* and *description*, as *Authority*, and the Patron thereof, *Antiquity*, are to be regarded: otherwise *such a work* might seem a *scholastick business and method*, rather than *a body of commanding Laws.*

APHO-

APHORISM LXIII.

In this *New Digest of Laws*, upon good advisement a caveat hath been put in; that the *Ancient volumes of Law* should not be utterly extinguisht, and perish in oblivion; but should at least remain in Libraries; though the common and promiscuous use thereof might be retain'd. For in Cases of weighty consequence, it will not be amiss to consult and look into the mutations and continuations of *Laws past :* and indeed it is usual to sprinkle modern matters with Antiquity. *And this new corps of Law,* must be confirmed only by such, who in every state have the power of making Laws; lest perchance under colour of *Digesting Ancient Laws, new Laws,* under-hand be conveyed in.

APHORISM LXIV.

It could be wisht that this *Instauration of Laws,* might fall out, and be undertaken in *such times,* as, for learning and experience excel *those more Ancient times,* whose Acts and Deeds they recognize: which fell out otherwise in the works of *Justinian.* For it is a great unhappines, when the works of the Ancient, are maimed, and recompiled, by the judgement and choice of a less wise and learned Age: but oft times that is necessary which is not the best.

Thus much be spoken of the Obscurity of Laws, arising from the excessive and confused accumulation thereof. Now let us speak of the dark and doubtful Description of them.

Of the Perplext and Obscure Descriptions of *LAWS.*

APHORISM LXV.

Obscure *Description of Laws* arises either from the *Loquacity or Verbosity* of them; or again from *extream Brevity;* or from the *Preamble of a Law* repugnant with the *Body of a Law.*

APHORISM LXVI.

It follows that we now speak of the *Obscurity of Law,* arising from a corrupt and crooked *description thereof.* The *Loquacity* and *Prolixity,* which hath been used in setting down Laws, *we dislike :* neither doth such a writer any way compass what he desires, and labours for; but rather the quite contrary. For while a man endeavours to pursue and express *every Particular case in apt and proper terms,* hoping to gain more Certitude thereby; contrariwise it falls out, that through *many words, multitude of Questions* are ingendred; so as a more sound and solid interpretation of Law, according to the genuine sense and mind thereof, is much intercepted through the noise of words.

APHO-

APHORISM LXVII.

And yet notwithstanding a *too Concise and affected Brevity* for Majesties sake, or as more Imperial, is not therefore to be approved, specially in these times; lest Law become perchance, a *Lesbian Rule.* Wherefore a *middle temper'd stile* is to be embraced; and a generality of words well stated to be sought out; which though it do not so throughly pursue cases comprehended, yet it excludes cases not comprehended clearly enough.

APHORISM LXVIII.

Yet in ordinary and Politick Laws and Edicts, wherein for most part no man adviseth with his Counsel, but trusteth to his own judgment, all should be more *amply explicated and pointed out, as it were, with the finger,* even to the meanest capacity.

APHORISM LXIX.

So neither should we allow of *Preambles* to Laws, which amongst the ancients were held impertinencies, and which introduce *Disputing* and not *commanding Laws*, if we could well away with ancient custom. But these *Prefaces* commonly (as the times are now) are necessarily prefixt, not so much for explication of Law, as for perswasion that such a Law may pass in the solemn meeting of a State; and again, to give satisfaction to the communalty. Yet so far as possible may be, *let Prologues be avoided, and the Law begin with a command.*

APHORISM LXX.

The Mind and Meaning of a Law, though sometimes it may be drawn not improperly from *Prefaces* and *Preambles* (*as they term them*); yet the latitude and extention thereof, must not be fetcht from thence. For a *Preamble* by way of example, sometimes fetcheth in, lays hold upon some of the plausible and most specious passages; when yet the Law compriseth many more: or on the contrary, the Law *restrains* and *limits* many Cases, the reason of which *limitations* to insert in the *Preface* were *superfluous.* Wherefore the *dimension* and *latitude* of a Law must be taken from the Body of a Law : *for a Preamble often falls either short, or over.*

APHORISM LXXI.

And there is a very *vitious manner of Recording of Laws*, that is, when the case at which the *Law* aimeth, is *exprest at large in the preamble,* afterward from the force of the word(*The like*) or some such *term of relation,* the *Body of a Law* is reverst into the *Preamble*; so as the *Preamble* is inserted and incorporated into the Law it self; which is

an

an obfcure and not fo fafe a courfe ; becaufe the fame diligence ufeth not to be taken in pondering and examining the words of a *Preamble*, as there ufeth to be done in the *Body of a Law* it felf. This part touching the *Incertainty of Laws* proceeding from an *ill Defcription of them* we fhall handle more at large hereafter, when we come to treat of the *Interpretation of Laws*. Thus much *of the obfcure Defcription of Laws*. Now let us fpeak of the ways of expounding Laws.

Of the divers ways of expounding Law and folving Doubts.

APHORISM LXXII.

THe ways of *expounding Law* and *folving Doubts*, are five. For this is done either by *Court-Rolls* and *Records* ; or by *Authentick Writs* ; or by *fubfidiary Books* ; or by *Prelections* ; or by *Refponfes* and *Refolutions of Wife men*. All thefe, if they be well inftituted and fet down, will be fingular helps at hand againft the *obfcurity* of Laws.

Of the reporting of Judgements.

APHORISM LXXIII.

ABove all, let *the Judgements* delivered in higher, and *Principal Courts* of Judicature, and in matters of *grave importance*, fpecially *Dubious*, and which have fome Difficulty and *Newnefs* in them, be taken with faith and diligence. For *Decrees are the Anchors of Law, as Laws are of the Republick*.

APHORISM LXXIV.

The manner of collecting fuch *Judgements* and *Reporting* them, let be this. *Regifter the cafe precifely* ; the *Judgements exactly* ; *annex the Reafons of the Judgements* alleadged by the Judges ; mingle not Authorities of *Cafes brought for example* with *Cafes Principal*. As for *Perorations of Pleaders*, unlefs there be fomething in them very remarkable, pafs them over with filence.

APHORISM LXXV.

The Perfons which fhould Collect *thefe Judgements*, Let them be of the order and rank of the *learnedft Advocates*, and let them receive a liberal Remuneration from the State. Let not the *Judges* themfelves meddle, at all, with thefe *Reports* ; left perchance, devoted to their own opinions, and fupported by their own Authority, they *tranfcend the limits of a Reporter*.

APHO.

APHORISM LXXVI.

Digeſt *theſe Judgments* according *to the order* and *continuation of time*, not according to *Method* and *Titles* : for *writings of this nature* are, as it were, the *Hiſtories* and *Reports of Laws* ; nor do the *Decrees* alone, but their *times* alſo give light to a wiſe Judge.

Of Authentick Writers.

APHORISM LXXVII.

L Et the *Body of Law* be built only upon the Laws themſelves, which conſtitute the *common Law* ; next of *Decrees* or *Statutes* ; in the third place of *Judgements enrolled* ; beſides theſe, either let there be no other *Authenticks* at all, or ſparingly entertain'd.

APHORISM LXXVIII.

Nothing ſo much imports *Certainty of Laws* (of which we now diſcourſe) as that *Authentick Writings* be confined within moderate bounds ; and that the *exceſſive multitude of Authors* and Doctors of the Laws, whereby the mind and ſentence of Laws are diſtracted ; the Judge confounded ; proceedings are made immortal ; and the Advocate himſelf, deſpairing to read over and conquer ſo many Books, betakes himſelf to Abridgements ; be diſcarded. It may be ſome good gloſs, and ſome few of Claſſick Writers, or rather ſome ſmall parcel of few Writers, may be received for *Authenticks*. Yet of the *reſt*, ſome uſe may be made in Libraries, where Judges or Advocates, may as occaſion is offered read their Diſcourſes : but in cauſes to be pleaded, let them not be permitted to be brought and alleaged in the Court, nor grow up into Autority.

Of Auxiliary Books.

APHORISM LXXIX.

L Et not the knowledge and practice of *Law* be deſtituted, but rather well provided of *Auxiliary Books*. They are in general ſix ſorts, Inſtitutes ; of the ſignification of Words ; of the Rules of Law ; Ancient Records ; Abridgements ; Forms of Pleading.

APHORISM LXXX.

Young Students and Novices are to be enter'd by *Inſtitutes* ; that they may the more profoundly and orderly draw and take in the knowledge and Difficulties of the *Laws*. Compoſe theſe *Inſtitutes* after a clear and perſpicuous manner. In theſe *elementary Books* run over the whole *private Law* ; not paſſing by ſome Titles, and dwelling too long upon others ; but briefly touching ſomething in all ; that
coming

coming to read through the *whole body of Laws*, nothing may be presented altogether ftrange; but what hath been tafted, and preconceiv'd by fome flight notion. Touch not the *Publick Law in Inftitutes*, but let that be deduced from the *Fountains of themfelves*.

APHORISM LXXXI.

Compile a Commentary upon the *Terms of Law*: Be not too curious and tedious in the explication thereof; and of rendring their fenfe; for the fcope here, is not exactly to feek out the *Definition of Words*, but fuch *explications* only, as may clear the paffage to the reading of the *Books of Law*. Digeft not this Treatife by the *letters of the Alphabet*: leave that to fome Index; but let fuch words as import the fame thing be forted together; that in the comprehenfion of the fenfe, one may adminifter help upon the other.

APHORISM LXXXII.

A found and well-labour'd Treatife of the *divers Rules of Law*, conduceth (if any thing doth) to the *certainty of Laws*. A work worthy the Pen of the greateft Wits, and wifeft Jurifts. Nor do we approve what is extant in this kind. And not only noted and common *Rules*, are to be collected, but alfo others more fubtil and abftrufe, which may be abftracted out of the *Harmony of Laws*, and *Judged Cafes*; fuch as are fometimes found in the *beft Rubrics*; and thefe are the general *Dictates of Reafon*, and the *Ballaft*, as it were of *Law*.

APHORISM LXXXIII.

But all *Decrees and Placits of Law*, muft not be taken for *Rules*, as is wont to be, abfurdly enough: for if this fhould be admitted, then fo many Laws, fo many Rules; for a Law is nothing elfe, than a *commanding Rule*. But accept thofe for *Rules* which cleave to the very *Form of Juftice*, from whence for moft part the fame *Rules* are commonly found through the *Civil Laws* of Different *States*; unlefs perhaps they vary for the reference to the *Forms of publick Governments*.

APHORISM LXXXIV.

After the *Rule* is divided in a brief and fubftantial comprehenfion of words; let there be, *for explication*, annext *examples*, and moft clear and luculent *Decifions of Cafes*; *Diftinctions* and *exceptions* for *limitations*; *Points concurrent in fence*, for *Amplification* of the fame *Rule*.

APHORISM LXXXV.

It is well given in Precept, *that a Law fhould not be drawn from Rules*; but the *Rule from the Law in force*. Neither is a *Proof* to be taken from the words of a *Rule*, as if it were a *Text of Law*: for a *Rule* (as the fea-man's needle doth the Poles) *indicates* only, not *Determines Laws*.

APHO.

Besides the *Body of Law*, it will avail also, to survey the *Antiquities or ancient Records of Laws*, whose Authority, though it be vanisht, yet their Reverence remains still. And let the *Writings* and *Judgements* concerning *Laws*, be received for the *Antiquities of Laws*, which in time preceded the *Body of Laws*; whether they were publisht or not : for these must not be lost. Therefore out of these *Records* select what ever is most useful (for there will be found much vain and frivolous matter in them)and digest them into one volume; lest *old fables*, (as *Trebonianus* calls them) be mixt with the *Laws* themselves.

APHORISM LXXXVII.

And it much imports the practick part of Laws, that the whole Law be *Digested into Places and Titles*; whereto a man may have (as occasion shall be given) a sudden recourse , as to a furnisht Promptuary for present practice. These *Books of Abridgements*, both reduce into *Order* what was dispersed, and *abreviate* what was diffused and *Prolix* in Law. But caution must be taken that these *Breviaries*, make not men prompt for the *practick part*, and slothful for the *knowledge it self* : for their proper use and office is this, that by them the *Law* may be tilled over again, and not throughly learned. And these *Summaries* must by all means be collected with great diligence, faith and judgement, lest they *commit Felony against the Law*.

APHORISM LXXXVIII.

Make a Collection of the *divers Forms of Pleading* in every kind : for this conduceth much to the practick Part : and certainly these *Forms* do discover the Oracles and secret Mysteries of Laws : for there are many things which lie hidden in Laws; But in *Forms* of Pleadings, they are better and more largely displayed; —*like the fist to the Palm*.

Of Responses and Resolutions of Doubts.

APHORISM LXXXIX.

SOme course must be taken for the *cutting off*, and satisfying *particular Doubts* which emerge from time to time : for it is a hard case that they which desire to secure themselves from error,should find no guide to the way : but that present businesses should be hazarded; and there should be no means to know the Law before the matter be dispatcht.

APHORISM XC.

That the Resolutions of the Wise , given to Clients touching *point of Law*, whether by *Advocates* or *Professors*, should be of such Authority, that it may not be lawful for the Judge to depart from their opinion, we cannot approve. *Let Law be derived from sworn Judges.*

APHORISM XCI.

To Feel and found Judgements by feigned Caufes and Perfons, that by this means, men might find out what the Courfe and proceeding of Law will be, we approve not: for it difhonoureth the Majefty of *Laws*, and is to be accounted a kind of *prevarication* or double dealing; *and it is a foul fight to fee places of Judicature to borrow any thing from the ftage.*

APHORISM XCII.

Wherefore let, as well the *Decrees*, as the *anfwers and Counfels* proceed from the Judges alone: thofe of fuits depending; thefe of difficult points of Law, in the general. Require not thefe *Decifions*, whether in caufes private or publick, from the Judges themfelves, (for this were to make the Judge an Advocate) but of the *Prince*, or of the *State. From thefe* let the order be directed unto the *Judges:* and let the *Judges* thus authorized, hear the *reafons on both fides;* both of the Advocates or of the Committees, deputed by the parties to whom the matter appertaineth; or of them affigned by the Judges themfelves; if neceffity fo require: and weighing the Caufe, let them deliver the Law upon the cafe and declare it. Let thefe *verdicts* and *counfels*, be recorded and notified amongft *Cafes adjudged*, and be of equal *authority.*

Of Prelections.

APHORISM XCIII.

Et the *Lectures of Law*, and the exercifes of thofe that addrefs themfelves to the ftudies of Law, be fo inftituted and ordered, that all may tend rather to the laying afleep, than the awaking of Queftions and Controverfies in Law. For (asthe matter is now carried) a School is fet up, and open amongft all, to the multiplying *of Altercations and Queftions in Law*; as if their aim was only to make oftentation of wit. And this is an old difeafe, for even amongft the Ancients, it was, as it were, a glory, by Sects and Factions, to *cherifh rather than extinguifh many queftions* concerning Law. Provide againft this inconvenience.

Of the Inftability of Judgements.

APHORISM XCIV.

Judgements become *incertain*, either through *immature and too precipitate proceeding to fentence*; or through *Emulation of Courts*; or through ill and *unfkilful regiftring of Judgements*; or becaufe there is a too *eafie and expedit way open of Reverfing and Refcinding them.* Wherefore it muft be provided, that *Judgements* iffue forth not without a *ftaid deliberation had afore-hand*; and that Courts bear a *Reverent*

rent *respect* to one another ; and that Decrees *be drawn up faithfully*
and wisely ; and that the *way to repeal Judgements be narrow*, rocky
and strewed, as it were, with sharp stones.

A P H O R I S M XCV.

If a *Judgement* have been awarded upon a *Case* in any Principal
Court; and the *like case* intervene in another Court; proceed not
to *sentence* before the matter be advised upon in some *solemn Assembly*
of Judges : for if *Judgements awarded must needs be repeal'd*, yet let
them be interred with Honour.

A P H O R I S M XCVI.

For Courts to be at debate and variance *about Jurisdictions* is a humane frailty ; and the more because this int●perance, through a
misprission and vain conceit *(that it is the part of a stout resolute Judge*
to enlarge the priviledges of the Court) is openly countenanced and
spur'd on, whereas it hath need of the Bridle.   But that out of this
heat of stomach, Courts should so easily *reverse* on both sides *Judge-*
ments awarded, which nothing pertain to *Jurisdiction*, is an insuffe-
rable evil, which by all means should be repres'd and punisht ; by
Kings or Counsels of State, or the form of Government.   For it is a
Presibent of the worst example, *That Courts, that should distribute*
Peace, should themselves practice Duels.

A P H O R I S M. XCVII.

Let there not be a too easie and free passage made to *the Repealing*
of Judgements by *Appellations*, and *writs of Error*, or *Re-examination,*
and the like.   It is maintained by some, that a Suit may be brought
into a Higher Court, as entire and untried, the Judgement past upon it, *set aside* and *absolutely suspended :* others are of opinion that the
Judgement it self may stand in force, but the execution thereof may be
staid : neither of these is to be allowed, unless the Courts wherein
the Judgement was awarded, were of a base and inferior order : but
rather that both the *Judgement stand*, and that the execution thereof go on ; so a Caveat be put in by the Defendant for Damages and
charges if the *Judgement* should be *reverst.*

But this *Title* touching the *Certainty of Laws* shall suffice for a president to the rest of a * *Digest*, which we with care and diligence
endeavour to contrive.   And now have we concluded *Civil Know-*
ledge (so far as we thought fit to entreat thereof) and together with it
Humane Philosophy, as also with *Humane Philosophy* ; *Philosophy in Ge-*
neral. Wherefore being now at length at some pause, and looking
back into that we have past through ; this our writing seems to us not
much unlike those sounds and Preludes, which *Musicians* make while
they are tuning their *Instruments* ; which is harsh and unpleasing to
hear , but yet is a cause why the *Musick* is sweeter afterwards.

* Digestum ju-
ris Anglicani ;
Sacrum Iustitiæ
Templum; Opus
sane Regium ;
sed nondum
conditum; quod
Tuo seculo Ex-
cellentissime
Principum, In-
staurandum :
Tui Nominis
Æternitati,
consecrandum
reservatur.

So

So have we been content to employ our pains in tuning the *Instrument of the Muses*, and to set it unto a true Harmony, that afterwards they may play who have better hands. *Surely*, when I set before me the condition of these times, in which *Learning* seems to have made her *third Circuit* to Men; and withal diligently behold, with what various supplies and supports being furnisht, she hath made her visitation; as are, the *height* and *vivacity* of *many Wits* in this our Age; *the excellent monuments of Ancient writers*, which as so many great lights shine before us; *the Art of Printing*, which communicates Books with a liberal hand to men of all fortunes; *the travel'd bosom of the Ocean* and of the world, opened on all parts, whereby multitudes of experiments unknown to the Ancients have been disclosed; and *Natural History*, by the access of an infinite Mass advanced : *the leasure* wherewith the Kingdoms and States of Europe every where abound, not imploying men so generally in *Civil Businesses*, as the States of *Græci* did in respect of their *Popularity*; or as the state of the *Romans* did in respect of their *Monarchy: the Peace* which at this present, Brittany, Spain, Italy, as also at this instant France and many other Countries enjoy : *The Consumption and Examinition* of all that can be imagined or said *in controversies of Religion*, which now so long have taken up so many Wits, and diverted them from the studies of *other Sciences : the Elevation and Perfection of Your Majesties Learning*; about whom (as the Birds about the Phænix) whose vollies of wits flock and assemble : *Lastly the inseparable property which attends time it self*, which is, *ever more and more to disclose truth :* when we think, I say, on these advantages; we cannot but be raised to this Perswasion, that this *third period of Learning*, will far surpass those two former of the *Grecian and Roman Learning*. Only if men will but well and wisely know their own strength and their own weakness both; and take, one from the other, *light of Inventions*; and not *Fire-brands of contradiction*; and esteem of the Inquisition of Truth, as a noble enterprise, and not as a delight or ornament ; and imploy wealth and magnificence to things of worth and excellency, and not to things vulgar and of popular estimation.

As for my Labours, if any man shall please himself or others in the reprehension of them, certainly they shall cause me put up that ancient request, but of great patience, *verbera, sed Audi*; *let men reprehend as they please, so they observe and weigh what is spoken*. Verily the Appeal is lawful (though, it may be, for this matter, not so needful) if it be made *from the first cogitations of men unto the second*; *and from the neerer times, to the times farther off*.

Now let us come unto the *Learning*, which those two ancient *Periods of time* were not so blest as to know, I mean *Sacred and Divinely inspired Theology*, the noblest *Saboath and Port of all mens Labours and Peregrinations*.

THE

Ninth Book

OF

FRANCIS L. VERULAM

Vicount St *ALBAN:*

OF THE

Dignity and Advancement

OF

LEARNING.

To the KING.

Chap. I.

The Partitions of Infpired Divinity *are omitted, only acceſs is made to* three *Deficients.* I. The Doctrine of the right uſe of Humane Reaſon in matters Divine. II. The Doctrine of the Degrees of Unity in the City of God. III. And the Emanations of SS. Scriptures.

AND now (*moſt excellent King*) we have with a ſmall Bark, ſuch as we were able to ſet out, ſail'd about the univerſal circumference, as well *of the old as the new* , *World of Sciences*; with how proſperous winds and courſe, we leave to Poſterity to Judge. What remains but that having accompliſht our Deſigns, we ſhould pay our vows? But there reſts yet behind *Sacred-inſpired-Divinity* ; whereof if we ſhould proceed to intreat, we ſhould depart out of the *Pinnace of Humane Reaſon* , and go into the *ſhip of the Church* , which muſt alone be governed by a *Divine ſea-needle* , to direct her courſe aright : for the *Stars of Philoſophy* which hitherto ſhined forth unto us, and were our chief guide, here fail us: it were then meet, we

R r 2   kept

kept filence in this facred fubject. Wherefore we fhall omit the *juſt partitions of this knowledge* ; yet notwithſtanding fomewhat we will caſt into this treafury, by way of good wifhes according to the proportion of our flender hability.   This we do the rather becaufe we find no coaſt or fpace of ground in the whole *Body of Divinity* lying vacant and untilled ; fo diligent have men been, either in fowing of *Good feed, or fowing of Tares.*

§ *Wherefore we* will propound *three Appendices of Theology*, treating, not of the matter *informed* of by *Divinity*, or to be *informed* of, but only of the *manner of information :* neither will we annex examples, or fet down precepts concerning thefe Tractates, as our manner was to do in the reſt ; that we refer to *Divines* ; for thefe are (as hath been faid) *like meer vows only.*

I. *The prerogative of God* comprehends the whole man ; and is extended as well to the *Reafon*, as to the *will of Man* ; that is, that man renounce himfelf wholly, and draw near unto God : wherefore as we are to *obey his law*, though we find a reluctation in our *will*, fo we are to *believe his word*, though we a find a reluctation in our *Reafon :* for if we believe only that which is agreeable unto our *Reafon*, we give affent to the *Matter*, not to the *Author* ; which is no more than we would do towards a fufpected and difcredited witnefs : but *that Faith which was accounted unto Abraham for Righteoufnefs*, was of fuch a point, as whereat *Sarah laughed*, who therein was an Image of *Natural Reafon.*   By how much therefore any *Divine Myſterie* is more difcondant, and incredible ; by fo much the more Honour is given to God in *Believing*, and the victory of our *Faith* is made more noble: Nay, even finners by how much the more they are furcharg'd in confcience, and yet repofe a truft in the mercies of God for their falvation, by this do more honour God, *for all defperation is a reproach of the Deity.*   Nay farther, (if we truly confider the point) it is an Act more great and high to *believe*, than to *know*, as we now *know :* for in *knowledge* man's mind fuffers from *fenfe*, which refults from things materiate ; but in *Belief* the fpirit fuffers from fpirit, which is the worthier Agent : the cafe is otherwife in the *ſtate of Glory*, for then *Faith ſhall ceafe, and we ſhall know, as we are known.*   Wherefore we may conclude, that *Sacred Theology* is grounded on, and muſt be deduced from the *Oracles of God* ; and not from the *light of Nature*, or the *Dictates of Reafon :* for it is written, *The Heavens declare the Glory of God*, but we never find it written, *The Heavens declare the will of God :* of the *will of God*, it is faid, *Ad legem & Teſtimonia* ; *ſi non fecerint fecundum illud*, &c.   This holds not only in thofe great Myſteries concerning the *Deity*, the *Creation*, the *Redemption*, but appertains alfo to a more perfect interpretation of the *Law Moral*, *Love your Enemies* ; *do good to them that hate you*, &c. *that you may be the children of your heavenly Father, who commands the rain to fall upon the juſt and unjuſt*, which words certainly deferve that applaufe, *Nec vox hominem fonat :* For it is a voice beyond the light of Nature.   So likewife we fee the Heathen Poets efpecially, when they fall upon a paffion, do ſtill expoſtulate with *Laws and Moralities* (which yet are far more free and indulgent than *di-*
vine

SOPHRON five de legitimo ufu RATIONIS humanæ in DIVINIS.

Gen. 18.

1 Cor. xiii.

Pfal. xix.

Mat. v.

vine Laws) as if in a kind of malignity, they were repugnant to the liberty of nature,

Plutar. in A-
lex. M.

——— *Et quod natura remittit*
	Invida jura negant ———

So said *Dendamis* the Indian, unto Alexanders Messengers, *That he had heard somewhat of the name of* Pythagoras, *and some other of the wise men of* Grecia, *and that he held them for excellent men ; but they had one fault, which was, that they had in too great Reverence and Veneration, an imaginary thing they called Law and Manners.* So it must be confest, that a great part of the *Law Moral* is of that perfection, whereunto the light of nature cannot aspire: yet notwithstanding, that men are said to have, even from the *Light and Law of Nature,* some notions and conceits of *virtue, vice, justice, injury, good and evil,* is most true and certain. Yet we must understand that this *light of Nature* is used in two several senses ; *first,* as it springs from sense, Induction, Reason, Arguments, according to the *Laws of Heaven and Earth;* *Secondly,* as it is imprinted and shines upon the spirit of Man by an inward instinct according to the *Law of Conscience,* which is a spark, and, as it were, the Remains of a Pristine and Primitive Purity : in which latter sense principally, the soul is participant of some light to behold and discern the perfection of the *Moral Law ;* which light is not altogether so clear, but such as in some measure rather reprehends *vices,* than fully informes us concerning Duties: So then the *Religion* as well *Moral* as *Mystical* depends upon *Divine Revelation.*

§ The *use, notwithstanding, of Humane Reason in matters spiritual,* is without question, manifold, very spacious, and general ; and it is not for nothing that the Apostle calls Religion, *our reasonable service of God,* Let it be remembred that the shadows and Figures of the old Law, *were full of Reason* and *signification,* much differing from the ceremonies of Idolatry and magick, which were sur ? and mute ; oftentimes instructing nothing, no not so much as insinuating any thing. *The Christian Faith especially, as in all things, so in this is eminent, and deserves highly to be magnified, that it holds a golden Mediocrity touching the use of Reason and Disputation, which is the off-spring of Reason ; between the Law of the Heathen and the Law of Mahomet, which have imbraced the two extremes ;* for the Religion of the *Heathen,* had no constant belief or confession ; on the contrary in the Religion of *Mahomet,* all Disputation was interdicted : so as one hath the very face of wandring and multifarious error ; the other of cunning and cautelous imposture ; whereas the *Holy Christian Faith* doth both admit and reject *Disputation,* but according to due bounds.

V. Doct. fi.
Hooker.um de
L. Eccl. Poli-
tæl. 3. v111.
1x.l.1. § v111
1x.
Rom. x11.

§ The *use of humane Reason in matter pertaining to Religion* is of two sorts ; the one in the *explication and conception of the Mistery;* the other in *Illations and Inferences derived from thence.* As touching the *Explication of Misteries,* we see that God vouchsafeth to descend to the weakness of our capacity , so expressing and unfolding his *Misteries* as they may be best comprehended by us ; *and inoculating*

*ting, as it were, his Revelations, upon the Conceptions and Notions of
our Reason;* and *so applying his inspirations to open our understanding,
as the form of the key is fitted to the ward of the lock.* In which respect notwithstanding, we ought not to be wanting to our selves;
for seeing God himself makes use of the faculty and function of *Reason* in his *Illuminations;* we ought also every way to imploy and improve the same, whereby we may become more capable to receive
and draw in such holy *Mysteries :* with this caution, that the mind
for its Module be dilated to the amplitude of the Mysteries; and
not the Mysteries be streightned and girt into the narrow compass of
the Mind.

§ *As for Illations,* we ought to know that there is allowed us a *use
of Reason* and Argument, in regard of *Mysteries,* Secondary and Respective; not Primitive and Absolute : for after the *Articles and
Principles of Religion* are placed in their seats, so as they stand altogether exempt from the examination of *Reason* , it is then indeed
permitted unto us to make derivations and inferences from them, according to the Analogy of them. *In things Natural* this holds not;
for both the Principles are liable to examination, by *Induction* I mean,
though not by *Syllogism;* and the same Principles have no repugnancy
with *Reason,* but that the first and middle Propositions may be derived from the same Fountain. But it is otherwise in the *Doctrine* of
Religion, where the first propositions are their own supporters and
subsistent by themselves; and again, they are not regulate by that
Reason, which inferreth consequent propositions. Nor holdeth this
in *Religion* alone, but also in other *Sciences,* both of greater and
smaller nature; namely *where the Primarie Propositions are Placita
not Posita;* because in *these* also the *use of Reason* cannot be absolute.
For *instance we see in Games , as Chess , or the like , that the first
Draughts and Laws of the Play are merely positive & ad placitum, which
must absolutely be accepted, and not disputed; but that thereupon you
may win the Game, and with the best advantage manage your Play, is
a thing artificial and rational.* So it is likewise in Humane Laws ,
wherein there be many *Maximes* (as they stile them) that is, mere
Placita Juris, grounded more *upon Authority than Reason;* neither
come they into disceptation : but what is *most just,* not absolutely
but relatively, (that is from the Analogie of *these Maximes*) that
indeed is *Rational,* and affords a large field of Disputation. Such
therefore is that *secondary Reason,* which hath place in *sacred Theology,*
that is, which is grounded upon the *Placits of God.*

§ And as there is a double *use of humane Reason in matters Divine;*
so in the same use there is a double excess; the one *where there is made
a more curious enquiry into the manner of the Mystery than is beseeming;*
the other *when equal Authority is attributed to Derivations , which is
to Principles.* For both he, may seem to be *Nicodemus Disciple,* who
pertinaciously enquires, *How can a man be born when he is old?* and
he in no wise can be accounted *Pauls Disciple,* which may not sometimes interlace his instructions with *Ego non Dominus,* or that, *According to my Judgment;* for to many *Illations* that stile is well applied :
wherefore to my understanding it would be a wholesome and very

Joan. III.

1 Cor VII.

pro-

profitable courſe, if there were a ſober and diligent Tractate compiled, which as a kind of *Divine Dialectick* might give directions,
concerning the true limits and uſe of Reaſon in matters Divine; which
would be a kind of *Opiate Medicine*, *not only to quiet and lay aſleep the
vanity of Aery ſpeculations, wherewith the Schools ſometime labour;
but likewiſe not a little calm, and mitigate the furies and rage of Controverſies, which raiſe ſidings and factions in the Church.* A Treatiſe
of this nature we ſet down as *Deficient*, and term it *Sophron* or *the
the right uſe of Humane Reaſon in matters Divine.*

II. It imports exceedingly the *Peace of the Church*, that the
League of Chriſtians, preſcribed by our Saviour in thoſe two clauſes
which ſeem to croſs one the other, were well and clearly expounded; whereof the one defines thus, *He that is not with us is againſt
us :* the other thus : *He that is not againſt us is with us.* From thoſe
two ſeveral aſſertions it plainly appears, *that there are ſome Articles
wherein whoſoever diſſenteth, is to be held as not comprehended in the
league : and there are other Articles, wherein a man may diſſent, and
yet the league be kept entire.* For the bounds of Chriſtian community
are ſet down ; *One Faith, one Baptiſm* ; and not, *one Rite, one Opinion.*
We ſee likewiſe the Coat of our Saviour *was entire without ſeam* ; but
the garment of the Church *was of divers Colours.* The *Chaff* muſt
be ſever'd from the corn in the ear ; but the *Tares* may not preſently be pull'd up from the Corn in the Field. When *Moſes* ſaw an
Egyptian fighting with an Iſraelite, he did not ſay, why ſtrive you ?
but drew his ſword and ſlew the Egyptian ; but when he ſaw two
Iſraelites fight, though it could not poſſible be that both parties had a
juſt cauſe ; yet he thus beſpeaks them both, *You are brethren, why ſtrive
you ?* Wherefore if theſe things be well obſerved, it will be found
a matter of great moment and uſe to define what, and of what latitude thoſe points are, which diſcorporate men from the body of
the Church, and caſt them out and quite caſhier them from the communion and fellowſhip of the faithful. And if any think that this
hath been done now long ago, let him ſeriouſly conſider with what
ſincerity, and moderation the ſame hath been perform'd. In the
mean ſpace it is very likely, that he that makes mention of *Peace*,
ſhall bear away that anſwer *Jehu* gave to the Meſſenger, *Is it Peace
Jehu ? What haſt thou to do with Peace ? turn and follow me.* *Peace*
is not the matter that many ſeek after, but parties and ſiding : Notwithſtanding we thought good to ſet down amongſt *Deficients*, as a
wholſome and profitable work, a Treatiſe touching *the Degrees of U-
nity in the City of God.*

III. Seeing the Parts of Sacred Scripture touching the *Information
of Theology*, are ſuch and ſo great; let us ſpecially conſider the Interpre-
tion thereof; nor do we here ſpeak of the *Authority* of interpreting
them, which is eſtabliſht by the conſent of the Church, but of the
manner of Interpreting. This is of two ſorts, *Methodical* ; and *Solute,*
or at large : for this divine water, which infinitely excels that
of *Jacobs well*, is drawn forth and deliver'd much after the ſame
manner as *Natural waters* uſe to be out of *Wells* ; for theſe at the firſt
draught are either receiv'd into *Ciſterns*, and ſo may be conveyed,
and

*
IRENÆUS,
five de Gra-
dibus unitatis
in Civitate
Dei.
Luc. c ix.
Luc. xi.

Epheſ. iv.
Joan. x y.
1 Cor. xiv.

Exod. ii.

1 Reg. ix.

*
UTRES
COELE-
STES, five
Emanationes
Scripturarum.

and deriv'd by many Pipes for publick and private use ; or is poured forth immeditately in Buckets and Veſſels, to be us'd out of hand,
as occaſion requires.

§ Now this former *Methodical manner* hath at length brought
forth unto us *Scholaſtical Theology*, whereby *Divinity* hath been collected into an *Art*, as into a *Ciſtern* ; and the ſtreams of *Axioms* and
Poſitions, diſtributed from thence into all parts.

§ But in *ſolute Manner of Interpreting*, *two extreams* intervene ;
the one preſuppoſeth ſuch a *perfection in Scriptures*, *as that all Philoſo-*
phy ought to be fetcht and deriv'd from thoſe ſacred Fountains ; *as if all*
other Philoſophy were an unhallowed and Heatheniſh thing. This di-
ſtemperature hath prevail'd eſpecially in the School of *Paracelſus*,
and ſome others ; the ſource and ſpring whereof flowed from the
Rabbins and Cabaliſts. But theſe men have not attain'd their purpoſe ; nor do they give honour (as they pretend) to *Scriptures*, but
rather embaſe and diſtain them. For to ſeek a *materiate Heaven* and
Earth in the Word of God, whereof it is ſaid *Heaven and Earth ſhall*
paſs, *but my word ſhall not paſs*, is indeed to purſue Temporary things
amongſt eternal : *for as to ſeek Divinity in Philoſophy*, *is as if you*
would ſeek the living amongſt the Dead ; ſo on the other ſide , *to ſeek*
Philoſophy in Divinity, *is all one as to ſeek the dead amongſt the*
living.

§ The other *manner of Interpreting*, which we ſet down as an exceſs, ſeems at firſt ſight ſober and chaſte ; yet notwithſtanding it
both diſhonoureth *Scriptures*, and is a great prejudice and detriment to the Church ; and it is, to ſpeak in a word, when *Divinely-in-*
ſpir'd Scriptures are expounded after the ſame manner that humane
writings are. For it muſt be remembred, that there are two points
known to God the Author of Scripture, which man's nature cannot
comprehend ; that is, *The ſecrets of the Heart* ; *and the ſucceſſion of*
Times. Wherefore ſeeing the Precepts and Dictates of Scriptures
were written and *directed to the Heart and Thoughts of men*, and comprehend the viciſſitudes of all Ages, with an eternal and certain
fore-ſight of all Hereſies, *Contradictions* ; differing and mutable e-
ſtates of the Church, as well in general , as of the Elect in ſpecial ; they are to be interpreted according to the Latitude and the
proper ſence of the place, and reſpectively toward that preſent
occaſion whereupon the words were utter'd ; or in preciſe congruity from the Context of the precedent and ſubſequent words ; or in
contemplation of the principal ſcope of the place ; but ſo as we conceive them to comprehend, not only totally or collectively, but di-
ſtributively, even in clauſes, and in every word, infinite ſprings and
ſtreams of Doctrine to water every part of the Church, and the ſpirits of the Faithful: For it hath been excellently obſerved, that the
Anſwers of *our Saviour*, to many of the queſtions which were propounded to him, ſeem not to the purpoſe, but, as it were, impertinent to the ſtate of the queſtion demanded. The Reaſons hereof
are two : the one, that being he knew the *thoughts* of thoſe that propounded the Queſtions, not from their words, as we men uſe to do,
but immediately, and of himſelf, he made anſwer to their *thoughts*,

               not

Mat.xxiv.

not to their *words.* The other Reafon is, that he fpake not only to them that were then prefent, but to us alfo who now live, and to men of every Age and Place to whom the Gofpel fhould be preacht: which fenfe in many places of Scripture muft take place.

§ Thefe thus briefly toucht and fore-tafted, come we now to that Treatife which we report as *Deficient.* There are found indeed a-mongft *Theological writings* too many *Books of Controverfies,* an in-finite Mafs of that *Divinity* which we call *Pofitive,* as *Common-places; Particular Treatife; Cafes of Confcience; Sermons; Homilies;* and many *Prolix Commentaries* upon the *Books of Scripture:* but the Form of writing *Deficient* is this, namely *fuccinct and found Collecti-on,* and that with judgement, of *Annotations and Obfervations upon particular Texts of Scripture;* not dilating into common-places; or chafing after Controverfies; or reducing them into method of Art: but which be altogether fcattered and Natural; a thing indeed now and then expreft in more learned Sermons, which for moft part vanifh; but which as yet, is not collected into Books that fhould be tranf-mitted to Pofterity. *Certainly* as Wines which at firft preffing run gently, yield a more pleafant tafte, than thofe where the Wine-prefs is hard wrought; becaufe thofe fomewhat relifh of the ftone and skin of the Grape; fo thofe obfervations are moft wholfome and fweet, which flow from Scriptures gently expreft, and naturally ex-pounded, and are wrefted or drawn afide to common places or Controverfies; fuch a Treatife we will name, *The Emanations of Scripture.*

" § Thus have we made, as it were, a *fmall Globe of the Intellectu-*
" *al world,* as faithfully as we could, together with a defignation
" and defcription of thofe parts which I find not conftantly occu-
" pate, or not well converted by the Induftry and Labours of men.
" In which work if I have any where receded from the opini-
" on of the Ancients, I defire that Pofterity would fo judge of my
" intentions, as that this was done with a mind of further *Progreffion,*
" and *Proficience in melius;* and not out of a humour of *Innovation,*
" or Tranfmigration *in aliud:* for I could not be true and conftant
" to my felf, or the Argument which I have in hand, if I had not re-
" folvedly determin'd, *To add to the Inventions of others,* fo far as I
" was able. And I am as willing, and as fincerely wifh, that later
" ages may go beyond me hereafter, as I have endeavoured to go
" beyond others now. And how faithfully I have dealt in this bu-
" finefs may appear even by this, that I have propounded my opini-
" ons every where naked and unarm'd, not feeking to prejudicate
" the liberty of others by the pugnacity of confutations. For in a-
" ny thing which I have well fet down, I am in good hope that it
" will come fo to pafs, that if in the firft reading a fcruple or objecti-
" on be mov'd, in the fecond reading an anfwer will be ready made;
" and in thofe things wherein I have chauc'd to err, I am fure I have
" not prejudiced the right by litigious arguments, which common-
" ly are of this nature, *that they procure Authority to error, and dero-*
" *gate from Good inventions;* for from *Dubitation Error acquires Ho-*

" *nour, Truth suffer repulse.* And now I call to mind an Anſwer *Themi-*
" *ſtocles* made, who, when an Ambaſſador in a ſet ſpeech had boaſted
" great matters of a ſmall Village, takes him up thus , *Friend, your*
" *words would require a City.* Surely I ſuppoſe it may be juſtly ob-
" jected to me, that *my words require an Age*, a whole Age perchance
" to prove them, and many Ages to perfect them. Notwithſtanding
" ſeeing the greateſt matters are owing unto their Principles, it is
" enough to me that I have *Sowen unto Poſterity, and the immortal*
" *God*, whoſe divine Majeſty I humbly implore through his Son and
" our Saviour , that he would vouchſafe graciouſly to accept theſe
" and ſuch *like ſacrifices of Humane underſtanding ſeaſoned with Reli-*
" *gion as with ſalt, and incenſed to his Glory.*

A

A

NEW WORLD

OF

SCIENCES:

OR THE

DEFICIENTS

THE
INDEX
OF
SACRED SCRIPTURES
Illuftrated or Alleged.

GEN.

Cap.	Verf.	Pag.
1	1,&c.	26
1	2	137
1	3	27
1	9,&c.	102
1	9	132
1	27	87
2	7	102
2	7	132
2	8	27
3	5	239
3	19	135
3	19	167
3	22	71
4	2	27
4	21	27
5	24	223
11	9	27
18	10	316
45	3	73
49	9	287

EXOD.

Cap.	Verf.	Pag.
2	13	319
7	1	180
7	12	48
24	18	223

LEVIT.

Cap.	Verf.	Pag.
13	12, 13	28

DEUT.

Cap.	Verf.	Pag.
12	16	117

I. REG.

Cap.	Verf.	Pag.
20	34	46

III. REG.

Cap.	Verf.	Pag.
4	29	2
4	29	247
4	33	28
4	33	247

IV. REG.

Cap.	Verf.	Pag.
9	30	130
9	18	319

ESTH.

Cap.	Verf.	Pag.
6	1	63

JOB

Cap.	Verf.	Pag.
9	9	28
10	10	28
13	9	5
26	7	28
26	13	28
		28

THE
INDEX
OF
HUMANE AUTHORS

Cenſured, Praiſed, Cited.

Dectori

LECTORI ACADEMICO S.

*C*Erte, Philofophia Naturalis *omnium Scientiarum nobiliffima eft, Certiffima ac ampliffima; utpote fuo ambitu Complectens volumen illud magnum & admirandum* Operum Dei ac Creaturarum; *eorumq; varietatem, Conftantiam ac ornatum.* Catalogus vero ifte, *qui Capita & fumma Rerum Continet, omnium qui unquam prodiere, perfectiffimus eft, maxime ordinatus ac definitus :* ad imaginem Mundi *compofitus ac* Rerum; *non* intellectus & fpeculationum, *quarum non eft ordo, numerus, neq; finis.* Catalogus *reverà ad menfuram univerfi & experimentorum ita accommodatus,* ut naturam in natura quærat, *eamq; in omnes ejus formas mutatam conftringat, omnefq; ejus ftatus comprehendat;* libertatem, errores, vincula; in fpeciebus fuis, in monftris, in mechanicis. *Deniq;* Index eft *incomparabilis, ac fummo judicio elaboratus. Ad fylvam & fupellectilem Hiftoriarum Naturalium Colligendam, nullus uberior; ad, fic collectam, in locos* Com. & *proprias claffes digerendam, nullus Concinnior; ad, fic digeftam, memoriter retinendam, nullus efficacior unquam extitit; vel humano ingenio ac induftria excogitari poteft.* Interpres *fic cogitavit? quod* Juventuti Academicæ ac veritatis amantibus *notum fieri, ipforum intereffe putavit. Erunt fortaffis Pedarii Senatores, qui, modernis methodis adfueti, aliam fententiam ferent; atque ferant aliam;* Sed juftificata eft fapientia à filiis fuis.

CATALOGUS
Hiſtoriarum Particularum.

Secundum Capita.

1 Iſtoria Cœleſtium; ſive Aſtronomica.
 2 Hiſtoria configurationis Cœli & partium ejus, versùs Terram & partes ejus; ſive Coſmographica.
 3 Hiſtoria Cometarum.
 4 Hiſtoria Meteororum ignitorum.
 5 Hiſtoria Fulgurum, Fluminum, Tonitruum, & Coruſcationum.
 6 Hiſtoria Ventorum, & Flatuum repentinorum, & Undulationum Aeris.
 7 Hiſtoria Iridum.
 8 Hiſtoria Nubium, prout ſupernè conſpiciuntur.
 9 Hiſtoria Expanſionis Cœruleæ, Crepuſculi, plurium Solium, plurium Lunarum, Halonum, Colorum variorum Solis & Lunæ; atq; omnis varietatis Cœleſtium ad aſpectum, quæ fit ratione Medii.
10 Hiſtoria Pluviarum Ordinariarum, Procelloſarum, & Prodigioſarum; etiam Cataractarum (quas vocant) Cœli, & ſimilium.
11 Hiſtoria Grandinis, Nivis, Gelú, Pruinæ, Nebulæ, Roris, & ſimilium.
12 Hiſtoria omnium aliorum Cadentium ſive Deſcendentium ex alto, & ſupernè generatorum.
13 Hiſtoria Sonituum in alto (ſi modò ſint aliqui) præter Tonitrua.
14 Hiſtoria Aeris, in Toto, ſive in Configuratione Mundi.
15 Hiſtoria Tempeſtatum, ſive Temperamentorum Anni, tam ſecundùm variationes Regionum, quàm ſecundùm accidentia Temporum, & periodos Annorum; Diluviorum, Fervorum, Siccitatum, & ſimilium.
16 Hiſtoria Terræ & Maris; Figuræ & Ambitûs ipſorum, & Configurationis ipſorum inter ſe, atq; Exporrectionis ipſorum in latum

aut

aut angustum; Insularum Terræ in Mari, Sinuum Maris, & Lacuum salsorum in Terrâ, Isthmorum, Promontoriorum.

17 Historia Motuum (si qui sint) globi Terræ & Maris; & ex quibus Experimentis illi colligi possunt.

18 Historia Motuum majorum & Perturbationum in Terrâ & Mari, nempè Terræ Motuum & Tremorum & Hiatuum, Insularum de novo enascentium, Insularum fluctuantium, Abruptionum Terrarum per ingressum Maris, Invasionum & Illuvionum, & contrà Desertionum Maris; Eruptionum ignium è terrâ, Eruptionum subitanearum Aquarum è Terrâ, & similium.

19 Historia Geographica Naturalis, Montium, Vallium, Sylvarum, Planitierum, Arenarum, Paludum, Lacuum, Fluviorum, Torrentium, Fontium, & omnis diversitatis scaturiginis ipsorum, & similium: missis Gentibus, Provinciis, Urbibus,& hujusmodi Civilibus.

20 Historia Fluxuum & Refluxuum Maris, Euriporum, Undulationum & Motuum Maris aliorum.

21 Historia cæterorum Accidentium Maris; Salsuginis ejus, Colorum diversorum, Profunditatis: & Rupium, Montium, Vallium submarinarum, & similium.

Sequuntur Historiæ Massarum majorum.

22 Historia Flammæ, & Ignitorum.
23 Historia Aeris, in substantiâ, non in Configuratione.
24 Historia Aquæ, in substantiâ, non in Configuratione.
25 Historia Terræ & diversitatis ejus in Substantiâ, non in Configuratione.

Sequuntur Historiæ Specierum.

26 Historia Metallorum perfectorum, Auri, Argenti,& Minerarum, Venarum, Marcasitarum eorundem: Operaria quoque in Mineris ipsorum.
27 Historia Argenti Vivi.
28 Historia Fossilium; veluti Vitrioli, & Sulphuris, &c.
29 Historia Gemmarum; veluti Adamantis, Rubini, &c.
30 Historia Lapidum; ut Marmoris, Lapidis Lydii, Silicis, &c.
31 Historia Magnetis.
32 Historia Corporum Miscellaneorum, quæ nec sunt Fossilia prorsus, nec Vegetabilia; ut Salium, Succini, Ambræ-griseæ, &c.
33 Historia Chymica circà Metalla & Mineralia.
34 Historia Plantarum, Arborum, Fruticum, Herbarum: & Partium eorum, Radicum, Caulium, Ligni, Foliorum, Florum, Fructuum, Seminum, Lachrymarum, &c.
35 Historia Chymica circa Vegitabilia.
36 Historia Piscium, & Partium ac Generationis ipsorum.
37 Historia Volatilium, & Partium ac Generationis ipsorum.

38 Historia

38 Hiſtoria Quadrupedum , & Partium ac Generationis ipſorum.

39 Hiſtoria Serpentum, Vermium, Muſcarum, & cæterorum Inſecto-
rum; & partium ac generationis ipſorum.

40 Hiſtoria Chymica circa ea quæ ſumuntur ab Animalibus.

Sequuntur Hiſtoriæ Hominis.

41 Hiſtoria Figuræ , & Membrorum externorum Hominis , Sta-
turæ , Compagis , Vultûs , Lineamentorum ; eorumq; varietatis ſecundùm Gentes & Climata , aut alias minores Differentias.

42 Hiſtoria Phyſiognomica ſuper ipſa.

43 Hiſtoria Anatomica, ſive Membrorum internorum Hominis; &
varietatis ipſorum, quatenùs invenitur in ipsâ naturali Compage
& Structurâ, non tantùm quoad Morbos & Accidentia præterna-
turalia.

44 Hiſtoria partium ſimilarium Hominis ; ut Carnis, Oſſium , Mem-
branarum, &c.

45 Hiſtoria Humorum in Homine; Sanguinis , Bilis , Spermatis,
&c.

46 Hiſtoria Excrementorum ; Sputi , Urinarum, Sudorum , Se-
dimentorum , Capillorum , Pilorum, Reduviarum, Unguium,
& ſimilium.

47 Hiſtoria Facultatum; Attractionis, Digeſtionis, Retentionis, Ex-
pulſionis, Sanguificationis, Aſſimilationis alimentorum in membra, Verſionis Sanguinis & Floris ejus in Spiritum, &c.

48 Hiſtoria Motuum Naturalium & Involuntariorum ; ut Motûs
Cordis, Motûs Pulſuum, Sternutationis, Motûs Pulmonum, Motûs Erectionis Virgæ, &c.

49 Hiſtoria Motuum mixtorum ex Naturalibus & voluntariis ; veluti Reſpirationis, Tuſſis, Urinationis, Sedis, &c.

50 Hiſtoria Motuum Voluntariorum; ut Inſtrumentorum ad voces
articulatas; ut Motuum Oculorum, Linguæ, Faucium, Manuum,
Digitorum; Deglutionis, &c.

51 Hiſtoria Somni & Inſomniorum.

52 Hiſtoria diverſorum Habituum Corporis; Pinguis , Macilenti;
Complexionum (quas vocant,) &c.

53 Hiſtoria Generationis Hominum.

54 Hiſtoria Conceptionis, Vivificationis, Geſtationis in utero, Par-
tûs, &c.

55 Hiſtoria Alimentationis Hominis, atq; omnis Edulii & Potabilis,
atq; omnis Diætæ; & Varietatis ipſorum, ſecundùm Gentes aut
minores differentias.

56 Hiſtoria Augmentationis & Incrementi Coporis in Toto & Partibus ipſius.

57 Hiſtoria Decursûs Ætatis; Infantiæ, Pueritiæ, Juventutis, Sene-
ctutis, Longævitatis, Brevitatis Vitæ, & ſimilium, ſecundum Gentes & minores differentias.

58 Hiſtoria

58 Historia Vitæ & Mortis.
59 Historia Medicinalis, Morborum, & Symptomatum & Signorum eorundem.
60 Historia Medicinalis, Curæ, & Remediorum, & Liberationum à Morbis.
61 Historia Medicinalis eorum quæ confervant Corpus & Sanitatem.
62 Historia Medicinalis eorum quæ pertinent ad Formam & Decus Corporis, &c.
63 Historia Medicinalis eorum quæ corpus alterant, & pertinent ad Regimen Alterativum.
64 Historia Pharmaco-polaris.
65 Historia Chirurgica.
66 Historia Chymica circa Medicinas.
67 Historia Visûs & visibilium, sive Optica.
68 Historia Picturæ, Sculptoria, Plastica, &c.
69 Historia Auditûs & Sonorum.
70 Historia Musica.
71 Historia Olfactûs, & Odorum.
72 Historia Gustûs & Saporum.
73 Historia Tactûs & ejus Objectorum.
74 Historia Veneris, ut speciei Tactûs.
75 Historia Dolorum corporeorum, ut speciei Tactûs.
76 Historia Voluptatis & Doloris in genere.
77 Historia Affectuum ; ut Iræ, Amoris, Verecundiæ, &c.
78 Historia Facultatum Intellectualium ; Cogitativæ, Phantasiæ, Discursûs. Memoriæ, &c.
79 Historia Divinationum Naturalium.
80 Historia Dignotionum, sive Diacrisium occultarum Naturalium,
81 Historia Coquinaria ; & Artium subfervientium, veluti Macellaria, Aviaria, &c.
82 Historia Pistoria, & Panificiorum ; & Artium subfervientium, ut Molendinaria, &c.
83 Historia Vinaria.
84 Historia Cellaria, & diversorum generum Potûs.
85 Historia Bellariorum & Confecturarum.
86 Historia Mellis.
87 Historia Sacchari.
88 Historia Lacticiniorum.
89 Historia Balneatoria, & Unguentaria.
90 Historia Miscellanea circa curam corporis ; Tonsorum, Odorariorum, &c.
91 Historia Auri-fabrilis, & Artium subfervientium.
92 Historia Lanificiorum, & Artium subfervientium.
93 Historia Opificiorum è Serico & Bombyce, & Artium subfervientium.
94 Historia Opificiorum ex Lino, Cannabio, Gossipio, Setis, & aliis Filaceis ; & Artium subfervientium.
95 Historia Plumificiorum.
96 Historia Textoria, & Artium subfervientium.

97 Historia

97 Hiſtoria Tinctoria.
98 Hiſtoria Coriaria, Alutaria; & Artium ſubſervientium:
99 Hiſtoria Culcitraria & Plumaria.
100 Hiſtoria Ferri-Fabrilis.
101 Hiſtoria Latomiæ ſive Lapicidarum.
102 Hiſtoria Lateraria, & Tegularia.
103 Hiſtoria Figularis.
104 Hiſtoria Cæmentaria, & Cruſtaria.
105 Hiſtoria Ligni-fabrilis.
106 Hiſtoria Plumbaria.
107 Hiſtoria Vitri & omnium Vitreorum, & Vitriaria.
108 Hiſtoria Architecturæ in genere.
109 Hiſtoria Plauſtraria Rhedaria, Lecticaria, &c.
110 Hiſtoria Typographica, Libraria, Scriptoria, Sigillatoria; Atra-
    menti, Calami, Papyri, Membranæ, &c.
111 Hiſtora Ceræ.
112 Hiſtoria Viminaria.
113 Hiſtoria Storearia, Opificiorum ex Stramine, Scirpis, & ſi-
    milibus.
114 Hiſtoria Lotricaria, Scoparia, &c.
115 Hiſtoria Agriculturæ, Paſcuariæ, Cultûs Sylvarum, &c.
116 Hiſtoria Hortulana.
117 Hiſtoria Piſcatoriá.
118 Hiſtoria Venationis & Aucupii.
119 Hiſtoria Rei Bellicæ, & Artium ſubſervientium; Armamenta-
    ria, Arcuaria, Sagittaria Sclopetaria, Tormentaria, Baliſtaria,
    Machinaria, &c.
120 Hiſtoria Rei Nauticæ, & Practicarum, & Artium ſubſervi-
    tium.
121 Hiſtoria Athletica, & omnis generis Exercitationum Ho-
    minis.
122 Hiſtoria Rei Equeſtris.
123 Hiſtoria Ludorum omnis generis.
124 Hiſtoria Præſtigiatorum & Circulatorum.
125 Hiſtoria Miſcellanea diverſarum Materiarum Artificialium; ut
    Eſmaltæ, Porcellanæ, complurium Cæmentorum, &c.
126 Hiſtoria Salium.
127 Hiſtoria Miſcellanea diverſarum Machinarum, & Mo-
    tuum.
128 Hiſtoria Miſcellanea Experimentorum Vulgarium, quæ non
    coaluërunt in Artem.

*Etiam Mathematicarum purarum Hiſtoriæ conſcribendæ ſunt, licèt ſint
    potiùs Obſervationes quàm Experimenta.*

129 Hiſtoria naturarum & poteſtatum Numerorum.
130 Hiſtoria naturarum & poteſtatum Figurarum.

NOn abs re fuerit admonere, quòd, cùm necesse sit multa ex Experimentis sub duobus Titulis vel pluribus cadere, (veluti Historia Plantarum & Historia Artis Hortulanæ multa habebunt ferè communia) commordior sit inquisitio per Artes, Dispositio verò per Corpora. Parùm enim nobis curæ est de Artibus ipsis Mechanicis, sed tantùm de iis quæ afferunt ad instruendam Philosophiam. Verùm hæc è re natâ meliùs regentur.

F I N I S.

Typographus Lectori.

UNâ aut alterâ Paginâ vacante in damnum Bibilopo-
læ, ad implendam areolam inanem, Nobiliff. Au-
thoris Literas, fuo Collegio miffas ac propriâ manu muni-
tas, fubjungere vifum eft. Quòd vivit Chartula hæc peri-
tura, id noftrum munus eft ; Tuum, Lector, fi vigeat. Suc-
cincta pagina eft, fed folida : & excellentium virorum etiam
Reliquiæ confervandæ. *Vale.*

F R A. De V E R U L A M I O
Vice-Comes Sᵃⁱ A L B A N I.

Percelebri Collegio Sanctæ & Individuæ Trinitatis.
IN
CANTABRIGIA. S.

R*Es omnes earumq; progreſſus initiis ſuis de-*
bentur : Itaq; cum initia Scientiarum è
Fontibus veſtris hauſerim, incrementa ip-
ſarum vobis rependenda exiſtimavi. Spero itidem fo-
re, ut hæc noſtra apud vos tanquam in Solo nativo Fe-
liciùs ſuccreſcant. Quamobrem & vos hortor, ut ſal-
vâ animi modeſtia, & erga veteres reverentiâ, ipſi
quoq; Scientiarum Augmentis non deſitis : verum
ut poſt volumina ſacra verbi Dei & Scripturarum,
ſecundo loco volumen illud magnum operum Dei &
Creaturarum, ſtrenuè, & præ omnibus libris, qui pro
Commentariis tantùm haberi debent, evolvatis.
Valete.

www.ingramcontent.com/pod-product-compliance
Lightning Source LLC
Chambersburg PA
CBHW021337110726
47900CB00005B/1502